Triumph 675
Service and Repair Manual

by Matthew Coombs

Models covered

(4876 - 1AO1 - 288)

Daytona. 674.8cc. 2006 to 2012
Daytona R. 674.8cc. 2011 and 2012
Street Triple. 674.8cc. 2007 to 2015
Street Triple R. 674.8cc. 2009 to 2016
Street Triple RX. 674.8cc. 2016

Special Edition versions included

© Haynes Publishing 2016

ABCDE
FGHIJ
KLMNO
P

A book in the **Haynes Service and Repair Manual Series**

ISBN 978 0 85733 924 9

British Library Cataloguing in Publication Data
A catalogue record for this book is available from the British Library

Library of Congress Control Number 2014958878

Printed in Malaysia

Haynes Publishing
Sparkford, Yeovil, Somerset BA22 7JJ, England

Haynes North America, Inc
859 Lawrence Drive, Newbury Park, California 91320, USA

Printed using NORBRITE BOOK 48.8gsm (CODE: 40N6533) from NORPAC; procurement system certified under Sustainable Forestry Initiative standard. Paper produced is certified to the SFI Certified Fiber Sourcing Standard (CERT - 0094271)

Contents

LIVING WITH YOUR TRIUMPH

Introduction

Pre-ride checks

MAINTENANCE

Routine maintenance and servicing

Contents

REPAIRS AND OVERHAUL

REFERENCE

A Phoenix from the ashes

by Julian Ryder

Where is the most modern motorcycle factory in the World? Tokyo? Berlin? Turin, maybe? No, it's in Hinckley, Leicestershire. Unlikely as it may seem, the Triumph factory in the Midlands of England is a more advanced production facility than anything the mighty Japanese industry, German efficiency or Italian flair can boast. Since the marquee was reborn in 1991, Triumph has grown into a big player on the world stage and is now the only volume manufacturer of automotive transport that can call itself truly British.

It's important to realise that the new Triumph company has very little to do with the company that was a giant on the world stage in the post-war years when British motorcycle makers dominated the global markets. It is true that new owner John Bloor bought the patents, manufacturing rights and, most importantly, trademarks when the old factory's assets were sold in 1983, but the products of the old and new companies bear no relation at all to one another. Apart, of course, from the name on the tanks. Bloor's research-and-development team started work in Collier Street, Coventry and in 1985 work started on the ten-acre green-field factory site, which was occupied for the first time the following year.

The 2007 Daytona

The reborn Triumphs

The R & D team soon dispensed with the old Meriden factory's project for a modern DOHC, eight-valve twin known within the factory as the Diana project (after Princess Di) but shown at the NEC International Bike Show in 1982 as the Phoenix. The world got to see the real new Triumphs for the first time at the Cologne Show in late 1990. The company was obviously anxious to distance itself from the old, leaky, unreliable image of the British motorcycle, but it was equally anxious not to engage in a head-on technology war with the big four Japanese factories. The watchword was 'proven technology', the new engines were in-line triples and housed in a universal steel chassis with a large-diameter tubular backbone. Seemingly contrary to the company's desire to distance itself from the past, the new bikes would all carry famous model names from Triumph's past.

But if Triumph's technology wasn't exactly path-breaking it was certainly very clever. The key concept was the modular design of the motor based around long and short-throw crankshafts in three and four-cylinder configurations. Every engine used the common 76 mm bore with either 55 or 65 mm throw cranks so that the short-stroke engine would be 750 cc in three-cylinder form and 1000 cc as a four. Put the long-stroke crank in and you get a 900 cc triple and a 1200 cc four. The first bike to hit the shops was the 1200 Trophy, a four-cylinder sports tourer which was immediately competitive in a very strong class. There was also a 900 cc, three-cylinder Trophy. The 750 and 1000 Daytonas used the short-stroke motor in three and four-cylinder forms in what were intended to be the sportsters of the range. The other two models, 750 and 900 cc three-cylinder Tridents, cashed in on the early-'90s fad for naked retro bikes that followed the world-wide success of the Kawasaki Zephyr.

The reborn Triumphs were received with acclaim from the motorcycle press – tinged with not a little surprise. They really were very good motorcycles, the big Trophy was a match for the Japanese opposition in a class full of very accomplished machinery. The fact it could live with a modern day classic like the Yamaha FJ1200 straight off the drawing board was a tribute to John Bloor's designers and production engineers. The bike was big, fast, heavy and quite high, but it worked and worked well. And it didn't leak oil or break down, it was obvious that whatever else people were going to say about Triumphs they weren't going to able to resurrect the old jokes about British bangers leaving puddles of lubricant under them. As the rest of the range arrived and tests of them got into print, the star of the show emerged; it was the long-stroke, three-cylinder, 900 cc motor. It didn't matter how it was dressed up, the big triple had that indefinable quality – character. It was the motor the Japanese would never have made,

The 2008 Street Triple

very torquey but with a hint of vibration that endears rather than annoys. Somewhere among the modern, water-cooled, multi-valve technology, the 900-triple had the genes of the old air-cooled OHV Triumph Tridents that appeared in 1969 and stayed in production until '75.

Model development

The range stayed basically unchanged until the Cologne Show of '92. Looking back at the first range it is now easy to see – hindsight again – that the identity of all the models was far too close. The sports tourer Trophy models were reckoned to be a little too sporting, the basic Tridents still had the handlebar and footrest positions of faired bikes. Triumph management later agreed that the first range evinced a certain lack of confidence; that was certainly not the case with the revamped 1993 range.

Visitors to the Cologne Show in September '92 agreed that the Triumphs were the stars, any lack of confidence there may have been two years earlier was completely gone. Any shyness the management may have felt about the Triumph name's past was shaken off as the new Tridents went retro style. Overall, the identities of the original bikes became more individual and more obviously separated; the Trophy models became more touring oriented, the Daytona more sporty looking and the Trident models more traditional. The factory even had the confidence to put small Union Flag emblems on the side panels of each

model, no more apologising for the imagined shortcomings of British engineering. Despite this spreading of the range's appeal, all these bikes were still built on the original modular concept.

There was, however, an exception to this rule of uniformity in the shape of a brand new bike, the Tiger 900. This model was in the enduro/desert-racer style much favoured in Continental Europe but not at all popular at home in the UK. Here was a Triumph with a 19-inch front tyre, wire wheels and a lower power output than the other 900s. Both the chassis and engine parts were slightly different from the rest of the range. Judging their market as cleverly as ever, the factory held back another new model for the International Bike Show at the Birmingham NEC. This was the Daytona 1200, an out and out speed machine with a hidden political agenda. Its high-compression, 147 PS engine gave it brutal straight-line performance in much the same way as the big Kawasakis of the mid-'80s, and like them it wasn't too clever in the corners because of its weight and length. The bike was built as much to show that Triumph could do it as to sell in big numbers, it also had the secondary function of thumbing the corporate nose at the UK importers' gentlemen's agreement not to bring in bikes of over 125 PS.

Next year's NEC show saw two more new Triumphs, both reworkings of what was now regarded as a modern classic, the 900 triple. The Speed Triple was a clever reincarnation of the British cafe racer style, complete with clip-on handlebars and rear-set footrests. The big three-cylinder engine in standard tune got an all-black finish with black chrome pipes and silencers for the appropriately mean look. Black wheel rims and new bodywork completed a superbly styled bike available with black or yellow bodywork, the Speed Triple was the star of the show, a bike with an attitude.

The other newcomer was a more radical project, the Daytona Super III. Externally the motor looked like the usual 900 cc three, but a lot of work by Cosworth Engineering was hidden under the cases. The result was 115 PS as opposed to the standard 900 Daytona's 98 PS.

Triumphs in America

Triumph's next big step was into the US market, where the old company was so strong in the post-war years when the only competition was Harley-Davidson and where there is considerable affection for the marque. The name Triumph chose to spearhead this new challenge was Thunderbird, a trademark sourced in Native American mythology. This time the famous name adorned yet another version of the 900 triple but this time heavily restyled and in a retro package. Dummy cooling fins give it the look of an air-cooled motor, the logo was cast into the clutch cover, and there were soft

edges and large expanses of polished alloy. Inside those restyled cases, the motor was retuned even more than the Tiger's for a very user-friendly dose of low-down punch and mid-range power. The cycle parts were given an equally radical redesign, although the retro style stopped short of giving the Thunderbird twin rear shock absorbers. But everything else, the shape of the tank, the chrome headlight and countless other details, harks back to the original Thunderbird and nothing does so as shamelessly as the 'mouth-organ' tank badge, a classic icon if ever there was one.

The first Thunderbird derivative, the Adventurer, appeared for 1996 with a different rear subframe and rear-end styling including a

The 2009 Street Triple R

sissy bar and single seat. That same year, the short-stroke 750 cc motor bowed out of the range, but it went with a bang not a whimper not in a final batch of Tridents but in a limited-edition run of 750 Speed Triples. The bigger Speed Triple's motor was inserted in the Sprint and the result called the Sprint Sport. The reason for using up all those motors was the advent of the new range of fuel-injected and heavily revised three-cylinder engines that first powered the T509 Speed Triple and T595 Daytona of 1997.

Fuel Injection

The first fuel-injected Triumph, the Daytona T595, was a major milestone for the Factory. It represented a change of policy, the first time Triumph would venture to confront their opposition on the cutting edge of technology. In early 1997, the Honda FireBlade and Ducati 916 ruled. The T595 was able to play in the same ball park. Only on a race track could the Japanese and Italian machines be shown to be better. In the real world the T595 was at least as good a bike. The old long stroke of 65 mm was retained but everything else was new, it was a radical departure from the modular concept that had dominated production until now. You could see how the new motor was a lightened version of the old triple, but fuel injection was new and the frame was a radical departure from previous practice. Serpentine tubing ran from steering head to swingarm pivot and it was aluminium. Bodywork looked tasty too. Despite what Triumph had said about not taking on the Japanese back in 1991, the T595 came out of comparative tests with the 'Blade and 916 on equal terms. The new bike was also given the Speed Triple treatment and adorned with bug-eyed twin headlights in the fashionable 'streetfighter' style.

The trouble with the Supersports end of the market is that the goal posts keep moving, so Triumph hedged their bets by softening the 955i's nominal 128 PS to 108, housing it in a simpler twin-beam frame and calling the result the Sprint ST. This continuation of the original Sprint concept was one of the hits of 1999. As a sports tourer, the fuel-injected Sprint ST was right up there with Honda's classic class leader, the VFR. Some magazines even preferred the British bike. High praise. The Tiger got the fuel-injected 855 cc motor in '99. The result was a much more svelte machine than the original carburetted model, but Britain still refused to fall in love with the concept. Not that development of the carburetted bikes was neglected. Triumph got a Thunderbird derivative right in 1998 with the Thunderbird Sport.

Up to 1999 Triumph concentrated on big bikes but then they took another giant step towards the big time by taking on the Japanese in the most competitive market sector of them all, Supersports 600, with the TT600. For 2001 the most famous name of all was bought out of retirement: Bonneville. And it was an air-cooled twin! From a standing start

in 1991, the Hinckley factory was competing in all the major motorcycle market sectors. Much bigger production volumes meant the original modular concept was no longer a necessity. By the dawn of the 21st Century Triumph had sold over 100,000 motorcycles.

Then the factory was struck by one of the biggest fires ever at a British industrial site. In March 2002 the production line, moulding shop and stores were destroyed and many other parts of the plant severely damaged. Just six months later the rebuilt factory was running at full capacity. The first new product out of the doors was the Daytona 600, a replacement for the TT600. Where the first Supersports 600 Triumph had failed to compete with the Japanese this one was good enough to win a TT in the hands of Kiwi Isle of Man hero Bruce Anstey.

With an eye on America Triumph then unleashed their most audacious bike yet: the Rocket III. (Whisper it, but Rocket III was actually a BSA model name back in the 1970s.) They call it a cruiser but behemoth would be a better description, it's the first production bike to boast a capacity of over two litres and the only thing on the roads that can make a Harley V-Rod look shy and retiring.

In total contrast to the Rocket III, Triumph got serious about the supersports sector in 2006 with the 675cc Daytona triple. Use of the hallmark three-cylinder layout allowed the bike to race against 600cc fours in Supersport competition despite its capacity advantage. The Daytona also dominated its sector in the annual Masterbike test that brings journalists all over the world to test the leading sports bikes from every manufacturer. It is by common consent one of the best middleweights on the market. This gave the factory the confidence to support a racing effort officially rather than surreptitiously. Aussie racer Glen Richards won the 2008 British Supersport Championship on a 675 Daytona against stiff opposition from Japanese importers. The following season Triumph achieved two rostrum finishes in the World Supersport Championship thanks to ex-500cc GP winner Garry McCoy. For 2010 the factory continued to back the Italian BE1 team and upped the effort to field four riders: Daytona 200 winner Chaz Davies from Great Britain, double class World Champion Stephane Charpentier of France, Spaniard David Salom and American Jason di Salvo. The split of riders' nationalities is significant from a marketing point of view, but this major effort shows how the company's attitude to racing has changed.

When the Triumph marque was reborn, one of the major planks of the factory's philosophy was that they were not going to take on the Japanese factories in their strongest sector – supersport bikes. The Daytona 675 demonstrates how much Triumph has achieved in a short period of time. Not surprisingly the universally-praised 675cc triple motor also found its way into a Speed Triple in 2007, swiftly followed by an 'R' version with lots of carbon fibre and trick suspension.

Acknowledgements

Our thanks are due to Fowlers Motorcycles of Bristol and Bridge Motorcycles of Exeter who supplied the machines featured in the illustrations throughout this manual, and Total Triumph of Taunton who provided technical assistance. We would also like to thank NGK Spark Plugs (UK) Ltd for supplying the colour spark plug condition photographs, the Avon Rubber Company for supplying information on tyre fitting, and Draper Tools for supplying many of the tools shown in the photographs.

Thanks are also due to Julian Ryder for providing the introductory copy – A Phoenix from the ashes. We would also like to extend thanks to Triumph Motorcycles, Hinckley, for permission to use pictures of the Triumph models. Triumph Motorcycles Limited bears no responsibility for the content of this book, having had no part in its origination or preparation.

About this manual

The aim of this manual is to help you get the best value from your motorcycle. It can do so in several ways. It can help you decide what work must be done, even if you choose to have it done by a dealer; it provides information and procedures for routine maintenance and servicing; and it offers diagnostic and repair procedures to follow when trouble occurs.

We hope you use the manual to tackle the work yourself. For many simpler jobs, doing it yourself may be quicker than arranging an appointment to get the motorcycle into a dealer and making the trips to leave it and pick it up. More importantly, a lot of money can be saved by avoiding the expense the shop must pass on to you to cover its labour and overhead costs. An added benefit is the sense of satisfaction and accomplishment that you feel after doing the job yourself.

References to the left or right side of the motorcycle assume you are sitting on the seat, facing forward.

We take great pride in the accuracy of information given in this manual, but motorcycle manufacturers make alterations and design changes during the production run of a particular motorcycle of which they do not inform us. No liability can be accepted by the authors or publishers for loss, damage or injury caused by any errors in, or omissions from, the information given.

Weights and dimensions

Daytona and Daytona R

Overall length . . . . .2020 mm
Overall width. . . . . .710 mm
Overall height . . . . .1105 mm
Wheelbase . . . . .1395 mm
Seat height . . . . .830 mm
Dry weight (no fuel and oil). . . . . .165 kg
Wet weight . . . . .185 kg
Max. payload (rider, passenger, luggage, accessories) . . . . . . .195 kg

Street Triple to VIN 560476

Overall length . . . . .2000 mm
Overall width. . . . . .735 mm
Overall height . . . . .1060 mm
Wheelbase . . . . .1390 mm
Seat height . . . . .800 mm
Dry weight (no fuel and oil). . . . . .167 kg
Wet weight . . . . .189 kg
Max. payload (rider, passenger, luggage, accessories) . . . . . . .195 kg

Street Triple from VIN 560477

Overall length . . . . .2055 mm
Overall width. . . . . .740 mm
Overall height . . . . .1060 mm
Wheelbase . . . . .1410 mm
Seat height . . . . .800 mm
Wet weight . . . . .182 kg
Max. payload (rider, passenger, luggage, accessories) . . . . .195 kg

Street Triple R to VIN 560476

Overall length . . . . .2030 mm
Overall width. . . . . .755 mm
Overall height . . . . .1110 mm
Wheelbase . . . . .1410 mm
Seat height . . . . .805 mm
Dry weight (no fuel and oil). . . . . .167 kg
Wet weight . . . . .189 kg
Max. payload (rider, passenger, luggage, accessories) . . . . . . .195 kg

Street Triple R from VIN 560477, Street Triple RX

Overall length . . . . .2055 mm
Overall width. . . . . .740 mm
Overall height . . . . .1110 mm
Wheelbase . . . . .1410 mm
Seat height . . . . .820 mm
Wet weight . . . . .182 kg
Max. payload (rider, passenger, luggage, accessories) . . . . . . .195 kg

Engine

Type	Liquid-cooled, 12 valve in-line three cylinder
Capacity (bore x stroke)	674.8 cc (74 x 52.3 mm)
Compression ratio	12.65 to 1
Camshafts	DOHC, chain-driven from the right-hand end of the crankshaft
Engine management system	Multipoint sequential fuel injection, digital inductive ignition
Clutch	Wet multi-plate, cable-operated
Gearbox	6-speed constant mesh
Final drive.	Chain and sprockets

Chassis

Frame type	Twin spar aluminium
Rake and trail	
Daytona	23.9°, 89.1 mm
Street Triple to VIN 560476	24.3°, 95.3 mm
Street Triple from VIN 560477	24.1°, 99.6 mm
Street Triple R to VIN 560476	23.9°, 92.4 mm
Street Triple R from VIN 560477, Street Triple RX	23.4°, 95 mm
Front suspension	
Daytona	
2006 to 2008	41 mm upside-down cartridge forks with spring preload, rebound and compression damping adjustment
2009-on	41 mm upside-down cartridge forks with spring preload, rebound and low and high speed compression damping adjustment
Daytona R	43 mm upside-down Ohlins cartridge forks with spring preload, rebound and compression damping adjustment
Street Triple	41 mm upside-down cartridge forks, non-adjustable
Street Triple R/RX	41 mm upside-down cartridge forks with spring preload, rebound and compression damping adjustment
Rear suspension	
Daytona	
2006 to 2008	Twin-sided swingarm, single shock with rising-rate linkage and rebound and compression damping adjustment
2009-on	Twin-sided swingarm, single shock with rising-rate linkage and rebound and low and high speed compression damping adjustment
Daytona R	Twin-sided swingarm, single shock with rising-rate linkage and rebound and compression damping adjustment
Street Triple	Twin-sided swingarm, single shock with rising-rate linkage, non-adjustable
Street Triple R/RX	Twin-sided swingarm, single shock with rising-rate linkage and rebound and compression damping adjustment
Wheels	5-spoke cast alloy – Front 17 x 3.5, Rear 17 x 5.5
Tyres*	Front – 120/70-17, Rear – 180/55-17
Front brakes	
Daytona	
2006 to 2008	2 x 308 mm discs with 4-piston radial calipers
2009-on	2 x 308 mm discs with 4-piston radial monobloc calipers
Daytona R	2 x 308 mm discs with Brembo 4-piston radial monobloc calipers
Street Triple to VIN 560476	2 x 308 mm discs with 2-piston sliding calipers
Street Triple from VIN 560477	2 x 310 mm discs with 2-piston sliding calipers
Street Triple R to VIN 560476	2 x 308 mm discs with 4-piston radial calipers
Street Triple R from VIN 560477, Street Triple RX	2 x 310 mm discs with 4-piston radial calipers
Rear brake (all models)	1 x 220 mm disc with single piston sliding caliper

* Refer to the owners handbook, the tyre information label on the swingarm, or your Triumph dealer or a tyre specialist for approved tyre brands and ratings.

Model development

Daytona 675

The Daytona 675 was introduced in October 2005, though marketed as a 2006 model. It superseded the four cylinder TT600, and took advantage of the extra 75cc allowed in the Supersports class for three-cylinder engines.

The Daytona had an all-new aluminium twin-spar frame. Suspension was by Kayaba, with fully adjustable upside-down telescopic forks at the front and a single shock with rising rate linkage at the rear that had adjustable damping. It had a twin-sided swingarm.

For 2008 a special edition SE model was available alongside the standard Daytona, with the same specification as standard models but with carbon fibre exhaust shield, front mudguard and rear hugger, heel guards, chain guard and cockpit trim panels.

For 2009 power output and engine rev limit was increased through modifications to the cylinder head and fuel mapping, and the 1st gear ratio was higher. The cam chain tensioner was hydraulic instead of mechanical. Front and rear suspension were now adjustable for both low and high speed compression damping. The front brake calipers were monobloc, meaning they were machined out of a single piece of aluminium. The fairing and bodywork were redesigned.

New colours and decals, plus revised instrumentation were the only changes for the standard model from 2010 to 2012. A special edition model was available in 2010 with a host of official Triumph accessories to personalise the bike.

For 2011 and 2012 Triumph issued the Daytona R, a 'race-spec' version carrying Ohlins suspension front and rear, and Brembo calipers and radial master cylinder at the front, along with various carbon fibre bits and a quickshifter, as standard. A race kit for the top end of the engine and including a programmable electronic control module were available as options.

Street Triple

The Street Triple was introduced in September 2007 as the smaller stablemate to the 1050 Speed Triple.

Although essentially a Daytona 675 without the fairing, the engine is de-tuned for more mid-range power. The Street Triple has one-piece handlebars, a different exhaust system, and lower spec suspension and brakes.

The Street Triple R, launched for 2009, featured the suspension and brakes of the Daytona 675, but retained the styling of the standard Street Triple.

For 2010 both models had a revised instrument display, lighter rear wheel and rear sprocket and the fuel injection was recalibrated.

For 2012 a new headlight was fitted.

The Street Triple models received a major restyle in 2013, with a new 3-into-1 underslung exhaust system, a new fuel tank and airbox, revised radiator panels, new seat and seat cowling, new tail light, a new swingarm and restyled wheels, an immobiliser and ABS, along with a Brembo rear caliper, and various detail changes to the handlebar, mirror and footrest mounts.

Frame and engine numbers

The engine number is stamped into the top of the crankcase (above the clutch) on the right-hand side of the engine. The VIN (vehicle identification number) is stamped into the right-hand side of the steering head and is duplicated on a plate riveted to the left-hand side of the frame just behind the steering head. These numbers should be recorded and kept in a safe place so they can be furnished to law enforcement officials in the event of a theft.

The VIN, engine number, and model code should be recorded and kept in a handy place (such as with your driver's licence) so that they are always available when purchasing or ordering parts for your machine.

The procedures in this manual distinguish between the bikes by model name. If a model has been modified during its production life, then either the VIN, engine number, or the model year is used to differentiate between the versions, as appropriate.

Buying spare parts

Once you have found the identification numbers, record them for reference when buying parts. Since the manufacturers change specifications, parts and vendors (companies that manufacture various components on the machine), providing the ID numbers is the only way to be reasonably sure that you are buying the correct parts.

Whenever possible, take the worn part to the dealer so direct comparison with the new component can be made. Along the trail from the manufacturer to the parts shelf, there are numerous places that the part can end up with the wrong number or be listed incorrectly.

The two places to purchase new parts for your motorcycle – the accessory store and the franchised dealer – differ in the type of parts they carry. While dealers can obtain virtually every part for your motorcycle, the accessory dealer is usually limited to normal high wear items such as shock absorbers, tune-up parts, various engine gaskets, cables, chains, brake parts, etc. Rarely will an accessory outlet have major suspension components, cylinders, transmission gears, or cases.

Used parts can be obtained for roughly half the price of new ones, but you can't always be sure of what you're getting. Once again, take your worn part to the breaker's yard for direct comparison.

Whether buying new, used or rebuilt parts, the best course is to deal directly with someone who specialises in parts for your particular make.

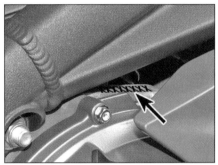

The engine number is stamped into the crankcase on the right-hand side of the engine

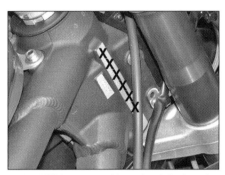

The VIN is stamped into the right-hand side of the steering head

The VIN is duplicated on an information plate (arrowed) on the frame

Professional mechanics are trained in safe working procedures. However enthusiastic you may be about getting on with the job at hand, take the time to ensure that your safety is not put at risk. A moment's lack of attention can result in an accident, as can failure to observe simple precautions.

There will always be new ways of having accidents, and the following is not a comprehensive list of all dangers; it is intended rather to make you aware of the risks and to encourage a safe approach to all work you carry out on your bike.

Asbestos

● Certain friction, insulating, sealing and other products - such as brake pads, clutch linings, gaskets, etc. - contain asbestos. Extreme care must be taken to avoid inhalation of dust from such products since it is hazardous to health. If in doubt, assume that they do contain asbestos.

Fire

● Remember at all times that petrol is highly flammable. Never smoke or have any kind of naked flame around, when working on the vehicle. But the risk does not end there - a spark caused by an electrical short-circuit, by two metal surfaces contacting each other, by careless use of tools, or even by static electricity built up in your body under certain conditions, can ignite petrol vapour, which in a confined space is highly explosive. Never use petrol as a cleaning solvent. Use an approved safety solvent.

● Always disconnect the battery earth terminal before working on any part of the fuel or electrical system, and never risk spilling fuel on to a hot engine or exhaust.

● It is recommended that a fire extinguisher of a type suitable for fuel and electrical fires is kept handy in the garage or workplace at all times. Never try to extinguish a fuel or electrical fire with water.

Fumes

● Certain fumes are highly toxic and can quickly cause unconsciousness and even death if inhaled to any extent. Petrol vapour comes into this category, as do the vapours from certain solvents such as trichloro-ethylene. Any draining or pouring of such volatile fluids should be done in a well ventilated area.

● When using cleaning fluids and solvents, read the instructions carefully. Never use materials from unmarked containers - they may give off poisonous vapours.

● Never run the engine of a motor vehicle in an enclosed space such as a garage. Exhaust fumes contain carbon monoxide which is extremely poisonous; if you need to run the engine, always do so in the open air or at least have the rear of the vehicle outside the workplace.

The battery

● Never cause a spark, or allow a naked light near the vehicle's battery. It will normally be giving off a certain amount of hydrogen gas, which is highly explosive.

● Always disconnect the battery ground (earth) terminal before working on the fuel or electrical systems (except where noted).

● If possible, loosen the filler plugs or cover when charging the battery from an external source. Do not charge at an excessive rate or the battery may burst.

● Take care when topping up, cleaning or carrying the battery. The acid electrolyte, evenwhen diluted, is very corrosive and should not be allowed to contact the eyes or skin. Always wear rubber gloves and goggles or a face shield. If you ever need to prepare electrolyte yourself, always add the acid slowly to the water; never add the water to the acid.

Electricity

● When using an electric power tool, inspection light etc., always ensure that the appliance is correctly connected to its plug and that, where necessary, it is properly grounded (earthed). Do not use such appliances in damp conditions and, again, beware of creating a spark or applying excessive heat in the vicinity of fuel or fuel vapour. Also ensure that the appliances meet national safety standards.

● A severe electric shock can result from touching certain parts of the electrical system, such as the spark plug wires (HT leads), when the engine is running or being cranked, particularly if components are damp or the insulation is defective. Where an electronic ignition system is used, the secondary (HT) voltage is much higher and could prove fatal.

Remember...

✗ **Don't** start the engine without first ascertaining that the transmission is in neutral.

✗ **Don't** suddenly remove the pressure cap from a hot cooling system - cover it with a cloth and release the pressure gradually first, or you may get scalded by escaping coolant.

✗ **Don't** attempt to drain oil until you are sure it has cooled sufficiently to avoid scalding you.

✗ **Don't** grasp any part of the engine or exhaust system without first ascertaining that it is cool enough not to burn you.

✗ **Don't** allow brake fluid or antifreeze to contact the machine's paintwork or plastic components.

✗ **Don't** siphon toxic liquids such as fuel, hydraulic fluid or antifreeze by mouth, or allow them to remain on your skin.

✗ **Don't** inhale dust - it may be injurious to health (see Asbestos heading).

✗ **Don't** allow any spilled oil or grease to remain on the floor - wipe it up right away, before someone slips on it.

✗ **Don't** use ill-fitting spanners or other tools which may slip and cause injury.

✗ **Don't** lift a heavy component which may be beyond your capability - get assistance.

✗ **Don't** rush to finish a job or take unverified short cuts.

✗ **Don't** allow children or animals in or around an unattended vehicle.

✗ **Don't** inflate a tyre above the recommended pressure. Apart from overstressing the carcass, in extreme cases the tyre may blow off forcibly.

✔ **Do** ensure that the machine is supported securely at all times. This is especially important when the machine is blocked up to aid wheel or fork removal.

✔ **Do** take care when attempting to loosen a stubborn nut or bolt. It is generally better to pull on a spanner, rather than push, so that if you slip, you fall away from the machine rather than onto it.

✔ **Do** wear eye protection when using power tools such as drill, sander, bench grinder etc.

✔ **Do** use a barrier cream on your hands prior to undertaking dirty jobs - it will protect your skin from infection as well as making the dirt easier to remove afterwards; but make sure your hands aren't left slippery. Note that long-term contact with used engine oil can be a health hazard.

✔ **Do** keep loose clothing (cuffs, ties etc. and long hair) well out of the way of moving mechanical parts.

✔ **Do** remove rings, wristwatch etc., before working on the vehicle - especially the electrical system.

✔ **Do** keep your work area tidy - it is only too easy to fall over articles left lying around.

✔ **Do** exercise caution when compressing springs for removal or installation. Ensure that the tension is applied and released in a controlled manner, using suitable tools which preclude the possibility of the spring escaping violently.

✔ **Do** ensure that any lifting tackle used has a safe working load rating adequate for the job.

✔ **Do** get someone to check periodically that all is well, when working alone on the vehicle.

✔ **Do** carry out work in a logical sequence and check that everything is correctly assembled and tightened afterwards.

✔ **Do** remember that your vehicle's safety affects that of yourself and others. If in doubt on any point, get professional advice.

● If in spite of following these precautions, you are unfortunate enough to injure yourself, seek medical attention as soon as possible.

Coolant level

Before you start:

✔ Make sure you have a supply of coolant available – a mixture of 50% distilled water and 50% corrosion inhibited ethylene glycol anti-freeze is needed. Triumph specify their HD4X Hybrid OAT coolant.
✔ Always check the coolant level when the engine is **cold**.
✔ Support the motorcycle in an upright position on level ground, using an auxiliary stand if required.

Bike care:

● Use only the specified coolant mixture. It is important that anti-freeze is used in the system all year round, and not just in the winter. Do not top the system up using only water, as the system will become too diluted.
● Do not overfill the reservoir. If the coolant is significantly above the MAX level line at any time, the surplus should be siphoned or drained off to prevent the possibility of it being expelled out of the overflow hose.
● If the coolant level falls steadily, check the system for leaks (see Chapter 1). If no leaks are found and the level continues to fall, it is recommended that the machine be taken to a Triumph dealer for a pressure test.

DAYTONA

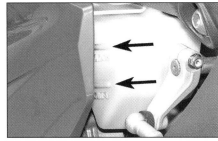

1 The reservoir is mounted behind the rear of the fairing side panel on the left-hand side. The coolant level should be between the MAX and MIN level lines (arrowed) marked on the reservoir.

3 . . . then remove the reservoir filler cap.

2 If the coolant level does not lie between the MAX and MIN level lines, to improve access carefully pull the fairing side panel away to free the peg from the grommet . . .

4 Top the coolant level up with the recommended coolant mixture, using a funnel if necessary. Fit the cap and push the fairing side panel peg into the grommet.

STREET TRIPLE – to VIN 560476

1 Remove the seat (see Chapter 7). The coolant level should be between the MAX and MIN level lines (arrowed) marked on the reservoir.

2 If the coolant level does not lie between the MAX and MIN level lines, remove the reservoir filler cap.

3 Top the coolant level up with the recommended coolant mixture, using a funnel if necessary. Fit the cap, then install the seat.

STREET TRIPLE – from VIN 560477

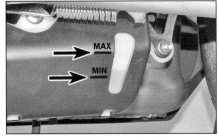

1 The reservoir is mounted low on the left-hand side of the bike, near the sidestand. The coolant level should be between the MAX and MIN level lines (arrowed) marked on the reservoir.

2 If the coolant level does not lie between the MAX and MIN level lines, remove the reservoir filler cap.

3 Top the coolant level up with the recommended coolant mixture, using a funnel if necessary. Fit the cap.

Engine oil level

Before you start:

✔ Support the motorcycle in an upright position on level ground – don't check the oil level with the bike on its sidestand.

✔ Start the engine and let it idle for several minutes to allow it to reach normal operating temperature.

Caution: Do not run the engine in an enclosed space such as a garage or workshop.

✔ Stop the engine and leave the motorcycle undisturbed for a few minutes to allow the oil level to stabilise.

Bike care:

● If you have to add oil frequently, you should check whether you have any oil leaks. If there is no sign of oil leakage from the joints and gaskets the engine could be burning oil (see *Fault Finding*).

● Check the oil on the dipstick – if there are signs of a white emulsion there could be a coolant leakage from one of the pipes running through the sump and into the water pump (this is likely to be the case if the oil level is too high, or seems to rise each time you check it). If this is the case remove the sump and the pipes, clean the sump and fit new O-rings to the pipes (see Chapter 2).

The correct oil

● Modern, high-revving engines place great demands on their oil. It is very important that the correct oil for your bike is used.

● Always top up with a good quality oil of the specified type and viscosity and do not overfill the engine. Triumph recommend using Mobil 1 Racing 4T oil.

● Refer to the **Note** at the beginning of Section 3 in Chapter 1 – over the production life of the models covered the engine oil volumes and dipsticks have changed, and unless you are aware of the changes and have owned the bike for a while it is possible (especially if you are the new owner of a second-hand machine) that you may have the wrong dipstick for the amount of oil in the engine.

Caution: Do not mix any chemical additives with the oil, however good they may sound, as they could cause clutch slip. Never use mineral, vegetable, non-detergent or castor based oils.

Oil type	Semi or fully synthetic motorcycle engine oil, API grade SH or higher and JASO MA
Oil viscosity	SAE 10W/40 or 15W/50

1 Unscrew the oil level dipstick from the right-hand side of the engine.

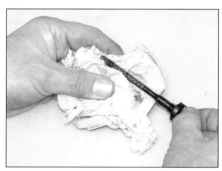

2 Wipe off the oil, screw the dipstick fully home, then unscrew it again . . .

3 . . . and check that the oil is between the upper and lower level lines (arrowed) in the hatched area at the bottom of the dipstick.

4 If topping up is necessary unscrew the filler cap from the top of the clutch cover . . .

5 . . . and top up the engine oil to the correct level with the recommended grade and type of oil, using a funnel if necessary. DO NOT top up via the hole for the dipstick.

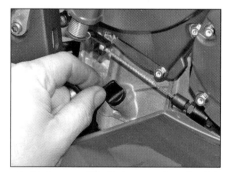

6 Make sure the O-rings on the dipstick and filler cap are in good condition and correctly located. Use new ones if necessary. Fit the dipstick and filler cap.

Brake fluid levels

> ⚠️ **Warning: Brake hydraulic fluid can harm your eyes and damage painted surfaces, so use extreme caution when handling and pouring it and cover surrounding surfaces with rag. Do not use fluid that has been standing open for some time, as it absorbs moisture from the air which can cause a dangerous loss of braking effectiveness.**

Before you start:

✔ Make sure you have the correct hydraulic fluid. DOT 4 is recommended.
✔ Support the motorcycle in an upright position, using an auxiliary stand if required.
✔ The front master cylinder reservoir is on the handlebar – turn the handlebars until reservoir is as level as possible.
✔ The rear master cylinder reservoir is located on the right-hand side.
✔ Wrap a rag around the reservoir being worked on to ensure that any spillage does not come into contact with painted surfaces.

Bike care:

● The fluid in the front and rear brake master cylinder reservoirs will drop slightly as the brake pads wear down.
● If any fluid reservoir requires repeated topping-up this is an indication of an hydraulic leak somewhere in the system, which should be investigated immediately.

● Check for signs of fluid leakage from the hydraulic hoses and brake system components – if found, rectify immediately (see Chapter 6).
● Check the operation of both brakes before taking the machine on the road; if there is evidence of air in the system (spongy feel to lever or pedal), it must be bled as described in Chapter 6.

FRONT BRAKE FLUID LEVEL – Daytona, Daytona R, and Street Triple R

1 The front brake fluid level is visible through the reservoir body – it must be between the UPPER and LOWER level lines (arrowed).

2 To top up on Daytona and Street Triple R models, undo the reservoir cap clamp screw and remove the clamp . . .

3 . . . then unscrew the cap and remove the plate and diaphragm.

4 To top up on Daytona R models, undo the reservoir cap screws (arrowed) and remove the cap, plate and diaphragm.

5 Top up with DOT 4 hydraulic fluid, until the level is between the LOWER and UPPER level lines – do not overfill. Take care to avoid spills (see **Warning** above).

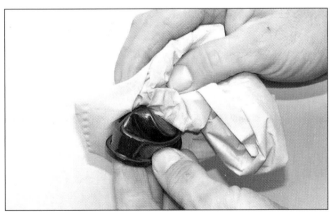

6 Wipe any moisture off the diaphragm, opening it out to access the folds.

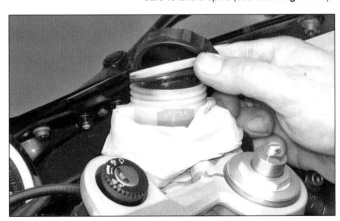

7 Ensure that the diaphragm is correctly seated before installing the plate and cap. Secure the cap with its clamp or screws, according to model.

FRONT BRAKE FLUID LEVEL – STREET TRIPLE

1 The front brake fluid level is visible through the window in the reservoir body – it must be above the LOWER level line (arrowed).

2 To top up, undo the reservoir cover screws (arrowed) and remove the cover and diaphragm.

3 Top up with DOT 4 hydraulic fluid . . .

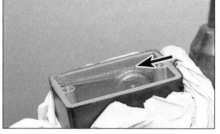

4 . . . until the level is up to the UPPER level line (arrowed) marked on the inside of the reservoir – do not overfill. Take care to avoid spills (see **Warning** on page 0•14).

5 Wipe any moisture off the diaphragm, opening it out to access the folds.

6 Fit the diaphragm onto the cover, then fit the cover, making sure the diaphragm is correctly seated before tightening the screws.

REAR BRAKE FLUID LEVEL

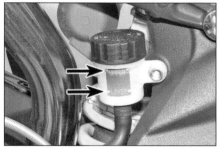

1 The rear brake fluid level is visible through the reservoir body – it must be between the UPPER and LOWER level lines (arrowed).

2 To top up, undo the reservoir cap and remove the plate and diaphragm – on Street Triple models from VIN 560477 you may have to slacken the nut on the reservoir mounting bolt and tilt the reservoir so the cap clears the frame.

3 Top up with DOT 4 hydraulic fluid, until the level is between the LOWER and UPPER level lines – do not overfill. Take care to avoid spills (see **Warning** on page 0•14).

4 Wipe any moisture off the diaphragm, opening it out to access the folds.

5 Ensure that the diaphragm is correctly seated before installing the plate and cap.

Tyres

The correct pressures

● The tyres must be checked when cold, not immediately after riding. Note that low tyre pressures may cause the tyre to slip on the rim or come off. High tyre pressures will cause abnormal tread wear and unsafe handling.

1 Remove the cap from the valve – if it is missing fit a new one.

● Use an accurate pressure gauge. Many garage forecourt gauges are wildly inaccurate. If you buy your own, spend as much as you can justify on a quality gauge.
● Correct air pressure will increase tyre life and provide maximum stability, handling capability and ride comfort.

Tyre care

● Check the tyres carefully for cuts, tears, embedded nails or other sharp objects and excessive wear. Operation of the motorcycle with excessively worn tyres is extremely hazardous, as traction and handling are directly affected. Also check the wheels for signs of damage and distortion.
● Check the condition of the tyre valve and ensure the dust cap is in place.
● Pick out any stones or nails which may have become embedded in the tyre tread. If

left, they will eventually penetrate through the casing and cause a puncture.
● If tyre damage is apparent, or unexplained loss of pressure is experienced, seek the advice of a tyre fitting specialist without delay.

Tyre tread depth

● At the time of writing UK law requires that tread depth must be at least 1 mm over 3/4 of the tread breadth all the way around the tyre, with no bald patches. Many riders, however, consider 2 mm tread depth minimum to be a safer limit. Triumph recommend a minimum of 2 mm for normal riding, or 3 mm on the rear tyre for high speed riding (over 80 mph, 130 km/h).
● Many tyres now incorporate wear indicators in the tread. Identify the triangular pointer or TWI mark on the tyre sidewall to locate the indicator bar. Fit a new tyre if the tread has worn down to the bar.

	Front	Rear
Daytona	34 psi (2.35 Bar)	36 psi (2.48 Bar)
Street Triple	34 psi (2.35 Bar)	42 psi (2.90 Bar)

2 Check the tyre pressures when the tyres are cold and keep them properly inflated.

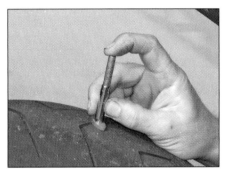

3 Measure tread depth at the centre of the tyre using a tread depth gauge.

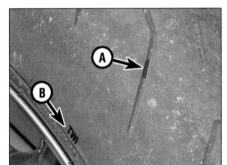

4 Tyre tread wear indicator bar A and its location marking B (usually either an arrow, a triangle or the letters TWI) on the sidewall.

Suspension, steering and final drive

Suspension and Steering

● Check that the front and rear suspension operates smoothly without binding. Check that there are no fluid leaks from the front fork seals or rear shock absorber.
● Check that the suspension is adjusted as required, where applicable (see Chapter 5).

● Check that the steering moves smoothly from lock-to-lock.

Final drive

● Check that the chain slack isn't excessive, and adjust it if necessary (see Chapter 1).
● If the chain looks dry, lubricate it (see Chapter 1).

Legal and safety

Lighting and signalling

● Take a minute to check that the headlight, tail light, brake light, instrument lights and turn signals all work correctly.
● Check that the horn sounds when the button is pushed.
● A working speedometer graduated in mph is a statutory requirement in the UK.

Safety

● Check that the throttle grip rotates smoothly and snaps shut when released, in all steering positions. Also check for the correct amount of freeplay (see Chapter 1).
● Check that the engine shuts off when the kill switch is operated.

● Check that sidestand return spring holds the stand securely up when retracted.
● Check the safety interlock circuit (see Chapter 1).
● Check that the clutch cable is working smoothly and with the correct freeplay (see Chapter 1).
● Check for any nuts and bolts that may have worked loose.

Fuel

● This may seem obvious, but check that you have enough fuel to complete your journey. Check for signs of fuel leakage – if any are found, rectify the cause immediately.
● Ensure you use the correct grade fuel – see Chapter 4 Specifications.

Chapter 1
Routine maintenance and Servicing

Contents

Degrees of difficulty

| Easy, suitable for novice with little experience | | Fairly easy, suitable for beginner with some experience | | Fairly difficult, suitable for competent DIY mechanic | | Difficult, suitable for experienced DIY mechanic | | Very difficult, suitable for expert DIY or professional | |

Engine

Spark plugs
- Type . . . . NGK CR9EK
- Electrode gap . . . . 0.7 mm

Engine idle speed. . . . . 1250 rpm
Cylinder identification. . . . . numbered 1 to 3 from left to right
SAIS solenoid valve resistance . . . . 20 to 25 ohms
Valve clearances (COLD engine)
- Intake valves. . . . . 0.10 to 0.20 mm
- Exhaust valves
  - Daytona models to VIN 381274 . . . . 0.275 to 0.325 mm
  - Daytona models from VIN 381275 . . . . 0.325 to 0.375 mm
  - Street Triple models to engine No. 452999 . . . . 0.275 to 0.325 mm
  - Street Triple models from engine No. 453000 . . . . 0.325 to 0.375 mm

Cycle parts

Brake pad minimum thickness. . . . . 1.5 mm
Drive chain slack . . . . 20 to 30 mm*
Chain stretch limit (see Section 2) . . . . 319 mm
Throttle opening cable freeplay (at twistgrip flange) . . . . 2 to 3 mm
Throttle closing cable freeplay (deflection). . . . . 2 to 3 mm
Clutch cable freeplay (at lever stock) . . . . 2 to 3 mm
Tyre pressures (cold). . . . . see *Pre-ride checks*

The range given is what we recommend and may differ from information in your handbook or on a sticker on the swingarm. If in doubt seek the advice of a Triumph service specialist within a dealership.

Lubricants and fluids

Engine oil type . . . . Semi or fully synthetic motorcycle engine oil, SAE 10W/40 or 15W/50, API grade SH or higher and JASO MA – Triumph recommend Mobil 1 Racing 4T oil

Engine oil capacity (see Text)
- Daytona models and Street Triple models to VIN 560476
  - Dry engine, new filter . . . . 3.5 litres
  - Wet fill with new filter . . . . 3.1 litres
  - Wet fill without new filter. . . . . 2.9 litres
- Street Triple models from VIN 560477
  - Dry engine, new filter . . . . 3.6 litres
  - Wet fill with new filter . . . . 3.2 litres
  - Wet fill without new filter. . . . . 3.0 litres

Coolant . . . . Triumph HD4X Hybrid OAT pre-mixed coolant **OR** a 50% distilled water / 50% corrosion inhibited ethylene glycol anti-freeze mix

Coolant capacity
- Daytona . . . . 2.4 litres
- Street Triple. . . . . 2.2 litres

Brake fluid . . . . DOT 4
Drive chain . . . . Chain lubricant suitable for O-ring chains – Triumph recommend Mobil Chain Spray or Mobilube HD 80
Steering head bearings . . . . Mobil Grease HP 222 or Lithium-based multi-purpose grease
Swingarm pivot and bearings, suspension linkage bearings. . . . . Mobil Grease HP 222 or Lithium-based multi-purpose grease
Wheel bearings and seal lips . . . . Mobil Grease HP 222 or Lithium-based multi-purpose grease
Gearchange lever/clutch and brake lever/brake pedal/sidestand pivots . . Mobil Grease HP 222 or Lithium-based multi-purpose grease
Cables . . . . Aerosol cable lubricant
Throttle grip . . . . Multi-purpose grease or dry film lubricant

Torque wrench settings

Coolant outlet pipe drain plug . . . . 10 Nm
Fork clamp bolts (top yoke) . . . . 26 Nm
Front footrest bracket bolts . . . . 24 Nm
Fuel pump mounting plate bolts . . . . 9 Nm
Handlebar clamp bolts – Daytona . . . . 26 Nm
Handlebar positioning bolts – Daytona . . . . 5 Nm
Oil drain plug . . . . 25 Nm
Oil filter . . . . 10 Nm
Rear axle nut . . . . 110 Nm
Secondary air injection reed valve cover bolts. . . . . 9 Nm
Spark plugs . . . . 12 Nm
Steering head bearing adjuster locknut . . . . 40 Nm
Steering head bearing adjuster nut (using the service tool)
- Initial (pre-load) setting. . . . . 40 Nm
- Final setting . . . . 15 Nm
Steering stem nut. . . . . 90 Nm

Note: *The Pre-ride checks outlined in the owner's manual, and described in detail at the front of this manual, covers those items which should be inspected on a daily basis. Always perform the pre-ride inspection at every maintenance interval (in addition to the procedures listed). The intervals listed below are the intervals recommended by the manufacturer.*

Pre-ride
☐ See *Pre-ride checks* at the beginning of this manual.

After the initial 500 miles (800 km)
Note: *This check is usually performed by a Triumph dealer after the first 500 miles (800 km) from new. Thereafter, maintenance is carried out according to the following intervals of the schedule.*

After the initial 12,000 miles (20,000 km)
☐ On Street Triple models from VIN 560477 check, and adjust if necessary, the camshaft timing (Chapter 2, Section 9)

Every 200 miles (300 km)
☐ Check, adjust, clean and lubricate the drive chain (Section 1)

Every 500 miles (800 km)
☐ Check the drive chain for wear and stretch and the sprockets for wear (Section 2)

Every 6000 miles (10,000 km) or 12 months (whichever comes sooner)
☐ Change the engine oil and filter and check the oil cooler (Section 3)
☐ Check the engine management system (Section 4)
☐ Check and adjust the throttle cables (Section 5)
☐ Check the cooling system (Section 6)
☐ Check the fuel system (Section 7)
☐ Check the suspension (Section 8)
☐ Check the brake pads (Section 9)
☐ Check the brake system and brake light switch operation (Section 10)
☐ Check the tightness of all nuts, bolts and fasteners (Section 11)
☐ Check the condition of the wheels and tyres (Section 12)
☐ Check the clutch (Section 13)
☐ Check the drive chain slider (Section 14)
☐ Check the spark plugs (Section 15)
☐ Check/adjust engine idle speed and throttle body synchronisation (Section 16)
☐ Check and adjust the steering head bearings (Section 17)

Every 12,000 miles (20,000 km) or two years (whichever comes sooner)
Carry out all the items under the 6000 mile (10,000 km) check, plus the following
☐ Renew the air filter element (Section 18)
☐ Check the secondary air injection system (Section 19)
☐ Check and adjust the valve clearances (Section 20)
☐ Lubricate the steering head bearings (Section 17)
☐ Check the wheel bearings (Section 21)
☐ Lubricate the clutch and brake levers, gearchange lever linkage, brake pedal pivot and sidestand pivots and the throttle and clutch cables (Section 22)
☐ Change the coolant (Section 23)
☐ Fit new spark plugs (Section 15)

Every two years
☐ Change the brake fluid (Section 10)

Every 18,000 miles (30,000 km) or three years (whichever comes sooner)
Carry out all the items under the 6000 mile (10,000 km) check, plus the following
☐ Check and adjust the exhaust control valve cables – Daytona models only (Section 24)

Every 24,000 miles (40,000 km) or four years (whichever comes sooner)
Carry out all the items under the 12,000 mile (20,000 km) check, plus the following
☐ Fit new EVAP system hoses – California models only (see Chapter 4)

Every 30,000 miles (50,000 km) or five years (whichever comes sooner)
☐ Change the front fork oil (Section 25)

Non-scheduled maintenance
☐ Fit new fuel system hoses (Section 7)
☐ Fit new brake master cylinder and caliper seals (see Section 10)
☐ Fit new brake hoses (Section 10)
☐ Lubricate the swingarm and suspension linkage bearings (Section 8)
☐ Check the sidestand and safety interlock circuit (Section 26)
☐ Check the battery (Section 27)
☐ Check and adjust the headlight aim (Chapter 8)
☐ Check the cylinder compression and engine oil pressure (Chapter 2, Section 3)

Daytona left side

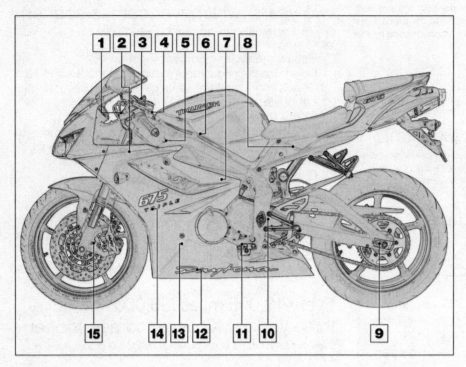

1 Clutch cable adjuster at upper end
2 Coolant pressure cap
3 Front fork pre-load and rebound damping adjuster
4 Steering head bearing adjuster
5 SAIS control valve
6 Air filter
7 Coolant reservoir
8 Battery
9 Drive chain adjuster
10 Drive chain slider
11 Sidestand switch
12 Engine oil drain plug
13 Engine oil filter
14 Radiator bottom hose disconnection point for coolant draining
15 Front fork compression damping adjuster

Daytona right side

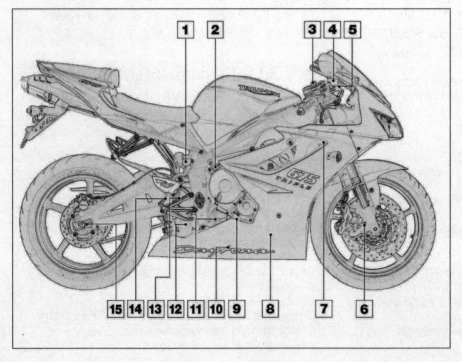

1 Rear brake fluid reservoir
2 Engine oil filler cap
3 Front fork pre-load and rebound damping adjuster
4 Front brake fluid reservoir
5 Throttle cable adjuster at upper end
6 Front fork compression damping adjuster
7 Coolant bleed hole screw in radiator
8 Drain plug in coolant outlet pipe
9 Clutch cable adjuster at lower end
10 Exhaust control valve
11 Engine oil dipstick
12 Exhaust control valve actuator
13 Rear brake light switch
14 Rear brake pedal height adjuster
15 Drive chain adjuster

Street Triple 2007 to 2012 left side

1 Coolant pressure cap
2 Clutch cable adjuster at upper end
3 Steering head bearing adjuster
4 SAIS control valve
5 Coolant bleed hole screw in top hose
6 Air filter
7 Rear shock compression damping adjuster (R model)
8 Coolant reservoir
9 Battery
10 Drive chain adjuster
11 Rear shock rebound damping adjuster (R model)
12 Drive chain slider
13 Sidestand switch
14 Engine oil drain plug
15 Engine oil filter
16 Radiator bottom hose disconnection point for coolant draining
17 Front fork pre-load and rebound damping adjuster (R model)
18 Front fork compression damping adjuster (R model)

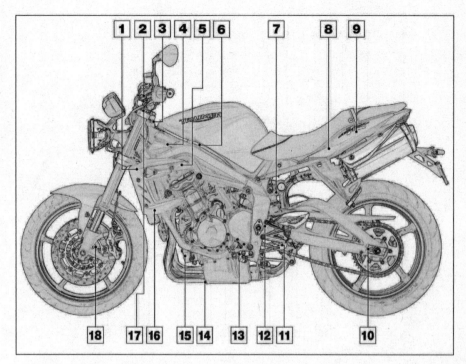

Street Triple 2007 to 2012 right side

1 Rear brake fluid reservoir
2 Engine oil filler cap
3 Front brake fluid reservoir (R type shown)
4 Throttle cable adjuster at upper end
5 Front fork pre-load and rebound damping adjuster (R model)
6 Front fork compression damping adjuster (R model)
7 Coolant bleed hole screw in radiator
8 Drain plug in coolant outlet pipe
9 Clutch cable adjuster at lower end
10 Engine oil dipstick
11 Rear brake light switch
12 Rear brake pedal height adjuster
13 Drive chain adjuster

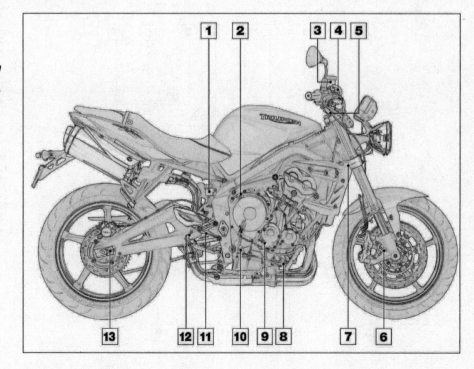

Component locations

Street Triple R 2013-on left side

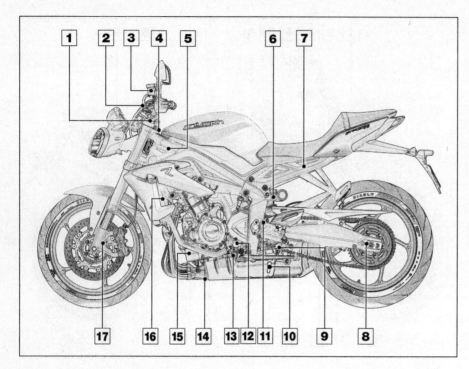

1 Front fork pre-load and rebound damping
   adjuster (R/RX model)
2 Clutch cable adjuster at upper end
3 Front brake fluid reservoir (R/RX model)
4 Steering head bearing adjuster
5 SAIS control valve
6 Rear shock compression damping adjuster
   (R/RX model)
7 Battery
8 Drive chain adjuster
9 Rear shock rebound damping adjuster
   (R/RX model)
10 Coolant reservoir level marks
11 Drive chain slider
12 Coolant reservoir filler cap
13 Sidestand switch
14 Engine oil drain plug
15 Engine oil filter
16 Radiator bottom hose disconnection point
   for coolant draining
17 Front fork compression damping adjuster
   (R model)

Street Triple 2013-on right side

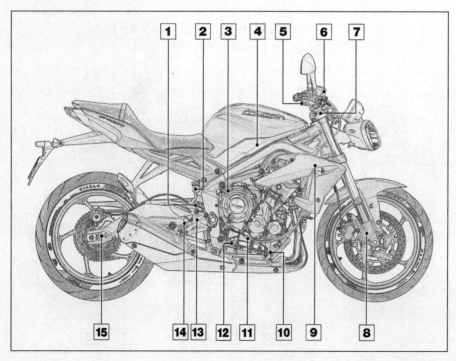

1 Rear shock pre-load adjuster (standard
   model)
2 Rear brake fluid reservoir
3 Engine oil filler cap
4 Air filter
5 Throttle cable adjuster at upper end
6 Front brake fluid reservoir (standard model)
7 Front fork pre-load and rebound damping
   adjuster (R/RX model)
8 Front fork compression damping adjuster
   (R/RX model)
9 Coolant pressure cap
10 Drain plug in coolant outlet pipe
11 Clutch cable adjuster at lower end
12 Engine oil dipstick
13 Rear brake light switch
14 Rear brake pedal height adjuster
15 Drive chain adjuster

1 This Chapter is designed to help the home mechanic maintain his/her motorcycle for safety, economy, long life and peak performance.

2 Deciding where to start or plug into the routine maintenance schedule depends on several factors. If the warranty period on your motorcycle has just expired, and if it has been maintained according to the warranty standards, you may want to pick up routine maintenance as it coincides with the next mileage or calendar interval. If you have owned the machine for some time but have never performed any maintenance on it, then you may want to start at the beginning and include all frequent procedures to ensure that nothing important is overlooked. If you have just had a major engine overhaul, then you

should start the engine maintenance routines from the beginning. If you have a used machine and have no knowledge of its history or maintenance record, you should combine all the checks into one large initial service and then settle into the maintenance schedule prescribed.

3 Before beginning any maintenance or repair, the machine should be cleaned thoroughly, especially around the oil filter, valve cover, side panels, etc. Cleaning will help ensure that dirt does not contaminate the engine and will allow you to detect wear and damage that could otherwise easily go unnoticed.

4 Many of the bolts used in the building of the engine are of the Torx type. Unless you are already equipped with a good range of

Torx bits, you are advised to obtain a set. Make sure you get bits that can be used in conjunction with a socket set so that a torque wrench can be applied – a Torx key set will not be adequate on its own, though will be useful in addition to the bits.

5 Certain maintenance information is sometimes printed on decals attached to the motorcycle. If any information on the decals differs from that included here, use the information on the decal.

6 Note that in many cases, Triumph use the machine's VIN number as a means of identification rather than the year of manufacture. Always check the VIN number against the details given in this manual to ensure you follow the correct procedure.

Maintenance procedures

1 Drive chain check, adjustment, cleaning and lubrication

Check

1 As the chain stretches with wear, adjustment will periodically be necessary. A neglected drive chain won't last long and can quickly damage the sprockets. Routine chain adjustment and lubrication isn't difficult and will ensure maximum chain and sprocket life.

2 To check the chain slack the bike should be supported upright with no extra weight on it. Make sure the transmission is in neutral.

3 Push up on the bottom run of the chain and measure the slack midway between the two sprockets **(see illustration)**. Compare your measurement to that listed in this Chapter's Specifications. Since the chain will rarely wear

evenly, resulting in a tight spot, move the bike so that another section of chain can be checked – do this several times to check the entire length of chain. Any adjustment should be based upon the measurement taken at the tightest point.

4 In some cases where lubrication has been neglected, corrosion and galling may cause the links to bind and kink, which effectively shortens the chain's length **(see illustration)**. Any such links should be thoroughly cleaned and worked free. If they are rusty or the links have seized together and cannot be freed replace the chain with a new one. If you find a tight area, clean off the oil and dirt, mark it with felt pen or paint, and repeat the measurement after the bike has been ridden. If the chain's still tight or kinked in the same area it can damage the transmission output shaft bearing, so replace it with a new one (see Chapter 6).

Adjustment

5 Make sure the transmission is in neutral. Position the bike so the tightest point of the chain is at the centre of its bottom run.

6 Slacken the axle nut **(see illustration)**.

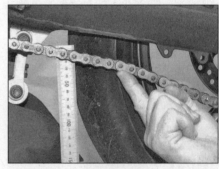

1.3 Push up on the chain and measure the slack

1.4 Neglect has caused the links in this chain to kink

1.6 Slacken the rear axle nut (arrowed)

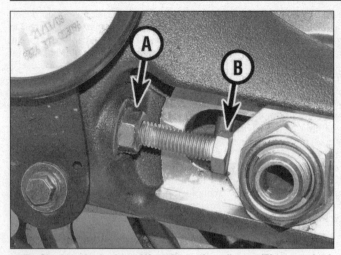

1.7a Slacken the locknut (A) and turn the adjuster (B) as required

1.7b Check the relative position of the back edge of each adjustment marker with the marks on the swingarm

7 Slacken the adjuster locknut on each side of the swingarm **(see illustration)**. Turn the adjusters evenly, anti-clockwise to reduce freeplay and clockwise to increase it, until the amount of freeplay specified at the beginning of the Chapter is obtained at the centre of the bottom run of the chain. Following chain adjustment, check that the back edge of each chain adjustment marker is in the same position in relation to the marks on the swingarm **(see illustration)**. It is important each adjuster aligns with the same mark; if not, the rear wheel will be out of alignment with the front. Also check that there is no clearance between the head of each adjuster and the front of each adjustment marker – push or kick the wheel forwards to eliminate any freeplay.

> **HAYNES HiNT** *Refer to Chapter 6 for information on checking wheel alignment.*

8 If there is a discrepancy in the chain adjuster positions, adjust one of them so that its position is exactly the same as the other. Check the chain freeplay as described above and readjust if necessary.
9 Check again that there is no clearance between the head of each adjuster and the front of each adjustment marker. Tighten the axle nut to the torque setting specified at the beginning of the Chapter **(see illustration)**. Tighten the adjuster locknuts **(see illustration 1.7a)**. Recheck the adjustment.

Cleaning and lubrication

10 If required, wash the chain in paraffin (kerosene), then wipe it off and allow it to dry, using compressed air if available **(see illustration)**. If the chain is excessively dirty remove it and soak it in a suitable

container filled with paraffin (see Chapter 5).
Caution: Don't use petrol (gasoline), solvent or other cleaning fluids which might damage the internal sealing properties of the chain. Don't use high-pressure water. The entire process shouldn't take longer than ten minutes – if it does, the O-rings in the chain rollers could be damaged.
11 The best time to lubricate the chain is after the motorcycle has been ridden - when the chain is warm, the lubricant will penetrate the joints between the side plates better than when cold. Use the specified chain lube, or if not available one which is marked as being suitable for O-ring chains; other types may contain solvents that could damage the O-rings. Apply the lubricant to the area where the side plates overlap – not the middle of the rollers (see

1.9 Tighten the axle nut to the specified torque setting

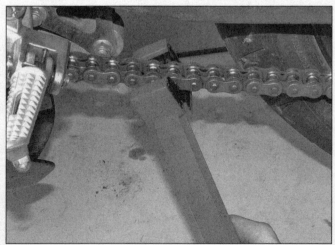

1.10 Specially-shaped chain cleaning brushes are available from good suppliers

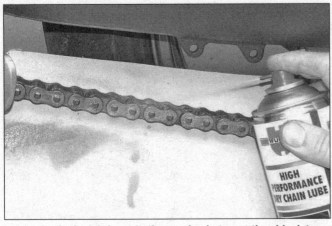

1.11 Apply the lubricant to the overlap between the sideplates

2.2 Undo the screws (arrowed) and remove the chainguard

illustration). Triumph recommend that the bike should not be ridden for 8 hours after applying lubricant to allow it to penetrate between the chain components, so it's a good idea to do this at the end of the day. Before riding the bike wipe off any excess lubricant.

> **HAYNES HiNT** *Apply the lubricant to the top of the lower chain run, so centrifugal force will work it into the chain when the bike is moving. After applying the lubricant, let it soak in for a few minutes, then wipe off any excess.*

2 Drive chain and sprockets wear and stretch check

1 Make sure the transmission is in neutral. Support the bike on its sidestand.
2 Remove the chainguard **(see illustration)**.
3 Check the entire length of the chain for damaged rollers, loose links and pins, and missing O-rings. Fit a new chain if damage is found (see Chapter 6). **Note:** *Never fit a new chain onto old sprockets, and never use the old chain if you fit new sprockets – replace the chain and sprockets as a set.*

4 To check the amount of chain wear (stretch), obtain a 10 to 20 kg (20 to 40 lb) weight and hang it from the middle of the bottom run of the chain. Measure along the top run the length of 20 links (from the centre of the 1st pin to the centre of the 21st pin) and compare the result with the service limit specified at the beginning of the Chapter. Rotate the wheel so that several sections of the chain are measured, then calculate the average. If the chain exceeds the service limit it must be replaced with a new one (see Chapter 6).
5 Remove the front sprocket cover (see Chapter 6). Check the teeth on the front and rear sprockets for wear **(see illustration)**.

3 Engine oil and filter change

> ⚠ *Warning: Be careful when draining the oil, as the exhaust pipes, the engine, and the oil itself can cause severe burns.*

Note: *The oil volume of the engine was increased by 0.5 litre for Daytona models from VIN 381275-on (and also on 2009 and later Street Triples) and a new shorter dipstick was fitted to accommodate this. The new oil volume can be applied retrospectively to all earlier Daytona*

models and all Street Triple models fitted with the longer dipstick – either replace your dipstick with the new shorter one, or use the upper level line on the old long dipstick as the lower level line for the increased oil volume. If you are in doubt as to which dipstick is fitted on your bike, or as to how much oil you should be putting in, ask your Triumph dealer for advice.

1 Consistent routine oil and filter changes are the single most important maintenance procedure you can perform on a motorcycle. The oil not only lubricates the internal parts of the engine, transmission and clutch, but it also acts as a coolant, a cleaner, a sealant, and a protector. Because of these demands, the oil takes a terrific amount of abuse and should be changed often with new oil of the recommended grade and type. Saving a little money on the difference in cost between a good oil and a cheap oil won't pay off if the engine is damaged. The oil filter should be changed with every oil change.
2 Before changing the oil, warm up the engine so the oil will drain easily. Place the motorcycle on its sidestand, making sure it is on level ground. Position a clean drain tray below the oil drain plug and filter on the front of the engine.
3 Unscrew the oil filler cap from the clutch cover to vent it and to act as a reminder that there is no oil in the engine **(see illustration)**.

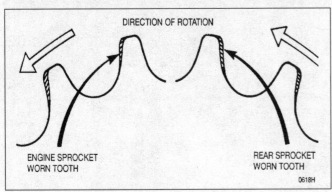

2.5 Check the sprockets in the areas indicated to see if they are worn excessively

DIRECTION OF ROTATION

ENGINE SPROCKET WORN TOOTH

REAR SPROCKET WORN TOOTH

0618H

3.3 Remove the oil filler cap from the clutch cover

3.4a Unscrew the oil drain plug . . .

3.4b . . . and allow the oil to drain

3.5a Unscrew the filter using a filter removal socket or strap . . .

3.5b . . . and drain it into the tray

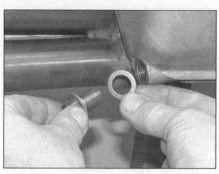

3.6 Fit the drain plug using a new sealing washer and tighten it to the specified torque

4 Unscrew the oil drain plug and allow the oil to flow into the drain tray **(see illustrations)**. Discard the sealing washer as a new one must be fitted.

5 Unscrew the filter using a filter removal socket or a strap wrench and tip any residual oil into the drain tray **(see illustrations)**. Triumph can supply an oil filter tool (Part No. T3880313).

6 When the oil has completely drained, fit the plug into the sump using a new sealing washer and tighten it to the torque setting specified at the beginning of the Chapter **(see illustration)**. Avoid overtightening, as you will damage the sump.

7 Smear some new engine oil onto the rubber seal on the filter, then screw the filter onto the engine until the seal just seats **(see illustrations)**. If a filter socket is available, tighten the filter to the torque setting specified at the beginning of the Chapter. Otherwise, tighten the filter as tight as possible by hand, or by the number of turns specified on the filter or its packaging. **Note:** *Do not use a strap or chain type removing tool to tighten the filter as you will damage the filter body.*

8 Refill the engine to the correct level using the recommended type and amount of oil (see Specifications and *Pre-ride checks,* and the **Note** at the beginning of this Section). Install

3.7a Smear some clean oil onto the seal . . .

3.7b . . . then thread the filter onto the engine and tighten it as described

the dipstick and filler cap, using new O-rings if the old ones are damaged, deformed or deteriorated **(see illustration 3.3)**. Start the engine and let it run for two or three minutes. Stop the engine, wait a few minutes, then check the oil level (see *Pre-ride checks*). If necessary, add more oil to bring the level up to the correct level on the dipstick. Check that there are no leaks around the filter and drain plug. If the filter is leaking tighten it some more. If the drain plug is leaking make sure it is tightened to the correct torque, and if it is you will need to drain the oil again and replace the sealing washer with a new one.

9 Refer to Chapter 2, Section 6, and check the oil cooler and its hoses for damage and leaks. Replace any components as necessary with new ones.

10 The old oil drained from the engine cannot be re-used and should be disposed of properly. Check with your local refuse disposal company, disposal facility or environmental agency to see whether they will accept the used oil for recycling. Don't pour used oil into drains or onto the ground. Remember to drain all the old oil from the filter (you can punch a hole in the filter to ensure it drains fully) into the drain pan. Note that the old filter should be taken to the oil disposal facility rather than disposed of with the household rubbish.

> **HAYNES HiNT** *Check the old oil carefully – if it is very metallic coloured, then the engine is experiencing wear from break-in (new engine) or from insufficient lubrication. If there are flakes or chips of metal in the oil, then something is drastically wrong internally and the engine will have to be disassembled for inspection and repair. If there are pieces of fibre-like material in the oil, the clutch is experiencing excessive wear and should be checked.*

Note: It is illegal and anti-social to dump oil down the drain. To find the location of your local oil recycling bank in the UK, call 03708 506 506 or visit www.oilbankline.org.uk
In the US note that any oil supplier must accept used oil for recycling.

4 Engine management system check

Note: *The idle speed is controlled by the idle air control valve, which in turn is controlled by the electronic control module (ECM). Idle speed cannot be manually adjusted – it can only be done using the diagnostic tool.*

1 The engine management system should be checked for any stored diagnostic fault codes. To do this, the Triumph diagnostic tool is essential. Take your machine to a dealer and have them check the system – it should not take them long. Note that this task is not an option for the DIY mechanic, not only because the diagnostic tool would be prohibitively expensive, but because an authorisation code is required to operate it and these are only available to Triumph dealers.

2 If any problems with the system occur during use, the malfunction indicator light (MIL) in the instrument cluster will illuminate. If this happens, the management system switches itself into 'limp home' mode, so that in theory you should not be left stranded. Depending on the problem, it is possible that you will notice no difference in the running of the motorcycle. In order to diagnose the fault and to turn the MIL off, the diagnostic tool is essential, so again the machine must be taken to a Triumph dealer.

3 Further information on the system, including all tests and checks that can be performed without the Triumph diagnostic tool, is contained in Chapter 4.

5 Throttle cable check

1 Make sure the throttle twistgrip rotates easily from fully closed to fully open with the front wheel turned at various angles. The twistgrip should return automatically from fully open to fully closed when released.

2 If the throttle sticks, this is probably due to a cable fault. Remove the cable (see Chapter 4) and lubricate it (see Section 22). If the inner cable still does not run smoothly in the outer cable, fit a new cable. With the cable removed, check that the twistgrip runs smoothly and freely around the handlebar – dirt and debris combined with a lack of lubrication can cause the action to be stiff. Install the lubricated or new cable, making sure it is correctly routed (see Chapter 4). If this fails to improve the operation of the throttle, the fault could lie in the throttle bodies. Remove the airbox and check the action of the throttle linkage and butterflies (see Chapter 4).

3 With the throttle operating smoothly, check for a small amount of freeplay in the opening cable. This is measured in terms of the amount of twistgrip rotation before the throttle opens **(see illustration)**. Compare the amount to that listed in this Chapter's Specifications. If it's incorrect, adjust the cables as follows.

4 An adjuster is incorporated at the twistgrip end of the opening cable – slide the rubber boots back to expose it **(see illustration)**. Slacken the locknut on the adjuster, then turn the adjuster until the specified amount of freeplay is obtained (see this Chapter's Specifications), then retighten the locknut.

5.3 Check for the specified amount of free rotation in the twistgrip

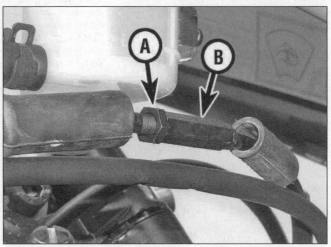

5.4 Pull back the rubber boots to expose the opening throttle cable adjuster locknut (A) and adjuster (B)

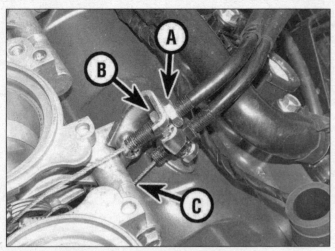

5.7 Throttle opening cable locknut (A) and adjuster nut (B). Throttle closing cable deflection measurement point (C)

6.3 Squeeze the hoses to check for cracks, deterioration and hardening

Turn the adjuster in to increase freeplay and out to reduce it.

5 If the opening cable adjuster has reached its limit of adjustment, reset it so that it is halfway along its adjustment limit, then adjust both cables at the throttle body end as follows.

6 Remove the fuel tank and the airbox (see Chapter 4).

7 Fully slacken the locknut holding the opening (upper) cable in the bracket to free the adjuster nut from its holding tabs **(see illustration)**. Thread the adjuster nut up the cable to increase freeplay, and down to decrease it, then draw it up against the bracket and check the freeplay, readjusting as required until the specified amount of freeplay is obtained. Tighten the locknut onto the bracket on completion. With the throttle fully closed, check that there is the specified amount of freeplay (measured as total deflection of the cable inner wire) in the closing (lower) cable and adjust it at the bracket in the same way.

8 Further adjustments can now be made at the twistgrip end. If the cables cannot be adjusted as specified, replace them with new ones (see Chapter 4).

9 Check that the throttle twistgrip operates smoothly and snaps shut quickly when released. Install the airbox and fuel tank (see Chapter 4).

⚠ **Warning: Turn the handlebars all the way through their travel with the engine idling. Idle speed should not change. If it does, the cable may be routed incorrectly. Correct this condition before riding the bike.**

6   Cooling system checks

⚠ **Warning: The engine must be cool before beginning this procedure.**

1 Check the coolant level in the reservoir (see Pre-ride checks).

2 On Daytona models remove both fairing side panels (see Chapter 7).

3 Check the entire cooling system for evidence of leaks. Examine each rubber coolant hose along its entire length. Look for cracks, abrasions and other damage. Squeeze each hose at various points **(see illustration)**. They should feel firm, yet pliable, and return to their original shape when released. If they are dried out or hard, replace them with new ones.

4 Check for evidence of leaks at each cooling system joint. If necessary, tighten the hose clips carefully to prevent future leaks.

5 To prevent leakage of water from the cooling system to the lubrication system and vice versa, two seals are fitted on the water pump shaft. There is a drain hole between the seals in the seal housing section of the pump. If either seal fails, the drain allows the coolant or oil to escape via a tube through a hole in the bottom of the sump and prevents them mixing **(see illustration)**. The seal on the water pump side is of the mechanical type which bears on the rear face of the impeller. The second seal, which is mounted behind the mechanical seal is of the normal feathered lip type. If on inspection the drain hole shows

signs of coolant leakage, remove the pump and replace it with a new one (see Chapter 3) – the seals are not available separately.

6 Check the radiator for leaks and other damage **(see illustration)**. Leaks in the radiator leave tell-tale scale deposits or coolant stains on the outside of the core below the leak. If leaks are noted, remove the radiator (see Chapter 3) and either have it repaired by a professional or replace it with a new one.

Caution: Do not use a liquid leak stopping compound to try to repair leaks.

7 Check the radiator fins for mud, dirt and insects, which may impede the flow of air through the radiator. If the fins are dirty, remove the radiator (see Chapter 3) and clean it using water or low pressure compressed air directed through the fins from the rear face of the radiator. If the fins are bent or distorted, straighten them carefully with a screwdriver. If airflow is restricted by bent or damaged fins over more than 30% of the radiator's surface area, fit a new radiator.

8 On Street Triple models to VIN 560476 displace the left-hand radiator cowl, and on Street Triple models from VIN 560477 remove the right-hand radiator cowl (see Chapter 7).

9 Remove the pressure cap from the filler neck

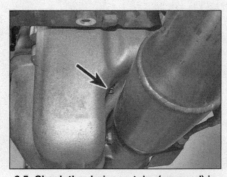

6.5 Check the drainage tube (arrowed) in the sump for signs of leakage

6.6 Check the radiator joints and fins for damage and leakage

in the radiator as follows: turn the cap anti-clockwise until it reaches a stop – if you hear a hissing sound (indicating there is still pressure in the system), wait until it stops; now press down on the cap and continue turning it until it can be removed **(see illustration)**. Check the condition of the coolant in the system. If it is rust-coloured or if accumulations of scale are visible, drain, flush and refill the system (See Section 23). Check the cap seals for cracks and other damage – maintaining a good seal to retain the pressure in the cooling system is essential to the efficient function of the system. If in doubt about the pressure cap's condition, have it tested by a Triumph dealer or replace it with a new one – the expense is minimal. Fit the cap by turning it clockwise until it reaches the first stop, then push down on it and continue turning until it reaches the main stop.

10 Check the antifreeze content of the coolant with an antifreeze hydrometer. Sometimes coolant looks like it's in good condition, but might be too weak to offer adequate protection. If the hydrometer indicates a weak mixture, drain, flush and refill the system (see Section 23).

11 Start the engine and let it reach normal operating temperature, then check for leaks again. As the coolant temperature increases beyond normal, the fan should come on automatically and the temperature should begin to drop. If it doesn't, refer to Chapter 3 and check the fan motor, relay and fan circuit carefully, then if the fan still does not work, refer to Chapter 4 and check the engine coolant temperature sensor and the engine management system, which control the fan. Note that if the engine is switched off while the fan is running, the fan should continue to run until the coolant temperature has dropped to a normal level.

12 If the coolant level is consistently low, and no evidence of leaks can be found, have the entire system pressure checked by a Triumph dealer.

7 Fuel system checks

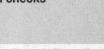

⚠ **Warning: Petrol (gasoline) is extremely flammable, so take extra precautions when you work on any part of the fuel system. Don't smoke or allow open flames or bare light bulbs near the work area, and don't work in a garage where a natural gas-type appliance is present. If you spill any fuel on your skin, rinse it off immediately with soap and water. When you perform any kind of work on the fuel system, wear safety glasses and have a fire extinguisher suitable for a Class B type fire (flammable liquids) on hand.**

General checks

1 Remove the fuel tank (see Chapter 4). Check the entire system for signs of leaks, deterioration or damage; in particular check that there are no leaks from the fuel feed hose and its connectors, the fuel rail and injectors, and from the fuel pump assembly sealing ring on the underside of the fuel tank. Also check the condition of the fuel tank drain and breather hoses and the airbox hoses. Replace any hoses which are cracked or have deteriorated with new ones (see below).

2 Refer to Chapter 4 for removal of the fuel rail if fuel leakage is evident.

3 If the tank has been leaking from the fuel pump seal, tightening the mounting plate bolts may help – remove the tank (see Chapter 4), then rest it upside down on some rag to do this. To ensure the plate is evenly seated, slacken the bolts a little first, then tighten them evenly and a little at a time in a criss-cross pattern to the torque setting specified at the beginning of the Chapter. If leaks persists, remove the pump assembly and replace the seal with a new one (see Chapter 4).

4 Check all throttle body hoses for loose connections, cracks and deterioration, and replace them with new ones if necessary.

5 Check the secondary air injection system hoses (see Section 19).

6 On California models, check the EVAP system hoses for loose connections, cracks and deterioration and replace them with new ones if necessary. At the specified service interval new hoses should be fitted whatever the apparent condition of the existing ones (see Chapter 4).

Fuel filter

7 A fuel filter is incorporated in the fuel pump assembly inside the tank.

8 If fuel starvation occurs and no other fault can be found it is possible the filter is blocked. The filter is part of the fuel pump assembly and is not available separately, so a new pump must be fitted (see Chapter 4).

Hose renewal

9 Remove the fuel tank, and if necessary the airbox, as required for access to the hose(s) being replaced (see Chapter 4). Refer to the procedure in the relevant Section of Chapter 4 and detach the hose at each end, noting how it is secured and its routing. When fitting the new hose make sure it is correctly routed and secured as before.

10 Run the engine and check that there are no leaks before taking the machine out on the road.

8 Suspension checks

1 The suspension components must be maintained in top operating condition to ensure rider safety. Loose, worn or damaged suspension parts decrease the motorcycle's stability and control.

Front suspension

2 While standing alongside the motorcycle, apply the front brake and push on the handlebars to compress the forks several times **(see illustration)**. Check they move up-and-down smoothly without binding. If binding is felt, the forks should be disassembled and inspected (see Chapter 5).

6.9 Remove the pressure cap from the radiator filler neck as described

8.2 Pump the forks to check their action

8.3 Check the fork inner tube (arrowed) below the seal for leaks, pitting and corrosion

8.5 Check for leakage on the damper rod (arrowed)

3 Inspect the fork inner tube for signs of scratches, corrosion and pitting, and oil leakage **(see illustration)**. Carefully lever the dust seal out of the outer tube using a flat-bladed screwdriver and inspect the area around the fork oil seal. Any scratches, corrosion and pitting in the area of fork travel will cause premature seal failure. If the damage is excessive new inner tubes should be installed (see Chapter 5). If oil leaks are evident, new oil seals must be fitted (see Chapter 5).

4 Check the tightness of all suspension nuts and bolts to be sure none have worked loose, referring to the torque settings specified at the beginning of Chapter 5.

Rear suspension

5 Check the rear shock absorber for fluid leaks on the damper rod **(see illustration)**. If leaks are found, a new shock should be installed (see Chapter 5).

6 With the aid of an assistant to support the bike, compress the rear suspension several times. It should move up and down freely without binding or rough spots or noises. If necessary the worn or faulty component must be identified and replaced with a new one. The problem could be due to the shock absorber, the suspension linkage components or the swingarm.

7 Support the motorcycle using an auxiliary stand so that the rear wheel is off the ground. Grab the swingarm and rock it from side to side – there should be no discernible movement at the rear **(see illustration)**. If there's a little movement or a slight clicking can be heard, inspect the tightness of all the rear suspension mounting bolts and nuts, referring to the torque settings specified at the beginning of Chapter 5, and re-check for movement. Next, grasp the top of the rear wheel and pull it upwards – there should be no discernible freeplay before the shock absorber begins to compress **(see illustration)**. Any freeplay felt in either check indicates worn bearings in the suspension linkage or swingarm, or worn shock absorber mountings. The worn components must be replaced with new ones (see Chapter 5).

8 To make an accurate assessment of the swingarm bearings, remove the rear wheel (see Chapter 6) and the bolt securing the suspension drop link to the swingarm (see Chapter 5). Grasp the rear of the swingarm with one hand and place your other hand at the junction of the swingarm and the frame. Try to move the rear of the swingarm from side-to-side. Any wear (play) in the bearings should be felt as movement between the swingarm and the frame at the front. If there is any play the swingarm will be felt to move forward and backward at the front (not from side-to-side). Next, move the swingarm up and down through its full travel. It should move freely, without any binding or rough spots or noises. If any play in the swingarm is noted or if the swingarm does not move freely, remove the swingarm and inspect the bearings (see Chapter 5).

9 Check the tightness of all suspension nuts and bolts to be sure none have worked loose, referring to the torque settings specified at the beginning of Chapter 5.

8.7a Checking for play in the swingarm bearings

8.7b Checking for play in the suspension linkage bearings

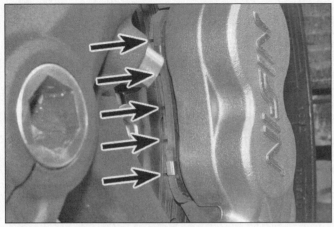

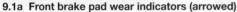

9.1a Front brake pad wear indicators (arrowed)

9.1b Rear brake pad wear indicator (arrowed)

Swingarm and suspension linkage bearing lubrication

10 Over a period of time the grease will harden and dirt will penetrate the bearings.

11 The rear suspension components are not equipped with grease nipples. Remove the swingarm and the suspension linkage as described in Chapter 5 for re-greasing of the bearings.

9 Brake pad wear check

1 Each brake pad has one or more wear indicators that can be viewed without removing the pads from the caliper. The groove(s) in the pad friction material form the wear indicators. On the front brake pads when the friction material has worn to the bottom of the grooves (i.e. the grooves are only just or no longer visible), the pads must be replaced with new ones **(see illustration)**. On the rear brake pads when the friction material has worn to the start of the groove the pads must be replaced with new ones **(see illustration)**. If required, remove the pads and measure the amount of friction material remaining – the

minimum is 1.5 mm. **Note:** *Some after-market pads may use different indicators.*

2 If the pads are dirty, or you are in doubt as to the amount of friction material remaining, remove them for inspection (see Chapter 6).

Caution: Do not allow the pads to wear beyond the wear limit indicator or minimum thickness.

3 Always renew brake pads in sets and renew the pads in both front brake calipers at the same time. If the pads appear to be wearing unevenly it is likely that a piston is sticking or has seized – remove the caliper and the pads and check the operation of each piston (see Chapter 6).

10 Brake system check

General check

1 A routine general check of the brake system will ensure that any problems are discovered and remedied before the rider's safety is jeopardised.

2 Check the brake lever and pedal for looseness, improper or rough action, excessive play, bends, and other damage. Replace any

damaged parts with new ones (see Chapter 5). Clean and lubricate the lever and pedal pivots if their action is stiff or rough (see Section 22).

3 If the lever or pedal action feels spongy bleed the brakes (see Chapter 6).

4 Make sure all brake component fasteners are tight. Check the brake pads for wear (see Section 9) and make sure the fluid level in the reservoirs is correct (see *Pre-ride checks*). Check that there is no sign of fluid leakage at the hose connections and that the hoses between the calipers and master cylinders are not cracked or damaged.

5 Make sure the brake light comes on when the front brake lever is pulled in. The front brake light switch, mounted on the underside of the lever bracket, is not adjustable. If it fails to operate properly, check it (see Chapter 8).

6 Make sure the brake light comes on just before the rear brake takes effect. The switch is operated mechanically by a spring connected to the brake pedal. If it fails to operate properly, first check that the spring is still attached to both the pedal and the switch pullrod **(see illustration)**. If adjustment is necessary, hold the switch and turn the adjuster nut on the switch body until the brake light is activated when required **(see illustration)**. If the brake light comes on too late, turn the nut clockwise.

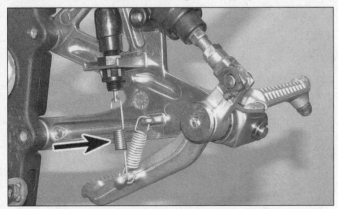

10.6a Make sure the brake light switch spring (arrowed) is secure at each end

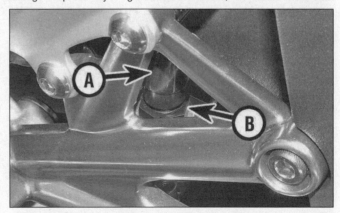

10.6b Hold the brake light switch (A) and turn the adjuster nut (B)

If the brake light comes on too soon or is permanently on, turn the nut anti-clockwise. If the switch doesn't operate the brake light, check it (see Chapter 8).

7 The front brake lever has a span adjuster which alters the distance of the lever from the handlebar to suit different hand sizes. On standard Daytona models and all Street Triples each setting is identified by a number on the adjuster which aligns with the arrow on the lever bracket. Pull the lever away from the handlebar and turn the adjuster ring until the setting which best suits the rider is obtained **(see illustration)**. There are six settings on Daytona models and four on Street Triples – setting 1 gives the largest span. When making adjustment ensure that the pin set in the lever bracket is engaged in its detent in the adjuster. On Daytona R models turn the adjuster screw clockwise to increase the span and anti-clockwise to reduce it.

Brake hoses

8 The hoses will deteriorate with age and in addition to the regular inspection described in Step 4, consideration should be given to renewing the hoses after a long period regardless of their apparent condition (see Chapter 6).
9 Always replace the banjo union sealing washers with new ones when fitting new hoses. Refill the system with new brake fluid and bleed the system as described in Chapter 6.

Brake caliper and master cylinder seals

10 Brake system seals will deteriorate with age and lose their effectiveness, leading to sticky operation of the brake master cylinders or the pistons in the brake calipers, or fluid loss. They should be replaced with new ones if fluid leakage or a sticking action is apparent.
11 Replace all the seals in each caliper and master cylinder as a set; master cylinder seals are supplied as a kit along with a new piston and spring (see Chapter 6).

Brake fluid change

12 The brake fluid should be changed at the prescribed interval or whenever a master cylinder or caliper overhaul is carried out.

Refer to Chapter 6, Section 10 for details. Ensure that all the old fluid is pumped from the hydraulic system and that the level in the fluid reservoir is checked and the brakes tested before riding the motorcycle.

11 Nuts and bolts tightness check

1 Since vibration of the machine tends to loosen fasteners, all nuts, bolts, screws, etc. should be periodically checked for proper tightness. If you feel the engine vibrating more than usual, check all engine mountings before assuming there are extensive internal problems.
2 Pay particular attention to the following:
● Spark plugs
● Engine oil drain plug
● Coolant drain plug
● Gearchange lever, brake and clutch lever, and brake pedal bolts
● Footrest and stand bolts
● Engine mounting bolts
● Shock absorber and suspension linkage bolts and swingarm pivot
● Handlebar clamp bolts
● Front axle and axle clamp bolts
● Front fork clamp bolts (top and bottom yoke)
● Rear axle nut
● Brake caliper mounting bolts
● Brake hose banjo bolts and caliper bleed valves
● Brake disc bolts
● Exhaust system bolts/nuts
3 If a torque wrench is available, use it along with the torque specifications at the beginning of this and other Chapters.

12 Wheels and tyres check

Tyres

1 Check the tyre condition and tread depth thoroughly – see *Pre-ride checks*.

Wheels

2 The cast wheels are virtually maintenance free, but they should be kept clean and checked periodically for cracks and other damage. Also check the wheel runout and alignment (see Chapter 6).
3 Never attempt to repair damaged cast wheels – they must be replaced with new ones. Check the valve rubber for signs of damage or deterioration and have it renewed by a motorcycle tyre fitting specialist if necessary. Also, make sure the valve stem cap is in place and tight.

13 Clutch check

1 Check that the clutch lever operates smoothly and easily.
2 If the lever action is heavy or stiff, remove the cable (see Chapter 2) and lubricate it (see Section 22). If the inner cable still does not run smoothly in the outer cable, replace it with a new one. Install the lubricated or new cable (see Chapter 2). If the action is still stiff, remove the lever and check for damage or distortion, or any other cause, and remedy as necessary. Clean and lubricate the pivot and contact areas (see Section 22). If the lever is good, refer to Chapter 2 and check the release mechanism in the cover and the clutch itself.
3 With the cable operating smoothly, check that it is correctly adjusted. Periodic adjustment is necessary to compensate for wear in the clutch plates and stretch of the cable. Check that the amount of freeplay in the cable is within the specifications listed at the beginning of the Chapter – freeplay is measured in terms of the clearance between the inner end of the lever (stock) and its bracket, before the clutch is actuated **(see illustration)**.
4 If adjustment is required, turn the adjuster in or out until the required amount of freeplay

10.7 Adjusting the front brake lever span on Street Triple and standard Daytona

13.3 Clutch cable freeplay is measured at gap between lever stock and bracket (arrowed)

13.4 Turn the adjuster to set the correct freeplay

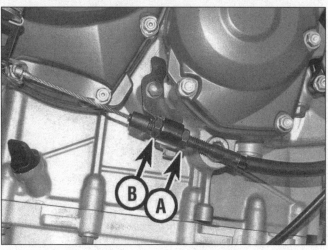

13.5 Front nut (A), rear nut (B)

is obtained **(see illustration)**. To increase freeplay, turn the adjuster clockwise (into the lever bracket). To reduce freeplay, turn the adjuster anti-clockwise (out of the lever bracket).

5 If all the adjustment has been taken up at the lever, reset the adjuster to give the maximum amount of freeplay by screwing it fully into the bracket (make sure the cable release slot

in the adjuster does not align with that in the bracket – turn it out some if necessary), then set freeplay to between 2 to 3 mm using the adjuster nuts on each end of the threaded section in the cable bracket on the right-hand side of the engine. To increase freeplay, slacken the front nut, then thread the rear nut up the cable until the freeplay is correct **(see illustration)**. To decrease freeplay, slacken the

rear nut, then thread the front nut down the cable towards the bracket until the freeplay is correct. Now use the adjuster at the clutch lever bracket to set the specified clearance between the clutch lever and its bracket.

Caution: The specified clearance is very small and care must be taken to ensure that there is actually some freeplay in the cable, albeit a small amount, otherwise the clutch may slip.

14.2a Move the top of the clip off . . .

14.2b . . . then draw it out . . .

14 Drive chain slider check

1 Remove the chainguard **(see illustration 2.2)**. Create maximum slack in the chain (see Section 1).

2 Detach the gearchange linkage rod from the lever **(see illustrations)**. Unscrew the footrest bracket bolts and remove the footrest/gear lever assembly **(see illustration)**.

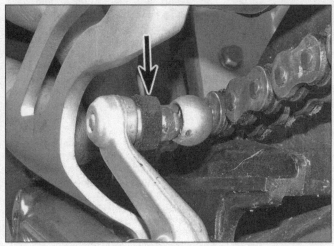

14.2c . . . and detach the rod from the lever. Note the seal (arrowed)

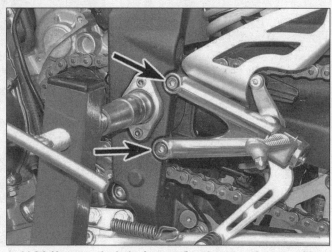

14.2d Unscrew the bolts (arrowed) and remove the assembly

14.3 Clean the chain slider (arrowed) and check for wear

15.3 Displace the valve, then unscrew the bolts (arrowed) and displace the bracket (early type bracket shown)

3 Clean the chain slider with a suitable solvent to remove all traces of grease and road dirt. Inspect the surface of the slider – if it is deeply grooved or damaged it must be replaced with a new one **(see illustration)**.
4 Unscrew the bolt securing the slider to the swingarm. Draw the slider back off the swingarm – note there is a collar for the bolt that fits into the inner side of the slider.
5 Installation is the reverse of removal. Tighten the footrest bracket bolts to the torque setting specified at the beginning of the Chapter. Make sure the ball joint seal is in place and smear the ball with grease before fitting the rod **(see illustration 14.2c)**.

15 Spark plugs

Check and adjustment

1 Make sure your spark plug socket is the correct size before attempting to remove the plugs – a suitable one is supplied in the motorcycle's toolkit. Make sure the ignition is switched OFF. On Daytona models remove the left-hand fairing side panel (see Chapter 7).
2 Remove the airbox (see Chapter 4).
3 Displace the SAIS solenoid valve (see illustration). Unscrew the bolts and displace or remove the bracket.
4 The ignition coils, one for each cylinder, are integral with the spark plug caps. Clean the area around each coil to prevent any dirt falling into the spark plug channels. Check that the cylinder location is marked on each ignition coil wiring connector and mark them accordingly if not.
5 Disconnect the ignition coil wiring connectors **(see illustration)**. Pull the coils off the spark plugs **(see illustration)**.
6 Using compressed air if available, clean the area around the base of the spark plugs to prevent any dirt falling into the engine when they are removed.
7 Using either the plug removing tool supplied in the bike's toolkit or a deep socket type wrench, unscrew the plugs from the cylinder head and remove them **(see illustrations)**. Lay each plug out in relation to its cylinder – if any plug shows up a problem it will then be easy to identify the troublesome cylinder.
8 Inspect the electrodes for wear. Both the centre and side electrodes should have square edges and the side electrodes should be of uniform thickness. Look for excessive deposits and evidence of a cracked or chipped insulator around the centre electrode. Compare your spark plugs to the colour spark plug reading chart on the inside rear cover of this manual. Check the threads, the washer and the ceramic insulator body for cracks and other damage.
9 If the electrodes are not excessively worn, and if the deposits can be easily removed with a wire brush, and there are no cracks or chips visible in the insulator, the plugs can be re-gapped and re-used. If in doubt concerning the condition of the plugs, replace them with new ones, as the expense is minimal.
10 Cleaning spark plugs by sandblasting is permitted, provided you clean the plugs with a high flash-point solvent afterwards.
11 Before installing the plugs, make sure they are the correct type and heat range

15.5a Disconnect the wiring connector from each coil . . .

15.5b . . . then pull the coils off the spark plug

15.7a Unscrew the plug . . .

15.7b . . . and remove it from the head

and check the gap between the electrodes **(see illustration)**. Compare the gap to that specified and adjust as necessary. If the gap must be adjusted, bend the side electrodes carefully and be very careful not to chip or crack the insulator nose **(see illustration)**. Make sure the sealing washer is in place on the plug before installing it.

12 Since the cylinder head is made of aluminium, which is soft and easily damaged, thread the plugs into the head turning the tool by hand **(see illustration 15.7b)**. Once the plugs have seated and are finger-tight, tighten them to the torque setting specified at the beginning of the Chapter using a torque wrench if available, or by 1/4 to 1/2 turn more using the tool supplied and a socket drive if not **(see illustration 15.7a)**. Do not over-tighten them.

> **HAYNES HiNT**
>
> *As the plugs are quite deeply recessed, you can slip a short length of hose over the end of the plug to use as a tool to thread it into place. The hose will grip the plug well enough to turn it, but will start to slip if the plug begins to cross-thread in the hole – this will prevent damaged threads.*

13 Fit the coils onto the spark plugs **(see illustration 15.5b)**. Connect the coil wiring connectors, making sure each goes to its correct cylinder **(see illustration 15.5a)**.

14 Fit the SAIS control valve bracket, then fit the valve onto it **(see illustration 15.3)**. Install the airbox (see Chapter 4).

> **HAYNES HiNT**
>
> *Stripped plug threads in the cylinder head can be repaired with a Heli-Coil thread insert – see 'Tools and Workshop Tips' in the Reference section.*

Renewal

15 Remove the old spark plugs as described above and install new ones.

16 Idle speed and throttle body synchronisation

Idle speed

1 The engine idle speed cannot be adjusted in the conventional way. It can only be adjusted using the Triumph engine management system diagnostic tool (see Section 4). If the idle speed is incorrect (see Specifications at the beginning of the Chapter), first check the idle air control valve (see Chapter 4). If that is good take the bike to a Triumph dealer.

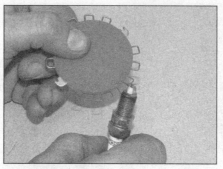

15.11a Using a wire type gauge to measure the spark plug electrode gap

Throttle body synchronisation

2 Throttle body synchronisation is the process of adjusting the throttle bodies so they pass the same amount of fuel/air mixture to each cylinder. Throttle bodies that are out of synchronisation will result in decreased fuel mileage, increased engine temperature, less than ideal throttle response and higher vibration levels.

3 The throttle bodies cannot be synchronised in the normal way by measuring the vacuum present in each throttle body using a set of vacuum gauges or a manometer. They can only be synchronised using the Triumph engine management system diagnostic tool. Take the bike to a Triumph dealer.

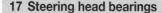

17 Steering head bearings

1 Steering head bearings can become dented, rough or loose during normal use of the machine – wear or damage will be noticeable in the way the bike handles. In extreme cases, worn or loose steering head bearings can cause steering wobble – a condition that is potentially dangerous. It is good practice to check the bearings on a regular basis and adjust them if necessary as described below.

Check

2 Using an auxiliary stand (not a front paddock stand), support the motorcycle in an upright position so that the front wheel is off the ground – on Daytona models first remove the fairing side panels (see Chapter 7), and on all models do not place the support under the exhaust system. On Daytona models remove the steering damper (see Chapter 5).

3 Point the front wheel straight-ahead and slowly move the handlebars from side-to-side. Any dents or roughness in the bearing races will be felt and the bars will not move smoothly and freely. Again point the wheel straight-ahead, and tap the front of the wheel to one side. The wheel should 'fall' under its own weight to the limit of its lock, indicating that the bearings are not too tight (take into

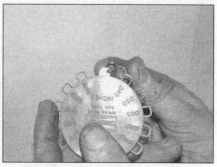

15.11b Adjust the electrode gap by bending the side electrode only

account the restriction that the cables, hose and wiring have). Check for similar movement to the other side.

4 Next, grasp the forks and try to pull and push them forward and backward **(see illustration)**. Any looseness in the steering head bearings will be felt as front-to-rear movement of the forks. If play is felt in the bearings, adjust the steering head as follows.

> **HAYNES HiNT**
>
> *Make sure you are not mistaking any movement between the bike and stand, or between the stand and the ground, for freeplay in the bearings. Do not pull and push the forks too hard – a gentle movement is all that is needed. Freeplay between the fork tubes due to worn bushes can also be misinterpreted as steering head bearing play – do not confuse the two.*

Adjustment

Caution: *Take great care not to apply excessive pressure when adjusting the bearings because this will cause premature bearing failure.*

5 Remove the fuel tank (see Chapter 4), and on Daytona models the fairing (see Chapter 7). **Note:** *Although it is not strictly necessary to remove the fuel tank and fairing, doing so will prevent the possibility of damage should a tool slip.*

17.4 Checking for play in the steering head bearings

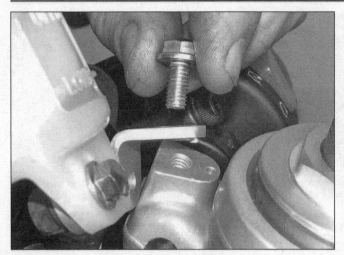

17.6a Displace the reservoir . . .

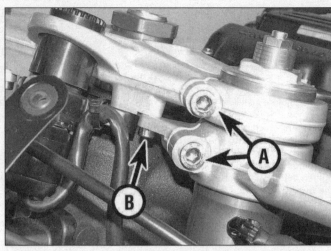

17.6b . . . then slacken the clamp bolts (A) and unscrew the positioning bolt (B) on each side of the yoke

6 On Daytona models unscrew the front brake fluid reservoir bracket bolt and displace the reservoir **(see illustration)**. Slacken the handlebar clamp bolts and the fork clamp bolts in the top yoke **(see illustration)**. Unscrew the handlebar positioning bolts.

7 On Street Triple models, displace the handlebars from the top yoke (see Chapter 5). Slacken the fork clamp bolts in the top yoke **(see illustration 17.6b)**.

8 Wrap some masking tap around the steering stem nut to protect its finish **(see illustration)**. Unscrew the nut **(see illustration)**.

9 Ease the top yoke up off the forks and lay it clear of the steering stem on some rag **(see illustration)**.

10 Using either the Triumph service tool (Part No. T3880024) or a C-spanner or suitable drift, unscrew the locknut, then lift off the tabbed washer **(see illustrations)**.

11 Triumph specify a torque setting for the adjuster nut, which can only be applied using their service tool (Part No. T3880024), or if you fabricate a tool to fit the adjuster nut slots **(see illustration)**. Slacken the adjuster nut slightly, then with the tool fitted to a torque wrench, apply a torque of 40 Nm to the adjuster nut – this will preload the bearings. Now slacken the nut and tighten it to the final torque setting of 15 Nm.

12 If the service tool isn't available slacken the adjuster nut slightly using a C-spanner until pressure is just released, then tighten it until all freeplay is removed, then tighten it a

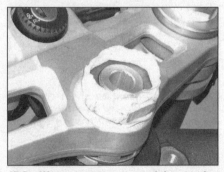

17.8a Wrap some tape around the steering stem nut . . .

17.8b . . . then unscrew it

17.9 Lift the top yoke up and rest it on some rag

17.10a Unscrew the locknut using a C-spanner . . .

17.10b . . . and remove the tabbed washer

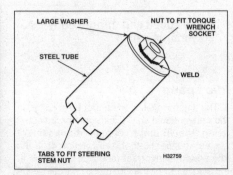

17.11 Home-made version of the Triumph service tool

17.12 Using a C-spanner to adjust the steering head bearings

17.14 Tighten the steering stem nut to the specified torque

little more **(see illustration)**. This pre-loads the bearings. Now slacken the nut, then tighten it again, setting it so that all freeplay is just removed yet the steering is able to move freely from side to side. To do this tighten the nut only a little at a time, and after each tightening repeat the checks outlined above (see Steps 3 and 4) until the bearings are correctly set. The object is to set the adjuster nut so that the bearings are under a very light loading, just enough to remove any freeplay.

13 Fit the tabbed washer, locating the tab in the slot **(see illustration 17.10b)**. Fit the locknut and tighten it to 40 Nm if the tool is available, or using a C-spanner if not – the tabbed lockwasher is there to prevent the adjuster nut turning with it.

14 Fit the top yoke onto the steering stem **(see illustration 17.9)**. Fit the steering stem nut and tighten it to the specified torque **(see illustration)**. Now tighten the fork clamp bolts to the specified torque **(see illustration 17.6b)**.

15 On Daytona models align the handlebars then fit the positioning bolts and tighten to the specified torque, then tighten the handlebar clamp bolts to the specified torque **(see illustration 17.6b)**. Fit

the brake fluid reservoir, locating the peg in the hole **(see illustration 17.6a)**.

16 On Street Triple models install the handlebars (see Chapter 5).

17 Install the fuel tank and fairing as required (see Chapters 4 and 7). On Daytona models install the steering damper (see Chapter 5).

Lubrication

18 Triumph specify that the steering head bearings must be re-greased at every second check and adjustment service interval. Re-greasing involves removing the steering stem – follow the procedure in Chapter 5 to remove and install the stem and adjust the bearings as described above on reassembly.

18 Air filter

Daytona models and Street Triple models to VIN 560476

1 Disconnect the battery (see Chapter 8).

2 Remove the fuel tank (see Chapter 4).

3 On Street Triple models unscrew the relay/fusebox bracket bolts **(see illustration)** and displace the assembly – there is no need to disconnect any wiring.

4 Disconnect the intake air temperature (IAT) sensor wiring connector **(see illustration)**. Disconnect the electronic control module (ECM) wiring connectors – they are colour coded and shaped so they cannot be re-connected the wrong way round **(see illustration)**.

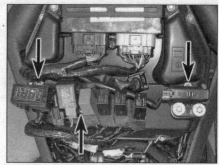

18.3 Undo the bolts (arrowed) and displace the bracket

18.4a Push the clip (arrowed) in and disconnect the IAT sensor wiring connector

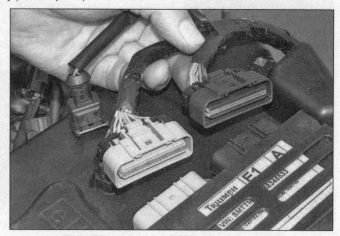

18.4b Disconnect the ECM wiring connectors

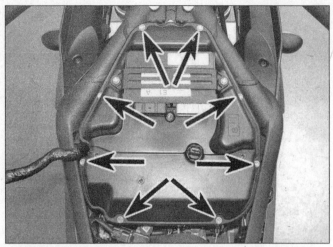

18.5a Undo the screws (arrowed) . . .

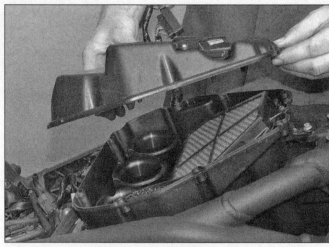

18.5b . . . and remove the cover

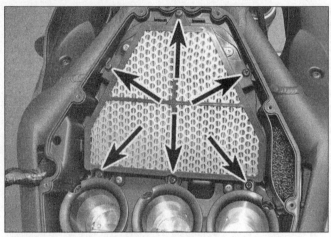

18.6a Undo the screws (arrowed) . . .

18.6b . . . and lift the filter out

5 Undo the screws securing the airbox cover and lift it off **(see illustrations)**.
6 Undo the screws securing the filter element then lift it out **(see illustrations)**.
7 Clean the inside of the airbox. Remove the crankcase breather mesh and clean it if necessary **(see illustration)**. Check the condition of the cover sealing ring and replace it with a new one if it is damaged, deformed or deteriorated.
8 Fit the new filter element into the airbox

and secure it with its screws **(see illustration 18.6b and a)**. Make sure the seal is seated in its groove in the cover **(see illustration)**. Fit the cover and secure it with the screws **(see illustrations 18.5b and a)**.
9 Connect the ECM and IAT sensor wiring connectors **(see illustrations 18.4b and a)**.
10 On Street Triple models fit the relay/fusebox bracket **(see illustration 18.3)**.
11 Install the fuel tank (see Chapter 4).

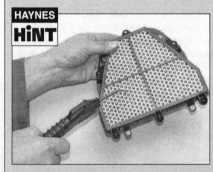

HAYNES HINT

If the motorcycle is constantly used in wet, dirty or dusty conditions, it is worth cleaning the element between renewal intervals. Remove it as described, and tap it on a hard surface to dislodge any large particles of dirt. If compressed air is available, use it to clean the element, directing the air in the opposite direction of normal flow. If the element is torn or cannot be cleaned, or is obviously beyond further use, replace it with a new one.

18.7 Check the mesh and clean if necessary

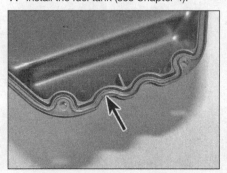

18.8 Make sure the seal (arrowed) is in place

18.13a Disconnect the connector

18.13b Undo the screw (arrowed) on the top . . .

18.13c . . . and the two screws (arrowed) on the back to free the ECM

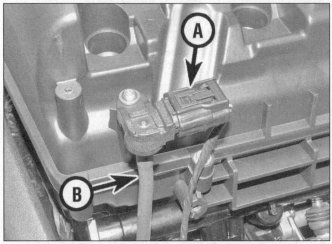

18.13d Disconnect the connector (A) and the hose (B)

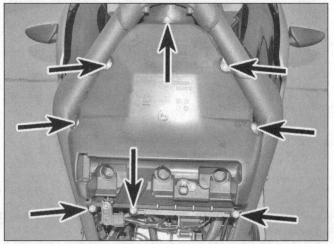

18.14 Airbox cover screws (arrowed)

Street Triple models from VIN 560477

12 Remove the fuel tank (see Chapter 4).

13 Disconnect the intake air temperature (IAT) sensor wiring connector **(see illustration)**. Displace the ECM from the airbox **(see illustrations)** – there is no need to disconnect the wiring. Disconnect the manifold absolute pressure (MAP) sensor wiring connector and hose **(see illustration)**.

14 Undo the screws securing the airbox cover and lift it off, noting the routing of the immobiliser ECM wiring **(see illustration)** – the air filter and the immobiliser ECM come away with the cover.

15 Remove the filter element from the cover **(see illustration)**.

16 Clean the inside of the airbox. Check the condition of the cover sealing ring and replace it with a new one if it is damaged, deformed or deteriorated **(see illustration 18.8)**.

17 Fit the new filter element into the airbox **(see illustration)** – it will only fit one way, so if it does not appear to fit correctly you have it the wrong way round. Make sure the seal is seated in its groove **(see illustration 18.8)**. Fit the cover, making sure the immobiliser ECM wiring routes correctly, and secure it with the screws **(see illustration)**.

18 Connect the MAP sensor hose and wiring connector **(see illustration 18.13d)**. Fit the ECM **(see illustrations 18.13c and b)**. Connect the IAT sensor wiring connector **(see illustration 18.13a)**.

19 Install the fuel tank (see Chapter 4).

18.15 Remove the filter from the cover

18.17a Fit the filter into the slots in the airbox

18.17b Make sure the wiring passes through the cut-out

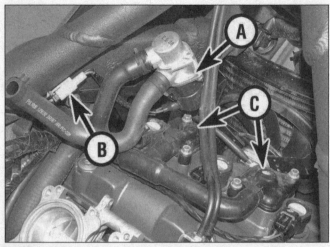

19.1 SAIS solenoid valve (A) and its wiring connector (B), and reed valve housings (C)

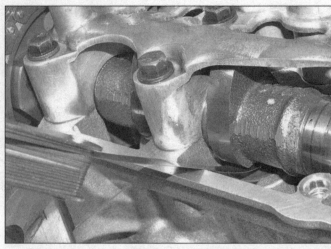

20.7 With the cam lobe pointing up use a feeler gauge to check the clearance

19 Secondary air injection system (SAIS) check

1 The system consists of an electrically actuated solenoid valve located under the front of the airbox and two reed valves in the top of the valve cover, with a hose system supplying air from the airbox via the solenoid valve to the reed valves **(see illustration)**. At certain engine speeds, the electronic control module (ECM) opens the solenoid valve and air is drawn into the exhaust ports via the reed valves. The introduced air promotes further combustion of the exhaust gases, reducing the level of pollutants. The reed valves prevent exhaust gases blowing back into the airbox.
2 Remove the airbox (see Chapter 4).
3 Check the system hoses for loose connections, cracks and deterioration, and replace them with new ones if necessary.
4 If there is a problem with the system, indicated either by the MIL lamp and a fault code (that can only be retrieved using Triumph's diagnostic tool), or by exhaust popping on throttle overrun refer to Chapter 4 to check the components in the system.

20 Valve clearance check and adjustment

Check

1 The engine must be completely cool for this maintenance procedure, so let the machine sit overnight before beginning.
2 Remove the spark plugs (see Section 15).
3 Remove the valve cover (see Chapter 2). The cylinders are numbered 1 to 3 from left to right. Make a chart or sketch of all valve positions so that a note of each clearance can be made against the relevant valve.
4 The clearance for a particular valve can be

measured when the cam lobe for that valve is pointing away from it, and there is one point during the engine cycle when all the lobes above the valves for a particular cylinder are pointing up – this is when the piston in that cylinder is at top dead centre (TDC) on the compression stroke, and all its valves are closed. To turn the camshafts, place the motorcycle on an auxiliary stand or stands so that the rear wheel is off the ground, select a high gear, and rotate the rear wheel by hand in its normal direction of rotation. A rear paddock stand is ideal, but axle stands can be used with care, using rag to cushion and protect components and prevent scratches.
5 Turn the rear wheel until all the camshaft lobes above the No. 1 cylinder are pointing away from the valves. The No. 1 cylinder is now at TDC on the compression stroke. Insert a feeler gauge of the same thickness as the correct valve clearance (see Specifications at the beginning of the Chapter) between the base of the camshaft lobe and the cam follower of each valve in turn and check that it is a firm sliding fit – you should feel a slight drag when the you pull the gauge out **(see illustration 20.7)**. If not, use the feeler gauges to obtain the exact clearance. Record the measured clearance on the chart. Note that there is a difference in the clearance between the intake valves and the exhaust valves.

6 Now turn the rear wheel until the camshaft lobes for the No. 2 cylinder are facing away from the valves. The No. 2 cylinder is now at TDC on the compression stroke. Measure the clearances of the valves using the method described in Step 5.
7 Now turn the rear wheel until the camshaft lobes for the No. 3 cylinder are facing away from the valves. The No. 3 cylinder is now at TDC on the compression stroke **(see illustration)**. Measure the clearances of the valves using the method described in Step 5.
8 When all clearances have been measured and charted, identify whether the clearance on any valve falls outside the range specified. If it does, the valve shim on that particular valve must be replaced with one of a thickness which will restore the correct clearance – see Step 9. If all clearances are good install the valve cover (see Chapter 2) and spark plugs (Section 15).

Shim adjustment

9 Remove the camshafts (see Chapter 2). Place rags over the spark plug holes and the cam chain tunnel to prevent a shim dropping into the engine on removal.
10 Remove the cam follower of the valve in question, using a suction tool or magnet if needed **(see illustration)**. Retrieve the shim from inside the follower **(see illustration)** – if

20.10a Lift out the cam follower . . .

20.10b . . . and retrieve the shim (arrowed)

it is not there pick it out of the top of the valve using a magnet or a small screwdriver with a dab of grease on it (the shim will stick to the grease) **(see illustration 20.16a)**. Do not allow the shim to fall into the engine.

11 The shim size may be marked on one face, but the shim should be measured with a micrometer to check that it has not worn **(see illustrations)**. If the shim has worn undersize, this must be taken into account when calculating the valve clearance.

12 The new shim thickness required can be calculated as follows – always aim to get the clearance at the mid-point of the specified range.

13 If the valve clearance is less than specified, subtract the measured clearance from the specified clearance, then deduct the result from the original shim thickness to obtain the required thickness of the new shim. For example:

Sample calculation – intake valve clearance too small

Specified clearance: 0.15 mm (0.10 to 0.20 mm)
Measured clearance: 0.08 mm
Difference: 0.07 mm
Shim thickness fitted: 2.575 mm
Correct shim thickness required is 2.575 – 0.07 = 2.505 mm

14 If the valve clearance is greater than specified, subtract the specified clearance from the measured clearance, and add the result to the thickness of the original shim to obtain the required thickness of the new shim. For example:

Sample calculation – exhaust valve clearance too large

Specified clearance: 0.30 mm (0.275 to 0.325 mm)
Measured clearance: 0.37 mm
Difference: 0.07 mm
Shim thickness fitted: 1.975 mm
Correct shim thickness required is 1.975 + 0.07 = 2.045 mm

15 Obtain the correct thickness shim(s) from a Triumph dealer. Where the required thickness is not equal to the available shim thickness, round off the measurement to the nearest available size. Shims are available in 0.025 mm increments from 1.70 mm to 3.00 mm. **Note:** *If the required replacement shim is greater than 3.00 mm (the largest available), the valve is probably not seating correctly due to a build-up of carbon deposits or valve damage. Remove the valve for checking (see Chapter 2).*

16 Lubricate the new shim with molybdenum disulphide oil (a 50/50 mixture of molybdenum disulphide grease and engine oil) and fit it into its recess in the top of the valve **(see illustration)**. Check that the shim is correctly seated, then lubricate the follower with molybdenum disulphide oil and fit it onto the valve **(see illustration)**. Repeat the procedure for any other valves as required, then install the camshafts (see Chapter 2).

20.11a The shim size is marked on one face . . .

20.11b . . . but measure it using a micrometer to confirm its size

20.16a Fit the shim into its recess . . .

20.16b . . . then fit the follower

17 Rotate the rear wheel several turns to seat the new shim(s), then check the clearances again.

18 Install the valve cover and spark plugs.

21 Wheel bearing check

1 Wheel bearings will wear over a period of time and result in handling problems.

2 Support the motorcycle upright using an auxiliary stand and so that the wheel being checked is off the ground. Check for any play in the bearings by pushing and pulling the wheel against the hub **(see illustration)**. Also spin the wheel and check that it rotates smoothly and quietly, taking into account any transmission or brake drag and noise – if in doubt displace the calipers (see Chapter 6).

3 If any play is detected in the wheel hub, or if the wheel does not rotate smoothly, freely and quietly, the wheel must be removed and the bearings inspected for wear or damage (see Chapter 6).

22 Stand, lever pivots and cable lubrication

1 Since the controls, cables and various other

components of a motorcycle are exposed to the elements, they should be lubricated periodically to ensure safe and trouble-free operation.

2 The footrests, clutch and brake levers, brake pedal, gearchange lever linkage and stand pivot should be lubricated frequently. In order for the lubricant to be applied where it will do the most good, the component should be disassembled (see Chapter 5), cleaned, and the recommended lubricant applied (see Specifications). However, if an aerosol spray lubricant is used, it can be applied to the pivot joint gaps and will usually work its way into the areas where friction occurs.

3 To lubricate the throttle and clutch cables, and on Daytona models the exhaust valve cables, disconnect the relevant cable at its upper end, then lubricate the cable with a pressure adapter

21.2 Checking for play in the wheel bearings

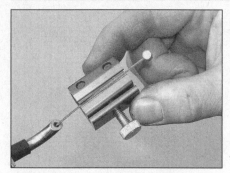

22.3a Fit the cable into the adapter . . .

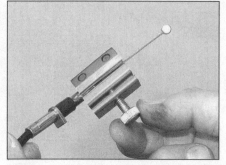

22.3b . . . and tighten the screw to seal it in . . .

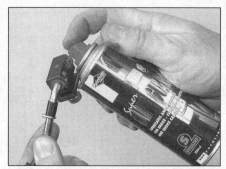

22.3c . . . then apply the lubricant using the nozzle provided inserted in the hole in the adapter

(see illustrations). See Chapter 4 for the throttle cable and exhaust valve cable removal procedures, and Chapter 2 for the clutch cable.

23 Coolant change

Warning: Allow the engine to cool completely before performing this maintenance operation. Also, don't allow antifreeze to come into contact with your skin or the painted surfaces of the motorcycle. Rinse off spills immediately with plenty of water. Antifreeze is highly toxic if ingested. Never leave antifreeze lying around in an open container or in puddles on the floor; children and pets are attracted by its sweet smell and may

drink it. Check with local authorities (councils) about disposing of antifreeze. Many communities have collection centres which will see that antifreeze is disposed of safely. Antifreeze is also combustible, so don't store it near open flames.

Draining

1 On Daytona models remove the fairing side panels (see Chapter 7).
2 On Street Triple models to VIN 560476 displace the radiator cowls, and on Street Triple models from VIN 560477 remove the right-hand radiator cowl (see Chapter 7).
3 Remove the pressure cap from the filler neck in the radiator by turning it anti-clockwise until it reaches a stop **(see illustration 6.9)**. If you hear a hissing sound (indicating there is still pressure in the system), wait until it stops. Now press down on the cap and continue

turning it until it can be removed. Also remove the filler cap from the coolant reservoir.
4 On Daytona models and Street Triple models to VIN 560476 unscrew the bleed-hole screw on the right-hand end of the radiator **(see illustration)**. On Street Triple models to VIN 560476 also remove the bleed-hole screw from the top hose coming from the radiator, noting the rubber sealing washer **(see illustration)**.
5 Position a suitable container beneath the left-hand end of the radiator. Slacken the clamp securing the bottom coolant hose to the radiator and detach it, then point it down into the container and allow the coolant to completely drain from both the radiator and the hose **(see illustrations)**.
6 Position the container beneath the coolant outlet pipe drain plug on the front of the engine. Unscrew the plug and allow the remaining coolant to completely drain **(see illustrations)**.

23.4a Remove the bleed screw (arrowed) from the top of the radiator . . .

23.4b . . . and on Street Triples from the top hose

23.5a Slacken the clamp (arrowed) . . .

23.5b . . . then detach the hose and allow the coolant to drain

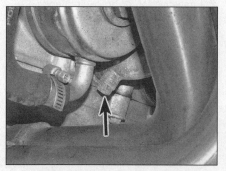

23.6a Unscrew the drain plug (arrowed) . . .

23.6b . . . and allow the coolant (arrowed) to drain

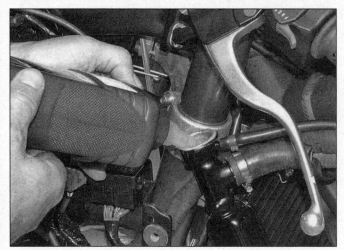

23.15 Fill the system using the correct mixture as described

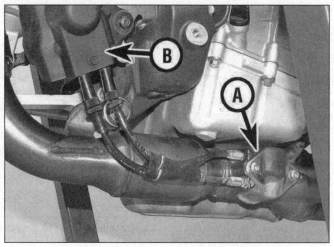

24.1 Exhaust control valve (A) and actuator (B)

If you are going to flush the system using a flushing compound retain the old sealing washer for use during flushing.

7 Run the radiator through with clean tap water by inserting a garden hose in the filler neck until the water flows out clear. If the radiator is extremely corroded, remove it (see Chapter 3) and have it cleaned professionally. Reconnect the hose and tighten the clamp, then continue to run the water through so it now comes out the drain plug in the outlet pipe. Remove, drain, and flush the reservoir, then refit it (see Chapter 3).

Flushing

8 Clean the outlet pipe drain hole then fit the plug using the old sealing washer.
9 Fill the cooling system with clean water mixed with a flushing compound **(see illustration 23.15)**. Make sure the flushing compound is compatible with aluminium components, and follow the manufacturer's instructions carefully.
10 Fit the pressure cap (where fitted) and the bleed-hole screw(s) **(see illustrations 23.4a and b)**. Start the engine and allow it to reach normal operating temperature. Let it run for about ten minutes.
11 Stop the engine and let it cool for a while. Cover the pressure cap with a heavy rag and turn it anti-clockwise to the first stop, releasing any pressure that may be present in the system. Once the hissing stops, push down on the cap and remove it completely.
12 Drain the system (Steps 3 to 6).
13 Fill the system with clean water and repeat the procedure in Steps 10 to 12.

Refilling

14 Fit a new sealing washer onto the outlet pipe drain plug and tighten it to the torque setting specified at the beginning of the Chapter **(see illustration 23.6a)**. Attach the

coolant hose to the radiator and tighten the clamp **(see illustration 23.5a)**.
15 Fill the system via the filler neck with the proper coolant mixture (see this Chapter's Specifications) **(see illustration)**. **Note:** *Pour the coolant in slowly to minimise the amount of air entering the system.* When the system appears full, squeeze the large bore hoses to dislodge air bubbles, then take the bike off its stand and shake it and lean it to dissipate the coolant, then place the bike back on the stand and top the system up.
16 On Daytona models and Street Triple models to VIN 560476 check that there is coolant visible in the bleed-hole(s). If there isn't, but the filler neck appears full, there is an air-lock somewhere. Try squeezing the pipes and shaking and leaning the bike again to disperse it. If that doesn't work you will need to siphon the coolant through the radiator using a vacuum pump – these are commercially available. Alternatively you may be able to form a sufficient seal using a piece of clear flexible tubing that fits tightly into the bleed hole, then sucking on the end of the tube – the reason the tube must be clear is so you can see the coolant when it exits the bleed hole and enters the tube, at which point stop sucking. DO NOT use tubing you can't see through – coolant does not taste very nice and is not good for you. If you cannot get coolant through to the bleed hole it is possible the radiator is blocked, and so must be replaced with a new one. Fit the bleed-hole screw(s), using a new rubber sealing washer with the screw for the top hose on Street Triples **(see illustrations 23.4a and b)**.
17 Fit the pressure cap.
18 Fill the coolant reservoir to the MAX level line (see *Pre-ride checks*).
19 Start the engine and allow it to idle for 2 to 3 minutes. Flick the throttle twistgrip part open 3 or 4 times, so that the engine speed rises to approximately 4000 – 5000 rpm, then stop the engine. Take the bike off its stand and shake it

and lean it to dissipate the coolant, then place the bike back on the stand. Any air trapped in the system should have bled back to the filler neck.
20 Let the engine cool then remove the pressure cap as described in Step 3. Check that the coolant level is still up to the top of the filler neck. If it's low, add the specified mixture until it reaches the top. Refit the pressure cap.
21 Check the coolant level in the reservoir and top up if necessary (see *Pre-ride checks*).
22 Check the system for leaks.
23 Do not dispose of the old coolant by pouring it down the drain. Instead pour it into a heavy plastic container, cap it tightly and take it into an authorised disposal site or service station – see **Warning** at the beginning of this Section.
24 On Daytona models install the fairing side panels (see Chapter 7). On Street Triple models install the radiator cowl(s) (see Chapter 7).

24 Exhaust control valve cable check

Note: *The exhaust control valve is fitted to Daytona models only.*
1 The exhaust control valve is located inside the single pipe section of the exhaust system just behind the joint of the three downpipes **(see illustration)**. The valve is connected by two cables to an actuator located near the joint of the downpipe assembly to the intermediate pipe. The actuator is controlled by the engine control module (ECM).
2 Remove the right-hand fairing side panel (see Chapter 7). Remove the covers from the actuator and the valve. Make sure the actuator is securely mounted and the cables are held securely.
3 Check the cables as follows: first check that there is 5 mm of the threaded section at the valve end of each cable on the front side

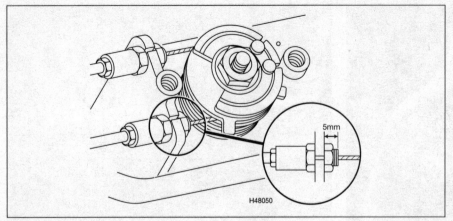

24.3a Measure distance from cable holder bracket to threaded end of adjuster

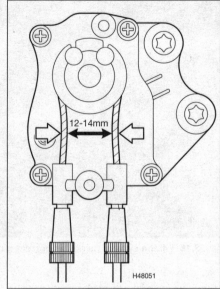

24.3b Measure the distance between the cables at this point when light finger pressure is applied

of the holding bracket **(see illustration)**. Next squeeze the exposed sections of the inner cables between the cable holder and pulley on the servo together using light finger pressure and measure the distance between the cables – it should be 12 to 14 mm **(see illustration)**. If the either condition is not as specified the cables need adjusting. To do this the control valve must be set in its middle position, which can only be done using the Triumph engine management system diagnostic tool. Take the bike to a Triumph dealer.

4 Refer to Section 22 and lubricate the cables.

5 Turn the ignition ON and observe the movement of the servo pulley, cables and valve (this is a function which occurs each time the ignition is turned on). If the servo pulley does not move, or if it tries to move but can't because the cables or the valve have seized, or if the cable action is stiff or juddery, check the condition of the cables and the operation of the valve (see Chapter 4).

25 Front fork oil change

1 Fork oil degrades over a period of time and loses its damping qualities.

2 Remove the front forks from the yokes as described in Chapter 5, Section 6, then change the oil as described in Chapter 5, Section 7.

3 Fork oil quantity, level and oil type are given in the Specifications at the beginning of Chapter 5.

26 Sidestand and safety interlock circuit

1 The sidestand return spring must be capable of retracting the stand fully and holding the stand retracted when the motorcycle is in use. If a spring is sagged or broken it must be replaced with a new one.

2 Lubricate the stand pivot regularly (see Section 22).

3 The sidestand switch prevents the motorcycle being started if it is in gear and the stand is down, and cuts the engine if the stand is put down while it is running and in gear. Check its operation by shifting the transmission into neutral, retracting the stand, pulling the clutch lever in and starting the engine. Pull in the clutch lever again and select a gear. Extend the sidestand. The engine should stop as the sidestand is extended. If the sidestand switch does not operate as described, check its circuit (see Chapter 8). The neutral and clutch switches are also part of the same circuit – to check them, make sure the engine can be started with the sidestand in either position, as long as the transmission is in neutral and the clutch is pulled in, and cannot be started with the transmission in gear, even with the stand up and the clutch

pulled in. If any of the situations are not as stated, check the circuit (see Chapter 8).

27 Battery checks

1 All models are fitted with a maintenance-free (sealed) battery which requires no maintenance. **Note:** *Do not attempt to remove the battery caps to check the electrolyte level or battery specific gravity. Removal will damage the caps, resulting in electrolyte leakage and battery damage.* All that should be done is to check that the terminals are clean and tight and that the casing is not damaged or leaking. See Chapter 8 for further details

Caution: Be extremely careful when handling or working around the battery. The electrolyte is very caustic and an explosive gas (hydrogen) is given off when the battery is charging.

2 If the machine is not in regular use, disconnect the battery and give it a refresher charge every month to six weeks (see Chapter 8).

Chapter 2
Engine, clutch and transmission

Contents

Degrees of difficulty

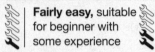

Easy, suitable for novice with little experience	**Fairly easy,** suitable for beginner with some experience	**Fairly difficult,** suitable for competent DIY mechanic	**Difficult,** suitable for experienced DIY mechanic	**Very difficult,** suitable for expert DIY or professional

Specifications

General

Capacity	674.8 cc
Bore	74.0 mm
Stroke	52.3 mm
Compression ratio	12.65 to 1
Cylinder numbering (from left side to right side of the bike)	1-2-3
Firing order.	1-2-3

Camshafts and cam chain

Camshaft runout.	0.15 mm max.
Camshaft end-float	
Standard.	0.23 to 0.33 mm
Maximum	0.4 mm
Camshaft bearing oil clearance	
Daytona to VIN 381274 and	
Street Triple models to engine No. 455109	0.070 to 0.121 mm
Daytona models from VIN 381275 and	
Street Triple models from engine No. 455110	0.040 to 0.081 mm
Service limit (max) – all models	0.17 mm
Camshaft journal diameter	
Daytona to VIN 381274 and	
Street Triple models to engine No. 455109	23.900 to 23.930 mm
Daytona models from VIN 381275 and	
Street Triple models from engine No. 455110	23.940 to 23.960 mm
Camshaft bearing bore diameter	24.000 to 24.021 mm
Cam chain stretch limit.	149.48 mm

Valves, guides and springs

Valve clearances	see Chapter 1
Valve head diameter	
Intake valve	30.5 mm
Exhaust valve	25.5 mm
Intake valve stem diameter	
Standard	3.975 to 3.990 mm
Service limit	3.965 mm
Exhaust valve stem diameter	
Standard	3.955 to 3.970 mm
Service limit	3.945 mm
Intake and exhaust valve guide bore diameter	
Standard	4.000 to 4.015 mm
Service limit	4.043 mm
Intake valve stem-to-guide clearance	
Standard	0.01 to 0.04 mm
Service limit	0.078 mm
Exhaust valve stem-to-guide clearance	
Standard	0.03 to 0.06 mm
Service limit	0.098 mm
Intake valve seat width (in head)	
Standard	0.8 to 1.2 mm
Service limit	1.5 mm
Exhaust valve seat width (in head)	
Standard	1.0 to 1.4 mm
Service limit	1.7 mm
Intake valve seat width (on valve)	
Daytona to VIN 381274	0.99 to 1.86 mm
Daytona models from VIN 381275	1.06 to 1.36 mm
Street Triple models	1.27 to 1.57 mm
Exhaust valve seat width (on valve)	
Daytona to VIN 381274 and	
Street Triple models to engine No. 452999	1.34 to 1.63 mm
Daytona models from VIN 381275 and	
Street Triple models from engine No. 453000	1.06 to 1.93 mm
Valve spring length	27.5 mm with 483 to 533 N

Cylinder liners

Cylinder liner ID	
Daytona models, and Street triple models to engine No. 454081	73.985 to 74.003 mm
Street triple models from engine No. 454082	74.030 to 74.050 mm
Service limit – all models	74.100 mm
Cylinder compression	150 to 180 psi (10.3 to 12.4 Bar)

Pistons

	Standard	Service limit
Piston OD (measured 8 mm up from skirt, at 90° to piston pin axis)		
Daytona	73.970 to 73.980 mm	73.920 mm
Street Triple	73.964 to 73.980 mm	73.920 mm
Piston pin bore diameter in piston	16.004 to 16.012 mm	16.040 mm
Piston pin diameter	15.995 to 16.000 mm	15.985 mm
Connecting rod small-end diameter	16.016 to 16.029 mm	16.039 mm

Piston rings

	Standard	Service limit
Ring-to-groove clearance		
Top ring – Daytona	0.04 to 0.08 mm	0.095 mm
Top ring – Street Triple	0.02 to 0.06 mm	0.075 mm
Second ring – all models	0.02 to 0.06 mm	0.075 mm
End gap (installed)		
Top ring		
Daytona models, and Street Triple models to engine No. 454081	0.10 to 0.25 mm	0.37 mm
Street Triple models from engine No. 454082	0.15 to 0.30 mm	0.42 mm
Second ring		
Daytona models, and Street Triple models to engine No. 454081	0.25 to 0.40 mm	0.52 mm
Street Triple models from engine No. 454082	0.30 to 0.45 mm	0.57 mm
Oil control ring side rails		
Daytona models, and Street Triple models to engine No. 454081	0.10 to 0.35 mm	
Street Triple models from engine No. 454082	0.20 to 0.70 mm	

Clutch

Friction plates
  Quantity 9
  Thickness
    Standard. . . . . 3.0 mm
    Service limit . . . . 2.8 mm
Plain plates
  Quantity 8
  Warpage (service limit) . . . . 0.20 mm
Clutch pack height . . . . 41.54 to 42.54 mm
Clutch cable freeplay . . . . see Chapter 1

Lubrication system

Oil pressure @ 5000 rpm . . . . 30 psi (2.1 Bar) @ 5000 rpm, oil at 80°C
Oil pump rotor tip-to-outer rotor clearance
  Standard. . . . . 0.15 mm
  Service limit . . . . 0.20 mm
Oil pump outer rotor-to-body clearance
  Standard. . . . . 0.15 to 0.22 mm
  Service limit . . . . 0.35 mm
Oil pump rotor end-float
  Standard. . . . . 0.04 to 0.09 mm
  Service limit . . . . 0.17 mm
Connecting rods and bearings
Connecting rod side clearance
  Standard. . . . . 0.15 to 0.30 mm
  Service limit . . . . 0.50 mm
Connecting rod big-end bearing oil clearance
  Standard. . . . . 0.035 to 0.065 mm
  Service limit . . . . 0.07 mm
Connecting rod big-end journal diameter
  Daytona models, and Street Triple models to VIN 560476
    Standard. . . . . 32.984 to 33.000 mm
    Service limit . . . . 32.960 mm
  Street Triple models from VIN 560477
    Standard. . . . . 33.010 to 33.026 mm
    Service limit . . . . 32.970 mm

Crankshaft and main bearings

Main bearing oil clearance
  Standard. . . . . 0.020 to 0.044 mm
  Service limit . . . . 0.07 mm
Main bearing journal diameter
  Standard. . . . . 32.984 to 33.000 mm
  Service limit . . . . 32.960 mm
Crankshaft end-float. . . . . 0.15 to 0.30 mm
Crankshaft run-out
  Standard. . . . . 0.02 mm or less
  Service limit . . . . 0.05 mm

Transmission

Primary reduction ratio. . . . . 1.848 to 1 (46/85)
Gear ratios (No. of teeth)
  First gear
    Daytona up to engine No. 330118 . . . . 2.615 to 1 (34/13)
    Daytona from engine No. 330119-on . . . . 2.313 to 1 (37/16)
    Street Triple. . . . . 2.615 to 1 (34/13)
  Second gear. . . . . 1.857 to 1 (39/21)
  Third gear . . . . 1.565 to 1 (36/23)
  Fourth gear. . . . . 1.350 to 1 (27/20)
  Fifth gear. . . . . 1.238 to 1 (26/21)
  Sixth gear. . . . . 1.136 to 1 (25/22)
Final reduction ratio . . . . 2.937 to 1 (47/16)

Selector drum and forks

	Standard	Service limit
Selector fork end width	5.9 to 6.0 mm	5.8 mm
Selector fork groove width in gears	6.1 to 6.17 mm	6.27 mm
Selector fork-to-groove clearance	0.47 mm maximum	

Torque settings

Balancer shaft end cover bolts . . . . 8 Nm
Cam chain support bolt . . . . 12 Nm
Cam chain tensioner – Daytona models to VIN 377509, Street Triple models to VIN 560476
 End bolt . . . . 7 Nm
 Tensioner mounting bolts . . . . 9 Nm
Cam chain tensioner – Daytona models from VIN 377510, Street Triple models from VIN 560477
 Tensioner mounting bolts . . . . 8 Nm
Camshaft holder bolts . . . . 10 Nm
Camshaft sprocket bolts
 Daytona models, and Street Triple models to VIN 560476 . . . . 15 Nm
 Street Triple models from VIN 560477 . . . . 22 Nm
Clutch centre nut . . . . 98 Nm
Clutch cover bolts . . . . 8 Nm
Clutch pressure plate bolts . . . . 10 Nm
Connecting rod cap bolts . . . . see Section 24
Coolant inlet and outlet pipe bolts . . . . 12 Nm
Crankcase 6 mm bolts (see text) . . . . 12 Nm
Crankcase 8 mm bolts (see text) . . . . 32 Nm
Crankcase breather baffle plate bolts . . . . 9 Nm
Crankcase breather tube screw . . . . 9 Nm
Cylinder head bolts
 Stage 1 . . . . 15 Nm
 Stage 2 . . . . 20 Nm
 Stage 3 . . . . Angle-tighten 120°
Cylinder head-to-crankcase screws . . . . 10 Nm
Engine mounting bolts
 Front and centre engine mounting adjusters . . . . 3 Nm
 Rear engine mounting adjusters . . . . 10 Nm
 Front mounting bolt nuts . . . . 48 Nm
 Centre mounting bolts . . . . 48 Nm
 Upper and lower rear mounting bolt nuts . . . . 48 Nm
Input shaft bearing housing bolts . . . . 12 Nm
Internal oil pipe bolts . . . . 12 Nm
Gearchange mechanism centralising spring
 locating pin . . . . 20 Nm
Oil cooler bolt . . . . 59 Nm
Oil pressure relief valve . . . . 15 Nm
Oil pump drive chain guide bolts . . . . 9 Nm
Oil pump driven sprocket bolt . . . . 14 Nm
Oil pump mounting bolts . . . . 12 Nm
Oil strainer bolts . . . . 12 Nm
Right-hand crankcase cover bolts . . . . 8 Nm
Selector drum cam plate screw . . . . 12 Nm
Selector fork shaft and drum bearing
 retainer screws . . . . 12 Nm
Starter clutch bolts . . . . 16 Nm
Stopper arm bolt . . . . 12 Nm
Sump bolts . . . . 10 Nm
Valve cover bolts . . . . 10 Nm

1 General information

The engine/transmission is a water-cooled, in-line three-cylinder design, fitted across the frame. The twelve valves are operated by double overhead camshafts, chain driven off the right-hand end of the crankshaft. The pistons run in removable liners, surrounded by a water jacket. A single balancer shaft is gear driven directly off the crankshaft.

The engine/transmission unit is constructed in aluminium alloy with the crankcase divided horizontally. The crankcase incorporates a wet sump, pressure fed lubrication system. The oil pump, which comes as an integrated assembly with the water pump, is chain driven off the back of the clutch housing.

The clutch is of the wet, multi-plate type and is gear driven off the crankshaft. The alternator is mounted on the left-hand end of the crankshaft.

The transmission is six-speed constant mesh. Final drive to the rear wheel is by chain and sprockets.

Many of the bolts used on Triumph motorcycles are of the Torx type. Unless you are already equipped with a good range of Torx bits, you are advised to purchase a set before attempting work on the engine. Make sure you get bits that can be used in conjunction with a socket set so that a torque wrench can be applied – a Torx key set will not be adequate on its own, though will be a useful addition to the bits.

2 Component access

Operations possible with the engine in the frame

The components and assemblies listed below can be removed without having to remove the engine/transmission assembly from the frame. However if a number of areas require attention at the same time, removal of the engine is recommended.

Valve cover
Cam chain tensioner
Camshafts and followers
Cam chain, tensioner blade and guide blade

Starter motor
Alternator and starter clutch
Clutch
Gearchange mechanism (selector arm/
  shaft, stopper arm and detent cam plate)
Oil pump/water pump
Oil cooler
Sump, oil strainer and pressure relief valve

Operations requiring engine removal

It is necessary to remove the engine/
transmission assembly from the frame to gain
access to the following components.
Cylinder head
Cylinder liners and pistons
Connecting rods and bearings
Crankshaft and bearings
Balancer shaft
Transmission shafts
Selector drum and forks

3 Engine wear assessment

Cylinder compression check

Note: *Turning the engine over with the ignition coils removed could generate a fault code in the engine management system – to clear this you will need to see a Triumph dealer equipped with the Diagnostic tool. See Chapter 4 for more information.*

1 Among other things, poor engine performance may be caused by leaking valves, incorrect valve clearances, a leaking head gasket, or worn pistons, rings and/or cylinder liners. A cylinder compression check will help pinpoint these conditions and can also indicate the presence of excessive carbon deposits in the cylinder heads.
2 The only tools required are a compression gauge and a spark plug wrench. A compression gauge with a threaded end (10 mm) to fit into the spark plug hole is preferable to one with a rubber cone end that has to held pressed against the hole. Depending on the outcome of the initial test, a squirt-type oil can may also be needed.
3 Make sure the valve clearances are correctly set (see Chapter 1).
4 Run the engine until it is at normal operating temperature. Remove the spark plugs (see Chapter 1) – when removing the airbox cover leave the wiring to the IAT sensor and the ECM connected and just lay the top to one side. Remove the MAP sensor from the airbox and reconnect the wiring and vacuum hose.
5 Fit the gauge into the No. 1 cylinder spark plug hole. If the rubber cone type is used keep the gauge pressed hard onto the hole throughout the test to maintain a good seal – it is a good idea to have an assistant to do this as you also need to pull the clutch lever in and hold the throttle wide open while turning

3.6 Checking cylinder compression

the engine over on the starter motor to do the test. Alternatively tie the clutch lever back to the handlebar.
6 With the ignition switch ON, the kill switch set to RUN, the clutch lever pulled in and the throttle held fully open, turn the engine over on the starter motor until the gauge reading has built up and stabilised **(see illustration).**
7 Record the reading, then repeat for the remaining cylinders.
8 Generally a range of 150 to 180 psi (10 to 12.5 Bar) is normal, while much above or below this can be considered high or low and should be investigated. Also, there should be no more than about 25 psi (1.7 Bar) difference between any of the cylinders, even if the figures for all cylinders are within the general limits.
9 If the reading is low, it could be due to a worn cylinder bore, piston or rings, failure of the head gasket, or worn valve seats. To determine which is the cause, pour a small quantity of engine oil into the spark plug hole to seal the rings, then repeat the compression test. If the figures are noticeably higher the cause is a worn cylinder, piston or rings. If there is no change the cause is a leaking head gasket or worn valve seats.
10 If the reading is high there could be a build-up of carbon deposits in the combustion chamber. Remove the cylinder head and scrape all deposits off the piston and the cylinder head.

Oil pressure check

11 To check the oil pressure, a suitable gauge and adapter that screws into the oil pressure switch will be needed. Triumph do not list an adapter as a spare part, but it is worth checking with a dealer as to availability. Otherwise, remove the pressure switch (see Chapter 8), and take it to an accessory dealer to match it up – if you are buying a pressure gauge, it may well come with a range of adapters. Refit the pressure switch before running the engine.
12 Warm the engine up to normal operating temperature then stop it. On Daytona models remove the right-hand fairing side panel (see Chapter 7).
13 Remove the oil pressure switch (see Chapter 8). Screw the adapter in its place.

Connect the gauge to the adapter. Install the throttle bodies, airbox and fuel tank (see Chapter 4).
14 Start the engine and increase the engine speed to 5000 rpm whilst watching the gauge reading. The oil pressure should be similar to that given in the Specifications at the start of this Chapter.
15 If the pressure is significantly lower than the standard, either the relief valve is stuck open, the oil pump is faulty, the oil pump pick-up strainer is blocked or there is other engine damage. Begin diagnosis by checking the oil pump pick-up strainer (see Section 18), then the oil pump. If those items check out okay, chances are the bearing oil clearances are excessive and the engine needs to be overhauled.
16 If the pressure is too high, the relief valve is stuck closed. To check it, see Section 18.
17 Stop the engine. Remove the fuel tank, then unscrew the gauge and adapter from the crankcase. Install the oil pressure switch (see Chapter 8).
18 On Daytona models install the fairing side panel (see Chapter 7).

4 Engine removal and installation

Caution: The engine is very heavy. Engine removal and installation should be carried out with the aid of at least one assistant. Personal injury or damage could occur if the engine falls or is dropped. An hydraulic or mechanical floor jack should be used to support and lower or raise the engine if possible.
Note: *Triumph specify that new nuts should be used on the engine mounting bolts on installation of the engine.*

Removal

1 Position the bike on an auxiliary stand or stands, so that it is supported in an upright position and is secure. Lock the front brake on by fitting a cable-tie around the handlebar and brake lever. Work can be made easier by raising the machine to a suitable height on an hydraulic ramp.
2 If the engine is dirty, particularly around its mountings, wash it thoroughly before starting any major dismantling. This will make work much easier and rule out the possibility of caked-on lumps of dirt falling into some vital component.
3 Remove the battery (see Chapter 8).
4 On Daytona models remove the fairing side panels and seat cowling (see Chapter 7).
5 On Street Triple models remove the side panels (see Chapter 7).
6 Remove the fuel tank, the airbox and the throttle bodies (see Chapter 4).
7 Disconnect the secondary air injection system solenoid valve wiring connector **(see**

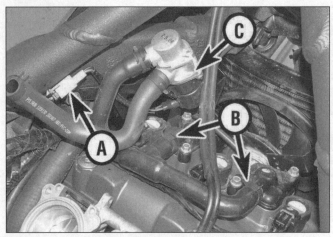

4.7 Disconnect the wiring connector (A), detach the hoses (B) and remove the valve (C)

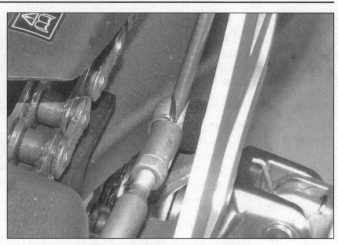

4.13a Move the top of the clip off . . .

illustration). Release the clips and disconnect the air hoses from the valve cover and remove the solenoid valve along with the hoses, noting how it locates.

8 Remove the ignition coils.

9 Drain the engine oil (see Chapter 1). If required remove the oil filter (see Chapter 1).

10 Drain the coolant (see Chapter 1).

11 Remove the radiator along with all the coolant hoses (i.e. detaching them from the engine rather than the radiator), noting their routing (see Chapter 3). It is advisable to tag the end of each hose using masking tape, then write the location of the hose on the tape. If required remove the oil cooler (see Section 6).

On Daytona models, and Street Triple models from VIN 560477, remove the coolant reservoir (see Chapter 3).

12 Remove the exhaust sysem (see Chapter 4).

13 Release the clip securing the linkage rod or quickshifter rod (according to model) to the gearchange lever **(see illustrations)**. Pry the rod off the lever **(see illustration)**. To improve access on Street Triple models remove the heel guard first. Note the alignment of the punch mark on the gearchange shaft end with the slit in the linkage arm clamp – if the punch mark is not visible make your own mark **(see illustration)**. Unscrew the pinch bolt and slide the arm off the shaft and draw the rod out of

the frame **(see illustration)**. Take care not to lose the ball-joint seal.

14 Remove the front sprocket (see Chapter 6).

15 Detach the clutch cable from the release lever on the clutch cover (see Section 17).

16 Remove the sidestand switch (see Chapter 8) – there is no need to detach the switch from the bracket.

17 Disconnect the wire from the coolant temperature sensor **(see illustration)**.

18 Disconnect the wiring connector from the oil pressure switch **(see illustration)**.

19 If required, remove the starter motor (see Chapter 8). If it is not being removed, pull back

4.13b . . . then draw it out . . .

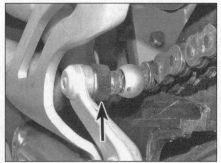

4.13c . . . and detach the rod from the lever. Note the seal (arrowed)

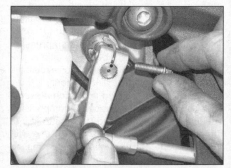

4.13d Note the alignment, then unscrew the bolt, slide the arm off the shaft . . .

4.13e . . . and draw the rod out

4.17 Press the clip in to release the ECT sensor wiring connector

4.18 Disconnect the oil pressure switch wiring connector

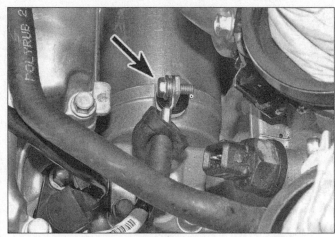

4.19 Unscrew the bolt (arrowed) and detach the lead from the starter motor

4.23 Unscrew the bolt (arrowed) and disconnect the earth leads from the crankcase

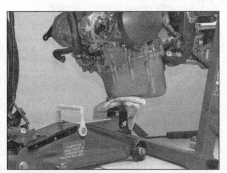

4.24 Place a jack under the engine

4.27a Unscrew the nut on the upper rear bolt . . .

4.27b . . . and the lower rear bolt . . . .

the rubber boot on the terminal, them unscrew the bolt, noting the spring washer, and detach the lead **(see illustration)**.

20 Trace the alternator and crankshaft position sensor wiring from the top of the alternator cover on the left-hand side of the engine and disconnect it at the connectors.

21 Trace the wiring from the speed sensor, which is in the top of the crankcase, and disconnect it at the connector.

22 Trace the wiring from the gear position sensor, which is on the left-hand side of the crankcase, and disconnect it at the connector.

23 Detach the earth leads from the engine **(see illustration)**.

24 At this point, position an hydraulic jack under the engine with a block of wood or some rag between the jack head and sump **(see illustration)**. Make sure the jack is centrally positioned so the engine will not topple in any direction when the last mounting bolt is removed. Take the weight of the engine on the jack, but make sure the jack is not trying to raise the whole bike.

25 Check that all wiring, cables and hoses are disconnected and clear of the engine.

26 When removing the engine mounting bolts, retrieve all nuts, washers and spacers from the mountings and slip them back on the bolts in their correct order for safekeeping, noting carefully where each fits.

27 Unscrew the nuts on the right-hand end of the upper and lower rear mounting bolts **(see illustrations)**. Withdraw the bolts **(see illustrations)**.

28 Unscrew the upper and lower rear engine mounting adjusters on the left-hand side using either the Triumph special tool Part No. T3880103 (which takes the form of a

4.27c . . . then withdraw the upper bolt . . .

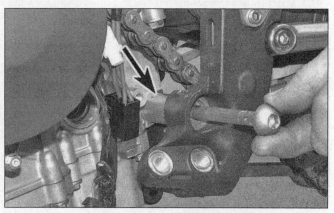

4.27d . . . and the lower bolt, noting the spacer (arrowed)

4.28a The engine mounting adjusters (arrowed) in the frame . . .

4.28b . . . can be undone using a tool such as this

very large flat-bladed screwdriver tip) or a suitable equivalent, until the adjusters no longer protrude from the inside of the frame (see illustrations). Retrieve the spacer(s) for the lower bolt, one on each side on Daytona models, and Street Triple models to VIN 560476, noting which fits where, and one on the left-hand side on Street Triples from VIN 560477 (see illustrations 4.39a and b).

29 Unscrew the left-hand centre mounting bolt (see illustration).

30 Unscrew the nut on the left-hand front mounting bolt, then withdraw the bolt (see illustration).

31 Unscrew the centre and front engine mounting adjusters on the left-hand side

using either the Triumph special tool Part No. T3880103 or equivalent until they no longer protrude from the inside of the frame (see illustrations 4.28a and b).

32 Have an assistant steady the engine then unscrew the right-hand centre mounting bolt (see illustration).

33 Unscrew the nut on the right-hand front mounting bolt, then withdraw the bolt (see illustration).

34 Lower the engine on the jack and slip the drive chain off the output shaft (see illustration). Remove the jack from under the engine and lower the engine until it rests, then manoeuvre the engine clear of the frame and onto the work surface.

 Warning: The engine is heavy and may cause injury if it falls.

35 Discard the nuts for the front and rear mounting bolts – new ones must be used when installing the engine.

Installation

36 Make sure the four engine mounting adjusters in the left-hand side do not protrude from the inside of the frame (see illustration). On Street Triple models from VIN 560477 lubricate the threads of the centre mounting bolts with a smear of copper grease.

37 With the aid of an assistant place the engine under the frame and carefully lift it onto the jack (see illustration 4.24). Raise

4.29 Unscrew and remove the left-hand centre bolt

4.30 Unscrew the nut and withdraw the left-hand front bolt

4.32 Unscrew and remove the right-hand centre bolt

4.33 Unscrew the nut and withdraw the right-hand front bolt

4.34 Slip the drive chain off the shaft

4.36 Make sure the adjusters are flush with the inside of the frame

4.39a Insert the bolt from the right and fit the short spacer (arrowed) . . .

4.39b . . . and the long spacer

4.40 Tighten the centre adjuster to the specified torque

the engine, slipping the drive chain around the output shaft as you do, until all the mounting holes align. Make sure no wires, cables or hoses become trapped between the engine and the frame. Now follow the correct procedure to install and tighten the mounting bolts as detailed below.

Caution: The engine mounting bolts must be tightened in the correct sequence. Failure to do so could leave the engine incorrectly aligned in the frame, placing undue stress on it, which could lead to severe damage.

38 Fit the right-hand centre mounting bolt and tighten it finger-tight **(see illustration 4.32)**.

39 Temporarily insert the lower rear mounting bolt from the **right**-hand side, on Daytona models and Street Triple models to VIN 560476 fitting the short spacer between the engine and frame on the right-hand side and the long spacer on the left, and on Street Triples from VIN 560477 fitting the spacer between the engine and frame on the left-hand side, inserting the bolt only far enough so the left-hand spacer is supported so the bolt does not prevent the tool being applied to the adjuster **(see illustrations)**. On Street Triples from VIN 560477 also insert the upper rear mounting bolt from the right-hand side, again leaving access to the adjuster.

40 Tighten the centre engine mounting adjuster on the left-hand side to the torque setting specified at the beginning of the Chapter using the Triumph tool or a suitable equivalent **(see illustration)**.

41 Fit the left-hand centre mounting bolt and tighten it finger-tight **(see illustration 4.29)**.

42 Tighten the upper and lower rear engine mounting adjusters on the left-hand side to the specified torque setting using the Triumph tool or equivalent **(see illustrations 4.28a and b)**.

43 Insert the right-hand front mounting bolt, then fit a new nut and tighten it to the specified torque **(see illustration 4.33)**.

44 Remove the left-hand centre mounting bolt **(see illustration 4.29)**, then re-check that the adjuster is tightened to its specified torque **(see illustration 4.40)**. Refit the bolt and tighten it to the specified torque.

45 Tighten the right-hand centre mounting

bolt to the specified torque **(see illustration 4.32)**.

46 Withdraw the lower rear mounting bolt from the right-hand side and insert it from the left **(see illustration 4.27d)** – the spacer(s) should remain in place. Fit a new nut and tighten it to the specified torque **(see illustration 4.27b)**.

47 Tighten the front engine mounting adjuster on the left-hand side to the torque setting specified at the beginning of the Chapter using the Triumph tool or equivalent **(see illustrations 4.28a and b)**.

48 On Street Triples from VIN 560477 withdraw the upper rear mounting bolt from the right-hand side. On all models insert the upper rear mounting bolt from the left-hand side, then fit a new nut and tighten it to the specified torque **(see illustrations 4.27c and a)**.

49 Insert the left-hand front mounting bolt, then fit a new nut and tighten it to the specified torque **(see illustration 4.30)**.

50 Lower the jack and remove it.

51 The remainder of the installation procedure is a direct reversal of the removal sequence, referring to the relevant Chapters where directed, and noting the following points.

● Tighten all nuts and bolts to the specified torque settings where directed.

● Clean any old grease off the linkage rod ball-joint and smear some fresh grease on. Align the slit in the gearchange linkage arm with the mark on the gearchange shaft end **(see illustration 4.13d)**. Make sure the ball-joint seal is fitted, the ball fits fully into the socket, and the clip locates correctly **(see illustrations 4.13c, b and a)**.

● Make sure all wires, cables and hoses are correctly routed and connected, and secured by any clips or ties.

● Use new gaskets on the exhaust pipe connections.

● Refill the engine with oil and coolant to the correct levels (see Chapter 1).

● Adjust the throttle and clutch cable freeplay (see Chapter 1).

● Adjust the drive chain slack (see Chapter 1).

● Start the engine and check that there are no oil or coolant leaks before installing the body panels.

5 Engine overhaul information

1 Before beginning the engine overhaul, read through the related procedures to familiarise yourself with the scope and requirements of the job. Overhauling an engine is not all that difficult, but it is time consuming. Check on the availability of parts and make sure that any necessary special tools are obtained in advance.

2 Most work can be done with a decent set of typical workshop hand tools, although a number of precision measuring tools are required for inspecting parts to determine if they are worn.

3 To ensure maximum life and minimum trouble from a rebuilt engine, everything must be assembled with care in a spotlessly clean environment.

Disassembly

4 Before disassembling the engine, thoroughly clean and degrease its external surfaces. This will prevent contamination of the engine internals, and will also make the job a lot easier and cleaner. A high flash-point solvent, such as paraffin (kerosene) can be used, or better still, a proprietary engine degreaser such as Gunk. Use old paintbrushes and toothbrushes to work the solvent into the various recesses of the casings. Take care to exclude solvent or water from the electrical components and intake and exhaust ports.

 Warning: The use of petrol (gasoline) as a cleaning agent should be avoided because of the risk of fire.

5 When clean and dry, position the engine on the workbench, leaving suitable clear area for working. Gather a selection of small containers, plastic bags and some labels so that parts can be grouped together in an easily identifiable manner. Also get some paper and a pen so that notes can be taken. You will also need a supply of clean rag, which should be as absorbent as possible.

6 Before commencing work, read through the appropriate section so that some idea of the necessary procedure can be gained. When removing components note that great force is seldom required, unless specified (checking the specified torque setting of the particular bolt being removed will indicate how tight it is, and therefore how much force should be needed). In many cases, a component's reluctance to be removed is indicative of an incorrect approach or removal method – if in any doubt, re-check with the text.

7 When disassembling the engine, keep 'mated' parts that have been in contact with each other during engine operation together – i.e. cylinder liners, pistons and rings, connecting rods, valves, etc). These 'mated' parts must not be mixed up and must be installed in their original location.

8 Engine/transmission disassembly should be done in the following general order with reference to the appropriate Sections.

   Remove the camshafts
   Remove the cam chain and blades
   Remove the cylinder head
   Remove the cylinder liners and pistons
   Remove the starter motor (see Chapter 8)
   Remove the clutch
   Remove the gearchange mechanism
   Remove the alternator (see Chapter 8)
   Remove the starter motor (see Chapter 8)
   Remove the sump
   Remove the oil/water pump
   Separate the crankcase halves
   Remove the crankshaft/connecting rods
   Remove the balancer shaft
   Remove the transmission shafts
   Remove the selector drum and forks

Reassembly

9 Reassembly is accomplished by reversing the general disassembly sequence.

6 Oil cooler

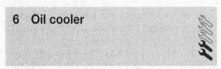

Note: *The oil cooler can be removed with the*

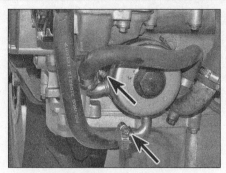

6.4 Slacken the clamps (arrowed) and detach the hoses

engine in the frame. If work is being carried out with the engine removed ignore the preliminary steps.

Removal

1 On Daytona models remove the fairing side panels (see Chapter 7).

2 Drain the engine oil (see Chapter 1). Keep the container below the sump to catch any residual oil in the cooler.

3 Either drain the coolant (see Chapter 1), or fit clamps to the hoses close to the unions on the cooler **(see illustration 6.4)**. Whichever method you choose, be prepared to catch any residual coolant in the hoses and cooler.

4 Slacken the hose clamp screws and detach the hoses from the cooler **(see illustration)**.

5 Unscrew the cooler bolt and remove the cooler, noting how it locates **(see illustration)**. Remove the sealing washer from the bolt and the O-ring from the cooler and discard them as new ones must be used **(see illustration 6.7a)**.

6 Check the cooler for leaks and other damage.

Installation

7 Installation is a reverse of the removal procedure, noting the following:

- Use a new O-ring and sealing washer **(see illustration)**.

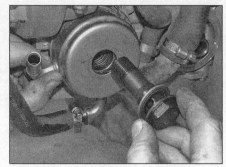

6.5 Unscrew the bolt and remove the cooler

- Make sure the cooler unions are correctly positioned and locate the tabs on each side of the lug on the crankcase **(see illustration)**.
- Tighten the cooler bolt to the torque setting specified at the beginning of the Chapter.
- Refill the engine with oil to the correct level (see Chapter 1 and Pre-ride checks). Make sure there are no leaks from the oil cooler hose unions when the engine is run.

7 Valve cover

Note: *The valve cover can be removed with the engine in the frame. If the engine has been removed, ignore the steps which do not apply.*

Removal

1 Disconnect the battery negative lead (see Chapter 8).

2 On Daytona models remove the fairing side panels (see Chapter 7).

3 Remove the fuel tank and the airbox (see Chapter 4).

4 On Street Triple models remove the right-hand radiator cowl (see Chapter 7).

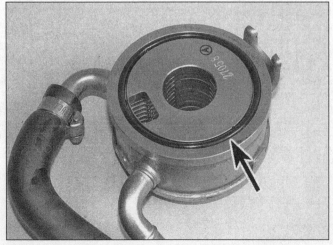

6.7a Fit a new O-ring (arrowed) into the groove

6.7b Locate the tabs (A) on each side of the lug (B)

7.6a Cut the cable-tie (arrowed) . . .

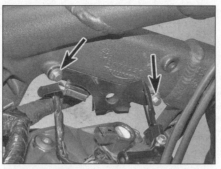

7.6b . . . then unscrew the bolts (arrowed) and remove the bracket from the left-hand side

7.6c . . . and from the right-hand side

5 Disconnect the secondary air injection system solenoid valve wiring connector **(see illustration 4.7)**. Release the clips and disconnect the air hoses from the reed valve housings on the valve cover and remove the valve along with the hoses, noting how it locates.

6 On Daytona models cut the cable-tie on the outside of the solenoid valve/fairing bracket **(see illustration)**. On all models remove the bracket from each side of the frame **(see illustrations)**.

7 Remove the ignition coils (see Chapter 4). Remove the reed valve covers, and if required the valves **(see illustration)**.

8 Undo the throttle cable bracket screws and detach the bracket from the throttle bodies **(see illustration)**.

9 Undo the valve cover bolts evenly and in the order shown, noting which fits where **(see illustration)**. Remove the bolts with their seals, then lift the valve cover off the cylinder head and remove from the right-hand side **(see illustration)**. **Note:** *If the cover is stuck, do not try to lever it off with a screwdriver. Tap it gently around the sides with a rubber hammer or block of wood to dislodge it.*

10 Note the location of the dowels in the secondary air holes **(see illustration 7.13)** – they may remain in the head or come off with the cover. Remove them for safekeeping if they are loose.

11 Examine the valve cover gasket for signs of damage or deterioration – remove the gasket and replace it with a new one if necessary **(see illustration 7.14)**. Check the seals on the cover bolts for cracks, hardening and deterioration and replace them with new ones if necessary.

Installation

12 Clean the mating surfaces of the cylinder head and the valve cover with a suitable solvent. If the original gasket is being used, remove any traces of old glue or sealant.

13 Fit the secondary air injection dowels if removed **(see illustration)**.

14 Fit the gasket onto the cylinder head, flat side up, making sure it locates correctly

around the rim, the plug bores and the dowels **(see illustration)**.

15 Position the valve cover on the cylinder head, making sure the gasket stays in

7.7 Remove the covers, and if required the reed valves (arrowed)

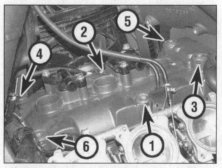

7.9a Unscrew the bolts in the order shown . . .

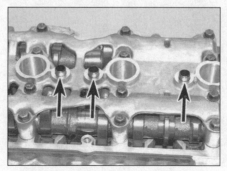

7.13 Fit the dowels (arrowed) if removed

place **(see illustration 7.9b)**. Lubricate the cover bolt seals with engine oil, fit them onto the bolts, then fit the bolts – the two shorter bolts fit at the cam chain end **(see**

7.8 Undo the screws (arrowed) and displace the bracket

7.9b . . . and remove the cover

7.14 Fit the gasket, making sure it locates correctly all around

7.15 Fit the seals onto the bolts then fit the bolts

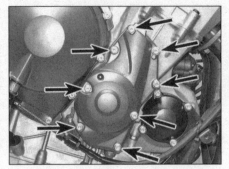

8.2 Unscrew the bolts (arrowed) and remove the cover

8.3a Turn the engine clockwise . . .

illustration). Tighten the bolts evenly in the same order as for removal, to the torque setting specified at the beginning of the Chapter **(see illustration 7.9a)**.
16 Install the remaining components in the reverse order of removal.

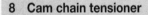

8   Cam chain tensioner

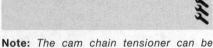

Note: *The cam chain tensioner can be removed with the engine in the frame. If the engine has been removed, ignore the steps which do not apply.*

Removal

1 Remove the valve cover (see Section 7). Remove the spark plugs (see Chapter 1).
2 Unscrew the right-hand crankcase cover bolts, noting the positions of the longer ones and the one fitted with a sealing washer **(see illustration)**. Remove the cover. Discard the gasket – a new one must be used. Remove the dowels if loose **(see illustration 8.16a)**. Check the condition of the sealing washer and replace it with a new one if necessary.
3 On Daytona models, and Street Triple models up to VIN 560476, rotate the crankshaft clockwise using a hex bit in the cam chain drive sprocket bolt or a socket on the nut, until the punch mark on the primary drive gear is aligned with the index mark on the crankcase, and the lines on the camshaft sprockets face

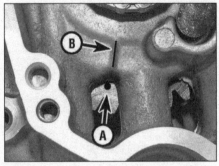

8.3b . . . until the punch mark (A) aligns with the index mark (B) . . .

inwards towards each other, parallel with the top of the cylinder head **(see illustrations)** – note that the sprockets used on some models (generally from around 2010-on, but only up to VIN 560476 on Street Triple models) have two lines on each sprocket, one plain and one marked with an '8'; align the plain lines as described, NOT the lines marked 8 **(see illustration)**. In this position, the No. 1 cylinder is at TDC. If the lines face away from each other when the punch mark aligns, turn the crankshaft clockwise one full turn so that the punch mark again aligns with the index mark – the lines on the camshaft sprockets will now be facing towards each other.
4 On Street Triple models from VIN 560477 rotate the crankshaft clockwise using a socket on the nut, until the punch mark (highlighted

8.3c . . . and the line on each sprocket points inwards and is parallel with the head mating surface

with paint) on the primary drive gear is aligned with the index mark (also highlighted) on the crankcase **(see illustrations 8.3a and b)**, and the lines (highlighted) on the camshaft ends face inwards towards each other, parallel with the top of the cylinder head **(see illustration)**. In this position, the No. 1 cylinder is at TDC. If the lines face away from each other when the punch mark aligns, turn the crankshaft clockwise one full turn so that the punch mark again aligns with the index mark – the lines on the camshaft sprockets will now be facing towards each other. Fit a locking pin (Triumph part No. T3880601 or a suitable equivalent, such as a punch of the correct diameter) through the holes in the crankcase and crankshaft web above the cam chain drive sprocket on the crankshaft to lock the crankshaft in position.

8.3d Alternative camshaft sprocket markings and alignment for some models

8.4 The line (arrowed) on each camshaft must point in and be parallel with the head mating surface

8.5 Cable-tie the chain to each sprocket to prevent the possibility of it jumping a tooth

8.6 Unscrew the end bolt (arrowed) and remove the sealing washer and spring

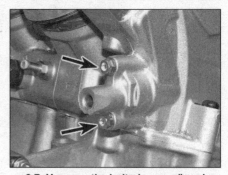

8.7 Unscrew the bolts (arrowed) and withdraw the tensioner from the head

8.9 Release the catch and check the plunger moves freely in and out

8.10a Cam chain tensioner assembly – Daytona from VIN 377510-on

1 Tensioner body
2 O-ring
3 Resister ring
4 Snap ring
5 Spring
6 Plunger
7 Snap ring groove

H48034

5 When the tensioner is withdrawn from the cylinder head, the cam chain will be un-tensioned, and could jump a tooth on the intake camshaft sprocket. To prevent this, fit a suitable wedge between the tensioner blade and the crankcase to keep the blade pressed against the chain, and as a back-up also fit a cable-tie through a hole and around the chain on each sprocket as shown **(see illustration)**.
6 On Daytona models up to VIN 377509 and Street Triple models up to VIN 560476 unscrew the large end bolt from the tensioner and withdraw the spring, noting that it will be under tension **(see illustration)**. Note the sealing washer on the bolt.
7 Unscrew the two mounting bolts, evenly and a little at a time, and withdraw the tensioner, noting that on Daytona models from VIN 377510 and Street Triple models from VIN

560477 the plunger will be pushed out under spring pressure **(see illustration)**. Remove the O-ring and discard it – a new one must be used **(see illustration 8.11a)**. On Daytona models from VIN 377510 and Street Triple models from VIN 560477 also remove and discard the gasket.

Inspection

8 Examine the tensioner components for signs of wear or damage.
9 On Daytona models up to VIN 377509 and Street Triple models up to VIN 560476 lift the catch on the tensioner body and move the plunger in and out – if it doesn't move smoothly and freely, replace the tensioner with a new one **(see illustration)**. Check the condition of the spring – if it is obviously deformed replace the tensioner with a new one.

10 On Daytona models from VIN 377510 and Street Triple models from VIN 560477 examine the tensioner for signs of wear or damage **(see illustration)**. Hold the ends of the resister spring together and withdraw the plunger and spring **(see illustration)**. Drain the oil out of the body. Clean all components. Make sure the resister ring and snap ring are correctly located in their grooves **(see illustration)**. Fit the spring back into the tensioner. Hold the ends of the resister ring together to expand it and push the plunger through it and all the way in **(see illustration 8.9b)** – when the snap ring aligns with the outer groove in the plunger keep it held there, release the resister ring, then move one end of the snap ring into the groove and hold it there, then slowly release the plunger so the snap ring holds it in the retracted position **(see illustration)**.

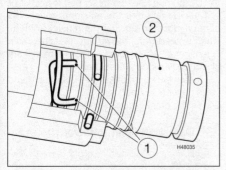

8.10b Hold the resister spring ends (1) together and withdraw the plunger (2) and spring

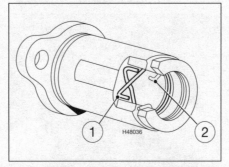

8.10c Make sure the resister ring (1) and snap ring (2) are correctly located

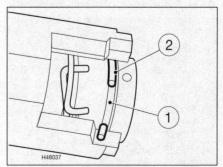

8.10d Locate the snap ring (2) in the groove (1) then release the plunger, which should lock in place

8.12a Fit a new O-ring (arrowed) into the groove . . .

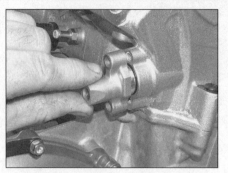

8.12b . . . then fit the tensioner

8.13 Fit the end bolt and spring, using a new sealing washer

Installation

Daytona models up to VIN 377509 and Street Triple models up to VIN 560476

11 Lift the catch and push the plunger in until it engages with the first tooth on the plunger ratchet in the fully retracted position **(see illustration 8.8)**.

12 Clean the threads of the tensioner mounting bolts. Fit a new O-ring into the groove on the tensioner body, then smear it with oil **(see illustration)**. Apply a suitable thread locking compound to the tensioner mounting bolt threads, then fit the tensioner and tighten the bolts to the torque setting specified at the beginning of the Chapter **(see illustration)**.

13 Make sure the sealing washer is on the end bolt. Fit the spring and end bolt into the tensioner body **(see illustration)**. Tighten the end bolt to the specified torque setting – as you fit the spring and tighten the bolt the plunger should be heard clicking over the ratchet mechanism as it extends against the tensioner

blade and takes up the slack in the chain.

14 Check that the tensioner plunger is correctly located in the middle of the tensioner blade when viewed from above, and that the chain is tensioned. Remove the cable-ties from around the sprockets **(see illustration 8.5)**.

15 Rotate the engine clockwise through four revolutions and recheck the timing marks (see Step 3) and tensioner plunger (see Step 13). If the cam chain has jumped whilst the tensioner was removed, remove the tensioner again to provide slack in the chain, then reposition the intake camshaft using a spanner on the hex behind the sprocket to turn it while feeding the chain around the sprocket, until the timing marks are correctly aligned.

16 Install the spark plugs (see Chapter 1) and valve cover (see Section 7).

17 Fit the crankcase cover dowels if removed, then fit a new gasket, locating it over the dowels **(see illustration)**. Fit the cover and tighten the bolts to the specified torque, making sure the two longer bolts are correctly

positioned and not forgetting the sealing washer with the centre top bolt, and using a new one if necessary **(see illustrations)**.

Daytona models from VIN 377510 and Street Triple models from VIN 560477

Note: *If a new tensioner is being fitted it will come with the plunger compressed into the body ready for installation – do not release the plunger before fitting.*

18 If the original tensioner is being refitted, and if not already done, refer to Step 9 and drain and clean the tensioner, then reset the plunger in the retracted position as described.

19 Clean the threads of the tensioner mounting bolts. Fit a new O-ring and gasket on the tensioner body. Apply a suitable thread locking compound to the tensioner mounting bolt threads, then fit the tensioner and tighten the bolts to the torque setting specified at the beginning of the Chapter.

20 Remove the wedge holding the tensioner blade and the cable-ties from around the sprockets **(see illustration 8.5)**.

21 On Street Triple models from VIN 560477 remove the crankshaft locking pin.

22 To release the tensioner plunger rotate the engine anti-clockwise a quarter turn, then turn it clockwise until the timing marks align as in Step 3 or 4, according to model. Check that the tensioner plunger is correctly located against the tensioner blade when viewed from above, and that the chain is tensioned. Make sure the timings marks are all correctly aligned (Step 3 or 4). Rotate the crankshaft clockwise through four full turns, then reset it to TDC on number 1 as described in Step 3 or 4. Check again that the tensioner plunger is correctly located against the tensioner blade when viewed from above, and that the chain is tensioned. Make sure the timings marks are all correctly aligned (Step 3 or 4).

23 Install the spark plugs (see Chapter 1) and valve cover (see Section 7).

24 Fit the crankcase cover (see Step 17).

8.17a Fit the new gasket onto the dowels

8.17b Fit the cover . . .

8.17c . . . positioning the longer bolts (arrowed) as shown . . .

8.17d . . . and using a new sealing washer on the top front bolt

9 Camshafts and followers

Note: *This procedure can be carried out with the engine in the frame.*

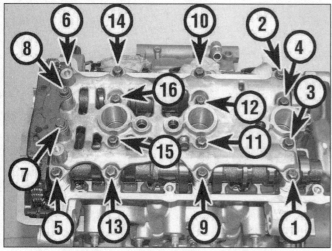

9.2 Slacken the bolts in the order shown

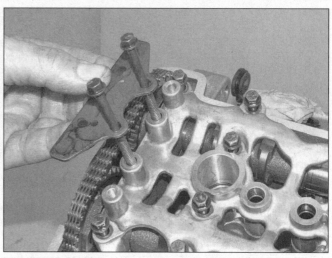

9.3a Remove the upper guide . . .

9.3b . . . then lift the holder off

9.3c Remove the small O-rings from the dowels (arrowed) . . .

9.3d . . . and the large ones from the plug bores

Removal

1 Remove the cam chain tensioner (see Section 8). Note that it is not necessary to fit the wedge or cable-tie the cam chain to the sprockets.
2 Undo the camshaft holder bolts evenly and a little at a time in the order shown (see illustration).
3 Remove the bolts and the cam chain upper guide, then lift the holder off (see illustrations). The two bolts that secure the guide are slightly longer than the rest. Remove the O-rings from around the dowels, and remove the dowels for

safekeeping if they are loose (see illustration). Remove the spark plug bore O-rings (see illustration). If the O-rings are damaged or deformed they must be replaced with new ones. *Caution: A camshaft could break if the holder bolts are not slackened as described and the pressure from a depressed valve causes the shaft to bend. Also, if the holder does not come squarely away from the head, the holder is likely to break. If this happens the cylinder head must be renewed; the holders are matched to the head and cannot be obtained separately.*

4 Lift the cam chain off the intake camshaft sprocket and remove the camshaft (see illustration 9.24).
5 Repeat the procedure for the exhaust camshaft (see illustration 9.23a).
6 The cam chain can be left to rest on its support bolt in the tunnel. Note that for identification the exhaust camshaft is marked with an 'E' on the right-hand end and the intake camshaft is marked with an 'I' (see illustration). Also the exhaust camshaft has a rib near its centre, which on the intake camshaft has been machined off (see illustration).

9.6a Exhaust camshaft mark (A), intake camshaft mark (B)

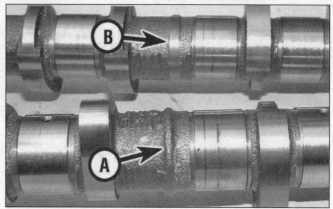

9.6b Exhaust camshaft rib (A), intake camshaft machined section (B)

9.8a Remove the cam follower . . .

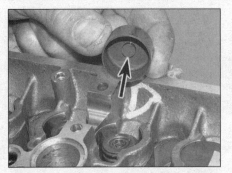

9.8b . . . and retrieve the shim (arrowed)

9.9 Inspect the bearing and lobe surfaces for scratches and wear – here's an example of damage requiring camshaft repair or renewal

7 If the followers and shims are being removed from the cylinder head, obtain a container which is divided into twelve compartments. Label each compartment with the location of a valve, i.e. cylinder identity (i.e. 1, 2 or 3), intake or exhaust valve (I or E), left or right valve (L or R). If a container is not available, use labelled plastic bags (egg cartons also work very well!).

8 Remove the cam follower of the first valve, using a suction tool or magnet if needed **(see illustration)**. Retrieve the shim from inside the follower **(see illustration)** – if it is not there pick it out of the top of the valve using a magnet or a small screwdriver with a dab of grease on it (the shim will stick to the grease) **(see illustration 9.21a)**. Do not allow the shim to fall into the engine. Repeat for all the valves.

Inspection

9 Inspect the bearing surfaces on the camshafts and in the cylinder head and camshaft holder. Look for score marks, deep scratches and evidence of spalling (a pitted appearance). Check the camshaft lobes for heat discoloration (blue appearance), score marks, chipped areas, flat spots and spalling **(see illustration)**.

 Refer to Tools and Workshop Tips (Section 3) in the Reference section for details of how to read a micrometer and dial gauge.

10 Check the amount of camshaft runout by supporting each end of the camshaft on V-blocks, and measuring any runout using a dial gauge. If the runout exceeds the specified limit the camshaft must be replaced with a new one.

11 Next, check the camshaft bearing oil clearances, using a product called Plastigauge. Check each camshaft in turn rather than both at the same time.

12 Clean the camshaft journals, the bearing surfaces in the cylinder head and the camshaft holder with a clean, lint-free cloth, then lay the camshaft in place in the cylinder head – there is no need to engage the chain on the sprocket. Ensure the crankshaft and camshaft are positioned as for removal (see Section 8, Step 3). Apply a thin smear of grease to each journal and silicone release agent to each bearing surface in the holder.

13 Cut strips of Plastigauge and lay one piece on each camshaft journal, parallel with the camshaft centreline **(see illustration)**. Make sure the dowels are installed then fit the camshaft holder **(see illustration 9.3c and b)**. Fit the holder bolts and the cam chain upper guide and tighten the bolts finger-tight – the longer bolts go with the guide **(see illustration 9.3a)**. Making sure the camshaft does not rotate, tighten the bolts evenly and a little at a time in the correct tightening sequence **(see illustration 9.28)**, to the torque setting specified at the beginning of the Chapter.

14 Now unscrew the bolts evenly and a little at a time in the removal sequence **(see illustration 9.2)** and carefully lift off the

holder, again making sure the camshaft does rotate.

15 To determine the oil clearance, compare the crushed Plastigauge (at its widest point) on each journal to the scale printed on the Plastigauge container **(see illustration)**. Compare the results to this Chapter's Specifications. If the oil clearance is greater than specified, measure the diameter of the camshaft journal with a micrometer **(see illustration)**. If the journal diameter is less than the specified limit, replace the camshaft with a new one and recheck the clearance. If the clearance is still too great, or if the camshaft journal is within its limit, replace the cylinder head and holder as a set with new ones – individual components are not available.

HAYNES HINT *Before renewing the camshafts, cylinder head/holders because of damage, check with local machine shops specialising in motorcycle engine work. In the case of the camshafts, it may be possible for cam lobes to be welded, reground and hardened, at a cost far lower than that of a new camshaft. If the bearing surfaces in the head or holders are damaged, it may be possible for them to be bored out to accept bearing inserts. Due to the cost of new components it is recommended that all options are explored!*

9.13 Lay a strip of Plastigauge across each bearing journal, parallel with the camshaft centreline

9.15a Compare the width of the crushed Plastigauge to the scale printed on the Plastigauge container

9.15b Measure the cam bearing journals with a micrometer

9.21a Fit each shim into the recess on the top of the valve assembly . . .

9.21b . . . then fit the follower

9.24a Keeping the front run of the chain taut, install the exhaust camshaft . . .

Note that if specialist measuring tools are available, the camshaft bearing bore inside diameter can be compared with the specified limit.

16 Repeat the oil clearance check on the other camshaft.

17 On Daytona models and Street Triple models up to VIN 560476 check the camshaft sprockets for wear, cracks and other damage, replacing them with new ones if necessary by unscrewing the bolts and removing the sprockets from the ends of the camshaft. The same design sprocket is used for each camshaft, but different bolt hole positions are provided for fitting to the intake or exhaust camshaft. When fitting the sprocket to the intake camshaft, the hole nearest to the IN marking and its corresponding opposite must be used; for the exhaust camshaft sprocket, the hole nearest to the EX marking and its opposite must be used **(see illustration 8.3)**. Clean the sprocket bolt threads then fit the sprockets as described, apply non-permanent thread locking compound to the bolts and tighten them to the specified torque setting. Follow the installation procedure below under the heading 'Daytona models and Street Triple models up to VIN 560476, and Street Triple models from VIN 560477 if the sprocket bolts have not been loosened'.

18 On Street Triple models from VIN 560477 check the camshaft sprockets for wear, cracks and other damage, replacing them with new ones if necessary – on these models the holes for the bolts are elongated, allowing adjustment of the position of the sprocket on the camshaft for fine tuning the valve timing, but this makes the set-up procedure complicated (see below). Unscrew the bolts and remove the sprockets only if absolutely necessary. The same design sprocket is used for each camshaft. Clean the sprocket bolt threads then fit the sprockets with the bolts in the elongated holes, but tighten the bolts finger-tight only at this stage so the sprocket can turn slightly within the restrictions of the holes. Make sure you follow the installation procedure below under the heading 'Street Triple models from VIN 560477 if the sprocket bolts have been loosened'. If the sprocket bolts on these models are not loosened at all, so the position of the sprocket on the

9.24b . . . with the line pointing rearwards parallel with the head

camshaft has not changed since removal of the camshaft, follow the installation procedure below under the heading 'Daytona models and Street Triple models up to VIN 560476, and Street Triple models from VIN 560477 if the sprocket bolts have not been loosened'.

19 If the sprockets are worn, it is likely the cam chain and sprocket on the crankshaft will be worn as well. Refer to Section 10 for details of how to check the cam chain for wear.

20 Inspect the outer surfaces of the followers and surfaces of the bores they run in for evidence of scoring, wear or other damage **(see illustration 9.8a)**. If necessary the followers and cylinder head must be replaced with new ones.

Installation

Note: It is important that the followers and shims are returned to their original valves otherwise the valve clearances will be inaccurate.

21 If removed, lubricate each shim with molybdenum disulphide oil and fit it into its recess in the top of the valve **(see illustration)**. Check that the shims are correctly seated, then lubricate and fit the followers **(see illustration)**.

22 Make sure the bearing surfaces in the cylinder head, on the camshafts and in the holder are clean, then liberally apply molybdenum disulphide oil (a 50/50 mixture of molybdenum disulphide grease and engine oil) to each of them. Also apply the oil to the camshaft lobes.

9.25 Lay the intake camshaft in the head, making sure the chain is taut between the sprockets

Daytona models, and Street Triple models up to VIN 560476, and Street Triple models from VIN 560477 if the sprocket bolts have not been loosened

23 Check that the crankshaft is positioned as described in Section 8, Step 3 or 4, according to model.

24 Lift the cam chain off the support bolt, and make sure that it is engaged around the drive sprocket on the crankshaft. Keeping the front run of the chain taut, lay the exhaust camshaft (marked with an 'E' and a rib) in position so that the line (the plain one, not the one marked 8 where present) on its sprocket faces rearwards and is parallel with the top mating surface of the cylinder head, then engage the chain on the sprocket teeth **(see illustrations)**.

25 Slip the intake camshaft (marked with an 'I') through the cam chain so that the line (the plain one, not the one marked 8 where present) on its sprocket faces forwards and is parallel with the head **(see illustration)**. Engage the chain fully on the sprocket teeth, making sure that the chain is tight between the camshafts, with any slack lying in the rear run where it will be taken up by the tensioner. Check that the punch mark on the primary drive gear is still aligned with the index mark on the crankcase.

26 Fit the spark plug bore O-rings, the dowels if removed, and the dowel O-rings **(see illustrations 9.3d and c)** – use new O-rings if necessary. Fit the holder onto the camshafts **(see illustration 9.3b)** – make sure it locates

9.26 Make sure the camshaft holder locates correctly

correctly over the raised section on each shaft **(see illustration)**. Clean and lightly oil the camshaft holder bolt threads. Fit the bolts, not forgetting the cam chain upper guide (which is secured by the two longer bolts) and tighten them finger-tight **(see illustration 9.3a)**.

27 In order to prevent the cam chain jumping a tooth as the camshafts are tightened down, fit cable-ties around the chain and through the sprockets **(see illustration 8.5)**.

28 Tighten the holder bolts evenly and a little at a time in the sequence shown until the specified torque setting is reached **(see illustration)**.

29 With all bolts tightened down, check that the timing marks still align (see Section 8, Step 3 or 4, according to model). If they don't, remove the cable-ties, then slip the cam chain off the sprockets (there should be enough slack in the rear run to do this easily without having to displace the camshafts). Turn the camshaft(s), and on Street Triple models to VIN 560476 the crankshaft, as required until their alignment is correct. With the timing set up correctly, check that each camshaft is not pinched by turning it a few degrees in each direction.

30 Install the cam chain tensioner (Section 8).
31 Check the valve clearances (see Chapter 1).

Street triple models from VIN 560477 if the sprocket bolts have been loosened

32 Check that the crankshaft is positioned as described in Section 8, Step 4. Make sure each sprocket is positioned so the bolts are central in their holes, and that the bolts are tight enough to hold them in that position, but not so tight that they can't be moved by hand.

33 Lift the cam chain off the support bolt, and make sure that it is engaged around the drive sprocket on the crankshaft. Keeping the front run of the chain taut, lay the exhaust camshaft (marked with an 'E' and a rib) in position so that the line on its end faces rearwards and is parallel with the top mating surface of the cylinder head, then engage the chain on the sprocket teeth **(see illustration 9.24a and 8.4)**. Slip the intake camshaft (marked with an 'I') through the cam chain so that the line on its end faces forwards and is parallel with the head **(see illustration 9.25 and 8.4)**. Engage the chain fully on the sprocket teeth, making sure that the chain is tight between the camshafts, with any slack lying in the rear run where it will be taken up by the tensioner.

34 On the left-hand end of the camshafts there are slots for aligning and locking the camshafts in the correct positions using either the Triumph tool, part No. T3880640, or a suitable piece of steel bar of the correct thickness to fit in the slots **(see illustration)**. Fit the tool or bar into the slots in both camshafts so they are locked in the correct position.

35 Fit the spark plug bore O-rings, and the dowels if removed **(see illustration 9.3c)** - use new O-rings if necessary. Fit the holder onto the camshafts **(see illustration 9.3b)** – make sure it locates correctly over the raised section on each shaft **(see illustration 9.26)**. Clean and lightly oil the camshaft holder bolt threads. Fit the bolts, not forgetting the cam chain upper guide (which is secured by the

two longer bolts) and tighten them finger-tight **(see illustration 9.3a)**.

36 In order to prevent the cam chain jumping a tooth as the camshafts are tightened down, fit cable-ties around the chain and through the sprockets **(see illustration 8.5)**.

37 Tighten the holder bolts evenly and a little at a time in the sequence shown to an initial torque setting of 5 Nm **(see illustration 9.28)**. Now tighten them in the same sequence to the final torque of 10 Nm.

38 With the camshafts and crankshaft locked with the bar tool and the pin respectively, the positions of the sprockets can now be set by pushing in on the back of the cam chain tensioner blade via the tensioner hole so the slack is taken up – again Triumph have a special tool for this, part No. T3880607, which fits in the place of the cam chain tensioner, and when the centre stud is tightened (a 6mm hex key is supplied with the tool to do this) to 0.6 Nm it sets the chain at exactly the correct tension so the sprockets are in exactly the right position. If you are not using the tool then just take up all the slack in the chain by pushing on the tensioner blade via the tensioner hole using a suitable tool so it is under some tension, but you do not have to push hard. With the chain tensioned remove the exposed camshaft sprocket bolt from each sprocket and apply some thread locking compound, then refit the bolts and tighten them to the specified torque.

39 Remove the camshaft locking bar and the crankshaft locking pin. Keeping the chain tensioned turn the crankshaft clockwise as before until the two other sprocket bolts are exposed. Remove the bolts and apply some thread locking compound, then refit the bolts and tighten them to the specified torque. Remove the tensioning tool.

40 Install the cam chain tensioner (Section 8).
41 Check the valve clearances (see Chapter 1).

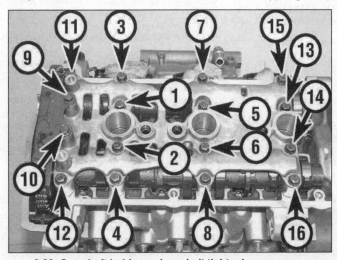

9.28 Camshaft holder and cap bolt tightening sequence

9.34 Fit the tool or piece of bar into the slots (arrowed) to align and lock the camshafts

10.5 Lift the front guide blade out

10.6 Unscrew and remove the support bolt . . .

10.7 . . . then remove the chain

10 Cam chain and tensioner/ guide blades

Note: *The cam chain and tensioner blade can be removed with the engine in the frame.*

Cam chain upper guide

1 Remove the valve cover (see Section 7).
2 Unscrew the bolts securing the upper guide and lift off **(see illustration 9.3a)**.
3 Installation is the reverse of removal. Tighten the bolts to the torque setting specified at the beginning of the Chapter for the camshaft holder bolts.

Cam chain

Removal

4 Remove the camshafts (see Section 9).
5 Lift the guide blade out of the front of the cam chain tunnel, noting how it locates **(see illustration)**.
6 Hold the cam chain and remove the support bolt from the centre of the right-hand side of the cylinder head **(see illustration)**. Note the seal on the bolt and replace it with a new one if it is worn or damaged.
7 Disengage the cam chain from the crankshaft sprocket and draw it out of the tunnel **(see illustration)**.

Inspection

8 Check the cam chain for binding, loose pins and worn or damaged plates and replace it with a new one if necessary.

9 Inspect the crankshaft and camshaft sprockets for worn, chipped or missing teeth. If the chain and sprockets show signs of extensive wear renew them as a complete set.
10 If the chain appears to be in good condition, check it for stretch as follows. Hang the chain from a hook and attach a 13 kg (28 lb) weight to its lower end.
11 Measure the length of 24 pins (from the outer edge of the 1st pin to the outer edge of the 24th pin) and compare the result to the stretch limit specified at the beginning of the Chapter. If the chain exceeds the service limit it must be replaced with a new one.

Installation

12 Installation is a reverse of removal. Make sure the chain is correctly engaged around the drive sprocket on the crankshaft. Fit the cam chain support bolt using a new sealing washer if necessary and tighten to the torque setting specified at the beginning of the chapter.

Cam chain tensioner blade

Removal

13 Remove the camshafts (see Section 9).
14 Withdraw the tensioner blade pivot pin and lift the blade out of the cam chain tunnel **(see illustrations)**.
15 Check the tensioner blade for wear, cracking and other damage, and replace it with a new one if necessary. On Daytona models from VIN 377510-on note the blade consists of three separate components – the tensioner plunger contact pad, the main

aluminium body of the blade, and the facing blade which the chain runs on – all of which are available separately.

Installation

16 Installation is the reverse of removal. Lubricate the pivot pin.

Cam chain guide blade

Removal

17 Remove the camshafts (see Section 9).
18 Lift the blade out of the cam chain tunnel, noting how it locates **(see illustration 10.5)**.
19 Check the guide blade for wear, cracking and other damage, and replace it with a new one if necessary.

Installation

20 Fit the cam chain guide blade into the front of the tunnel and locate it correctly in its seat and in its cut-out in the top of the cylinder head **(see illustration 10.5)**.
21 Install the camshafts (see Section 9).

11 Starter clutch and gears

Note: *The starter clutch can be removed with the engine in the frame. If the engine has been removed, ignore the steps which do not apply.*

Starter clutch check

1 If you suspect the starter clutch of being faulty, a simple check can be performed as follows.
2 Remove the starter motor (see Chapter 8).
3 Using a finger, check that the starter idle/ reduction gear turns clockwise, and locks when turned anti-clockwise, when looked at via the starter motor aperture. If not, remove the starter clutch for further investigation.

Removal

4 Remove the alternator rotor (see Chapter 8) – the starter clutch is bolted to the back of it. If the starter driven gear does not come away with the rotor slide it off the crankshaft.

Inspection

5 With the alternator face down on a

10.14a Withdraw the pivot pin . . .

10.14b . . . and lift the blade out

11.5 Starter clutch gear should turn freely anti-clockwise

11.6 Lift the gear out of the starter clutch body

11.7a Check the surface of the hub (A) and the sprags (B) for wear and damage

11.7b Starter clutch bolts (arrowed)

workbench, check that the starter driven gear rotates freely anti-clockwise and locks against the rotor clockwise **(see illustration)**. If it doesn't, the starter clutch should be dismantled for further investigation.

6 Withdraw the starter driven gear from the starter clutch, rotating it anti-clockwise as you do **(see illustration)**.

7 Examine the outer bearing surface of the gear hub and the condition of the sprags inside the housing **(see illustration)**. If the hub or sprags show signs of excessive wear or are damaged, replace them with new parts. To remove the starter clutch assembly, hold the alternator rotor using a holding strap and unscrew the six bolts inside the rotor **(see illustration)**. The sprag housing and sprag assembly are available separately. Lift the sprag assembly out of the housing, noting which

way round it fits. Install the new assembly in a reverse sequence – the sprag assembly fits into the lipped side of the housing, and the lipped side faces the alternator rotor. Tighten the bolts evenly and a little at a time in the sequence shown in illustration 11.7b to the torque setting specified at the beginning of the Chapter. Go round all the bolts two more times in sequence checking that all remain tightened to the correct torque.

8 Check the condition of the needle bearing on the crankshaft and fit a new bearing if necessary **(see illustration)** – refer to *Tools and Workshop Tips* in the Reference Section for details of bearing checks and removal and installation methods.

9 Also check the inner bearing surface in the starter driven gear hub, and if the bearing has been removed the bearing surface on the crankshaft, for wear and damage, particularly if the bearing itself was worn or damaged.

10 Examine the teeth of the idle/reduction gear and the corresponding teeth of the starter driven gear and starter motor driveshaft. Replace the gears and/or starter motor with new ones if worn or chipped teeth are discovered on related gears. Also check the idle/reduction gear shaft for damage.

Installation

11 Lubricate the outside of the starter driven gear hub, the needle bearing and the clutch sprags with molybdenum disulphide oil (a

50/50 mixture of molybdenum disulphide grease and engine oil).

12 Fit the gear into the clutch, rotating it clockwise as you do so to spread the sprags and allow the hub to enter **(see illustration 11.6)**.

13 Install the alternator rotor (see Chapter 8).

12 Cylinder head removal and installation

Note: *To remove the cylinder head the engine must be removed from the frame.*

Removal

1 Remove the engine from the frame (see Section 4).

2 Remove the camshafts and followers (see Section 9).

3 Remove the cam chain blades (see Section 10).

4 Remove the cam chain support bolt from the right-hand side of the cylinder head **(see illustration 10.6)**. Either remove the cam chain, or let it drop down the tunnel.

5 Release the coolant bypass hose clamp and detach the hose from the back of the head **(see illustration)**.

6 Undo the two screws from the right-hand end of the cylinder head **(see illustration)**.

7 Slacken the eight cylinder head bolts evenly and a little at a time in the sequence shown

11.8 Check the bearing (arrowed)

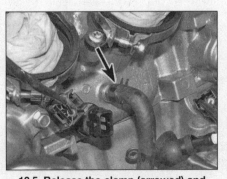

12.5 Release the clamp (arrowed) and detach the hose

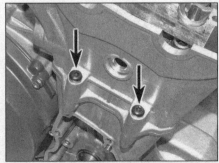

12.6 Remove the two screws (arrowed) from the right-hand end of the head

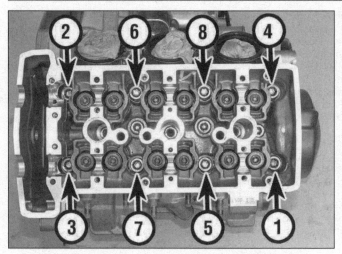

12.7 Sequence for loosening the cylinder head bolts

12.9 Carefully lift the cylinder head up off the engine

(see illustration). When all are loose, remove the bolts and their washers. Triumph specify to use new bolts and washers on installation.

8 Tap around the joint of the cylinder head and the crankcase with a soft-faced mallet to free the head. Don't attempt to free it by inserting a screwdriver in the joint – you'll damage the sealing surfaces.

9 Carefully lift the head off and remove it (see illustration). Remove the head gasket and the two dowels if they are loose (see illustrations 12.15).

10 If the crankshaft is rotated with the head off it is possible that the liners may move and the seal between them and the crankcase be broken, causing coolant from the cylinder block water jacket to seep into the crankcase. If this happens the cylinder liners must be removed and resealed. Refer to Section 14 for liner removal and installation details. Alternatively clamp them in place using the bolt, nut and washer arrangement described and shown in Section 14 (see illustration 14.10b).

11 Inspect the cylinder head gasket and the mating surfaces for signs of leakage, which could indicate that the head is distorted. If necessary, check the cylinder head for warpage using a straight-edge (see Section 13, Step 15). Discard the old head gasket as a new one must be fitted on reassembly.

Installation

12 If disturbed fit and seal the liners in the cylinder block (see Section 14). Remove the clamping bolts once the sealant has set.

13 Clean the mating surfaces of the cylinder head and crankcase with a suitable solvent to remove all traces of old gasket. If a scraper is used, take care not to scratch or gouge the soft aluminium. Ensure none of the old gasket material falls into the cylinders or water jacket.

HAYNES HiNT *Refer to Tools and Workshop Tips for details of gasket removal methods.*

14 Check that the bolt holes in the crankcase are clean and dry. Clean the threads and under the heads of the head bolts. Lubricate the threads with a smear of clean engine oil, then wipe them with lint free cloth so most but not all the oil is removed. Lubricate under the heads of the bolts with molybdenum disulphide grease.

15 If removed, fit the two dowels into the crankcase (see illustration). Fit the new head gasket over the dowels – it should be obvious which way round it fits, but check that all the holes are correctly aligned.

16 Carefully fit the cylinder head, locating it on the dowels (see illustration 12.9).

12.15 Fit the dowels (arrowed) then lay the head gasket on

17 Fit the new cylinder head bolts with their new washers and tighten them finger-tight only at this stage (see illustration).

18 Tighten the cylinder head bolts in the correct numerical sequence to the stage 1 torque setting (see illustration). Repeat to the stage 2 torque setting. Finally, attach a degree disc to the torque wrench and angle-tighten each bolt 120° following the same sequence (see illustration).

19 Fit the screws into the right-hand end of the cylinder head and tighten them to the specified torque setting (see illustration 12.6).

20 Fit the coolant bypass hose and tighten the clamp hose (see illustration 12.5).

12.17 Fit the bolts with their washers . . .

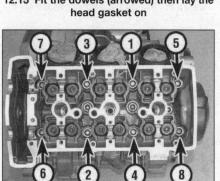

12.18a . . . then tighten them in the sequence shown and in stages as described . . .

12.18b . . . using a degree disc for the final stage

21 Install the cam chain if removed, or lift it out of the tunnel if not – in each case make sure it is correctly engaged around the drive sprocket on the crankshaft. Fit the cam chain support bolt using a new sealing washer if necessary and tighten to the torque setting specified at the beginning of the chapter **(see illustration 10.6)**.

22 Install the remaining components in the reverse order of removal.

13 Cylinder head and valve overhaul

1 Because of the complex nature of this job and the special tools and equipment required,

most owners leave servicing of the valves, valve seats and valve guides to a Triumph dealer or head specialist. However, you can make an initial assessment of whether the valves are seating correctly, and therefore sealing, by pouring a small amount of solvent into each of the valve ports. If the solvent leaks past any valve into the combustion chamber area the valve is not seating correctly and sealing.

2 With the correct tools (a valve spring compressor is essential – make sure it is suitable for motorcycle work), you can also remove the valves and associated components from the cylinder head, clean them and check them for wear to assess the extent of the work needed, and, unless seat cutting or guide replacement is required, reassemble them in the head.

3 A dealer service department or specialist can replace the guides and re-cut the valve seats.

4 After the valve service has been performed, be sure to clean it very thoroughly before installation on the engine to remove any metal particles or abrasive grit that may still be present from the valve service operations. Use compressed air, if available, to blow out all the holes and passages.

Disassembly

5 Remove the followers and their shims if you haven't already done so (see Section 9, Steps 7 and 8). Store the components as specified that they can be returned to their original locations without getting mixed up.

6 Carefully scrape all carbon deposits out of the combustion chamber area. A hand held wire brush or a piece of fine emery cloth can be used once the majority of deposits have been scraped away. Do not use a wire brush mounted in a drill motor, or one with extremely stiff bristles, as the head material is soft and may be eroded away or scratched by the wire brush.

7 Arrange to label and store the valves and their related components in the same way as the followers and shims (or with them if there is room) so they can be reinstalled in the same valve guides they are removed from.

8 Compress the valve spring on the first valve with a spring compressor, then remove the collets **(see illustrations)**. **Note:** *Take great care not to mark the follower bore with the spring compressor.* Do not compress the springs any more than is necessary. Carefully release the valve spring compressor, then remove the spring retainer and the spring **(see illustrations)**. Push the valve stem down and draw the valve out from the underside of the head **(see illustration)** – if the valve binds in the guide (won't pull through), push it back into the head and deburr the area around the collet groove with a very fine file or whetstone **(see illustration)**.

9 Pull the valve stem seal off the top of the valve guide with pliers and discard it (the old

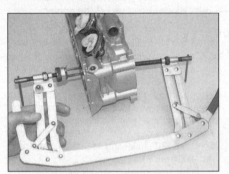

13.8a Compressing the valve springs using a valve spring compressor

13.8b Make sure the compressor is a good fit both on the top . . .

13.8c . . . and the bottom of the valve assembly

13.8d Remove the collets with needle-nose pliers, tweezers, a magnet or a screwdriver with a dab of grease on it

13.8e Remove the spring retainer and the spring . . .

13.8f . . . then push the valve down and draw it out

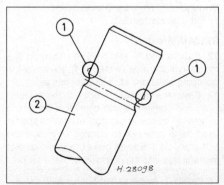

13.8g If the valve stem (2) won't pull through the guide, deburr the area above the collet groove (1)

13.9a Pull the seal off the top of the guide . . .

13.9b . . . then remove the spring seat

13.16 Measure the valve seat width with a ruler (or for greater precision use a Vernier caliper)

seal should never be reused) **(see illustration)**. Remove the spring seat – using a magnet is the easiest way to lift the seat off the head **(see illustration)**.

10 Repeat the procedure for the other valves. Keep the parts for each valve together so they can be reinstalled in the same location.

11 Next, clean the cylinder head with solvent and dry it thoroughly. Compressed air will speed the drying process and ensure that all holes and recessed areas are clean. Clean any traces of old gasket material from the cylinder head. If a scraper is used, take care not to scratch or gouge the soft aluminium.

 HAYNES HiNT *Refer to Tools and Workshop Tips (Section 7) for details of gasket removal methods.*

12 Clean all of the valve springs, collets, retainers and spring seats with solvent and dry them thoroughly. Do the parts from one valve at a time so that no mixing of parts between valves occurs.

13 Scrape off any deposits that may have formed on each valve face, head and stem. Again, make sure the valves do not get mixed up.

Inspection

14 Inspect the head very carefully for cracks and other damage. If cracks are found, a new head will be required. Check the cam bearing surfaces for wear and evidence of seizure. Check the camshafts for wear as well (see Section 9).

13.17a Measure the valve stem diameter with a micrometer

15 Using a precision straight-edge and a feeler gauge, check the head gasket mating surface for warpage. Refer to *Tools and Workshop Tips* (Section 3) in the Reference section for details of how to use the straight-edge. If the head is warped, but not excessively so, a specialist repair shop may be able to resurface it. If the head is excessively warped, replace it with a new one.

16 Examine the valve seats in the combustion chamber. If they are pitted, cracked or burned, the head will require work beyond the scope of the home mechanic. Measure the valve seat width and compare it to this Chapter's Specifications **(see illustration)**. If it exceeds the service limit, or if it varies around its circumference, valve seat overhaul is required.

17 Measure the valve stem diameter **(see**

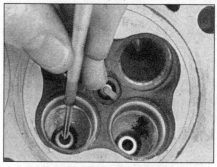

13.17b Insert a small hole gauge into the valve guide and expand it so there's a slight drag when it's pulled out

illustration). Clean the valve guides to remove any carbon build-up, then measure the inside diameters of the guides (at both ends and the centre of the guide) with a small hole gauge and micrometer **(see illustrations)**. The guides are measured at the ends and at the centre to determine if they are worn in a bell-mouth pattern (more wear at the ends). Subtract the stem diameter from the valve guide diameter to obtain the valve stem-to-guide clearance. If the stem-to-guide clearance is greater than listed in this Chapter's Specifications, and fitting new valves will restore the clearance,

 HAYNES HiNT *Refer to Tools and Workshop Tips in the Reference Section for details on how to use a micrometer.*

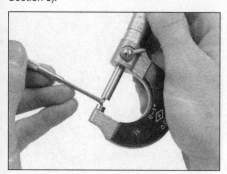

13.17c Measure the small hole gauge with a micrometer

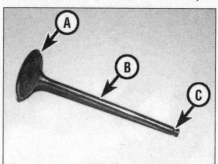

13.18 Check the valve face (A), stem (B) and collet groove (C) for signs of wear and damage

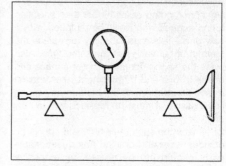

13.19 Check the valve stem for runout using V-blocks and a dial gauge

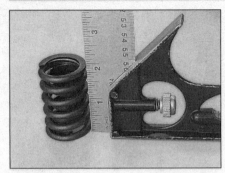

13.20 Check the valve springs do not tilt

13.24a Fit the valve stem seal . . .

13.24b . . . and carefully push it on until it clicks into place

13.25 Lubricate the stem and slide the valve into its guide

13.26a Fit the valve spring with the closer-wound coils facing down . . .

13.26b . . . then fit the spring retainer

fit new valves. If the guides are excessively worn, or worn unevenly, a new head will have to be fitted.

18 Carefully inspect each valve face, stem and collet groove area for cracks, pits and burned spots (see illustration).

19 Rotate the valve and check for any obvious indication that it is bent. Use V-blocks and a dial gauge if available (see illustration). If the valve is bent, it must be replaced with a new one. Check the end of the stem for pitting and excessive wear. The presence of any of the above conditions indicates the need for valve servicing. The stem end can be ground down, provided that the amount of stem above the collet groove after grinding is sufficient.

20 Check the end of each valve spring for wear and pitting. Measure the spring length with the specified load on it (see Specifications) and compare it to that listed. If any spring compresses further than specified it has sagged and must be replaced with a new one – it is a good policy to replace the springs on all valves at the same time. Also place the spring upright on a flat surface and check it for bend by placing a ruler against it (see illustration). If the bend in any spring is excessive, it must be replaced with a new one.

21 Check the spring retainers and collets for obvious wear and cracks. Any questionable parts should not be reused, as extensive damage will occur in the event of failure during engine operation.

22 If the inspection indicates that no overhaul

work is required, the valve components can be reinstalled in the head.

Reassembly

23 Working on one valve at a time, lay the spring seat in place in the cylinder head (see illustration 13.9b).

24 Fit a new seal onto the guide (see illustration). Use an appropriate size deep socket to push the seal over the end of the valve guide, then push further until it is felt to clip into place (see illustration). Don't twist or cock the seal, or it will not seal properly against the valve stem. Also, don't remove it again or it will be damaged.

25 Coat the valve stem with molybdenum disulphide oil (a 50/50 mixture of molybdenum

disulphide grease and engine oil), then fit it into its guide (see illustration). Check that the valve moves up and down freely.

26 Fit the spring with its closer-wound coils facing down into the cylinder head (see illustration). Now fit the spring retainer, with its shouldered side facing down so that it fits into the top of the springs (see illustration).

27 Apply a small amount of grease to the inside of the collets – this will help to help hold them in place as the pressure is released from the spring (see illustration). Compress the spring with the valve spring compressor and fit the collets (see illustration). When compressing the spring, do so only as far as is necessary to slip the collets into place. Make certain that the collets are securely locked

13.27a A small dab of grease will help to keep the collets in place on the valve while the spring is released

13.27b Compress the springs and install the collets, making sure they locate in the groove

13.27c Make sure the collets lock as you remove the compressor . . .

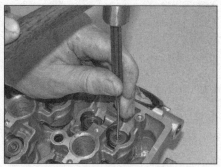

13.28 . . . then tap the valve stem to make sure

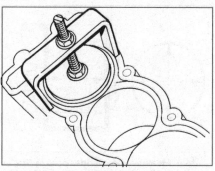

14.3 Extracting a liner using the Triumph tool

in the retaining groove when releasing the compressor **(see illustration)**.
28 Support the cylinder head on blocks so the valves can't contact the workbench top, then very gently tap the top of the valve stem to help seat the collets in the groove **(see illustration)**.
29 Repeat the procedure for the remaining valves. Remember to keep the parts for each valve together and separate from the other valves so they can be reinstalled in the same location.

> **HAYNES HiNT** *Check for proper sealing of the valves by pouring a small amount of solvent into each of the valve ports. If the solvent leaks past any valve into the combustion chamber area the valve grinding operation on that valve should be repeated.*

14 Cylinder liners

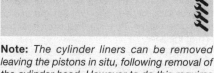

Note: *The cylinder liners can be removed leaving the pistons in situ, following removal of the cylinder head. However to do this requires the use of Triumph special tools, Part Nos. T3880315 and 3880101, to extract the liners. It may be possible to purchase a universal liner extractor from a good automotive tool supplier, but first make sure it is suitable for the size of the engine. A suitable home-made tool can be used to release the liners, but as it uses the drawbolt principle it is necessary to separate the crankcase halves and remove the crankshaft, connecting rods and pistons before it can be applied. If the liners are being removed as part of a complete engine overhaul anyway, then no extra work is involved, apart from making up the tool.*

Removal

1 If the Triumph special tool or a liner extractor is being used, just remove the cylinder head (see Section 12). Otherwise, separate the crankcase halves, then remove the crankshaft and connecting rods and pistons, referring to the relevant Sections of this Chapter.

2 Before removing the liners, mark the top edge of each liner at the front with a felt marker pen or similar, which will not damage the gasket surfaces. Indicate the cylinder number (1 to 3 from left to right) and the front face of each liner.
3 If the Triumph tool or a liner extractor is being used, turn the engine so that the piston in the liner being removed is at bottom dead centre (i.e. the bottom of its stroke). Gently draw each liner out of the cylinder block **(see illustration)**. The purpose of the extractor is to break the seal between the liner and the crankcase; once this has been achieved, the liner can be lifted out by hand – Support the piston and rod so they do not fall against the crankcase. Do not attempt to lever the liners out because the gasket surfaces will be damaged. As each liner is removed, stuff the crankcase aperture with clean rag to cushion the piston and prevent anything falling into the crankcase.
4 If the home-made drawbolt tool is being used (see **Tool Tip**), assemble the tool as shown. The bottom plate must be accurately fitted so that is bears on the bottom edge of the liner only – there must be no danger of it cocking sideways or slipping off the edge and scratching the inner surface of the liner **(see illustration)**. Also note that the bottom plate must locate inside the crankcase bore for the liner and have no sharp edges that will score the crankcase as the liner is drawn out. Tighten the top nut and gently draw the liner out of the cylinder block **(see illustration)**. Do not attempt to lever the liners out.

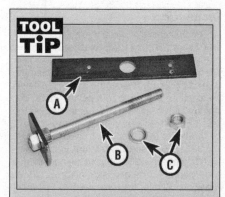

> **TOOL TIP**
>
> *Components of the home-made drawbolt tool: steel strap (A), drawbolt and bottom plate (B) and top nut and washer (C). The drawbolt tool can be made using a section of steel plate, accurately cut and chamfered so that it bears on the bottom edge of the liner, just inside the outside diameter of the liner. You will also need a length of flat steel bar of a suitable thickness, a length of threaded rod (15 mm diameter x 200 mm length), some washers and two nuts, and two pieces of wood (see illustration 14.4b). The thickness of the pieces of wood will determine by how much the liners can be extracted before they contact the flat steel bar, so make sure they are thick enough to allow the seal on the liner to be broken, and thus enable the liners to be removed by hand. Assemble the tool as described in Step 4.*

14.4a Make sure the bottom plate is accurately cut and fitted

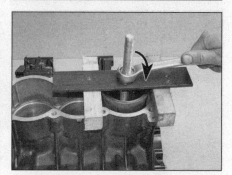

14.4b Turn the top nut clockwise and draw the liner up until the seal is broken

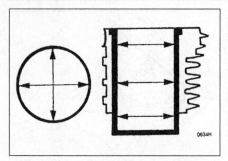

14.5 Measure the cylinder bore in the directions shown with a telescoping gauge, then measure the gauge with a micrometer

14.10a Carefully fit the liner down over the piston, making sure the rings enter correctly

14.10b Assemble a bolt, nut and washers as shown to clamp the liners

Inspection

5 Check the liner walls carefully for scratches and score marks. Using telescoping gauges and a micrometer (see Section 3 of *Tools and Workshop Tips*), check the internal diameter of each liner to assess the amount of wear. Measure near the top (but below the level of the top piston ring at TDC), centre and bottom (but above the level of the oil ring at BDC) of the bore, both parallel to and across the crankshaft axis **(see illustration)**. Compare the results to the specifications at the beginning of the Chapter. If the precision measuring tools are not available, take the liners to a Triumph dealer or specialist motorcycle repair shop for assessment and advice. If the liners are worn beyond the service limit, or badly scratched, scuffed or scored, replace them with new ones. The liners cannot be re-bored.
6 Note that the cylinder liners must not be honed.

Installation

Note: *If the crankcases were separated and the piston/connecting rod assemblies removed in order to remove the liners, you can either fit the piston/connecting rod assemblies into the liners before the liners are installed, then install them as an assembly (method 2) – or you can install the liners, then fit the piston/connecting rod assemblies into them afterwards (method 3).*
7 Remove all traces of old sealant from the mating surfaces of the liners and the crankcase. If the connecting rods and pistons are still in situ, this will be tricky because you must avoid old sealant dropping into the

sump. Remove any rag from the crankcase and make sure the mating surfaces of the liner and crankcase are clean, oil-free and dry. Check that the piston rings are correctly positioned in relation to the front of the engine **(see illustration 15.28)**.

Method 1 – piston/connecting rod assemblies in situ

8 Apply a continuous bead of a suitable silicone sealant (Triumph use ThreeBond 1215) to the liner mating surface as shown, following any instructions on the sealant package regarding use **(see illustration 14.14)**.
9 Lubricate the bore surface of the liner with engine oil. Make sure that the No. 1 liner is matched with the No. 1 piston/connecting rod assembly and so on, and that it is installed with the previously made mark at the front (see Step 2). Make sure that the piston is at top dead centre (i.e. at the top of its stroke).
10 Slip the liner over the piston, compressing each ring with your fingers as it enters the liner, and use a gentle rocking motion as the liner is pushed downwards **(see illustration)**. The liner has a chamfered lead-in to enable the piston to be installed without the use of ring compressors. Press the liner fully down until it is felt to seat. Clamp the liner in place using suitable bolts, nuts and soft washers threaded into the head bolt holes as shown to prevent it lifting **(see illustration)** – do not overtighten the clamps and do not use steel washers as the mating surface of the head could be indented, causing leakage and compression problems.
11 Turn the crankshaft to position the next piston at TDC, then install the other liners in

the same way. As the crankshaft is rotated, make sure that the installed liner does not lift off its seating. If this happens, the liner must be removed, cleaned and fresh sealant applied. After fitting the second and third liners make sure that there is an even gap between the flat side of the centre liner and each outer liner – you should be able to fit a 0.1 mm feeler gauge blade into the gap and slide it all the way along.

Method 2 – piston/connecting rod assemblies removed

12 Lubricate the bore surface of the liner with engine oil. Make sure that the No. 1 piston/ connecting rod assembly is matched with the No. 1 liner and so on, and that they are installed the correct way round – the arrow or dot or EX mark on the piston crown must point to the front of the liner and the front of the engine.
13 Slip the piston into the bottom of the liner, compressing each ring with your fingers as it enters, and use a gentle rocking motion as the liner is pushed downwards **(see illustration)**. The liner has a chamfered lead-in to enable the piston to be installed without the use of ring compressors. Position the piston near the top of the liner.
14 Apply a continuous bead of a suitable silicone sealant (Triumph use ThreeBond 1215) to the liner mating surface as shown, following any instructions on the sealant package regarding use **(see illustration)**.
15 Fit the No. 1 liner into the left-hand side of the crankcase, with the previously made mark at the front (see Step 2), and press it down until it is felt to seat **(see illustration)**.

14.13 Carefully feed the piston into the liner, making sure the rings enter correctly

14.14 Apply the silicone sealant as shown . . .

14.15 . . . then fit the liner into the crankcase

14.20a Carefully lower the connecting rod and piston into the liner . . .

14.20b . . . feeding each ring in as you do

14.21 Check that the liners are all flush using a straight-edge

Clamp the liner in place using suitable bolts, nuts and soft washers threaded into the head bolt holes as shown to prevent it lifting **(see illustration 14.10b)** – do not overtighten the clamps and do not use steel washers as the mating surface of the head could be indented, causing leakage and compression problems.

16 Install the other liners in the same way, with No. 2 in the middle and No. 3 on the right. Note that if the cylinder head is being installed immediately, there is no need to clamp the individual liners in place. After fitting the second and third liners make sure that there is an even gap between the flat side of the centre liner and each outer liner – you should be able to fit a 0.1 mm feeler gauge blade into the gap and slide it all the way along.

Method 3 – piston/connecting rod assemblies removed

17 Apply a continuous bead of a suitable silicone sealant (Triumph use ThreeBond 1215) to the liner mating surface as shown, following any instructions on the sealant package regarding use **(see illustration 14.14)**.

18 Fit the No. 1 liner into the left-hand side of the crankcase, with the previously made mark at the front (see Step 2), and press it down until it is felt to seat. Fit the No. 2 liner into the middle, then the No. 3 into the right-hand side, again with the marks at the front. After fitting the second and third liners make sure that there is an even gap between the flat side of the centre liner and each outer liner – you should be able to fit a 0.1 mm feeler gauge blade into the gap and slide it all the way along. Clamp the liners in place using suitable bolts, nuts and soft washers threaded into the head bolt holes as shown to prevent them lifting **(see illustration 14.10b)** – do not overtighten the clamps and do not use steel washers as the mating surface of the head could be indented, causing leakage and compression problems.

19 Lubricate the bore surface of each liner with engine oil. Make sure that the No. 1 piston/connecting rod assembly is matched with the No. 1 liner and so on, and that they are installed the correct way round – the arrow or dot or EX mark on the piston crown must point to the front of the liner and the front of the engine.

20 Slip the piston into the liner, making sure

the connecting rod does not scratch the surface, then carefully compress and feed each piston ring into the liner until the piston crown is flush with the top **(see illustrations)**. If available, a piston ring compressor makes installation a lot easier.

All methods

21 When all liners are installed, check that their top surfaces are all exactly level with the cylinder block using a precision straight-edge as shown **(see illustration)**.

22 Install the cylinder head soon after installing the liners to avoid crankshaft movement accidentally breaking the seals.

23 Install the remaining components in the reverse order of removal, referring to the relevant Sections of the Chapter.

15 Pistons and piston rings

Removal

1 Remove the cylinder head (see Section 12).

2 If the crankcases are not being separated and a cylinder liner extractor is available, remove the cylinder liners (see Section 14). Make sure that all apertures into the crankcase are well blocked with clean rag. Rotate the crankshaft so that the best access is obtained for each piston, and on the outer pistons extract the pins inwards.

3 If the crankcases are being separated, do so now (see Section 22), then follow the

15.5b . . . to lever out the circlip

procedure in Section 25 and separate the connecting rods from the crankshaft, and remove the rods with the pistons from the tops of the liners. Now remove the liners (see Section 14).

4 Before removing the pistons, mark the cylinder number on the crown of each piston. Also note the arrow or dot or EX mark on each crown which points to the front of the engine – if the mark is not visible, make your own as the piston must be installed the correct way round. If the connecting rods have been removed, check that the marks you made across the front are the same way as the piston mark.

5 Carefully prise out the circlip on one side of the piston using needle-nose pliers or a small flat-bladed screwdriver inserted into the notch **(see illustrations)**. Push the piston pin out from the other side to free the piston from the connecting rod **(see illustration)**.

15.5a Use a small screwdriver or pointed instrument inserted in the notch (arrowed) . . .

15.5c Withdraw the pin and remove the piston

15.7 Removing the piston rings using a ring removal and installation tool

15.13 Measure the piston ring-to-groove clearance with a feeler gauge

15.14 Measure the piston diameter with a micrometer at the specified distance from the bottom of the skirt

Remove the other circlip and discard them as new ones must be used. When the piston has been removed, fit its pin back into its bore so that related parts do not get mixed up. Remember the importance of the rag in preventing dropped circlips from falling into the crankcase.

HAYNES HINT *If a piston pin is a tight fit in the piston bosses, use a heat gun to expand the alloy piston sufficiently to release its grip of the pin. Alternatively purchase (or make up) a piston pin drawbolt tool – see 'Tools and Workshop Tips' in the Reference section.*

HAYNES HINT *To prevent the circlip from pinging away, pass a rod or screwdriver, which has a diameter greater than the gap between the circlip ends, through the piston pin. This will trap the circlip if it springs out.*

Inspection

Pistons

6 Before the inspection process can be carried out, remove the piston rings and clean the pistons.
7 Using your thumbs or a piston ring removal and installation tool, carefully remove the rings from the pistons **(see illustration)**. Do

not nick or gouge the pistons in the process. Carefully note which way up each ring fits and in which groove as they must be installed in their original positions and the same way up if being re-used. The upper surface of the top and second rings should be marked T1 and T2 or N and N2 respectively – if the mark on each ring is different, note which mark is for the top ring and which is for the second. The rings can also be distinguished by their different profiles **(see illustration 15.26a)**.
8 Scrape all traces of carbon from the tops of the pistons. A hand-held wire brush or a piece of fine emery cloth can be used once most of the deposits have been scraped away. Do not, under any circumstances, use a wire brush mounted in a drill motor to remove deposits from the pistons; the piston material is soft and will be eroded away by the wire brush.
9 Use a piston ring groove cleaning tool to remove any carbon deposits from the ring grooves. If a tool is not available, a piece broken off an old ring will do the job. Be very careful to remove only the carbon deposits. Do not remove any metal and do not nick or gouge the sides of the ring grooves.
10 Once the deposits have been removed, clean the pistons with solvent and dry them thoroughly. Make sure the oil return holes below the oil ring groove are clear.
11 Carefully inspect each piston for cracks around the skirt, at the pin bosses and at the ring lands. Normal piston wear appears as even, vertical wear on the thrust surfaces of the piston and slight looseness of the top ring

in its groove. If the skirt is scored or scuffed, the engine may have been suffering from overheating and/or abnormal combustion, which caused excessively high operating temperatures. The oil pump and cooling systems should be checked thoroughly.
12 A hole in the piston crown, an extreme to be sure, is an indication that abnormal combustion (pre-ignition) was occurring. Burned areas at the edge of the piston crown are usually evidence of spark knock (detonation). If any of the above problems exist, the causes must be corrected or the damage will occur again.
13 Measure the piston ring-to-groove clearance by laying a new piston ring in the ring groove and slipping a feeler blade in beside it **(see illustration)**. Check the clearance at three or four locations around the groove. If the clearance is greater than that specified, the piston is worn. **Note:** *Make sure you have the correct ring for the groove – the two compression rings can be identified by their markings and profile (see illustration 15.26a).*
14 Measure the piston diameter 8 mm up from the bottom of the skirt and at 90° to the piston pin axis **(see illustration)**. If outside of the specified figure, the piston must be replaced with a new one.
15 If the necessary measuring equipment is available, measure the connecting rod small-end bore diameter, the piston pin outside diameter and the inside diameter of the pin bores in the piston **(see illustrations)**. Replace any component that has worn beyond the specified limits with a new one.

15.15a Measure the internal diameter of the small-end bore . . .

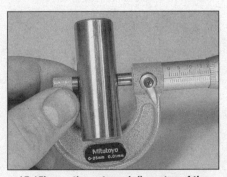

15.15b . . . the external diameter of the pin . . .

15.15c . . . and the internal diameter of the bore in the piston

15.18 Measuring piston ring installed end gap

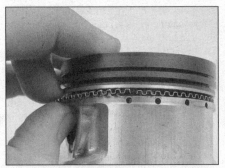

15.24a Fit the oil ring expander in its groove . . .

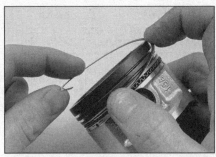

15.24b . . . then fit the lower side rail and the upper side rail each side of it. The oil ring components must be installed by hand

Piston rings

16 It is good practice to use new piston rings when an engine is being overhauled. Before fitting the new rings, the ring end gaps must be checked.

17 Lay out the pistons and the new ring sets so the rings will be matched with the same piston and cylinder during the end gap measurement procedure and engine assembly.

18 Fit the top ring into the top of the first liner and square it up with the cylinder walls by pushing it in with the top of the piston until the third ring on the piston is level with and parallel all the way round to the top of the liner. To measure the end gap, slip a feeler blade between the ends of the ring and compare the measurement to the Specification **(see illustration)**.

19 If the gap is larger or smaller than specified, double check to make sure that you have the correct rings before proceeding.

20 If the gap is too small, check the liner for distortion (see Section 14). If the liner is good you can try to carefully increase the end gap by filing the ends of the rings with a fine file, but note that rings are very brittle, and it is better to get another set from your dealer, who should exchange them if you explain the circumstances, as they should really fit correctly.

21 If the end gap exceeds the service limit specified with the old rings, fit new rings and check again. If it is still excessive check the liner for wear (see Section 14).

22 Repeat the procedure for each ring that will be installed in the first cylinder and for each ring in the remaining cylinders. Remember to keep the rings, pistons and cylinders matched up.

23 Once the ring end gaps have been checked/corrected, the rings can be fitted onto the pistons.

24 The oil control ring (lowest on the piston) is installed first. It is composed of three separate components, the expander and the upper and lower side rails. First slip the expander into the groove, making sure the ends butt against each other and do not overlap. Next fit the lower side rail, then the upper **(see illustrations)**. New side rails can be fitted either way up, but if the removed

ones are being reused they must be installed the same way up as they were removed. Do not use a piston ring installation tool on the side rails as they may be damaged. Instead, place one end of the side rail into the groove between the expander and the ring land. Hold it firmly in place and slide a finger around the piston while pushing the rail into the groove.

25 After the three oil ring components have been installed, check to make sure that both the upper and lower side rails can be turned smoothly in the ring groove.

26 Fit the second (middle) ring next – it should be marked T2 at one end, and this mark must face up. If no mark is visible, the second ring and top rings can be distinguished by their different profiles **(see illustration)** – make sure you have the correct ring. **Note:** *From new the top ring has a blue mark on its outer*

edge, and the second ring has a yellow mark and an overall bronze appearance. Fit the ring into the middle groove on the piston. Either use your thumbs to hold the ring ends apart when installing the ring over the piston, or slip sections of old feeler gauge blades between the ring and piston to guide it into its groove **(see illustration)**, or use a ring removal/installation tool **(see illustration 15.7)**.

Caution: Do not expand the ring any more than is necessary to slide it into place – the ring material is brittle and is easily broken if overstressed.

27 Finally, fit the top ring in the same manner. Make sure the T1 mark near the end gap is facing up.

28 Position the ring end gaps around the piston as shown **(see illustration)**.

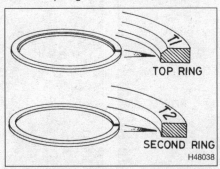

15.26a The rings can be identified by their different profiles – the T1 or T2 mark must face up

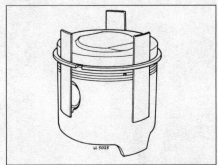

15.26b Old pieces of feeler gauge blade can be used to guide the ring over the piston

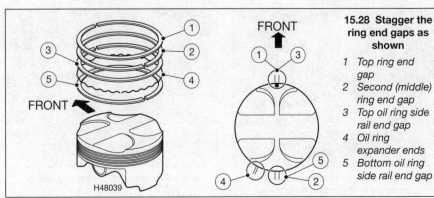

15.28 Stagger the ring end gaps as shown

1 *Top ring end gap*
2 *Second (middle) ring end gap*
3 *Top oil ring side rail end gap*
4 *Oil ring expander ends*
5 *Bottom oil ring side rail end gap*

Installation

29 If the connecting rods have not been removed from the engine, stuff clean rag into the crankcase mouth to prevent any dropped circlips falling in. Lubricate the connecting rod small-end bore with engine oil.

30 Fit a new circlip into the groove in one side of the piston bore (the outer side for the outer pistons if the connecting rods have not been removed). Locate the piston on its rod so that the arrow or dot or EX mark on its crown is facing forwards, the same way as the mark you made on the rod if removed. Push the piston pin fully into the piston and secure with

16.2a **Unscrew the bolt (arrowed) . . .**

a second new circlip – make sure the circlip is fully seated in its groove **(see illustrations 15.5c, b and a)**.

31 Install the other pistons in the same way. If the connecting rods have not been removed from the engine, rotate the crankshaft to gain the best access.

32 Check that the piston rings are still correctly positioned in relation to the front of the engine **(see illustration 15.28)**.

33 Install all components and assemblies according to your removal procedure, referring to the relevant Sections of the Chapter.

16 Clutch

Note: *The clutch can be removed with the engine in the frame. If the engine has already been removed, ignore the steps which don't apply.*

Removal

1 On Daytona models remove the right-hand fairing side panel (see Chapter 7).
2 Unscrew the clutch cable bracket bolt

then detach the cable end from the release mechanism arm on the clutch cover **(see illustrations)**.

3 Working in a criss-cross pattern, slacken the clutch cover bolts evenly, noting the bolt with the sealing washer, and the position of the fairing side panel bracket on Daytona models **(see illustration)**.

4 Lift the cover away from the engine, being prepared to catch any residual oil **(see illustration 16.31b)**.

5 Remove the gasket and discard it. Note the two locating dowels and remove them for safe-keeping if loose **(see illustration 16.31a)**.

6 Working in a criss-cross pattern, gradually and evenly slacken the clutch spring retaining bolts until spring pressure is released, then remove the bolts and springs **(see illustration)**. Remove the pressure plate and the pull-rod **(see illustrations)**.

7 Grasp the complete set of clutch plates and remove them as a pack – you may have to hook the inner plates out using a piece of wire **(see illustration)**. Unless the plates are being replaced with new ones, keep them in their original order. Note that the outer plate is slightly darker in colour, and that the inner friction plate is also slightly darker and

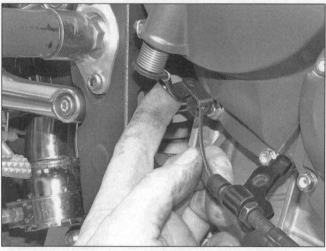

16.2b **. . . and detach the cable end**

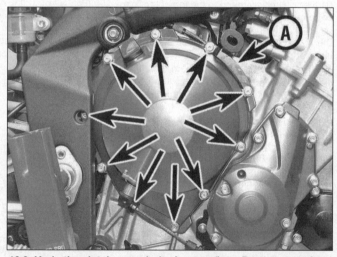

16.3 **Undo the clutch cover bolts (arrowed); on Daytona note how the two bolts secure the bracket (A)**

16.6a **Unscrew the bolts (arrowed) as described and remove the springs**

16.6b **Remove the pressure plate . . .**

16.6c **. . . and withdraw the pull-rod**

16.7 Draw the clutch plates out

16.8 Using a commercially-available tool to hold the clutch centre while unscrewing the nut

16.10 Draw the bearing and sleeve out as described . . .

has a larger internal diameter. Remove the anti-judder spring and spring seat, noting how they fit **(see illustrations 16.26b and a)**.

8 The transmission input shaft must be locked to enable the clutch nut to be slackened. This can be done in several ways. If the engine is in the frame, engage 2nd gear and have an assistant hold the rear brake on hard with the rear tyre in firm contact with the ground. Alternatively, and if the engine is out of the frame, either the Triumph service tool (Part No. T3880026), or a commercially available (and not expensive) equivalent holding tool can be used as shown (do not fit it too tightly), to hold the clutch centre whilst the nut is slackened **(see illustration)**. Unscrew the nut and remove the Belleville washer and plain washer from the input shaft **(see illustrations 16.25c, b and a)**. Discard the Belleville washer as a new one must be used on installation.

9 Slide the clutch centre off the input shaft, followed by the large thrust washer **(see illustrations 16.24b and a)**.

10 Jiggle the clutch housing backwards and forwards and draw out the bearing and sleeve, using a magnet or a pair of pliers to help, then support the housing and slide the bearing and sleeve off the shaft **(see illustration)**.

11 Slide the clutch housing off the shaft, noting how the primary driven gear on the back of the housing engages with the primary drive gear on the crankshaft, and manoeuvre it out of the crankcase **(see illustration)**. Note how the oil pump drive pegs locate in the holes in the back of the clutch housing.

Inspection

12 After an extended period of service the clutch friction plates will wear and promote clutch slip. Measure the thickness of each friction plate using a Vernier caliper **(see illustration)**. If any plate has worn to or beyond the service limit given in the Specifications, the friction plates must be replaced with a new set – don't forget there are two different thicknesses of plate.

13 If the plates are good, but the clutch has been slipping, it could be that the springs have sagged. As no specification is available for the spring free length, the only way to check them is to compare them with new ones. If the springs have sagged, replace them as a set.

14 The plain plates should not show any signs of excess heating (bluing). Check for warpage using a flat surface and feeler blades

16.11 . . . then draw the clutch housing out

(see illustration). If any plate exceeds the maximum permissible amount of warpage, or shows signs of bluing, all plain plates must be renewed as a set.

15 Inspect the clutch assembly for burrs and indentations on the edges of the protruding tangs of the friction plates and/or the slots in the edge of the outer drum with which they engage **(see illustration)**. Similarly check for wear between the inner tongues of the plain plates and the slots in the clutch centre **(see illustration)**. Wear of this nature will cause clutch drag and slow disengagement during gear changes, as the plates will snag when the pressure plate is lifted. With care a small amount of wear can be corrected by dressing with a fine file, but if this is excessive the worn components should be replaced with new ones.

16 Inspect the clutch housing needle bearing and the bearing surfaces of the sleeve and

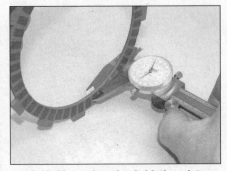

16.12 Measuring clutch friction plate thickness

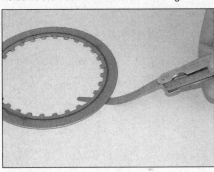

16.14 Check the plain plates for warpage

16.15a Check for wear of the friction plate tabs and the clutch housing slots . . .

16.15b . . . and of the plain plate tongues and clutch centre slots

16.16 Inspect the needle bearing, the sleeve and the bearing surface in the housing

16.18 Check the pull-rod, pressure plate, and bearing (arrowed) for wear

16.19a Withdraw the shaft . . .

housing **(see illustration)**. Check the springs in the back of the clutch housing and check the teeth on the primary driven gear. If any components are worn of damaged, replace them with new ones.

17 Inspect the anti-judder spring and spring seat for wear. If the spring is flattened, replace the spring and seat as a set **(see illustration 16.26b)**.

18 Check the pull-rod, the pressure plate and the bearing for signs of damage and wear **(see illustration)**. Ensure that the inner race of the bearing spins freely without any sign of notchiness. Push the bearing out of the pressure plate if a new one is needed.

19 Check the clutch release mechanism in the clutch cover for smooth operation. Note how the return spring ends locate, then withdraw the shaft from the cover, noting the washer **(see illustration)**. Check the shaft, oil

seal and bearings for wear and replace them with new ones if necessary **(see illustration)**.

20 Check the pull-rod end and its locating cut-out in the shaft for signs of wear and damage, and replace them with new ones if necessary. Clean all components and lubricate the seal and bearings with grease.

Installation

21 Remove all traces of gasket material from the crankcase and clutch cover mating surfaces.

22 Lubricate the clutch housing needle bearing and sleeve with clean engine oil **(see illustration 16.16)**.

23 Get a suitable piece of steel rod to fit into the hole in the primary drive gear. Using a screwdriver between the sprung and main sections of the primary drive gear teeth, twist it until the gear teeth align, then fit the rod into

the hole so it holds them in this position **(see illustration)**. Slide the clutch housing over the input shaft and manoeuvre it into the crankcase so that the primary driven gear engages with the primary drive gear on the crankshaft, then push the housing on so that it is fully engaged with the primary drive gear and the holes in the clutch housing engage with the pegs on the oil pump drive sprocket – if necessary, turn the oil pump driven sprocket until the holes align and the clutch housing is felt to engage with the pegs **(see illustrations)**. Fit the bearing and the sleeve into the housing, with the grooved face of the sleeve outwards **(see illustration)**. When correctly fitted the bearing sleeve should be flush with the outer face of the clutch housing. With everything correctly aligned withdraw the rod from the hole in the gear **(see illustration)**.

24 Slide the large thrust washer over the

16.19b . . . and check the seal and the bearings (arrowed) for wear

16.23a Align the gear teeth sections as described and fit the rod to hold them

16.23b When fitting the housing align the pegs on the oil pump drive sprocket with the holes in the back of the clutch housing . . .

16.23c . . . and jiggle the sprocket until they are felt to engage . . .

16.23d . . . then slide the bearing and sleeve into the housing

16.23e Withdraw the rod from the hole

16.24a Fit the large thrust washer . . .

16.24b . . . and slide the clutch centre onto the shaft

16.25a Fit the plain washer . . .

16.25b . . . the Belleville washer . . .

16.25c . . . and the nut . . .

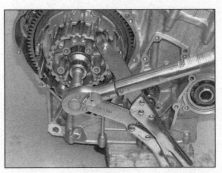

16.25d . . . and tighten it to the specified torque

input shaft, then slide the clutch centre onto the input shaft splines (see illustrations).
25 Fit the plain washer and the new Belleville washer with its OUT marking facing outwards, then thread the clutch nut on (see illustrations). Using the method employed on removal to lock the input shaft, tighten the nut to the torque setting specified at the beginning of the Chapter (see illustration). **Note:** *When the nut has been tightened, check that the clutch centre rotates freely with the transmission in neutral.*
26 The standard clutch pack comprises nine friction plates and eight plain plates. There are three different types of friction plate – the outermost and innermost plates are different to the rest and the innermost has a larger internal diameter. There are two different thicknesses of plain plate (2.0 mm and 1.6 mm), and as standard there are six 2.0 mm plates and two 1.6 mm plates, and the 1.6 mm plates fit outermost.

27 If new clutch plates are being fitted the assembled height of the pack must be measured, and if necessary adjusted, before they are installed. Assemble the pack in the order described in Step 26 and measure its free height using a Vernier caliper (see illustration) – if the height is not within the range specified at the beginning of the Chapter, either replace the outermost 2.0 mm plate with a 1.6 mm plate, or replace the inner most 1.6 mm plate with a 2.0 mm plate, as required to bring the height within the specified range. The 1.6 mm plate(s) must always be fitted outermost, and there must be no less than one and no more than three.
28 Fit the anti-judder spring seat into the clutch centre, followed by the anti-judder spring, fitting the spring so that its outer edge is raised off the spring seat (see illustrations).
29 Coat each clutch plate with engine oil prior to installation. Identify the inner friction plate – it has a larger internal diameter (i.e.

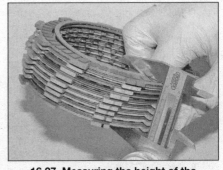

16.27 Measuring the height of the assembled clutch plate pack

the plate is narrower) and is slightly darker. Build up the clutch plates, starting with the inner friction plate that is narrower, seating it around the anti-judder spring seat and spring (see illustration). Next fit a plain plate, then

16.28a Fit the spring seat and the spring . . .

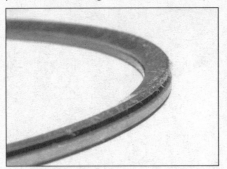

16.28b . . . making sure they are the correct way round

16.29a Fit the inner friction plate . . .

16.29b ... then a plain plate, and so on

16.30 Fit the pressure plate making sure it engages correctly

16.31 Fit the springs and the bolts then tighten them evenly in a criss-cross sequence

16.33a Smear a bit of sealant onto the joint (arrowed) on each side

16.33b Locate a new gasket over the dowels (arrowed)

16.33c Fit the cover, making sure the shaft and pull-rod engage

alternate normal friction and plain plates until all but the last friction plate are installed (see illustration). Fit the outer friction plate (slightly darker).

30 Insert the pull-rod into the end of the shaft (see illustration 16.6c). Fit the pressure plate, engaging the notches on its inner rim with the slots in the inside of the clutch centre (see illustration).

31 Fit the springs and bolts and tighten the bolts evenly and a little at a time in a criss-cross sequence to the specified torque setting (see illustration).

32 If removed, make sure the spring and washer are on the shaft then fit it into the cover (see illustration 16.19a). Make sure the spring ends locate correctly.

33 Apply a dab of sealant to the crankcase joints (see illustration). Fit the dowels into the crankcase if removed, then fit a new gasket,

locating it over the dowels (see illustration). Fit the cover, angling the release shaft arm so it engages with the pull-rod (see illustration).

34 Fit the cover bolts, using a new sealing washer with the second bolt up at the front (see illustration), and not forgetting to secure the bracket on Daytona models (see illustration 16.3). Tighten the bolts evenly in a criss-cross sequence to the specified torque setting. Operate the release lever and make sure it picks up the end of the pull-rod correctly – it should come up solid when it is pointing towards the engine.

35 Attach the clutch cable end to the release lever on the clutch cover, then fit the cable bracket and tighten its bolt (see illustrations 16.2b and a). Check and adjust cable freeplay (see Chapter 1).

36 On Daytona models install the right-hand fairing side panel (see Chapter 7).

17 Clutch cable
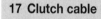

1 On Daytona models remove the right-hand fairing side panel (see Chapter 7).

2 Slacken the locknuts securing the cable in the bracket on the clutch cover and thread the rear locknut off (see illustration).

3 Slip the cable end out of the retainer on the clutch arm, noting how it fits (see illustration 16.2b). Draw the cable out of the bracket, collecting the rear locknut as you do.

4 Thread the cable adjuster into the lever bracket on the handlebar (see illustration). Align the slot in the adjuster with the slot in the bracket.

5 Pull the outer cable end from the socket in the adjuster and release the inner cable from

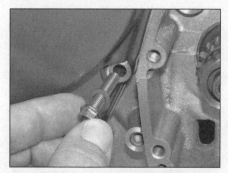

16.34 Use a new sealing washer

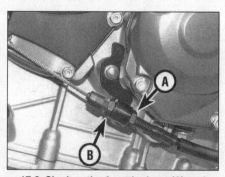

17.2 Slacken the front locknut (A) and thread the rear locknut (B) off the cable

17.4 Turn the adjuster into the lever bracket

the lever **(see illustrations)**. Remove the cable from the machine, noting its routing and releasing any guides, ties or clips.

> **HAYNES HiNT** *Before removing the cable from the bike, tape the lower end of the new cable to the upper end of the old cable. Slowly pull the lower end of the old cable out, guiding the new cable down into position. Using this method will ensure the cable is routed correctly.*

6 Unless a new cable is being fitted check the cable ends for security of the nipples and any loose strands and fraying. Make sure the inner cable slides smoothly and freely in the outer cable. If required lubricate the cable using a pressure adapter (see Chapter 1).
7 Turn the clutch release mechanism arm to check for smooth operation of the shaft in the cover and any signs of wear or damage. Remove it for inspection if required (see Section 16).
8 Installation is the reverse of removal. Apply grease to the cable ends. Make sure the cable is correctly routed. Make sure the cable lower end is properly located in the retainer on the release mechanism arm.
9 Adjust the clutch lever freeplay (see Chapter 1). On Daytona models install the fairing side panel (see Chapter 7).

18 Sump, oil strainer and pressure relief valve

Note: *The sump can be removed with the engine in the frame. If work is being carried out with the engine removed ignore the steps which don't apply.*

Removal

1 On Daytona models remove the fairing side panels (see Chapter 7).
2 Drain the engine oil, and if required remove the oil filter (see Chapter 1).
3 Remove the exhaust system (see Chapter 4).
4 Unscrew the sump bolts, slackening them evenly in a criss-cross sequence to prevent distortion **(see illustration)**. Remove the sump. Discard the sump gasket as a new one must be fitted – if the sump gasket on your model is shaped so that the internal oil pipe passes through a hole in it **(see illustration 18.6)**, either cut the gasket free of the pipe, or remove the gasket after removing the pipe (Step 6). Remove the dowels if loose.
5 Remove the drain tube for the water pump – it may have come away with the sump, or otherwise will be in the pump **(see illustration)**. Discard its O-rings – new ones must be used.
6 Unscrew the internal oil pipe bolts and remove the pipe **(see illustration)**. Discard the O-rings – new ones must be used.

17.5a Draw the outer cable end from the adjuster and slip the inner cable out via the slots . . .

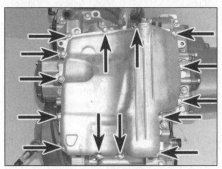
18.4 Sump bolts (arrowed)

7 Unscrew the oil strainer bolts and remove the strainer **(see illustration)**. Remove the O-ring and discard it – a new one must be used.

18.6 Unscrew the bolts (arrowed) and remove the pipe

18.8 Unscrew the relief valve

17.5b . . . then detach the inner cable end from the lever

18.5 Remove the tube (arrowed) and discard its O-rings

8 Unscrew the pressure relief valve **(see illustration)**.
9 Undo the crankcase breather drain tube screw and remove the tube **(see illustration)**.

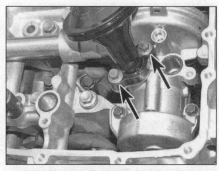
18.7 Unscrew the bolts (arrowed) and remove the strainer

18.9 Undo the screw (arrowed) and remove the tube

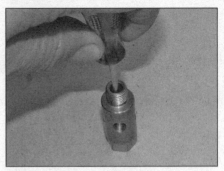

18.11a Check the plunger moves smoothly and freely

18.11b Remove the circlip (arrowed) to release the spring and plunger

18.14 Fit the tube using a new O-ring (arrowed)

Remove the O-ring and discard it – a new one must be used.

Inspection

10 Clean through the water pump drain tube, the internal oil pipe and the breather drain tube with solvent, and blow them through, with compressed air if available.

11 Push the relief valve plunger into the valve body and check that it moves smoothly and freely against the spring pressure **(see illustration)**. If not, remove the circlip, noting that it is under spring pressure, and remove the spring seat, spring and plunger **(see illustration)**. Clean all the components in solvent and check them for scoring, wear or damage. If any is found, fit a new relief valve – individual components are not available. Otherwise, coat the inside of the valve body and the plunger with clean engine oil, then insert the plunger, spring and spring seat and

secure them with the circlip. Check the action of the valve plunger again – if it is still suspect, replace the valve with a new one.

12 Clean the strainer in solvent and remove any debris caught in the gauze, blowing through it with compressed air if available. The presence of metal caught in the strainer, or in the bottom of the sump, is indicative of engine wear that should be investigated.

Installation

13 Remove all traces of gasket material from the sump and crankcase mating surfaces. Clean the threads of all bolts that had threadlock applied.

14 Fit the crankcase breather drain tube using a new O-ring **(see illustration)**. Apply a drop of non-permanent thread locking compound to the screw threads and tighten it to the torque setting specified at the beginning of the Chapter.

15 Apply a drop of non-permanent thread locking compound to the pressure relief valve threads and tighten the valve to the specified torque setting **(see illustration 18.8)**.

16 Fit the strainer using a new O-ring **(see illustration)**. Apply a drop of non-permanent thread locking compound to the bolts and tighten them to the specified torque **(see illustration)**.

17 Fit the internal oil pipe using new O-rings – if the new sump gasket is shaped so the pipe has to pass through it, fit the O-rings first, then the gasket, then the pipe **(see illustrations)**. If not then fit the gasket as in Step 19. Apply a drop of non-permanent thread locking compound to the pipe bolts and tighten them to the specified torque.

18 Fit new O-rings onto each end of the water pump drain tube **(see illustration)**. Fit the tube into the pump.

19 Fit the sump dowels if removed **(see**

18.16a Fit a new O-ring into the groove . . .

18.16b . . . then fit the strainer and threadlock the bolts

18.17a Fit new O-rings (arrowed) . . .

18.17b . . . then lay the gasket onto the sump . . .

18.17c . . . then fit the pipe

18.18 Fit two new O-rings onto each end of the tube

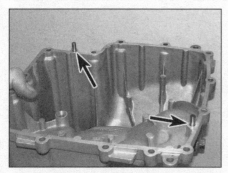

18.19a Make sure the dowels (arrowed) are in place . . .

18.19b . . . then fit the sump

illustration). If not done in Step 17, place a new gasket onto the sump if the engine is in the frame, or onto the crankcase if the engine has

been removed and is upside down on the bench – use a smear of grease to hold the gasket in place if required. Fit the sump and tighten the

bolts evenly in a criss-cross sequence to the specified torque setting (see illustration).

20 Install the exhaust system (see Chapter 4).

21 If removed install a new oil filter. Fill the engine with the correct type and quantity of oil (see Chapter 1 and *Pre-ride checks*). Start the engine and check that there are no leaks.

22 On Daytona models install the fairing side panels (see Chapter 7).

19 Oil and water pump

Note: *The oil/water pump can be removed with the engine in the frame.*

Removal

1 Drain the engine oil and coolant (see Chapter 1).

2 Remove the clutch (see Section 16).

3 Remove the sump, then remove the internal oil pipe and the oil strainer (see Section 18).

4 Unscrew the coolant inlet pipe bolt on the left-hand side of the crankcase and displace or remove the pipe – release the clamps and detach the hoses first if you want to remove it (see illustration). Discard the O-ring – a new one must be used.

5 Release the clamps and detach the hoses from the coolant outlet pipe bolt on the front of the crankcase (see illustration). Unscrew the bolt and withdraw the pipe. Discard the O-rings – new ones must be used.

6 Unscrew the pump drive chain guide bolts and remove the guide (see illustration).

7 Slide the drive sprocket and chain off the bearing and sleeve, using a small screwdriver to keep them in place (see illustration).

8 Unscrew the pump mounting bolts and remove the driven sprocket cover (see illustration). Disengage the chain from the driven sprocket and remove the chain and drive sprocket (see illustration). Slide the drive sprocket bearing, sleeve and spacer off the shaft (see illustrations 19.18b and a).

9 Withdraw the roll pin from the front mounting bolt hole to release the pump from the

19.4 Unscrew the bolt and displace or remove the pipe

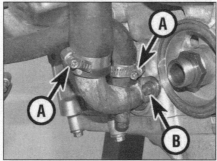

19.5 Slacken the clamps (A) and detach the hoses, then unscrew the bolt (B) and withdraw the pipe

19.6 Unscrew the bolts (arrowed) and remove the guide

19.7 Draw the sprocket off the bearing and sleeve to get some slack in the chain

19.8a Unscrew the bolts (arrowed) and remove the cover

19.8b Disengage the chain and remove it along with the drive sprocket

19.9a Hook the roll pin out . . .

19.9b . . . and remove the pump

19.10 Counter-hold the sprocket and unscrew the bolt (arrowed)

crankcase – to do this locate a hooked tool under the stepped section of the split in the pin and draw it out **(see illustrations)** – also grip the side of the pin with pliers if necessary. Remove the O-ring from the coolant inlet sleeve

19.11 Unscrew the bolts (arrowed) and remove the body

to the water pump and discard it – a new one must be used **(see illustration 19.16a)**.

Inspection

Note: *Individual parts are not available for the combined oil and water pump; if the checks described below (and those in Chapter 3 for the water pump) indicate that the oil pump is worn, it must be replaced with a complete new unit.*
10 Counter-hold the pump driven sprocket and unscrew the bolt, then remove the sprocket and washer **(see illustration)**.
11 Unscrew the three bolts and remove the oil pump body **(see illustration)**.
12 Remove the inner and outer rotors, noting which way round they fit. Clean them with solvent. Examine them for scoring and wear.
13 Fit the outer rotor into the body and measure the clearance between them **(see illustration)**. Fit the inner rotor over the shaft

and locate the cut-outs over the drive pin **(see illustration)**. Fit the outer rotor over the inner rotor, then position them as shown and measure the clearance between the inner rotor tip and the outer rotor tip with a feeler gauge, and record the measurement **(see illustrations)**. Fit both rotors into the body, then lay a straight-edge across the body and measure the rotor end-float (gap between the rotors and straight-edge) with a feeler gauge. If any of the results are outside the limits listed in this Chapter's Specifications, replace the pump with a new one.
14 Before reassembling the pump, make sure that all parts are clean. Lubricate the rotors with new engine oil. Make sure the drive pin is in place **(see illustration)**. Fit the inner and outer rotors. **(see illustrations 19.13b and c)**. Fit the pump body and tighten the bolts securely **(see illustration)**. Fit the washer onto

19.13a Measuring outer rotor-to-body clearance

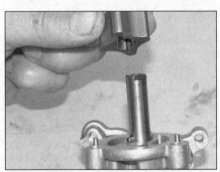

19.13b Fit the inner rotor . . .

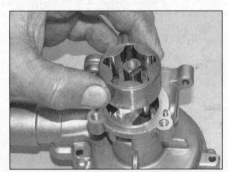

19.13c . . . and the outer rotor . . .

19.13d . . . and measure rotor tip clearance

19.14a Set the drive pin (arrowed) centrally

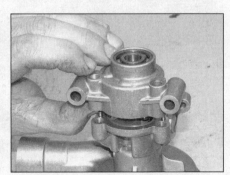

19.14b Fit the body onto the locating pins

19.14c Fit the washer onto the shaft . . .

19.14d . . . then fit the sprocket

19.16a Fit a new O-ring (arrowed) into the groove

19.16b Prime the pump as described

19.17a Fit the roll pin . . .

19.17b . . . and tap it in

the end of the shaft then locate the driven sprocket, OUT mark facing out and aligning the flats (see illustrations). Apply a thread locking compound to the bolt threads, then counter-hold the sprocket and tighten the bolt to the specified torque (see illustration 19.10).
15 Inspect the oil pump drive and driven sprockets and chain for damage and wear – the drive sprocket and chain are available separately, but the driven sprocket is part of the pump. Check the needle bearing and sleeve and replace them with new ones if they are worn.

Installation

Note: A revised oil pump is fitted to all models from engine No. 472611. If a new oil pump is required on models with an engine number up to 472610 you will be supplied with the revised oil pump – the old one is not available. If you are fitting the revised pump to an old engine you

may find that it will not fit properly – this is most likely to occur on models with a VIN number containing F2. If this is the case you need to remove about 2 mm of metal from the protruding boss on the crankcase that is preventing the correct seating of the pump using a suitable tool such as a Dremel. After doing this it is essential that all traces of removed metal are cleaned from inside the crankcase.
16 Fit a new O-ring into the coolant inlet sleeve to the water pump (see illustration). Pour some new engine oil into the pump and turn the sprocket so the rotors are liberally coated (see illustration).
17 Locate the pump on the crankcase (see illustration 19.9b). Insert the roll pin and tap it in until it seats using a punch (see illustrations).
18 Slide the spacer onto the shaft, followed by the sleeve with its collared end innermost,

then fit the bearing onto the sleeve (see illustrations). Fit the drive sprocket into the chain and slide the sprocket onto the shaft, but not onto the bearing, then slip the chain around the driven sprocket and slide the drive sprocket onto the bearing (see illustration 19.8b). Check the chain is correctly engaged around each sprocket. Fit the driven sprocket cover then tighten the pump mounting bolts to the torque setting specified at the beginning of the Chapter (see illustration 19.8a).
19 Clean the pump drive chain guide bolts. Apply some fresh threadlock, fit the guide and tighten the bolts to the specified torque (see illustration 19.6).
20 Fit new O-rings onto the coolant outlet pipe (see illustration). Insert the pipe, locating it in the pump, and tighten its bolt to the specified torque. Connect the hoses and tighten the clamps (see illustration 19.5).

19.18a Slide the spacer on . . .

19.18b . . . then fit the sleeve and bearing

19.20 Fit new O-rings (arrowed) before inserting the pipe

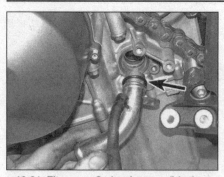

19.21 Fit a new O-ring (arrowed) before fitting the pipe

20.2 Unscrew the bolts (arrowed) and remove the plate

20.4 Remove the E-clip and the washer behind it

20.5 Withdraw the gearchange shaft

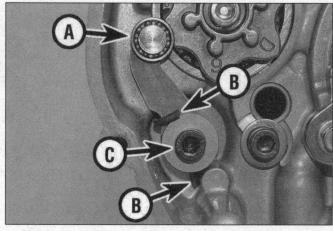

20.6 Note how the roller (A) and spring ends (B) locate, then unscrew the bolt (C) and remove the arm

21 Fit a new O-ring onto the coolant inlet pipe **(see illustration)**. Fit the pipe and tighten its bolt to the specified torque. If detached connect the hoses and tighten the clamps.

22 Install the oil strainer, the internal oil pipe, and the sump (see Section 18).

23 Install the clutch (see Section 16).

24 Replenish the engine oil and coolant (see Chapter 1).

20 Gearchange mechanism

Note: *The gearchange mechanism can be removed with the engine in the frame. If the engine has been removed, ignore the steps which don't apply.*

Removal

1 Make sure the transmission is in neutral. Remove the clutch (see Section 16).

2 Unscrew the crankcase breather baffle plate bolts and remove the plate **(see illustration)**.

3 Remove the front sprocket cover (see (Chapter 6).

4 Remove the E-clip and washer from the shaft **(see illustration)**. Wrap a single layer of thin insulating tape around the shaft splines to protect the oil seal lips as the shaft is removed.

5 Note how the gearchange shaft centralising spring ends fit on each side of the locating pin in the casing, and how the pawls on the selector arm locate onto the pins on the cam plate end of the selector drum. Grasp the shaft/arm assembly and withdraw it from the crankcase, noting the washer **(see illustration)**.

6 Note how the stopper arm roller locates in the neutral detent on the selector drum cam, and how the spring ends locate **(see illustration)**. Unscrew the stopper arm bolt and remove the collar, then arm, the washer and the spring, noting how they fit.

7 If required, undo the cam plate bolt, locking the selector drum with a holding tool or using a suitable tool wedged between the plate and the crankcase **(see illustration)**. Remove the plate, using a screwdriver to help ease it off if necessary. Note that there is a locating pin in the end of the selector drum – it should be tight, but take care as it could drop out. Remove it from the drum for safekeeping if it is loose.

Inspection

8 Check the selector arm for cracks, distortion and wear of its pawls, and check for any corresponding wear on the pins on the selector drum cam plate **(see illustration)**. Also check the stopper arm roller and the

20.7 Counter-hold the drum as described and unscrew the bolt (arrowed)

20.8 Check the pawls on the arm and the pins on the plate

20.12a Check the bearings (arrowed) and
their seals

20.12b Draw the bearing out . . .

20.12c . . . then draw the seal out

20.12d Fit the new seal with the marked
side facing in . . .

20.12e . . . and drive it in . . .

20.12f . . . then drive the new bearing in

detents in the cam plate for any wear or damage, and make sure the roller turns freely. Replace any components that are worn or damaged with new ones. If required (and not already done), refer to Step 7 for removal of the cam plate, and to Step 12 for installation.

9 Inspect the shaft centralising spring and the stopper arm return spring for fatigue, wear or damage (see illustration 20.8). If any is found, they must be replaced with new ones. To replace the shaft spring release the circlip, then slide the spring off the shaft. Fit the new spring, locating the ends on each side of the tab, then fit the circlip, using a new one if the old one distorted on removal.

10 Make sure the locating pin in the crankcase around which the centralising spring ends locate is tightened to the specified torque setting – if loose, remove it, clean the threads and apply fresh threadlock, then tighten it to the correct torque.

11 Check the gearchange shaft is straight and look for damage to the splines. If the shaft is bent you can attempt to straighten it, but if the splines are damaged the shaft must be replaced with a new one.

12 Check the condition of the shaft bearings and oil seals in the crankcase (see illustration). If the bearings are worn or the seals are damaged, deteriorated or showing signs of leakage they must be replaced with new ones. Draw the bearings out using a puller, then draw out the seals (see illustrations). Do not reuse the bearings once removed. Drive the new seals squarely into place with the marked side facing in using a suitable socket that bears only on the outer rim, not on the inner lip (see illustration). Drive the new bearings into place (see illustration).

Installation

13 If removed, fit the cam plate locating pin into the end of the selector drum. Locate the

cam plate onto the pin, carefully using a drift to tap it into place if necessary. Clean the threads of the bolt, then apply a suitable non-permanent thread locking compound and tighten it to the torque setting specified at the beginning of the Chapter (see illustration 20.7) – lock the drum with a holding tool as on removal.

14 Clean the threads of the stopper arm bolt. Assemble the stopper arm, spring and collar, then slide the bolt through and fit the washer, positioning the spring ends correctly (see illustrations). Apply a suitable non-permanent thread locking compound to the bolt threads. Fit the stopper arm assembly, locating the roller in the neutral detent in the cam plate, and tighten the bolt to the torque setting specified at the beginning of the Chapter (see illustration) – make sure the collar locates correctly in the arm, the roller remains aligned in its detent, and the spring ends remain correctly located as you tighten the bolt (see illustration 20.6).

20.14a Assemble the spring, arm and
collar . . .

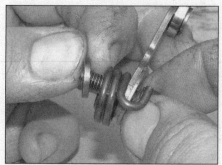

20.14b . . . then fit the bolt and washer

20.14c Fit the stopper arm assembly onto
the crankcase

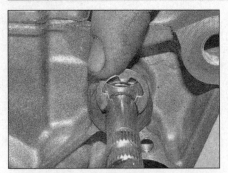

20.15 Fit the washer and press the E-clip into the groove

20.16 Make sure everything is correctly in place

15 Check that the centralising spring is properly positioned on the shaft **(see illustration 20.8)**. Apply some oil to the gearchange shaft bearings, and some grease to the lips of the oil seals **(see illustration 20.12a)**. Slide the shaft into place and push it all the way through the case until the splined end comes out the other side, and locate the selector arm pawls onto the pins on the selector drum cam plate and the centralising spring ends onto each side of the locating pin in the crankcase **(see illustration 20.5)**. Fit the washer and E-clip onto the left-hand end of the shaft **(see illustration)**.

16 Check that all components are correctly positioned **(see illustration)**. Clean the

21.3 Unscrew the bolts (arrowed) and remove the cover

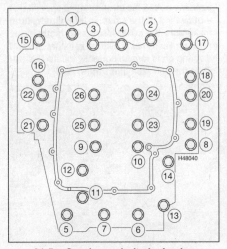

21.5a Crankcase bolt slackening sequence

threads of the crankcase breather baffle plate bolts. Apply some fresh threadlock, then fit the plate and tighten the bolts to the specified torque **(see illustration 20.2)**.

17 Install the clutch (see Section 16).

18 Remove the insulating tape from around the gearchange shaft splines. Install the front sprocket cover (see Chapter 6).

21 Crankcase separation and reassembly

Separation

1 To access the crankshaft and connecting rods, balancer shaft, transmission shafts, selector drum and forks, and all related bearings, the crankcases must be split.

2 Remove the engine from the frame (see Section 4). Remove the following components, referring to the relevant Sections.

Camshafts and followers (Section 9)*
Cam chain, tensioner blade and guide blade (Section 10)*
Cylinder head (Section 12)*
Cylinder liners and pistons (Sections 14 and 15)*
Alternator and starter clutch (see Chapter 8)*
Clutch (see Section 16)
Starter motor (Chapter 8)
Sump, oil strainer, oil pipe and drain tubes (see Section 18)
Oil/water pump and its drive chain (see Section 19)
Gearchange mechanism (see Section 20)

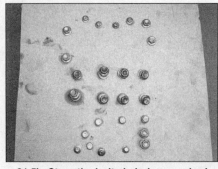

21.5b Store the bolts in holes punched into a piece of card as shown

* If the crankcase halves are being separated just to examine the crankshaft, balancer shaft or transmission components without removing them, or to just remove the transmission shafts and/or selector drum and forks, then there is no need to remove the camshafts, cam chain, cylinder head, liners and pistons, and alternator, though the right-hand crankcase cover and alternator cover must be removed. The gearchange mechanism need only be removed if the transmission is being removed.

3 Unscrew the balancer shaft end cover bolts, noting the bracket **(see illustration)**. Remove the cover and discard the gasket.

4 Turn the crankcase upside down, supporting it as required using blocks of wood so it is stable.

5 Slacken and remove all bolts from the lower crankcase half following the numbered sequence **(see illustration)**. **Note:** *As each bolt is removed, store it in its relative position in a cardboard template of the lower crankcase half* **(see illustration)**. *This will ensure that all bolts are installed in the correct location on reassembly. Also, take note of the washers on the eight crankshaft journal bolts and store them with the bolts to ensure correct reassembly.*

6 Carefully lift the lower crankcase half off the upper half, leaving the crankshaft, balancer shaft and transmission shafts in the upper half of the crankcase **(see illustration)**. As the lower half is lifted away take care not to dislodge or lose any main bearing shells and the three dowels. **Note:** *If the halves don't separate easily, make sure all fasteners have been removed. Don't lever between the crankcase mating surfaces or they will leak; initial separation can be achieved by tapping gently around the joint with a soft-faced mallet.*

7 Remove the three locating dowels if they are loose – they could be in either crankcase half **(see illustration 21.11)**.

Reassembly

8 Remove all traces of sealant from the crankcase mating surfaces.

9 Ensure that all components are in place in the upper and lower crankcase halves. If the transmission shafts have not been removed, remove the oil seal from the left-hand end of the output shaft and replace it with a new one (see Section 27). Check the position of

21.6 Lift the lower crankcase half off carefully so as not to dislodge components

21.11 Make sure the dowels (arrowed) are
in place

21.12a Apply sealant . . .

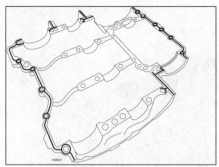

21.12b . . . to the shaded area as shown

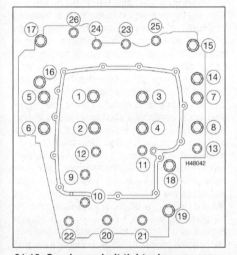

21.16 Crankcase bolt tightening sequence
– all bolts, first stage

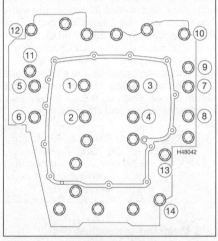

21.17 Crankcase bolt tightening sequence
– M8 bolts, second stage

21.19 Fit the cover using a new gasket

the selector drum and forks and transmission shafts – make sure they're in the neutral position (i.e. the transmission shafts rotate independently of each other).

10 Lubricate the transmission shaft pinions, selector drum and forks, and crankshaft journals with clean engine oil, then use a rag soaked in high flash-point solvent to wipe over the mating surfaces of both crankcase halves to remove all traces of oil.

11 If removed, fit the three locating dowels into the upper crankcase half **(see illustration)**.

12 Apply a small amount of suitable silicone sealant (Triumph use ThreeBond 1215) to the indicated areas of the mating surface of the lower crankcase half **(see illustrations)**.

Caution: Take care not to apply an excessive amount of sealant, as it will ooze out when the case halves are assembled and may obstruct oil passages and prevent the bearings from seating.

13 Make sure that the main bearing shells are in position, then carefully fit the lower crankcase half onto the upper half, making sure it locates onto the dowels **(see illustration 21.6)**.

14 Check that the lower crankcase half is correctly seated and that all shafts are free to rotate. **Note:** *If the cases are not correctly*

seated, remove the lower crankcase half and investigate the problem. Do not attempt to pull them together using the crankcase bolts as the case will crack and be ruined.

15 Clean the threads of the lower crankcase bolts and insert them in their original locations, making sure the washers are fitted with the eight crankshaft journal bolts **(see illustration 21.5b)**. Secure all bolts finger-tight at this stage.

Caution: Note that two sizes of bolt are used, 6 mm and 8 mm. Care must be taken to distinguish between them during the tightening sequence as the larger 8 mm bolts are set tighter, and if a 6 mm bolt is mistaken for an 8 mm bolt, it may shear or strip threads.

16 Tighten the crankcase bolts as follows: tighten all crankcase bolts to 12 Nm, tightening them in the correct numbered sequence **(see illustration)**.

17 Now tighten the M8 size crankcase bolts (Nos. 1 to 8) to 32 Nm in the correct sequence **(see illustration)**. Finally tighten the M8 size crankcase bolts (Nos. 9 to 14) to 32 Nm in the correct sequence **(see illustration 21.17)**.

18 With all crankcase fasteners tightened, check that the crankshaft, balancer shaft and transmission shafts rotate smoothly and easily. If there are any signs of undue stiffness or of

any other problem, the fault must be rectified before proceeding further.

19 Fit the balancer shaft end cover using a new gasket and tighten the bolts to the specified torque **(see illustration)** – do not forget to secure the bracket with the front two bolts **(see illustration 21.3)**.

20 Install all removed assemblies in the reverse of the sequence in Step 2.

22 Crankcase inspection

1 After the crankcases have been separated remove the crankshaft and connecting rods, balancer shaft, transmission shafts and oil pipe, selector drum and forks, and all related bearings, referring to the relevant Sections. Also remove the speed sensor (see Chapter 4) and the oil pressure switch (see Chapter 8). Unscrew the breather chamber cover screws and remove the cover **(see illustration)**.

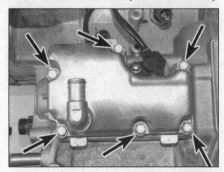

22.1a Breather chamber bolts (arrowed)

22.1b Remove the oil gallery plugs (arrowed) . . .

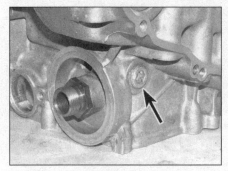

22.1c . . . and the oil gallery plug

Discard the gasket – a new one must be used. Remove the oil gallery plugs **(see illustrations)**.

2 Remove all traces of old gasket sealant from the mating surfaces. Minor damage to the surfaces can be cleaned up with a fine sharpening stone or grindstone.

3 Clean the crankcases and oil passages thoroughly with new solvent and dry them with compressed air, blowing through all oil passages and jets **(see illustrations)**.

4 Small cracks or holes in aluminium castings may be repaired with an epoxy resin adhesive as a temporary measure. Permanent repairs can be effected by argon-arc welding, and only a specialist in this process is in a position to advise on the economy or practical aspect of such a repair. Alternatively you could try one of the low temperature aluminium welding kits available. If any damage is found that can't be repaired, renew the crankcase halves as a set.

5 Damaged threads can be economically reclaimed by using a diamond section wire insert, of the Helicoil type, which is easily fitted after drilling and re-tapping the affected thread.

6 Sheared studs or screws can usually be removed with screw extractors, which consist of a tapered, left thread screws of very hard steel. These are inserted into a pre-drilled hole in the stud, and usually succeed in dislodging the most stubborn stud or screw. If a problem arises which seems beyond your scope, it is worth consulting a professional engineering firm before condemning an otherwise sound casing. Many of these firms advertise regularly in the motorcycle press.

7 Fit the breather chamber using a new

gasket, and apply some threadlock to the bolts **(see illustration 22.1a)**. Apply some thread lock to the oil gallery plugs and tighten them **(see illustrations 22.1b and c)**.

8 Install the speed sensor (see Chapter 4) and the oil pressure switch (see Chapter 8).

Caution: Be very careful not to nick or gouge the crankcase mating surfaces or leaks will result. Check both crankcase halves very carefully for cracks and other damage.

HAYNES HiNT *Refer to 'Tools and Workshop Tips' in the Reference section for details of how to install a thread insert and use a screw extractor.*

23 Main and connecting rod bearing information

1 Even though main and connecting rod bearings are generally replaced with new ones during the engine overhaul, the old bearings should be retained for close examination as they may reveal valuable information about the condition of the engine.

2 Bearing failure occurs mainly because of lack of lubrication, the presence of dirt or other foreign particles, overloading the engine and/or corrosion. Regardless of the cause of bearing failure, it must be corrected before the engine is reassembled to prevent it from happening again.

3 When examining the bearings, remove the

main bearings from the crankcase halves and the rod bearings from the connecting rods and caps and lay them out on a clean surface in the same general position as their location on the crankshaft journals. This will make it possible for you to match any noted bearing problems with the corresponding crankshaft journal.

4 Dirt and other foreign particles get into the engine in a variety of ways. It may be left in the engine during assembly or it may pass through filters or breathers. It may get into the oil and from there into the bearings. Metal chips from machining operations and normal engine wear are often present. Abrasives are sometimes left in engine components after reconditioning operations, especially when parts are not thoroughly cleaned using the proper cleaning methods. Whatever the source, these foreign objects often end up imbedded in the soft bearing material and are easily recognised. Large particles will not imbed in the bearing and will score or gouge the bearing and journal. The best prevention for this cause of bearing failure is to clean all parts thoroughly and keep everything spotlessly clean during engine reassembly. Frequent and regular oil and filter changes are also recommended.

5 Lack of lubrication or lubrication breakdown has a number of interrelated causes. Excessive heat (which thins the oil), overloading (which squeezes the oil from the bearing face) and oil leakage or throw off from excessive bearing clearances, worn oil pump or high engine Streets all contribute to lubrication breakdown. Blocked oil passages will also starve a bearing and destroy it. When lack of lubrication is the cause of bearing failure, the bearing material is wiped or extruded from the steel backing of the bearing. Temperatures may increase to the point where the steel backing and the journal turn blue from overheating.

6 Riding habits can have a definite effect on bearing life. Full throttle low Street operation, or labouring the engine, puts very high loads on bearings, which tend to squeeze out the oil film. These loads cause the bearings to flex, which produces fine cracks in the bearing face (fatigue failure). Eventually the bearing material will loosen in pieces and tear away from the steel backing. Short trip riding leads to corrosion of bearings, as insufficient engine heat is produced to drive off the condensed water and corrosive gases produced. These products collect in the engine oil, forming acid and sludge. As the oil is carried to the engine bearings, the acid attacks and corrodes the bearing material.

7 Incorrect bearing installation during engine assembly will lead to bearing failure as well. Tight fitting bearings which leave insufficient bearing oil clearances result in oil starvation. Dirt or foreign particles trapped behind a bearing insert result in high spots on the bearing which lead to failure.

8 To avoid bearing problems, clean all parts thoroughly before reassembly, double check all bearing clearance measurements and lubricate the new bearings with clean engine oil during installation.

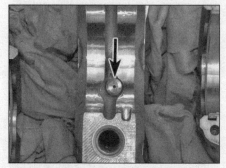

22.3a Clean through the piston oil jets (one of which arrowed) . . .

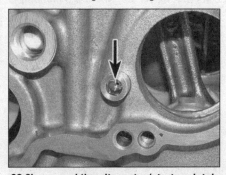

22.3b . . . and the alternator/starter clutch oil jet

24.4 Measure the connecting rod side clearance using a feeler gauge

24 Connecting rods and big-end bearings

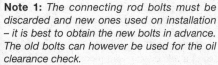

Note 1: *The connecting rod bolts must be discarded and new ones used on installation – it is best to obtain the new bolts in advance. The old bolts can however be used for the oil clearance check.*

Note 2: *There are a number of different ways in which the connecting rods can be removed, and your best approach will depend on what other work, if any, you are doing on the engine.*

● *If the liners have been removed and the pistons have already been separated from the rods, then you can either remove the crankshaft with the rods still attached, and then separate them afterwards, or you can leave the crankshaft in situ, remove the rod caps and then remove the rods from the top of the crankcase.*

● *If the pistons have not been separated from the rods, they cannot be removed along with the crankshaft as the pistons will not fit through the crankcase main bearing webs. Remove the rod caps first, then remove the rod and piston assemblies from the top of the crankcase.*

Note 3: *If the crankshaft and transmission shafts are left in situ, take great care not to dislodge them when the rods/pistons are being removed.*

Removal

1 Remove the engine from the frame (see Section 4).

24.7 ... and remove the connecting rod cap

2 Remove the cylinder head (see Section 12).
3 Separate the crankcase halves (see Section 21).
4 Before separating the rods from the crankshaft, measure the side clearance on each rod with a feeler gauge **(see illustration)**. If the clearance on any rod is greater than the service limit listed in this Chapter's Specifications, replace that rod with a new one.
5 Using paint or a marker pen, mark the relevant cylinder identity across the join between each connecting rod and cap at the front – these ensure that the cap and rod are fitted correctly on reassembly **(see illustration)**. Cylinders are numbered 1 to 3, from the left to the right-hand side of the engine.
6 Working on one connecting rod at a time, unscrew the connecting rod cap bolts and remove them **(see illustration)**.
7 Separate the cap, complete with the lower bearing shell, from the crankpin **(see illustration)**. If the cap appears stuck, tap it lightly on one end with a hammer while pulling it. If necessary thread the bolts part-way back in and tap the heads lightly to dislodge the rod from the cap.
8 Lift the crankcase and support it with sufficient clearance for the rods or rod and piston assemblies to be removed through the top of the crankcase.
9 Support the rod to prevent it marking the liner bore or block, and detach it, complete with the upper bearing shell, from the crankpin, then remove the rod or rod and piston assembly **(see illustration)**.

24.5 Mark the cylinder number across the front of the rod and cap

24.9 Push the rod off the crankpin and withdraw it from the top

24.6 Working on one rod at a time, unscrew the cap bolts ...

> **HAYNES HINT** *If required, to ease removal of the pistons from the tops of the liners, carefully remove any ridge of carbon built up on the top of each liner bore using a scraper. If there is a pronounced wear ridge, remove it using a ridge reamer.*

Caution: Do not try to remove the piston/connecting rod from the bottom of the crankcase. The piston will not pass the crankcase main bearing webs.
10 Fit the relevant bearing shells (if removed), cap, bolts on each piston/connecting rod assembly so that they are all kept together as a matched set.
11 If required and not already done, separate the pistons from the connecting rods (see Section 15). If the cylinder liners weren't clamped in place after removing the cylinder head, remove them for resealing (see Section 14).

Inspection

12 Check the connecting rods for cracks and other obvious damage. Refer to Section 15 and check the piston pin and connecting rod small-end bore dimensions for wear. Replace any components that are worn beyond the specified limit with new ones.
13 Refer to Section 23 and examine the connecting rod bearing shells. If they are scored, badly scuffed or appear to have seized, new shells must be installed. Always replace the shells in the connecting rods as a set. If they are badly damaged, check the corresponding crankpin. Evidence of extreme heat, such as discoloration, indicates that lubrication failure has occurred. Be sure to thoroughly check the oil pump and pressure relief valve as well as all oil holes and passages before reassembling the engine.
14 Have the rods checked for twist and bending by a Triumph dealer if you are in doubt about their straightness.

Oil clearance check

15 Whether new bearing shells are being fitted or the original ones are being re-used, the connecting rod bearing oil clearance should be checked prior to reassembly. Work on one rod at a time when checking the clearances.

24.17 To remove a big-end bearing shell, push it sideways and lift it out

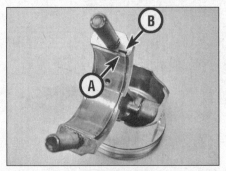

24.18 Make sure the tab (A) locates in the notch (B)

24.22 Measure the crushed Plastigauge using the appropriate scale on the pack

16 If it is in situ, lift the crankshaft out of the upper crankcase half, taking care not to dislodge the main bearing shells. Ensure that the crankshaft is securely supported on the work surface.

17 Remove the bearing shells from the rod and cap, keeping them in order (see illustration). Clean the backs of the shells and the bearing locations in both the connecting rod and cap, and the crankpin journal.

18 Press the bearing shells into their locations, making sure that the tab on each shell engages the notch in the connecting rod/cap (see illustration). Make sure the bearings are fitted in the correct locations and take care not to touch any shell's bearing surface with your fingers. Apply a smear of grease to each crankpin and a smear of silicone release agent to each bearing shell in the rod and cap.

19 Cut a length of the appropriate size Plastigauge (it should be slightly shorter than the width of the crankpin). Place a strand of Plastigauge on the crankpin journal for the rod being checked. Fit the rod onto its crankpin, then fit the cap, making sure it is fitted the correct way around so the previously made markings align. Note that the accuracy of this check is dependant on the rod not turning on the crankpin while it is installed and tightened – if it does, the Plastigauge will be disturbed and an inaccurate reading will result. Apply a smear of molybdenum disulphide grease to the bolt threads and to the underside of the heads and tighten them finger-tight.

20 Tighten the bolts in five stages, using a torque wrench and a degree disc, as follows.

First tighten them to 22 Nm, then slacken them by 120°. Now tighten them to 10 Nm, then to 14 Nm, and finally tighten them by 120° (see Haynes Hint on page 2•47).

21 Slacken the bolts and remove the connecting rod cap, again taking great care not to rotate the crankshaft.

22 Compare the width of the crushed Plastigauge on the crankpin to the scale printed on the Plastigauge envelope to obtain the connecting rod bearing oil clearance (see illustration). Be sure to use the appropriate scale as both imperial and metric scales are shown.

23 On completion carefully scrape away all traces of the Plastigauge material from the crankpin and bearing shells using a fingernail or other object which will not score the bearing surfaces.

24 If the clearance is within the range listed in this Chapter's Specifications and the bearing shells are in perfect condition, they can be reused.

25 If the clearance is beyond the specified service limit, first measure the diameter of the crankpin with a micrometer and compare the result with the Specifications at the beginning of this Chapter (see illustration 24.28). If the journal diameter is larger than the service limit, new bearing shells can be fitted (see Steps 27 to 29). If the journal diameter is smaller than the service limit, the crankshaft must be replaced with a new one.

26 Repeat the procedure for the remaining connecting rods. If the oil clearance is too great on any one, replace all of the shells (on all three rods) at the same time.

Bearing shell selection

27 The connecting rod big-end bearing oil clearance is controlled in production by selecting one of two grades of bearing shell. The grades are indicated by a colour-coding marked on the edge of each shell (see illustration). New bearing shells are selected as follows according to the crankpin journal diameter.

28 Measure the crankpin journal diameter using a micrometer and record the result (see illustration).

29 Match the measured journal diameter to the required bearing shells using the following table, according to model.

Daytona models, and Street Triple models to VIN 560476		
Con-rod big-end bore diameter	Crankpin journal diameter	Shell colour
36.000 to 36.009 mm	32.992 to 33.000 mm	White
36.000 to 36.009 mm	32.984 to 32.991 mm	Red

Street Triple models from VIN 560477		
Con-rod big-end bore diameter	Crankpin journal diameter	Shell colour
36.000 to 36.009 mm	33.018 to 33.026 mm	White
36.000 to 36.009 mm	33.010 to 33.017 mm	Red

Installation

Note 1: *New connecting rod bolts must be used for final assembly.*

Note 2: *There are a number of different ways in which the connecting rods can be installed, and your best approach will depend on what other work, if any, you are doing on the engine.*

● *If the pistons have been separated from the rods and the crankshaft has been removed, then you can either fit the rods onto the crankshaft and then install the crankshaft, or you can install the crankshaft and then install the rods from the top of the crankcase.*

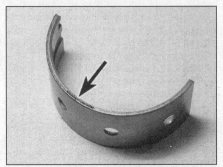

24.27 The colour code is marked on the side of the shell (arrowed)

24.28 Measure the crankpin width using a micrometer

● If the pistons have not been separated from the rods, the rod and piston assemblies cannot be installed attached to the crankshaft as the pistons will not fit through the crankcase main bearing webs. Install the rod and piston assemblies from the top of the crankcase then install the crankshaft. You will also have to make a decision regarding installation of the liners, as the rod and piston assemblies can be installed before them, with them or after them – see Section 14 for details.

● If it makes no difference, we advise fitting the pistons onto the rods first, then fitting the rod and piston assemblies into the liners, then installing the liners. At this point the cylinder head can be installed to avoid the risk of disturbing the liner seals when installing the crankshaft.

30   Remove the bearing shells from the rods and caps, keeping them in order **(see illustration 24.17)**. Clean the backs of the shells and the bearing locations in both the connecting rod and cap, and the crankpin journal. If new shells are being fitted, ensure that all traces of the protective grease are cleaned off using paraffin (kerosene). Wipe the shells, cap and rod dry with a clean lint free cloth.

31   Press the bearing shells into their locations, ensuring that the tab on each shell engages the notch in the connecting rod/cap **(see illustration 24.18)**. Make sure the bearings are fitted in the correct locations and take care not to touch any shell's bearing surface with your fingers.

32   Decide upon your installation procedure, then assemble the rods, pistons, cylinder liners and crankshaft as required, referring to the relevant Sections. **Note:** When installing the connecting rods on the crankshaft, refer to the previously made marks to ensure they are fitted in the correct positions (see Step 5).

33   Lubricate the shells with molybdenum disulphide oil (a 50/50 mixture of molybdenum disulphide grease and engine oil). Fit the rod onto its crankpin, then fit the cap, making sure it is the correct way around so the previously made markings align **(see illustration and 24.7)**. Apply a smear of molybdenum disulphide grease to the bolt threads and to the underside of the heads **(see illustration 24.6)**. Fit the bolts and tighten them

finger-tight at this stage. Check to make sure that all components have been returned to their original locations using the marks made on disassembly.

34   Tighten the bolts in five stages, using a torque wrench and a degree disc, as follows. First tighten them to 22 Nm, then slacken them by 120°. Now tighten them to 10 Nm, then to 14 Nm, and finally tighten them by 120°.

 HAYNES HiNT   *If a degree disc is not available, the angle can be determined by using the points on the connecting rod bolt. There are six points on the bolt, so the angle between each point is 60°. Select one point as a reference and mark it with paint or a marker. Now select the second point clockwise from it and mark its position on the connecting rod cap. Tighten the nut – when the mark on the first point aligns with the mark made on the connecting rod cap, it will have turned through 120°.*

35   Install the other connecting rods in the same way. Check to make sure that all components have been returned to their original locations using the marks made on disassembly.

36   **Note:** If the cylinder liners are installed, ensure appropriate measures have been taken to prevent them lifting off their seals (see Section 14). Check that the crankshaft rotates freely and that the rods rotate smoothly and freely on the crankpins. If there are any signs of roughness or tightness, remove the rods and re-check the bearing clearance. Sometimes tapping the bottom of the connecting rod cap will relieve tightness, but if in doubt, recheck the clearances.

37   Reassemble the crankcase halves and the rest of the engine according to your removal procedure, referring to the relevant Sections.

25   Crankshaft and main bearings

Removal

1   Remove the engine from the frame (see Section 4) and separate the crankcase halves (see Section 21).

2   Refer to Section 24 and separate the connecting rods from the crankshaft (unless the pistons have been removed, in which case the rods can remain attached for now, and removed later if required). **Note:** If no work is to be carried out on the piston/connecting rod assemblies there is no need to remove them from the bores (unless the liners have been removed), but, making sure the liners are secure (see Section 14), you can push them up to the top of the bores so that the big-ends are clear of the crankshaft.

3   Before removing the crankshaft, check the amount of end-float using a dial gauge. If it exceeds the limit specified, the crankshaft and/or the crankcases must be replaced with new ones.

4   Align then remove the balancer shaft (see Section 26). Lift the crankshaft out of the upper crankcase half, taking care not to dislodge the main bearing shells **(see illustration)**.

5   If required, remove the bearing shells from the crankcase halves by pushing their centres to the side, then lifting them out **(see illustration)**. Keep the shells in order.

Inspection

6   Clean the crankshaft with solvent, squirting it through all oil passages. If available, blow it through and dry with compressed air. Check the balancer shaft drive gear teeth and the cam chain drive sprocket teeth for wear and damage, referring to Sections 26 and 10 to also check the driven gear and sprockets and the cam chain.

7   Refer to Section 23 and examine the main bearing shells. If they are scored, badly scuffed or appear to have been seized, new shells must be installed. Always renew the main bearings as a set. If they are badly damaged, check the corresponding crankshaft journals. Evidence of extreme heat, such as discoloration, indicates that lubrication failure has occurred. Be sure to thoroughly check the oil pump and pressure relief valve as well as all oil holes and passages before reassembling the engine.

8   Inspect the crankshaft journals, paying particular attention where damaged bearing shells have been discovered. If the journals are scored or pitted in any way a new crankshaft will be required. Note that oversize shells are not available, precluding the option of re-grinding the crankshaft.

24.33 Pull the rod up onto its crankpin

25.4 Carefully lift the crankshaft out of the crankcase

25.5 To remove a main bearing shell, rotate it and lift it out

Oil clearance check

9 Whether new bearing shells are being fitted or the original ones are being re-used, the main bearing oil clearance should be checked prior to reassembly.

10 If not already done, remove the bearing shells from the crankcase halves by pushing their centres to the side, then lifting them out **(see illustration 25.5)**. Keep the shells in order. Clean the backs of the shells and their locations in both the crankcase halves.

11 Press the bearing shells back into their locations, making sure that the tab on each shell engages in the notch **(see illustration)**. Make sure the shells are fitted in the correct locations and take care not to touch any shell's bearing surface with your fingers. Apply a smear of grease to each journal and a smear of silicone release agent to each bearing shell.

12 Lay the crankshaft in position in the upper crankcase **(see illustration 25.4)**. Cut several lengths of the appropriate size Plastigauge (they should be slightly shorter than the width of the crankshaft journal). Place a strand of Plastigauge on each crankshaft journal.

13 If removed, fit the three locating dowels into the upper crankcase half **(see illustration 21.11)**. Carefully fit the lower crankcase half onto the upper half, making sure it locates onto the dowels **(see illustration 21.6)**. Check that the lower crankcase half is correctly seated. **Note:** *If the casings are not correctly seated, remove the lower crankcase half and investigate the problem. Do not attempt to pull them together using the crankcase bolts as the casing will crack and be ruined.* Install the eight M8 crankshaft journal bolts with their washers in their original locations and tighten them in the correct numerical sequence (1 to 8) in the two stages and to the torque settings as described in Section 21 **(see illustration 21.16)**. Make sure that the crankshaft is not rotated as the bolts are tightened.

14 Slacken and remove the bolts, working in a criss-cross pattern from the outside in, then carefully lift off the lower crankcase half, making sure the Plastigauge is not disturbed.

15 Compare the width of the crushed Plastigauge on each crankshaft journal to the scale printed on the Plastigauge envelope to obtain the main bearing oil clearance **(see illustration 24.22)**.

16 On completion carefully scrape away all traces of the Plastigauge material from the journals and bearing shells using a fingernail or other object which will not score the bearing surfaces.

17 If the clearance is within the range listed in this Chapter's Specifications and the bearing shells are in perfect condition, they can be reused. If the clearance is beyond the specified service limit, first measure the diameter of the crankshaft journals with a micrometer and compare the results with the Specifications at the beginning of this Chapter **(see illustration)**. If the journal diameters are larger than the service limit, new bearing shells can be fitted

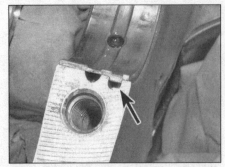

25.11 Press each shell into place, locating the tab in the notch (arrowed)

(see Steps 18 and 19). If the journal diameters are smaller than the service limit, the crankshaft must be replaced with a new one.

Bearing shell selection

18 The main bearing oil clearance is controlled in production by selecting one of four grades of bearing shell. The grades are indicated by a colour-coding marked on the edge of each shell **(see illustration 24.27)**. New shells are selected with reference to the following chart, having first measured the crankshaft journal diameter and the crankshaft bore diameter.

19 Measure the diameter of each crankshaft journal with a micrometer and record the results **(see illustration 25.17)**. Next, assemble the crankcase halves with the bearing shells and crankshaft removed, and tighten the eight M8 crankshaft journal bolts in the correct numerical sequence in the two stages and to the torque settings as described in Section 21. Measure each crankshaft journal bore diameter using a bore gauge and micrometer and record the results. Refer to *Tools and Workshop Tips* in the Reference Section for details on how to use the measuring equipment.

Crankcase bore diameter	Crankshaft journal diameter	Shell colour
35.973 to 35.982 mm	32.993 to 33.000 mm	White
35.973 to 35.981 mm	32.984 to 32.992 mm	Red
35.981 to 35.989 mm	32.993 to 33.000 mm	Red
35.981 to 35.988 mm	32.984 to 32.992 mm	Blue
35.989 to 35.997 mm	32.993 to 33.000 mm	Blue
35.989 to 35.997 mm	32.984 to 32.992 mm	Green

Installation

20 Clean the backs of the bearing shells and the bearing recesses in both crankcase halves. If new shells are being fitted, make sure that all traces of the protective grease are cleaned off using paraffin (kerosene). Wipe the shells and crankcase halves dry with a lint-free cloth.

21 Press the bearing shells into their

25.17 Measure the crank journals width using a micrometer

locations, making sure that the tab on each shell engages in the notch **(see illustration 25.11)**. Make sure the bearings are fitted in the correct locations and take care not to touch any shell's bearing surface with your fingers. Lubricate the shells with molybdenum disulphide oil (a 50/50 mixture of molybdenum disulphide grease and engine oil).

22 Identify the tooth on the balancer drive gear on the crankshaft marked with a dot – this tooth must align with the marked tooth on the balancer shaft driven gear when it is installed **(see illustration 26.2)**. Lower the crankshaft into position in the upper crankcase, with the marked tooth facing forwards **(see illustration 25.4)**. Install the balancer shaft, making sure that it is correctly timed to the crankshaft (see Section 26).

23 If removed, install the connecting rods (see Section 24), then reassemble the crankcase halves and the rest of the engine according to your removal procedure, referring to the relevant Sections.

26 Balancer shaft

Removal

1 Remove the engine from the frame and separate the crankcase halves (see Sections 4 and 22).

2 The balancer shaft is gear driven off the right-hand end of the crankshaft – the crankshaft drive gear and the balancer shaft driven gear are marked so that precise timing

26.2 Balancer shaft driven gear and crankshaft drive gear alignment marks

26.3 Carefully lift the balancer shaft out of the crankcase

26.5a Remove the circlip . . .

26.5b . . . and the wave washer

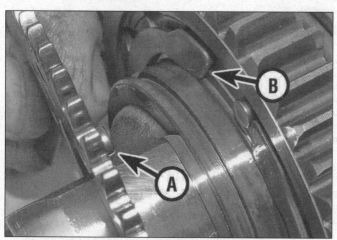

26.5c Note how the pin (A) locates against the end of the backlash spring (B)

26.6 Remove the circlip (arrowed) and the washer behind it

of the two shafts can be achieved. Rotate the crankshaft until the teeth marked with dots align **(see illustration)**.

3 Note how the retaining rings on the bearings on each end of the balancer shaft locate in the grooves in the crankcase, and how the bearing locating pins sit in the cut-outs. Carefully lift the balancer shaft out **(see illustration)**. The balancer shaft driven gear incorporates an inner spring-loaded backlash eliminator gear – as the shaft is lifted out, the backlash eliminator gear will spring out of alignment with the main gear.

Inspection, disassembly and reassembly

4 Inspect the teeth of both inner and main driven gears for signs of wear or damage, and check the teeth of the drive gear on the crankshaft. Only the inner backlash eliminator gear is available – if the main outer gear is damaged a complete new shaft must be fitted.

5 The shaft can be disassembled if required – all other components except the main outer gear and the shaft itself are available individually. Slide the needle bearing off the left-hand end of the shaft. Remove the circlip securing the inner gear, then remove the wave washer and the gear, noting how the pin on the inside face locates against one end of the

backlash spring **(see illustrations)**. Remove the spring, noting it how it locates against the pin in the main gear **(see illustration 26.7a)** – check it for damage and deformation and replace it with a new one if necessary.

6 Check the bearings for wear and damage. If they do not run smoothly and freely, or if there is excessive freeplay between the needle bearing and its sleeve, or between the ball bearing races, replace them with new ones if necessary. To remove the ball bearing remove the circlip and washer, then use a puller to draw the bearing off the shaft or a press to push the shaft out of the bearing **(see illustration)**. Discard the circlip and use a new one. When fitting the new bearing make sure the retaining ring faces the main gear, and

either drive it on using a suitable tubular drift that bears only on the inner race, or support the bearing on its inner race and press the shaft into it. In either case make sure the bearing seats against the lip on the shaft. Fit the washer and a new circlip, making sure it locates in the groove.

7 Fit the backlash eliminator gear spring, locating the ends on each side of the pin on the inner face of the main gear **(see illustrations)**. Fit the inner gear, aligning it so its pin is to the left of the main gear pin, and so that both pins are between the spring ends **(see illustration 26.5c)**. Fit the wave washer and the circlip, making sure it locates in the groove **(see illustrations 26.5b and a)**.

26.7a Fit the spring . . .

26.7b . . . positioning it as shown

26.9 Make sure the dot on the drive gear is correctly positioned

26.10a Inner face of main gear is marked with a dot, inner gear with a line – these must be aligned

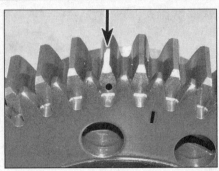

26.10b Mark the top of the tooth (arrowed) with paint

8 Lubricate the needle bearing with clean engine oil, then slide it onto the sleeve with its retaining ring to the outside.

Installation

9 Before installing the balancer shaft, ensure the tooth on the drive gear on the crankshaft marked with a dot is facing forwards (see illustration).

10 Now you must align the tooth on the inner face of the main gear marked with a dot with the tooth on the inner gear marked with a line (see illustration). To do this, first mark the top edge of the main gear tooth with paint so that it can be identified when the two gears are aligned (see illustration). Use a holding tool inserted in the holes in the inner gear and a large spanner to draw the gears into position against the tension of the backlash spring

(see illustrations). Lock the gears together – Triumph provides a special tool to do this (Part No. T3880016), or alternatively use a piece of crushed tube or similar between the gear teeth, or make a locking plate out of aluminium as shown (see illustration). Note that the tool must be positioned so that it is not in the way when the balancer shaft is installed in the crankcase (see illustration 26.11a).

11 Lay the shaft in the crankcase (see illustration) – make sure that the tooth marked with a dot on the outer face of the main (driven) gear aligns with the tooth marked with a dot on the crankshaft drive gear (see illustration 26.2). Check that the bearing retaining rings locate in their grooves and the locating pins seat in the cut-outs (see illustrations).

12 Remove the locking tool.

 Warning: If the balancer shaft and crankshaft gears are not correctly aligned, severe engine vibration will occur leading to damage to engine components.

13 Reassemble the crankcase halves and the rest of the engine according to your removal procedure, referring to the relevant Sections.

27 Transmission shaft removal and installation

Removal

1 Remove the engine from the frame and separate the crankcase halves (see Sections 4 and 21).

26.10c Use the set-up shown . . .

26.10d . . . to align the marked gears as described . . .

26.10e . . . then lock them together

26.11a Lay the balancer shaft in the crankcase as described

26.11b Make sure the retaining ring and locating pin are correctly seated . . .

26.11c . . . on each end

27.2 Lift out the transmission output shaft

27.4a Unscrew the bolts (arrowed) and where fitted remove the plate

27.4b Thread two bolts into the housing as shown . . .

27.4c . . . and use them to draw the housing out

2 Lift the output shaft out of the crankcase, noting how the selector forks locate in their pinion grooves, and how the ball bearing retaining ring and oil seal lip locate in the grooves and the needle bearing pin locates in the hole **(see illustration)**. Remove the oil seal from the left-hand end and discard it – a new one must be used **(see illustration 27.10a)**.

3 Remove the selector drum and forks (see Section 29).

4 Undo the input shaft ball bearing housing bolts, and on engines from No. 330119-on remove the plate **(see illustration)**. Thread two of the bolts into the threaded holes in the housing and continue to screw them in evenly and a little at a time after they have contacted the crankcase – this will draw the bearing housing and shaft out **(see illustrations)**. Once the housing is free of the crankcase draw the shaft out.

5 If required withdraw the transmission oil pipe, levering it carefully out with a screwdriver **(see illustration)**. New O-rings must be used, but leave the old ones on for the time being so they can be used as a guide for fitting the new ones – on some models two different sizes are

used, and on others three different sizes are used.

6 If necessary, the transmission shafts can be disassembled and inspected for wear or damage as described in Section 28.

Installation

Note: *Triumph specify to use new bolts for the bearing housing on the input shaft, but to retain the old bolts for use when drawing the housing into the crankcase – once the housing seats remove the old bolts and replace them with the new bolts, tightening them to the specified torque. This is because the new bolts come pre-treated with a thread locking compound. If necessary you can clean the threads of the old bolts and apply some fresh threadlock to them.*

7 If removed clean the transmission oil pipe with solvent and blow through it, with compressed air if available. Fit the new O-rings onto the pipe in accordance with the layout of the old ones and smear them with oil – note that some early Daytona models were fitted with two O-rings exactly the same size (9.1 x 1.6), but on others, and on all later

models (and on all Street Triples) the one nearest the flanged (right-hand) end of the pipe is slightly larger (10.1 x 1.6). Check the O-rings that have been supplied and fit accordingly. Fit the pipe into the crankcase, locating the tab in the cut-out **(see illustration 27.5)**.

8 Slide the input shaft into the crankcase, aligning the ball bearing housing bolt holes with those in the crankcase, locating the inner end in its needle bearing in the crankcase, and pushing the ball bearing housing in as far

27.5 Remove the oil pipe if required

27.8a Slide the shaft into the crankcase

27.8b Make sure the tabs do not become disengaged from the slots and out of alignment as shown

27.8c On engines from No. 330119-on fit the plate

27.8d Fit the bolts . . .

27.8e . . . and tighten them as described to draw the housing in

as it will go by hand **(see illustration)**. Make sure the tabs on the washer behind the 2nd gear pinion remain engaged in the slots in the slotted washer and do not fall out of alignment as shown **(see illustration)** – if they do, the pinions will be pressed tightly together and jam as the bearing housing is pressed in. Clean the threads of the original housing bolts (see **Note** above). If the original bolts are being reused for final assembly apply some fresh threadlock. On engines from No. 330119-on fit the plate **(see illustration)**. Fit the bolts and tighten them evenly and a little at a time in a criss-cross pattern to draw the housing squarely in if it wouldn't push in all the way

(see illustrations). When the housing seats, if the original bolts are being used for final assembly tighten them to the torque setting specified at the beginning of the Chapter, or if new ones are being used for final assembly remove the original ones, fit the new ones, and tighten them to the specified torque.

9 Install the selector drum and forks (see Section 29).

10 Make sure the bearing retaining ring is in place on the ball bearing on the left-hand end of the output shaft, then fit a new oil seal onto the sleeve **(see illustration)**. Install the output shaft, making sure the needle bearing pin locates in its hole **(see illustration 27.2)**, the

retaining ring and locating pin locate correctly **(see illustration)**, and the selector forks locate in their pinion grooves.

11 Ensure that the gears of both shafts mesh correctly and that they're in the neutral position i.e. the input shaft can be turned whilst the output shaft is held stationary.

12 Reassemble the crankcase halves and the rest of the engine according to your removal procedure, referring to the relevant Sections.

28 Transmission shaft overhaul

1 Remove the shafts from the crankcase as described in Section 27.

> **HAYNES HINT**
> *When disassembling the transmission shafts, place the parts on a long rod or thread a wire through them to keep them in order and facing the proper direction.*

Input shaft disassembly

2 Slide the thrust washer off the left-hand end of the shaft **(see illustrations 28.18b)**. Make a paint mark on the outer face of the

27.10a Fit the retaining ring (arrowed) if removed, then fit a new oil seal onto the shaft

27.10b Make sure the ring locates in the groove and the pin in the cut-out

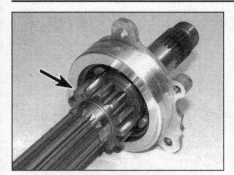

28.6 1st gear pinion (arrowed)

28.12a Check the bearing on the shaft . . .

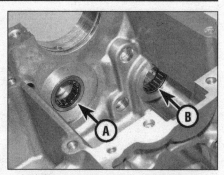

28.12b . . . and the bearing (A) in the crankcase. Selector drum bearing (B)

2nd gear pinion then slide it off the shaft (see illustrations 28.18a).

3 Slide the tabbed washer off the shaft, noting how its tabs locate in the slotted washer (see illustrations 28.17c). Turn the slotted washer to align the splines, then slide it off the shaft (see illustrations 28.17b and a).

4 Slide the 6th gear pinion and its splined bush off the shaft, followed by the splined washer (see illustrations 28.16c, b and a).

5 Remove the circlip securing the combined 3rd/4th gear pinion then slide the pinion off the shaft (see illustrations 28.15b and a).

6 Remove the circlip securing the 5th gear pinion, then slide the splined washer, the pinion and its bush off the shaft (see illustrations 28.14d, c, b and a). The 1st gear pinion is integral with the shaft (see illustration).

Input shaft inspection

7 Wash all of the components in clean solvent and dry them off.

8 Check the gear teeth for cracking and other obvious damage. Check the 5th and 6th gear bushes and the surface in the inner diameter of the gears for scoring or heat discoloration. If the gear or bush is damaged, replace it with a new one.

9 Inspect the dogs and the dog holes in related gears for excessive wear. Renew the paired gears as a set if necessary.

10 Measure the selector fork groove width in the 3rd/4th gear pinion as described in Section 29.

11 The shaft is unlikely to sustain damage unless the engine has seized, placing an unusually high loading on the transmission, or the machine has covered a very high mileage.

Check the surface of the shaft, especially where a pinion turns on it, and the edges of the splined sections, and replace the shaft with a new one if it has scored or picked up. Damage of any kind can only be cured by renewal.

12 The ball bearing on the left-hand end of the shaft is a press fit on the shaft, and the housing is a press fit on the bearing (see illustration). On engines up to No. 330118 a circlip also secures the bearing in its housing. First remove the circlip and discard it – a new one must be used. Press the shaft out of the bearing, then press the bearing out of the housing, from the outside on engines up to No. 330118 and from the inside on all others – note which way round the bearing fits. The bearing cannot be reused. Refer to *Tools and Workshop Tips* in the Reference Section for more information on bearing checks and removal and installation methods. When fitting the new bearing press it into the housing until it seats, from the inside on engines up to No.

330118 and from the outside on all others, locating the press only on the outer race. Press the bearing onto the shaft until it seats using a suitable tube that locates only on the inner race. On engines up to No. 330118 fit a new circlip. Replace the needle bearing in the crankcase with a new one if it is worn or damaged, or does not run freely (see illustration).

Input shaft reassembly

13 During reassembly, always use new circlips. Lubricate the components with the correct grade of engine oil before assembling them.

14 Slide on the 5th gear pinion bush, then slide the pinion, with its dogs facing away from the integral 1st gear pinion, onto the bush (see illustrations). Slide the splined washer against the pinion (see illustration). Fit the circlip, making sure it locates in its groove (see illustrations).

28.14a Slide the 5th gear pinion bush on the shaft . . .

28.14b . . . then fit the 5th gear pinion on the bush

28.14c Slide on the splined washer . . .

28.14d . . . then fit the circlip . . .

28.14e . . . making sure it locates in its groove

28.15a Slide the 3rd/4th gear pinion onto the shaft, making sure the oil holes (arrowed) do not align . . .

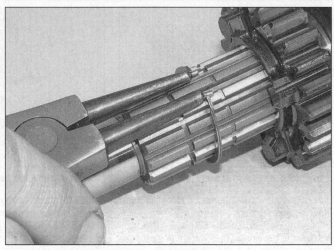

28.15b . . . then fit the circlip . . .

28.15c . . . making sure it locates in its groove

15 Slide the combined 3rd/4th gear pinion with the larger (4th) gear facing the 5th gear pinion, making sure the oil hole does NOT align with the oil hole in the shaft (see illustration). Fit the circlip, making sure it locates in its groove (see illustrations).

16 Slide the splined washer against the circlip, then fit the 6th gear pinion bush making sure the oil hole does NOT align with the oil hole in the shaft (see illustrations). Slide the 6th gear pinion onto the bush with its dogs facing the 3rd gear (see illustration).

17 Slide the slotted washer onto the shaft to its groove then turn it to misalign the splines so the washer is locked (see illustrations). Slide

the tabbed washer onto the shaft, locating the tabs into the slots of the slotted washer (see illustration).

18 Fit the 2nd gear pinion with its previously marked side facing away from the 6th gear pinion (see illustration). Slide on the thrust washer (see illustration). The assembled input shaft should be as shown (see illustration).

Output shaft disassembly

19 Slide the needle bearing and thrust washer off the right-hand end of the shaft (see illustrations 28.40b and a).

20 Slide the 1st gear pinion off the shaft, followed its bush, the thrust washer and the

28.16a Slide the splined washer on . . .

28.16b . . . followed by the bush, making sure the oil holes (arrowed) do not align . . .

28.16c . . . then fit the 6th gear pinion onto the bush

28.17a Slide the slotted washer to its groove . . .

28.17b . . . then turn it to lock it against the splines . . .

28.17c . . . then slide on the tabbed washer and fit the tabs in the slots

28.18a Slide the 2nd gear pinion onto the shaft . . .

28.18b . . . followed by the thrust washer

28.18c The assembled input shaft should be as shown

5th gear pinion (see illustrations 28.39b, a, 28.38b, a).

21 Remove the circlip, then slide off the splined washer, the 4th gear pinion, and its bush (see illustrations 28.37d, c, b and a).

22 Slide the tabbed washer off the shaft, noting how its tabs locate in the slotted washer (see illustrations 28.36c). Turn the slotted washer to align the splines, then slide it off the shaft (see illustrations 28.36b and a).

23 Slide the 3rd gear pinion and its bush off the shaft, and the splined washer (see illustrations 28.35c, b and a).

24 Remove the circlip and slide off the 6th gear pinion (see illustrations 28.34b and a).

25 Remove the circlip, then slide off the splined washer, the 2nd gear pinion and its bush (see illustrations 28.33d, c, b and a).

Output shaft inspection

26 Wash all of the components in clean solvent and dry them off.

27 Check the gear teeth for cracking and other obvious damage. Check the bushes and the surface in the inner diameter of their gears for scoring or heat discoloration. If a gear or bush is damaged, replace them both with new ones.

28 Inspect the dogs and the dog holes in related gears for excessive wear. Renew the paired gears as a set if necessary.

29 Measure the selector fork groove width in the 5th and 6th gear pinions (see Section 29).

30 The shaft is unlikely to sustain damage unless the engine has seized, placing an unusually high loading on the transmission, or the machine has covered a very high mileage. Check the surface of the shaft, especially where a pinion turns on it, and the edges of the splined sections, and replace the shaft with a new one if it has scored or picked up. Damage of any kind can only be cured by renewal.

31 The ball bearing and sleeve on the left-hand end of the shaft are a press fit (see illustration). Support the bearing and press the shaft out of

it and the sleeve – note which way round they fit. The bearing cannot be reused. Refer to Tools and Workshop Tips in the Reference Section for more information on bearing checks and removal and installation methods. Press the bearing onto the shaft until it seats using a suitable tube that locates only on the inner race. Press the sleeve on, chamfered (narrow) end facing out, until it seats against the bearing. Replace the needle bearing with a new one if it is worn or damaged, or does not run freely.

Output shaft reassembly

32 During reassembly, always use new circlips. Lubricate the components with engine oil before assembling them.

33 Slide the 2nd gear pinion bush onto the shaft, then slide the pinion onto the bush, with its chamfered rim facing away from the ball bearing, followed by the splined washer (see illustrations). Fit the circlip, making sure it locates in its groove (see illustration).

28.31 Check the bearing and replace with a new one if necessary

28.33a Slide the 2nd gear pinion bush onto the shaft . . .

28.33b . . . then fit the pinion onto the bush

28.33c Slide on the splined washer . . .

28.33d . . . then fit the circlip . . .

28.33e . . . making sure it locates in its groove

28.34a Slide the 6th gear pinion onto the shaft, making sure the oil holes (arrowed) do not align . . .

28.34b . . . then fit the circlip . . .

28.34c . . . making sure it locates in its groove

34 Slide 6th gear pinion onto the shaft with its selector fork groove facing away from the 2nd gear pinion, making sure the oil holes in the gear do NOT align with the oil hole in the shaft **(see illustration)**. Secure the gear with the circlip, making sure it locates in the shaft groove **(see illustrations)**.
35 Slide the splined washer onto the shaft, followed by the 3rd gear pinion bush, making sure the oil hole in the bush does NOT align with the hole in the shaft **(see illustrations)**. Slide the 3rd gear pinion onto the bush with

its recessed side facing the 6th gear pinion **(see illustration)**.
36 Slide the slotted washer onto the shaft to its groove then turn it to misalign the splines so the washer is locked **(see illustrations)**. Slide the tabbed washer onto the shaft, locating the tabs into the slots of the slotted washer **(see illustration)**.
37 Slide on the 4th gear pinion splined bush, making sure the oil holes do NOT align, then slide the pinion onto the bush, with its recessed side facing away from the 3rd gear, followed by the splined

28.35a Slide the splined washer on . . .

28.35b . . . followed by the bush, making sure the oil holes (arrowed) do not align . . .

28.35c . . . then fit the 3rd gear pinion onto the bush

28.36a Slide the slotted washer to its groove . . .

28.36b . . . then turn it to lock it against the splines . . .

28.36c . . . then slide on the tabbed washer and fit the tabs in the slots

28.37a Slide the 4th gear pinion bush onto the shaft, making sure the oil holes (arrowed) do not align . . .

28.37b . . . then fit the 4th gear pinion onto the bush

28.37c Slide on the splined washer . . .

28.37d . . . then fit the circlip . . .

28.37e . . . making sure it locates in its groove

28.38a Slide the 5th gear pinion onto the shaft, making sure the oil holes (arrowed) do not align . . .

washer **(see illustrations)**. Fit the circlip, making sure it locates in its groove **(see illustrations)**.
38 Slide the 5th gear pinion onto the shaft with its selector fork groove facing the 4th gear pinion, making sure the oil holes in the

gear do NOT align with the hole in the shaft **(see illustration)**. Fit the thrust washer **(see illustration)**.
39 Slide the 1st gear pinion bush onto the shaft, again making sure the oil holes do NOT align, then fit the 1st gear pinion onto the

bush, with the deeper recessed side facing the 5th gear pinion **(see illustrations)**.
40 Fit the thrust washer and needle bearing **(see illustrations)**.
41 The assembled output shaft should be as shown **(see illustration)**.

28.38b . . . followed by the thrust washer . . .

28.39a . . . the bush, making sure the oil holes (arrowed) do not align . . .

28.39b . . . then fit the 1st gear pinion onto the bush

28.40a Fit the thrust washer . . .

28.40b . . . and the needle bearing . . .

28.41 The assembled output shaft should be as shown

29.5 Unscrew the bolts (arrowed) and remove the retainers

29.6 Withdraw the shaft and remove the forks

29 Selector drum and forks

Note: *The selector drum and forks can be removed without separating the crankcases, though the engine must be removed from the frame and the sump removed.*

Removal

1 Remove the engine from the frame and separate the crankcase halves (see Sections 4 and 21).

2 Remove the gear position sensor (see Chapter 4).
3 Remove the transmission output shaft (see Section 27).
4 Mark each selector fork for identification using paint or a felt pen, i.e. 1 to 3 from left to right, with the marks facing the left-hand side of the engine, as an aid to installation. Note how the guide pin on each fork locates in the groove in the selector drum.
5 Unscrew the bolts securing the selector fork shaft/selector drum bearing retainers and remove them, noting how they fit **(see illustration)**.

6 Support the output shaft selector forks and withdraw their shaft from the right-hand side of the crankcase, then remove the forks **(see illustration)**. Slide the forks back on the shaft in their correct order and way round.
7 Withdraw the input shaft selector fork shaft, then move the fork guide pin out of its track in the selector drum **(see illustration)**. Withdraw the selector drum **(see illustration)**. Remove the input shaft selector fork **(see illustration)**. Slide the fork the correct way round back on the shaft.

Inspection

8 Check the selector forks and shaft for wear and damage.
9 Locate each selector fork in its corresponding gear pinion groove and measure the fork-to-groove clearance using a feeler gauge **(see illustration)**. If the clearance is outside the service limit, measure the selector fork end widths and the groove in the gear using a Vernier caliper. Replace any component that is worn beyond the service limit with a new one (see Specifications).
10 Check the fit of each fork on the shaft – they should slide freely but with no freeplay between them **(see illustration)**. Check the selector fork shaft for bend by rolling it along

29.7a Withdraw the shaft and displace the fork . . .

29.7b . . . then withdraw the drum . . .

29.7c . . . and remove the fork

29.9 Measure the fork-to-groove clearance using a feeler gauge

29.10 Check the fit of each fork on the shaft

29.11 Check the fork guide pins and the grooves they run in

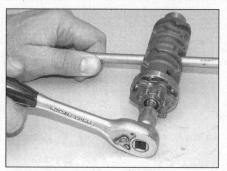

29.12 Use a rod through the drum to hold it while unscrewing the cam plate bolt

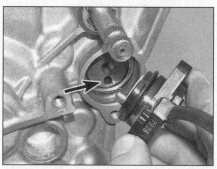

29.15 Align the hole (arrowed) as shown

a flat surface. A bent shaft will cause difficulty in selecting gears and make the gearchange action heavy. Replace the shaft with a new one if necessary.

11 Inspect the selector drum grooves and selector fork guide pins for wear and damage **(see illustration)**. If they show signs of wear or damage the selector fork(s) and drum must be replaced with new ones.

12 Check that the selector drum ball bearing rotates freely and has no sign of freeplay between its inner and outer race. Fit a new bearing if necessary – refer to Section 20, Step 7 to remove the cam plate, holding the drum as shown **(see illustration)**. Also check the needle bearing in the crankcase.

Installation

13 Clean the fork shaft/selector drum bearing retainer plate screw threads to remove all old threadlock. Apply molybdenum disulphide oil (a 50/50 mixture of molybdenum disulphide grease and engine oil) to the selector fork ends, guide pins and shafts and to the tracks in the selector drum before installing them. Lubricate the drum bearings with oil.

14 Fit the input shaft selector fork into its pinion groove, making sure it is the correct way round – see Step 3 **(see illustration 29.7c)**.

15 Slide the selector drum into the crankcase **(see illustration 29.7b)**. Rotate the drum so the hole for the gear position sensor pin is aligned a shown **(see illustration)**.

16 Pivot the input shaft selector fork to locate its guide pin the in its track in the selector drum then insert the fork shaft **(see illustration 29.7a)**.

17 Slide the output shaft selector fork shaft into its bore in the crankcase and through each fork in turn, making sure they are correctly fitted (see Step 3), locating each fork guide pin in its track in the selector drum **(see illustration 29.6)**.

18 Fit the selector fork shaft/selector drum bearing retainers and bolts, applying a suitable non-permanent thread locking compound to the threads and tightening them to the torque setting specified at the beginning of the Chapter **(see illustration 29.5)**.

19 Install the transmission output shaft (see Section 27).

20 Install the gear position sensor (see Chapter 4).

30 Recommended running-in procedure

1 Make sure the engine oil and coolant levels are correct (see Pre-ride checks).

2 Make sure there is fuel in the tank.

3 Start the engine and let it run at a moderately fast idle until it reaches normal operating temperature.

> ⚠ **Warning: If the oil pressure warning light doesn't go off, or it comes on while the engine is running, stop the engine immediately.**

4 Check carefully that there are no oil or coolant leaks, and make sure the transmission and controls, especially the brakes, function properly before road testing the machine.

5 Treat the machine gently for the first few miles to make sure oil has circulated throughout the engine and any new parts installed have started to seat.

6 Upon completion of the road test, and after the engine has cooled down completely, recheck the valve clearances and check the engine oil and coolant levels (see Pre-ride checks).

> **HAYNES HiNT** *If a lubrication failure is suspected, stop the engine immediately and try to find the cause. If an engine is run without oil, even for a short period of time, severe damage will occur.*

7 If new pistons and liners or new main and/ or big-end bearings have been installed, the bike will have to be run in as if when new. This means greater use of the transmission and a restraining hand on the throttle. There's no point in keeping to any set road speed limit – it's the engine revs and load that are important. For the first 500 miles (800 km) the main idea is to keep from labouring the engine and to gradually increase performance, but do not exceed 3/4 of maximum engine speed – and allow the engine to warm up gently. It is best to vary engine and road speed as much as possible, so use the gearbox. Between 500 and 1000 miles (800 and 1600 km) gradually work engine speed up to the maximum, again avoiding labouring or straining the engine, or being in the wrong gear. Experience is the best guide, since it's easy to tell when an engine is running freely.

Chapter 3
Cooling system

Contents

Degrees of difficulty

Easy, suitable for novice with little experience	Fairly easy, suitable for beginner with some experience	Fairly difficult, suitable for competent DIY mechanic	Difficult, suitable for experienced DIY mechanic	Very difficult, suitable for expert DIY or professional

Specifications

Coolant
Mixture type and capacity ....   see Chapter 1

Radiator
Cap valve opening pressure..................................   16 psi (1.1 Bar)

Cooling fan
Cooling fan cut-in temperature ....   103°C

Thermostat
Opening temperature......................................   66 to 76°C

Torque wrench settings
Coolant inlet union bolts..................................   8 Nm
Thermostat housing bolts...................................   9 Nm

1 General information

The cooling system uses a water/antifreeze coolant to carry away excess energy in the form of heat. The cylinders are surrounded by a water jacket from which the heated coolant is circulated by thermo-syphonic action in conjunction with a water pump. The water pump is an integral unit with the oil pump and is driven by a chain running off the back of the clutch. The hot coolant passes upwards to the thermostat and through to the radiator. The coolant then flows across the radiator core, where it is cooled by the passing air, to the water pump and back to the engine where the cycle is repeated.

A thermostat is fitted in the system to prevent the coolant flowing through the radiator when the engine is cold, therefore accelerating the speed at which the engine reaches normal operating temperature. A coolant temperature sensor transmits information to the engine management system. This information is used to help optimise the fuelling of the engine at all temperatures. The engine management system also controls the temperature gauge and the cooling fan, via a relay. Because the control side of these cooling system functions is integral with the engine management system, they are dealt with in Chapter 4. The function side of the cooling fan and relay are in this Chapter, while the function of the temperature gauge is in Chapter 8.

The complete cooling system is partially sealed and pressurised, the pressure being controlled by a valve contained in the spring-loaded radiator cap. By pressurising the coolant the boiling point is raised, preventing premature boiling in adverse conditions. The overflow pipe from the system is connected to a reservoir into which excess coolant is expelled under pressure. The discharged coolant automatically returns to the radiator when the engine cools.

 Warning: Do not remove the pressure cap from the radiator when the engine is hot. Scalding hot coolant and steam may be *blown out under pressure, which could cause serious injury. When the engine has cooled, place a thick rag, like a towel over the pressure cap; slowly rotate the cap anti-clockwise to the first stop. This procedure allows any residual pressure to escape. When the steam has stopped escaping, press down on the cap while turning it anti-clockwise and remove it. Do not allow antifreeze to come into contact with your skin or painted surfaces of the motorcycle. Rinse off any spills immediately with plenty of water. Antifreeze is highly toxic if ingested. Never leave antifreeze lying around in an open container or in puddles on the floor; children and pets are attracted by its sweet smell and may drink it. Check with the local authorities about disposing of used antifreeze. Many communities will have collection centres which will see that antifreeze is disposed of safely.*

Caution: At all times use the specified type of antifreeze, and always mix it with distilled water in the correct proportion. The antifreeze contains corrosion inhibitors which are essential to avoid damage to the cooling system. A lack of these inhibitors could lead to a build-up of corrosion which would block the coolant passages, resulting in overheating and severe engine damage. Distilled water must be used as opposed to tap water to avoid a build-up of scale which would also block the passages.

Many of the bolts used on Triumph motorcycles are of the Torx type. Unless you are already equipped with a good range of Torx bits, you are advised to obtain a set. Make sure you get bits that can be used in conjunction with a socket set so that a torque wrench can be applied – a Torx key set will not be adequate on its own, though will be useful in addition to the bits.

2 Radiator pressure cap

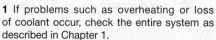

1 If problems such as overheating or loss of coolant occur, check the entire system as described in Chapter 1.

2 On Daytona models remove the left-hand cockpit trim panel (see Chapter 7). On Street Triple models displace the left-hand radiator cowl (see Chapter 7).

3 Remove the pressure cap from the filler neck in the radiator as follows: turn the cap anti-clockwise until it reaches a stop – if you hear a hissing sound (indicating there is still pressure in the system), wait until it stops; now press down on the cap and continue turning it until it can be removed **(see illustration)**. Check the cap seals – if you are in any doubt as to their effectiveness replace the cap with a new one – maintaining a good seal to retain the pressure in the cooling system is essential to the efficient function of the system.

4 If no obvious problems can be found have the radiator cap opening pressure checked by a Triumph dealer equipped with the special tester required for the job. If the cap is defective, replace it with a new one. If you are unable to get the cap tested fit a new one anyway – the cost is minimal.

3 Coolant reservoir

Removal

1 On Daytona models, remove the left-hand fairing side panel (see Chapter 7) and the fuel tank (see Chapter 4). Detach the hoses from the top of the reservoir, noting which fits where. Unscrew the reservoir bolt and nut and remove the reservoir and fairing bracket **(see illustration)**. Remove the filler cap and tip the contents into a suitable container

2 On Street Triple models to VIN 560476 remove the seat and displace the left-hand radiator cowl (see Chapter 7). Release the clamp and detach the hose from the top of the reservoir **(see illustration)**. Hold a container suitable to collect the contents of the reservoir, then release the clamp and detach the hose from the radiator filler neck, hold the hose in the container below the level of the bottom of the reservoir and allow the coolant to drain

2.3 Remove the pressure cap as described

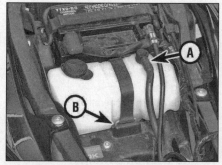
3.1 Unscrew the nut and the bolt (arrowed) and remove the reservoir

3.2a Detach the hose (A). Reservoir retaining strap (B)

(see illustration). Unhook the strap. Lift the reservoir, then release the clamp and detach the hose from the bottom.

3 On Street Triple models from VIN 560477 unscrew the bolt and release the cover from the reservoir, noting how it hooks over the tabs on the underside (see illustration). Draw the top hose union out of the reservoir (see illustration). Hold a container suitable to collect the contents of the reservoir, then release the clamp and detach the hose from the bottom and allow the coolant to drain (see illustration). Unscrew the bolt and remove the reservoir.

Installation

4 Installation is the reverse of removal. Make sure the hoses are correctly installed and secured with their clamps, where fitted – the hose from the radiator filler neck goes to the rear union on Daytona models and the bottom union on Street Triples. On completion refill the reservoir (see Pre-ride checks).

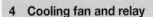
4 Cooling fan and relay

Cooling fan

Check

1 If the engine is overheating and the cooling fan isn't coming on, first check the fan fuse (see Chapter 8). Next check the fan relay as described in Steps 7 to 9.

2 If the fuse and relay are good and the fan still does not come on, the fault could lie in either the cooling fan motor itself, or the relevant wiring and connectors. Test all the wiring and connections, referring to Electrical system fault finding at the beginning of Chapter 8 and to the Wiring Diagram for your model at the end of it.

3 To access the cooling fan wiring connector, on Daytona models remove the left-hand fairing side panel (see Chapter 7), and on Street Triple models remove the airbox (see Chapter 4). Trace the wiring from the fan

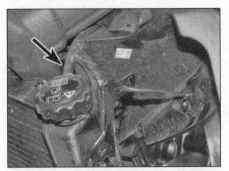
3.2b Detach the hose (arrowed) from the filler neck and drain the reservoir as described

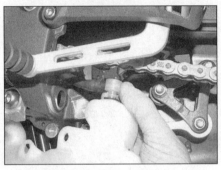
3.3b Draw the union out with the hose connected

motor and disconnect it at the connector (see illustrations).

4 Using a 12 volt battery and two jumper wires, connect the positive (+) battery lead to the blue/white wire terminal on the fan wiring connector and the negative (-) lead to the black wire terminal. Once connected the fan should operate. If it does not, and the wiring is all good, then the fan motor is faulty. Replace the fan assembly with a new one (Step 5) – individual components are not available. If all tests so far have shown no problems, test the coolant temperature sensor (see Chapter 4).

Renewal

5 Remove the radiator (see Section 6). Undo the screws securing the fan assembly to the radiator and remove it (see illustration).

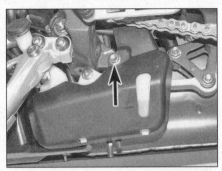
3.3a Reservoir cover bolt (arrowed)

3.3c Bottom hose (A), mounting bolt (B)

6 Installation is the reverse of removal.

Cooling fan relay

Check

Note: Refer to the Wiring Diagrams at the end of Chapter 8 for relay terminal identification.

7 If the engine is overheating and the cooling fan isn't coming on, first check the fan fuse (see Chapter 8). If the fuse is blown, check the fan circuit for a short to earth (see the wiring diagrams at the end of this book).

8 If the fuse is good, on Daytona models remove the left-hand cockpit trim panel (see Chapter 7), on Street Triple models to VIN 560476 raise and support the fuel tank (see Chapter 4), and on Street Triple models from VIN 560477 remove the seat (see Chapter 7). Disconnect the relay from its connector block

4.3a Cooling fan wiring connector – Daytona

4.3b Cooling fan wiring connector – Street Triple

4.5 Fan motor screws (arrowed)

4.8a Cooling fan relay (arrowed) – Daytona

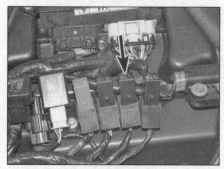

4.8b Cooling fan relay (arrowed) – Street Triple up to VIN 560476

4.8c Cooling fan relay (arrowed) – Street Triple models from VIN 560477

4.9a On Street Triple models from VIN 560477 release the relay holder clips . . .

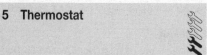

4.9b . . . and displace the holders to match wire colours to terminals

(see illustrations). Check the terminals and sockets for damage and corrosion.

9 Refer to the Wiring Diagrams at the end of Chapter 8 and to the wires going into the relay socket for terminal identification (see illustrations). Connect a continuity tester or a multimeter set to the ohms x 1 scale between the No. 3 and No. 5 wire terminals on the relay – there should be no continuity or infinite resistance. If there is continuity or zero resistance replace the relay with a new one. Using a fully-charged 12 volt battery and two insulated jumper wires, connect the positive (+) terminal of the battery to the No. 1 wire terminal on the relay, and the negative (–) terminal to the No. 2 wire terminal on the relay. At this point the relay should be heard to click and there should be continuity or zero resistance. If this is the case the relay is proved good. If the relay does not click when battery voltage is applied and the tester or meter

indicates no continuity (infinite resistance), the relay is faulty and must be replaced with a new one. If the relay is good, test the fan motor (see Step 4).

Renewal

10 On Daytona models remove the left-hand cockpit trim panel (see Chapter 7), and on Street Triple models raise and support the fuel tank (see Chapter 4).

11 Disconnect the relay from its connector block (see illustration 4.8a or b).

12 Plug the new relay into its connector.

5 Thermostat

1 The thermostat is automatic in operation and should give many years service without requiring attention. In the event of a failure, the valve will

probably jam open, in which case the engine will take much longer than normal to warm up. Conversely, if the valve jams shut, the coolant will be unable to circulate and the engine will overheat. Neither condition is acceptable, and the fault must be investigated promptly.

Removal

2 Drain the cooling system (see Chapter 1).
3 Remove the throttle bodies (see Chapter 4).
4 Unscrew the bolts securing the thermostat housing, then detach it from the cylinder head and remove the thermostat, noting how it fits (see illustrations). Discard the seal as a new one must be used (see illustration 5.7).

Check

5 Examine the thermostat visually before carrying out the test. If it remains in the open position at room temperature, it should be replaced with a new one.

6 Suspend the thermostat by a piece of wire in a container of cold water. Place a thermometer in the water so that the bulb is close to the thermostat, and not in contact with the container (see illustration). Heat the water, noting the temperature when the thermostat opens, and compare the result with the specified opening temperature given at the beginning of the Chapter. If the thermostat opens at a different temperature, does not open at all, or is permanently open, it is faulty and must be replaced with a new one.

Note: In the event of thermostat failure, as an emergency measure only, it can be removed and the machine used without it. Take care

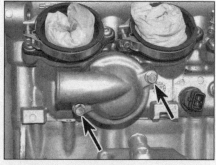

5.4a Unscrew the bolts (arrowed), detach the cover . . .

5.4b . . . and withdraw the thermostat

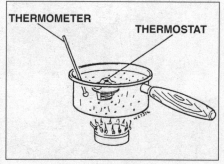

5.6 Thermostat testing set-up

5.7 Fit a new seal over the rim of the thermostat

when starting the engine from cold as it will take much longer than usual to warm up. Ensure that a new unit is installed as soon as possible.

Installation

7 Fit a new seal onto the thermostat **(see illustration)**.
8 Fit the thermostat into the cylinder head with the toggle pin at the top, then fit the housing and tighten the bolts to the specified torque setting **(see illustrations 5.4b and a)**.
9 Refill the cooling system (see Chapter 1 and *Pre-ride checks*).

6 Radiator

⚠ *Warning: The engine must be completely cool before carrying out this procedure.*

Removal

1 On Daytona models remove the fairing side panels. On Street Triple models remove the airbox (see Chapter 4) and the radiator cowls (see Chapter 7).
2 Drain the cooling system (see Chapter 1).
3 On Daytona models unscrew the intake air duct vacuum reservoir bolt and displace the reservoir from the left-hand side of the radiator, noting the clamp **(see illustration)**. Free the wiring connector and clutch cable from the right-hand side **(see illustration)**.
4 On Street Triple models disconnect the horn wiring connectors and move the wiring aside

6.7a Unscrew the bolt (arrowed) on the left . . .

6.3a Release the hose and wiring, then unscrew the bolt

(see illustration). On models to VIN 560476 free the clutch cable from the right-hand side **(see illustration)**.
5 Slacken or release (according to type) the clamps securing all the radiator hoses and detach them from the radiator, noting which fits where **(see illustrations)**.

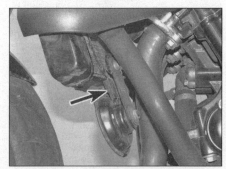

6.4a Disconnect the horn wiring connectors (arrowed)

6.5a Left-hand side radiator hoses (arrowed)

6.7b . . . and the bolts (arrowed) on the right . . .

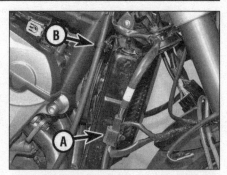

6.3b Detach the wiring connector (A) and clutch cable guide (B)

6 Trace the wiring from the fan motor and disconnect it at the connector **(see illustration 4.3a or b)**.
7 Unscrew the bolts securing the radiator, noting the arrangement of the collars and rubber grommets, and remove the radiator **(see illustrations)**.

6.4b Detach the clutch cable guide (arrowed)

6.5b Right-hand side radiator hose (arrowed)

6.7c . . . and remove the radiator

6.9 Make sure the collars and grommets are in good condition

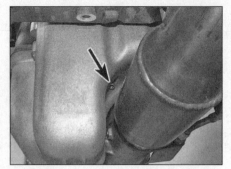

7.2 Water pump drain tube (arrowed)

7.6 Water pump cover bolts (arrowed)

8 If necessary, remove the cooling fan from the radiator (see Section 4).

9 Check the radiator for signs of damage and clear any dirt or debris that might obstruct air flow and inhibit cooling. If the radiator fins are badly damaged or broken the radiator must be replaced with a new one. Also check the rubber mounting grommets, and replace them with new ones if necessary **(see illustration)**.

Installation

10 Installation is the reverse of removal, noting the following.
- *Make sure the collars and grommets are correctly installed with the mounting bolts (see illustration 6.9).*
- *Make sure that the wiring connector is correctly connected (see illustration 4.3a or b).*
- *Ensure the coolant hoses are in good condition (see Chapter 1), and are retained by their clamps, using new ones if necessary.*
- *On completion refill the cooling system as described in Chapter 1 and Pre-ride checks.*

7 Water pump

Check

1 The water pump is located on the left-hand side of the engine.

2 To prevent leakage of water from the cooling system to the lubrication system and vice versa, two seals are fitted on the water pump shaft. There is a drain hole between the seals in the seal housing section of the pump. If either seal fails, the drain allows the coolant or oil to escape via a tube through a hole in the bottom of the sump and prevents them mixing **(see illustration)**. The seal on the water pump side is of the mechanical type which bears on the rear face of the impeller. The second seal, which is mounted behind the mechanical seal is of the normal feathered lip type. If on inspection the drain hole shows signs of

coolant leakage, remove the pump assembly and replace it with a new one (see Step 5) – the seals are not available separately.

3 Remove the oil/water pump (see Chapter 2, Section 19). Remove the pump cover (see Step 6). Wiggle the water pump impeller back-and-forth and in-and-out, and spin it by hand. If there is excessive movement, or the pump is noisy or rough when turned, or if any damage is found, replace the pump assembly with a new one – individual components are not available.

4 Check the pump housing and cover, and the impeller and shaft for cracks, deformation and any other damage. Check that the shaft is straight – if it is bent, replace the pump assembly with a new one. Also check for corrosion or a build-up of scale in the pump body and clean or renew the pump as necessary.

Removal and installation

5 The water pump is an integral assembly with the oil pump, and no individual components are available. Refer to Chapter 2, Section 19 for removal and installation of the pump assembly.

6 If you just want to remove the cover to inspect the pump, unscrew the bolts, then hold the housing and detach the cover **(see illustration)**. Note that the cover seal is not listed as being available separately.

7 Installation is the reverse of removal.

8 Coolant hoses, pipes and unions

Removal

1 Before removing a hose, pipe or union, drain the coolant (see Chapter 1).

2 Use a screwdriver to slacken the larger-bore hose clamps, then slide them back along the hose and clear of the union spigot. The smaller-bore hoses are secured by spring clamps which can be expanded by squeezing their ears together with pliers.

Caution: The radiator unions are fragile. Do not use excessive force when attempting to remove the hoses.

3 If a hose proves stubborn, release it by rotating it on its union before working it off. If all else fails, cut the hose with a sharp knife then slit it at each union so that it can be peeled off in two pieces. Whilst this means renewing the hose, it is preferable to buying a new radiator.

4 Remove the coolant inlet union on the engine by detaching the hose (see above), then unscrewing the bolts **(see illustration)**. Discard the O-ring as new one must be used.

Installation

5 Slide the clamp onto the hose and then work it on to its respective union.

> **HAYNES HINT** *If the hose is difficult to push on its union, it can be softened by soaking it in very hot water, or alternatively a little soapy water can be used as a lubricant.*

6 Rotate the hose on its union to settle it in position before sliding the clamp into place and tightening it securely.

7 If the inlet union has been removed, fit a new O-ring into the groove and tighten the bolts to the torque setting specified at the beginning of the Chapter **(see illustration 8.4)**.

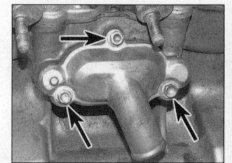

8.4 Coolant inlet union bolts (arrowed)

Chapter 4
Engine management system (fuel and ignition)

Contents

Degrees of difficulty

Easy, suitable for novice with little experience 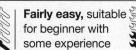	**Fairly easy,** suitable for beginner with some experience	**Fairly difficult,** suitable for competent DIY mechanic
Difficult, suitable for experienced DIY mechanic	**Very difficult,** suitable for expert DIY or professional	

Specifications

Fuel
Grade
  Daytona models
    Europe . . . . Unleaded, minimum 95 RON (Europe Research Octane Number)
    US. . . . . Unleaded, minimum 89 (R+M)/2 (US CLC or AKI Octane rating)
  Street Triple models
    Europe . . . . Unleaded, minimum 91 RON (Europe Research Octane Number)
    US. . . . . Unleaded, minimum 87 (R+M)/2 (US CLC or AKI Octane rating)
Fuel tank capacity . . . . 17.4 litres
Fuel quantity remaining when low level warning
  light comes on . . . . 4.0 litres

Engine management system
Type . . . . Electronic
Control sensors . . . . Atmospheric pressure, engine coolant temperature, crankshaft position, gear position, manifold absolute pressure, intake air temperature, throttle position, oxygen content (lambda), speed (road), tip-over

Coolant temperature sensor resistance
  Warm engine. . . . . 200 to 400 ohms
  Cold engine
    20°C ambient . . . . 2.35 to 2.65 K-ohms
    15°C ambient . . . . 2.9 to 3.3 K-ohms
    -10°C ambient . . . . 8.5 to 10.25 K-ohms
Intake air temperature sensor resistance
  80°C ambient . . . . 200 to 400 ohms
  20°C ambient . . . . 2.35 to 2.65 K-ohms
  -10°C ambient . . . . 8.5 to 10.25 K-ohms

Fuel injection system

Operating pressure (nominal)	
Daytona models, and Street Triple models to VIN 560476.........	43.5 psi (3.0 Bar) @ 1250 rpm
Street Triple models from VIN 560477	50.75 psi (3.5 Bar) @ 1250 rpm
Idle air control unit stepper motor resistance....................	4 to 12 ohms
Fuel injector resistance.............................	11 to 12.5 ohms
Fuel pump resistance.............................	2 to 6 ohms
Secondary air injection system solenoid valve resistance	20 to 25 ohms
Intake air flap solenoid valve resistance (Daytona models)	40 to 50 ohms
EVAP system purge valve resistance (California models)	24 to 28 ohms

Ignition system

Type	Digital inductive
Firing order...	1–2–3
Cylinder identification................................	1–2–3, from left to right
Spark plugs	see Chapter 1
Ignition coil resistance	0.8 to 1.2 ohms
Crankshaft position sensor (pick-up coil) resistance	0.21 K-ohms ± 10% @ 20°C
Rev limiter cut-in	
Daytona models	14,000 rpm
Street Triple models	13,000 rpm

Torque settings

Air intake duct bolts in airbox.............................	6 Nm
Crankshaft position sensor bolts	6 Nm
Exhaust system	
Daytona	
Silencer mounting bolt	27 Nm
Silencer-to-intermediate pipe clamp bolt...................	10 Nm
Intermediate pipe mounting bolt.........................	22 Nm
Intermediate pipe-to-downpipe assembly clamp bolt......................................	10 Nm
Downpipe assembly nuts, models to VIN 381274 (see Text)	
Initial setting	2 Nm
Final setting.......................................	19 Nm
Downpipe assembly nuts, models from VIN 381275 (see Text)	
Initial setting	2 Nm
Final setting.......................................	15 Nm
Downpipe assembly rear mounting bolt.....................	19 Nm
Exhaust control valve servo mounting bolts.................	12 Nm
Street Triple models to VIN 560476	
Silencer mounting bolt	15 Nm
Silencer-to-intermediate pipe clamp bolt...................	10 Nm
Intermediate pipe mounting bolt.........................	22 Nm
Intermediate pipe-to-downpipe assembly clamp bolt......................................	10 Nm
Downpipe assembly nuts (see Text)	
Initial setting	2 Nm
Final setting.......................................	19 Nm
Downpipe assembly rear mounting bolt.....................	15 Nm
Rear sub-frame bolt nuts	48 Nm
Street Triple models from VIN 560477	
Silencer front mounting bolt	19 Nm
Silencer rear mounting bolt nut	27 Nm
Silencer-to-downpipe clamp nut	8 Nm
Downpipe assembly nuts (see Text)	
Initial setting	2 Nm
Final setting.......................................	15 Nm
Fuel pump mounting plate bolts	9 Nm
Fuel rail screws.....................................	3.5 Nm
Fuel tank bolts	9 Nm
Idle air control unit mounting screws	3.5 Nm
Intake stub screws	
Daytona models, and Street Triple models to VIN 560476.........	12 Nm
Street Triple models from VIN 560477	8 Nm
Oxygen sensor	25 Nm
Throttle position sensor screws	2 Nm

1 General information and precautions

General information

All models are fitted with an electronic engine management system which controls both the fuel and ignition system functions. The system is controlled by an electronic control module, or ECM. The ECM receives information from various sensors around the motorcycle, which it uses to determine the optimum fuel requirements for the fuel injection system and the optimum timing for the ignition system for all engine speeds and loads.

The sensors used are for atmospheric pressure, crankshaft position, engine coolant temperature, manifold absolute pressure, intake air temperature, oxygen (lambda), road speed, throttle position, gear position, and tip-over. Information on the function of these sensors is in Section 14.

The fuel system consists of the fuel tank, the fuel pump with integral filter, pressure regulator and level sensor, the fuel hose, fuel rail and injectors, the throttle bodies and throttle control cables, and the air intake system. The fuel pump is housed inside the tank. There is an injector for each cylinder, housed in the throttle body. The low fuel warning circuit is operated by a level sensor that is an integral part of he fuel pump. Cold starting and idle speed is controlled by the ECM which reacts to the information sent by the intake air temperature sensor and the coolant temperature sensor, and adjusts the fuel requirements accordingly via a throttle stepper motor on the right-hand end of the throttle bodies – there is no manual method (i.e. a choke) for assisting cold starting, or for adjusting engine idle speed.

On Daytona models a flap inside the intake air duct controls air flow to improve throttle response at low engine speeds. The flap is actuated by a vacuum, and the vacuum is controlled by a solenoid valve which operates on a signal from the ECM. The flap is closed at engine speeds up to 4500 rpm and throttle angles less than 12°, otherwise it is open.

The exhaust system is a three-into-one design on Daytona models and Street Triples from VIN 560477, and a three-into-one-into-two design on Street Triples to VIN 560476. On Daytona models a valve inside the rear of the downpipe assembly controls gas flow to maximise performance at different engine speeds. The valve is controlled by a servo which operates on a signal from the ECM.

The ignition system type is digital inductive, which due to its lack of mechanical parts is totally maintenance-free. The coil for each spark plug is incorporated in the spark plug cap. The system incorporates an electronic advance system controlled by the ECM, which reacts to the information sent to it from the various sensors to provide the spark at the optimum time. A rev limiter prevents the engine exceeding its maximum rpm. The system incorporates a safety interlock circuit which will cut the ignition if the sidestand is put down whilst the engine is running and in gear, or if a gear is selected whilst the engine is running and the sidestand is down. The tip-over sensor will cut the ignition if it detects that the machine has fallen over.

The engine management system has an in-built two-stage diagnostic function. The initial stage is fault detection, whereupon the system notes the fault and counts the occurrences, looking for repetition. If the fault was a temporary glitch that does not reoccur, no DTC (diagnostic trouble code, or fault code) is registered. If the fault continues a DTC is registered, and the ECM records and stores all engine and system data at that moment, and the malfunction indicator lamp (MIL) in the instrument cluster illuminates. Recorded faults can then be checked using Triumph's diagnostic tool, which reads the data and lists a code to indicate the exact fault. If this happens, the management system in most cases switches itself into 'limp home' mode, so that in theory you should not be left stranded, or in some cases switches itself off, in which case you will be left stranded, depending on the severity of the fault – with minor faults it is possible that you will notice no difference in the running of the motorcycle. If after the DTC has been logged and the MIL comes on the fault clears itself, the MIL will remain on until the engine has been through three engine warm-up and system power-down cycles without the fault recurring, and the DTC will self-erase after forty such cycles. If the fault does not clear itself but is repaired the DTC can be erased using Triumph's tool and the MIL will turn itself off.

Because of their nature, the individual system components can be checked but not repaired. If system troubles occur, and the faulty component can be isolated, the only cure for the problem is to replace the part with a new one. Keep in mind that most electrical parts, once purchased, cannot be returned. To avoid unnecessary expense, make very sure the faulty component has been positively identified before buying a new part.

Many of the bolts used on Triumph motorcycles are of the Torx type. Unless you are already equipped with a good range of Torx bits, you are advised to obtain a set. Make sure you get bits that can be used in conjunction with a socket set so that a torque wrench can be applied – a Torx key set will not be adequate on its own, though will be useful in addition to the bits.

Precautions

⚠️ **Warning: Petrol (gasoline) is extremely flammable, so take extra precautions when you work on any part of the fuel system. Don't smoke or allow open flames or bare light bulbs near the work area, and don't work in a garage where a natural gas-type appliance is present. If you spill any fuel on your skin, rinse it off immediately with soap and water. When you perform any kind of work on the fuel system, wear safety glasses and have a fire extinguisher suitable for a class B type fire (flammable liquids) on hand.**

● Always perform fuel-related procedures in a well-ventilated area to prevent a build-up of fumes.

● Never work in a building containing a gas appliance with a pilot light, or any other form of naked flame. Ensure that there are no naked light bulbs or any sources of flame or sparks nearby.

● Do not smoke (or allow anyone else to smoke) while in the vicinity of petrol (gasoline) or of components containing it. Remember the possible presence of vapour from these sources and move well clear before smoking.

● Check all electrical equipment belonging to the house, garage or workshop where work is being undertaken (see the *Safety first!* section of this manual). Remember that certain electrical appliances such as drills, cutters etc. create sparks in the normal course of operation and must not be used near petrol (gasoline) or any component containing it. Again, remember the possible presence of fumes before using electrical equipment.

● Always mop up any spilt fuel and safely dispose of the rag used.

● Any stored fuel that is drained off during servicing work must be kept in sealed containers that are suitable for holding petrol (gasoline), and clearly marked as such; the containers themselves should be kept in a safe place. Note that this last point applies equally to the fuel tank if it is removed from the machine; also remember to keep its filler cap closed at all times.

● Read the *Safety first!* section of this manual carefully before starting work.

● Owners of machines used in the US, particularly California, should note that their machines must comply at all times with Federal or State legislation governing the permissible levels of noise and of pollutants such as unburnt hydrocarbons, carbon monoxide etc. that can be emitted by those machines. All vehicles offered for sale must comply with legislation in force at the date of manufacture and must not subsequently be altered in any way which will affect their emission of noise or of pollutants.

● In practice, this means that adjustments may not be made to any part of the fuel, ignition or exhaust systems by anyone who is not authorised or mechanically qualified to do so, or who does not have the tools, equipment and data necessary to properly carry out the task. Also if any part of these systems is to be replaced it must be replaced with only genuine Triumph components or by components which are approved under the relevant legislation. The machine must never be used with any part of these systems removed, modified or damaged.

2.2 A prop (arrowed) for the tank is clipped to the seat

2.4a Unscrew the bolts (arrowed)

2.4b Fuel tank shown propped using a piece of wood

2 Fuel tank

Warning: Refer to the precautions given in Section 1 before starting work.

Raise

1 On Daytona models remove the rider's seat (see Chapter 7). Get a suitable prop such as a piece of 4 x 2 wood to place between the front of the tank and the frame.

2 On Street Triple models remove the seat (see Chapter 7). On models to VIN 560476 release the tank support from its clips on the underside of the seat (see illustration). On models from VIN 560477 get a suitable prop such as a piece of 4 x 2 wood.

3 Disconnect the battery (see Chapter 8).

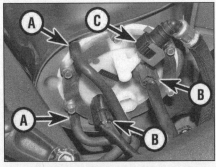

2.7 Disconnect the hoses (A), the wiring connectors (B) and the fuel hose (C)

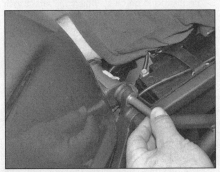

2.11b ... then withdraw the sleeve

4 Make sure the fuel cap is secure. Unscrew the bolts securing the front of the tank **(see illustration)**. Raise the tank and support it, on Street Triple models to VIN 560476 using the prop provided located in the holes in the frame and tank bracket **(see illustration)**.

Removal

Note: *If the tank is full of fuel it will be quite heavy, and supporting it while disconnecting the hoses and wiring connectors will be more difficult – either make sure the tank is nearly empty, or siphon any excess fuel out and into a suitable container before removal (siphons are cheaply available from a good automotive store), or have an assistant to help.*

5 Make sure the fuel cap is secure. Have some rag to hand to catch any residual fuel in the connector and its union as the fuel hose is disconnected – the tank and hose are both self-sealing so there won't be much.

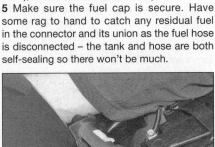

2.11a Unscrew the bolt . . .

2.12 Carefully lift the tank off the frame and remove it

6 Raise and support the tank (Steps 1 to 4).

7 If required mark or tag the drain and breather hoses (but note that on some models with hoses of the same diameter there may already be a dot marked on the hose to the left-hand union, while on others the hoses are a different diameter so there should be no point) so they can be installed the correct way round, then detach them **(see illustration)**.

8 Disconnect the wiring connectors – one is for the fuel pump and the other for the fuel level sensor **(see illustration 2.7)**.

9 On models up to engine No. 296220 press in the clips on the fuel hose connector and pull the hose off its union.

10 On models from engine No. 296221-on slide the orange fuel hose connector cover down to reveal the clips, then press the clips in and pull the hose off its union **(see illustration 2.7)**.

11 Unscrew the bolt securing the rear of the tank **(see illustration)**. Withdraw the sleeve from the rear mount **(see illustration)**.

12 Carefully lift the tank off the bike and remove it **(see illustration)**.

13 Inspect the tank support rubbers and the mounting bolt rubbers for signs of damage or deterioration and replace them with new ones if necessary – note the collars fitted in the front mounting bolt rubbers.

Installation

14 Installation is the reverse of removal, noting the following:

● Check the condition of all the rubber grommets and supports and replace them with new ones if they are damaged, deformed or deteriorated. Fit the collars into the front mounting bolt grommets. Make sure all components are correctly located before fitting the tank and stay located while fitting it.

● Each end of the fuel hose is colour-coded – the orange end connects to the fuel pump, the grey end to the fuel rail. Make sure the connector is fully pushed onto the union until the clips locate, then where fitted push the connector cover up to cover the clips – if the cover won't push up the connector is not properly located.

● Make sure the electrical connectors are secure – the brown or green one (according

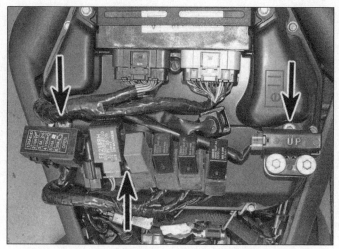

3.2 Unscrew the bolts (arrowed) and displace the bracket

3.3a On models up to VIN 451398 push in the clip (arrowed) to release the connector

to model) goes into the right hand socket on the pump, the black into the left.
● Make sure the drain and breather hoses are secure and fitted to the correct unions (see Step 7).
● Make sure the mounting bolt collars and sleeve are correctly fitted. Tighten the fuel tank mounting bolts to the torque setting specified at the beginning of the Chapter.
● Before installing the seat, switch the ignition ON and check that there are no leaks around the hose unions as the pump pressurises the system.

Cleaning and repair

15 All repairs to the fuel tank should be carried out by a professional who has experience in this critical and potentially dangerous work. Even after cleaning and flushing of the fuel system, explosive fumes can remain and ignite during repair of the tank.
16 If the fuel tank is removed from the bike, it should not be placed in an area where sparks

or open flames could ignite the fumes coming out of the tank. Be especially careful inside garages where a natural gas-type appliance is located, because the pilot light could cause an explosion.

3 Airbox

Daytona models, and Street Triple models to VIN 560476

Removal

1 Remove the fuel tank (see Section 2).
2 On Street Triple models unscrew the relay/fusebox bracket bolts and displace the assembly – there is no need to disconnect any wiring **(see illustration)**.
3 Disconnect the intake air temperature (IAT) sensor wiring connector **(see illustration)**. Disconnect the electronic control module

3.3b Disconnect the ECM connectors

(ECM) wiring connectors **(see illustration)** – they are colour coded and shaped so they cannot be re-connected the wrong way round. Disconnect the manifold absolute pressure (MAP) sensor wiring connector and hose **(see illustration)**. On models with a quickshifter disconnect the wiring connector.
4 Undo the screws securing the airbox cover and lift it off **(see illustration)**.

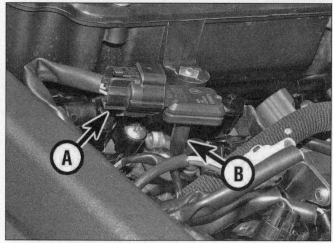

3.3c Disconnect the wiring connector (A) and the hose (B)

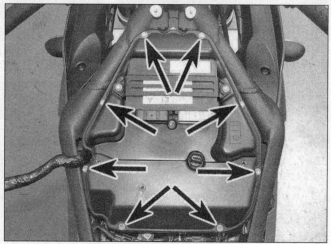

3.4 Undo the screws (arrowed) and remove the cover

3.5a Unscrew the bolts (arrowed) . . .

3.5b . . . and remove the ducts

3.6 Unscrew the bolt (arrowed)

3.7a Disconnect the crankcase breather hose . . .

3.7b . . . and the SAIS hose

3.9 Check the foam seal (arrowed) around the front

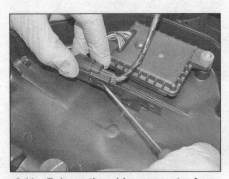

3.11a Release the wiring connector from the bracket . . .

3.11b . . . and disconnect it

5 Unscrew the air intake duct bolts and remove the ducts **(see illustrations)**.

6 Unscrew the bolt securing the front of the airbox to the frame **(see illustration)**.

7 Lift the airbox, then release the clips and disconnect the crankcase breather hose from the right-hand side and the secondary air injection hose from the left **(see illustrations)**. Note how the front of the airbox locates against the air duct in the frame. Block the throttle bodies with a clean rag to prevent anything falling in.

8 If required remove the air filter (see Chapter 1), and the IAT sensor and MAP sensor (see Section 14).

Installation

9 Installation is the reverse of removal, noting the following:

● Do not forget to remove the rag from the throttle bodies.

● Make sure the foam seal around the front intake duct is in good condition and has not come away at any point **(see illustration)**.

● Tighten the air intake duct bolts before the front mounting bolt, and tighten them to the torque setting specified at the beginning of the Chapter.

● Make sure all hoses and wiring connectors are correctly and securely attached.

Street Triple models from VIN 560477

Removal

10 Remove the air filter (see Chapter 1).

11 Release the immobiliser ECM wiring connector from its bracket and disconnect it and remove the cover **(see illustrations)**. Remove the immobiliser from the cover if required (see Section 18).

12 Unscrew the air intake duct bolts and remove the ducts **(see illustration)**.

13 Unscrew the bolt securing the front of the airbox to the frame **(see illustration 3.12)**.

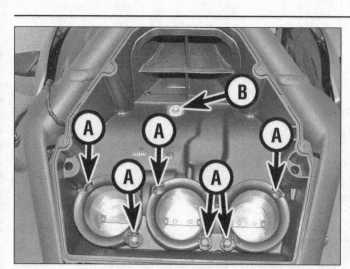

3.12 Intake duct bolts (A), airbox bolt (B)

3.14 Disconnect the SAIS hose and the crankcase breather hose (arrowed)

14 Lift the airbox, then release the clip(s) and disconnect the secondary air injection hose from the left-hand side and the crankcase breather hose from the right **(see illustration)** – note that the clip securing the air injection hose is no longer fitted on models from VIN 587665. Note how the air duct on the front of the airbox locates in the frame. Block the throttle bodies with a clean rag to prevent anything falling in.

15 If required remove the IAT sensor and MAP sensor (see Section 14).

Installation

16 Installation is the reverse of removal, noting the following:
- Do not forget to remove the rag from the throttle bodies.
- Make sure the air duct on the front of the box locates correctly in the frame
- Tighten the air intake duct bolts before the front mounting bolt, and tighten them to the torque setting specified at the beginning of the Chapter.
- Make sure all hoses and wiring connectors are correctly and securely attached.

4 Fuel pump and relay

⚠ **Warning: Refer to the precautions given in Section 1 before starting work.**

Fuel pump

Check

1 The fuel pump is located inside the fuel tank.

2 The fuel pump runs for a few seconds when the ignition is switched ON, then cuts out when the system is up to operating pressure, and cuts in again when the engine is started. If you can't hear anything, first check the No. 6 fuse on Daytona models and Street Triple

models to VIN 560476, and the No. 4 fuse on (see Chapter 8). Next check the wiring and wiring connectors in the fuel pump and relay circuit, referring to *Electrical system fault finding* at the beginning of Chapter 8 and to the Wiring Diagram for your model at the end of it. Next, check the relay (see below). If they are all good, remove the pump (see below) and check the internal connections **(see illustration)**.

3 If the pump still does not work, using a fully charged 12 volt battery and two insulated jumper wires, connect the negative (-) lead to the black wire terminal, then briefly touch the positive (+) lead to the purple/white or purple (according to model) wire terminal – the pump should operate. If the pump does not operate, replace it with a new one. The pump is controlled by the ECM and the EMS (engine management system) relay, so if the pump, its relay and the wiring are all good, it is possible the ECM or the EMS relay are faulty – first check the relay (see Section 13). Refer to Section 12 for further information on the ECM.

4 If the pump operates but is thought to be delivering an insufficient amount of fuel, first check that the fuel tank breather hose is unobstructed, and that the fuel hose is in good condition and not pinched or trapped. If all is good, check the fuel pressure (see Section 5).

Removal

5 Make sure the ignition is switched OFF. Using a siphon pump, drain the fuel from the tank into a suitable container. Remove the fuel tank (see Section 2). Turn the tank upside down and rest it on some rag.

6 Note the orientation of the fuel pump and its mounting plate. Unscrew the bolts, then remove the plate and withdraw the pump assembly, then on Street Triple models from VIN 560477 disconnect the fuel level sensor internal wiring connector **(see illustrations)**. Remove the pump seal, noting which way

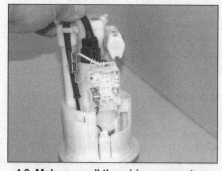

4.2 Make sure all the wiring connectors are secure

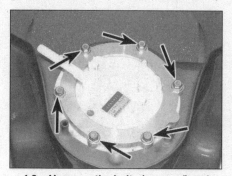

4.6a Unscrew the bolts (arrowed) and remove the plate . . .

4.6b . . . then carefully withdraw the pump . . .

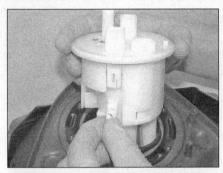

4.6c ... and on Street Triples from VIN 560477 disconnect the sensor wiring connector

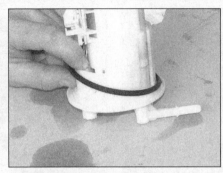

4.8a Fit a new seal and make sure it is the correct way up

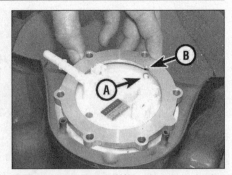

4.8b Locate the tab (A) on the pump in the cut-out (B) in the plate

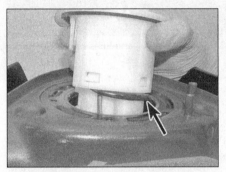

4.8c Make sure the wiring (arrowed) is looped around the pump under the rim

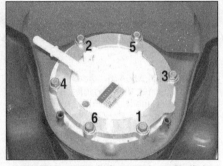

4.8d Tighten the bolts evenly and a little at a time in the sequence shown to the specified torque

4.9a Fuel pump relay (arrowed) – Daytona

round it fits, and discard it as a new one must be used (see illustration 4.8a).

7 The pump assembly comes as a sealed unit for which no individual parts are available. If the pump or one of its components fails the complete unit must be replaced with a new one.

Installation

8 Installation is the reverse of removal, noting the following:
● Make sure the fuel tank and pump mounting plate mating surfaces are clean.
● Fit a new seal onto the pump with the raised lip facing up (see illustration 4.8a).
● The pump and its mounting plate can only fit one way – the pump has a tab that locates in a cut-out in the plate, and the plate has an offset mounting bolt hole (see

illustration 4.8b). Manoeuvre the pump into the tank, on Street Triple models from VIN 560477 making sure the level sensor wiring is looped all the way around the narrower section of the body as shown (see illustration 4.8c), and on all models making sure the seal remains in place and seats correctly (see illustration 4.6b).
● Make sure everything is correctly aligned and seated, then tighten the mounting plate bolts evenly and a little at a time in the sequence shown to the torque setting specified at the beginning of the Chapter (see illustration 4.8d).
● On completion, start the engine and check carefully that there is no leakage from around the pump mounting plate and from the hose connection.

Fuel pump relay

Check

Note: *Daytona models in the VIN range 249504 to 300525 were not originally fitted with a fuel pump relay, but it was found that shutting the engine off using the kill switch could damage the fuel pump driver on the ECM circuit board. As a result a relay kit including sub-harness was made available for retrospective fitting.*

9 On Daytona models remove the left-hand fairing side panel (see Chapter 7), on Street Triple models to VIN 560476 raise and support the fuel tank (see Chapter 4), and on Street Triple models from VIN 560477 remove the seat (see Chapter 7). Disconnect the relay from its connector block (see illustrations). Check the terminals and sockets for damage and corrosion.

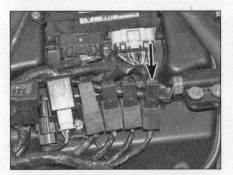

4.9b Fuel pump relay (arrowed) – Street Triple to VIN 560476

4.9c Fuel pump relay (arrowed) – Street Triple from VIN 560477

4.9d Pull the relay off its connector

4.10a Depress the tab to free the relay . . .

4.10b . . . and identify the terminals from the wire colours

10 Refer to the Wiring Diagrams at the end of Chapter 8 and to the wires going into the relay socket for terminal identification **(see illustrations)**. Connect a continuity tester or a multimeter set to the ohms x 1 scale between the No. 3 and No. 5 wire terminals on the relay – there should be no continuity or infinite resistance. If there is continuity or zero resistance replace the relay with a new one. Using a fully-charged 12 volt battery and two insulated jumper wires, connect the positive (+) terminal of the battery to the No. 1 wire terminal on the relay, and the negative (–) terminal to the No. 2 wire terminal on the relay. At this point the relay should be heard to click and there should be continuity or zero resistance. If this is the case the relay is proved good. If the relay does not click when battery voltage is applied and the tester or meter indicates no continuity or infinite resistance, the relay is faulty and must be replaced with a new one. If the relay is good, test the pump (see above).

Removal and installation

11 On Daytona models remove the left-hand fairing side panel (see Chapter 7), and on Street Triple models raise and support the fuel tank (see Chapter 4).
12 Disconnect the relay from its connector block **(see illustration 4.9a, b, and c)**.
13 Fit the new relay in reverse order.

5 Fuel pressure check

Warning: Refer to the precautions given in Section 1 before starting work.

1 To check the fuel pressure, the Triumph tool (Pt. No. T3880001) is needed. The tool comprises a gauge and two adapter hoses, one marked A, the other marked B – use adapter hose B. A commercial pressure gauge will not be of any use. If required you

can also use the wiring harness adapter (Pt. No. 3880123) that allows the fuel pump to be connected to the wiring loom with the fuel tank removed and supported next to the bike – this allows easier connection and use of the gauge and hose adapter, but is not essential.
2 Make sure the ignition switch is in the OFF position. If the wiring harness adapter is not being used, refer to Section 2 and detach the fuel hose from the fuel pump mounting plate and rest the fuel tank on the frame. If the wiring harness adapter is being used, refer to Section 2 and remove the tank and place it on a suitable support next to the bike.
3 Connect the adapter hose between the bike's fuel hose and the fuel pump union on the underside of the tank. Press each connector onto its union until it is felt and heard to click into place. Fit the pressure gauge into its union, again until it is felt to click into place.
4 If the tank has been removed connect the pump using the wiring harness adapter.
5 Turn the ignition switch ON and check the pressure reading on the gauge. Start the engine and allow it to idle. The pressure should be as specified at the beginning of the Chapter.
6 Turn the ignition OFF. Have some rag ready to catch residual fuel in the adapter hose. Release the pressure gauge by sliding its outer ferrule down – the gauge will spring out of the union. Release the adapter hose by pressing the clips on the connectors in. Install the fuel tank (see Section 2).
7 If the pressure is too low, either the pressure regulator is stuck open, the fuel pump is faulty, the strainer or filter is blocked, or there is a leak in the system, probably from a hose joint. Firstly check the system for leaks. If none are found, fit a new fuel pump – all other possible causes are due to components within the pump assembly, which is a sealed unit.
8 If the pressure is too high, there could be a blockage somewhere in the system, and/or the pressure regulator could be stuck closed,

or the fuel pump check valve could be faulty. First check the fuel rail and injectors for a blockage (see Section 8). Next fit a new fuel hose. If the pressure is still too high fit a new fuel pump – all other possible causes are due to components within the pump assembly, which is a sealed unit.

6 Fuel level sensor

Warning: Refer to the precautions given in Section 1 before starting work.

Check

1 If the low fuel level warning light fails to come on either when the ignition is first turned on or if the fuel level is low, first check the level sensor and instrument cluster wiring connectors (see Section 2 and Chapter 8 respectively), then check the wiring between the sensor and the instrument cluster for continuity, referring to 'Electrical system fault finding' at the beginning of Chapter 8 and to the wiring diagrams at the end of it.
2 Triumph provide no test data or procedure for checking the operation of the sensor, but it is safe to assume that if you connect a multimeter set to read resistance (ohms) to the sensor wiring connector, then as the float in the sensor moves up and down the resistance will change – there should be infinite resistance when the float is at the top of the sensor, and little or no resistance when it is at the bottom. To perform this test you will have to start with an empty fuel tank, then gradually fill it while watching the reading on the ohmmeter. Raise the fuel tank to gain access to the sensor wiring connector (see Section 2).
3 If the sensor does not behave as described, on Daytona models, and Street Triple models to VIN 560476 fit a new fuel pump – the sensor is an integral part of it. On Street Triple models

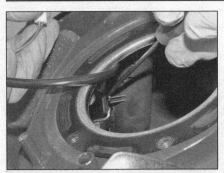

6.6a Release the retaining clip . . .

6.6b . . . and remove the sensor as described

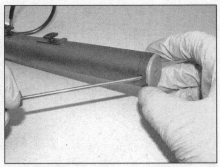

6.7a Release and remove the cap

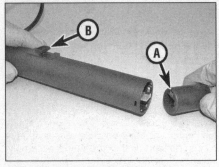

6.7b The magnet cover (A) must be on the same side as the tabs (B)

from VIN 560477 replace the sensor with a new one (see Steps 5 to 8 below). Alternatively take the bike to Triumph dealer for further assessment. If everything appears to be working correctly it is possible the fault lies in the instrument cluster – refer to Chapter 8.

Removal and installation

Daytona models and Street Triple models to VIN 560476

4 The level sensor is incorporated in the fuel pump assembly inside the fuel tank, and is not available separately Refer to Section 4 to remove the fuel pump.

Street Triple models from VIN 560477

5 Refer to Section 4 and remove the fuel pump.
6 Reach inside the tank and carefully push the retaining clip securing the sensor to its bracket towards the rear of the tank using a long but small headed screwdriver, then tilt the centre towards the opening to release the middle tab from the bracket, then lift the sensor to release the bottom tab and manoeuvre the sensor out (see illustrations).
7 No individual parts are available fro the sensor, but there is a removable float inside the body, which could be stuck. Release the cap and check the float is able to move freely on its slider (see illustration). If you remove the float note which way up its fits as it can fit either way, but will give an incorrect reading if fitted the wrong way – the magnet cover on the face must fit down into the sensor body and be on the same side as the retaining tabs (see illustration).
8 Fit the new sensor onto the bracket, locating the bottom clip first, then the middle, making sure the retaining clip is heard to click into place.
9 Refer to Section 4 and install the fuel pump.

7 Throttle body

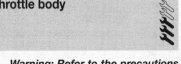

Warning: Refer to the precautions given in Section 1 before starting work.

Removal

1 Before removing the throttle body, disconnect the fuel pump wiring connector (see Section 2), then turn the engine over on the starter for a few seconds – this reduces any pressure in the fuel rail.
2 Remove the fuel tank and the airbox (see Sections 2 and 3).
3 Disconnect the fuel injector wiring connectors (see illustration).
4 Disconnect the idle air control unit wiring connector (see illustration 7.3).
5 Disconnect the throttle position sensor wiring connector (see illustration 7.3).
6 On Daytona models detach the intake air flap vacuum hose from its union on the left-hand end (see illustration). On ST models cut the cable-tie securing the wiring to the fuel rail.
7 Release the clamps securing the throttle

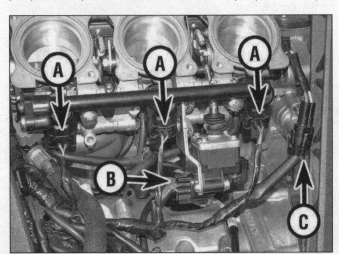

7.3 Disconnect the injector wiring connectors (A), the idle unit wiring connector (B) and the throttle sensor wiring connector (C)

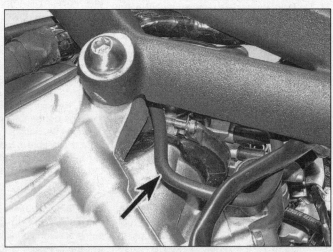

7.6 Detach the vacuum hose (arrowed) from its union

7.7a Slacken the left-hand clamp (arrowed) . . .

7.7b . . . and the middle and right-hand clamps (arrowed) . . .

7.7c . . . and displace the throttle body

body assembly, then ease the assembly out of the intake stubs **(see illustrations)**.

8 Undo the throttle cable bracket screws and detach the cable ends from the cam **(see illustrations)**.

9 Unless you are removing the intake stubs (Step 13) plug them with clean rags to prevent anything dropping inside. Note the location of the clamps on the stubs to aid reassembly.

10 If required, remove the fuel rail and injectors (see Section 8), but read the **Note** under the removal heading first.

11 If required, detach and remove the MAP sensor hoses, noting which fits where **(see illustration)**.

12 Do not remove the throttle position sensor

or idle air control unit from the throttle body unless you know there is a fault and are fitting a new one, or unless you are renewing the throttle body assembly **(see illustrations)**. If you do need to remove either or both, note that correct set-up is essential and can only be done using the Triumph diagnostic tool. There is no alternative, unless you want to run the risk of having the bike running incorrectly. Refer to Section 12 for further information on the engine management section, and to Section 14 for the throttle position sensor and Section 15 for the idle air control valve.

13 If required undo the screws securing each intake stub to the cylinder head and remove them **(see illustration)**. On Daytona models,

7.8a Undo the screws (arrowed) and detach the bracket . . .

7.8b . . . then free the cable ends from the cam

7.11 Remove the MAP sensor hose assembly (arrowed) if required

7.12a Throttle position sensor (arrowed)

7.12b Idle air control unit (arrowed)

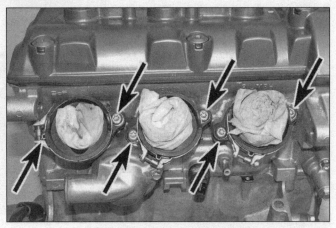

7.13 Intake stub screws (arrowed)

and Street Triple models to VIN 560476 remove the O-rings – new ones must be used. On Street Triple models from VIN 560477 check the condition of the sealing bead on each stub and if it is damaged replace the stub with a new one. Plug the intakes in the cylinder head with clean rag.

Cleaning

Caution: Use only a dedicated spray cleaner (such as a carburettor and injector cleaner) for throttle body cleaning.

14 Spray the cleaner over the throttle bodies to remove any dirt and grime, paying particular attention to the throttle cam assembly and spring. Use a nylon brush if required, but be careful not to embed dirt particles into the cam assembly as this could cause the throttles to stick. Ensure no dirt is lodged in the bores for the throttle body synchronising screws. Take great care not to disturb any screw settings.

15 If you have removed the intake stubs clean them and their mating surfaces on the cylinder head.

Inspection

16 Check the throttle bodies for cracks or any other damage which may result in air getting in.

17 Check that the throttle butterflies move smoothly and freely in the bodies, and make sure that the inside of each body is completely clean.

18 Check that the throttle cable cam moves smoothly and freely, taking into account spring pressure. Clean any grit and dirt from around the cam. Check the spring for signs of damage and distortion.

19 If a body or the butterfly linkage assembly is damaged, the whole assembly must be replaced as individual components are not available.

Installation

20 Installation is the reverse of removal, noting the following:

● Do not forget to remove the rag from the intakes.
● On Daytona models, and Street Triple models to VIN 560476, if removed, fit the intake stubs using new O-rings and tighten the screws to the torque setting specified at the beginning of the Chapter **(see illustration 7.13)**.
● On Street Triple models from VIN 560477, if removed, clean the threads of the intake stub screws and apply some fresh threadlock. Fit the intake stubs and tighten the screws to the torque setting specified at the beginning of the Chapter for your engine number **(see illustration 7.13)**.
● If removed fit the fuel injectors and fuel rail onto the throttle bodies as described in Section 8 before installing the throttle bodies.
● If removed connect each MAP sensor hose to its union as noted on removal **(see illustration 7.11)**.

● Ensure that the throttle bodies are fully engaged with the intake stubs before tightening the clamps.
● Make sure the wiring connectors are reconnected **(see illustration 7.3)**.
● Check the operation of the throttle cables and adjust as necessary (see Chapter 1).

8 Fuel rail and injectors

Warning: Refer to the precautions given in Section 1 before proceeding.

Check

1 If the MIL light has come on, and you suspect an injector to be faulty, you can either have a Triumph dealer confirm this using the diagnostic tool, or, if the engine runs, start it and allow it to idle, then check the operation of each injector in the throttle bodies using a sounding rod; an injector will emit a 'clicking' noise when functioning. If any injector is silent, either the injector or its wiring harness is faulty.

2 If the engine does not run, remove the fuel tank (Section 2). Disconnect the wiring connector from each injector in turn **(see illustration)**. Connect an ohmmeter between the terminals of the injector and measure the resistance **(see illustration)**. Compare each reading to that given in the Specifications. If

8.2a Disconnect the wiring connector . . .

8.4 Disconnect the fuel hose

the resistance of any injector differs greatly from that specified replace it with a new one.

3 If the injectors are good check for continuity in the wiring from each injector to the ECM and the EMS (engine management system) relay, referring to electrical system fault finding at the beginning of Chapter 8 and to the wiring diagram for your model at the end of it. If all is good check the EMS fuse (see Chapter 8), the EMS relay (Section 13), then the ECM (Section 12).

Removal

Note: The fuel injectors have an O-ring on each end to seal them in the fuel rail and throttle bodies to prevent fuel leakage under pressure. Removal of the injectors could cause the seals to lose their effectiveness, and Triumph do not list them as being available separately from the injectors themselves, which are expensive (but see Step 7). It is therefore best not to remove the fuel rail and injectors from the throttle bodies unless you have to fit a new injector.

4 Remove the throttle body assembly (see Section 7). Disconnect the fuel hose from its union on the fuel rail **(see illustration)** – see Section 2, Step 11 or 12 (according to engine number) for details if required.

5 Undo the fuel rail screws, then ease the fuel rail and injectors off the throttle bodies **(see illustration)**.

6 If required carefully pull the injector(s) out of the fuel rail.

7 Check the condition of the injector O-rings

8.2b . . . and measure the resistance between the terminals

8.5 Undo the screws (arrowed) and carefully remove the fuel rail with the injectors attached

8.10 Align the fuel injectors and ensure they seat correctly

9.2 Fully slacken the locknuts (arrowed) and free the cables from the bracket

9.3a Pull back the rubber boot . . .

9.3b . . . then undo the screws (arrowed) . . .

9.3c . . . separate the housing halves . . .

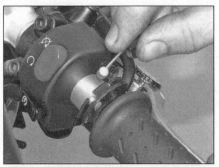

9.3d . . . then free the cable ends from the throttle pulley and the elbows from the housings

– if they are damaged or deformed they must be replaced with new ones, but note that they are not listed as being available separately from the injectors themselves. It is best to consult a Triumph dealer, who may be able to supply them separately, or alternatively take the old O-rings to a good aftermarket O-ring supplier and have them matched for size.

8 Modern fuels contain detergents which should keep the rail injectors clean and free of gum or varnish from residue fuel. Clean the rail in a dedicated cleaner and blow it through with compressed air. If an injector is suspected of being blocked, flush it through with injector cleaner.

Installation

9 Fit new O-rings onto each injector. Push each injector into its socket in the fuel rail, aligning the tab on the injector with the slot in the socket, and making sure you do not turn it whilst doing so, and that it is properly seated.
10 Fit the fuel rail and injector assembly onto the throttle bodies, making sure each injector seats correctly **(see illustration)**. Fit the fuel rail screws and tighten them to the torque setting specified at the beginning of the Chapter **(see illustration 8.5)**.
11 Connect the fuel hose: each end of the hose is colour-coded – the grey end connects to the fuel rail, the orange end to the fuel pump. Make sure the connector is fully pushed onto the union until the clips locate, then where fitted push the connector cover up to cover the clips **(see illustration 8.4)** – if

the cover won't push up the connector is not properly located.
12 Install the throttle body (see Section 7).

9 Throttle cables

> ⚠ **Warning: Refer to the precautions given in Section 1 before proceeding.**

Removal

1 Remove the fuel tank and the airbox (see Sections 2 and 3). Note the routing of the cables and mark them according to their location at each end.
2 Slacken the locknuts securing the opening and closing cables in the bracket and thread them up **(see illustration)**. Slip the outer cables out of the bracket and detach the inner cable ends from the throttle cam **(see illustration 7.8b)** – move the throttle cam round by hand to improve access as required, and if necessary displace the throttle bodies from the intake stubs (see Section 7) – there should be no need to disconnect the wiring.
3 Pull the rubber boot off the throttle pulley housing on the handlebars, then undo the housing screws **(see illustration)**. Separate the halves, then detach the inner cable ends from the pulley and free the cable elbows, noting how it all fits **(see illustrations)**.
4 Remove the cables from the machine noting their correct routing.

Installation

5 Installation is the reverse of removal. If necessary, lubricate the cables (see Chapter 1). Make sure the cables are correctly routed – they must not interfere with any other component and should not be kinked or bent sharply. Lubricate the end of each inner cable with multi-purpose grease.
6 Adjust the cables as described in Chapter 1. Turn the handlebars back and forth to make sure the cables don't cause the steering to bind.
7 Install the airbox and fuel tank (Sections 3 and 2).
8 Start the engine and check that the engine speed does not rise as the handlebars are turned. If it does, correct the problem before riding the motorcycle.

10 Exhaust system

> ⚠ **Warning: If the engine has been running the exhaust system will be very hot. Allow the system to cool before carrying out any work.**
> **Caution: The exhaust downpipe assembly incorporates a catalytic converter and oxygen sensor. Take care when handling it, and do not strike or drop it because the delicate catalytic converter element could be damaged.**

10.2 Disconnect the wiring connector

10.3a Unscrew the bolts (arrowed) . . .

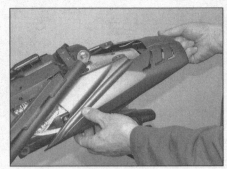

10.3b . . . and remove the cover

Daytona

Silencer

1 Remove the seat cowling (see Chapter 7).

2 Disconnect the turn signal and licence plate light wiring connector (see illustration).

3 If required (this can be done now, after the silencer has been removed, or not at all) unscrew the top cover bolts and remove the cover (see illustrations). Note the routing of the wiring, then unscrew the turn signal/licence plate bracket bolts and remove it (see illustration).

4 Note the orientation of the clamp securing the silencer to the intermediate pipe, then slacken the bolt (see illustration).

5 Unscrew and remove the nut on the silencer mounting bolt (see illustration). Support the silencer and withdraw the bolt, then draw the silencer out of the intermediate pipe (see illustration). Remove the mounting bolt rubber bushes for safekeeping if required (see illustration).

6 Check the condition of the sealing ring between the silencer and intermediate pipe and replace it with a new one if necessary (see illustration) – unless it is obviously in need of renewal it is best to leave it in place as it will be ruined after digging it out.

7 Installation is the reverse of removal. Check the condition of the rubber bushes and replace them with new ones if hardened or cracked (see illustration 10.5c). Fit a new sealing ring into the intermediate pipe if necessary (see illustration 10.6). When inserting the silencer make sure it does not catch on the rim of the sealing ring as it is easily damaged. Make sure the clamp is correctly orientated and located (see illustration 10.4). Tighten the silencer mounting bolt nut to the torque setting specified at the beginning of the Chapter, then tighten the clamp bolt to the specified torque. Run the engine and check that there are no leaks from the exhaust system.

Intermediate pipe

8 Remove the silencer (see above). Displace the exhaust control valve servo (see Step 16).

9 Note the orientation of the clamp securing the intermediate pipe to the downpipe

10.3c Unscrew the bolts (arrowed) on each side and remove the assembly

10.4 Slacken the clamp bolt (arrowed)

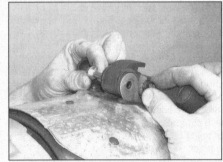

10.5a Unscrew the nut, then withdraw the bolt . . .

10.5b . . . and remove the silencer

10.5c Note the rubber bushes and take care not to lose them

10.6 Check the sealing ring (arrowed)

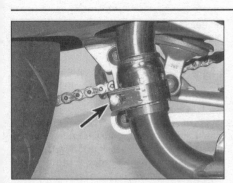

10.9 Slacken the clamp bolt (arrowed)

10.10a Unscrew the bolt (arrowed) . . .

10.10b . . . and manoeuvre the pipe out

assembly, then slacken the bolt **(see illustration)**.
10 Unscrew the bolt securing the intermediate pipe, noting the rubber bushes **(see illustration)**. Ease the intermediate pipe off the downpipe and manoeuvre it out from the bottom **(see illustration)**.
11 Check the condition of the sealing ring between the intermediate pipe and downpipe and replace it with a new one if necessary **(see illustration 10.21)** – leave it in place if still serviceable.
12 Installation is the reverse of removal. Fit a new sealing ring into the intermediate pipe if necessary. When fitting the pipe make sure the downpipe does not catch on the rim of the sealing ring as it is easily damaged. Make sure the clamp is correctly orientated and located. Tighten the mounting bolt and the clamp bolt

to the specified torque. Run the engine and check that there are no leaks from the exhaust system.

Downpipe assembly
13 Remove the fairing side panels (see Chapter 7).
14 Remove the radiator (see Chapter 3).
15 Trace the wiring from the Lambda (oxygen) sensor, freeing it from its guides and any ties, and disconnect it at the wiring connector **(see illustration)**. Feed the wiring back down to the sensor, noting its routing. If required remove the sensor (see Section 14).
16 Unscrew the exhaust control valve servo mounting bolts and displace it, then disconnect the wiring connector **(see illustrations)**. Do not disconnect the cables from either the servo or the valve on the

downpipe unless new parts are being fitted – if detached, the cables must be adjusted using the Triumph diagnostic tool, which means taking the bike to a Triumph dealer. Refer to the next sub-section below for details on the exhaust valve system.
17 Note the orientation of the clamp securing the downpipe assembly to the intermediate pipe, then slacken the bolt **(see illustration 10.9)**.
18 Unscrew the six downpipe assembly nuts from the cylinder head **(see illustration)**.
19 Unscrew the bolt securing the rear of the downpipe assembly, noting the arrangement of the collars and rubber bushes **(see illustration)**. Draw the downpipes off the cylinder head and the intermediate pipe, and remove the assembly **(see illustration)**.
20 Remove the gasket from each port in

10.15 Oxygen sensor (arrowed)

10.16a Unscrew the bolts (arrowed) and displace the servo . . .

10.16b . . . then disconnect the wiring connector

10.18 Unscrew the nuts (arrowed) . . .

10.19a . . . then unscrew the bolt . . .

10.19b . . . and remove the downpipe assembly

10.21 Check the sealing ring (arrowed)

10.22 Fit new gaskets

the cylinder head and discard them as new ones must be fitted **(see illustration 10.22)**. Remove the collars and bushes from the rear mounting for safekeeping if required. Check the condition of the rubber bushes and replace them with new ones if hardened or cracked.

21 Check the condition of the sealing ring between the intermediate pipe and downpipe and replace it with a new one if necessary **(see illustration)** – leave it in place if still serviceable.

22 Installation is the reverse of removal. Fit a new gasket into each of the cylinder head ports **(see illustration)** – they should have little tabs on them to keep them in place (fit these innermost), but if not apply a smear of grease to keep them in place. If removed, fit the bushes and collars into the rear mounting **(see illustration 10.19a)**.

23 Manoeuvre the assembly into position so that the head of each downpipe is located in

its port in the cylinder head, then fit the rear of the assembly in the intermediate pipe, taking care not to damage the sealing ring, and install the rear mounting bolt, but do not yet tighten it **(see illustrations)**. Fit the flanges onto the studs, then fit the downpipe nuts and tighten them in the sequence shown (1 to 6), first to the initial torque setting specified at the beginning of the Chapter, then in the same sequence to the final setting **(see illustrations)**.

24 Connect the exhaust valve servo wiring connector, then fit the servo and tighten its bolts to the specified torque **(see illustrations 10.16b and a)**.

25 Install the oxygen sensor if removed (Section 14). Reconnect the sensor wiring connector – make sure the wiring is correctly routed and secured.

26 Install the radiator (see Chapter 3). Refill the cooling system (see Chapter 1).

27 Run the engine and check that there are

no leaks from the exhaust system before installing the fairing side panels.

Exhaust control valve

28 A valve inside the rear of the downpipe assembly controls gasflow to maximise performance at different engine speeds. The valve is controlled via cables by an actuator which operates on a signal from the ECM. When the ignition is switched on the actuator moves the valve and sets it at its starting point.

29 To check the actuator and valve are functioning remove the right-hand fairing side panel (see Chapter 7). Turn the ignition on and check the actuator moves the valve.

30 If there are any problems with the system take the bike to a Triumph dealer – although you can remove the actuator, replace the cables and generally work on the system, all work requires the cables to be detached, and any time the cables are detached the system must be reset and adjusted using the Triumph diagnostic tool.

Street Triple models to VIN 560476

Silencers

31 Remove the side panel (see Chapter 7).

32 Note the orientation of the clamp securing the silencer to the intermediate pipe, then slacken the bolt **(see illustration)**.

33 Unscrew the nut on the silencer mounting bolt **(see illustration)**. Support the silencer, then withdraw the bolt and draw the silencer out of the intermediate pipe. Remove the collars and rubber bushes for safekeeping if required.

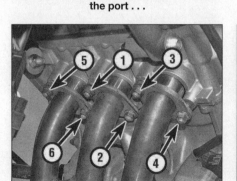

10.23a Make sure header pipes locate in the port . . .

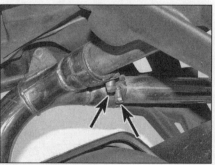

10.23b . . . and the rear pipe does not foul the sealing ring

10.23c Fit the flanges and the nuts . . .

10.23d . . . and tighten them as described in the sequence shown

10.32 Silencer clamp bolts (arrowed)

10.33 Silencer mounting bolt nut (arrowed)

10.39 Unscrew the bolt (arrowed)

34 Check the condition of the sealing ring between the silencer and intermediate pipe and replace it with a new one if necessary **(see illustration 10.6)** – unless it is obviously in need of renewal it is best to leave it in place as it will be ruined after digging it out.

35 Installation is the reverse of removal. Fit a new sealing ring into the intermediate pipe if necessary. When inserting the silencer make sure it does not catch on the rim of the sealing ring as it is easily damaged. Make sure the clamp is correctly orientated and located, and the cover locates correctly. Tighten the silencer mounting bolt to the torque setting specified at the beginning of the Chapter, then tighten the clamp bolt to the specified torque. Run the engine and check that there are no leaks from the exhaust system.

Intermediate pipe

36 Remove the silencers (see above).

37 Note the orientation of the clamp securing the intermediate pipe to the downpipe assembly, then slacken the bolt **(see illustration 10.9)**.

38 Slacken the rear sub-frame lower bolt on each side. Support the sub-frame, then unscrew the upper bolt on each side. Raise the sub-frame and either have an assistant support it or tie it up to the roof.

39 Unscrew the bolt securing the intermediate pipe, noting the rubber bushes **(see illustration)**. Ease the intermediate pipe off the downpipe and manoeuvre it out. Lower the

sub-frame, fit the upper bolts and tighten them finger-tight.

40 Check the condition of the sealing ring between the intermediate pipe and downpipe and replace it with a new one if necessary **(see illustration 10.21)**.

41 Installation is the reverse of removal. Fit a new sealing ring into the downpipe assembly if necessary. When fitting the pipe make sure it does not catch on the rim of the sealing ring as it is easily damaged. Make sure the clamp is correctly orientated and located. Tighten the mounting bolt then the clamp bolt to the specified torque. Tighten the rear sub-frame bolts to the specified torque. Run the engine and check that there are no leaks from the exhaust system.

Downpipe assembly

42 Remove the radiator (see Chapter 3). If fitted remove the belly pan (see Chapter 7).

43 Trace the wiring from the Lambda (oxygen) sensor, freeing it from its guides and any ties, and disconnect it at the wiring connector **(see illustration 10.15)**. Feed the wiring back down to the sensor, noting its routing. If required remove the sensor (see Section 14).

44 Note the orientation of the clamp securing the downpipe assembly to the intermediate pipe, then slacken the bolt **(see illustration 10.9)**.

45 Unscrew the six downpipe assembly nuts from the cylinder head **(see illustration 10.18)**.

46 Unscrew the bolt securing the rear of the downpipe assembly, noting the arrangement of the collars and rubber bushes **(see illustration 10.19a)**. Draw the downpipes off the cylinder head and the intermediate pipe, and remove the assembly **(see illustration 10.19b)**.

47 Remove the gasket from each port in the cylinder head and discard them as new ones must be fitted **(see illustration 10.22)**. Remove the collars and bushes from the rear mounting for safekeeping if required. Check the condition of the rubber bushes and replace them with new ones if hardened or cracked.

48 Check the condition of the sealing ring between the intermediate pipe and downpipe and replace it with a new one if necessary

(see illustration 10.21) – leave it in place if still serviceable.

49 Installation is the reverse of removal. Fit a new gasket into each of the cylinder head ports **(see illustration 10.22)** – they should have little tabs on them to keep them in place (fit these innermost), but if not apply a smear of grease to keep them in place. If removed, fit the bushes and collars into the rear mounting **(see illustration 10.19a)**.

50 Manoeuvre the assembly into position so that the head of each downpipe is located in its port in the cylinder head, then fit the rear of the assembly onto the intermediate pipe, taking care not to damage the sealing ring, and install the rear mounting bolt, but do not yet tighten it **(see illustrations 10.23a and b)**. Fit the flanges onto the studs, then fit the downpipe nuts and tighten them in the sequence shown (1 to 6), first to the initial torque setting specified at the beginning of the Chapter, then in the same sequence to the final setting **(see illustrations 10.23c and d)**.

51 Install the oxygen sensor if removed (Section 14). Reconnect the sensor wiring connector – make sure the wiring is correctly routed and secured.

52 Install the radiator (see Chapter 3). Refill the cooling system (see Chapter 1).

53 Run the engine and check that there are no leaks from the exhaust system. Install the belly pan if fitted (see Chapter 7).

Street Triple models from VIN 560477

Silencer

54 Remove the belly pan if fitted (see Chapter 7).

55 Remove the heat shield from the silencer **(see illustration)**.

56 Note the orientation of the clamp securing the silencer to the rear of the downpipe assembly, then slacken the nut **(see illustration)**.

57 Unscrew the nut on the silencer rear mounting bolt and withdraw the bolt **(see illustration)**. Support the silencer, then unscrew the front mounting bolt and draw the

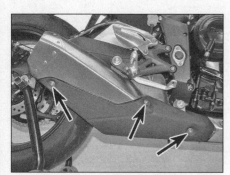

10.55 Undo the screws (arrowed) and remove the shield

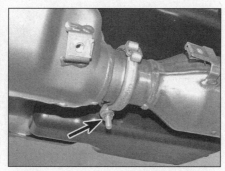

10.56 Slacken the clamp nut (arrowed)

10.57a Silencer rear mounting bolt nut (arrowed)

10.57b Silencer front mounting bolt (arrowed)

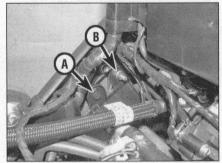

10.62a Trim clip (A) and nut (B) . . .

10.62b . . . securing the frame trim piece

silencer out of the downpipe **(see illustration)**. Remove the collars and rubber bushes for safekeeping if required.

58 Check the condition of the sealing ring between the silencer and downpipe and replace it with a new one if necessary **(see illustration 10.6)** – unless it is obviously in need of renewal it is best to leave it in place as it will be ruined after digging it out.

59 Installation is the reverse of removal. Use new rubber bushes if necessary. Fit a new sealing ring into the intermediate pipe if necessary. When inserting the silencer make sure it does not catch on the rim of the sealing ring as it is easily damaged. Make sure the clamp is correctly orientated and located, and the cover locates correctly. Fit the silencer mounting bolts and nut finger-tight only at first, then tighten the clamp bolt to the torque setting specified at the beginning of the Chapter, then tighten the silencer mounting bolts to the specified torques. Run the engine and check that there are no leaks from the exhaust system. Apply some copper grease to the heat shield bolt threads.

Downpipe assembly

60 Remove the silencer (Steps 54 to 58).
61 Remove the radiator (see Chapter 3).
62 Remove the fuel tank (see Section 2). Unscrew the nut and release the trim clip securing the frame trim piece, and manoeuvre it out **(see illustrations)**.
63 Remove the front sprocket cover (see Chapter 6). Trace the wiring from the Lambda

(oxygen) sensor, freeing it from its guides and any ties, and disconnect it at the wiring connector **(see illustration)**. Feed the wiring back down to the sensor, noting its routing. If required remove the sensor (see Section 14).
64 Unscrew the six downpipe assembly nuts from the cylinder head **(see illustration 10.18)**. Draw the downpipes off the head and remove the assembly **(see illustration 10.19b)**.
65 Remove the gasket from each port in the cylinder head and discard them as new ones must be fitted **(see illustration 10.22)**.
66 Installation is the reverse of removal. Fit a new gasket into each of the cylinder head ports **(see illustration 10.22)** – they should have little tabs on them to keep them in place (fit these innermost), but if not apply a smear of grease to keep them in place.
67 Manoeuvre the assembly into position so that the head of each downpipe is located in its port in the cylinder head **(see illustrations 10.23a and b)**. Fit the flanges onto the studs, then fit the downpipe nuts and tighten them in the sequence shown (1 to 6), first to the initial torque setting specified at the beginning of the Chapter, then in the same sequence to the final setting **(see illustrations 10.23c and d)**.
68 Install the oxygen sensor if removed (Section 14). Reconnect the sensor wiring connector **(see illustration 10.63)** – make sure the wiring is correctly routed and secured. Install the front sprocket cover (see Chapter 6).
69 Install the fuel tank (see Section 2). Fit the frame trim piece and secure it with the trim clip and nut **(see illustrations 10.62b and a)**.

70 Install the radiator (see Chapter 3). Refill the cooling system (see Chapter 1).
71 Install the silencer (Step 59).
72 Run the engine and check that there are no leaks from the exhaust system. Install the belly pan if fitted (see Chapter 7).

11 Ignition coils

⚠ *Warning: The energy levels in electronic systems can be very high. On no account should the ignition be switched on whilst the coils are connected and being held. Shocks from the HT circuit can be most unpleasant. Secondly, it is vital that the plugs are soundly earthed (grounded) when the system is checked for sparking. The ignition system components can be seriously damaged if the HT circuit becomes isolated.*

Removal

1 On Daytona models remove the left-hand fairing side panel (see Chapter 7). On all models remove the airbox (see Section 3).
2 Displace the SAIS solenoid valve, then unscrew the bolts and displace or remove the bracket **(see illustration)**.
3 Working on one coil at a time, disconnect the wiring connector **(see illustration)**.

10.63 Oxygen sensor wiring connector (arrowed)

11.2 Displace the valve, then unscrew the bolts (arrowed) and displace the bracket

11.3 Disconnect the wiring connector . . .

11.4 . . . and pull the coil off the spark plug

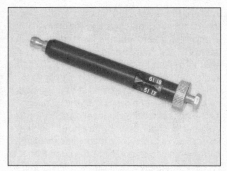

11.7 A typical ignition spark gap testing tool

4 Pull the coil off the spark plug **(see illustration)**.

Ignition system check

5 Remove the coil (Steps 1 to 4), then reconnect the wiring connector. Fit a new spark plug into the cap and hold the coil so the plug threads are in contact with the engine. Do not hold the plug against an engine cover that is magnesium coated as the coating could be damaged.

⚠️ *Warning: Do not remove any of the spark plugs from the engine to perform this check – atomised fuel being pumped out of the open spark plug hole could ignite, causing severe injury!*

6 Check that the kill switch is in the RUN position and the transmission is in neutral, then turn the ignition switch ON, pull the clutch lever in and turn the engine over on the starter motor. If the system is in good condition a regular, fat blue spark should be evident at the plug electrodes. If the spark appears thin or yellowish, or is non-existent, further investigation will be necessary. Turn the ignition OFF. Repeat the check for the other coils.

7 The ignition system must be able to produce a spark which is capable of jumping a particular size gap. Triumph provide no specification, but a healthy system should produce a spark capable of jumping at least 6 mm. Ignition spark gap testing tools are available from good suppliers **(see illustration)** – follow the manufacturer's instructions.

8 If the system is in good condition a regular, fat blue spark should be seen to jump the gap on the tool. If the test results are good the

entire ignition system can be considered good. If the spark appears thin or yellowish, or is non-existent, further investigation is necessary.

9 Using an ohmmeter or multimeter set to the ohms x 1 scale, measure the primary circuit resistance between the terminals on the coil **(see illustration)**. The resistance should be as specified at the beginning of the Chapter. If not, the coil is faulty and must be replaced with a new one. Set the ohmmeter or multimeter to the K-ohms scale and measure the secondary circuit resistance between one of the terminals on the coil and the plug contact in the base **(see illustration)**. Triumph do not specify a resistance but the coil we tested showed just over 11 K-ohms. If the value deviates from this figure by +/- 10%, the coil is faulty and must be replaced with a new one. The coil is a sealed unit and cannot therefore be repaired.

10 If the coils and spark plugs are good, then there is a fault elsewhere in the system. The likely faults are listed below, starting with the most probable source of failure. Work through the list systematically, referring to the subsequent sections for full details of the necessary checks and tests. **Note:** *Before checking the following items ensure that the battery is fully charged and that all fuses are in good condition.*

● Loose, corroded or damaged wiring connections, broken or shorted wiring between any of the component parts of the ignition system – refer to 'Electrical system fault finding' at the beginning of Chapter 8 and to the wiring diagram for your model at the end of it.

● Faulty spark plug, dirty, worn or corroded

plug electrodes, or incorrect gap between electrodes (see Chapter 1).
● Blown EMS fuse (see Chapter 8) or faulty EMS relay (see Section 13).
● Faulty ignition switch or engine kill switch (see Chapter 8).
● Faulty clutch, neutral or sidestand switch (see Chapter 8).
● Faulty crankshaft position sensor, incorrect air gap, or damaged triggers.
● Faulty ECM.

11 If the above checks don't reveal the cause of the problem, have the engine management system tested by a Triumph dealer. Triumph produce a diagnostic tool which can perform a complete analysis of the engine management system. Refer to Sections 1 and 12 for more information.

Installation

12 Fit the coils onto the spark plugs **(see illustration 11.4)**. Connect the coil wiring connectors, making sure each goes to its correct cylinder **(see illustration 11.3)**.

13 Fit the SAIS solenoid valve bracket, then fit the valve onto it **(see illustration 11.2)**.

14 Install the airbox (see Section 3). On Daytona models install the left-hand fairing side panel (see Chapter 7).

12 Engine management system and electronic control module (ECM)

⚠️ *Warning: Refer to the precautions given in Section 1 before starting work.*

1 For a general description of the system, see Section 1.

Diagnostic tool and fault codes

2 To diagnose the exact cause of a failure in the system, either the Triumph diagnostic tool or an EOBD (OBD2) fault code reader is essential **(see illustration)** – both of these plug into the socket under the seat **(see illustration 12.4)**.

3 The ECM has in-built diagnostic functions which record and store all data should a permanent fault occur. Diagnostic trouble codes (DTCs) can then be read using the diagnostic tool, which lists a P-code to

11.9a Testing the coil primary resistance

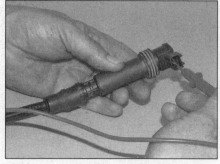

11.9b Test the coil secondary resistance

12.2 After-market EOBD (OBD2) fault code reader

12.4 Diagnostic tool socket is under seat

indicate the exact fault. Should a fault occur, the malfunction indicator light or symbol (MIL) in the instrument cluster illuminates. If this happens, the management system switches itself into 'limp home' mode, so that in theory you should not be left stranded. Depending on the problem, it is possible that you will notice no difference in the running of the motorcycle.
4 The socket for the diagnostic tool is located under the seat (see illustration). With the ignition off, plug the code reader into the socket. Turn the ignition on and allow the code reader to process any stored fault codes – these will be displayed as a four digit number prefixed by the letter P. Turn off the ignition and disconnect the

code reader once the P-code has been noted. Refer to the accompanying table to link the code with the faulty circuit. Once the fault has been rectified the code reader can be used to delete the stored code from the ECM's memory.
5 If you don't have access to a code reader it is possible to perform certain tests and checks to identify a particular fault, but the difficulty is knowing in which part of the system the fault has occurred, and therefore where to start checking. Further details on the functions of and checks that can be made to the individual sensors and components and the wiring between them are detailed below and in other Sections of this Chapter.

P-code	Circuit affected
P0030	Oxygen sensor heater – circuit fault
P0031	Oxygen sensor heater – open circuit to battery/short to earth
P0032	Oxygen sensor heater – short circuit to battery
P0078	Exhaust control valve actuator circuit fault
P0107	MAP sensor low voltage
P0108	MAP sensor high voltage
P0112	Intake air temperature too high
P0113	Intake air temperature too low
P0117	Engine coolant temperature too high – sensor short circuit to earth
P0118	Engine coolant temperature too low – sensor open circuit or short circuit to battery+
P0122	Throttle position sensor low input – short to earth or open circuit
P0123	Throttle position sensor high input – short circuit to sensor supply
P0130	Oxygen sensor circuit fault
P0136	Oxygen sensor circuit fault
P0201/P1201	Injector cyl 1 circuit fault – misfire = open circuit, flooding = short circuit
P0202/P1202	Injector cyl 2 circuit fault – misfire = open circuit, flooding = short circuit
P0203/P1203	Injector cyl 3 circuit fault – misfire = open circuit, flooding = short circuit
P0335	Crankshaft position sensor circuit fault
P0351	Ignition coil circuit fault cyl 1
P0352	Ignition coil circuit fault cyl 2
P0353	Ignition coil circuit fault cyl 3
P0413	SAIS valve short circuit to earth or open circuit
P0414	SAIS valve short circuit to battery
P0444	EVAP purge control valve short circuit to earth or open circuit
P0445	EVAP purge control valve short circuit to battery
P0460	Fuel level sensor circuit fault
P0500	Speed (speedometer) sensor fault or ABS sensor fault
P0505	Idle speed control system fault
P0560	Motorcycle voltage system fault
P0603	EEPROM fault
P0616	Starter relay coil short circuit to earth or open circuit
P0617	Starter relay short circuit to battery+

P-code	Circuit affected
P0630	EEPROM fault
P0654	Tachometer circuit fault
P0705	Gear position sensor fault
P1078	Exhaust control valve actuator position sensor low voltage
P1079	Exhaust control valve actuator position sensor high voltage
P1080	Exhaust control valve actuator mechanism fault
P1105	MAP sensor vacuum hose fault
P1107	Ambient air pressure sensor circuit low voltage
P1108	Ambient air pressure sensor circuit high voltage
P1115	Temperature gauge circuit fault
P1231	Fuel pump relay short circuit to earth or open circuit
P1232	Fuel pump relay short circuit to battery+
P1500	Speedometer circuit fault
P1508	Immobiliser (or tyre pressure sensor system) and ECM unmatched
P1520	ABS modulator ID incompatible
P1521	No signal to ABS modulator
P1552	Cooling fan – short or open circuit
P1553	Cooling fan – short to battery voltage/over temperature
P1602	Tunelock
P1604	ECM tamper detected
P1605	ECM locked by Tunelock
P1610	Low fuel output circuit fault
P1614	ECM and instruments incorrect matched
P1619	Headlight relay circuit fault
P1620	Headlight relay short circuit to battery
P1628	Fuel pump short circuit to earth or open circuit
P1629	Fuel pump short circuit to battery
P1631	Tip-over sensor circuit low voltage
P1632	Tip-over sensor circuit high voltage
P1650	No communication with immobiliser ECM
P1659	Ignition voltage input circuit fault
P1670	Intake air flap short circuit to earth or open circuit
P1671	Intake air flap short circuit to battery+
P1685	EMS relay fault
P1690	CAN-bus network communication fault between ECM and instruments
P1695	No communication with instruments
P1698	5 volt sensor supply circuit fault

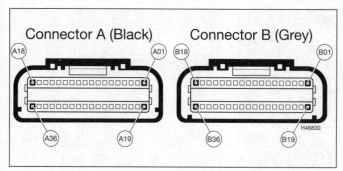

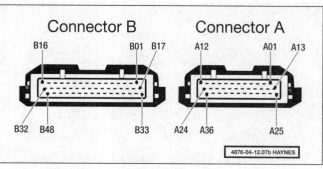

12.7a ECM wiring connector pin identification – Daytona model, and Street Triple model to VIN 560476

12.7b ECM wiring connector pin identification – Street Triple model from VIN 560477

Fault tracing

Note: Refer to 'Electrical system fault finding' at the beginning of Chapter 8 and to the wiring diagram for your model at the end of it.

6 If a fault is indicated, check the wiring and connectors to and from the ECM (electronic control module) and the various sensors and all their related components – raise or remove the fuel tank for access to the ECM and its connectors (see Section 2). It may be that a connector is dirty or corroded or has come loose – a dirty or corroded terminal or connector will affect the resistance in that circuit, which will upset the information going to the ECM, and therefore affect the decisions it makes in controlling the system. Electrical contact cleaners are available in aerosol cans from good suppliers.

7 A wire could be pinched and is shorting out – a continuity test of all wires from connector to connector will locate this. Albeit a fiddly and laborious task, the only way to determine any wiring faults is to systematically work through the Wiring Diagram (at the end of Chapter 8) and test each individual wire and connector for continuity – all wires are colour-coded. When making continuity checks, isolate the wire being tested by disconnecting the wiring connectors at each end. The Wiring Diagrams show the terminal identification for each wire on the ECM with the letter given on the wiring diagram indicating the relevant ECM connector, and the number referring to the terminal within that connector, as shown **(see illustrations)** – match these to the terminals on the ECM connector(s) when making the tests.

8 If all the wiring and connectors appear good, remove the relevant sensor and make sure its sensing tip or head is clean and undamaged, as this can often be the cause of inaccurate signals being sent to the ECM.

ECM removal and installation

Note: Before removing the ECM, make sure the ignition has been switched OFF for at least one minute to allow the system to power down.

9 Disconnect the battery (see Chapter 8).

10 Raise or remove the fuel tank for access to the ECM (see Section 2).

11 On Daytona models and Street Triple models to VIN 560476 disconnect the ECM wiring connectors **(see illustration 3.3b)**. Unscrew the retaining bracket bolts and remove the bracket, then remove the ECM **(see illustration)**.

12 On Street Triple models from VIN 560477 unscrew the ECM holder bolts and displace the ECM assembly **(see illustrations)**. Disconnect the wiring connectors by pushing the retaining tabs in and pivoting the locking bars up **(see illustration)**. Remove the ECM.

13 Installation is the reverse of removal. Check the terminal pins and connectors for damage and corrosion. The connectors cannot be re-connected the wrong way round. On Street Triple models from VIN 560477 make sure the wiring connector locking bars are in the released position, then push the connectors into the sockets until they are heard to click into place.

13 EMS relay

Note: Before disconnecting the relay, make sure the ignition has been switched OFF for at least one minute to allow the system to power down, then disconnect the battery (see Chapter 8). Refer to the Wiring Diagrams at the end of Chapter 8 for relay terminal identification.

1 The engine management system (EMS) has its own power relay which is designed to provide a steady voltage supply to the ECM. The ECM holds the relay open after the ignition is switched off to enable it perform various power-down functions, such as writing data to the memory, referencing the position of the idle air control valve, and if necessary, running the cooling fan.

12.11 ECM bracket bolts (arrowed) – Daytona model, and Street Triple model to VIN 560476

12.12b ...and the two screws (arrowed) on the back to free the ECM

12.12a Undo the screw (arrowed) on the top ...

12.12c Push the tab in and flip the bar up

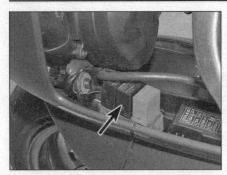

13.2a EMS relay (arrowed) – Daytona

13.2b EMS relay (arrowed) – Street Triple to VIN 560476

13.2c EMS relay (arrowed) – Street Triple from VIN 560477

Check

2 On Daytona models remove the left-hand fairing side panel (see Chapter 7), on Street Triple models to VIN 560476 raise and support the fuel tank (see Chapter 4), and on Street Triple models from VIN 560477 remove the seat (see Chapter 7). Disconnect the relay from its connector block (see illustrations). Check the terminals and sockets for damage and corrosion.

3 Refer to the Wiring Diagrams at the end of Chapter 8 and to the wires going into the relay socket for terminal identification (see illustrations 4.10a and b). Connect a continuity tester or a multimeter set to the ohms x 1 scale between the No. 3 and No. 5 wire terminals on the relay – there should be no continuity or infinite resistance. If there is continuity or zero resistance replace the relay with a new one. Using a fully-charged

12 volt battery and two insulated jumper wires, connect the positive (+) terminal of the battery to the No. 1 wire terminal on the relay, and the negative (–) terminal to the No. 2 wire terminal on the relay. At this point the relay should be heard to click and there should be continuity or zero resistance. If this is the case the relay is proved good. If the relay does not click when battery voltage is applied and the tester or meter indicates no continuity or infinite resistance, the relay is faulty and must be replaced with a new one.

Removal and installation

4 On Daytona models remove the left-hand cockpit trim panel (see Chapter 7). On Street Triple models raise and support the fuel tank (see Chapter 4).

5 Disconnect the relay from its connector block (see illustration 13.2a or b).

6 Plug the new relay into its connector.

14 Sensors

Note: *Before disconnecting the wiring connector from any sensor, make sure the ignition is switched OFF, and disconnect the battery (see Chapter 8).*

Atmospheric pressure sensor

Function

1 The sensor reads the pressure of the atmospheric (barometric) pressure (i.e. air density). The ECM combines this with other information to determine fuelling requirements.

Removal and installation

2 On Daytona models the sensor is located on the intake air duct in the fairing (see illustration) – remove the fairing (see Chapter 7), and for best access the instrument cluster (see Chapter 8). On Street Triple models to VIN 560476 the sensor is located at the back of the bike (see illustration) – remove the tail light for access (see Chapter 8), then move the wiring aside. On Street Triple models from VIN 560477 the sensor is located on the left-hand side of the rear sub-frame (see illustration) – remove the seat for access (see Chapter 7).

3 Disconnect the wiring connector from the sensor, then unscrew the bolt securing it. Installation is the reverse of removal.

Crankshaft position sensor

Function

4 The sensor reads the position of the crankshaft and how fast it is turning; this information is used by the ECM to determine which cylinder is on its ignition stroke and when it should fire. The ECM combines engine speed with information from other sensors to determine fuelling and ignition requirements.

Test, removal and installation

5 The crankshaft position sensor is mounted in the alternator cover and is part of the alternator stator assembly (see illustration).

6 To check the sensor, first make sure the ignition is switched OFF, then on Daytona models and Street Triple models to VIN 560476

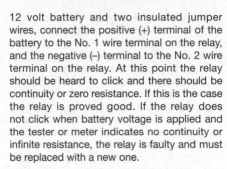

14.2a Atmospheric pressure sensor (arrowed) – Daytona

14.2b Atmospheric pressure sensor (arrowed) – Street Triple to VIN 560476

14.2c Atmospheric pressure sensor (arrowed) – Street Triple from VIN 560477

14.5 Crankshaft position sensor (arrowed)

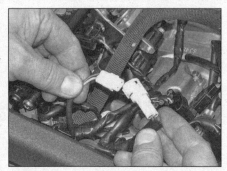

14.6a Disconnect the wiring connector . . .

14.6b . . . then measure the resistance of the sensor

14.10 ECT sensor (arrowed)

raise or remove the fuel tank (see Section 2), and on Street Triple models from VIN 560477 remove the throttle body (see Section 7). Trace the wiring from the sensor and disconnect it at the connector **(see illustration)**. Using an ohmmeter or multimeter set to the K-ohms scale, measure the resistance between the terminals on the sensor side of the connector **(see illustration)**. If the result is as specified, check that there is no continuity between each terminal and earth (ground).

7 Remove the alternator cover (see Chapter 8). Inspect the sensor and the sensor triggers on the alternator rotor for damage. Make sure the sensor head is clean, and the bolts are tight.

8 If the sensor is faulty, replace the alternator stator/sensor assembly with a new one (see Chapter 8) – the sensor is not available separately.

Engine coolant temperature sensor

Function

9 The sensor reads the temperature of the engine coolant, and the ECM uses the information to determine fuelling requirements, particularly for hot and cold starting.

Test

10 The sensor is located in the back of the cylinder head **(see illustration)**.

11 Make sure the ignition is switched OFF. Depending on your tools and dexterity you may be able to access the sensor sufficiently from the right-hand side of the bike – on Daytona models first remove the right-hand

fairing side panel (see Chapter 7). If not remove the airbox, and if required the throttle bodies (see Sections 3 and 7).

12 To test the sensor resistance, disconnect the wiring connector **(see illustration)**. Measure the resistance between the sensor terminals using an ohmmeter or multimeter set to the relevant scale for the temperature of the engine if warm, or the air if the engine is cold – see Specifications. If the result is not as specified, the sensor is faulty.

Removal and installation

13 The sensor is located in the back of the cylinder head **(see illustration 14.10)**. Depending on your tools and dexterity you may be able to access the sensor sufficiently from the right-hand side of the bike – on Daytona models first remove the right-hand fairing side panel (see Chapter 7). If not remove the airbox, and if required the throttle bodies (see Sections 3 and 7). Drain the cooling system (see Chapter 1). Disconnect the wiring connector **(see illustration 14.12)**.

14 Unscrew the sensor from the cylinder head. Discard the sealing washer as a new one must be used. Fit a new sealing washer onto the sensor, then thread it into the head and tighten it.

15 Reconnect the wiring connector, then fill the cooling system (see Chapter 1).

16 Install the throttle bodies and airbox as required.

Gear position sensor

Function

17 The sensor tells the ECM which gear the

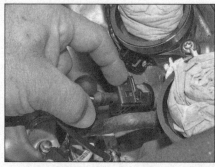

14.12 Push the clip in to release the wiring connector

engine is in, and the ECM then operates the neutral light and gear position indicator in the instrument cluster.

Check

18 Remove the sensor (see below), and check that the contact pin is not damaged, and that the switch plate turns freely in the body.

Removal and installation

19 The sensor is on the left-hand side of the engine **(see illustration)**. Remove the front sprocket cover (see Chapter 5).

20 Raise or remove the fuel tank (see Section 2). Trace the wiring from the sensor and disconnect it at the wiring connector.

21 Undo the screws and detach the sensor **(see illustration)**. Discard the O-ring as a new one should be used **(see illustration)**.

22 Install the sensor using a new O-ring and tighten the screws.

14.19 Gear position sensor (arrowed)

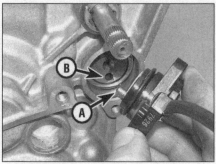

14.21a Remove the sensor, noting how the pin (A) locates in the hole (B)

14.21b Discard the O-ring and fit a new one

14.25 IAT sensor (arrowed) – Street Triple shown

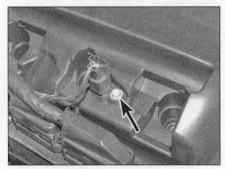

14.27 IAT sensor screw (arrowed) – models from VIN 451399

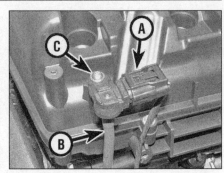

14.29 MAP sensor wiring connector (A), hose (B) and screw (C) – Street Triple from VIN 560477

23 Connect the wiring connector. Check the operation of the neutral light. Install the fuel tank (see Section 2) and the sprocket cover (see Chapter 5).

Intake air temperature sensor

Function

24 The sensor reads the temperature of the air in the airbox. As changes in temperature affect air density, the ECM uses the information to determine fuelling requirements.

Test, removal and installation

25 The sensor is mounted in the airbox cover **(see illustration)**. Make sure the ignition is switched OFF. Raise or remove the fuel tank (see Section 2).
26 To test the sensor resistance, disconnect the wiring connector **(see illustration 3.3a)**. Measure the resistance between the sensor terminals using an ohmmeter or multimeter set to the K-ohms scale. If the result is not as specified for the relevant temperature, the sensor is faulty.
27 To remove the sensor, disconnect the wiring connector **(see illustration 3.3a)**. On models up to VIN 451398 unscrew the sensor from the airbox, and on models from VIN 451399 undo the screw and remove the sensor from the airbox **(see illustration)**. Installation is the reverse of removal.

Manifold absolute pressure sensor

Function

28 The sensor reads the pressure of the air in the throttle bodies. The ECM combines this with other information to determine engine load and adjusts fuelling requirements accordingly.

Removal and installation

29 The sensor is mounted on the airbox **(see illustration 3.3c)**. Make sure the ignition is switched OFF. On Daytona models, and Street Triple models to VIN 560476 remove the airbox (see Section 3). On Street Triple models from VIN 560477 disconnect the intake air temperature (IAT) sensor wiring connector **(see illustration 14.27)**, displace the ECM from the airbox **(see illustrations 12.12a and**

b) – there is no need to disconnect the wiring, then disconnect the (MAP) sensor wiring connector and hose **(see illustration)**. On all models undo the screw securing the sensor to the airbox. Installation is the reverse of removal.

Oxygen (lambda) sensor

Function

30 The sensor measures oxygen left in the unburnt exhaust gases and generates a signal voltage which is fed back to the ECM. In this way the ECM can correct the mixture supplied to the engine to ensure that the oxygen content of the exhaust gases remains within a narrow range and suitable for the operation of the catalytic converter. This type of system is called closed-loop control.

Removal and installation

31 The sensor is located at the 3-into-1 junction in the exhaust downpipe assembly **(see illustration 10.15)**. On Daytona models remove the right-hand fairing side panel (see Chapter 7). On Street Triple models remove the sensor cover.
32 Trace the wiring from the sensor, freeing it from its guides and any ties, and disconnect it at the wiring connector. Feed the wiring back down to the sensor, noting its routing.
33 Unscrew and remove the sensor – the sensor is fragile so care must be taken not to apply undue force. If the sensor is difficult to unscrew or the area around it is badly corroded, apply a penetrating fluid.

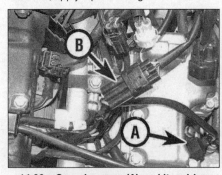

14.36a Speed sensor (A) and its wiring connector (B)

34 When installing the sensor, apply copper grease to the sensor threads and tighten it to the torque setting specified at the beginning of the Chapter – a special tool is required for this because of the wiring. Reconnect the sensor wiring connector – make sure the wiring is correctly routed and secured. On Street Triple models fit the sensor cover. On Daytona models install the right-hand fairing side panel (see Chapter 7).

Speed sensor

Function

35 The sensor reads the road speed of the bike by counting the rate at which the transmission output shaft is turning. This information is used by the ECM in conjunction with engine speed information to determine which gear the bike is in, and controls fuelling and ignition accordingly. The information also helps to determine the idle air control valve setting.

Removal and installation

36 The speed sensor is located in the top of the crankcase **(see illustration)**. Make sure the ignition is switched OFF. Raise or remove the fuel tank to access the wiring connector (see Section 2) – trace the wiring from the sensor to locate it. Disconnect the wiring connector, then unscrew the bolt and remove the sensor **(see illustration)**. Installation is the reverse of removal – check the condition of the O-ring and replace it with a new one if it is deformed

14.36b Unscrew the bolt and remove the sensor

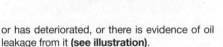
14.36c Fit a new O-ring if necessary

14.43a Tip-over sensor (arrowed) – Daytona

14.43b Tip-over sensor (arrowed) – Street Triple to VIN 560476

or has deteriorated, or there is evidence of oil leakage from it **(see illustration)**.

Throttle position sensor

Function

37 The sensor reads the amount of throttle being used, and the ECM uses this in conjunction with the information from other sensors to determine fuelling and ignition requirements.

Removal and installation

38 The sensor is located on the left-hand end of the throttle body **(see illustration 7.12a)**. Do not remove the throttle position sensor unless you know it is faulty and are replacing it with a new one, or unless you are replacing the throttle body with a new one. If you do remove it, it has to be set up using the Triumph diagnostic tool. There is no alternative, unless you want to run the risk of having the bike running incorrectly.

39 Remove the throttle body (see Section 7). Undo the screws, then rotate the sensor 45° clockwise and draw it off the end of the throttle shaft, noting the position of the O-ring.

40 Fit the O-ring onto the sensor, using a new one if necessary. Locate the sensor onto the end of the throttle shaft, making sure the O-ring seats correctly, then turn it anti-clockwise 45° to align the screw holes finger-tight.

41 Install the throttle body (see Section 7). The sensor must now be set up correctly using the Triumph diagnostic tool. On completion tighten the screws to the torque setting specified at the beginning of the Chapter.

Tip-over sensor

Function

42 The sensor is basically a safety switch that tells the ECM if the bike has fallen over, in which case the ECM will shut down the fuel pump and stop the engine. The switch can be reset by picking the bike up and turning the ignition off, then on again.

Removal and installation

43 On Daytona models the sensor is mounted on the air duct in the fairing **(see illustration)** – remove the fairing for access (see Chapter 7). On Street Triple models to

14.43c Tip-over sensor (arrowed) – Street Triple from VIN 560477

VIN 560476 the sensor is mounted on the airbox **(see illustration)** – raise or remove the fuel tank for access (see Section 2). On Street Triple models from VIN 560477 the sensor is located next to the battery **(see illustration)** – remove the seat for access (see Chapter 7).

44 Disconnect the wiring connector. Unscrew the bolts and remove the sensor.

45 Install the sensor with the UP mark at the top.

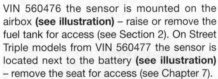

15 Idle air control unit

Check

1 The idle air control unit, located on the throttle body, is actuated by the ECM and set according to information received by the ECM from the various sensors **(see illustration 7.12b)**. The unit is used to control the engine idle speed, to adjust the air supply on engine overrun, to correct for altitude, and for cold starting. The idle speed cannot be adjusted manually.

2 The ECM actuates a stepper motor which moves an arm connected to a lever that contacts the throttle cam and varies the closed throttle position setting. If a fault in the valve is suspected check the wiring connector for loose, corroded or damaged terminals, and the wiring between the valve and the ECM for continuity, referring to 'Electrical system fault

15.7 Unscrew the nut (arrowed) and remove the washers

finding' at the beginning of Chapter 8 and the wiring diagrams at the end of it.

3 Remove the fuel tank and the airbox (see Sections 2 and 3).

4 To test the stepper motor resistance, first make sure the ignition is switched OFF. Disconnect the control valve wiring connector **(see illustration 7.3)**. First measure the resistance between the orange/brown and orange/white wire terminals in the sensor side of the connector using an ohmmeter or multimeter set to the ohms x 10 scale. Next, measure the resistance between the orange/blue and orange/pink wire terminals in the sensor side of the connector. If either of the results is not as specified, the stepper motor is faulty.

Removal

5 The idle air control unit is located on the throttle body **(see illustration 7.12b)**. Do not remove it unless you know it is faulty and are replacing it with a new one, or unless you are replacing the throttle body assembly with a new one. If you do remove it, it has to be set up using the Triumph diagnostic tool. There is no alternative, unless you want to run the risk of having the bike running incorrectly.

6 Remove the throttle body (see Section 7). Make a careful note of the how the actuating lever locates in relation to the throttle cam.

7 Unscrew the nut securing the arm in the lever and remove the metal and plastic washers **(see illustration)**.

8 Undo the screws securing the valve to its bracket, then draw the sensor down to free the arm from the lever **(see illustration)**. Note the plastic collar and spring on the arm, and leave them there.

Installation

9 Make sure the spring and plastic collar are in place on the arm, then fit the unit, locating the arm in the lever, and tighten the screws to the torque setting specified at the beginning of the Chapter. Fit the plastic and metal washers and the nylon nut to secure the arm in the lever. Make sure everything is correctly positioned.

10 Install the throttle body (see Section 7). The sensor must now be set up correctly using the Triumph diagnostic tool.

16 Intake air duct and flap (Daytona models)

Check

1 The intake air duct fits between the front of the fairing and the steering head. A flap inside the duct controls airflow to improve throttle response at low engine speeds. The flap is actuated by a rod coming from a diaphragm unit that responds to a vacuum, and the vacuum is sourced from the intake to the engine, via a reservoir, and is controlled by

15.8 Undo the screws (arrowed) and remove the unit

a solenoid valve which operates on a signal from the ECM **(see illustrations)**. The flap is closed at engine speeds up to 4500 rpm and throttle angles less than 12°, otherwise it is open.

2 If a fault in the flap is suspected remove the left-hand fairing side panel and the fairing (see Chapter 7). Check the solenoid wiring connector for loose, corroded or damaged terminals, and the wiring between the solenoid and the ECM for continuity, referring to 'Electrical system fault finding' at the beginning of Chapter 8 and the wiring diagrams at the end of it. Also check the vacuum reservoir for damage and cracks, and check the hoses to and from the reservoir, and from the solenoid to the flap, are in good condition and secure

at each end. Make sure the lever between the diaphragm and the flap is secure and not bent or damaged.

3 To test the solenoid resistance, first make sure the ignition is switched OFF. Disconnect the wiring connector. Measure the resistance between the terminals in the solenoid side of the connector using an ohmmeter or multimeter set to the ohms x 10 scale. If the result is not as specified, the solenoid is faulty.

Removal and installation

4 To remove the duct, remove the fairing (see Chapter 7). Displace the instrument cluster bracket along with the tip-over sensor and support them aside **(see illustration)**. Displace the atmospheric pressure sensor (see Section 14). Detach the vacuum hose from the diaphragm unit **(see illustration 16.1a)**. Unscrew the duct bolts and remove it **(see illustration)**.

5 To remove the diaphragm unit, remove the fairing (see Chapter 7). Detach the vacuum hose **(see illustration 16.1a)**. Remove the grille from the air duct **(see illustration)**. Turn the diaphragm unit a quarter turn clockwise to release it from the duct, then detach the rod from the flap.

6 To remove the reservoir, remove the left-hand fairing side panel (see Chapter 7). Detach the vacuum hoses, noting which fits

16.1a Intake air duct flap (A) and diaphragm unit (B) . . .

16.1b . . . vacuum reservoir (arrowed) . . .

16.1c . . . and solenoid valve (arrowed)

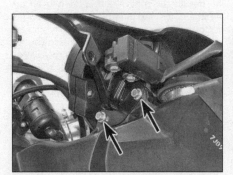

16.4a Unscrew the two bolts (arrowed) on each side and displace the instrument assembly

16.4b Unscrew the bolts (arrowed) on each side and remove the duct

16.5 Remove the grille

16.6 Release the hose and wiring and unscrew the bolt (arrowed)

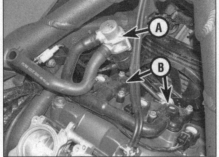

17.1 SAIS control valve (A) and reed valves (B)

17.5 Disconnect the wiring connector

where. Unscrew the bolt and remove the reservoir **(see illustration)**.

7 To remove the solenoid, remove the left-hand fairing side panel (see Chapter 7). Detach the vacuum hoses, noting which fits where **(see illustration 16.1c)**. Disconnect the wiring connector. Release and remove the solenoid.

Installation

8 Installation is the reverse of removal. Make sure the hoses are in good condition, correctly fitted and routed, and secure at each end. The vacuum hose from the throttle bodies fits onto the union marked A on the reservoir. The vacuum hose from the B union on the reservoir fits onto the lower union on the solenoid. The vacuum hose from the upper union on the solenoid fits onto the diaphragm unit.

17 Secondary air injection system (SAIS)

1 The system consists of an electrically actuated solenoid valve located under the front of the airbox and two reed valves in the top of the valve cover, with a hose system supplying air from the airbox via the solenoid valve to the reed valves **(see illustration)**. At certain engine speeds, the electronic control module (ECM) opens the solenoid valve and air is drawn into the exhaust ports via the reed

valves. The introduced air promotes further combustion of the exhaust gases, reducing the level of pollutants. The reed valves prevent exhaust gases blowing back into the airbox.

Solenoid valve and hoses

2 Remove the airbox (see Chapter 4).

3 Check the system hoses for loose connections, cracks and deterioration, and replace them with new ones if necessary.

4 A faulty solenoid valve should be indicated by the malfunction indicator lamp in the instrument cluster, although it is impossible to access fault codes without the use of the Triumph engine management system diagnostic tool.

5 If a fault is indicated trace the wiring from the valve and disconnect it at the connector **(see illustration)**. Check for continuity in the wiring between the loom side of the connector and the ECM. Measure the resistance of the solenoid windings using an ohmmeter connected across the terminals in the valve side of the connector – it should be as specified at the beginning of the Chapter.

6 Release the clip and disconnect the air outlet hose. Remove the valve, noting how it locates.

7 Blow into the valve inlet union – air should flow through the valve and out the outlet union. Now, using a fully charged 12 volt battery and two insulated jumper wires, connect the positive (+) battery terminal to the brown/pink wire terminal in the valve wiring connector and the negative (-) battery terminal to the yellow/

orange wire terminal. Check that the valve has closed by again blowing into the inlet union – no air should flow through the valve. If the valve does not function as described, replace it with a new one.

8 Installation is the reverse of removal. Ensure that the wiring connector terminals are clean and that the connector is secure.

Reed valves

9 Remove the airbox (see Chapter 4).

10 Remove the ignition coils (see Section 11).

11 Release the air hose clips and pull the hoses off the unions on the reed valve covers **(see illustration 17.1)**.

12 Undo the bolts securing the reed valve covers and lift off the covers **(see illustration)**. Lift the reed valves out carefully, noting which way round they fit **(see illustration)**.

13 If required, clean any carbon deposits off the reeds and stopper plates with a suitable solvent, taking care not to distort the reeds. Inspect the seats – if they are damaged or deteriorated, renew the reed assemblies. Hold each valve up to the light and check that there is no gap between the reed and the seat **(see illustration)**.

14 Installation is the reverse of removal. Ensure the reeds are fitted the correct way round and tighten the cover bolts securely.

15 Ensure the air hoses are clipped securely to the cover unions and correctly positioned before the airbox is installed.

17.12a Unscrew the bolts and remove the cover . . .

17.12b . . . and lift the reed valve out

17.13 Make sure there is no gap between the reed and its seat (arrowed)

18 EVAP system –
California market models

1 This system prevents the escape of fuel vapour into the atmosphere by storing it in a charcoal-filled canister located on the frame right-hand side at the rear.

2 When the engine is stopped, fuel vapour from the tank is directed into the canister where it is absorbed and stored whilst the motorcycle is standing. When the engine is started, the purge control valve opens, thus drawing vapours which are stored in the canister into the throttle body to be burned during the normal combustion process.

3 The tank vent pipe also incorporates a roll-over valve which closes and prevents any fuel from escaping through it in the event of the bike falling over. The tank filler cap has a one-way valve which allows air into the tank as the volume of fuel decreases, but prevents any fuel vapour from escaping.

4 The system is not adjustable and can be properly tested only by a Triumph dealer, as the diagnostic tool is required. However the owner can check that all the hoses are in good condition and are securely connected at each end. Replace any hoses that are cracked, split or generally deteriorated with new ones.

5 You can also check the purge valve by disconnecting the wiring connector and measuring the resistance of the valve using an ohmmeter. If the result is not as specified at the beginning of the Chapter, in particular if there is infinite or no resistance, replace the valve with a new one.

19 Catalytic converter

General information

1 The catalytic converter minimises the level of exhaust pollutants released into the atmosphere. It consists of a canister containing a fine mesh impregnated with a catalyst material, over which the hot exhaust gases pass. The catalyst speeds up the oxidation of harmful carbon monoxide, unburned hydrocarbons and soot, effectively reducing the quantity of harmful products released into the atmosphere via the exhaust gases.

2 The catalytic converter is housed in the exhaust downpipe assembly.

3 It operates under closed-loop control with an oxygen (Lambda) sensor feeding back gas oxygen content information to the ECM; information on the sensor can be found in Section 14.

Precautions

4 The catalytic converter is a reliable and simple device which needs no maintenance in itself, but there are some precautions the owner should note if the converter is to function properly for its full service life.

● DO NOT use leaded or lead replacement petrol (gasoline) – the additives will coat the precious metals, reducing their converting efficiency and will eventually destroy the catalytic converter.

● Always keep the ignition and fuel systems well-maintained in accordance with the manufacturer's schedule – if the fuel/air mixture is suspected of being incorrect have it checked on an exhaust gas analyser.

● If the engine develops a misfire, do not ride the bike at all (or at least as little as possible) until the fault is cured.

● DO NOT use fuel or engine oil additives – these may contain substances harmful to the catalytic converter.

● DO NOT continue to use the bike if the engine burns oil to the extent of leaving a visible trail of blue smoke.

● Remember that the catalytic converter is FRAGILE – do not strike it with tools during servicing work.

20 Immobiliser

General information

Note: *The immobiliser is fitted to Street Triple models from VIN 560477. The control unit also controls the tyre pressure monitoring system (TPMS), if fitted. Refer to Chapter 6 for details on the TPMS.*

1 The immobiliser will only allow the engine to be started if the signal sent from a transponder in the ignition key is recognised by the ECM. The signal from the transponder is picked up and transmitted by a receiver fitted around the top of the ignition switch to the immobiliser control unit, which in turn corresponds with the ECM. The system has its own self-diagnostic function. The immobiliser system components must be paired with the ECM and this can only be done using the Triumph diagnostic tool. The bike comes from the factory with two paired keys. A further two keys can be paired with the system.

2 An immobiliser light in the instrument cluster flashes for twenty-four hours when the immobiliser is active. When the ignition is turned on, and the key transponder is recognised by the ECM, the light goes out.

3 If the light comes on and stays on when the ignition is turned on there is a fault in the system. The Triumph diagnostic tool is required for fault code retrieval.

Immobiliser control unit

4 The immobiliser control unit is mounted inside the airbox. Remove the air filter (see Chapter 1).

5 Release the immobiliser ECM wiring connector from its bracket and disconnect it **(see illustrations 3.11a and b)**.

6 Undo the two screws and remove the control unit **(see illustration)**.

7 Installation is the reverse of removal.

Immobiliser receiver

8 The receiver is an integral part of the ignition switch and is not available separately. Refer to Chapter 8 for removal and installation of the switch.

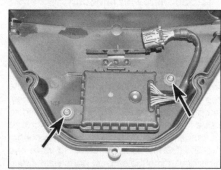

20.6 Immobiliser control unit screws (arrowed)

Chapter 5
Frame and suspension

Contents

Degrees of difficulty

Easy, suitable for novice with little experience 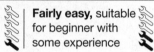	**Fairly easy,** suitable for beginner with some experience	**Fairly difficult,** suitable for competent DIY mechanic	**Difficult,** suitable for experienced DIY mechanic	**Very difficult,** suitable for expert DIY or professional

Specifications

Front forks

Fork oil type
Daytona and all Street Triple models	Kayaba KHL 15-10 or equivalent 5W fork oil
Daytona R	Ohlins fork oil 10309-01

Fork oil capacity
Daytona	
Up to VIN 381274	495 cc
From VIN 381275-on	492 cc
Daytona R	497 cc
Street Triple	
Up to VIN 560476	465 cc
From VIN 560477-on	505 cc
Street Triple R	
Up to VIN 560476	484 cc
From VIN 560477-on	483 cc

Fork oil level*
Daytona	
Up to VIN 381274	72 mm
From VIN 381275-on	89 mm
Daytona R	130 mm
Street Triple	
Up to VIN 560476	107 mm
From VIN 560477-on	86 mm
Street Triple R	
Up to VIN 560476	93 mm
From VIN 560477-on	89 mm

* Oil level is measured from the top of the tube with the fork spring removed and the leg fully compressed.

Torque wrench settings

Clutch lever bracket clamp bolts	12 Nm
Clutch lever pivot bolt locknut	3.5 Nm
Fork clamp bolts	
Top yoke	26 Nm
Bottom yoke – Daytona	20 Nm
Bottom yoke – Street Triple	22 Nm
Fork damper cartridge bolt	24 Nm

Torque wrench settings (continued)

Fork top bolt	
Daytona and Street Triple models	22 Nm
Daytona R	20 Nm
Front brake lever pivot bolt	1 Nm
Front brake lever pivot bolt locknut	6 Nm
Front brake master cylinder bracket clamp bolts	15 Nm
Front footrest bracket bolts	24 Nm
Gearchange lever pivot bolt	22 Nm
Handlebar bolts	
Daytona	
Positioning bolts	3 Nm
Clamp bolts	26 Nm
Street Triple	
Clamp bolts	26 Nm
Holder bolt nuts	35 Nm
Handlebar end-weight screws	3 Nm
Rear brake pedal pivot bolt	22 Nm
Rear shock absorber bolts/nuts	48 Nm
Rear suspension linkage bolts/nuts	48 Nm
Sidestand bracket bolts	45 Nm
Sidestand pivot bolt	20 Nm
Steering damper bolts	18 Nm
Steering head bearing adjuster locknut	40 Nm
Steering head bearing adjuster nut	
Initial (pre-load) setting	40 Nm
Final setting	
Daytona models and Street Triple models to VIN 560476	15 Nm
Street Triple models from VIN 560477	10 Nm
Steering stem nut	90 Nm
Swingarm	
Adjuster bolt	6 Nm
Pivot bolt nut	110 Nm

1 General information

All models have a twin spar aluminium frame that uses the engine as a stressed member.

Front suspension is by a pair of upside-down oil-damped telescopic forks with a cartridge-type damper. The forks are adjustable for spring pre-load, rebound damping and compression damping on 2006 to 2008 Daytona models (up to VIN 377509) and Street Triple R models, and for spring pre-load, rebound damping and both low and high speed compression damping on 2009 and later Daytona models (from VIN 377510-on). On standard Street Triples the forks are not adjustable.

At the rear, an aluminium alloy twin-sided swingarm acts on a single shock absorber via a three-way linkage. The shock absorber is adjustable for rebound damping and compression damping on 2006 to 2008 Daytona models (up to VIN 377509) and Street Triple R models, and for rebound damping and both low and high speed compression damping on 2009 and later Daytona models (from VIN 377510-on). On standard Street Triples the shock absorber is not adjustable.

Many of the bolts used on Triumph motorcycles are of the Torx type. Unless you are already equipped with a good range of Torx bits, you are advised to obtain a set. Make sure you buy bits that can be used in conjunction with a socket set so that a torque wrench can be applied – a Torx key set will not be adequate on its own, though will be useful in addition to the bits.

2 Frame

1 The frame should not require attention unless accident damage has occurred. In most cases, fitment of a new frame is the only satisfactory remedy for such damage. A few frame specialists have the jigs and other equipment necessary for straightening the frame to the required standard of accuracy, but even then there is no simple way of assessing to what extent the frame may have been over stressed.

2 After the machine has accumulated a lot of miles, the frame should be examined closely for signs of cracking or splitting at the welded joints. Loose engine mounting bolts can cause ovaling or fracturing of the mounts themselves. Minor damage can often be repaired by welding, depending on the extent and nature of the damage, but this is a task for an expert.

3 Remember that a frame which is out of alignment will cause handling problems. If misalignment is suspected as the result of an accident, it will be necessary to strip the machine completely so the frame can be thoroughly checked.

3 Footrests, brake pedal and gearchange lever

Footrests

1 Remove the E-clip from the bottom of the footrest pivot pin, then withdraw the pivot pin and remove the footrest (see illustration). On the rider's footrests, note the fitting of the return spring. On the passenger footrests, note

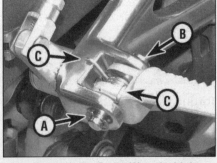

3.1a Remove the E-clip (A) and withdraw the pivot pin (B) – note the return spring ends (C) . . .

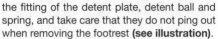

3.1b . . . and on the passenger footrest the detent plate, ball and spring (arrowed)

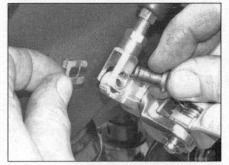

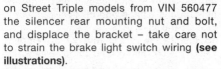

3.4 Remove the clip, withdraw the pin and detach the pushrod

3.5a Unscrew the bolts (arrowed) and displace the bracket to access the pivot bolt

the fitting of the detent plate, detent ball and spring, and take care that they do not ping out when removing the footrest **(see illustration)**.
2 On all models, the bank angle indicators on the end of the footrests can be replaced with new ones.
3 Installation is the reverse of removal.

Brake pedal

Removal

4 Remove the clevis pin retaining clip, then withdraw the pin and separate the pedal from the pushrod **(see illustration)** – on Street Triple models from VIN 560477 for best access do this after completing Steps 5 to 7, and if necessary displace the master cylinder from the bracket.
5 Unscrew the footrest bracket bolts, and

on Street Triple models from VIN 560477 the silencer rear mounting nut and bolt, and displace the bracket – take care not to strain the brake light switch wiring **(see illustrations)**.
6 Unhook the brake pedal return spring and the brake light switch spring **(see illustration)**.
7 Hold the bracket, unscrew the pivot bolt and remove the pedal **(see illustration 3.6)**.

Installation

8 Installation is the reverse of removal, noting the following:
● Apply grease to the brake pedal pivot and the bush in the pedal. Tighten the pedal pivot bolt to the torque setting specified at the beginning of the Chapter.
● Clean the threads of the footrest bracket

bolts, then apply some fresh threadlock and tighten them to the specified torque.
● If necessary use a new retaining clip on the clevis pin securing the brake pedal to the master cylinder pushrod.
● Check the operation of the rear brake light switch (see Chapter 1, Section 10).

Gearchange lever

Removal

9 Release the clip securing the linkage rod or quickshifter to the gearchange lever **(see illustrations)**. Pry the rod or quickshifter off the lever **(see illustration)**. To improve access on Street Triple models remove the heel guard first. Take care not to lose the ball-joint seal.
10 Unscrew the footrest bracket bolts and displace the bracket **(see illustration)**.

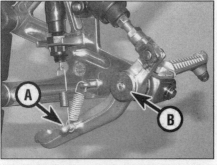

3.5b Silencer rear mounting nut/bolt (arrowed) – Street Triple from VIN 560477

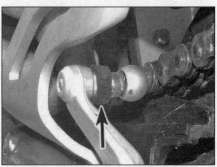

3.6 Unhook the springs (A) from the pedal. Brake pedal pivot bolt (B)

3.9a Move the top of the clip off . . .

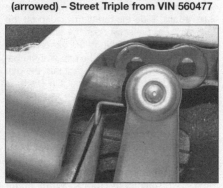

3.9b . . . then draw it out . . .

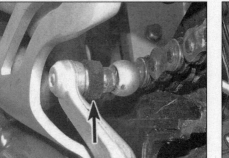

3.9c . . . and detach the rod from the lever. Note the seal (arrowed)

3.10 Unscrew the bolts (arrowed) and displace the bracket . . .

3.11 . . . to access the pivot bolt (arrowed)

3.13a Quickshifter wire connector

3.13b Quickshifter sensor

11 Hold the bracket, unscrew the pivot bolt and remove the lever **(see illustration)**.

Installation

12 Installation is the reverse of removal, noting the following:

- Apply grease to the gear lever pivot and the bush in the lever. Tighten the pivot bolt to the specified torque.
- Clean the threads of the front footrest bracket bolts, apply threadlock and tighten to the specified torque.
- Check the condition of the ball joint seal.

Quickshifter

13 Raise the fuel tank (see Chapter 4). Disconnect the quickshifter wiring connector **(see illustration)**. Feed the connector down to the quickshifter, noting its routing. To improve access on Street Triple models remove the heel guard **(see illustration)**.
14 Release the clips securing the quickshifter

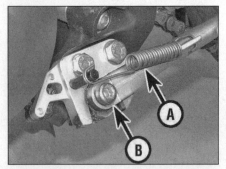

4.2 Unhook the springs (A), then unscrew the pivot bolt (B) and remove the stand

5.4 Remove the end-weight (arrowed) from each side

rod to the gearchange lever and linkage arm and pry the rod off the lever and arm **(see illustrations 3.9a, b and c)**. Take care not to lose the ball-joint seals.
15 Installation is the reverse of removal. Check the condition of the ball joint seals.

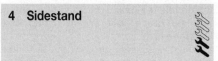

4   Sidestand

1 Support the motorcycle on an auxiliary stand.
2 Unhook the stand springs **(see illustration)**.
3 Unscrew the pivot bolt and remove the stand, noting how it locates against the switch plunger **(see illustration 4.2)**.
4 If required refer to Chapter 8, Section 19 and remove the sidestand bracket and switch.
5 On installation grease the pivot section of the bolt and the contact surfaces of the stand

5.3 Clutch lever bracket clamp bolts (arrowed)

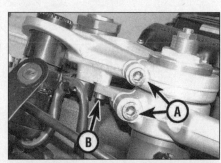

5.5a Slacken the clamp bolts (A) and unscrew the positioning bolt (B) on each side of the yoke

and bracket. Tighten the stand pivot bolt and the bracket bolts, to the specified torque settings. Reconnect the sidestand springs and check the stand is held securely up.
6 Check the operation of the sidestand switch (see Chapter 8).

5   Handlebars and levers

Handlebars

Removal

Note: *The handlebars can be displaced from the forks or top yoke without having to remove the lever or switch assemblies.*

1 On Daytona models, to prevent the possibility of damage, remove the fairing, fairing side panels and fuel tank (see Chapters 7 and 4). On Street Triple models, remove the mirrors (see Chapter 7).
2 On the right-hand side, displace the front brake master cylinder and reservoir (see Chapter 6). There is no need to disconnect the hydraulic hose, just keep the reservoir upright. Displace the handlebar switch housing (see Chapter 8) and disconnect the throttle cables from the twistgrip (see Chapter 4).
3 On the left-hand side, displace the handlebar switch housing (see Chapter 8). Unscrew the two bolts securing the clutch lever bracket to the handlebar **(see illustration)**; there is no need to detach the clutch cable.
4 Remove the handlebar end-weights **(see illustration)**. Slide the throttle twistgrip off the right-hand bar. Either slit open the left grip using a sharp blade and peel it off the bar or work a small screwdriver between the grip and the bar and spray some aerosol lubricant into the gap (take care to shield your eyes). On Daytona models, if required release the clip securing the internal weight in each handlebar using suitable pliers, then withdraw the weight with its rubber dampers; a new clip must be fitted.
5 On Daytona models slacken the handlebar clamp bolts and the fork clamp bolts in the top yoke **(see illustration)**. Unscrew the handlebar positioning bolts. Wrap some masking tap around the steering stem nut to protect its finish **(see illustration 9.4)**.

5.5b Unscrew the steering stem nut

5.5c Lift the top yoke up and rest it on some rag

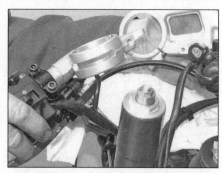

5.5d Slide the handlebar up and off the fork

Unscrew the nut **(see illustration)**. Ease the top yoke up off the forks and lay it clear of the steering stem on some rag **(see illustration)**. Ease the handlebar up and off the fork and either remove it, or displace it and lay it aside on some rag **(see illustration)**.

6 On Street Triple models, unscrew the handlebar holder clamp bolts, then remove the clamp(s) and either remove the handlebars, or displace them and lay them on some rag **(see illustration)**. If required unscrew the handlebar holder nuts on the underside of the top yoke and remove the holders, on models to VIN 560476 noting the washers and the arrangement of the rubber dampers and sleeves **(see illustration)**.

Installation

7 On Daytona models, installation is the reverse of removal, noting the following.
● Fit the handlebars loosely on the forks, then fit the top yoke **(see illustrations 5.5d and c)**. Tighten the steering stem nut first, then the fork clamp bolts, then align the handlebars and tighten the positioning bolt, followed by the clamp bolt, tightening them all to the torque settings specified at the beginning of the Chapter **(see illustrations 5.5b and a)**.
● If removed fit a new clip onto the outer end of each inner weight, then slide the weight, with its rubber dampers, into each handlebar so the clip tabs locate in the holes.
● Apply some rubber adhesive to the left-hand bar before fitting the grip. Apply some grease to the right-hand bar before sliding on the throttle twistgrip. Fit the end-weights.
● Refer to the relevant Chapters as directed for the installation of the handlebar mounted assemblies.
● Fit the clutch lever bracket and front brake master cylinder clamps with the UP mark facing up, and align the clutch lever clamp/bracket mating surfaces with the punch mark on the handlebar, and the master cylinder/clamp mating surfaces with the punch mark on Daytona, and with the L mark on Daytona R. Tighten the upper clamp bolt first, then the lower bolt, to the specified torque setting.
● Adjust throttle and clutch cable freeplay (see Chapter 1).

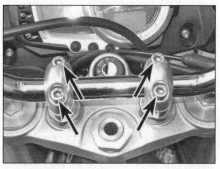

5.6a Handlebar holder clamp bolts (arrowed)

● Check the operation of the switches, the throttle, the front brake and the clutch before taking the machine on the road.
8 On Street Triple models, installation is the reverse of removal, noting the following
● If you removed the handlebar holders from the top yoke tighten the nuts on the underside to the torque setting specified at the beginning of the Chapter, on models to VIN 560476 making sure the sleeves and rubber dampers are correctly fitted – use new dampers if necessary. Make sure the handlebars are central in the holders, and align the mark in the front of the handlebar with the mating surfaces of the right-hand clamp and holder **(see illustration)**. Tighten the front clamp bolts first, then the rear, to the torque setting specified at the beginning of the Chapter.
● Apply some rubber adhesive to the left-hand bar before fitting the grip. Apply some grease to the right-hand bar before

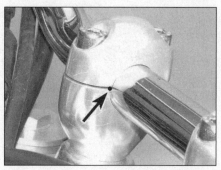

5.8 Align the punch mark with the clamp mating surfaces

5.6b Handlebar holder nut (arrowed)

sliding on the throttle twistgrip. Fit the end-weights.
● Refer to the relevant Chapters as directed for the installation of the handlebar mounted assemblies.
● Fit the clutch lever bracket and front brake master cylinder clamps with the UP mark facing up and align the clamp/bracket mating surfaces with the punch marks on the handlebar. Tighten the upper clamp bolt first, then the lower bolt, to the specified torque setting.
● Adjust throttle and clutch cable freeplay (see Chapter 1).
● Check the operation of the switches, the throttle, the front brake and the clutch before taking the machine on the road.

Clutch lever

9 Thread the clutch cable adjuster fully into the bracket to provide maximum freeplay in the cable **(see illustration)**. Unscrew the lever

5.9a Thread the adjuster fully in

5.9b Clutch lever pivot bolt locknut (arrowed)

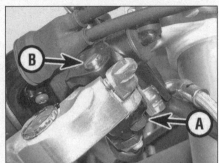

5.11 Brake lever pivot bolt locknut (A), pivot bolt (B)

pivot bolt locknut (see illustration). Tap the pivot bolt up and withdraw it, then remove the lever, detaching the cable nipple as you do so.
10 Installation is the reverse of removal. Apply grease to the pivot bolt shaft and the contact areas between the lever and its bracket, and to the clutch cable nipple. Fit the pivot bolt, then fit the locknut and tighten it to the torque setting specified at the beginning of the Chapter. Adjust the clutch cable freeplay (see Chapter 1).

Front brake lever

11 Unscrew the lever pivot bolt locknut, then unscrew the pivot bolt and remove the lever (see illustration).
12 Installation is the reverse of removal. Apply grease to the pivot bolt shaft and the contact areas between the lever and its bracket. Tighten the pivot bolt to the torque setting specified at

the beginning of the Chapter, then fit the locknut and tighten it to the specified torque.

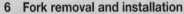

6 Fork removal and installation

Removal

Caution: Although not strictly necessary, and where applicable, before removing the forks it is recommended that the fairing side panels and/or fairing are removed (see Chapter 7). This will prevent accidental damage to the paintwork should a tool slip.
1 On Daytona models remove the fairing side panels, and if required the fairing (see Chapter 7).
2 Displace the front brake calipers (see

Chapter 6). There is no need to disconnect the hydraulic hoses.
3 Remove the front wheel (see Chapter 6).
4 Remove the front mudguard (see Chapter 7).
5 Work on each fork individually. Mark each fork to denote on which side it fits. Note the routing of the various cables and hoses around the forks, and release any cable-ties that secure them.
6 On Daytona models, when removing the right-hand fork, unscrew the front brake fluid reservoir bracket bolt and displace the reservoir, noting how the pin on the underside locates in the hole (see illustration). Slacken the handlebar clamp bolt and the fork clamp bolt in the top yoke (see illustration).
7 On Street Triple models slacken the fork clamp bolt in the top yoke (see illustration 6.6b).
8 If the forks are to be overhauled, or if the fork oil is being changed, on Daytona and Street Triple models wrap some masking tape around the fork top bolt to protect the finish, then slacken the bolt now whilst it is still clamped in the bottom yoke (see illustrations). On Daytona R models slacken the top bolt using the Triumph Special tool, part No. T3880161.
9 Measure the protrusion of the tops of the fork tube with the top yoke. Slacken but do not remove the fork clamp bolts in the bottom yoke (see illustration). Remove the fork by twisting it and pulling it downwards (see illustration).

6.6a Displace the reservoir to give access to the clamp bolts – note how the pin locates in the hole

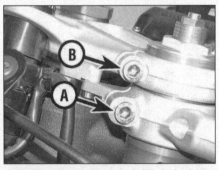

6.6b Handlebar clamp bolt (A), fork clamp bolt (B)

6.8a If required wrap some tape around the fork top bolt . . .

6.8b . . . and slacken the bolt now

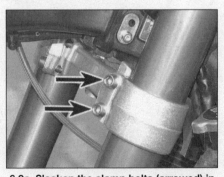

6.9a Slacken the clamp bolts (arrowed) in the bottom yoke . . .

6.9b . . . then draw the fork down and out of the yokes

6.11a Fork position measurement –
Daytona models, and Street Triple models
to VIN 560476

6.11b Fork position measurement – Street
Triple models from VIN 560477

If the fork legs are seized in the yokes, spray the area with penetrating oil and allow time for it to soak in before trying again.

Installation

10 Remove all traces of corrosion from the fork tubes and the yokes. Make sure you fit the fork to its correct side as noted on removal.

11 Slide the fork up through the bottom yoke, and the handlebar on Daytona models, and up into the top yoke, making sure the wiring, cables and hoses are the correct side of the fork as noted on removal **(see illustration 6.9c)**. Set the fork in the top yoke so the distance between the fork top bolt and the top of the fork tube is 4 mm above the top surface of the top yoke on all Daytona models and Street Triple models to VIN 560476, and 28 mm above the bottom

surface of the top yoke on Street Triple models from VIN 560477 **(see illustrations)**. Note that this is the standard setting specified by Triumph – if the setting you measured on removal is different because you have knowingly altered it, and you are aware of the implications this has on the geometry and handling of the bike, then set the forks as you prefer.

12 Tighten the fork clamp bolts in the bottom yoke to the torque setting specified at the beginning of the Chapter; tighten the upper bolt first, then the lower, and retighten the upper bolt **(see illustration 6.9b)**. If the fork leg has been dismantled or if the fork oil has been changed, tighten the fork top bolt to the specified torque setting **(see illustration 6.8b)**. Now tighten the fork clamp bolt in the top yoke, and the handlebar clamp bolt on Daytona models, to the specified torque settings **(see illustration 6.6b)**.

13 Install the front mudguard (see Chapter 7),

front wheel (see Chapter 6), and brake calipers (see Chapter 6).

14 On Daytona models, install the brake fluid reservoir **(see illustration 6.6a)**, the fairing if removed, and the fairing side panels (see Chapter 7).

15 Check the operation of the front forks and brakes before taking the machine out on the road.

7 Fork oil change

Daytona (except R) and all Street Triple models

Special Tool: *A special holding tool is needed to disassemble the forks – see Step 4. Triumph produces a service tool kit, comprising a spacer holder and stopper plate (Pt. No. TT3880067) to do this. Alternatively, use the set-up shown – the inner end of each handle locates in a hole in the spacer, and the slotted washer locates around the damper rod and under the locknut, so must be sized accordingly (see illustration 7.4a).*

1 After a high mileage the fork oil will deteriorate and its damping and lubrication qualities will be impaired. Always change the oil in both forks. Work on one fork at a time. On Daytona and Street Triple R models note the spring pre-load setting (see Section 13).

2 Remove the fork – make sure the top bolt is loosened while the leg is still clamped in the bottom yoke (see Section 6).

3 Support the fork upright and unscrew the top bolt from the top of the outer tube **(see illustration)**. Slide the outer tube down over the inner tube.

4 With the aid of an assistant and using a suitable tool **(see illustration)**, pull up on the fork top bolt, then press down on the spacer to compress the spring and expose the locknut on the bottom of the top bolt **(see illustration)**. Insert the stopper plate or slotted washer under the locknut **(see illustration)**. Carefully release the pressure on the spacer and allow the plate or slotted washer to rest against the underside of the locknut under spring pressure.

5 Counter-hold the locknut and loosen the top bolt, then thread the top bolt assembly off the damper rod **(see illustration)**. On Daytona and

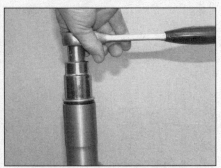

7.3 Unscrew the top bolt

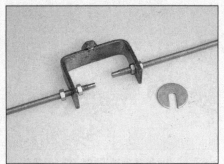

7.4a Tool for dismantling forks

7.4b Using the tool . . .

7.4c . . . push the spacer down and fit the washer under the locknut

7.5a Hold the locknut and thread the top bolt off

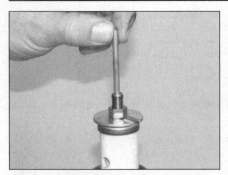

7.5b Withdraw the adjuster rod where fitted

7.9 Pour in the correct type and quantity of oil and pump the damper rod to circulate it

7.10 Measure the oil level and adjust if necessary

Street Triple R models withdraw the damping adjuster rod **(see illustration)**. Thread the locknut up to the top of the damping rod, but not off it **(see illustration 7.14a)** – this makes compressing the spring easier. **Note:** *The top bolt assembly should not be disassembled.*

6 Compress the spacer and remove the plate or slotted washer, then carefully allow the spring to relax. Remove the shaped washer where fitted, and the spacer **(see illustrations 7.13b and a)**. Withdraw the spring from the tube, noting which way up it fits **(see illustration 7.12)**.

7 Invert the fork leg over a suitable container and pump the fork and damper rod to expel as much oil as possible.

8 Support the leg and allow it to drain for several minutes, pumping it again. Wipe any excess oil off the spring and spacer. If the fork oil contains metal particles inspect the fork components for signs of wear (see Section 8).

9 Slowly pour in the correct quantity and type of fork oil as specified at the beginning of this Chapter **(see illustration)**. Draw the damper rod out of the fork using long-nosed pliers and pump the rod several times to circulate the oil and expel air from the damper cartridge. Secure the fork leg upright and allow it to stand for several minutes to allow all the air to escape. Now pump the rod several times again – once all the air is expelled you should feel stiff resistance when pumping the rod. Take great care to ensure that all air is expelled from the damper cartridge at this stage.

10 Fully compress the fork and damper rod and measure the oil level from the top of the tube **(see illustration)**. Add or subtract oil until it is at the level specified at the beginning of this Chapter for your model.

11 Draw the damper rod out. Fit a piece of thin wire around the rod under the locknut to help keep it extended **(see illustration)**.

12 Fit the spring into the fork with the closer-wound coils at the top, passing it over the wire **(see illustration)**.

13 Fit the spacer into the top of the spring, then fit the washer where removed **(see illustrations)**, sliding them over the wire.

14 Keeping the damper rod fully extended, press down on the spacer to compress the spring (see Step 4), then remove the wire and insert the stopper plate or slotted washer under the locknut **(see illustration 7.4b and c)**. Now thread the locknut back down **(see illustration)** – make sure the locknut is positioned so the amount of exposed thread above it as follows according to model **(see illustration)**: 12 mm on Daytona models to VIN 381274, 11 mm on Daytona models from

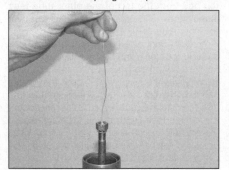

7.11 Wrap some thin wire under the locknut to hold the damper rod up

7.12 Fit the spring with the closer-wound coils at the top

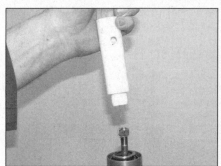

7.13a Fit the spacer onto the spring . . .

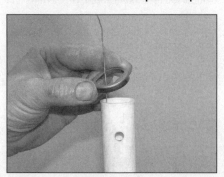

7.13b . . . then fit the washer onto the spacer

7.14a Thread the locknut down . . .

7.14b . . . and on Daytona set it to the correct position

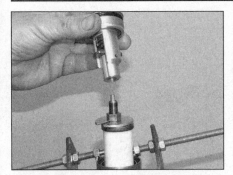

7.15 Thread the top bolt onto the rod

7.16 Make sure the spacer seats correctly over the top bolt and against the bar

VIN 381275 and Street Triple R models to VIN 560476, and 13 mm on Street Triple models from VIN 560477. On Street Triple models the locknut should be at the bottom of the threads.

15 Make sure the top bolt O-ring is in good condition then smear some fork oil onto it. On Daytona and Street Triple R models slide the damping adjuster rod into the damper rod **(see illustration 7.5b)**. Fit the top bolt and thread it all the way down to the locknut on Daytona and Street Triple R models, and as far as it will go on Street Triple models **(see illustration)**. Counter-hold the top bolt and tighten the locknut against it **(see illustration 7.5a)**.

16 Press down on the spacer to compress the spring and remove the plate or slotted washer, then carefully release the spring pressure, making sure the spacer seats correctly against the horizontal bar in the top bolt **(see illustration)**. Remove the holding tool.

17 Pull the outer tube all the way out of the inner tube and carefully screw the top bolt into the tube making sure it is not cross-threaded **(see illustration 7.3)**. Tighten the top bolt to the specified torque when the fork leg has been installed and is securely clamped in the bottom yoke.

18 Install the fork (see Section 6).

Daytona R

Special Tool: *Two special tools, a pin socket, part No. T3880161, for the fork top bolt, and a deep-set open spanner, part No. T3880162, for the locknut, are needed to disassemble the forks – see Steps 22 and 23. Due to the cost of these tools, and the relatively little use you will get from them, you may want to consider having the oil changed by a Triumph dealer or an Ohlins service centre – ask them for a cost comparison.*

19 After a high mileage the fork oil will deteriorate and its damping and lubrication qualities will be impaired. Always change the oil in both forks. Work on one fork at a time. Note the spring pre-load setting (see Section 13).

20 Remove the fork – make sure the top bolt is loosened while the leg is still clamped in the bottom yoke (see Section 6).

21 Refer to Section 13 and set the spring pre-load to its minimum setting, noting the number of turns.

22 Support the fork upright and unscrew the top bolt from the top of the outer tube using the special tool T3880161. Slide the outer tube down over the inner tube.

23 Counter-hold the locknut using tool T3880162 and loosen the top bolt using tool T3880161, then thread the top bolt off the damper rod. Thread the locknut off the top of the damping rod and remove the upper seat and the spring, noting which way up it fits. Draw the spacer out using a piece of wire as a hook.

24 Invert the fork leg over a suitable container, and pump the damper rod to expel as much oil as possible – make sure the damping adjuster rod does not come out of the damper rod as there is a sprung valve under it. Support the leg and allow it to drain for several minutes, pumping the damper rod again. Wipe any excess oil off the spring and spacer. If the fork oil contains metal particles inspect the fork components for signs of wear (see Section 8).

25 Slowly pour in the correct quantity and type of fork oil as specified at the beginning of this Chapter **(see illustration 7.9)**. Draw the damper rod out and pump it several times to circulate the oil and expel air from the damper cartridge. Secure the fork leg upright and allow it to stand for several minutes to allow all the air to escape. Now pump the rod several times again – once all the air is expelled you should feel stiff resistance when pumping the rod. Take great care to ensure that all air is expelled from the damper cartridge at this stage.

26 Fully compress the fork and damper rod and measure the oil level from the top of the tube **(see illustration 7.10)**. Add or subtract oil until it is at the level specified at the beginning of this Chapter.

27 Draw the damper rod out and fit the spacer into the fork – after fitting the spacer keep a hold of the top of the damper rod to prevent it sinking down.

28 Fit the spring into the fork – you will have to let go of the damper rod, but grab a hold of it as soon as the spring is seated using a pair of long-nosed pliers inserted from the side between the coils of the spring.

29 Fit the upper seat then thread the locknut onto the rod – you can now let go of the rod.

30 Now thread the locknut all the way down – make sure the spring is correctly seated on the underside of the seat.

31 Make sure the top bolt O-ring is in good condition then smear some fork oil onto it. Fit the top bolt and thread it all the way down to the locknut – do not thread the locknut up to the top bolt. Counter-hold the top bolt and tighten the locknut securely against it.

32 Pull the outer tube all the way out of the inner tube and carefully screw the top bolt into the tube making sure it is not cross-threaded. Tighten the top bolt to the specified torque when the fork leg has been installed and is securely clamped in the bottom yoke.

33 Install the fork (see Section 6).

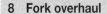

8 Fork overhaul

Disassembly

1 Remove the fork – make sure that the top bolt is loosened while the leg is still clamped in the bottom yoke (see Section 6). Always dismantle the fork legs separately to avoid interchanging parts. Store all components in separate, clearly marked containers. Remove the axle clamp bolts from the bottom of the right- or left-hand fork, according to model (not necessary on Daytona R).

2 On models except the Daytona R, if you want to remove the damper cartridge from the fork (this is not necessary if for example you are just fitting new seals) slacken the damper cartridge bolt in the bottom of the fork, then lightly re-tighten it to prevent oil coming out **(see illustration)**. If the bolt does not loosen, turn the leg upside down and compress the fork so that the spring exerts maximum pressure on the damper cartridge assembly to prevent it turning, then try to loosen the bolt. If you still have no luck, and an air wrench is not available, carry on and obtain a holding tool as described in Step 5. On Daytona R models there should be no need to ever remove the damper cartridge from the fork – neither it nor the inner tube into which it threads are available separately from the complete fork,

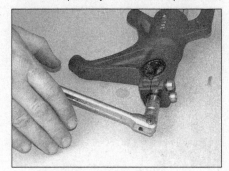

8.2 Slacken the damper rod bolt

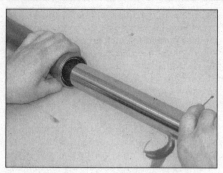

8.4 Draw the inner tube out

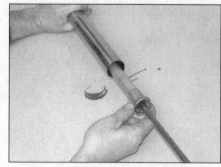

8.6 Withdraw the damper

8.7a Prise out the dust seal using a flat-bladed screwdriver . . .

and no individual components of the damper cartridge are available, so if there is a problem with any of the components the complete fork will have to be replaced with a new one.

3 Refer to Section 7, Steps 3 to 8 for models except the Daytona R, and Steps 19 to 24 for Daytona R models, and drain the fork oil.

4 Draw the inner tube out of the outer tube **(see illustration)**.

5 On models except the Daytona R, if required remove the previously loosened damper cartridge bolt and its sealing washer from the bottom of the inner tube **(see illustration 8.2)**. Discard the washer as a new one must be fitted on reassembly. If the damper cartridge bolt was impossible to slacken as described in Step 2, note that a Triumph service tool (Pt. No. T3880028) is available to hold the damper cartridge while the bolt is unscrewed – the tool passes down over the damper rod and engages the top of the cartridge body.

6 On models except the Daytona R withdraw the damper cartridge assembly from inside the inner tube **(see illustration)**.

7 Carefully prise the dust seal from the bottom of the outer tube **(see illustration)**. Remove the retaining clip **(see illustration)**. Discard the seal as a new one must be fitted on reassembly.

8 Carefully prise out the oil seal using a seal hook, taking great care not to damage the rim of the tube – on the fork photographed the seal was not tight, but if it is you may need to use an internal puller with slide-hammer attachment **(see illustrations)**. Remove the oil seal washer **(see illustration 8.15)**. Discard the seals as new ones must be fitted on reassembly.

Inspection

9 Clean all parts in a suitable solvent and blow them dry with compressed air, if available.

10 Check the outer surface of the fork inner

tube for score marks, scratches, pitting and flaking of the finish, and excessive or abnormal wear. Look for creases and dents. Check the tube for runout using V-blocks and a dial gauge. If the condition of the inner tube is suspect have it checked by a Triumph dealer or suspension specialist. Triumph provides no specifications for runout.

11 Inspect the inside surface of the outer tube and the working surface of each bush for score marks, scratches and signs of excessive wear (in which case the grey Teflon outer surface will have worn away to reveal the copper inner surface) **(see illustration)**. They are not available separately, so if necessary a new outer tube will have to be fitted.

12 Check the fork oil seal seat for nicks, gouges and scratches. If damage is evident, leaks will occur. Also check the oil seal washer for damage or distortion and replace it with a new one if necessary.

13 Check the spring for cracks and other damage. If the spring is defective or has sagged, fit new springs in both forks. Never fit only one new spring.

14 Check the damper cartridge for damage and wear. Hold the cartridge and gently pump the rod in and out. If the rod does not move smoothly, on models except the Daytona R the damper must be replaced with a new one, and on Daytona R the complete fork must be replaced with a new one.

Reassembly

15 Fit the oil seal washer into the bottom of the outer tube **(see illustration)**.

8.7b . . . then remove the retaining clip

8.8a Fit the puller under the seal and expand it . . .

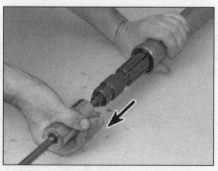

8.8b . . . then jar the seal out using a slide-hammer attachment

8.11 Check the working surface of each bush

8.15 Fit the washer

8.16a Fit the new seal and press it in

8.16b Fit the old seal on top . . .

8.16c . . . to protect the new one as you drive it in . . .

8.17 Fit the retaining clip

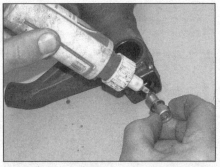

8.18 Apply a thread locking compound to the damper rod bolt and use a new sealing washer

8.19 Slide the dust seal on, making sure it is the correct way up

16 Fit the new oil seal into the tube and tap it into place until it seats and the retaining clip groove is visible – tap it in using a suitable socket with walls thin enough so it sits only on the hard outer rim of the seal and not on the spring rim on the top **(see illustration)**. If necessary you can use the old seal as an interface between the socket and the new seal, especially if your socket is not the ideal size **(see illustrations)**.

17 Fit the retaining clip, making sure it locates correctly in its groove **(see illustration)**.

18 On models except the Daytona R, if removed insert the damper cartridge into the inner tube until it contacts the bottom **(see illustration 8.6)**. Fit a new sealing washer onto the damper cartridge bolt and apply a few drops of a suitable non-permanent thread locking compound, then fit the bolt into the bottom of the inner tube, thread it

into the bottom of the damper cartridge and tighten it to the torque setting specified at the beginning of this Chapter **(see illustration)**. If the damper cartridge rotates inside the tube, the Triumph service tool described in Step 5 can be used to hold the head of the cartridge body. Alternatively fit the slotted washer under the damper rod locknut and use it to pull up on the rod which should help the bolt to tighten, or wait until the fork is fully reassembled and tighten it then (the pressure of the spring on the cartridge should prevent it from turning, especially if you compress the fork).

19 Slide the dust seal onto the inner tube **(see illustration)**. Lubricate the inner tube, the inner surfaces of the oil seal and the bushes inside the outer tube with fork oil. Carefully insert the inner tube into the outer tube using a twisting motion – it is important to keep

the tubes parallel or the seal lips could be damaged and will leak **(see illustration 8.4)**.

20 Press the dust seal into the outer tube **(see illustration)**.

21 Pour in the correct quantity and type of fork oil, and finish assembling the fork (see Section 7, Steps 9 to 17 for models except the Daytona R, and Steps 25 to 32 for Daytona R models).

22 Install the fork (see Section 6). Check and adjust the fork settings as required (see Section 13).

9   Steering stem

Removal

1 On Daytona models remove the fairing side panels, and if required the fairing (see Chapter 7). On all models it is advisable to remove the fuel tank to avoid the possibility of scratching it (see Chapter 4).

2 On all Daytona models remove the steering damper (see Section 16) and the horn (see Chapter 8). On Daytona R models release the front brake hoses from their guides on the bottom yoke.

3 On Street Triple models, displace the handlebars from the top yoke (see Section 5).

4 Wrap some masking tape around the steering stem nut for protection. Slacken the nut **(see illustration)**.

5 Remove the front forks (see Section 6).

8.20 Press the dust seal into the tube

9.4 Wrap some tape around the steering stem nut, then slacken it

9.6a Unscrew the steering stem nut . . .

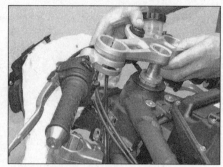

9.6b . . . then displace the top yoke and lay it aside

9.7 Unscrew the locknut and remove the washer, noting how it locates

6 Remove the steering stem nut **(see illustration)**. Ease the top yoke, along with the handlebars on Daytona models, up off the forks and lay it clear of the steering stem on some rag **(see illustration)**.

7 Using either the Triumph service tool (Part No. T3880024) or a C-spanner, unscrew the locknut, then lift off the tabbed washer **(see illustration)**.

8 Support the bottom yoke, then unscrew the bearing adjuster nut and gently lower the bottom yoke and steering stem out of the frame **(see illustrations)**.

9 Remove the bearing cover, the inner race and upper bearing from the top of the steering head **(see illustration)**. Remove the lower bearing from the bottom of the steering stem **(see illustration)**.

10 Remove all traces of old grease from the bearings and races and check them for wear or damage as described in Section 10. **Note:** *Do not attempt to remove the outer races from the steering head or the lower bearing inner race from the steering stem unless they are to be replaced with new ones.*

Installation

11 Smear a liberal quantity of lithium-based grease (see Chapter 1 Specifications) on the bearing outer races in the steering head. Work grease well into the upper and lower bearings. Fit the lower bearing over the steering stem **(see illustration 9.9b)**.

12 Carefully lift the steering stem/bottom yoke up through the steering head and support it **(see illustration 9.8b)**. Fit the upper bearing and its inner race, then fit the bearing cover **(see illustrations)**. Clean any traces of grease off the threads on the steering stem.

13 If separated fit the trim plate onto the

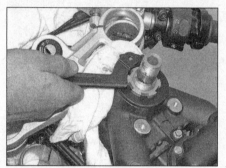

9.8a Unscrew the adjuster nut . . .

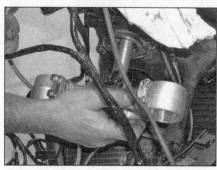

9.8b . . . then lower the bottom yoke and draw the stem out of the head

9.9a Remove the cover, inner race and bearing from the top of the head . . .

9.9b . . . and the lower bearing from the base of the stem

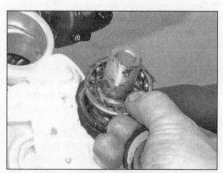

9.12a Fit the upper bearing . . .

9.12b . . . its inner race . . .

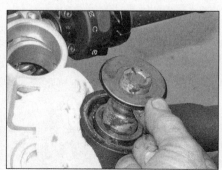

9.12c . . . and the bearing cover

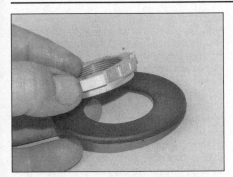

9.13a Make sure the plate is fitted to the underside . . .

9.13b . . . then fit the adjuster nut

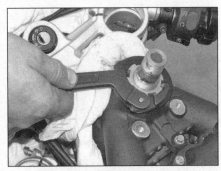

9.15 Tightening the adjuster nut using a C-spanner

bottom of the adjuster nut **(see illustration)**. Thread the nut onto the steering stem and tighten it finger-tight **(see illustration)**.

14 Triumph specify a torque setting for the adjuster nut, which can only be applied using their service tool (Part No. T3880024), or a suitable peg spanner, either bought commercially or fabricated by cutting castellations into an old socket of the correct size. With the tool fitted to a torque wrench, apply a torque of 40 Nm to the adjuster nut – this will preload the bearings. Now slacken the nut and tighten it to the final torque setting of 15 Nm.

15 If a tool isn't available tighten the adjuster nut using a C-spanner until all freeplay is removed, then tighten it a little more **(see illustration)**. This pre-loads the bearings. Now slacken the nut, then tighten it again, setting it so that all freeplay is just removed yet the steering is able to move freely from side to side. To do this tighten the nut only a little at a time, and after each tightening repeat the checks for freeplay and freedom of movement until the bearings are correctly set. The object is to set the adjuster nut so that the bearings are under a very light loading, just enough to remove any freeplay.

16 Fit the tabbed washer, locating the tab in the slot **(see illustration)**. Fit the locknut and tighten it to 40 Nm if the tool is available, or using a C-spanner if not **(see illustration)**.

17 Fit the top yoke onto the steering stem **(see illustration 9.6b)**. Fit the steering stem nut and tighten it finger-tight **(see illustration 9.6a)**.

18 Install the forks (see Section 6), but leave the clamp bolts in the top yoke loose. Install the front wheel (see Chapter 6). Tighten the steering stem nut to the specified torque setting, then tighten the fork clamp bolts.

19 On Daytona models, if the handlebars were detached from the top yoke, align them and tighten the positioning bolts to the specified torque **(see illustration 5.5a)**. Tighten the handlebar clamp bolts to the specified torque.

20 On Street Triple models install the handlebars (see Section 5).

21 Carry out a final check of the steering head bearing freeplay as described in Chapter 1, and if necessary re-adjust – this is especially important if the correct torque settings were not applied to the adjuster nut and locknut

9.16a Locate the tab in the slot . . .

9.16b . . . then fit the locknut

because the extra weight and inertia of the forks, front wheel and handlebars will make a difference to the feel of the freeplay and movement checks.

22 On Daytona models install the steering damper (see Section 16) and the horn (see Chapter 8).

10 Steering head bearing overhaul

Inspection

1 Remove the steering stem (see Section 9).

2 Remove all traces of old grease from the bearings and races and check them for wear or damage, referring to *Tools and Workshop Tips* in the Reference Section for information on bearing checks.

3 The bearing races should be polished and

10.3 Check the inner and outer races for wear and damage

free from indentations **(see illustration)**. Inspect the bearing rollers for signs of wear, damage or discoloration, and examine their cage for signs of cracks or splits. Spin the bearings by hand. They should spin freely and smoothly. If there are any signs of wear on any of the above components both upper and lower bearing assemblies should be renewed as a set, complete with new outer races. Only remove the outer races in the steering head and the lower bearing from the steering stem if new ones are being fitted – do not re-use them once they have been removed.

Renewal

4 Remove the steering stem (see Section 9).

5 The bearing outer races are an interference fit in the steering head and can be tapped from position with a suitable drift located on the rim of the race – there are two cut-outs in each race seat to make this easy **(see illustrations)**.

10.5a Drive the outer races from the steering head using a drift . . .

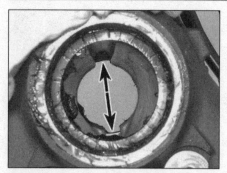

10.5b ... located in the cut-outs provided

Move the drift from one cut-out to the other so that the race is driven out squarely.
6 Alternatively, the races can be removed using a slide-hammer type bearing extractor – these can often be hired from tool shops.
7 The new outer races can be pressed into the steering head using a drawbolt arrangement **(see illustration)**, or by using a large diameter tubular drift. Ensure that the drawbolt washer or drift (as applicable) bears only on the outer edge of the race and does not contact the working surface.

 Installation of new bearing outer races is made much easier if they are left overnight in the freezer. This causes them to contract slightly making them a looser fit. Alternatively, use a freeze spray.

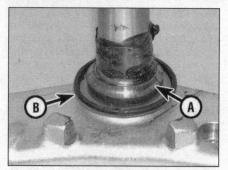

10.8a Lower bearing inner race (A) and seal (B)

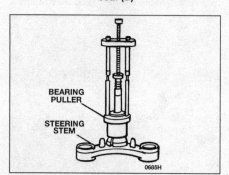

10.8d If necessary remove the inner race using a puller

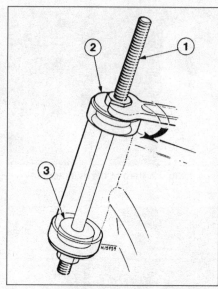

10.7 Drawbolt arrangement for fitting steering stem bearing races

1 Long bolt or threaded bar
2 Thick washer
3 Guide for lower race

8 The lower bearing inner race should only be removed from the steering stem if a new one is being fitted **(see illustration)**. To remove the race from the steering stem, thread a suitable nut onto the top of the stem to protect the threads, then place the stem on its side and tap under the race using a cold chisel to dislodge it, then use two screwdrivers placed

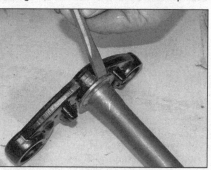

10.8b Dislodge the race using a cold chisel . . .

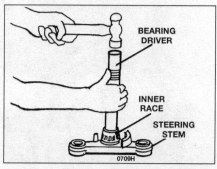

10.9 Drive the new bearing on using a suitable driver or a length of pipe

on opposite sides of the race to work it fully free, using blocks of wood to improve leverage and protect the yoke **(see illustrations)**. If the race is firmly in place it will be necessary to use a puller **(see illustration)**, or a press. Take the steering stem to a Triumph dealer if required. Remove the dust seal and discard it.
9 Fit a new dust seal onto the steering stem **(see illustration 10.8a)**. Fit the new race onto the stem and drive it into place using a length of tubing with an internal diameter slightly larger than the steering stem but not so large it contacts the bearing surface **(see illustration)**.
10 Install the steering stem (see Section 9).

11 Rear shock absorber

Note: *Locknuts are used on all shock absorber and suspension linkage bolts. Triumph specify that the nuts should only be used once, so new ones are needed for installation. If new nuts are not available, clean the threads of the old nuts and apply some fresh threadlock.*

Removal

1 On Daytona models remove the right-hand fairing side panel (see Chapter 7). Unscrew the exhaust valve servo mounting bolts and displace it, then disconnect the wiring connector. On Street Triple models from VIN 560477 remove the silencer (see Chapter 4).
2 Unscrew the rear brake fluid reservoir bolt **(see illustration)**.

10.8c . . . and work it up with screwdrivers

11.2 Unscrew the bolt (arrowed) and displace the reservoir

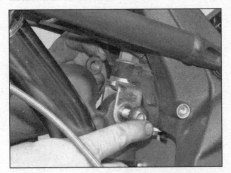

11.4 Unscrew the nut and withdraw the upper bolt

11.5 Ease the shock out of the upper mount

11.6a Unscrew the nut and withdraw the lower bolt . . .

3 Support the motorcycle securely in an upright position using an auxiliary stand or stands under the frame, footrest brackets or engine (do not use a rear paddock stand), so the rear wheel is about 50 mm off the ground. Position a support (such as a block of wood) under the rear wheel so that it does not drop when the shock absorber upper bolt is removed, but also making sure that the weight of the machine is off the rear suspension so that the shock is not compressed. Note which side the bolts are fitted before removal.

4 Unscrew the nut on the shock absorber upper mounting bolt, then withdraw the bolt **(see illustration)**.

5 Remove the support from under the rear wheel and lower it to the ground, freeing the shock upper mount from its bracket **(see illustration)**.

6 Unscrew the nut on the bolt securing the bottom of the shock absorber to the drop link plates **(see illustration)**. Withdraw the bolt and manoeuvre the shock up and out from the left-hand side **(see illustration)**.

7 Discard the nuts – new ones should be used.

Inspection

8 Inspect the shock absorber for obvious physical damage and the coil spring for looseness, cracks or signs of fatigue. Inspect the damper rod for signs of bending, pitting and oil leakage **(see illustration)**.

9 Remove the sleeve from the lower mounting bearing **(see illustration)**. Check the condition of the lower mounting seals and the bearing – if the bearing is dirty or rusty, meaning the seals have failed, lever them out, then after checking and if necessary fitting a new bearing (see Step 10), replace them with new ones **(see illustrations)**. Also check the bush in the upper mounting, and check the mountings themselves for cracks **(see illustration)**. Refer to Section 12 and check the bearings and seals in the drag link and swingarm. Triumph do not list the upper mounting bush as being available separately, but the lower mounting bearing, sleeve and seals are available.

10 To check the needle bearing, and for details of removal and installation methods, refer to *'Tools and workshop tips' (Section 5)* in the Reference section at the end of the book – note that once a needle bearing has been removed it cannot be re-used. Worn bearings can be driven out of their bores,

11.6b . . . then lift the shock out

but note that removal will destroy them; new bearings should be obtained before work commences. The new bearings should be pressed or drawn into their bores rather than driven into position. In the absence of a press,

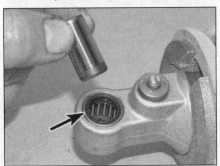

11.9a Withdraw the sleeve and check the bearing and seals (arrowed)

11.9c . . . and drive new ones in using a suitable socket

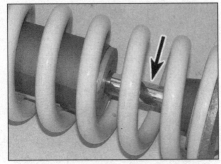

11.8 Look for cracks, pitting and oil leakage on the damper rod (arrowed)

a suitable drawbolt tool can be made up as described in the Reference section.

11 Replacement parts for the shock absorber itself are not available from Triumph. If it is worn or damaged, it must be replaced with a new one.

11.9b Lever the seals out . . .

11.9d Upper mounting bush (arrowed)

12.3a Detach the drop link plates from the drag link . . .

12.4a Detach the drag link from the frame . . .

Installation

12 Installation is the reverse of removal, noting the following:

● Apply lithium-based grease (see Chapter 1 Specifications) to the shock absorber and linkage bearings, sleeves and seals.

● Insert all bolts from the right-hand side. Use new nuts (see *Note*).

● Where fitted install the shock with the reservoir at the back. Fit the lower mounting bolt and new nut loosely **(see illustration 11.6a)**, then raise and support the wheel so the upper mounting aligns, insert the upper mounting bolt and fit a new nut **(see illustration 11.4)**. Tighten the nut on the lower bolt to the torque setting specified at the beginning of the chapter. Take the bike off the stand so the weight is through the suspension, then tighten the upper mounting bolt nut to the specified torque setting.

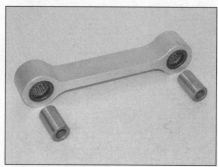

12.5a Withdraw the sleeves from the bearings in the drag link . . .

12.3b . . . and the swingarm

12.4b . . . and remove the sleeve

● Check the operation of the rear suspension and adjust the shock absorber settings as required before taking the machine on the road.

12 Rear suspension linkage

Note: *Locknuts are used on all shock absorber and suspension linkage bolts. Triumph specify that the nuts should only be used once, so new ones are needed for installation. If new nuts are not available apply some threadlock to the threads of the old nuts.*

Removal

1 Support the motorcycle securely in an upright position using an auxiliary stand or stands under the frame, footrest brackets or engine (do not use a rear paddock stand),

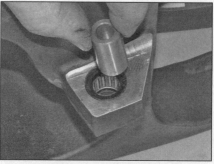

12.5b . . . and the swingarm

so the rear wheel is off the ground. Position a support under the rear wheel so that it does not drop when the shock absorber is detached, but also making sure that the weight of the machine is off the rear suspension so that the shock is not compressed. Note which side the bolts are fitted before removal.

2 On Daytona models and Street Triple models to VIN 560476 remove the exhaust intermediate pipe (see Chapter 4). On Street Triple models from VIN 560477 remove the silencer (see Chapter 4).

3 Unscrew the nuts and withdraw the bolts securing the drop link plates to the bottom of the shock absorber **(see illustration 11.6a)**, the drag link and the swingarm, and remove the plates **(see illustrations)** – note that they are marked on the right-hand side for correct installation.

4 Unscrew the nut and withdraw the bolt securing the drag link to the frame and remove the link, noting which way round it fits **(see illustration)**. Remove the sleeve for the bolt in the frame **(see illustration)**.

Inspection

5 Withdraw the bearing sleeves from the drag link and the drop link mount on the swingarm **(see illustrations)**. Thoroughly clean all components, removing all traces of dirt, corrosion and grease. If the bearings are dirty or rusty, meaning the seals have failed, lever them out, and after checking and if necessary fitting new bearings (see Steps 6 and 7), replace them with new ones **(see illustration)**.

6 Inspect all components closely, looking for obvious signs of wear such as heavy scoring, or for damage such as cracks or distortion. Slip each sleeve back into its bearing and check that there is not an excessive amount of freeplay between the two components. Replace any components as required with new ones.

7 To check the needle bearings, and for details of removal and installation methods, refer to *'Tools and workshop tips' (Section 5)* in the Reference section at the end of the book – note that once a needle bearing has been removed it cannot be re-used. Worn bearings can be driven out of their bores, but note that removal will destroy them; new

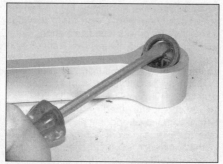

12.5c If required lever the seals out

bearings should be obtained before work commences. The new bearings should be pressed or drawn into their bores rather than driven into position. In the absence of a press, a suitable drawbolt tool can be made up as described in the Reference section.

8 Lubricate the needle roller bearings with grease.

9 Press new grease seals squarely into place **(see illustration)**. Lubricate the sleeves and fit them into the bearings **(see illustrations 12.5a and b)**.

Installation

10 Installation is the reverse of removal, noting the following:

● If not already done clean off old grease and apply new grease to all sleeves, bearings and seals, as described in Inspection. Make sure the sleeves are correctly fitted.

● Do not forget to fit the sleeve for the drag link-to-frame bolt **(see illustration 12.4b)**. Insert all bolts from the right-hand side. Use new nuts (see **Note**).

● Fit the drop link plates with the marked side facing to the right, and with the hole marked S/A fitted to the swingarm and that marked RSU fitted to the shock absorber **(see illustration)**.

● Install the bolts and new nuts finger-tight at first until all components are in position, then tighten the nuts to the torque setting specified at the beginning of the Chapter.

● Check the operation of the rear suspension before taking the machine on the road.

13 Suspension adjustment

Note: *Refer to the owners handbook supplied with the machine for recommended front and rear suspension settings to suit loading.*

Front forks – Daytona

1 The forks are adjustable for spring pre-load, rebound damping and compression damping on 2006 to 2008 models (up to VIN 377509), and for spring pre-load, rebound damping and both low and high speed compression damping on 2009 and later models (from VIN 377510-on).

12.9 Press the new seals into place, or drive them in with a socket if necessary

2 Spring pre-load is adjusted using a suitable spanner on the adjuster flats on the top of each fork **(see illustration)**. On models to VIN 381274 the amount of pre-load is indicated by lines on the adjuster, and the standard position is with the 5th line just visible above the top bolt hex. On models from VIN 381275 the amount of pre-load is indicated by the number of turns out from the fully screwed-in position, and the standard position is seven and a half turns out. Turn the adjuster clockwise to increase pre-load and anti-clockwise to decrease it. Always make sure both adjusters are set equally – this is easy to judge using the lines on each adjuster.

3 Rebound damping is adjusted using a screwdriver in the slot in the adjuster protruding from the pre-load adjuster **(see illustration)**. The amount of damping is indicated by the number of turns or clicks out from the fully screwed-in position. The standard position is six turns out on models to VIN 377509, nine clicks out on models from VIN 377510 to 381274, and twelve clicks out on models from VIN 381275. Turn the adjuster clockwise to increase damping and anti-clockwise to decrease it. To establish the current setting, turn the adjuster in (clockwise) until it stops, counting the number of turns or clicks, then reset it as required by turning it out. Always make sure both adjusters are set equally.

4 Compression damping (up to VIN 377509) is adjusted using a screwdriver in the slot in the adjuster in the bottom of the fork **(see illustration)**. The amount of damping is

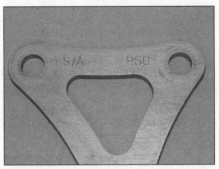

12.10 Make sure the plates are correctly fitted as described according to the marks

indicated by the number of turns out from the fully screwed-in position. The standard position is seven turns out. Turn the adjuster clockwise to increase damping and anti-clockwise to decrease it. To establish the current setting, turn the adjuster in (clockwise) until it stops, counting the number of turns, then reset it as required by turning it out. Always make sure both adjusters are set equally.

5 Low speed compression damping (from VIN 377510) is adjusted using a screwdriver in the slot in the centre of the adjuster in the bottom of the fork **(see illustration 13.4)**. The amount of damping is indicated by the number of clicks out from the fully screwed-in position. The standard position is nine clicks out on models to VIN 381274, and twelve clicks out on models from VIN 381275. Turn the adjuster clockwise to increase damping and anti-clockwise to decrease it. To establish the current setting, turn the adjuster in (clockwise) until it stops, counting the number of clicks, then reset it as required by turning it out. Always make sure both adjusters are set equally.

6 High speed compression damping (from VIN 377510) is adjusted by turning the outer ring of the adjuster in the bottom of the fork. **Note:** *When turning the high speed adjuster ring the low speed adjuster will turn with it – this is normal and does alter the low speed setting.* The amount of damping is indicated by the number of turns out from the fully turned-in position. The standard position is three turns out. Turn the adjuster clockwise to increase damping and anti-clockwise to

13.2 Spring pre-load adjuster (arrowed)

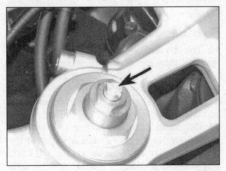

13.3 Rebound damping adjuster (arrowed)

13.4 Compression damping adjuster (arrowed)

13.8 Spring pre-load adjuster (A), damping adjuster (B)

13.15 Rebound damping adjuster (arrowed)

13.16 Compression damping adjuster (arrowed)

decrease it. To establish the current setting, turn the adjuster in (clockwise) until it stops, counting the number of turns, then reset it as required by turning it out. Always make sure both adjusters are set equally.

Front forks – Daytona R

7 Both forks have adjustable spring pre-load. The right-hand fork has adjustable rebound damping and the left-hand fork has adjustable compression damping.

8 Spring pre-load is adjusted using a suitable spanner on the adjuster flats on the top of each fork **(see illustration)**. The amount of pre-load is indicated by the number of turns clockwise from the fully anti-clockwise position, and the standard position is four turns clockwise. Turn the adjuster clockwise to increase pre-load and anti-clockwise to decrease it. To establish the current setting, turn the adjuster anti-clockwise until it stops, counting the number of turns, then reset it as required by turning it clockwise. Always make sure both adjusters are set equally.

9 Damping is adjusted using a 3 mm hex key in the adjuster set within the pre-load adjuster **(see illustration 13.8)**. The amount of damping is indicated by the number of clicks out from the fully screwed-in position, but note that the first click must be counted as zero, not one. The standard position for **rebound damping** in the right-hand fork is fourteen clicks out. The standard position for **compression damping** in the left-hand fork is sixteen clicks out. Turn the adjuster clockwise to increase damping and anti-clockwise to decrease it. To establish the current setting, turn the adjuster in (clockwise) until it stops, counting the number of clicks, then reset it as required by turning it out, remembering the first click is counted zero.

Front forks – Street Triple R

10 The forks are adjustable for spring pre-load, rebound damping and compression damping. On standard Street Triples the forks are not adjustable.

11 Spring pre-load is adjusted using a suitable spanner on the adjuster flats on the top of each fork **(see illustration 13.2)**. The amount of pre-load is indicated by the number of turns out from the fully screwed-in position.

The standard position is seven turns out on models to VIN 560476, and seven and a half turns out on models from VIN 560477. Turn the adjuster clockwise to increase pre-load and anti-clockwise to decrease it. Always make sure both adjusters are set equally – this is easy to judge using the lines on each adjuster.

12 Rebound damping is adjusted using a screwdriver in the slot in the adjuster protruding from the pre-load adjuster **(see illustration 13.3)**. The amount of damping is indicated by the number of clicks out from the fully screwed-in position. The standard position is four clicks out on models to VIN 560476, and ten clicks out on models from VIN 560477. Turn the adjuster clockwise to increase damping and anti-clockwise to decrease it. To establish the current setting, turn the adjuster in (clockwise) until it stops, counting the number of clicks, then reset it as required by turning it out. Always make sure both adjusters are set equally.

13 Compression damping is adjusted using a screwdriver in the slot in the adjuster in the bottom of the fork **(see illustration 13.4)**. The amount of damping is indicated by the number of clicks out from the fully screwed-in position. The standard position is four clicks out on models to VIN 560476, and ten clicks out on models from VIN 560477. Turn the adjuster clockwise to increase damping and anti-clockwise to decrease it. To establish the current setting, turn the adjuster in (clockwise) until it stops, counting the number of clicks, then reset it as required by turning it out. Always make sure both adjusters are set equally.

Rear shock absorber – Daytona

14 The shock absorber is adjustable for rebound damping and compression damping on 2006 to 2008 models (up to VIN 377509), and for rebound damping and both low and high speed compression damping on 2009 and later models (from VIN 377510-on).

15 Rebound damping is adjusted using a screwdriver in the slot in the adjuster in the base of the shock absorber on the left-hand side **(see illustration)**. The amount of damping is indicated by the number of turns/clicks out from the fully screwed-in position. The

standard position is six turns out on models up to VIN 377509 , nine clicks out on models from VIN 377510 to 381274, and twelve clicks out on models from VIN 381275. Turn the adjuster clockwise to increase damping and anti-clockwise to decrease it. To establish the current setting, turn the adjuster in (clockwise) until it stops, counting the number of turns, then reset it as required by turning it out.

16 Compression damping (up to VIN 377509) is adjusted using a screwdriver in the slot in the adjuster in the top of the shock absorber on the left-hand side **(see illustration)**. The amount of damping is indicated by the number of turns out from the fully screwed-in position. The standard position is eleven turns out. Turn the adjuster clockwise to increase damping and anti-clockwise to decrease it. To establish the current setting, turn the adjuster in (clockwise) until it stops, counting the number of turns, then reset it as required by turning it out.

17 Low speed compression damping (from VIN 377510) is adjusted using a screwdriver in the slot in the centre of the adjuster in the top of the shock absorber on the left-hand side **(see illustration 13.16)**. The amount of damping is indicated by the number of clicks out from the fully screwed-in position. The standard position is nine clicks out on models to VIN 381274, and twelve clicks out on models from VIN 381275. Turn the adjuster clockwise to increase damping and anti-clockwise to decrease it. To establish the current setting, turn the adjuster in (clockwise) until it stops, counting the number of clicks, then reset it as required by turning it out.

18 High speed compression damping (from VIN 377510) is adjusted by turning the outer ring of the adjuster in the top of the shock absorber on the left-hand side. **Note:** *When turning the high speed adjuster ring the low speed adjuster will turn with it – this is normal and does alter the low speed setting.* The amount of damping is indicated by the number of turns out from the fully turned-in position. The standard position is three turns out. Turn the adjuster clockwise to increase damping and anti-clockwise to decrease it. To

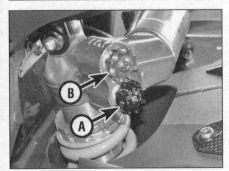

13.20 Rebound damping adjuster (A),
compression damping adjuster (B)

establish the current setting, turn the adjuster in (clockwise) until it stops, counting the number of turns, then reset it as required by turning it out.

Rear shock absorber – Daytona R

19 The shock absorber has adjustable rebound damping and compression damping.
20 **Rebound damping** is adjusted by turning the lower (black) adjuster on the top of the shock absorber on the left-hand side **(see illustration)**. The amount of damping is indicated by the number of clicks out from the fully screwed-in position, but note that the first click must be counted as zero, not one. The standard position is sixteen clicks out. Turn the adjuster clockwise to increase damping and anti-clockwise to decrease it. To establish the current setting, turn the adjuster in (clockwise) until it stops, counting the number of clicks, then reset it as required by turning it out, remembering the first click is counted zero.
21 **Compression damping** is adjusted by turning the upper (gold) adjuster on the top of the shock absorber on the left-hand side **(see illustration 13.20)**. The amount of damping is indicated by the number of clicks out from the fully screwed-in position, but note that the first click must be counted as zero, not one. The standard position is sixteen clicks out. Turn the adjuster clockwise to increase damping and anti-clockwise to decrease it. To establish the current setting, turn the adjuster in (clockwise) until it stops, counting the number of clicks, then reset it as required

by turning it out, remembering the first click is counted zero.

Rear shock absorber – Street Triple from VIN 560477

22 The shock absorber has adjustable spring pre-load. Pre-load is adjusted by turning the spring seat on the top of the shock absorber using the C-spanner provided in the bike's tool kit. There are five settings, each identified by an indent that seats under a lug on the shock body. Turn the adjuster clockwise to reduce spring pre-load and anti-clockwise to increase it. The standard setting is in position one, i.e. minimum pre-load.

Rear shock absorber – Street Triple R

23 The shock absorber is adjustable for rebound damping and compression damping. Note that pre-load is set at the factory and should not be adjusted.
24 **Rebound damping** is adjusted using a screwdriver in the slot in the adjuster in the base of the shock absorber on the left-hand side **(see illustration 13.15)**. The amount of damping is indicated by the number of clicks out from the fully screwed-in position. The standard position is eight clicks out on models to VIN 560476, and nine clicks out on models from VIN 560477. Turn the adjuster clockwise to increase damping and anti-clockwise to decrease it. To establish the current setting, turn the adjuster in (clockwise) until it stops, counting the number of clicks, then reset it as required by turning it out.
25 **Compression damping** is adjusted using a screwdriver in the slot in the adjuster in the top of the shock absorber on the left-hand side **(see illustration 13.16)**. The amount of damping is indicated by the number of clicks out from the fully screwed-in position. The standard position is eight clicks out on models to VIN 560476, and nine clicks out from VIN 560477. Turn the adjuster clockwise to increase damping and anti-clockwise to decrease it. To establish the current setting, turn the adjuster in (clockwise) until it stops, counting the number of clicks, then reset it as required by turning it out.

14 Swingarm removal and installation

Note 1: *Before removing the swingarm, it is advisable to perform the rear suspension checks described in Chapter 1 to assess the extent of any wear.*
Note 2: *Locknuts are used on all shock absorber and suspension linkage bolts. Triumph specify that the nuts should only be used once, so new ones are needed for installation. If new nuts are not available apply some threadlock to the threads of the old nuts.*

Removal

1 On Daytona models and Street Triple models to VIN 560476 remove the exhaust intermediate pipe (see Chapter 4). On Street Triple models from VIN 560477 remove the silencer (see Chapter 4).
2 Remove the rear wheel (see Chapter 6).
3 Remove the shock absorber (see Section 11). Place a support under the rear of the swingarm.
4 Unscrew the nut and withdraw the bolt securing the drop link plates to the swingarm, then pivot the linkage down **(see illustration 12.3b)**.
5 Remove the front sprocket cover (see Chapter 6). Slip the drive chain off the sprocket **(see illustration 14.15)**. If required remove the drive chain (see Chapter 6).
6 Release the brake hose guides from the swingarm **(see illustration)**. Position the brake caliper clear, making sure no strain is placed on the hose.
7 Before removing the swingarm it is advisable to re-check for play in the bearings (see Chapter 1). Any problems which may have been overlooked with the other suspension components attached to the frame are highlighted with them loose.
8 Where fitted remove the swingarm pivot caps **(see illustration)**. Counter-hold the swingarm pivot bolt head, then unscrew the nut on the left-hand end of the bolt and remove the washer **(see illustration)**. Discard the nut as a new one should be used. Push the pivot bolt in so it is clear of the adjuster bolt in the left-hand side of the frame.

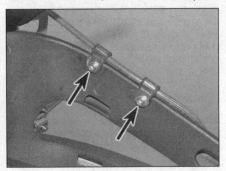

14.6 Unscrew the bolts (arrowed) to free the hose

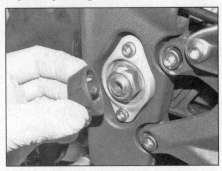

14.8a Pull the pivot cap off

14.8b Unscrew the nut and remove the washer

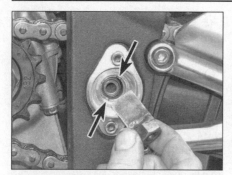

14.9 Home-made tool locates in the cut-outs (arrowed) in the adjuster

14.10 Withdraw the bolt and remove the swingarm

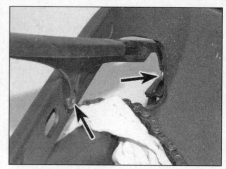

14.11a Chainguard screws (arrowed)

14.11b Chain slider screw (arrowed)

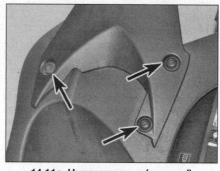

14.11c Hugger screws (arrowed)

14.14 Set the adjuster (arrowed) flush with the frame so it is not in the way

9 Using the Triumph special tool (Pt. No. T3880104), which is basically like a very large flat-bladed screwdriver tip, or a suitable equivalent, thread the adjuster bolt out of the frame until it no longer protrudes on the inside (see illustration).

10 Support the swingarm, then withdraw the pivot from the right-hand side, using a drift to knock it through if required, and remove the swingarm, making sure the drive chain does not drag on the floor (see illustration).

11 Remove the chain guard and chain slider, and on Daytona models the hugger, from the swingarm if necessary, noting how they fit (see illustrations). If the chain slider is badly worn or damaged, replace it with a new one.

12 Inspect all components for wear or damage as described in Section 15.

Installation

13 If not already done (see Section 15), remove the bearing spacer from the right-hand side and the sleeve from the left, and lubricate the bearings, spacer, sleeve and swingarm pivot with grease (see illustrations 15.1a and b). Refit the spacer and sleeve.

14 If removed, install the chain guard, slider and hugger (see illustrations 14.11a, b and c). Make sure the adjuster is in the frame, but not protruding from it on the inside (see illustration).

15 Offer up the swingarm and have an assistant hold it in place, making sure drive chain is looped over the chain slider at the front (see illustration). Slide the pivot bolt

through from the right-hand side, leaving it recessed from the head of the adjuster bolt on the right (see illustration 14.10).

16 Using the Triumph special tool (Pt. No. T3880104) or a suitable equivalent (see Step 9) (see illustration 14.9), tighten the adjuster bolt to the torque setting specified at the beginning of the Chapter (see illustration). Push the pivot bolt all the way through.

17 Fit the washer and a new nut on the left-hand end of the pivot bolt (see illustration 14.8). Counter-hold the bolt on the right-hand end and tighten the nut to the specified torque.

18 Install all remaining components and assemblies in a reverse of the removal procedure, referring to the relevant Sections and Chapters where necessary. Fit a new nut onto the drop link bolt and tighten it to the specified torque (see illustration 12.3b).

19 Check and adjust the drive chain slack (see Chapter 1). Check the operation of the rear suspension and brake before taking the machine on the road.

15 Swingarm bearings

Inspection

1 After removing the swingarm remove the bearing spacer from the right-hand side and

14.15 Make sure the drive chain is correctly looped over at the front

14.16 Tighten the adjuster to the specified torque

15.1a Remove the spacer . . .

15.1b . . . and withdraw the sleeve

15.4a Withdraw the long central spacer

15.4b Lever out the grease seal on each side

15.4c Remove the circlip from the right-hand side

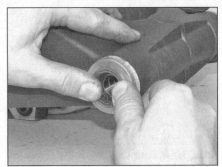

15.6 Press the new seals into place

the sleeve from the left (see illustrations). Thoroughly clean the swingarm, removing all traces of dirt, corrosion and grease.

2 Inspect all components closely, looking for obvious signs of wear such as heavy scoring, and cracks or distortion due to accident damage. Check the condition of the grease seals, and check the bearings for roughness, looseness and any other damage, referring to *Tools and Workshop Tips* (Section 5) in the Reference section. Any damaged or worn component must be replaced with a new one.

3 Check the swingarm pivot bolt is straight by rolling it on a flat surface such as a piece of plate glass (first wipe off all old grease and remove any corrosion using wire wool). If the equipment is available, place the pivot in V-blocks and measure the runout using a dial gauge. If the pivot is bent, replace it with a new one.

Seal and bearing renewal

4 If not already done remove the bearing spacer from the right-hand side and the sleeve from the left (see illustrations 15.1a and b). Withdraw the long central spacer through the needle bearing (see illustration). Lever out the grease seal from each side (see illustration). Discard the seals as new ones must be used. Remove the circlip securing the ball bearings (see illustration).

5 Refer to *Tools and Workshop Tips*

(Section 5) in the Reference section for more information on bearing checks and removal and installation methods. The needle bearing can be drawn or driven out of its bore, but note that removal will make it unusable; a new bearing should be obtained before work commences. To drive it out pass a long drift with a hooked end through the right-hand side of the swingarm and locate it on the inner edge of the bearing. Tap the drift around the bearing's inner edge to ensure that it leaves its bore squarely. Use the same method to drive out the ball bearings, but from the opposite side. Alternatively, and if available, a slide-hammer with knife-edged bearing puller attached can be used, and is better than using a drift, to extract the bearings. Note that there is a central spacer between the inner ball bearing and the needle bearing.

6 Fit the bearings with the marked side facing out. The new needle bearing should be pressed or drawn into its bore rather than driven into position. In the absence of a press, a suitable drawbolt arrangement can be made up as described in *Tools and Workshop Tips* (Section 5) in the Reference section. The ball bearings can be driven in using a driver or socket that bears only on the outer race, or they can be drawn or pressed in as with the needle bearing. Fit the long central spacer through the needle bearing so it sits between the two bearings (see illustration 15.4a). Press the new seals in using your fingers, or tap them in using a suitable socket (see

illustration). Lubricate the bearings, spacer, sleeve and seal lips with the recommended grease (see Chapter 1 Specifications) on installation.

16 Steering damper (Daytona models)

Removal

1 Remove the left-hand fairing side panel (see Chapter 7).

2 Pull the rubber boot off the rear mount (see illustration). Unscrew the bolt and collect the

16.2a Pull back the boot, then unscrew the bolt (arrowed) . . .

16.2b ... and retrieve the washer

16.3a Unscrew the bolt (arrowed) ...

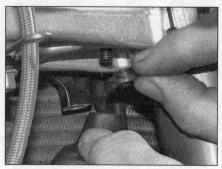

16.3b ... and retrieve the flanged sleeve

16.5 Use the cut-out (arrowed) to drive the bearing out

washer from between the damper rod and the bracket **(see illustration)**.

3 Unscrew the damper body bolt from the top of the bottom yoke and remove the damper, collecting the flanged sleeve from between the body and the underside of the yoke **(see illustrations)**. Note the bearing fitted in the top of the yoke **(see illustration 16.5)**.

Inspection

4 Clean the damper rod and inspect it for wear, score marks, oil leakage and corrosion. Damage to the surface of the rod will lead to oil loss and lack of damping. Pump the rod all the way in and out of the damper body. Movement should be slow and progressive and the rod should move smoothly. If the rod

binds, or there is no resistance, or if there is oil leakage, fit a new damper.

5 Check the bearings in the yoke and rod end – the yoke bearing is available separately, the rod bearing is not. If necessary drive the yoke bearing out from the underside using a drift located in the cut-out **(see illustration)**.

Installation

6 Installation is the reverse of removal, noting the following:

● Lubricate the damper body bearings with grease.

● Tighten the mounting bolts to the torque setting specified at the beginning of the Chapter.

Chapter 6
Brakes, wheels and final drive

Contents

Degrees of difficulty

| Easy, suitable for novice with little experience 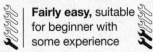 | Fairly easy, suitable for beginner with some experience | Fairly difficult, suitable for competent DIY mechanic | Difficult, suitable for experienced DIY mechanic | Very difficult, suitable for expert DIY or professional |

Specifications

Brakes

Brake fluid type . . . . DOT 4
Brake pad minimum thickness . . . . 1.5 mm
Front caliper piston OD
  Daytona up to VIN 381274 and Street Triple R and RX
    Large bore. . . . . 33.96 mm
      Small bore. . . . . 30.23 mm
  Daytona from VIN 381275 . . . . 32.03 mm
  Daytona R. . . . . 33.96 mm
  Street Triple. . . . . 27.00 mm
Front disc thickness
  Standard. . . . . 4.0 mm
  Service limit . . . . 3.5 mm
Front disc maximum runout . . . . 0.3 mm
Front master cylinder bore ID
  Daytona and Street Triple R . . . . 19.05 mm
  Street Triple. . . . . 14.00 mm
Rear caliper piston OD
  Daytona models and Street Triple models to VIN 560476 . . . . 38.18 mm
  Street Triple models from VIN 560477 . . . . 34 mm
Rear disc thickness
  Standard. . . . . 5.0 mm
  Service limit . . . . 4.5 mm
Rear disc maximum runout . . . . 0.3 mm
Rear master cylinder bore ID
  Daytona models and Street Triple models to VIN 560476 . . . . 14.0 mm
  Street Triple models from VIN 560477 . . . . 12.7 mm

ABS components

Wheel speed sensor air gap................................. 0.1 to 1.5 mm

Wheels

Runout (max)
    Axial (side-to-side) .... 0.5 mm
    Radial (out-of round)..................................... 0.5 mm

Tyres

Tyre pressures .... see *Pre-ride checks*
Tyre sizes*
    Front 120/70-17
    Rear 180/55-17

Refer to the owners handbook, the tyre information label on the swingarm, or your Triumph dealer or a tyre specialist for approved tyre brands and ratings.

Final drive

Chain type .... 525 (RK O-ring type as standard)
No. of links
    Daytona models and Street Triple models to VIN 560476 116
    Street Triple models from VIN 560477 117
Drive chain slack and stretch limit .... see Chapter 1

Torque wrench settings

ABS components
    Brake pipe nuts on modulator (models)...................... 15 Nm
    Front wheel pulse ring/brake disc bolts..................... 22 Nm
    Rear wheel pulse ring /brake disc bolts..................... 22 Nm
    Wheel speed sensor bolt .... 9 Nm
Brake caliper bleed valves
    Front calipers, all models .... 6 Nm
    Rear caliper
        Daytona models and Street Triple models to VIN 560476 .... 6 Nm
        Street Triple models from VIN 560477 .... 14 Nm
Brake hose banjo bolts.................................... 25 Nm
Front brake caliper joining bolts (Daytona
    to VIN 381274 and Street Triple R and RX) .... 22 Nm
Front brake caliper mounting bolts
    Daytona to VIN 381274 and Street Triple R and RX.............. 35 Nm
    Daytona from VIN 381275 and Daytona R .... 55 Nm
    Street Triple to VIN 486467............................... 28 Nm
    Street Triple from VIN 486468 .... 21 Nm
Front brake disc bolts .... 22 Nm
Front brake master cylinder clamp bolts
    Daytona R.. 8 Nm
    All other models .... 12 Nm
Front brake pad retaining pin............................... 18 Nm
Front sprocket nut .... 85 Nm
Front wheel axle... 65 Nm
Front wheel axle clamp bolts
    Daytona and Street Triple models .... 22 Nm
    Daytona R.. 19 Nm
Rear brake caliper mounting bolts
    Front .... 27 Nm
    Rear .... 22 Nm
Rear brake disc bolts..................................... 22 Nm
Rear brake master cylinder bolts............................ 18 Nm
Rear brake pad retaining pin .... 18 Nm
Rear sprocket nuts....................................... 55 Nm
Rear wheel axle nut .... 110 Nm

1 General information

All models are fitted with cast alloy wheels designed for tubeless tyres only.

Both front and rear brakes are hydraulically operated disc brakes. On Daytona and Street Triple R models the front brake has two opposed-piston calipers, each with four pistons. On Street Triple models the front brake has a sliding caliper with two pistons. On all models the rear brake has a single piston sliding caliper.

The drive to the rear wheel is by chain and sprockets.

Caution: Disc brake components rarely require disassembly. Do not disassemble components unless absolutely necessary. If an hydraulic brake line is loosened, the system must be thoroughly bled. Do not use solvents on internal brake components. Solvents will cause the seals to swell and distort. Use only clean brake fluid or denatured alcohol for cleaning. Use care when working with brake fluid as it can injure your eyes and it will damage painted surfaces and plastic parts.

Many of the bolts used on Triumph motorcycles are of the Torx type. Unless you are already equipped with a good range of Torx bits, you are advised to obtain a set. Make sure you get bits that can be used in conjunction with a socket set so that a torque wrench can be applied – a Torx key set will not be adequate on its own, though will be useful in addition to the bits.

2 Brake pad renewal

⚠️ *Warning: The dust created by the brake system may contain asbestos, which is harmful to your health. Never blow it out with compressed air and don't inhale any of it. An approved filtering mask should be worn when working on the brakes.*

Front pads – Daytona, Daytona R, and Street Triple R

1 On Daytona models up to VIN 381274 and Street Triple R and RX models, remove the R-clip from the inner end of the pad retaining pin **(see illustration)**. Slacken the pad retaining pin **(see illustration)**. Unscrew the caliper mounting bolts and slide the caliper off the disc **(see illustration 3.1a)**. Free the brake hose(s) from the clip(s) on the mudguard to give more freedom of movement if required (see illustration 3.1c). Unscrew the pad retaining pin and remove the pad spring, noting how it fits, and the pads **(see illustration)**.
2 On Daytona models from VIN 381275 slacken the pad retaining pin **(see illustration)**.

2.1a Remove the R-clip . . .

2.1b . . . then slacken the pad pin

2.1c Unscrew the pin and remove the spring . . .

2.1d . . . then remove the pads

Unscrew the caliper mounting bolts and slide the caliper off the disc **(see illustration 3.1a)**. Free the brake hose(s) from the clip(s) on the mudguard to give more freedom of movement

if required **(see illustration 3.1c)**. Unscrew the pad retaining pin and remove the pads, and if required the pad spring, noting how it fits **(see illustrations)**.

2.2a Slacken the pad pin (arrowed)

2.2b Unscrew the pin . . .

2.2c . . . and remove the pads

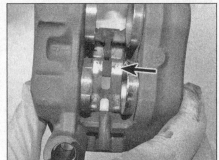

2.2d Pad spring (arrowed) – if the pistons are in the way remove the spring after they have been pushed back in (Step 8)

2.3 Caliper mounting bolts (A) and pad spring (B) – Daytona R

2.8a Push the pistons in using finger pressure, a piece of wood . . .

2.8b . . . or a proper tool

3 On Daytona R models unscrew the caliper mounting bolts and slide the caliper off the disc **(see illustration)**. Free the brake hose(s) from the clip(s) on the mudguard to give more freedom of movement if required **(see illustration 3.1c)**. Slide each pad in turn to the centre of the caliper until its ends clear the lugs then remove it. If required remove the pad spring, noting how it fits.

4 Inspect the surface of each pad for contamination and check that the friction material has not worn beyond its service limit (see Chapter 1, Section 9). If either pad is worn down to or beyond the service limit wear indicator or the minimum thickness specified, is fouled with oil or grease, or is heavily scored or damaged by dirt and debris, both pads in each caliper must be replaced with new ones. Note that it is not possible to fully degrease the friction material; if the pads are contaminated in any way new ones must be fitted. Check that the wear on each pad is even – uneven wear between the pads or across one pad is a sign of a sticking or seized piston or pistons (see Steps 8 and 9).

5 If the pads are in good condition clean them carefully, using a fine wire brush which is completely free of oil and grease, to remove all traces of road dirt and corrosion. Using a pointed instrument, clean out the groove in the friction material and dig out any embedded particles of foreign matter. Spray with a dedicated brake cleaner to remove any dust.

6 Check the condition of the brake disc (see Section 4).

7 Remove all traces of corrosion from the pad pin. Check for signs of damage and wear.

8 Clean around the exposed section of each piston to remove any dirt or debris that could cause the seals to be damaged. If new pads are being fitted, now push the pistons all the way back into the caliper to create room for them; if the old pads are still serviceable push the pistons in a little way. To push the pads back use finger pressure or a piece of wood as leverage, or place the old pads back in the caliper and use a metal bar or a screwdriver inserted between them, or use grips and a piece of wood, rag or card to protect the caliper body **(see illustration)**. Alternatively obtain a proper piston-pushing tool from a good tool supplier **(see illustration)**. If there is too much brake fluid in the reservoir it may be necessary to remove the cap, plate and diaphragm and siphon out some fluid (see Pre-ride checks). If the pistons are difficult to push back, remove the bleed valve cap, then attach a length of clear hose to the bleed valve and place the open end in a suitable container, then open the valve and try again (see Section 10). Take great care not to draw any air into the system. If in doubt, bleed the brakes afterwards.

9 If a piston appears seized (uneven wear in the pad(s) is a sure sign of this), apply the brake lever and check whether the piston in question moves at all – first block or hold the other pistons using wood or cable-ties. If it moves out but can't be pushed back the chances are there is some hidden corrosion stopping it. If it doesn't move at all, or to fully

clean and inspect the pistons, overhaul the caliper (see Section 3).

10 Where shims are fitted to the backs of the pads, make sure they are clean and correctly seated. Where no shims are fitted lightly smear the backs of the pads with copper-based grease, making sure that none gets on the front or sides of the pads. On all models lightly smear the pad pin with copper-based grease.

11 On Daytona models up to VIN 381274 and Street Triple R and RX models, insert the pads into the caliper so that the friction material on each pad faces the other **(see illustration 2.1d)**. Fit the pad spring onto the pads, making sure it is the correct way up **(see illustration 2.1c)**. Slide the pad retaining pin through the hole in the outer pad, then press down on the pad spring and slide the pin over the spring and through the hole in the inner pad **(see illustration)**. Tighten the pin finger-tight. Slide the caliper onto the disc making sure the pads locate correctly on each side **(see illustration 3.20a)**. Fit the caliper mounting bolts and tighten them to the torque setting specified at the beginning of this Chapter. Fit the brake hose(s) into the clip(s) if removed. Tighten the pad pin to the torque setting specified at the beginning of the Chapter. Fit the R-clip, using a new one if necessary **(see illustration 2.1a)**.

12 On Daytona models from VIN 381275 fit the pad spring if removed **(see illustration 2.2d)**. Insert the pads into the caliper so that the friction material on each pad faces the other **(see illustration 2.2c)**. Press the pads against the spring to align the holes and slide the pin through the holes in the pads **(see illustration 2.2b)**. Tighten the pin finger-tight. Make sure the dowels are in place then slide the caliper onto the disc, making sure the pads locate correctly on each side **(see illustration)**. Clean the caliper mounting bolt threads and smear the lower four threads with copper grease. Fit the bolts and tighten them to the torque setting specified at the beginning of this Chapter. Fit the brake hose(s) into the clip(s) if removed. Tighten the pad pin to the torque setting specified at the beginning of the Chapter.

13 On Daytona R models fit the pad spring if removed, making sure the arrow points in the same direction as that on the caliper

2.11 Make sure the pad pin locates correctly over the spring

2.12 Seat the caliper squarely onto the dowels (arrowed)

2.16a Remove the plug . . .

2.16b . . . then slacken the pad pin

2.18a Unscrew the pin . . .

2.18b . . . then remove the pads

2.20a Slide the caliper off the bracket and check the boots (arrowed)

2.20b Remove the spring (arrowed) . . .

(see illustration 2.3). Insert each pad into the caliper in turn, pressing it against the spring and seating its ends on the lugs then sliding it against the pistons, so that the friction material on each pad faces the other. Make sure the dowels are in place then slide the caliper onto the disc, making sure the pads locate correctly on each side. Clean the caliper mounting bolt threads and smear the lower four threads with copper grease. Fit the bolts and tighten them to the torque setting specified at the beginning of this Chapter. Fit the brake hose(s) into the clip(s) if removed.

14 Operate the brake lever until the pads contact the disc. Check the level of fluid in the hydraulic reservoir (see Pre-ride checks).

15 Check the operation of the brakes before riding the motorcycle.

Front pads – Street Triple

16 Unscrew the pad retaining pin plug (see illustration). Slacken the pad retaining pin (see illustration).

17 Unscrew the caliper mounting bolts and slide the caliper off the disc (see illustration 3.1b). Free the brake hose(s) from the clip(s) to give more freedom of movement if required (see illustration 3.1c).

18 Unscrew the pad retaining pin and remove the pads (see illustrations).

19 Refer to Steps 4, 5, 6 and 7 above and inspect the pads and caliper components.

20 Separate the bracket from the caliper by sliding them apart (see illustration). Clean off all traces of corrosion and hardened grease. Check the rubber boots. If they are damaged or deteriorated, they should be replaced with new ones (but check with a Triumph dealer as they do not list them as being available separately). Note how the pad spring is fitted

and remove it for cleaning if required (see illustration). Also note the pad guide on the bracket (see illustration).

21 Clean around the exposed section of the pistons to remove any dirt or debris that could cause the seals to be damaged. If new pads are being fitted, now push the pistons all the way back into the caliper to create room for them; if the old pads are still serviceable push the pistons in a little way. To push the pistons back use finger pressure or a piece of wood as leverage, or place the old pads back in the caliper and use a metal bar or a screwdriver inserted between them, or use grips and a piece of wood, with rag or card to protect the caliper body (see illustration). Alternatively obtain a proper piston-pushing tool from a good tool supplier (see illustration). If there is too much brake fluid in the reservoir it may be necessary to remove the cover

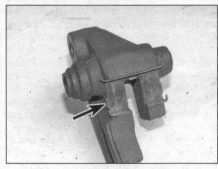

2.20c . . . and the guide (arrowed) if required

2.21a Push the pistons in using finger pressure, a piece of wood . . .

2.21b . . . or a proper tool

2.24 Make sure the pad ends locate correctly in the guide

2.28 Remove the plug then slacken the pad pin (arrowed)

2.30 Unscrew the pin and remove the pads

and diaphragm and siphon some out (see Pre-ride) checks. If a piston is difficult to push back, remove the bleed valve cap, then attach a length of clear hose to the bleed valve and place the open end in a suitable container, then open the valve and try again (see Section 10). Take great care not to draw any air into the system. If in doubt, bleed the brake afterwards.

22 If a piston appears seized, apply the brake lever and check whether the piston in question moves at all – first block or hold the other piston using wood or cable-ties. If it moves out but can't be pushed back in the chances are there is some hidden corrosion stopping it. If it doesn't move at all, or to fully clean and inspect the pistons, disassemble the caliper and overhaul it (see Section 3).

23 If removed, fit the pad spring into the caliper, making sure it is clean and correctly located (see illustration 2.20b). Make sure the guide is clean and correctly fitted on the bracket (see illustration 2.20c). Apply a smear of silicone based grease to the slider pins and inside the boots. Slide the bracket back onto the caliper (see illustration 2.20a). Check that the caliper is able to slide freely.

24 Lightly smear the pad retaining pin with copper grease. Fit the pads into the caliper (see illustration 2.18b) – make sure their ends locate against the guide on the bracket (see illustration). Press the pads against the spring and slide the pad pin through (see illustration 2.20a). Make sure the pin passes through the hole in each pad. Tighten the pin finger-tight.

25 Slide the caliper onto the disc, making

sure the pads sit squarely on each side (see illustration 3.20b). Install the caliper mounting bolts and tighten them to the torque setting specified at the beginning of the Chapter. Now tighten the retaining pin to the specified torque (see illustration 2.16b). Smear the pad pin plug threads with copper grease and fit the plug (see illustration 2.16a).

26 Operate the brake pedal several times to bring the pads into contact with the disc. Top up the master cylinder reservoir if necessary (see Pre-ride checks).

27 Check the operation of the brake before riding the motorcycle.

Rear pads – Daytona models, and Street Triple models to VIN 560476

28 Unscrew the pad retaining pin plug (see illustration). Slacken the pad retaining pin.

29 Unscrew the caliper mounting bolts and slide the caliper off the disc (see illustration 6.2).

30 Unscrew and remove the pad pin, then remove the pads, noting how they fit (see illustration).

31 Refer to Steps 4, 5, 6 and 7 above and inspect the pads and caliper components.

32 Clean off all traces of corrosion and hardened grease from the bolts and boots, and from the sleeve in the caliper boot (see illustration). Replace the rubber boots with new ones if they are damaged, deformed or deteriorated. Note how the pad spring is fitted and remove it for cleaning if required (see illustration). Also note the pad guide on the bracket (see illustration).

33 Clean around the exposed section of the piston to remove any dirt or debris that could cause the seals to be damaged. If new pads are being fitted, push the piston all the way back into the caliper to create room for them; if the old pads are still serviceable push the piston in a little way. To push the piston back use finger pressure or a piece of wood as leverage, or two pieces of wood and a metal bar or a screwdriver inserted between them, or use grips and a piece of wood, with rag or card to protect the caliper body (see illustration). Alternatively obtain a proper

2.32a There is a boot (arrowed) with a sleeve in the caliper and one in the bracket

2.32b Remove the spring (arrowed) . . .

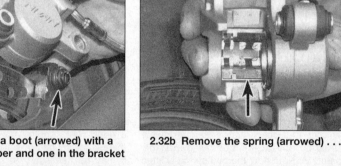

2.33a Push the pistons in using finger pressure, a piece of wood . . .

2.32c . . . and the guide (arrowed) if required

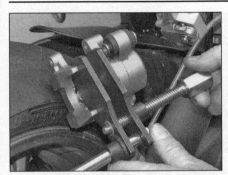

2.33b ... or a proper tool

2.40 Push the caliper against the disc to force the piston in

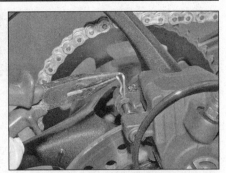

2.42a Remove the clip ...

piston-pushing tool from a good tool supplier **(see illustration)**. If there is too much brake fluid in the reservoir it may be necessary to remove the cap, plate and diaphragm and siphon some out (see Pre-ride checks). If the piston is difficult to push back, remove the bleed valve cap, then attach a length of clear hose to the bleed valve and place the open end in a suitable container, then open the valve and try again (see Section 10). Take great care not to draw any air into the system. If in doubt, bleed the brake afterwards.

34 If the piston appears seized, apply the brake pedal and check whether the piston moves at all. If it moves out but can't be pushed back in the chances are there is some hidden corrosion stopping it. If it doesn't move at all, or to fully clean and inspect the piston, disassemble and overhaul the caliper (see Section 6).

35 If removed, fit the pad spring into the caliper, making sure it is clean and correctly located **(see illustration 2.32b)**. Make sure the guide is clean and correctly fitted on the bracket **(see illustration 2.32c)**. Lightly smear the pad retaining pin with copper grease. Apply a smear of silicone based grease to the bolts and inside the boots and sleeve **(see illustration 2.32a)**.

36 Fit the pads into the caliper and slide the pad pin through **(see illustration 2.30)**. Tighten the pin finger-tight.

37 Slide the caliper onto the disc, making sure the pads sit squarely on each side and

locate correctly in the bracket and against the guide **(see illustration 6.14a and b)**. Fit the bolts and tighten them to the torque settings specified at the beginning of the Chapter **(see illustration 6.2)**. Now tighten the pad pin to the specified torque **(see illustration 2.28)**. Smear the pad pin plug threads with copper grease and fit the plug.

38 Operate the brake pedal until the pads contact the disc. Check the level of fluid in the hydraulic reservoir and top-up if necessary (see Pre-ride checks).

39 Check the operation of the rear brake before riding the motorcycle.

Rear pads – Street Triple models from VIN 560477

40 Push the caliper against the disc to push the piston in **(see illustration)** – if new pads are being fitted, push the piston all the way in to create room for them. If there is too much brake fluid in the reservoir it may be necessary to remove the cap, plate and diaphragm and siphon some out (see Pre-ride checks). If the piston is difficult to push back, remove the bleed valve cap, then attach a length of clear hose to the bleed valve and place the open end in a suitable container, then open the valve and try again (see Section 10). Take great care not to draw any air into the system. If in doubt, bleed the brake afterwards.

41 If the piston appears seized, apply the brake pedal and check whether the piston moves at all. If it moves out but can't be

pushed back in the chances are there is some hidden corrosion stopping it. If it doesn't move at all, or to fully clean and inspect the piston, remove the caliper (see Section 6).

42 Remove the pad retaining pin clip **(see illustration)**. Drive the pad retaining pin out using a suitable punch **(see illustration)**.

43 Remove the pads, noting how they fit **(see illustration)**.

44 Refer to Steps 4, 5, 6 and 7 above and inspect the pads and caliper components.

45 Check the condition of the rubber boots and replace them with new ones if they are damaged, deformed or deteriorated – to do this refer to Section 6, remove the caliper and slide it off the bracket. Note how the pad spring is fitted and remove it for cleaning if required **(see illustration 6.24a)**. Also note the pad guide on the bracket **(see illustration 6.24b)**.

46 Smear the pad pin with copper grease. Fit the pads into the caliper, making sure their front ends seat correctly against the guide on the bracket **(see illustration 2.43)**. Push the pads up against the spring to align the holes and slide the pad pin through, making sure the hole for the clip is vertical, and seating it using a punch **(see illustration)**. Fit the clip into the hole in the pin **(see illustration 2.42a)**.

47 Operate the brake pedal until the pads contact the disc. Check the level of fluid in the hydraulic reservoir and top-up if necessary (see Pre-ride checks).

48 Check the operation of the rear brake before riding the motorcycle.

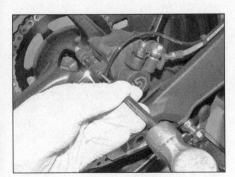

2.42b ... then drive out the pin ...

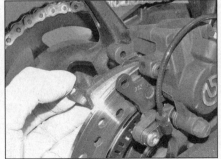

2.43 ... and slide out the pads

2.46 Push the pads up against the spring to align the holes

3.1a Caliper mounting bolts (arrowed) on Daytona and Street Triple R

3.1b Caliper mounting bolts (arrowed) on Street Triple

3 Front brake calipers

⚠ **Warning: If a caliper indicates the need for an overhaul (usually due to leaking fluid or sticky operation), all old brake fluid should be flushed from the system. Also, the dust created by the brake system may be harmful to your health. Never blow it out with compressed air and don't inhale any of it. An approved filtering mask should be worn when working on the brakes. Do not, under any circumstances, use petroleum-based solvents to clean brake parts. Use DOT 4 brake fluid, dedicated brake cleaner or denatured alcohol only, as described.**

Removal

1 If the calipers are just being displaced from the forks as part of the wheel removal procedure, unscrew the caliper mounting bolts and slide the caliper off the disc **(see illustrations)**. Free the brake hose from its clip(s) to give more freedom of movement if required **(see illustration)**. Secure the caliper to the bike with a cable-tie to avoid straining the brake hose. **Note:** *Do not operate the brake lever while either caliper is off the disc.*

2 If the caliper is being completely removed or overhauled, place some rag around the brake hose banjo bolt, then unscrew the bolt and detach the banjo union, noting its alignment with the caliper, and catching any residual fluid with the rag **(see illustrations)**. When working on the right-hand caliper, note the double hose arrangement (except on Daytona R models) **(see illustration)**. Wrap clingfilm around the banjo union and secure the hose in an upright position to minimise fluid loss. Discard the sealing washers, as new ones must be fitted on reassembly. Remove the brake pads (see Section 2) – this involves detaching the caliper.

Overhaul

Note: *If the caliper is being overhauled (usually due to sticking pistons or fluid leaks) read through the entire procedure first and make sure that you have obtained all the new parts required, including some new DOT 4 brake fluid.*

3 On Street Triple models separate the bracket from the caliper by sliding them apart **(see illustration 2.20a)**. Remove the pad spring from the caliper, noting how it fits **(see illustration 2.20b)**.

3.1c Release the brake hose(s) from the clip(s) if required

4 Clean all dirt and dust off the caliper with denatured alcohol or brake system cleaner. Have some clean rag ready to catch any spilled brake fluid.

5 Mark the inside of each piston with its location in the caliper using a felt marker to ensure that the pistons can be matched to their original bores on reassembly. Note that on Daytona models (up to VIN 377509) and Street Triple R models two sizes of piston are used in each caliper (see Specifications at the beginning of this Chapter).

6 On Daytona models up to VIN 381274 and

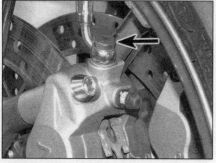

3.2a Brake hose banjo bolt (arrowed) – Daytona and Street Triple R

3.2b Brake hose banjo bolt (arrowed) – Street Triple

3.2c Note the arrangement of the hoses and sealing washers on the right caliper

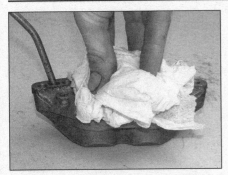

3.6a Apply compressed air to the fluid passage . . .

3.6b . . . until the pistons are displaced

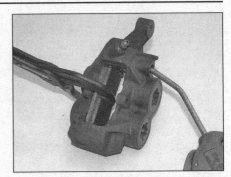

3.7a Hold the pistons on one side in using wood and grips . . .

Street Triple R and RX models, unscrew the caliper body joining bolts and separate the body halves, catching any residual fluid with the rag **(see illustration 3.17b)**. Remove the O-ring and discard it **(see illustration 3.17a)**. Place one half of the caliper piston side up on a bench. Get a wad of rag and hold it against the pistons as a cushion to protect your hand as the pistons are forced out. Apply compressed air gradually and progressively, starting with a fairly low pressure, to the fluid passage and allow the pistons to ease evenly out of their bores, controlling them with hand pressure and the rag **(see illustrations)**. Repeat the procedure for the other caliper half.

7 On Daytona models from VIN 381275 and Daytona R models, due to the construction of these calipers it is easier to overhaul one

side of the caliper completely and refit the components and then do the other side, rather than removing all components in both sides. Push the pistons on one side of the caliper fully into their bores until they are flush with the body **(see illustration 2.8a or b)**. Hold the pistons in place using a piece of wood about 10 to 15 mm thick and a pair of good grips, protecting the caliper with some rag **(see illustration)**. Apply compressed air gradually and progressively, starting with a fairly low pressure, to the brake fluid inlet until the pistons on the other side contact the piece of wood or tool **(see illustration)**. Remove the wood or tool, then remove the pistons from their bores **(see illustration)**. Have some clean rag ready to catch the shower of hydraulic fluid.

8 On Street Triple models get a wad of rag

and hold it against the pistons as a cushion to protect your hand as the pistons are forced out. Apply compressed air gradually and progressively, starting with a fairly low pressure, to the fluid inlet on the caliper body and allow the pistons to ease evenly out of their bores, controlling them with hand pressure and the rag **(see illustration)**.

9 If a piston is stuck in its bore due to corrosion the caliper should be replaced with a new one. Do not try to remove a piston by levering it out or by using pliers or other grips.

10 Remove the dust seals and the piston seals from the piston bores using a soft wooden or plastic tool to avoid scratching the bores **(see illustration)**. Discard the seals as new ones must be fitted on reassembly.

11 Clean the pistons and bores with DOT 4 brake fluid. If compressed air is available,

3.7b . . . then displace the pistons from the other side . . .

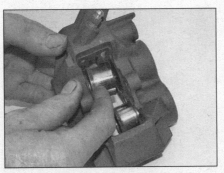

3.7c . . . and remove them from their bores

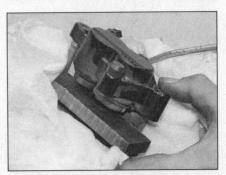

3.8a Position the wood as shown then apply compressed air . . .

3.8b . . . until both pistons are displaced . . .

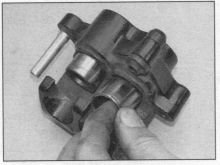

3.8c . . . then remove the wood and withdraw the pistons

3.10 Remove the seals and discard them

3.13a Lubricate the new piston seals with brake fluid . . .

3.13b . . . then fit them into their grooves . . .

3.14 . . . followed by the new dust seals

blow it through the fluid galleries in the caliper to ensure they are clear (make sure it is filtered and unlubricated).

Caution: Do not, under any circumstances, use a petroleum-based solvent to clean brake parts.

12 Inspect the caliper bores and pistons for signs of corrosion, nicks and burrs and loss of plating. If surface defects are present, the pistons and/or the caliper assembly must be replaced with new ones. If the caliper is in poor condition, the other front caliper and the master cylinder should also be checked.

13 Lubricate the new piston seals with clean brake fluid and fit them in their grooves in the caliper bores (see illustrations). Remember that on Daytona (up to VIN 381274) and Street Triple R and RX models there are two sizes of bore in each caliper and care must therefore be taken to ensure that the correct size seals are fitted to the correct bores (see

Specifications). The same applies when fitting the new dust seals and pistons. Note that on Daytona models from VIN 381275 and Daytona R models the upper piston in each half of the caliper has a matt finish (Nymfron); the lower pistons are nickel-plated.

14 Lubricate the new dust seals with clean brake fluid and install them in their grooves in the caliper bores (see illustration).

15 Lubricate the pistons with clean brake fluid and install them, closed-end first, into the caliper bores, taking care not to displace the seals (see illustration). Using your thumbs, push the pistons all the way in, making sure they enter the bore squarely.

16 On Daytona models from VIN 381275 and Daytona R models now block the side of the caliper that has been overhauled and displace the pistons from the other side, repeating the procedure.

17 On Daytona models up to VIN 381274 and

Street Triple R and RX models clean the threads of the caliper body joining bolts. Lubricate the new caliper body O-ring with clean brake fluid and fit it into the appropriate half of the caliper body (see illustration). Join the two halves of the caliper body, ensuring that the O-ring stays in place (see illustration). Apply a threadlock to the joining bolts and tighten them evenly to the torque setting specified at the beginning of this Chapter.

18 On Street Triple models clean off all traces of corrosion and hardened grease from the slider pins and rubber boots. Check the rubber boots – if they are damaged or deteriorated, they should be replaced with new ones (but check with a Triumph dealer as they do not list them as being available separately). Fit the pad spring into the caliper, making sure it is correctly located (see illustration 2.20b). Apply a smear of copper or silicone based grease to the slider pins. Slide the caliper back onto the bracket (see illustration 2.20a). Check that the caliper is able to slide freely.

Installation

19 If the caliper has been overhauled install the brake pads (see Section 2) – this procedure involves installing the caliper.

20 If the calipers have just being displaced slide the caliper onto the brake disc, making sure the pads fit on each side of the disc (see illustrations). Fit the caliper mounting bolts and tighten them to the torque setting specified at the beginning of the Chapter.

21 If detached, connect the brake hose(s) to the caliper, using new sealing washers on

3.15 Fit the pistons and push them all the way in

3.17a Fit the O-ring into its recess . . .

3.17b . . . then join the caliper halves and tighten the bolts

3.20a Fitting the caliper on Daytona and Street Triple R

3.20b Fitting the caliper on Street Triple

each side of each banjo fitting. Align the fitting as noted on removal **(see illustration 3.2a or b)**. Tighten the banjo bolt to the specified torque setting. Top up the hydraulic reservoir with DOT 4 brake fluid (see Pre-ride checks) and bleed the system as described in Section 10. Check that there are no fluid leaks and test the operation of the brake before riding the motorcycle.

22 Fit the brake hose into its clip(s) if removed **(see illustration 3.1c)**.

4 Front brake discs

Inspection

1 Inspect the surface of the disc for score marks and other damage. Light scratches are normal after use and won't affect brake operation, but deep grooves and heavy score marks will reduce braking efficiency and accelerate pad wear. If a disc is badly grooved replace both discs with new ones – never fit only one new disc.

2 The disc must not be allowed to wear down to a thickness less than the service limit as listed in this Chapter's Specifications. The minimum thickness is also stamped on the disc **(see illustration)**. Check the thickness of the disc with a micrometer and replace both discs with new ones **(see illustration)**.

3 To check if the disc is warped, position the bike on an auxiliary stand with the front wheel raised off the ground. Mount a dial gauge to the fork leg, with the gauge plunger touching the surface of the disc about 10 mm from the outer edge **(see illustration)**. Rotate the wheel and watch the gauge needle, comparing the reading with the limit listed in the Specifications at the beginning of this Chapter. If the runout is greater than the service limit, check the wheel bearings for play (see Chapter 1). If the bearings are worn,

4.2a The minimum thickness is marked on the disc

4.2b Using a micrometer to measure disc thickness

install new ones (see Section 15) and repeat this check. If the disc runout is still excessive, a new pair of discs will have to be fitted – never fit only one new disc.

Removal

4 Remove the wheel (see Section 13).

Caution: Do not lay the wheel down and allow it to rest on the disc – the disc could become warped. Set the wheel on wood blocks so the disc doesn't support the weight of the wheel.

5 Mark the relationship of the discs to the wheel, so they can be installed in the same position (unless you are fitting new discs). Also mark the discs according to their side as the discs are different. If you are installing new discs, match them to the old ones so they can be installed correctly.

6 Unscrew the disc bolts, loosening them evenly and a little at a time in a criss-cross pattern to avoid distorting the disc, then remove the disc from the wheel **(see illustration)** – note that on models with ABS the left-hand disc bolts also secure the wheel sensor pulse ring (see Section 21). Triumph specify that new bolts should be used as they are pre-treated with a threadlock, but if necessary clean the threads of the old bolts and apply some fresh threadlock to them on installation.

Installation

7 Before installing the disc, make sure there is no dirt or corrosion where the disc seats on the hub, particularly right in the angle of the seat, as this will not allow the disc to sit flat when it is bolted down and it will appear to be warped when checked or when using the front brake.

8 Mount the disc on the wheel making sure it is the correct way round, and on the correct side (see Step 5). Align the previously applied matchmarks (if you're reinstalling the original disc). On models with ABS fit the pulse ring onto the left-hand disc.

9 Install new or threadlocked bolts and tighten them evenly and a little at a time in a criss-cross pattern to the torque setting specified at the beginning of the Chapter **(see illustration 4.6)**. Clean off all grease from the brake disc using acetone or brake system cleaner. If new discs have been installed, remove any protective coating from its working surfaces. Always fit new brake pads when installing new discs.

10 Install the front wheel (see Section 13).

11 Operate the brake lever several times to bring the pads into contact with the disc. Check the operation of the brake carefully before riding the bike.

4.3 Set up a dial gauge with the probe contacting the brake disc, then rotate the wheel to check for runout

4.6 Unscrew the bolts (arrowed) and remove the disc

5.1a Brake light switch wiring connectors (arrowed) – Daytona and Street Triple R

5.1b Brake light switch wiring connectors (arrowed) – Street Triple

5.2a On Daytona and Street Triple R unscrew the reservoir bolt (arrowed)

5.2b Master cylinder bolts (arrowed) – Daytona and Street Triple R

5.2c Master cylinder bolts (arrowed) – Street Triple

5.4a Undo the screw (arrowed) and remove the clamp

5 Front brake master cylinder

⚠️ **Warning: If the brake master cylinder is in need of an overhaul all old brake fluid should be flushed from the system. Overhaul of the brake master cylinder must be done in a spotlessly clean work area to avoid contamination and possible failure of the brake hydraulic system components. Do not, under any circumstances, use petroleum-based solvents to clean brake parts. Use DOT 4 brake fluid, dedicated brake cleaner or denatured alcohol only, as described. To prevent damage from spilled**

brake fluid, always cover paintwork when working on the braking system.

Note: *On Daytona R models it is not possible to overhaul the master cylinder as no parts are available for it – a new master cylinder must be fitted.*

Removal

1 Disconnect the wiring connectors from the brake light switch **(see illustrations)**.

2 If the master cylinder is just being displaced, ensure the fluid reservoir cover or cap is secure. On Daytona and Street Triple R models undo the bolt securing the reservoir to the bracket **(see illustration)**. Unscrew the master cylinder clamp bolts and remove the back of the clamp, noting how it fits, then position the master cylinder and reservoir assembly clear

of the handlebar **(see illustrations)**. Ensure no strain is placed on the hydraulic hose. Keep the reservoir upright to prevent air entering the system.

3 If the master cylinder is being overhauled, remove the brake lever (see Chapter 5).

4 On Daytona and Street Triple R models remove the reservoir cap clamp screw and clamp **(see illustration)**. On Daytona R slacken the reservoir cap screws **(see illustration)**. Undo the bolt securing the reservoir to the bracket **(see illustration 5.2a)**.

5 Place some rag under the brake hose banjo bolt, then unscrew the bolt and detach the banjo union, noting its alignment with the master cylinder, and catching any spilled fluid in the rag **(see illustrations)**. Wrap clingfilm around the banjo union and secure the hose

5.4b Slacken the screws (arrowed)

5.5a Brake hose banjo bolt (arrowed) – Daytona and Street Triple R

5.5b Brake hose banjo bolt (arrowed) – Street Triple

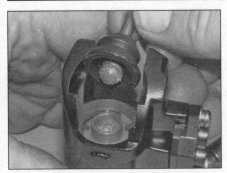

5.9a Remove the boot and pushrod from the end of the master cylinder . . .

5.9b . . . then depress the piston and remove the circlip . . .

5.9c . . . then draw out the piston . . .

in an upright position to minimise fluid loss. Discard the sealing washers as new ones must be fitted on reassembly.

6 Unscrew the master cylinder clamp bolts and remove the back of the clamp, noting how it fits, then lift the master cylinder and reservoir away from the handlebar **(see illustration 5.2b or c)**.

7 Remove the reservoir cover or cap and remove the diaphragm plate where fitted and the diaphragm. Drain the brake fluid from the master cylinder and reservoir into a suitable container. Wipe any remaining fluid out of the reservoir with a clean rag. On Daytona and Street Triple R models, if required release the clip securing the reservoir hose to the union on the master cylinder and detach the hose.

8 If required, undo the screw securing the brake light switch to the bottom of the master cylinder and remove the switch **(see illustration 5.1a or b)**.

Overhaul

Note: *If the master cylinder is being overhauled (usually due to sticking or poor action, or fluid leaks) read through the entire procedure first and make sure that you have obtained the rebuild kit (which includes the boot, circlip, piston, cup, seal and spring), as the old parts should not be reused once removed. Also get some new DOT 4 brake fluid.*

9 On Daytona and Street Triple R models carefully remove the dust boot and pushrod from the master cylinder, noting how they locate. Using circlip pliers, remove the circlip

5.9d . . . and the spring

and slide out the piston assembly and the spring, noting how they fit **(see illustrations)**. If they are difficult to remove, apply low pressure compressed air to the fluid outlet. Lay the parts out in the proper order to prevent confusion during reassembly.

10 On Street Triple models carefully remove the dust boot, along with the pushrod on Daytona and Street Triple R models, from the master cylinder, noting how it locates. Using circlip pliers, remove the circlip and slide out the piston assembly and the spring, noting how they fit **(see illustrations)**. If they are difficult to remove, apply low pressure compressed air to the fluid outlet. Lay the parts out in the proper order to prevent confusion during reassembly.

11 Clean the master cylinder with clean

5.10a Remove the rubber boot from the end of the master cylinder . . .

brake fluid. If compressed air is available, use it to dry the cylinder thoroughly (make sure it's filtered and unlubricated).

Caution: Do not, under any circumstances, use a petroleum-based solvent to clean brake parts.

12 Check the master cylinder bore for corrosion, scratches, nicks and score marks. If damage or wear is evident, the master cylinder must be replaced with a new one. If the master cylinder is in poor condition, then the calipers should be checked as well. Check that the fluid inlet and outlet ports are clear.

13 The dust boot, circlip, piston, cup, seal and spring are included in the rebuild kit. Use all of the new parts, regardless of the apparent condition of the old ones. Fit them according to the layout of the old piston assembly **(see**

5.10b . . . then depress the piston and remove the circlip . . .

5.10c . . . draw out the piston . . .

5.10d . . . then the spring

5.13a On Daytona and Street Triple R make sure the cup and seal are correctly installed on the piston

5.13b On Street Triple make sure the seal is correctly installed on the piston

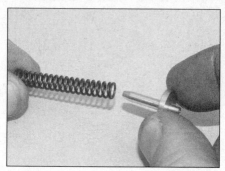

5.14a Fit the guide into the end of the spring

5.14b Push the piston into the bore . . .

5.14c . . . and hold it there while fitting the circlip

5.14d Feed the rim of the boot into the bore

illustrations). Lubricate the cup and seal with new brake fluid before fitting them.

14 On Daytona and Street Triple R models make sure the guide is fitted up inside the

spring **(see illustration)**. Lubricate the piston with clean brake fluid and slide it into the master cylinder **(see illustration)**. Make sure the lips on the cup and seal do not turn inside

out. Depress the piston and install the new circlip, making sure it locates properly in its groove **(see illustration)**. Fit the pushrod into the new rubber boot, seating the boot outer lip in the groove. Fit the boot and carefully push the inner lip in against the circlip using a blunt tool **(see illustration)**.

15 On Street Triple models fit the cup onto the narrow end of the spring and lubricate it with new brake fluid **(see illustration)**. Fit the spring wide-end first into the master cylinder and push the cup in, making sure its lip does not turn inside out **(see illustrations)**. Lubricate the piston with clean brake fluid and slide it into the master cylinder and up against the cup and spring **(see illustration)**. Make sure the lip on the seal does not turn inside out. Depress the piston and install the new

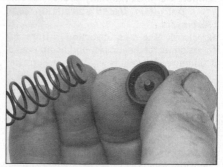

5.15a Fit the cup onto the spring . . .

5.15b . . . then fit the spring . . .

5.15c . . . and push the cup into the bore

5.15d Insert the piston . . .

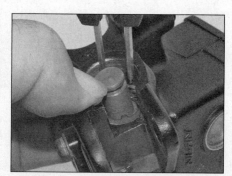

5.15e . . . then push it in and fit the circlip . . .

5.15f . . . pressing it into place using a small screwdriver

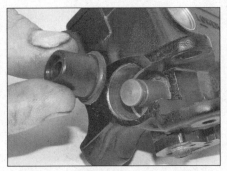

5.15g Make sure the boot locates correctly in the bore and around the piston

5.18 Align the mating surfaces of the clamp with the punch mark on the handlebar

circlip, making sure it locates properly in its groove (see illustrations). Fit the new rubber dust boot and carefully push the inner lip in against the circlip using a blunt tool. make sure the outer lip is seated correctly in the groove in the piston.

16 Check the reservoir diaphragm and replace it with a new one it if it is damaged or deteriorated. On Daytona and Street Triple R models also check the reservoir hose for cracks or splits and fit a new one if necessary.

Installation

17 If removed, fit the brake light switch onto the bottom of the master cylinder and tighten the screw (see illustration 5.1a or b).

18 Attach the master cylinder to the handlebar, aligning the clamp joint with the 'L' mark on the handlebar on Daytona R models, and the punch mark on all other models (see illustration), then fit the back of the clamp with its UP mark facing up (see illustration 5.2b or c). Tighten the upper bolt to the torque setting specified at the beginning of this Chapter, followed by the lower bolt.

19 On Daytona and Street Triple R models locate the fluid reservoir on the bracket and secure it with the nut and bolt (see illustration 5.2a). If detached connect the reservoir hose to the union on the master cylinder and secure it with the clip.

20 Connect the brake hose to the master cylinder, using new sealing washers on each side of the banjo fitting. Align the hose as noted on removal (see illustration 5.5a or b). Tighten the banjo bolt to the torque setting specified at the beginning of this Chapter – if you can't get a socket and torque wrench onto the bolt on Daytona models due to the angle with the fork, slacken the clamp bolts and reposition the master cylinder as required, then lightly retighten the bolts, tighten the banjo bolt, then move the master cylinder back to its correct position.

21 Install the brake lever (see Chapter 5).

22 Connect the brake light switch wiring (see illustration 5.1a or b).

23 Fill the fluid reservoir with new DOT 4 brake fluid (see Pre-ride checks). Refer to Section 10 and bleed the air from the system.

24 Check the operation of the brake before riding the motorcycle.

6 Rear brake caliper

⚠ **Warning: If a caliper is in need of an overhaul all old brake fluid should be flushed from the system. Also, the dust created by the brake system may be harmful to your health. Never blow it out with compressed air and do not inhale any of it. An approved filtering mask should be worn when working on the brakes. Overhaul of the brake caliper must be done in a spotlessly clean work area to avoid contamination and possible failure of the brake hydraulic system components. Do not, under any circumstances, use petroleum-based solvents to clean brake parts. Use DOT 4 brake fluid, dedicated brake cleaner or denatured alcohol only, as described. To prevent damage from spilled brake fluid, always cover paintwork when working on the braking system.**

Daytona models, and Street Triple models to VIN 560476

Removal

1 If required unscrew the brake hose guide bolts (see illustration).

2 If the caliper is just being displaced, unscrew the caliper mounting bolts and slide the caliper off the disc (see illustration). Tie or support it clear, making sure no strain is placed on the hose. **Note:** *Do not operate the brake pedal while the caliper is off the disc.*

3 If the caliper is being completely removed or overhauled, place some rag around the brake hose banjo bolt, then unscrew the bolt and detach the banjo union, noting its alignment with the caliper, and catching any residual fluid with the rag (see illustration). Wrap clingfilm around the banjo union and secure the hose in an upright position to minimise fluid loss. Discard the sealing washers as new ones must be fitted on reassembly. Remove the brake pads (see Section 2) – this involves detaching the caliper.

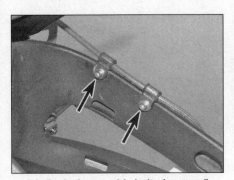

6.1 Brake hose guide bolts (arrowed)

6.2 Unscrew the bolts and slide the caliper off the disc

6.3 Brake hose banjo bolt (arrowed)

6.5a Fit the wood, then apply the compressed air as described . . .

6.5b . . . until the piston is displaced

6.7 Remove the seals and discard them

Overhaul

Note: *If the caliper is being overhauled (usually due to a sticking piston or fluid leak) read through the entire procedure first and make sure that you have obtained all the new parts required, including some new DOT 4 brake fluid.*

4 Clean the exterior of the caliper with denatured alcohol or brake system cleaner. Clean off all traces of corrosion and hardened grease from the bolts and from the boots in the caliper and bracket – remove the sleeve from the boot in the caliper. Replace the rubber boots with new ones if they are damaged, deformed or deteriorated – they come as a set along with the sleeve and mounting bolts **(see illustration 2.32a)**.

5 Place a piece of wood between the piston and the caliper body – it should be

just thick enough to stop the piston leaving the bore. Apply compressed air gradually and progressively, starting with a fairly low pressure, to the fluid inlet on the caliper body and allow the piston to ease out of its bore **(see illustrations)**.

6 If the piston is stuck due to corrosion, find a suitable bolt to block the fluid inlet banjo bolt bore and thread it in, then unscrew the bleed valve and apply the air to this in the same way – the narrower bore will allow more air pressure to be applied to the piston as less can escape. Do not try to remove the piston by levering it out or by using pliers or other grips. If the piston has completely seized you may have to replace the caliper with a new one.

7 Remove the dust seal and the piston seal from the piston bore using a soft wooden or

plastic tool to avoid scratching the bores **(see illustration)**. Discard the seals as new ones must be fitted.

8 Clean the piston and bore with clean DOT 4 brake fluid. Blow through the fluid galleries in the caliper to ensure they are clear.

Caution: Do not, under any circumstances, use a petroleum-based solvent to clean brake parts.

9 Inspect the caliper bore and piston for signs of corrosion, nicks and burrs and loss of plating. If surface defects are present, the piston and/or the caliper assembly must be replaced with new ones.

10 Lubricate the new piston seal with clean brake fluid and fit it into the inner groove in the caliper bore **(see illustrations)**.

11 Lubricate the new dust seal with silicone grease and fit it into the outer groove in the caliper bore **(see illustration)**.

12 Lubricate the piston with clean brake fluid and fit it, closed-end first, into the caliper bore, taking care not to displace the seals **(see illustration)**. Using your thumbs, push the piston all the way in, making sure it enters the bore squarely **(see illustration)**.

13 Apply a smear of silicone-based grease to the boots and sleeve, and fit them if removed or if new ones are being used **(see illustration 2.32a)**.

Installation

14 If the caliper was just displaced, refer to Section 2 and make sure the pads and all caliper components are in good functioning order. Slide the caliper onto the disc making

6.10a Lubricate the new piston seal with brake fluid . . .

6.10b . . . then fit it into its groove . . .

6.11 . . . followed by the new dust seal

6.12a Fit the piston . . .

6.12b . . . and push it all the way in

6.14a Slide the caliper onto the disc . . .

6.14b . . . making sure the pads locate correctly against the guide

6.20 Brake hose banjo bolt (arrowed)

sure the pads locate correctly on each side **(see illustrations)**. Install the caliper mounting bolts and tighten them to the torque settings specified at the beginning of the Chapter **(see illustration 6.2)**.

15 If the caliper has been overhauled refer to Section 2 and install the brake pads and caliper.

16 If detached, connect the brake hose to the caliper, aligning it as noted on removal, and using new sealing washers on each side of the fitting **(see illustration 6.3)**. Tighten the banjo bolt to the torque setting specified at the beginning of the Chapter.

17 If detached fit the rear brake hose guides onto the swingarm **(see illustration 6.1)**.

18 Top up the hydraulic reservoir with DOT 4 brake fluid (see Pre-ride checks) and bleed the system as described in Section 10. Check that there are no fluid leaks and test the operation of the brake before riding the motorcycle.

Street Triple models from VIN 560477

Note: *It is not possible to fully overhaul the caliper as not all parts are available for it – if a new piston or seals are required a new caliper must be fitted. The only parts available are the rubber boots for the slider pins, the pad pin and clip and the bleed valve and cap.*

Removal

19 Unscrew the brake hose guide bolts on the swingarm. On models with ABS, either displace the wheel speed sensor from the caliper bracket (see Section 21), or release the sensor wire from the clips joining it to the brake hose, as required.

20 If the caliper is being completely removed, place some rag around the brake hose banjo bolt, then unscrew the bolt and detach the banjo union, noting its alignment with the caliper, and catching any residual fluid with the rag **(see illustration)**. Seal the banjo union and secure the hose upright to minimise fluid loss and prevent air getting in. New sealing washers must be fitted on reassembly.

21 Remove the brake pads (see Section 2). Remove the rear wheel (see Section 14) – this leaves the caliper assembly free.

Overhaul

22 Slide the caliper and bracket apart **(see illustration)**.

23 Clean the caliper and bracket with denatured alcohol or brake system cleaner. Clean off all traces of corrosion and hardened grease from the slider pins and their boots. Replace the rubber boots with new ones if they are damaged, deformed or deteriorated.

24 Note how the pad spring is fitted and remove it for cleaning if required **(see illustration)**. Also clean the pad guide on the bracket **(see illustration)**.

25 Make sure the pad spring and guide are correctly located **(see illustrations 6.24a and b)**. Apply a smear of silicone grease to the slider pins and inside the boots **(see illustration 6.22)**. Slide the caliper onto the bracket, making sure the boot rims seat correctly in the groove in the slider pin.

Installation

26 Install the rear wheel (see Section 14). Install the brake pads (see Section 2).

27 If detached, connect the brake hose to the caliper, aligning it as noted on removal, and using new sealing washers on each side of the fitting **(see illustration 6.20)**. Tighten the banjo bolt to the torque setting specified at the beginning of the Chapter.

28 Secure the brake hose, and where fitted the ABS wheel speed sensor wire, or fit the sensor if displaced (Section 21).

29 Check the fluid level in the reservoir (see Pre-ride checks), and if required bleed the system as described in Section 10. Check that there are no fluid leaks and test the operation of the brake before riding the motorcycle.

7 Rear brake disc

Inspection

1 Refer to Section 4 of this Chapter, noting that the dial gauge should be attached to the swingarm.

Removal

2 Remove the rear wheel (see Section 14).

3 Mark the relationship of the disc to the wheel so it can be installed in the same position (unless you are fitting a new disc).

4 Unscrew the disc bolts, loosening them

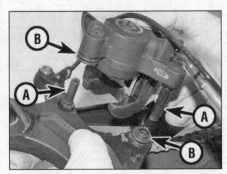

6.22 Slide the caliper and bracket apart. Slider pins (A), rubber boots (B)

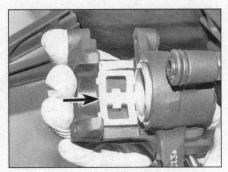

6.24a Pad spring (arrowed)

6.24b Pad guide (arrowed)

7.4 Rear brake disc bolts (arrowed)

8.1 Reservoir mounting bolt (arrowed)

8.2 Unscrew the banjo bolt and detach the hose

evenly and a little at a time in a criss-cross pattern to avoid distorting the disc, then remove the disc from the wheel **(see illustration)** – note that on models with ABS the disc bolts also secure the wheel sensor pulse ring (see Section 21). Triumph specify that new bolts should be used as they are pre-treated with a threadlock, but if this is not practicable clean the threads of the old bolts and apply some fresh threadlock to them on installation.

Installation

5 Before installing the disc, make sure there is no dirt or corrosion where the disc seats on the hub, particularly right in the angle of the seat, as this will not allow the disc to sit flat when it is bolted down and it will appear to be warped when checked or when using the rear brake.
6 Mount the disc on the wheel making sure it is the correct way round **(see illustration 7.4)**. Align the previously applied matchmarks (if you're reinstalling the original disc). On models with ABS fit the pulse ring onto the disc.
7 Fit the new or threadlocked bolts, then tighten them evenly and a little at a time in a criss-cross pattern to the torque setting specified at the beginning of the Chapter. Clean off all grease from the brake disc using acetone or brake system cleaner. If a new brake disc has been fitted, remove any protective coating from its working surfaces.
8 Install the rear wheel (see Section 14).
9 Operate the brake pedal several times to bring the pads into contact with the disc.

Check the operation of the brake carefully before riding the motorcycle.

8 Rear brake master cylinder

⚠️ **Warning: If the brake master cylinder is in need of an overhaul all old brake fluid should be flushed from the system. Overhaul of the brake master cylinder must be done in a spotlessly clean work area to avoid contamination and possible failure of the brake hydraulic system components. Do not, under any circumstances, use petroleum-based solvents to clean brake parts. Use clean DOT 4 brake fluid, dedicated brake cleaner or denatured alcohol only, as described. To prevent damage from spilled brake fluid, always cover paintwork when working on the braking system.**

Removal

1 Unscrew the bolt securing the reservoir to the frame **(see illustration)**.
2 Place some rag around the brake hose banjo bolt, then unscrew the bolt and detach the banjo union, noting its alignment, and catching any residual fluid with the rag **(see illustration)**. Discard the two sealing washers as they must be replaced with new ones. Wrap the end of the hose or pipe in clingfilm to prevent excessive loss of brake fluid, fluid spills and system contamination.

3 On Daytona models, and Street Triple models to VIN 560476, remove the retaining clip from the clevis pin securing the master cylinder pushrod to the brake pedal **(see illustration)**. Withdraw the clevis pin and separate the pushrod from the pedal. Unscrew the bolts securing the master cylinder and remove it along with the reservoir, noting how the bolts secure the heel guard **(see illustration)**.
4 On Street Triple models from VIN 560477 slacken the bolts securing the master cylinder – note the position of the brake pipe bracket. Refer to Chapter 5 and remove the brake pedal, then remove the master cylinder.
5 Remove the reservoir cap, diaphragm plate and diaphragm, and drain the fluid in the reservoir into a suitable container. If required release the clamp securing the reservoir hose to the union on the master cylinder and detach the hose.

Overhaul

Note: *If the master cylinder is being overhauled (usually due to sticking or poor action, or fluid leaks) read through the entire procedure first and make sure that you have obtained the rebuild kit (which includes the piston, cup, seal and spring), as the old parts should not be reused once removed. Also get some new DOT 4 brake fluid.*
6 Dislodge the rubber dust boot from the base of the master cylinder to reveal the pushrod retaining circlip **(see illustration)**.
7 Depress the pushrod and, using circlip

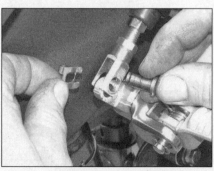

8.3a Remove the retaining clip and withdraw the clevis pin

8.3b Master cylinder bolts (arrowed)

8.6 Pull the boot out . . .

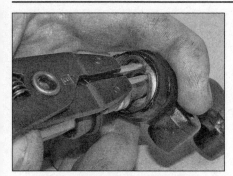

8.7a ... then release the circlip ...

8.7b ... and remove the pushrod assembly ...

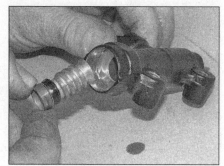

8.7c ... the piston ...

pliers, remove the circlip **(see illustration)**. Remove the pushrod, then slide out the piston assembly and spring **(see illustrations)**. If they are difficult to remove, apply low pressure compressed air to the fluid outlet. Lay the parts out in the proper order to prevent confusion during reassembly.

8 Clean the master cylinder with clean brake fluid.

Caution: Do not, under any circumstances, use a petroleum-based solvent to clean brake parts. If compressed air is available, use it to dry the parts thoroughly (make sure it's filtered and unlubricated).

9 Check the master cylinder bore for corrosion, scratches, nicks and score marks. If damage is evident, the master cylinder must be replaced with a new one. If the master cylinder is in poor condition, then the caliper should be checked as well.

10 Inspect the reservoir hose for cracks or splits and replace it with a new one if necessary **(see illustration 8.15)**. If required, remove the hose union from the master cylinder **(see illustration)**. Discard the O-ring as a new one must be used.

11 The piston, cup, seal and spring are included in the rebuild kit. Use all of the new parts, regardless of the apparent condition of the old ones. Fit them according to the layout of the old piston assembly. If the seal is not already fitted onto the piston, lubricate it with new brake fluid before fitting it, and make sure the wider end will fit into the master cylinder first **(see illustration)**.

12 Fit the cup onto the narrow end of the spring **(see illustration)**. Fit the spring, wide-end

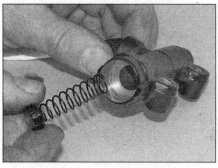

8.7d ... and the spring

first, into the master cylinder, and push the cup in, making sure the lip does not turn inside out **(see illustrations)**.

13 Lubricate the piston with clean brake fluid

8.10 Remove the circlip (arrowed) to release the union

and push it into the master cylinder up against the spring, making sure the lip on the seal does not turn inside out **(see illustration)**.

14 Fit the rubber boot and circlip on the rod

8.11 Make sure the seal is correctly fitted on the piston

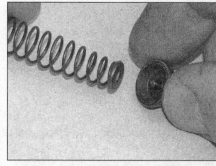

8.12a Fit the cup onto the spring ...

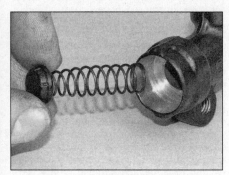

8.12b ... then fit the spring into the cylinder ...

8.12c ... and push the cup in

8.13 Fit the piston into the cylinder

8.14a Locate the pushrod and push
it in . . .

8.14b . . . then fit the circlip . . .

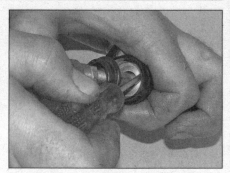

8.14c . . . and push it into its groove

8.14d Make sure the boot lips locate
correctly

8.15 Fit the reservoir hose and its clamp

Hold the master cylinder upright and tighten the banjo bolt to the torque setting specified at the beginning of the Chapter (**see illustration 8.16b**). Displace the footrest bracket and master cylinder, then refer to Chapter 5 for installation of the brake pedal, fitting the master cylinder along with the heel plate and the brake pipe bracket.

18 Install the reservoir, making sure the hose is correctly routed, and secure it with the bolt (**see illustration 8.1**).

19 Fill the fluid reservoir with new DOT 4 brake fluid (see Pre-ride checks) and bleed the system following the procedure in Section 10.

20 Fit the rubber diaphragm, making sure it is correctly seated, the diaphragm plate and the cap onto the master cylinder reservoir.

21 Check the operation of the brake carefully before riding the motorcycle.

9 Brake hoses and fittings

Inspection

1 Brake hose condition should be checked regularly and the hoses replaced with new ones at the specified interval (see Chapter 1). Twist and flex the hoses while looking for cracks, bulges and seeping hydraulic fluid. Check extra carefully around the areas where the hoses connect with the banjo fittings, as these are common areas for hose failure.

2 Inspect the banjo fittings connected to the brake hoses. If the fittings are rusted, scratched or cracked, fit new ones.

Removal and installation

3 The brake hoses have banjo fittings on each end. Cover the surrounding area with plenty of rags. Unscrew the banjo bolt at each end of the hose, noting the alignment of the fitting with the master cylinder or brake caliper. Free the hose from any clips or guides and remove it, noting its routing. Discard the sealing washers. **Note:** *Do not operate the brake lever or pedal while a brake hose is disconnected.*

4 Position the new hose, making sure it isn't twisted or otherwise strained, and ensure that it is correctly routed through any clips or guides and is clear of all moving components.

if removed and locate the lower rim of the boot in its groove. Locate the pushrod against the piston and push it in, then fit the circlip, making sure it is properly seated in the groove (**see illustrations**). Fit the upper rim of the boot into the groove in the master cylinder (**see illustration**).

15 If removed, fit a new reservoir hose union O-ring, then push the union into the master cylinder and secure it with the circlip (**see illustration 8.10**). Connect the reservoir hose to the union and secure it with the clamp (**see illustration**).

Installation

16 On Daytona models, and Street Triple models to VIN 560476 locate the master cylinder and the heel guard, fit the lower bolt only and tighten it finger-tight. Connect the brake hose to the master cylinder, using new

sealing washers on each side of the union, and aligning it as noted on removal (**see illustration**). Hold the master cylinder upright and tighten the banjo bolt to the torque setting specified at the beginning of the Chapter (**see illustration**). Now position the master cylinder correctly, fit the upper bolt and tighten both bolts to the torque setting specified at the beginning of the Chapter. Align the brake pedal with the master cylinder pushrod clevis, then slide in the clevis pin, and secure it with the retaining clip (see illustration 8.3a).

17 On Street Triple models from VIN 560477, temporarily fit the master cylinder onto the bracket using the bottom bolt only, then fit the footrest bracket to the frame and tighten the bolts. Connect the brake hose to the master cylinder, using new sealing washers on each side of the union, and aligning it as noted on removal (**see illustration 8.16a**).

8.16a Fit the hose using new sealing
washers . . .

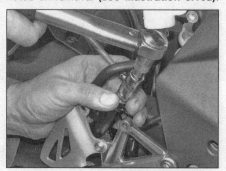

8.16b . . . and tighten the bolt to the
specified torque

10.5a Front brake caliper bleed valve (arrowed) – Daytona and Street Triple R

10.5b Front brake caliper bleed valve (arrowed) – Street Triple

10.5c Rear brake caliper bleed valve (arrowed)

5 Check that the fittings align correctly, then install the banjo bolts, using new sealing washers on both sides of the fittings **(see illustration 8.17a)**. Tighten the banjo bolts to the torque setting specified at the beginning of this Chapter.

6 Flush the old brake fluid from the system, refill with new DOT 4 brake fluid (see Pre-ride checks) and bleed the air from the system (see Section 10).

7 Check the operation of the brakes before riding the motorcycle.

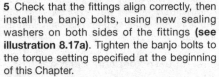

10 Brake bleeding and fluid change

Note 1: *On ABS models, before draining the brake fluid from the system, changing the fluid, or disconnecting any brake hoses or pipes from the master cylinders and ABS modulator or between them, bear in mind that the system must be bled on completion of work, and although this is done initially in the same way as models without ABS, to complete the procedure effectively the Triumph Diagnostic tool must be used to open and close the solenoids within the ABS modulator, and this can only be carried out by a dealer with the diagnostic tool. The bike should be transported, not ridden, to the dealer. It is OK to disconnect*

the hoses from the calipers, provided they are supported upright to minimise fluid loss and air ingress, as they come after the modulator in the system and so any air that gets into the end of the hose or caliper does not have to bleed through the modulator.

Note 2: *If bleeding the system using the conventional method (or one-man kit) described does not work sufficiently well, it is advisable to obtain a vacuum-type brake bleeding tool, following the manufacturer's instructions **(see illustration 10.18)**.*

Bleeding

1 Bleeding the brakes is simply the process of removing air from the master cylinder, the hose, and the brake caliper. Bleeding is necessary whenever a brake system hydraulic connection is loosened, after a component or hose is replaced with a new one, or when the master cylinder or caliper is overhauled. Leaks in the system may also allow air to enter, but leaking brake fluid will reveal their presence and warn you of the need for repair.

2 To bleed the brakes, you will need some new DOT 4 brake fluid, a length of clear vinyl or plastic hose that fits snugly over the bleed valve, a small container partially filled with clean brake fluid, some rags, a spanner (preferably a ring spanner) to fit the brake caliper bleed valve, and help from an assistant. One-man brake bleeding kits, consisting of a container

and hose arrangement with one-way valve, are available from good automotive suppliers, and negate the need for an assistant.

3 Cover painted components to prevent damage in the event that brake fluid is spilled.

4 Refer to Pre-ride checks and remove the reservoir cover or cap, diaphragm plate (where fitted) and diaphragm, and slowly pump the brake lever (front brake) or pedal (rear brake) a few times, until no air bubbles can be seen floating up from the bottom of the reservoir. This bleeds the air from the master cylinder end of the line. Temporarily refit the reservoir cap or cover.

5 Pull the dust cap off the bleed valve on the caliper **(see illustrations)**. Loosen then lightly retighten the bleed valve – if you have a ring spanner, use this and leave it fitted over the valve during the procedure. Attach one end of the clear vinyl or plastic hose to the bleed valve and submerge the other end in the clean brake fluid in the container **(see illustration)**. If you're using a one-man type brake bleeder, there is no need for fluid in the container.

6 Check the fluid level in the reservoir. Do not allow the fluid level to drop below the low level mark during the procedure.

7 Carefully pump the brake lever or pedal three or four times, then hold it in (front) or down (rear) and open the bleed valve **(see illustration)**. When the valve is opened, brake fluid will flow out of the caliper into the

10.5d Set the kit, comprising container, hose and spanner, up as shown . . .

10.7 . . . and bleed the brake as described

10.9 Front master cylinder bleed valve (arrowed) – Daytona and Street Triple R

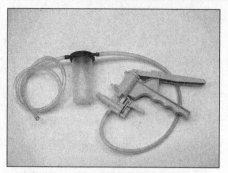

10.18 A commercially available vacuum tool that can be used for drawing brake fluid out

clear tubing, and the lever will move toward the handlebar, or the pedal will move down. If there is air in the system there will be air bubbles in the brake fluid coming out of the caliper.

8 Tighten the bleed valve, then release the brake lever or pedal gradually. Top-up the reservoir and repeat the process until no air bubbles are visible in the brake fluid leaving the caliper, and the lever or pedal is firm when applied. On completion, disconnect the hose, then tighten the bleed valve to the torque setting specified at the beginning of this Chapter and install the dust cap.

9 On Daytona and Street Triple R models the front brake master cylinder is fitted with a bleed valve **(see illustration)** – after bleeding the calipers bleed the master cylinder in the same way.

 If it is not possible to produce a firm feel to the lever or pedal, the fluid may be aerated. Let the brake fluid in the system stabilise for a few hours and then repeat the procedure when the tiny bubbles in the system have settled out.

10 Top-up the reservoir to the correct level, then install the diaphragm, diaphragm plate (where fitted), and cap or cover (see Pre-ride checks). Wipe up any spilled brake fluid. Check the entire system for fluid leaks.

11 On models with ABS refer to the Note above and if necessary take the bike to a Triumph dealer to complete the bleeding of the modulator. Check the operation of the brakes before riding the motorcycle.

Fluid change

12 Changing the brake fluid is a similar process to bleeding the brakes and requires the same materials plus a suitable tool for siphoning the fluid out of the reservoir. Also ensure that the container is large enough to take all the old fluid when it is flushed out of the system.

13 Follow Steps 2, 3 and 5, then remove the reservoir cap, diaphragm plate (where fitted)

and diaphragm and siphon the old fluid out of the reservoir. Fill the reservoir with new brake fluid, then carefully pump the brake lever or pedal three or four times and hold it in (front) or down (rear) while opening the caliper bleed valve. When the valve is opened, brake fluid will flow out of the caliper into the clear tubing, and the lever will move toward the handlebar, or the pedal will move down.

14 Tighten the bleed valve, then release the brake lever or pedal gradually. Keep the reservoir topped-up with new fluid to above the LOWER level at all times or air may enter the system and greatly increase the length of the task. Repeat the process until new fluid can be seen emerging from the caliper bleed valve.

 Old brake fluid is invariably much darker in colour than new fluid, making it easy to see when all old fluid has been expelled from the system.

15 Disconnect the hose, then make sure the bleed valve is tightened to the specified torque setting and fit the dust cap.

16 Top-up the reservoir to the correct level, then install the diaphragm, diaphragm plate (where fitted), and cap or cover (see *Pre-ride*

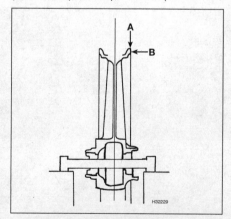

11.2 Check the wheel for radial (out-of-round) runout (A) and axial (side-to-side) runout (B)

checks). Wipe up any spilled brake fluid. Check the entire system for fluid leaks.

17 On models with ABS refer to the Note above and if necessary take the bike to a Triumph dealer to complete the bleeding of the modulator. Check the operation of the brakes before riding the motorcycle.

Draining the system for overhaul

18 Draining the brake fluid is again a similar process to bleeding the brakes. The quickest and easiest way is to use a commercially available vacuum-type brake bleeding tool **(see illustration)** – follow the manufacturer's instructions. Otherwise follow the procedure described above for changing the fluid, but quite simply do not put any new fluid into the reservoir – the system fills itself with air instead.

11 Wheel inspection and repair

1 In order to carry out a proper inspection of the wheels, it is necessary to support the bike upright so that the wheel being inspected is raised off the ground. Position the motorcycle on an auxiliary stand. Clean the wheels thoroughly to remove mud and dirt that may interfere with the inspection procedure or mask defects. Make a general check of the wheels (see Chapter 1) and tyres (see Pre-ride checks).

2 Attach a dial gauge to the fork or the swingarm and position its tip against the side of the wheel rim. Spin the wheel slowly and check the axial (side-to-side) runout of the rim **(see illustration)**.

3 In order to accurately check radial (out of round) runout with the dial gauge, remove the wheel from the machine, and the tyre from the wheel. With the axle clamped in a vice and the dial gauge positioned on the top of the rim, the wheel can be rotated to check the runout **(see illustration 11.2)**.

4 An easier, though slightly less accurate, method is to attach a stiff wire pointer to the fork or the swingarm and position the end a fraction of an inch from the wheel rim where the wheel and tyre join. If the wheel is true, the distance from the pointer to the rim will be constant as the wheel is rotated. **Note:** *If wheel runout is excessive, check the wheel bearings very carefully before renewing the wheel.*

5 The wheels should also be inspected for cracks, flat spots on the rim and other damage. Look very closely for dents in the area where the tyre bead contacts the rim. Dents in this area may prevent complete sealing of the tyre against the rim, which leads to deflation of the tyre over a period of time. If damage is evident, or if runout in either direction is excessive, the wheel will have to be renewed. Never attempt to repair a damaged cast alloy wheel.

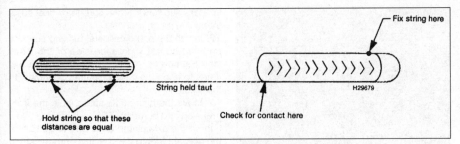

12.5 Wheel alignment check using string

12 Wheel alignment check

1 Misalignment of the wheels, which may be due to a cocked rear wheel or a bent frame or fork yokes, can cause strange and possibly serious handling problems. If the frame or yokes are at fault, repair by a frame specialist or replacement with new parts are the only alternatives.

2 To check the alignment you will need an assistant, a length of string or a perfectly straight piece of wood or metal bar and a ruler. A plumb bob or other suitable weight will also be required.

3 In order to make a proper check of the wheels it is necessary to support the bike in an upright position, using an auxiliary stand. First ensure that the chain adjuster markings coincide on each side of the swingarm (see Chapter 1, Section 1). Measure the width of both tyres at their widest points. Subtract the smaller measurement from the larger measurement, then divide the difference by two. The result is the amount of offset that should exist between the front and rear tyres on both sides.

4 If a string is used, have your assistant hold one end of it about halfway between the floor and the rear axle, touching the rear sidewall of the tyre.

5 Run the other end of the string forward and pull it tight so that it is roughly parallel to the floor **(see illustration)**. Slowly bring the string into contact with the front sidewall of the rear tyre, then turn the front wheel until it is parallel with the string. Measure the distance from the front tyre sidewall to the string.

6 Repeat the procedure on the other side of the motorcycle. The distance from the front tyre sidewall to the string should be equal on both sides.

7 As previously mentioned, a perfectly straight length of wood or metal bar may be substituted for the string **(see illustration)**. The procedure is the same.

8 If the distance between the string and tyre is greater on one side, or if the rear wheel appears to be out of alignment, have your machine checked by a Triumph dealer or frame specialist.

9 If the front-to-back alignment is correct, the wheels still may be out of alignment vertically.

10 Using a plumb bob, or other suitable weight, and a length of string, check the rear wheel to make sure it is vertical. To do this, hold the string against the tyre upper sidewall and allow the weight to settle just off the floor. When the string touches both the upper and lower tyre sidewalls and is perfectly straight, the wheel is vertical. If it is not, place thin spacers under one leg of the stand until it is.

11 Once the rear wheel is vertical, check the front wheel in the same manner. If both wheels are not perfectly vertical, the frame and/or major suspension components are bent.

13 Front wheel

Removal

1 Support the motorcycle securely in an upright position on level ground using an auxiliary stand so the front wheel is off the ground.

2 Displace the front brake calipers (see Section 3). Support them with a piece of wire, string, a cable-tie or a bungee cord so that no strain is placed on the hoses. There is no need to disconnect the hoses. **Note:** *Do not operate the front brake lever with the calipers removed.*

3 Slacken the axle clamp bolts on the bottom of the right- or left-hand fork, according to model **(see illustration)**. Unscrew the axle – you'll need a dedicated motorcycle axle bit, readily available from good suppliers, or a large hex bit or car sump key.

4 Support the wheel, then withdraw the axle and lower the wheel to the ground **(see illustration)**. Use a drift to drive the axle out if required. Roll the wheel out from between the forks.

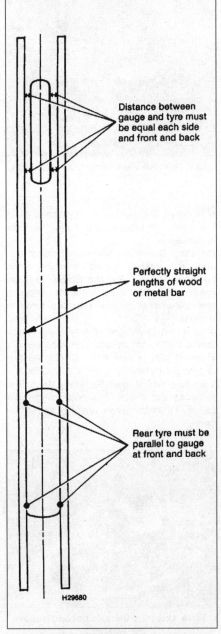

12.7 Wheel alignment check using a straight-edge

13.3 Slacken the clamp bolts (A) then unscrew the axle (B) using a large hex bit

13.4 Withdraw the axle and remove the wheel

13.5 Remove the spacer from each side

13.11 Tighten the axle to the specified torque

5 Remove the spacer from each side of the wheel for safekeeping if required **(see illustration)**.

Caution: Don't lay the wheel down and allow it to rest on a disc – the disc could become warped. Set the wheel on wood blocks so the disc doesn't support the weight of the wheel, or keep it upright.

6 Clean off all old grease from the axle and spacers and remove any corrosion using a scouring pad or wire wool. Check the axle is straight by rolling it on a flat surface. If the equipment is available, place the axle in V-blocks and check for runout using a dial gauge. If the axle is bent, replace it with a new one.

7 Check the condition of the wheel bearings (see Section 15).

Installation

8 Apply lithium-based grease to the lips of the bearing seals, to the axle and to the spacers. Fit a spacer into each side of the wheel – they are the same **(see illustration 13.5)**.

9 Manoeuvre the wheel into position.

10 Lift the wheel into place between the forks, making sure the spacers remain in position, and slide the axle in from the left-hand side **(see illustration 13.4)**.

11 Tighten the axle to the torque setting specified at the beginning of the Chapter **(see illustration)**. Wipe any excess grease off the

spacers and forks. Make sure the wheel spins freely.

12 Install the brake calipers, making sure the pads sit squarely on each side of the discs (see Section 3). Apply the front brake a few times to bring the pads back into contact with the discs.

13 Move the bike off its stand, hold the front brake on and pump the forks a few times. Now tighten the axle clamp bolts on the bottom of the relevant fork to the specified torque setting (see illustration 13.3).

14 Check for correct operation of the front brake before riding the motorcycle.

---

14 Rear wheel

Removal

1 Support the motorcycle securely in an upright position on level ground using an auxiliary stand so the rear wheel is off the ground.

2 Refer to Chapter 1 and slacken the drive chain.

3 Displace the rear brake caliper (see Section 6). Support it with a piece of wire, string, a cable-tie or a bungee cord so that no strain is placed on the hose. There is no need to disconnect the hose from the caliper. **Note:** *Do not operate the brake pedal with the caliper removed.*

4 Unscrew the nut from the left-hand end of the axle and remove the washer and the adjustment position marker **(see illustrations)**.

5 Support the wheel then withdraw the axle along with the right-hand adjustment position marker and lower the wheel to the ground **(see illustration)**. Remove the caliper bracket, noting how it locates between the wheel and the swingarm **(see illustration)**. Disengage the chain from the sprocket and remove the wheel from between the swingarm ends **(see illustration)**.

6 Remove the plain spacer from the left-hand

14.4a Unscrew the axle nut and remove the washer . . .

14.4b . . . and adjustment position marker

14.5a Withdraw the axle and lower the wheel . . .

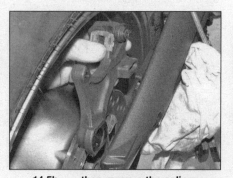

14.5b . . . then remove the caliper bracket . . .

14.5c . . . and slip the chain off the sprocket

side of the wheel and the shouldered spacer from the right-hand side for safekeeping if required **(see illustrations)**.

7 Clean off all old grease from the axle and spacers and remove any corrosion using a scouring pad or wire wool. Check the axle is straight by rolling it on a flat surface. If the equipment is available, place the axle in V-blocks and check for runout using a dial gauge. If the axle is bent, replace it with a new one.
8 Check the wheel bearings and sprocket coupling bearings (see Section 15).

Installation

9 Apply a thin coat of lithium-based grease to the lips of each grease seal, and also to the spacers and the axle.
10 Fit the plain spacer into the left-hand side of the wheel and the shouldered spacer into the right-hand side **(see illustrations 14.6a and b)**.
11 Manoeuvre the wheel into place between the ends of the swingarm. Fit the drive chain around the sprocket **(see illustration 14.5c)**. Fit the brake caliper bracket onto the swingarm, locating the lug in the groove **(see illustration 14.5b)**.
12 Slide the right-hand adjustment position marker (the one with the raised sections, which must face out) onto the axle. Lift the wheel into position, making sure the caliper bracket and the spacers remain in place, and slide the axle through from the right-hand side **(see illustration 14.5a)**. Make sure it passes through the caliper bracket. Make sure the adjustment marker is correctly positioned with the raised sections horizontal and fit the flats on the axle head between them **(see illustration)**.
13 Check that everything is correctly aligned, then fit the left-hand adjustment position marker **(see illustration 14.4b)**. Fit the washer and the axle nut **(see illustration 14.4a)**. Adjust the chain slack as described in Chapter 1. Tighten the axle nut to the torque setting specified at the beginning of the Chapter, making sure the adjustment markers are butted against the adjuster bolt heads **(see illustration)**.
14 Install the brake caliper, making sure the pads sit squarely on each side of the disc (see Section 6).
15 Operate the brake pedal several times to bring the pads into contact with the disc. Check the operation of the rear brake before riding the bike.

14.6a Remove the plain spacer . . .

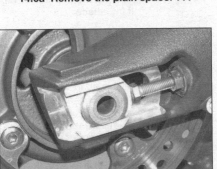
14.6b . . . and the shouldered spacer

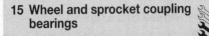
14.12 Make sure the axle head and adjustment marker locate correctly

15 Wheel and sprocket coupling bearings

Front wheel bearings

Note: *Always renew the wheel bearings in pairs, never individually. Avoid using a high pressure cleaner on the wheel bearing area.*
1 Remove the wheel (see Section 13). A caged ball bearing is fitted in each side of the wheel.
2 Lever out the bearing seal from each side

15.2 Lever out the grease seals

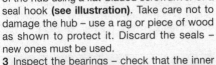
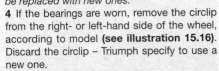
14.13 Tighten the axle nut to the specified torque

of the hub using a flat-bladed screwdriver or a seal hook **(see illustration)**. Take care not to damage the hub – use a rag or piece of wood as shown to protect it. Discard the seals – new ones must be used.
3 Inspect the bearings – check that the inner race turns smoothly and that the outer race is a tight fit in the hub (see *Tools and Workshop Tips* in the Reference Section). **Note:** *Do not remove the bearings unless they are going to be replaced with new ones.*
4 If the bearings are worn, remove the circlip from the right- or left-hand side of the wheel, according to model **(see illustration 15.16)**. Discard the circlip – Triumph specify to use a new one.
5 Move the bearing spacer aside to expose the inner race **(see illustration)**. Using a metal rod (preferably a brass punch) inserted through the centre of the upper bearing drive the lower bearing from the hub, moving the spacer

15.5a Move the spacer to the side to expose the inner race (arrowed) . . .

15.5b ... then locate the drift on it and drive the bearing out

15.10 Fit the grease seal and press or tap it into place

15.14 Lever out the grease seal

around and relocating the drift so it's driven out squarely **(see illustration)**. The bearing spacer will also come out. Turn the wheel over so that the remaining bearing faces down. Drive the bearing out of the wheel. Alternatively use an internal expanding puller on a slide-hammer attachment draw the bearings out, holding the wheel securely down as you do **(see illustrations 15.17a and b)**.

6 Thoroughly clean the hub area of the wheel and inspect the bearing seats for scoring and wear. If the seats are damaged, consult a Triumph dealer or wheel specialist before reassembling the wheel.

7 Drive the new bearing, marked side facing out, into one side of the hub until it seats using a bearing driver or suitable socket located on the outer race – do not drive it in using the inner race **(see illustration 15.19)**.

15.16 Remove the circlip

15.17a Locate the knife edge of the puller in the gap between the bearing and the spacer, then expand it ...

Alternatively draw it in using a drawbolt arrangement (see Tools and Workshop Tips). Ensure the bearing is fitted squarely and all the way onto its seat.

8 Turn the wheel over then fit the bearing spacer and the other new bearing.

9 Fit a new circlip into its groove outside the relevant bearing **(see illustration 15.16)**.

10 Apply a smear of grease to the lips of the new seals, then press them into the hub **(see illustration)**. Level the seals with the rim of the hub with a small block of wood if necessary **(see illustration 15.22b)**.

11 Clean the brake discs using acetone or brake system cleaner, then install the wheel (see Section 13).

Rear wheel bearings

12 Remove the wheel (see Section 14). Lift the sprocket coupling out of the wheel, noting how it fits, and remove the spacer inside it **(see illustrations 15.24a and b)**. A caged ball bearing is fitted in each side of the wheel.

13 Set the wheel on wood blocks with the disc (right-hand side) facing up.

14 Lever out the bearing seal on the right-hand side of the hub using a flat-bladed screwdriver or a seal hook **(see illustration)**. Take care not to damage the hub – use a rag or piece of wood as shown to protect it. Discard the seal – a new one must be used.

15 Inspect the bearings – check that the inner race turns smoothly and that the outer race is a tight fit in the hub (see Tools and Workshop Tips in the Reference Section). **Note:** *Do not*

15.17b ... and use the slide-hammer to dislodge the bearing

remove the bearings unless they are going to be replaced with new ones.

16 If the bearings are worn, remove the circlip securing the right-hand bearing **(see illustration)**. Discard the circlip – Triumph specify to use a new one.

17 Move the bearing spacer aside to expose the inner race **(see illustration 15.5a)**. Using a metal rod (preferably a brass punch) inserted through the centre of the upper bearing drive the lower bearing from the hub, moving the spacer around and relocating the drift so it's driven out squarely **(see illustration 15.5b)**. The bearing spacer will also come out. Turn the wheel over so that the remaining bearing faces down. Drive the bearing out of the wheel. Alternatively use an internal expanding puller on a slide-hammer attachment draw the bearings out, holding the wheel securely down as you do **(see illustrations)**.

18 Thoroughly clean the hub area of the wheel and inspect the bearing seats for scoring and wear. If the seats are damaged, consult a Triumph dealer or wheel specialist before reassembling the wheel.

19 Drive the new bearing, marked side facing out, into one side of the hub until it seats using a bearing driver or suitable socket located on the outer race **(see illustration)** – do not drive it in using the inner race. Alternatively draw it in using a drawbolt arrangement (see Tools and Workshop Tips). Ensure the bearing is fitted squarely and all the way onto its seat.

20 Turn the wheel over then fit the bearing spacer and the other new bearing.

15.19 A socket can be used to drive in the bearing

15.22a Fit the grease seal and press or tap it into place . . .

15.22b . . . using a block of wood as shown levels it with the rim

15.24a Lift the sprocket coupling out of the wheel . . .

15.24b . . . and remove the spacer from inside it

15.25 Lever out the grease seal

15.27 Remove the circlip (arrowed)

21 Fit a new circlip into its groove outside the right-hand bearing **(see illustration 15.16)**.

22 Apply a smear of grease to the lips of the new seal, then press it into the right-hand side of the hub **(see illustration)**. Level the seal with the rim of the hub with a small block of wood if necessary **(see illustration)**.

23 Make sure the spacer is in place, then fit the sprocket coupling into the wheel **(see illustrations 15.24b and a)**. Clean the brake disc using acetone or brake system cleaner, then install the wheel (see Section 14).

Sprocket coupling bearing

24 Remove the rear wheel (see Section 14). Lift the sprocket coupling out of the wheel, noting how it fits, and remove the spacer inside it **(see illustrations)**.

25 Lever out the bearing seal from the outside of the coupling using a large flat-bladed screwdriver or seal hook **(see illustration)**. Take care not to damage the hub – use a rag or piece of wood as shown to protect it. Discard the seal – a new one must be used.

26 Inspect the bearing – check that the inner race turns smoothly and that the outer race is a tight fit in the hub (see Tools and Workshop Tips in the Reference Section). **Note:** *Do not remove the bearing unless it is going to be replaced with a new one.*

27 If the bearing is worn, remove the circlip **(see illustration)**. Discard the circlip – Triumph specify to use a new one.

28 Support the coupling on blocks of wood and drive the bearing out from the inside using a bearing driver or socket **(see illustration)**.

29 Thoroughly clean the bearing recess in the

coupling then fit the bearing from the outside of the coupling, with the marked or sealed side facing out. Using a bearing driver or a socket large enough to contact the outer race of the bearing, drive it in until it is completely seated **(see illustration)**. Fit a new circlip into its groove.

30 Apply a smear of grease to the lips of the new seal, then press it into the coupling **(see illustration)**. Level the seal with the rim of the hub with a small block of wood if necessary **(see illustration 15.22b)**.

31 Check the sprocket coupling/rubber dampers (see Section 19).

32 Fit the spacer, then fit the sprocket coupling into the wheel **(see illustrations 15.24b and a)**. Clean the brake disc using acetone or brake system cleaner then install the wheel (see Section 14).

15.28 Drive the bearing out from the inside

15.29 A socket can be used to drive in the bearing

15.30 Press or drive the seal into the coupling

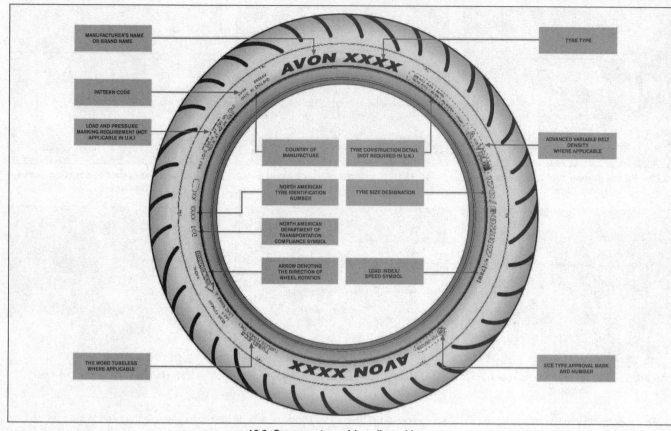

MANUFACTURER'S NAME OR BRAND NAME

PATTERN CODE

LOAD AND PRESSURE MARKING REQUIREMENT (NOT APPLICABLE IN U.K.)

TYRE TYPE

ADVANCED VARIABLE BELT DENSITY WHERE APPLICABLE

COUNTRY OF MANUFACTURE

TYRE CONSTRUCTION DETAIL (NOT REQUIRED IN U.K.)

NORTH AMERICAN TYRE IDENTIFICATION NUMBER

TYRE SIZE DESIGNATION

NORTH AMERICAN DEPARTMENT OF TRANSPORTATION COMPLIANCE SYMBOL

ARROW DENOTING THE DIRECTION OF WHEEL ROTATION

LOAD INDEX/ SPEED SYMBOL

THE WORD TUBELESS WHERE APPLICABLE

ECE TYPE APPROVAL MARK AND NUMBER

16.3 Common tyre sidewall markings

16 Tyre information and fitting

General information

1 The wheels fitted to all models are designed to take tubeless tyres only. Tyre sizes are given in the Specifications at the beginning of this chapter.
2 Refer to the Pre-ride checks listed at the beginning of this manual for tyre maintenance.

Fitting new tyres

3 When selecting new tyres, refer to the tyre information in the Owner's Handbook. Ensure that front and rear tyre types are compatible, the correct size and correct speed rating; if necessary seek advice from a Triumph dealer or tyre fitting specialist **(see illustration)**.
4 It is recommended that tyres are fitted by a motorcycle tyre specialist rather than attempted in the home workshop. This is because the force required to break the seal between the wheel rim and tyre bead is substantial, and is usually beyond the capabilities of an individual working with normal tyre levers. Additionally, the specialist will be able to balance the wheels after tyre fitting.
5 Note that punctured tubeless tyres can in

some cases be repaired. Repairs must be carried out by a motorcycle tyre fitting specialist.

17 Drive chain removal, cleaning and installation

Note: *The drive chain, which passes through the swingarm brace, has a riveted-type soft (joining) link so it can be split using one of several commercially-available chain cutting/ staking tools (Triumph can supply one, part No. T3880027). The soft joining link can be recognised by the side plate's different colour, as well as by the riveted ends of the link's two pins which look as if they have been deeply centre-punched, instead of peened over as with all the other pins.*
1 Remove the front sprocket cover (see Section 18).
2 Identify the soft link and move it to a suitable position to work on by rotating the back wheel **(see illustration)**.
3 Slacken the drive chain as described in Chapter 1.
4 Split the chain at the soft link using a chain breaker tool – refer to Section 8 'Chains' of Tools and Workshop Tips in the Reference section at the end of this manual for details of how to use the tool and how to rivet the

new soft link securely, or follow the tool manufacturer's instructions. Note that it is essential to use a new soft link when re-joining the chain. Never install a clip-type master link.
5 After riveting, check the soft link and pin ends for any signs of cracking. If there is any evidence of cracking, the soft link, O-rings (or X-rings), and side plate must be replaced with new ones. Measure the diameter of the riveted pin ends in two directions and check that each pin has been evenly riveted.
6 Install the sprocket cover.
7 On completion, adjust and lubricate the chain following the procedures described in Chapter 1.

17.2 The soft link (arrowed) should be easy to identify

18.1a Move the top of the clip off . . .

18.1b . . . then draw it out . . .

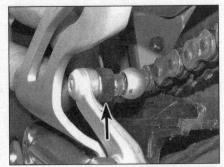

18.1c . . . and detach the rod from the lever. Note the seal (arrowed)

Caution: Don't use gasoline (petrol), solvent or other cleaning fluids which might damage its internal sealing properties. Don't use high-pressure water. Remove the chain, wipe it off, then blow dry it with compressed air immediately. The entire process shouldn't take longer than ten minutes – if it does, the sealing rings in the chain rollers could be damaged.

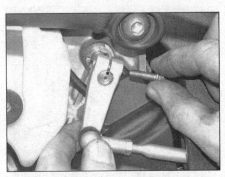

18.1d Note the alignment, then unscrew the bolt, slide the arm off the shaft . . .

18.1e . . . and draw the rod out

18 Sprockets

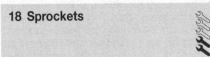

Front sprocket cover

1 Release the clip securing the linkage rod or quickshifter to the gearchange lever **(see illustrations)**. Pry the rod or quickshifter off the lever **(see illustration)**. To improve access on Street Triple models remove the heel guard first. Note the alignment of the punch mark on the gearchange shaft end with the slit in the linkage arm clamp – if the punch mark is not visible make your own mark **(see illustration)**. Unscrew the pinch bolt and slide the arm off the shaft and draw the rod or quickshifter out of the frame **(see illustration)**. Take care not to lose the ball joint seal.

2 Unscrew the front sprocket cover bolts securing and remove the cover **(see illustration)** – note the routing of any wiring and hoses through the front of the cover, according to model.

3 Installation is the reverse of removal. Clean any old grease off the linkage rod ball joint

and smear some fresh grease on. Align the slit in the linkage arm with the mark on the shaft. Make sure the ball joint seal is fitted, the ball fits fully into the socket, and the clip locates correctly.

Sprocket check

4 Remove the front sprocket cover (Steps 1 and 2).

5 Check the wear pattern on both sprockets (see Chapter 1, Section 2). If the sprocket teeth are worn excessively, replace the chain and both sprockets as a set. Whenever the sprockets are inspected, the drive chain should be inspected also (see Chapter 1). Always replace the chain and sprockets as a set – worn sprockets can ruin a new drive chain and vice versa.

6 Adjust and lubricate the chain following the procedures described in Chapter 1.

Front sprocket

Note: *Slacken the front sprocket nut before disengaging the chain from the rear sprocket so the rear brake can be used to prevent the front sprocket turning.*

7 Remove the front sprocket cover (Steps 1 and 2).

8 Bend down the tab(s) on the sprocket nut lockwasher **(see illustration)**. Have an assistant apply the rear brake hard, then unscrew the nut and remove the washer **(see illustration 18.11b)**. Discard the washer as a new one should be used. Refer to Chapter 1 and adjust the chain so that it is fully slack.

9 If the sprocket is not being replaced with a new one, mark the outside with a scratch or dab of paint so that it can be installed the same way round. Slide the sprocket and chain off the shaft and slip the sprocket out of the chain **(see illustration)**. If there is not enough

18.2 Unscrew the bolts and remove the cover

18.8 Bend back the lockwasher tab(s) then unscrew the nut and remove the washer

18.9 Slide the sprocket off the shaft and remove it

18.10 Align the splines and slide the sprocket onto the shaft

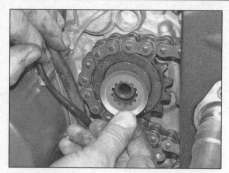

18.11a Fit the new lockwasher . . .

18.11b . . . and the nut, and tighten it to the specified torque

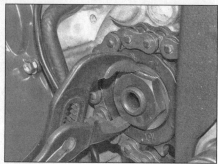

18.11c Bend the tabs up against the nut

slack in the chain to remove the sprocket, disengage the chain from the rear wheel.

10 Engage the new sprocket with the chain and slide it on the shaft **(see illustration)**. Take up the slack in the chain (see Chapter 1).

11 Slide on the new lockwasher, locating it on the splines **(see illustration)**. Fit the nut with its shouldered side facing in and tighten it to the torque setting specified at the beginning of the Chapter, applying the rear brake to prevent the sprocket from turning **(see illustration)**. Bend up the tabs of the lockwasher against the nut **(see illustration)**.

12 Install the front sprocket cover and gearchange linkage (Steps 3, 2 and 1).

Rear sprocket

13 Remove the rear wheel (see Section 14).

14 Unscrew the nuts securing the sprocket to the coupling **(see illustration)**. Remove the sprocket, noting which way round it fits.

15 Fit the sprocket onto the coupling with the

stamped mark facing out, then fit the nuts. Tighten the nuts evenly and in a criss-cross sequence to the torque setting specified at the beginning of the Chapter.

16 Install the rear wheel (see Section 14).

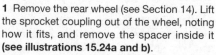

19 Rear sprocket coupling/ rubber damper

1 Remove the rear wheel (see Section 14). Lift the sprocket coupling out of the wheel, noting how it fits, and remove the spacer inside it **(see illustrations 15.24a and b)**.

2 Check the coupling for cracks or any obvious signs of damage.

3 Lift the rubber damper piece from the wheel hub, noting how it fits. Check it for cracks, hardening and general deterioration **(see illustration)**. Replace the damper piece with a new one if necessary.

18.14 Rear sprocket nuts (arrowed)

19.3 Lift the damper piece out and check the segments

4 Checking and replacement procedures for the sprocket coupling bearing are described in Section 15.

5 Installation is the reverse of removal. Make sure the damper assembly is correctly fitted.

20 TPMS (Tyre Pressure Monitoring System)

General information

1 A tyre pressure monitoring system (TPMS) may be fitted as an optional extra on Street Triple models from VIN 560477. A sensor inside each wheel measures the pressure of air in the tyre and transmits to a read-out on the instrument panel via the immobiliser/TPMS control unit (covered in Section 20, Chapter 4). The system will only transmit a read-out when the bike reaches a speed of 12 mph (20 km/h) – until then the read-out will only show two dashes. Each sensor is powered by its own internal battery, but as the sensors are sealed units new sensors must be fitted when the batteries run out.

2 The system monitors real-time pressures, so as the tyre warms up with use the pressure displayed will increase. Tyre pressures should always be checked and set when the tyres are cold, so do not re-adjust the pressure when the tyre is warm because the read-out says it is higher than it should be. The cold pressures specified by Triumph take into account the fact that pressures will increase as the tyres warm.

3 Triumph advise that cold tyre pressures should only be set using an accurate tyre gauge, and not using the TPMS read-out. Refer to the Pre-ride checks listed at the beginning of this manual for tyre pressure check details and tyre maintenance.

4 The system performs its own self-diagnosis, and in the event of a fault the read warning light will come on and the tyre symbol will flash. The Triumph diagnostic tool is required for fault code retrieval.

5 It is advisable to inform whoever may be fitting new tyres of the presence of a sensor in each wheel, as they are easily damaged – an adhesive label on each wheel rim identifies the position of the sensor, but the label may well have come off, or been taken off. Note that the use of 'get-you-home' puncture repair sealants injected via the valve may well damage the sensor beyond use.

21 ABS (Anti-lock brake system)

General information

⚠️ *Warning: The ABS system works by comparing the relative speed of the wheels, and is programmed using the wheel and tyre sizes specified and fitted as standard. If non-specified wheels or tyres are fitted the control unit may become confused and the system will not function correctly.*

1 The anti-lock braking system (ABS), fitted on Street Triple models from VIN 560477, prevents the wheels from locking up under hard braking or on uneven road surfaces. A sensor on each wheel picks up information about the speed of wheel rotation from a pulse ring mounted on the wheel and transmits to an electronic control unit in the modulator, and if it senses that a wheel is about to lock, it activates the solenoids in the modulator which releases brake pressure momentarily to that wheel, preventing a skid. When the system is active a pulsing can be felt through the lever or pedal as the fluid pressure is released and reapplied as required. The front and rear systems are entirely independent of each other, even though they function through the same control module and modulator.

2 The ABS system is self-checking, and is automatically switched on with the ignition. ABS will not function at speeds of less than 6 mph (10 km/h), with the ignition off, if a fault is indicated (ABS warning light remains on after start-up or comes on during use), or if the battery is flat.

3 When the ignition switch is turned on, the ABS indicator light on the instrument panel flashes, then goes off when a speed of 6 mph (10 km/h) is reached. If the indicator light stays on, or comes on while riding, then there is probably a fault in the system, in which case it will record a fault code. Stop the motorcycle and switch the ignition switch off. Switch it on again, start the engine and ride the bike – if the light goes off then the system is OK and will work, but the fault code is till stored. Depending on the severity or continuity of a fault the system may or may not switch itself off, but if it doesn't and the fault still exists, when the bike is next ridden it will not switch itself on. If the light remains on or comes on again, take the machine to a Triumph dealer for testing – fault codes can only be read and diagnosed by the Triumph special tool, and every main dealer has one.

4 Note that under certain conditions, the indicator light could come on and a fault code could be registered, even though there is no actual problem with the system. This is when the effects of the conditions themselves simulate an actual fault. This can occur if the machine is ridden continuously on very bumpy roads, or if the rider does a wheelie, or if the air pressure on one tyre is extremely low, or if the machine is placed on the centrestand or an auxiliary stand with the engine running and the rear wheel is turning when the front is not. If this happens stop the bike and turn the engine off, then restart and ride the bike – the light may not come on again when the system confirms everything is OK, but if it does the fault code must be retrieved and then erased before the indicator light will go out.

5 The only actions the owner can take in the case of a fault, and the only maintenance that can be applied, is firstly to make sure there is no dirt or debris on each wheel speed sensor tip or between the poles on the sensor rotor **(see illustration 21.9 or 21.13)**. Secondly

check the air gap between the sensor tip and one of the poles on the rotor, though once set, this is unlikely to change. Check the gap by inserting a feeler gauge between the sensor and the tip of one of the poles. Check the gap in different places by rotating the wheel. If the gap is not within the range specified at the beginning of the Chapter, remove the sensor (see below) and adjust the air gap by inserting a shim of the required thickness to bring the gap within specifications. Shims are available in sizes of 0.5, 1.0, 1.5 and 2.0 mm. On completion tighten the bolt to the specified torque setting.

6 Also make a check of all the system wiring and connectors, looking for chafed wires or broken connector pins, damp or corroded terminals, and if required refer to electrical system fault finding at the beginning of Chapter 8 and to the wiring diagrams at the end of it and check all wiring for continuity. Make sure the ignition is OFF before disconnecting any wiring connectors or making any tests.

7 If the indicator light does not come on when the ignition is switched on, check the ABS fuses (see Chapter 8) and the instrument panel and the control unit wiring connectors. If all is good, take the machine to a Triumph dealer for testing.

8 Fault diagnosis and any other work on the system, including the final stage of bleeding it and changing the brake fluid, must be undertaken by a Triumph dealer.

Component removal and installation

Front wheel sensor

9 The sensor is mounted in the bottom of the left-hand fork **(see illustration)**.

10 Remove the airbox (see Chapter 4). Disconnect the sensor wiring connector. Free the wiring from any ties and the clips and feed it down to the sensor, noting its routing.

11 Unscrew the bolt securing the sensor and withdraw it from the fork, collecting any shim fitted behind the sensor plate.

12 Installation is the reverse of removal. Make sure the sensor tip is clean and undamaged, and that the mounting plate is not distorted. Make sure any shim previously fitted is positioned between the mounting plate and the fork. Tighten the bolt to the torque setting

21.9 Front wheel speed sensor (arrowed)

specified at the beginning of the Chapter. Check the air gap (see Step 5).

Rear wheel sensor

13 The sensor is mounted in the rear brake caliper bracket **(see illustration)**.

14 Raise or remove the fuel tank (see Chapter 4). Disconnect the sensor wiring connector **(see illustration)**. Free the wiring from any ties and the clips and feed it down to the sensor, noting its routing.

15 Unscrew the bolt securing the sensor and withdraw it from the bracket, collecting any shim fitted behind the sensor plate.

16 Installation is the reverse of removal. Make sure the sensor tip is clean and undamaged, and that the mounting plate is not distorted. Make sure any shim previously fitted is positioned between the mounting plate and the caliper bracket. Tighten the bolt to the torque setting specified at the beginning of the Chapter. Check the air gap (see Step 5).

Front wheel pulse ring

17 Remove the wheel (see Section 13). Support the wheel using wooden blocks so no weight is on the disc.

18 Unscrew the bolts securing the pulse ring and lift it off – note that the bolts also secure the brake disc.

19 Before installing the ring, make sure there is no dirt or corrosion between the mating surfaces as this will not allow the ring to sit flat when bolted down and it will be warped and could cause the ABS system to indicate a fault. Tighten the bolts evenly in a criss-cross pattern to the torque setting specified at the beginning of the Chapter.

21.13 Rear wheel speed sensor (arrowed)

21.14 Rear wheel speed sensor wiring connector

21.25a Release the clips . . .

21.25b . . . and displace the relays

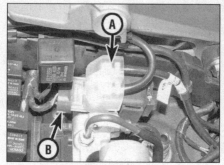

21.26a Displace the relay (A) and disconnect the connector (B)

Rear wheel pulse ring

20 Remove the wheel (see Section 14).

21 Unscrew the bolts securing the pulse ring and lift it off – note that the bolts also secure the brake disc.

22 Before installing the ring, make sure there is no dirt or corrosion between the mating surfaces as this will not allow the ring to sit flat when bolted down and it will be warped and could cause the ABS system to indicate a fault. Tighten the bolts evenly in a criss-cross pattern to the torque setting specified at the beginning of the Chapter.

Modulator

Note: *Before removing the modulator, bear in mind that the system must be bled on completion of work, and although this is done initially in the same way as models without ABS, to complete the procedure the Triumph Diagnostic tool must be used to open and close the solenoids within the modulator, and this can*

only be carried out by a dealer. The bike should be transported, not ridden, to the dealer.

23 Have some clean rag to hand to catch any spilled brake fluid and some clingfilm to wrap around the end of each pipe as it is disconnected. Drain the brake fluid from the system (see Section 10).

24 Remove the battery (Chapter 8). Remove the airbox (see Chapter 4).

25 Release and displace the relay mounting blocks **(see illustrations)**.

26 Displace the starter relay and disconnect the wiring connector **(see illustration)**. Remove the relay bracket **(see illustration)**.

27 Disconnect the wiring connector from the control unit by pushing the retaining tab in and pivoting the locking bar forwards **(see illustrations)**.

28 Unscrew the brake pipe nuts, being prepared with some rag to catch any residual fluid **(see illustration)**.

29 Unscrew the modulator bracket mounting bolts **(see illustrations)**. Carefully manoeuvre the modulator out, taking great care not to bend the pipes.

30 If required remove the bracket from the modulator. Make sure the grommets in the bracket are in good condition.

31 Installation is the reverse of removal. Make sure the collars are fitted in the mounting bracket grommets. If the correct tools are available tighten the brake pipe nuts to the torque setting specified at the beginning of the Chapter. Make sure the modulator wiring connector locking bar is in its released position, then push the connector into the socket until it is heard to click into place.

32 Bleed the hydraulic system following the procedure in Section 10, then transport the bike to a Triumph dealer for bleeding of the modulator. Check the operation of both front and rear brakes carefully before riding the motorcycle.

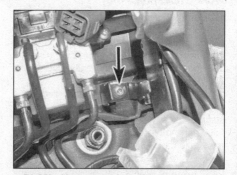

21.26b Unscrew the bolt (arrowed) and remove the bracket

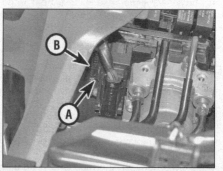

12.27a Push the tab (A) in and the bar (B) forwards . . .

21.27b . . . and disconnect the connector

21.28 Unscrew the pipe nuts (arrowed)

21.29a Unscrew the bolt (arrowed) . . .

21.29b . . . and the bolts (arrowed)

Chapter 7
Bodywork

Contents

Degrees of difficulty

Easy, suitable for novice with little experience	**Fairly easy,** suitable for beginner with some experience	**Fairly difficult,** suitable for competent DIY mechanic	**Difficult,** suitable for experienced DIY mechanic	**Very difficult,** suitable for expert DIY or professional

1 General information

This Chapter covers the procedures necessary to remove and install the body parts. Since many service and repair operations on these motorcycles require their removal the procedures are grouped here and referred to from other Chapters.

In the case of damage to the body parts, it is usually necessary to remove the broken component and replace it with a new (or used) one. The material that the body panels are composed of doesn't lend itself to conventional repair techniques. There are however some shops that specialise in 'plastic welding', so it may be worthwhile seeking the advice of one of these specialists before scrapping an expensive component. There are also DIY kits available for making small repairs.

When attempting to remove any body panel, first study it closely, noting any fasteners and associated fittings, to be sure of returning everything to its correct place on installation. In some cases the aid of an assistant will be required when removing panels, to help avoid the risk of damage to paintwork. Once the evident fasteners have been removed, try to withdraw the panel as described but DO NOT FORCE IT – if it will not release, check that all fasteners have been removed and try again. Where a panel engages another by means of tabs, be careful not to break the tab or its mating slot or to damage the paintwork. Remember that a few moments of patience at this stage will save you a lot of money in replacing broken fairing panels! To undo trim clip fasteners, turn them 90° anti-clockwise.

When installing a body panel, first study it closely, noting any fasteners and associated fittings removed with it, to be sure of returning everything to its correct place. Check that all fasteners and damping/rubber mounts are in good condition; any of these must be replaced with new ones if faulty before the panel is reassembled. Check also that all mounting brackets are straight and repair or renew them if necessary before attempting to install the panel. Where assistance was required to remove a panel, make sure your assistant is on hand to install it. To install trim clip fasteners, turn them 90° clockwise.

Tighten the fasteners securely, but be careful not to overtighten any of them or the panel may break (not always immediately) due to the uneven stress.

2.1a Turn the key, then lift the rear of the seat and remove it . . .

2.1b . . . noting how the tab (arrowed) locates

2.1c Unscrew the bolt (arrowed) and remove the seat . . .

2.1d . . . noting how the tab (arrowed) locates

2 Seat(s)

1 On Daytona models, to remove the rider's seat insert the ignition key into the seat lock located on the left-hand side of the bike, and turn it anti-clockwise **(see illustration)**. Lift up the rear of the seat and draw it backwards, noting how the tab at the front locates **(see illustration)**. To remove the pillion seat lift the front to expose the bolt, undo it, and remove the seat, noting how it locates **(see illustrations)**.

2 On Street Triple and Street Triple R models, insert the ignition key into the seat lock located on the left-hand side of the bike, and turn it

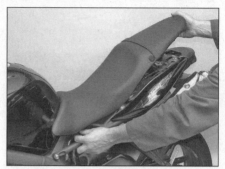

2.2a Turn the key, then lift the rear of the seat and remove it . . .

2.2b . . . noting how the tab (arrowed) locates

2.3a Operate the lock and raise the cover

2.3b Seat cover tabs (arrowed) locate under bodywork

2.3c Rider's seat is retained by a screw on each side

2.3d Seat tab locates under fuel tank

3.2a Undo the screws (arrowed) . . .

anti-clockwise (see illustration). Lift up the rear of the seat and draw it backwards, noting how the tab at the front locates (see illustration).

3 On Street Triple RX models, to remove the pillion seat (or seat cover) insert the ignition key into the seat lock located on the left-hand side of the bike, and turn it anti-clockwise (see illustration). Lift up the seat and disengage its locating tabs (see illustration). To remove the rider's seat lift each side in turn to expose the screw, undo them, and remove the seat, noting how the tab at the front locates under the fuel tank (see illustrations).

4 Installation is the reverse of removal. Push down on the seat to engage the latch.

3 Fairing and body panels

Daytona
Seat cowling

1 Remove the seats (see Section 2).
2 Undo the four screws securing the seat cowling (see illustration). Carefully pull the sides away at the front and lift the seat cowling, disconnect the tail light wiring connector when accessible, and remove the cowling (see illustrations).
3 Installation is the reverse of removal.

3.2b . . . then displace the cowling, disconnect the wiring connector . . .

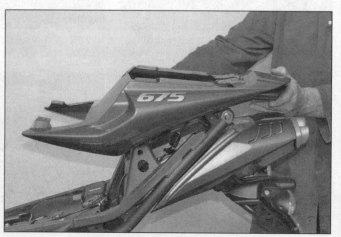

3.2c . . . and lift the cowling away

3.4a Undo the screws (arrowed) . . .

3.4b . . . and remove the panel

3.7 Release the trim clips (arrowed)

3.8a Release the trim clips (arrowed) . . .

3.8b . . . and remove the inner panel

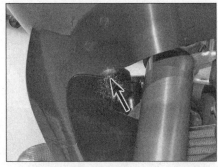

3.9 Release the trim clip (arrowed)

Cockpit trim panels

4 Undo the two screws and remove the panel **(see illustrations)**.
5 Installation is the reverse of removal.

Fairing side panels

6 Remove the cockpit trim panel (Step 4). On models from VIN 381275 remove the regulator/rectifier (see Chapter 8).
7 Release the four trim clips securing the panels to each other on the underside **(see illustration)**. Note how the panels fit together.
8 When removing the left-hand fairing side panel, release the two trim clips and two screws securing the inner panel and detach it from the side panel **(see illustrations)**.
9 When removing the right-hand fairing side panel, release the trim clip securing the inner panel to the fairing **(see illustration)**.
10 Undo the screws securing the panel to its brackets and to the fairing **(see illustration)**. Carefully pull the panel away to release the

pegs from the grommets – for the left-hand panel there is one below the back of the frame beam, one at the top front into the fusebox/relay holder, and one into the centre panel (if both panels are being removed, detach the first from the centre panel, then remove the second panel with the centre panel attached,

and if required remove it afterwards); for the right-hand panel there is one below the back of the frame beam, and one into the centre panel **(see illustrations)**. Detach the panel from the fairing and the other side panel, then disconnect the turn signal wiring connectors and remove the panel **(see illustration)**.

3.10a Undo the screws (arrowed) . . .

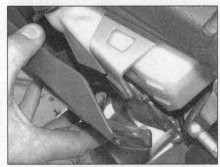

3.10b . . . then release the pegs from the grommets . . .

3.10c . . . according to side . . .

3.10d . . . detaching the first panel from the centre panel

3.10e Disconnect the wiring connectors

3.11a Release the trim clips (arrowed) to remove the inner panel

3.11b Free the centre panel grommet from the peg

3.12a Make sure the tabs engage correctly with the fairing . . .

3.12b . . . and with the other panel

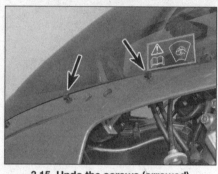

3.15 Undo the screws (arrowed)

3.17 Undo the screw (arrowed)

11 If required remove the inner panel from the right-hand fairing side panel, and the centre panel **(see illustrations)**. If required remove the turn signal from each panel (see Chapter 8).

12 Installation is the reverse of removal. Make sure the panels engage correctly with the fairing, the centre panel, and each other **(see illustrations)**.

Fairing

13 Release the trim clip securing the fairing to each inner panel **(see illustration 3.9)**.

14 Remove the mirrors (see Section 4).

15 On models to VIN 381274 undo the two windshield screws immediately to the front and rear of each mirror mount **(see illustration)**.

16 Remove the cockpit trim panels (Step 4).

17 Undo the remaining screw securing the fairing to the fairing side panel on each side **(see illustration)**.

18 Unscrew the bolts, one on each side, securing the fairing to the fairing stay **(see illustration)**.

19 Release the fusebox/relay holder from its peg, disconnect the headlight wiring connector, and free the wiring from below the headlight, noting its routing **(see illustrations)**.

20 Draw the fairing forwards, noting how the pegs locate, and remove the fairing **(see illustrations)**. Note the rubber pads for the mirror and remove them for safekeeping if required.

3.18 Unscrew the bolt (arrowed) on each side

3.19a Release the holder . . .

3.19b . . . disconnect the wiring connector . . .

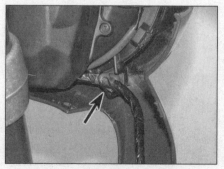

3.19c . . . release the wiring clamp (arrowed)

3.20a Note how the pegs locate . . .

3.20b . . . and remove the fairing

3.23a Windshield screws (arrowed) –
models to VIN 381274

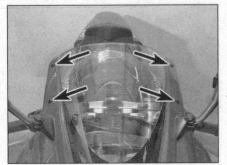

3.23b Windshield screws (arrowed) –
models from VIN 381275

3.26a Undo the screws (arrowed) . . .

3.26b . . . then free the peg from the
grommet . . .

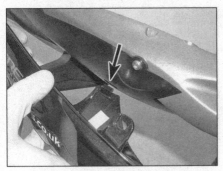

3.26c . . . or the tab from the slot,
according to models

21 Installation is the reverse of removal. Do not forget the mirror pads, if removed. Make sure the front wiring room locates correctly inside the fairing.

Windshield

22 On models from VIN 381275 and R models remove the mirrors (see Section 4).

23 Undo the screws securing the windshield to the fairing and lift it off **(see illustration)**. Make sure none of the rubber wellnuts drop out of the fairing, and check that they are all in good condition.

24 Installation is the reverse of removal. Do not overtighten the screws.

Street Triple and Street Triple R

Side panels

25 Remove the seat (see Section 2).

26 Undo the two screws, then on models to VIN 560476 free the peg from the grommet, and on models from VIN 560477 free the tab from the slot and disconnect the seat lock cable from the left-hand panel, and remove the panel **(see illustrations)**.

27 Installation is the reverse of removal.

Tail light cover

28 On models to VIN 560476 remove the side panels (Steps 25 and 26). Slacken the bolt on the underside of the mudguard, then draw the cover back off the tail light, noting how the tab locates between the mudguard and the bolt's captive nut **(see illustrations)**.

29 On models from VIN 560477 refer to Chapter 8 and remove the tail light assembly from the bike, then remove the light from the cover.

30 Installation is the reverse of removal.

Radiator cowls – models to VIN 560476

Note: *To avoid removing the air filter housing, the cowls can be displaced from their mounts leaving the wiring connected – this will give enough room to access the radiator pressure cap, coolant hose and hose bleed screw on the left-hand side, and the coolant hose, radiator bleed screw and clutch cable guide on the right. Support the cowl so no strain is placed on the wiring.*

31 Remove the airbox.

32 Disconnect the turn signal wiring connectors **(see illustration)**. Feed the wiring through to the cowl, noting its routing.

33 Undo the screws securing the cowl and

3.28a Slacken the bolt (arrowed) . . .

3.28b . . . then draw the cover back, noting where the tab locates (arrowed)

3.32 Turn signal wiring connectors (arrowed)

3.33a Undo the screws and the bolt (arrowed)

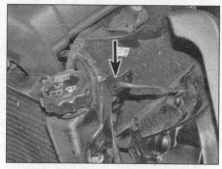

3.33b Note the routing of the wiring through the hole (arrowed)

3.36a Unscrew the bolt (arrowed)

3.36b Free the bracket from the turn signal . . .

3.36c . . . and the slot from the grommet

Radiator cowls – models from VIN 560477

36 Undo the turn signal bolt **(see illustration)**. Free the bracket on the front of the outer cowl from the turn signal then slide it forwards to free the slot at the back from around the grommet **(see illustrations)**.

37 Release the two trim clips on the inner side of the inner panel **(see illustration)**. Release the turn signal wiring from the clip on the inner edge of the cowl and disconnect the connectors **(see illustration)**. Undo the two screws on the outside of the middle cowl, then draw the turn signal wiring out and remove the cowl **(see illustrations)**. If required remove the turn signal from the cowl **(see illustration)**.

38 If required undo the inner cowl screws and remove it from the radiator **(see illustration)**.

39 Installation is the reverse of removal.

the turn signal and either displace or remove the cowl as required **(see illustration)** – if removing it take care not to snag the turn signal wiring connectors as you draw them through the hole in the bracket, and note the routing of the horn wiring behind the left-hand cowl **(see illustration)**.

34 If required remove the turn signal from the cowl.

35 Installation is the reverse of removal.

3.37a Release the trim clips (arrowed)

3.37b Turn signal wiring connectors (arrowed)

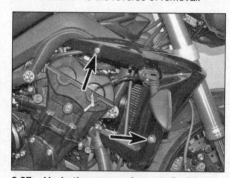

3.37c Undo the screws (arrowed), displace the cowl . . .

3.37d . . . and draw the wiring out

3.37e Note the routing of the wiring and how it is secured

3.38 Inner cowl screws (arrowed)

3.40a Undo the screws (arrowed – models to VIN 560476 shown, there are four on models from VIN 560477) . . .

3.40b . . . and remove the cowl

3.42 Undo the screws (arrowed) on each side

Instrument cowl (if fitted)

40 Undo the screws and draw the cowl off the instrument cluster (see illustrations). If required remove the instrument cluster (see Chapter 8), then remove the cowl face plate from the bracket, noting how it locates.
41 Installation is the reverse of removal.

Belly pan (if fitted)

42 Undo the two screws on each side and remove the belly pan (see illustration).
43 Installation is the reverse of removal.

Street Triple RX

Side panels, licence plate bracket and undertray

44 Remove the seats (see Section 2).
45 Remove the tail light cover screws and manoeuvre the cover out, noting how its

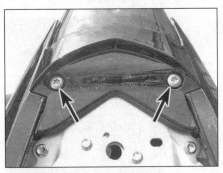

3.45a Remove the two screws (arrowed) . . .

front tabs locate under the side panels (see illustrations).
46 Undo the four screws from the side panels, then free each panel separately, noting the tab at the front and rear points; the support brackets fit under the front mountings (see illustrations).

3.45b . . . and free the front tabs of the tail light cover from under the side panels

If working on the left side panel, disconnect the seat lock cable (see illustrations).
47 Remove the four bolts and the single Allen bolt to free the seat latch bracket, then manoeuvre its front tang out from under the tool tray (see illustration). Trace the tail light

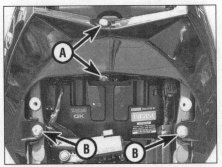

3.46a Side panels are held by joining screws (A) and screws to sub-frame (B)

3.46b Brackets locate under each front mounting to support the rider's weight

3.46c On the left side panel pull the cable out of the bracket . . .

3.46d . . . and disconnect the trunnion from the seat lock

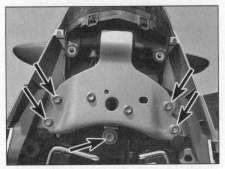

3.47a Seat latch bracket bolts (arrowed)

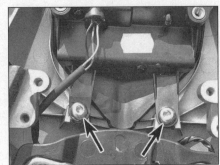

3.47b Tail light is retained by two screws (arrowed) . . .

3.47c . . . and its lower tab fits under the undertray tab

3.48a Licence plate bracket bolts (arrowed)

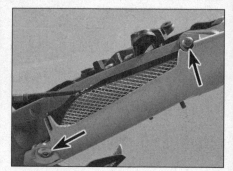

3.48b Undertray bolts to sub-frame by two screws on each side

4.1a Unscrew the nuts (arrowed) . . .

4.1b . . . and remove the mirror

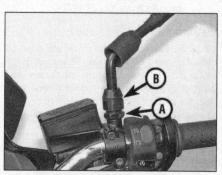

4.2 Lift the boot to access the hex (A). Conical adjustment nut (B)

wiring to the connector and disconnect it, then remove the two screws and remove the tail light, noting how its lower tab locates under the undertray tab on each side **(see illustrations)**.

48 Trace the licence plate and rear turn signal wiring to its connector and disconnect it. Remove the four bolts to free the licence plate bracket from the sub-frame, noting the headed spacers **(see illustration)**. Draw the bracket and wiring down through the undertray. The undertray is secured to the sub-frame by two screws on each side **(see illustration)**; note how the seat lock cable is routed on the left side.

49 Installation is the reverse of removal.

Radiator cowls

50 See Steps 36 to 39.

Instrument cowl

51 See Steps 40 and 41.

Belly pan

52 See Steps 42 and 43.

4 Mirrors

1 On Daytona models, where fitted remove the caps from the mirror nuts on the inside of the fairing, then unscrew the nuts and remove the mirror **(see illustrations)**.

2 On Street Triple models to VIN 560476, lift the rubber cover off the base of the mirror, then unscrew it from its mount using the bottom hex **(see illustration)**.

3 On Street Triple models from VIN 560477, unscrew the bolt securing it, noting the arrangement of the washers and rubber sleeve.

4 Installation is the reverse of removal. To adjust the position of the mirror on Street Triple models, counter-hold the base hex, then slacken the conical nut above it, reposition the mirror as required, then tighten the nut **(see illustration 4.2)**.

5 Front mudguard

1 Remove the front wheel (see Chapter 6).

2 If not already done when displacing the brake calipers, free the brake hoses from the mudguard **(see illustration)**.

3 Undo the two screws on each side, then tilt the mudguard and draw it down from between the forks **(see illustrations)**.

4 Installation is the reverse of removal.

5.2 Release the brake hose from the clip(s) on each side

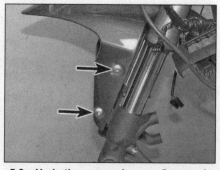

5.3a Undo the screws (arrowed) on each side . . .

5.3b . . . and remove the mudguard as described

Chapter 8
Electrical system

Contents

Degrees of difficulty

Easy, suitable for novice with little experience | **Fairly easy,** suitable for beginner with some experience | **Fairly difficult,** suitable for competent DIY mechanic | **Difficult,** suitable for experienced DIY mechanic | **Very difficult,** suitable for expert DIY or professional

Specifications

Battery

Daytona up to VIN 381274
  Type . . . . Yuasa YT 7B-BS
  Capacity 12V, 6.5Ah
Daytona models from VIN 381275 and Street Triple models
  Type . . . . Yuasa YTX9-BS
  Capacity 12V, 8Ah
Current leakage . . . . 1 mA (max)
Charging rate
  Daytona . . . . 0.65A (max)
  Street Triple. . . . . 0.8A (max)
Charging time (flat battery). . . . . see Section 4

Alternator

Nominal output. . . . . 33.5A @ 4000 rpm
Regulated output . . . . 13.5 to 15 volts DC
Stator coil resistance . . . . 0.4 to 0.6 ohms

Bulbs

Headlight
  Daytona
    Right-hand bulb (main beam) 12V 65W H9
    Left-hand bulb (dip beam) 12V 55W H7
  Street Triple. . . . . 12V 60/55W H4 x 2
Sidelights
  Daytona . . . . 5W x 2
  Street Triple. 4W x2
Brake/tail light . . . . LED
Turn signal light . . . . 12V 10W (orange) x 4
Instrument lights. . . . . LED

Fuses

Fuse identity is marked on the fusebox lid

Daytona

Fuse 1	15A (starter circuit relay, headlights)
Fuse 2	10A (ignition switch, starter circuit)
Fuse 3	5A (side lights, tail light)
Fuse 4	10A (Turn signals, brake light, horn, alarm where fitted)
Fuse 5	15A (cooling fan)
Fuse 6	20A (engine management)
Main fuse (in starter relay)	30A

Street Triple models to VIN 560476

Fuse 1	20A (starter circuit relay, headlights)
Fuse 2	10A (ignition switch, starter circuit)
Fuse 3	5A (side lights, tail light)
Fuse 4	10A (Turn signals, brake light, horn, alarm where fitted)
Fuse 5	15A (cooling fan)
Fuse 6	20A (engine management)
Main fuse (in starter relay)	30A

Street Triple models from VIN 560477

Fuse 1	10A (side light, tail light, license plate light)
Fuse 2	15A (cooling fan)
Fuse 3	10A (ignition switch, starter circuit relay)
Fuse 4	15A (engine management)
Fuse 5	10A (heated grips, where fitted)
Fuse 6	20A (headlights)
Main fuse (in starter relay)	30A
ABS fuse (in separate box)	20A

Torque wrench settings

Alternator cover bolts	8 Nm
Alternator rotor bolt	120 Nm
Alternator stator bolts	12 Nm
Alternator stator/CKP sensor wiring clamp bolt	6 Nm
CKP sensor bolts	6 Nm
Fork clamp bolts – top yoke	26 Nm
Handlebar bolts	
Daytona	
Positioning bolts	5 Nm
Clamp bolts	26 Nm
Street Triple	
Clamp bolts	26 Nm
Holder bolt nuts	35 Nm
Oil pressure switch	13 Nm
Sidestand bracket bolts	45 Nm
Starter motor mounting bolts	10 Nm
Steering stem nut	90 Nm

1 General information

All models have a 12 volt electrical system charged by a three-phase alternator, with the rotor mounted on the left-hand end of the crankshaft and the stator located in the alternator cover.

The system incorporates a combined regulator/rectifier. The regulator maintains the charging system output within the specified range to prevent overcharging, and the rectifier converts the ac (alternating current) output of the alternator to dc (direct current) to power the lights and other components and to charge the battery.

The starter motor is mounted on the top of the crankcase, and the starter clutch is mounted on the back of the alternator rotor. The starting system includes the motor, the battery, the relay and the various wires and switches.

Note: *Keep in mind that electrical parts, once purchased, cannot be returned. To avoid unnecessary expense, make very sure the faulty component has been positively identified before buying a replacement part.*

Many of the bolts used on Triumph motorcycles are of the Torx type. Unless you are already equipped with a good range of Torx bits, you are advised to obtain a set. Make sure you get bits that can be used in conjunction with a socket set so that a torque wrench can be applied – a Torx key set will not be adequate on its own, though will be useful in addition to the bits.

2 Electrical system fault finding

1 A typical electrical circuit consists of an electrical component, the switches, relays, etc, related to that component and the wiring and connectors that link the component to the battery and the frame.

2 Before tackling any troublesome electrical circuit, first study the wiring diagram thoroughly to get a complete picture of what makes up that individual circuit. Trouble spots, for instance, can often be narrowed down by noting if other components related to that circuit are operating properly or not. If several components or circuits fail at one time, chances are the fault lies either in the fuse or

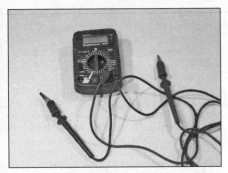

2.4a A digital multimeter can be used for all electrical tests

2.4b A battery-powered continuity tester

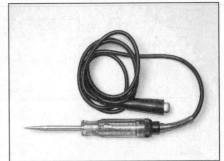

2.4c A simple test light is useful for voltage tests

in the common earth (ground) connection, as several circuits are often routed through the same fuse and earth (ground) connections.

3 Electrical problems often stem from simple causes, such as loose or corroded connections or a blown fuse. Prior to any electrical fault finding, always visually check the condition of the fuse, wires and connections in the problem circuit. Intermittent failures can be especially frustrating, since you can't always duplicate the failure when it's convenient to test. In such situations, a good practice is to clean all connections in the affected circuit, whether or not they appear to be good – where possible use a dedicated electrical cleaning spray along with sandpaper, wire wool or other abrasive material to remove corrosion, and a dedicated electrical protection spray to prevent further problems. All of the connections and wires should also be wiggled to check for looseness which can cause intermittent failure.

4 If you don't have a multimeter it is highly advisable to obtain one – they are not expensive and will enable a full range of electrical tests to be made. Go for a modern digital one with LCD display as they are easier to use. A continuity tester and/or test light are useful for certain electrical checks as an alternative, though are limited in their usefulness compared to a multimeter **(see illustrations)**.

Continuity checks

5 The term continuity describes the uninterrupted flow of electricity through an electrical circuit. Continuity can be checked with a multimeter set either to its continuity function (a beep is emitted when continuity is found), or to the resistance (ohms / Ω) function, or with a dedicated continuity tester. Both instruments are powered by an internal battery, therefore the checks are made with the ignition OFF. As a safety precaution, always disconnect the battery negative (–) lead before making continuity checks, particularly if ignition switch checks are being made.

6 If using a multimeter, select the continuity function if it has one, or the resistance (ohms) function. Touch the meter probes together and check that a beep is emitted or the meter reads zero, which indicates continuity. If there

is no continuity there will be no beep or the meter will show infinite resistance. After using the meter, always switch it OFF to conserve its battery.

7 A continuity tester can be used in the same way – its light should come on or it should beep to indicate continuity in the switch ON position, but should be off or silent in the OFF position.

8 Note that the polarity of the test probes doesn't matter for continuity checks, although care should be taken to follow specific test procedures if a diode or solid-state component is being checked.

Switch continuity checks

9 If a switch is at fault, trace its wiring to the wiring connectors. Separate the connectors and inspect them for security and condition. A build-up of dirt or corrosion here will most likely be the cause of the problem – clean up and apply a water dispersant such as WD40, or alternatively use a dedicated contact cleaner and protection spray.

10 If using a multimeter, select the continuity function if it has one, or the resistance (ohms) function, and connect its probes to the terminals in the connector **(see illustration)**. Simple ON/OFF type switches, such as brake light switches, only have two wires whereas combination switches, like the handlebar switches, have many wires. Study the wiring diagram to ensure that you are connecting to the correct pair of wires. Continuity should be

indicated with the switch ON and no continuity with it OFF.

Wiring continuity checks

11 Many electrical faults are caused by damaged wiring, often due to incorrect routing or chaffing on frame components. Loose, wet or corroded wire connectors can also be the cause of electrical problems.

12 A continuity check can be made on a single length of wire by disconnecting it at each end and connecting the meter or continuity tester probes to each end of the wire **(see illustration)**. Continuity (low or no resistance – 0 ohms) should be indicated if the wire is good. If no continuity (high resistance) is shown, suspect a broken wire.

13 To check for continuity to earth in any earth wire connect one probe of your meter or tester to the earth wire terminal in the connector and the other to the frame, engine, or battery earth (–) terminal. Continuity (low or no resistance – 0 ohms) should be indicated if the wire is good. If no continuity (high resistance) is shown, suspect a broken wire or corroded or loose earth point (see below).

Voltage checks

14 A voltage check can determine whether power is reaching a component. Use a multimeter set to the dc voltage scale, or a test light. The test light is the cheaper component, but the meter has the advantage of being able to give a voltage reading.

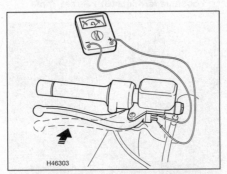

2.10 Continuity should be indicated across switch terminals when lever is operated

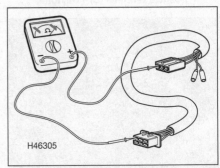

2.12 Wiring continuity check. Connect the meter probes across each end of the same wire

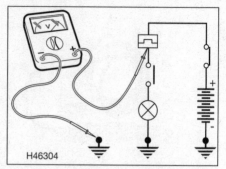

2.15 Voltage check. Connect the meter positive probe to the component and the negative probe to earth

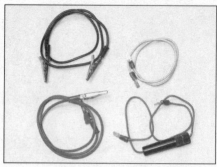

2.23 A selection of insulated jumper wires

15 Connect the meter or test light in parallel, i.e. across the load **(see illustration)**.
16 First identify the relevant wiring circuit by referring to the wiring diagram at the end of this Chapter. If other electrical components share the same power supply (i.e. are fed from the same fuse), take note whether they are working correctly – this is useful information in deciding where to start checking the circuit.
17 If using a meter, check first that the meter leads are plugged into the correct terminals on the meter (red to positive (+), black to negative (–). Set the meter to the dc volts function, where necessary at a range suitable for the battery voltage – 0 to 20 vdc. Connect the meter red probe (+) to the power supply wire and the black probe to a good metal earth (ground) on the motorcycle's frame or directly to the battery negative terminal. Battery voltage should be shown on the meter

with the ignition switch, and if necessary any other relevant switch, ON.
18 If using a test light, connect its positive (+) probe to the power supply terminal and its negative (–) probe to a good earth (ground) on the motorcycle's frame. With the switch, and if necessary any other relevant switch, ON, the test light should illuminate.
19 If no voltage is indicated, work back towards the fuse continuing to check for voltage. When you reach a point where there is voltage, you know the problem lies between that point and your last check point.

Earth (ground) checks

20 Earth connections are made either directly to the engine or frame (such as neutral switch, oil pressure switch etc. which only have a positive feed) or by a separate wire into the earth circuit of the wiring harness. Alternatively

a short earth wire is sometimes run from the component directly to the motorcycle's frame.
21 Corrosion is a common cause of a poor earth connection, as is a loose earth terminal fastener.
22 If total or multiple component failure is experienced, check the security of the main earth lead from the negative (–) terminal of the battery, the earth lead bolted to the engine, and the main earth point(s) on the frame. If corroded, dismantle the connection and clean all surfaces back to bare metal. Remake the connection and prevent further corrosion from forming by smearing battery terminal grease over the connection.
23 To check the earth of a component, use an insulated jumper wire to temporarily bypass its earth connection **(see illustration)** – connect one end of the jumper wire to the earth terminal or metal body of the component and the other end to the motorcycle's frame. If the circuit works with the jumper wire installed, the earth circuit is faulty.
24 To check an earth wire first check for corroded or loose connections, then check the wiring for continuity (Step 13) between each connector in the circuit in turn, and then to its earth point, to locate the break.

3 Battery removal and installation

Caution: Be extremely careful when handling or working around the battery. The electrolyte is very caustic and an explosive gas (hydrogen) is given off when the battery is charging.

Removal and installation

1 On Daytona models remove the rider's seat (see Chapter 7). On Street Triple models remove the seat (see Chapter 7).
2 Unscrew the negative (–) terminal bolt first and disconnect the lead from the battery **(see illustrations)**. Lift up the insulating cover to access the positive (+) terminal, then unscrew the bolt and disconnect the lead.
3 Release the battery strap **(see illustration)**.
4 Carefully lift the battery from the bike **(see illustration)**.
5 On installation, clean the battery terminals and lead ends with a wire brush, fine sandpaper or steel wool. Reconnect the leads, connecting the positive (+) terminal first.

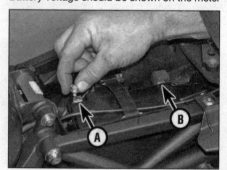

3.2a Battery negative terminal (A), and positive terminal (B) – Daytona

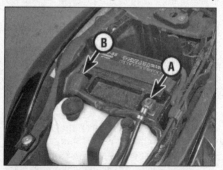

3.2b Battery negative terminal (A), and positive terminal (B) – Street Triple

HAYNES HiNT *Battery corrosion can be kept to a minimum by applying a layer of petroleum jelly (Vaseline) or dielectric grease (available as a spray) to the terminals after the cables have been connected. DO NOT use a mineral based grease.*

Inspection and maintenance

6 The battery fitted on all models is of the maintenance-free (sealed) type, therefore

3.3 Unhook the strap (arrowed)

3.4 Carefully lift the battery out – it is quite heavy

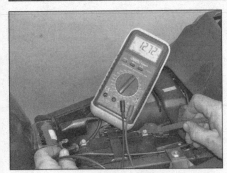

3.11 Checking battery voltage – connect the meter as shown

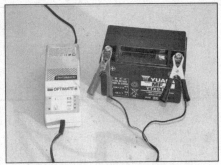

4.2 Battery connected to a charger

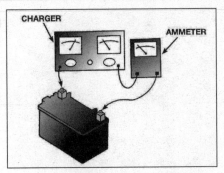

4.3 If the charger doesn't have an ammeter built in, connect one in series as shown. DO NOT connect the ammeter between the battery terminals or it will be ruined

requiring no specific maintenance. However, the following checks should still be regularly performed.

7 Check the battery terminals and leads for tightness and corrosion. If corrosion is evident, unscrew the terminal bolts and disconnect the leads from the battery, disconnecting the negative (–) terminal first, and clean the terminals and lead ends with a wire brush or knife and emery paper. Reconnect the leads, connecting the negative (+) terminal first, and apply a thin coat of petroleum jelly or battery terminal (dielectric) grease to the connections to slow further corrosion. DO NOT use a standard mineral based grease.

8 Keep the battery case clean to prevent current leakage, which can discharge the battery over a period of time (especially when it sits unused). Wash the outside of the case with a solution of baking soda and water. Rinse the battery thoroughly, then dry it.

9 Look for cracks in the case and renew the battery if any are found. If acid has been spilled on the frame or battery box, neutralise it with a baking soda and water solution, dry it thoroughly, then touch up any damaged paint.

10 If the motorcycle sits unused for long periods of time, disconnect the leads from the battery terminals, negative (–) terminal first. Refer to Section 4 and charge the battery once every month to six weeks.

11 The condition of the battery can be assessed by measuring the voltage present

at the battery terminals **(see illustration)**. Connect the voltmeter positive (+) probe to the battery positive (+) terminal, and the negative (–) probe to the battery negative (–) terminal. When fully charged there should be 12.8 volts (or more) present. If the voltage falls below 12.3 volts the battery must be removed, disconnecting the negative (–) terminal first, and recharged as described in Section 4.

4 Battery charging

Caution: Be extremely careful when handling or working around the battery. The electrolyte is very caustic and an explosive gas (hydrogen) is given off when the battery is charging.

1 Remove the battery (see Section 3).

2 Connect the charger to the battery, making sure that the positive (+) lead on the charger is connected to the positive (+) terminal on the battery, and the negative (–) lead is connected to the negative (–) terminal **(see illustration)**.

3 The battery should be charged at the specified rate for up to 12 hours if it is completely flat, or until the voltage across the terminals reaches 12.8V – disconnect the charger and allow the battery to stabilise for 30 minutes after charging before taking a voltage reading. The actual time required depends on the initial voltage present

(Section 3, Step 11). Exceeding this can cause the battery to overheat, buckling the plates and rendering it useless. It is best to use a dedicated motorcycle battery charger, preferably one of the 'intelligent' ones that constantly monitors the state of charge and controls its output accordingly. If a normal car type charger is used check that after a probable initial peak, the charge rate falls to a safe level consistent with the charge rate specified for your model at the beginning of the Chapter – if the charger does not have an ammeter, you can connect one as shown if required **(see illustration)**. If the battery becomes hot during charging **stop**. Further charging will cause damage. There are many bike-specific chargers available from good suppliers that are designed for the maintenance and recovery of motorcycle batteries, in particular catering for the requirements of heavily discharged MF batteries. They are not too expensive, and are a worthwhile investment, especially if the bike is not used over winter. Follow the manufacturer's instructions.

4 If the recharged battery discharges rapidly when left disconnected it is likely that an internal short caused by physical damage or sulphation has occurred. A new battery will be required. A sound battery will tend to lose its charge at about 1% per day.

5 Install the battery (see Section 3).

6 If the motorcycle sits unused for long periods of time, charge the battery once every month to six weeks and leave it disconnected.

5 Fuses

1 The electrical system is protected by fuses of different ratings. The main fuse is housed in the starter relay, which on Daytona models is under the back of the fuel tank, and on Street Triple models is under the seat **(see illustrations)**. All other fuses are housed in a fusebox, which on Daytona models is under the left-hand cockpit trim panel, and on Street

5.1a Starter relay (arrowed) – Daytona

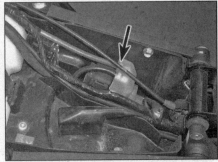

5.1b Starter relay (arrowed) – Street Triple

5.1c Fusebox (arrowed) – Daytona

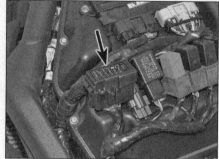

5.1d Fusebox (arrowed) – Street Triple

5.2 Main fuse (arrowed)

Triple models is under the fuel tank **(see illustrations)**.

2 To access the main fuse, on Daytona models raise or remove the fuel tank (see Chapter 4), and on Street Triple models remove the seat (see Chapter 7). Remove the plastic cover from the starter relay **(see illustration 5.1a)**. The fuse is between the wiring connector and the leads **(see illustration)**. A spare main fused is housed in the relay sleeve.

3 To access the fusebox fuses, on Daytona models remove the left-hand cockpit trim panel (see Chapter 7). On Street Triple models raise or remove the fuel tank (see Chapter 4). Unclip the fusebox lid **(see illustration)**. A spare fuse of each rating is housed in the fusebox.

4 The fuses can be removed and checked visually. If you can't pull the fuse out with your fingertips, use a suitable pair of pliers. A blown fuse is easily identified by a break in the element **(see illustration)**, or can be tested for continuity using an ohmmeter or continuity tester – if there is no continuity, it has blown. Each fuse is clearly marked with its rating and must only be replaced by a fuse of the same rating. If a spare fuse is used, always replace it with a new one so that a spare of each rating is carried on the bike at all times.

⚠️ *Warning: Never put in a fuse of a higher rating or bridge the terminals with any other substitute, however temporary it may be. Serious damage may be done to the circuit, or a fire may start.*

5 Sometimes fuses blow for no specific reason, in which case replacing it with a new one is the only action required. Also corrosion of the fuse ends and fusebox terminals may occur and cause poor fuse contact. If this happens, remove the corrosion with a wire brush or emery paper, then spray the fuse end and terminals with electrical contact cleaner.

6 If the new fuse blows, you need to check the relevant circuit and its components carefully for evidence of a short-circuit. Look for bare wires and chafed, melted or burned insulation.

6 Lighting system check

Note: *Refer to Electrical system fault finding (Section 2) and to the Wiring Diagrams at the end of the Chapter when making electrical tests on any part of the system.*

1 If none of the lights work, check battery voltage (see Section 3) – low voltage indicates either a faulty battery or a defective charging system. Refer to Sections 3 and 4 for battery checks and Section 26 for charging system tests. If there is a problem with more than one circuit at the same time, or with all circuits, it is likely to be a fault relating to a multi-function component, such as the fuse or the ignition switch. When checking for a blown filament in a bulb, it is advisable to back up a visual check with a continuity test of the filament as it is not

always apparent that a bulb has blown. When testing for continuity, remember that on single terminal bulbs it is the metal body of the bulb that is the earth (ground).

Headlight

2 If a headlight fails to work, check the bulb(s) and the bulb terminals and wiring connectors first (see Section 7), then the circuit fuse (see Section 5). If they are all good, check for battery voltage at the blue/white (high beam) or blue/red (low beam) supply wire terminal in the headlight wiring connector, with the ignition switch ON, and the dip beam/main beam switch set appropriately. If voltage is present, check for continuity between the black (earth or ground) wire terminal and the battery negative (–) terminal. If there is no continuity, check the earth (ground) circuit for an open or poor connection.

3 If no voltage is indicated, check the wiring and connectors between the headlight, dimmer switch, fusebox, and the ignition switch, and check the dimmer switch and ignition switch (see Sections 18 and 17).

4 If no problem can be found refer first to Section 16 and check the headlight relay on Street Triple models from VIN 560477, and the starter circuit relay on all other models. Make sure the relay is secure in its connector and that the terminals are corrosion free and not bent or broken. Then check the function of the relay itself as described.

Tail light

Note: *The tail and brake lights consist of a number of LEDs. If an individual LED fails it cannot be replaced with a new one (the only solution is to fit a complete new tail light unit), but the rest should continue to function. If none of them work, it is more likely to be a circuit problem – follow Steps 5 and 6.*

5 If the tail light fails to work, check the wiring connector first (see Section 10), then the circuit fuse (see Section 5). If they are all good, check for battery voltage at the yellow wire terminal in the loom side of the tail light wiring connector, with the ignition switch ON. If voltage is present, check for continuity between the black (earth or ground) wire terminal and the battery negative (–) terminal. If there is no continuity, check the earth (ground) circuit for an open or poor connection.

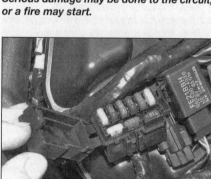

5.3 Unclip the lid to access the fusebox fuses – the identity, location and rating of each fuse is marked on or in the lid

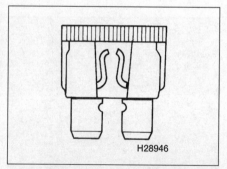

H28946

5.4 A blown fuse can be identified by a break in its element

6 If no voltage is indicated, check the wiring and connectors between the tail light and the ignition switch, then check the switch (see Section 17).

Sidelight and licence plate light

7 If the sidelight and/or licence plate light fails to work, check the bulb and the bulb terminals and wiring connectors first (see Section 7 or 10), then the circuit fuse. If they are all good, check for battery voltage at the yellow wire terminal in the loom side of the wiring connector, with the ignition switch ON. If voltage and continuity are present, check for continuity between the black (earth or ground) wire terminal and the battery negative (–) terminal. If there is no continuity, check the earth (ground) circuit for an open or poor connection.

8 If no voltage is indicated, check the wiring and connectors between the sidelight and the ignition switch, then check the switch (see Section 17).

Brake light

Note: *The tail and brake lights consist of a number of LEDs. If an individual LED fails it cannot be replaced with a new one (the only solution is to fit a complete new tail light unit), but the rest should continue to function. If none of them work, it is more likely to be a circuit or switch problem – follow Steps 9 and 10.*

9 If the brake light fails to work, check the wiring connector first (see Section 10), then the circuit fuse (see Section 5). If they are all good, check for battery voltage at the green/purple wire terminal in the loom side of the tail light wiring connector, with the ignition switch ON, and the brake lever or pedal applied. If voltage is present, check for continuity between the black (earth or ground) wire terminal and the battery negative (–) terminal. If there is no continuity, check the earth (ground) circuit for an open or poor connection.

10 If no voltage is indicated, check the brake light switches (see Section 14), then the wiring and connectors between the tail light and the switches.

Turn signal lights

11 If one light fails to work, check the bulb

7.2a Remove the cover . . .

7.2c Release the clips . . .

and the bulb terminals first, then the wiring connectors (see Section 13). If none of the turn signals work, first check the signal circuit fuse (see Section 5).

12 If the fuse is good, see Section 12 for the turn signal circuit check.

7 Headlight and sidelight bulbs

Note: *The headlight bulbs are of the quartz-halogen type. Do not touch the bulb glass as skin acids will shorten the bulb's service life. If the bulb is accidentally touched, it should be wiped carefully when cold with a rag soaked in methylated spirit and dried before fitting.*

⚠ **Warning: Allow the bulb time to cool before removing it if the headlight has just been on.**

7.2b . . . and disconnect the wiring connector

7.2d . . . and remove the bulb

Daytona

Headlight

1 The right-hand bulb is for the main beam, the left-hand for the dipped beam. To access the bulbs remove the cockpit trim panel on the relevant side (see Chapter 7).

2 To remove the dipped beam bulb, undo the screws and remove the cover **(see illustration)**. Disconnect the wiring connector from the bulb **(see illustration)**. Release the bulb retaining clips, then remove the bulb **(see illustrations)**.

3 To remove the main beam bulb, undo the screws and remove the cover. Disconnect the wiring connector from the bulb **(see illustrations)**. Turn the bulb unit anti-clockwise and withdraw it **(see illustration)**.

4 Fit the new bulb in reverse order, bearing in mind the information in the Note above.

5 Install the trim panel(s). Check the operation of the headlight.

7.3a Remove the cover . . .

7.3b . . . and disconnect the wiring connector

7.3c Release and remove the bulb

7.6 Remove the cover

7.7 Pull the bulbholder out of the headlight . . .

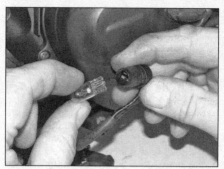

7.8 . . . then pull the bulb out of the holder

Sidelight

6 Undo the screws and remove the cover **(see illustration)**.

7 Carefully pull the bulbholder out – do not pull it out by the wires **(see illustration)**.

8 Carefully pull the bulb out of the holder **(see illustration)**.

9 Fit the new bulb in reverse order.

10 Check the operation of the sidelight.

Street Triple up to VIN 480781, Street Triple R up to VIN 482181

Headlight

11 Undo the headlight rim clamp screw, taking care not to lose the nut, then support the headlight and remove the rim **(see illustrations)**. Carefully draw the light unit out of the shell, noting how it fits **(see illustration)**. Note the seat for the light unit in the housing **(see illustration 7.17)**.

12 Disconnect the wiring connector from the headlight bulb **(see illustration)**. Carefully pull the rubber sidelight bulbholder out – do not pull it out by the wires **(see illustration)**. Place the headlight on a bench.

13 Remove the rubber dust cover, noting how it fits **(see illustration)**.

14 Release the bulb retaining clip, noting how it fits, then remove the bulb **(see illustrations)**.

7.11a Undo the screw and collect the nut . . .

7.11b . . . then remove the rim . . .

7.11c . . . and displace the light unit

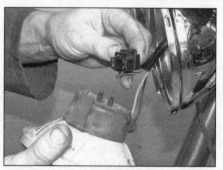

7.12a Disconnect the headlight wiring connector . . .

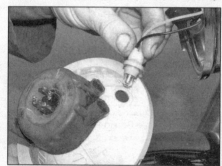

7.12b . . . and pull the sidelight out

7.13 Remove the cover

7.14a Release the clip . . .

7.14b . . . and remove the bulb

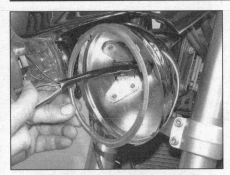

7.17 Make sure the seat is correctly in place

7.21 Carefully pull the bulb out of the holder

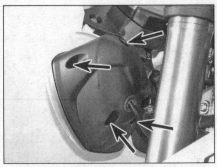

7.24a Undo the screws (arrowed) . . .

15 Fit the new bulb, bearing in mind the information in the Note above. Make sure the tabs on the bulb fit correctly in the slots in the bulb housing, and secure it in position with the retaining clip.
16 Fit the dust cover then connect the wiring connector.
17 Make sure the light unit seat is correctly fitted in the housing (see illustration), and the unit locates correctly, then fit the rim and tighten the clamp (see illustrations 7.11c, b and a).
18 Check the operation of the headlight.

Sidelight

19 Undo the headlight rim clamp screw, taking care not to lose the nut, then support the headlight and remove the rim (see illustrations 7.11a and b). Carefully draw the light unit out of the shell, noting how it fits (see illustration 7.11c). Note the seat for the light unit in the housing (see illustration 7.17).

20 Carefully pull the rubber bulbholder out (see illustration 7.12b) – do not pull it out by the wires.
21 Carefully pull the bulb out of the holder (see illustration).
22 Fit the new bulb in reverse order.
23 Check the operation of the sidelight.

Street Triple from VIN 480782, Street Triple R from VIN 482182, Street Triple RX

Headlight

24 Undo the screws on the back of the headlight, draw the beam unit out the front and disconnect the wiring (see illustrations).
25 Disconnect the wiring connector and remove the rubber dust cover (see illustrations).
26 Release the bulb retaining clip, noting how it fits, then remove the bulb (see illustrations).

27 Fit the new bulb, bearing in mind the information in the Note above. Make sure the tabs on the bulb fit correctly in the slots in the bulb housing, and secure it in position with the retaining clip (see illustrations 7.26b and a).
28 Fit the dust cover and connect the wiring (see illustrations 7.25b and a).
29 Connect the wiring connector, fit the beam unit into the housing and tighten the screws (see illustrations 7.24b and a).
30 Check the operation of the headlight.

Sidelight

31 Undo the screws on the back of the headlight, draw the beam unit out the front and disconnect the wiring (see illustrations 7.24a and b).
32 Carefully pull the rubber bulb holder out (see illustration) – do not pull it out by the wires.

7.24b . . . displace the beam unit and disconnect the connector

7.25a Pull the connector off . . .

7.25b . . . and remove the cover

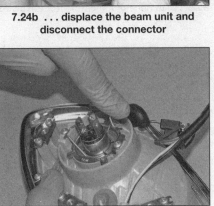

7.26a Release the clip . . .

7.26b . . . and remove the bulb

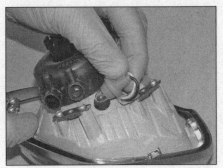

7.32 Pull the bulb holder out of the headlight . . .

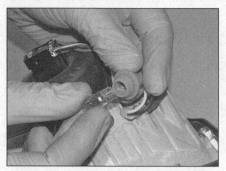

7.33 . . . and the bulb out of the holder

33 Carefully pull the bulb out of the holder **(see illustration)**.
34 Fit the new bulb in reverse order.
35 Check the operation of the sidelight.

8 Headlight assembly

Removal

Daytona

1 Remove the fairing (see Chapter 7).
2 Unscrew the bolts securing the headlight assembly and remove it from the fairing **(see illustration)**.
3 If required, remove the headlight and sidelight bulbs (see Section 7).

8.4a Headlight wiring connectors (arrowed) – Street Triple to VIN 480781, R to VIN 482181

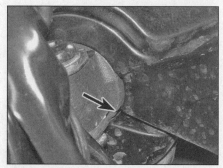

8.5a Make an alignment mark between the centre piece and the holder

8.2 Headlight mounting bolts (arrowed) – Daytona

Street Triple

4 On the Street Triple up to VIN 480781 and Street Triple R up to VIN 482181 remove the airbox (see Chapter 4), then trace the wiring from the headlight(s) and disconnect it at the connector(s) **(see illustration)**. On the Street Triple from VIN 480782 and Street Triple R from VIN 482182 pull the cover off the back of the instrument cluster, then disconnect the headlight wiring connector **(see illustrations)**.
5 To remove the complete headlight assembly, first make an alignment mark between the centre pivot piece and the holder so the headlights can be installed with the same vertical alignment **(see illustration)**. Support the headlight assembly, then unscrew the two clamp bolts and remove the clamp and the headlights **(see illustration)**.
6 To remove an individual light, unscrew the nut and withdraw the bolt securing it to the

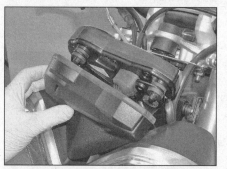

8.4b On all other Street triples pull the cover off . . .

8.5b Headlight assembly clamp bolts (arrowed) – Street Triple models

central mounting piece and remove the light **(see illustration)**.

Installation

7 Installation is the reverse of removal. Make sure all the wiring is correctly connected and secured. Check the operation of the headlight and sidelight. Check the headlight aim (see Section 9).

9 Headlight aim

Note: *An improperly adjusted headlight may cause problems for oncoming traffic or provide poor, unsafe illumination of the road ahead. Before adjusting the headlight aim, be sure to consult with local traffic laws and regulations – for UK models refer to MOT Test Checks in the Reference section.*
1 The headlight beams can be adjusted both horizontally and vertically. Before making any adjustment, check that the tyre pressures are correct and the suspension is adjusted as required. Make any adjustments to the headlight aim with machine on level ground, with the fuel tank half full, with an assistant sitting on the seat, and with the headlight on and shining against a dark vertical surface such as a garage wall, and set to main or dipped beam as required. If the bike is usually ridden with a passenger on the back, have a second assistant do this.

8.4c . . . to access the connector (arrowed)

8.6 Individual headlight mounting bolt and nut (arrowed)

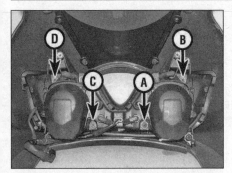

9.2 Main beam vertical adjuster (A), main beam horizontal adjuster (B); dipped beam vertical adjuster (C), dipped beam horizontal adjuster (D)

Daytona

2 To raise either beam turn the vertical adjuster screw clockwise, and to lower it turn it anti-clockwise **(see illustration)**.

3 To move the main (right-hand) beam to the right turn the adjuster screw anti-clockwise, and to move it to the left turn it clockwise **(see illustration 9.2)**.

4 To move the dipped (left-hand) beam to the right turn the adjuster screw clockwise, and to move it to the left turn it anti-clockwise **(see illustration 9.2)**.

Street Triple

5 Vertical adjustment of the headlight is made by slackening the clamp bolts on the headlight mounting and by pivoting the lights up or down as required – the beams can only

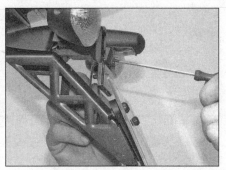

10.2 Undo the bolt and displace the light

be moved as a pair and are not individually adjustable **(see illustration 8.5b)**. Tighten the bolts on completion.

6 Horizontal adjustment is made by slackening the nut on the bottom of the pivot bolt on each individual headlight mounting and by pivoting the light to the right or left as required – each beam can be adjusted independently of the other **(see illustration 8.6)**. Tighten the nut on completion.

10 Brake/tail LEDs and licence plate bulb

Brake/tail lights

1 The brake and tail lights consist of a number of LEDs. If an individual LED fails it cannot be replaced with a new one (the only solution is to

fit a complete new tail light unit), but the rest should continue to function. If none of them work, it is more likely to be a circuit problem (see Section 6).

Licence plate bulb

2 On Daytona models and Street Triple models to VIN 560476, counter-hold the nut and unscrew the bolt securing the licence plate light and detach it **(see illustration)**. On Street Triple models from VIN 560477 unscrew the bolt securing the licence plate light and detach it.

3 Ease the bulbholder out of the back of the licence plate light, and pull the bulb out of the holder **(see illustrations)**.

4 Fit the new bulb in reverse order.

11 Tail light assembly

1 On Daytona models remove the seat cowling (see Chapter 7). Unscrew the tail light bolts and draw the light out **(see illustration)**.

2 On Street Triple and Street Triple R models to VIN 560476 remove the side panels and tail light cover (see Chapter 7). Unscrew the tail light bolts then draw the light out and disconnect the wiring connector **(see illustrations)**.

3 On Street Triple and Street Triple R models from VIN 560477 remove the side panels (see Chapter 7). Remove the seat support **(see illustration)**. Unscrew the tail light assembly bolts then draw the assembly out

10.3a Release the bulbholder . . .

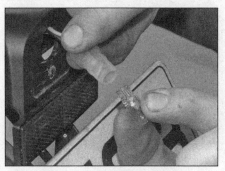

10.3b . . . then pull the bulb out

11.1 Unscrew the bolts (arrowed)

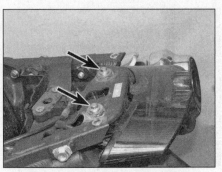

11.2a Unscrew the bolts (arrowed) . . .

11.2b . . . then draw out the light and disconnect the wiring

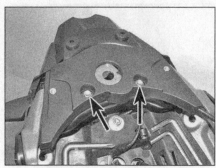

11.3a Unscrew the bolts (arrowed) and remove the seat support

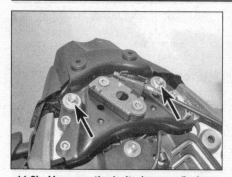

11.3b Unscrew the bolts (arrowed), draw the assembly out . . .

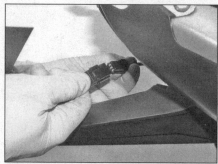

11.3c . . . and disconnect the wiring

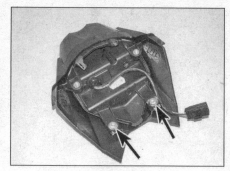

11.3d Tail light bolts (arrowed)

and disconnect the wiring connector **(see illustrations)**. Unscrew the tail light bolts and draw it out of the cover **(see illustration)**.

4 On Street Triple RX models refer to the side panels, licence plate bracket and undertray removal procedure in Chapter 7, Section 3.

5 Installation is the reverse of removal. Check the operation of the tail and brake lights.

12 Turn signal circuit check and relay

1 Most turn signal problems are the result of a burned out bulb or corroded socket. This is especially true when the turn signals function properly in one direction, but fail to flash in

the other direction. Check the bulbs, sockets and wiring connectors (see Section 13). Also, check the turn signal circuit fuse (see Section 5) and the switch (see Section 18).

2 If the bulbs, sockets, connectors, fuse, switch and battery are good, check the turn signal relay – to access it on Daytona models remove the left-hand fairing side panel (see Chapter 7), and on Street Triple models raise or remove the fuel tank (see Chapter 4).

3 Disconnect the relay wiring connector then free it from its mount **(see illustrations)**. Triumph do not provide any specific test data for the relay itself, so the easiest way to test it is by substituting the suspect one with a known good one. You can however test the wiring to and from the relay as follows.

4 Check for voltage at the orange/green wire in the relay wiring connector with the ignition ON. Turn the ignition OFF when the check is complete. If no voltage is present, using the appropriate wiring diagram at the end of this Chapter check the wiring between the relay and the ignition switch and the fusebox. If voltage was present, check for continuity in the wiring between the relay, turn signal switch and turn signal lights for continuity. If all the wiring and connectors are good, replace the relay with a new one.

13 Turn signal bulbs and assemblies

Turn signal bulbs

1 Undo the turn signal lens screw and remove the lens, noting how it fits **(see illustrations)**.

2 Push the bulb into the holder and twist it anti-clockwise to remove it **(see illustration)**. Check the socket terminals for corrosion and clean them if necessary. Line up the pins of the new bulb with the slots in the socket, then push the bulb in and turn it clockwise until it locks into place.

3 Fit the lens, making sure the tab locates

12.3a Turn signal relay (arrowed) – Daytona

12.3b Turn signal relay (arrowed) – Street Triple

13.1a On some models the screw goes in from the front . . .

13.1b . . . and on others from the back

13.2 Release and remove the bulb

13.3 Make sure the tab locates correctly when fitting the lens

13.4a Unscrew the bolt (arrowed) . . .

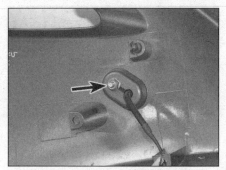

13.4b . . . counter-holding the nut (arrowed) where fitted

13.5a Disconnect the relevant wiring connectors (arrowed)

13.5b Front turn signal bolt (arrowed)

13.6 Note the routing of the wiring and how it is secured

correctly **(see illustration)**. Do not overtighten the screw as the lens or threads could be damaged.

Front turn signals

4 On Daytona models release the fairing inner panel trim clips and remove the panel (see Chapter 7). Disconnect the turn signal wiring connectors. Unscrew the bolt on the outside, counter-holding the nut on the inside where fitted (models up to VIN 381274), then withdraw the bolt and remove the turn signal, taking care not to snag the wiring **(see illustrations)**.
5 On Street Triple models to VIN 560476 remove the airbox (see Chapter 4). Disconnect the turn signal wiring connectors **(see illustration)**. Unscrew the bolt and remove

the turn signal, taking care not to snag the wiring as you draw it through the radiator cowl bracket **(see illustration)**.
6 On Street Triple models from VIN 560477 remove the outer and middle radiator cowls (see Chapter 7). Release the wiring from the clips and remove the turn signal from the middle cowl, taking care not to snag the wiring as you draw it through **(see illustration)**.
7 Installation is the reverse of removal. Make sure the wiring is correctly routed and securely connected. Check the operation of the turn signals.

Rear turn signals

8 On Daytona models unscrew the bolt on the outside, counter-holding the nut on the inside

where fitted (models up to VIN 381274), then displace the turn signal **(see illustration)**. Disconnect the wiring connectors and withdraw the turn signal, taking care not to snag the wiring.
9 On Street Triple models to VIN 560476 remove the tail light (see Section 11). Disconnect the turn signal and licence plate light wiring connectors **(see illustration)**. Unscrew the turn signal bracket bolts and remove the assembly. Unscrew the bolt and remove the turn signal, taking care not to snag the wiring and noting its routing.
10 On Street Triple models from VIN 560477 remove the seat (see Chapter 7). Disconnect the turn signal and licence plate light sub-loom wiring connector **(see illustration)**. Unscrew the tail hanger bolts and remove the assembly

13.8 Rear turn signal bolt (arrowed)

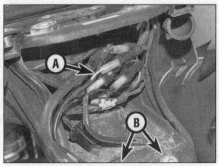

13.9 Disconnect the wiring connectors (A). Turn signal bracket bolts (B)

13.10a Disconnect the connector (arrowed) and release the wire from the clip

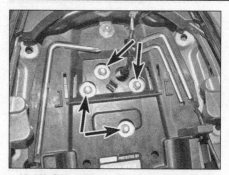

13.10b Unscrew the bolts (arrowed) . . .

13.10c . . . and remove the tail hanger

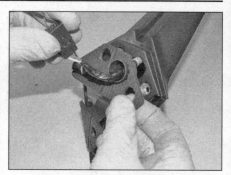

13.10d Note how the gasket fits

13.10e Release the clips and remove the reflector

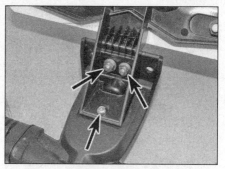

13.10f Unscrew the bolt and nuts (arrowed) and remove the bracket

13.10g Unscrew each turn signal bolt . . .

13.10h . . . and split the halves . . .

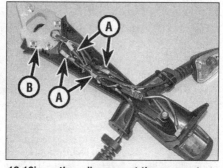

13.10i . . . then disconnect the connectors (A). Note how the plate (B) locates

13.11 Push the clips on using a socket

(see illustrations). Remove the rubber gasket (see illustration). Ease the rear reflector clips up off the pegs using a small screwdriver and remove the reflector (see illustration). Remove the license plate bracket from the hanger (see illustration). Unscrew the bolts and detach the turn signals from the hanger,

then split the hanger into its upper and lower sections (see illustrations). Disconnect the turn signal wiring connectors and remove the turn signal, taking care not to snag the wiring and noting its routing (see illustration).
11 Installation is the reverse of removal. Make sure the wiring is correctly routed and

securely connected. On Street Triple models from VIN 560477 make sure the metal plate and rubber gasket are correctly located in and on the hanger respectively (see illustrations 13.10i and d), and secure the reflector by pushing the clips down over the pegs using a small socket (see illustration). Check the operation of the turn signals.

14 Brake light switches

Circuit check

1 Before checking the switches, check the brake light circuit (seeSection 6).
2 The front brake light switch is mounted on the underside of the brake master cylinder. Disconnect the wiring connectors from the switch (see illustrations). Using a continuity tester, connect the probes to the terminals of

14.2a Front brake light switch wiring connectors (A) and screw (B) – Daytona

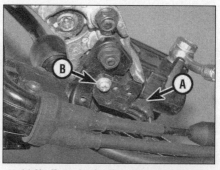

14.2b Front brake light switch wiring connectors (A) and screw (B) – Street Triple

14.3 Rear brake light switch (arrowed)

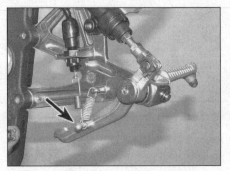

14.8a Unhook the spring (arrowed) . . .

14.8b . . . then hold the adjuster nut (arrowed) and unscrew the switch

the switch. With the brake lever at rest, there should be no continuity. With the brake lever applied, there should be continuity. If the switch does not behave as described, replace it with a new one.

3 The rear brake light switch is mounted on the right-hand side, above the brake pedal (see illustration). Raise or remove the fuel tank (see Chapter 4). Trace the wiring from the switch and disconnect it at the connector. Using a continuity tester, connect the probes to the terminals on the switch or the wiring connector, according to model. With the brake pedal at rest, there should be no continuity. With the brake pedal applied, there should be continuity. If the switch does not behave as described, replace it with a new one.

4 If the switches are good, check for voltage at one of the connectors (it could be either one) for the front brake switch, and at the orange/green wire terminal in the connector for the rear brake switch, with the ignition switch ON – there should be battery voltage. If there's no voltage present, check the wiring between the switch and the ignition switch (refer to Section 2 at the beginning of this chapter and the *Wiring Diagrams* at the end of it). If there is voltage check the wiring from the switch to the tail light assembly.

Switch renewal

Front brake light switch

5 The switch is mounted on the underside of the brake master cylinder. Disconnect the wiring connectors from the switch (see illustration 14.2a or b).

6 Remove the single screw securing the switch to the bottom of the master cylinder and remove the switch.

7 Installation is the reverse of removal. The switch isn't adjustable.

Rear brake light switch

8 The rear brake light switch is mounted on the inside of the right-hand footrest bracket (see illustration 14.3). Raise or remove the fuel tank (see Chapter 4). Trace the wiring from the switch and disconnect it at the connector. Free the wiring from any clips or ties and feed it through to the switch. Detach the lower end of the switch spring from the brake pedal (see illustration). Unscrew and remove the switch from the adjuster nut in the bracket (see illustration).

9 Installation is the reverse of removal. Make sure the brake light is activated just before the rear brake pedal takes effect. If adjustment is necessary, hold the switch and turn the adjuster nut on the switch body until the brake light is activated when required (see illustration 14.8b).

15 Instrument cluster

Check

1 Specific test data for the instruments is not available. Refer below for access to the wiring connector and check that it is securely connected to the instrument cluster, and also refer to the relevant Section of this Chapter or to other Chapters and check that the other end

of the wiring is securely connected to its source (i.e. neutral switch, oil pressure switch, fuel level sensor, coolant temperature sensor etc). Check all wires for continuity from pin to pin, referring to electrical system fault finding (Section 2) and to the wiring diagrams at the end of the Chapter.

2 Check that all earth wires have a good connection. If all the wiring is good, it is possible that there are faults in the switches or sensors or the electronic control module (ECM) of the engine management system which provide much of the information to the instruments. Refer to Chapter 4 for details. If all checks point at faulty instruments rather than wiring or the engine management system, take the instrument cluster to a Triumph dealer for further assessment.

3 All of the warning and instrument lights are LEDs. If the cause of any problem (i.e. neutral light not coming on) cannot be traced it is possible the LED has failed, in which case a new instrument cluster must be fitted.

Removal

4 Disconnect the battery negative (–) terminal (see Section 3).

5 On Daytona models remove the fairing (see Chapter 7). Unscrew the fairing/instrument bracket bolts and displace it from the air duct – note how the right-hand bolts secure the tip-over sensor bracket (see illustration). Pull the rubber boot back and disconnect the wiring connector (see illustration). Unscrew the bolt, collect the washer, and detach the instrument cluster from the bracket, noting how the pegs locate in the grommets (see illustration).

15.5a Unscrew the bolts (arrowed) on each side and displace the assembly . . .

15.5b . . . then disconnect the wiring connector

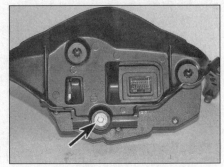

15.5c Unscrew the bolt and detach the instrument cluster

15.6 Disconnect the wiring connector (A) then unscrew the bolt (B) and remove the instruments

6 On Street Triple models, either remove the cover from the back of the instrument cluster – it is a push fit with pegs locating in grommets, or remove the instrument cowl if fitted (see Chapter 7). Pull back the rubber boot and disconnect the wiring connector **(see illustration)**. Unscrew the bolt, collect the washer, and detach the instrument cluster from the bracket, noting how the pegs locate in the grommets.

Installation

7 Installation is the reverse of removal. Check the rubber grommets for cracks and deterioration and replace them with new ones if necessary. Make sure the wiring connector is secure. On Street Triple models not fitted with a cowl make sure the instrument cluster cover seal is correctly fitted before fitting the cover.

16 Relays

Note: *Refer to the Wiring Diagrams at the end of the Chapter for relay terminal identification.*
1 The following circuit relays are fitted: turn signal relay (see Section 12), starter circuit relay, starter motor relay (see Section 24), cooling fan relay (see Chapter 3), engine management system (EMS) relay (see Chapter 4) and fuel pump relay (see Chapter 4) **(see illustrations)**. Street Triple models from VIN 560477 also have a headlight relay, and where fitted a heated grip relay.
2 On Daytona models remove the right-hand

16.1a Cooling fan relay (A), EMS relay (B), starter circuit relay (C) – Daytona

16.1c Fuel pump relay (A), cooling fan relay (B), EMS relay (C), starter circuit relay (D), turn signal relay (E) – Street Triples to VIN 560476

fairing side panel to access the turn signal and fuel pump relays, and the left-hand cockpit trim panel to access the rest (see Chapter 7). On Street Triple models to VIN 560476 raise or remove the fuel tank to access all relays (see Chapter 4). On Street Triple models from VIN 560477 remove the seat to access all relays (see Chapter 7).
3 Before removing a relay disconnect the battery negative (–) terminal (see Section 3). The starter circuit relay, cooling fan relay, EMS relay, and fuel pump relay have terminals on their underside which plug directly into sockets – simply pull the relay out of its socket **(see illustration)**.
4 Refer to the Wiring Diagrams at the end of Chapter 8 and to the wire colours into the relay socket to identify the activating power in

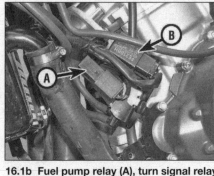

16.1b Fuel pump relay (A), turn signal relay (B) – Daytona

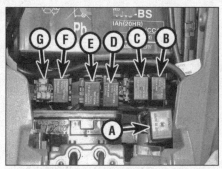

16.1d Turn signal relay (A), EMS relay (B), headlight relay (C), fuel pump relay (D), cooling fan relay (E), starter circuit relay (F), heated grip relay socket (G) – Street Triples from VIN 560477

and out terminals, and the main power in and out terminals that provide the power to the appropriate electrical component (you can also refer to the relevant Chapter or Section within this Chapter where given in Step 1 for more specific information on the individual relays) **(see illustrations)**. Using an ohmmeter or continuity tester, connect the positive (+) probe to the relay's main power in terminal, and the negative (–) probe to the relay's main power out terminal. There should be no continuity. Leaving the meter connected, and using a fully charged 12 volt battery and two insulated jumper wires, connect the positive (+) terminal of the battery to the activating power in terminal, and the negative (–) terminal to the activating power out terminal. At this point the relay should close and

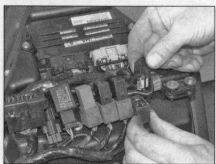

16.3 Removing a relay from its connector block

16.4a On Street Triple models from VIN 560477 release the relay holder clips . . .

16.4b . . . and displace the holders to match wire colours to terminals

17.1a Ignition switch and left-hand switch housing wiring connectors – Daytona

17.1b Ignition switch and left-hand switch housing wiring connectors – Street Triple

17.4 Remove the trim piece (arrowed)

the multimeter read 0 ohms (continuity) – there should be an audible click as the relay closes.

5 The starter circuit relay performs a load relief function for the headlight circuit. In its normal position, the relay completes the power supply circuit to the headlight. When the starter button is pressed, the relay switches its supply from the headlight circuit to the starter relay, thus enabling full battery power to be available for operation of the starter motor. Testing of the starter circuit relay can be carried out as described in Step 4, noting the different circuits connected by the two 'power out' terminals (see Wiring Diagrams at the end of this Chapter).

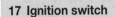

17 Ignition switch

⚠️ **Warning: To prevent the risk of short circuits, remove the seat(s) and disconnect the battery negative (–) lead before making any ignition switch checks.**

Check

1 On Daytona models release the fairing inner panel trim clips and remove the panel (see Chapter 7). On Street Triple models remove the airbox (see Chapter 4). Trace the wiring from the base of the ignition switch and disconnect it at the connector **(see illustrations)**. Make the checks on the switch side of the connector.
2 Using an ohmmeter or a continuity tester, check the continuity of the connector terminal pairs (see the *Wiring Diagrams* at the end of

this Chapter). Continuity should exist between the terminals connected by a solid line on the diagram when the switch key is turned to the indicated position.
3 If the switch fails any of the tests, replace it with a new one.

Removal

4 Refer to Step 1 and disconnect the switch wiring connector. On Street Triple models from VIN 560477 undo the screws and remove the left-hand trim piece from the front of the frame **(see illustration)**. Feed the wiring back to the switch, freeing it from all clips and ties and noting its correct routing.
5 Refer to Chapter 1, Section 17, Steps 6 to 8 (according to model) and remove the top yoke to a work bench.
6 Two shear-head bolts mount the ignition switch to the underside of the top yoke **(see illustration)**. The heads of the bolts must be driven round using a suitable punch or drift, or drilled off, before the switch can be removed. Mount the yoke in a vice equipped with soft jaws and padded out with rags to do this. Remove the bolts with their oval washers and withdraw the switch from the top yoke. The immobiliser receiver (later models) is integral with the switch.

Installation

7 Obtain new shear-head bolts. Fit the switch onto the top yoke. Fit the oval washers and tighten the bolts until their heads shear off **(see illustration 17.6)**.
8 Fit the top yoke onto the steering stem. Route the wiring back to the connector, securing it with any clips and ties, and reconnect it **(see**

illustration 17.1a or b). On Street Triple models from VIN 560477 fit the left-hand trim piece onto the front of the frame **(see illustration 17.4)**.
9 Refer to Chapter 1, Section 17, Steps 14 to 16 (according to model) and install the top yoke and handlebars
10 On Daytona models install the inner panel. On Street Triple models install the airbox (see Chapter 4).

18 Handlebar switches

1 Most problems are caused by dirty or corroded contacts, but wear and breakage of internal parts is a possibility that should not be overlooked. If breakage does occur, the entire switch and related wiring harness will have to be replaced with a new one, as individual parts are not available.
2 The switches can be checked for continuity using an ohmmeter or a continuity test light (see Section 2).
3 On Daytona models, to access the connector for the left-hand switches release the fairing inner panel trim clips and remove the panel (see Chapter 7) **(see illustration 17.1a)**, and to access the connector for the right-hand switches remove the right-hand fairing side panel (see Chapter 7) **(see illustration)**. On Street Triple models remove the airbox (see Chapter 4). Trace the wiring from the switch and disconnect it at the connector **(see illustration and 17.1b)**. Make the checks on the switch side of the connector.

17.6 Ignition switch bolts (arrowed)

18.3a Right-hand switch wiring connector (arrowed) – Daytona

18.3b Right-hand switch wiring connector (arrowed) – Street Triple

18.8 Press in the clip (arrowed) and withdraw the switch

18.9a Right-hand switch housing screws (arrowed) – Daytona

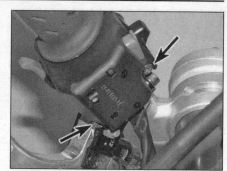

18.9b Left-hand switch housing screws (arrowed)

4 Check for continuity between the terminals of the switch harness with the switch in the various positions (i.e. switch off – no continuity, switch on – continuity) – see the *Wiring Diagrams* at the end of this Chapter.

5 If the continuity check indicates a problem exists, split the switch housing (see Step 9) and spray the switch contacts with electrical contact cleaner. If they are accessible, the contacts can be scraped clean with a knife or polished with crocus cloth. If switch components are damaged or broken, it should be obvious when the switch is disassembled.

Removal

6 If the switch is to be removed from the bike, rather than just displaced from the handlebar, refer to Step 3 and disconnect the wiring connector. On Street Triple models from VIN 560477 undo the screws and remove the left-hand trim piece from the front of the frame **(see illustration 17.4)**. Feed the wiring back to the switch, freeing it from all clips and ties and noting its correct routing.

7 When displacing or removing the right-hand switch disconnect the wiring connectors from the front brake light switch **(see illustration 14.2a or b)**.

8 When displacing or removing the left-hand switch first release the clutch switch from the lever bracket – use a small screwdriver to release the clip on the underside of the switch and pull it out **(see illustration)**.

9 Unscrew the handlebar switch screws and free the switch from the handlebar by separating the halves **(see illustrations)**.

Installation

10 Installation is the reverse of removal. Where present make sure the locating pin in the switch housing locates in the hole in the handlebar. Make sure the wiring connectors are correctly routed and securely connected. Make sure the clutch switch tabs are aligned with the cut-outs in the lever bracket and the retaining clip engages in its hole.

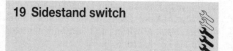

19 Sidestand switch

Check

1 The sidestand switch is mounted on the sidestand bracket. The switch is part of the safety circuit which stops the engine running if the transmission is put into gear whilst the sidestand is down. Before checking the electrical circuit, check the starter circuit fuse (see Section 5).

2 Trace the wiring from the switch and disconnect it at the connector **(see illustration)** – raise or remove the fuel tank if required (see Chapter 4), or alternatively on Daytona models remove the left-hand fairing side panel (see Chapter 7).

3 Check the operation of the switch using an ohmmeter or continuity test light. Connect the meter probes to the terminals on the switch side of the connector. With the sidestand up there should be continuity (zero resistance)

between the terminals, and with the stand down there should be no continuity (infinite resistance).

4 If the switch does not perform as expected, it is defective and must be replaced with a new one.

5 If the switch is good, check the other components in the starter circuit as described in the relevant sections of this Chapter. If all components are good, check the wiring between the various components, referring to Section 2 at the beginning of this Chapter and to the wiring diagrams at the end of it.

Removal and installation

6 Trace the wiring from the switch and disconnect it at the connector **(see illustration 19.2)** – raise or remove the fuel tank if required (see Chapter 4), or alternatively on Daytona models remove the left-hand fairing side panel (see Chapter 7). Feed the wiring down, freeing it from any clips and ties and noting its routing.

7 Unscrew the bolts securing the sidestand bracket and remove the stand assembly **(see illustration)**.

8 Undo the screws securing the switch and remove it, noting how it fits **(see illustration)**.

9 Fit the new switch and tighten the screws.

10 Install the sidestand assembly and tighten the bracket bolts to the torque setting specified at the beginning of the Chapter.

11 Feed the wiring up to the connector and reconnect it. Check the operation of the switch.

12 Install the fuel tank.

19.2 Disconnect the switch wiring connector

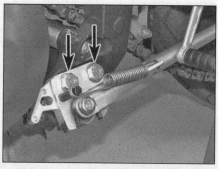

19.7 Unscrew the bolts (arrowed) and remove the bracket . . .

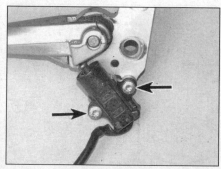

19.8 . . . then undo the screws (arrowed) and remove the switch

20 Clutch switch

Check

1 The clutch switch is mounted in the clutch lever bracket. The switch is part of the safety circuit which prevents or stops the engine running if the transmission is in gear whilst the sidestand is down, and prevents the engine from starting unless the transmission is in neutral, the sidestand is up and the clutch lever is pulled in.

2 To check the switch, refer to Section 18 and disconnect the left-hand switch assembly wiring connector. Connect the probes of an ohmmeter or a continuity tester to the black and black/yellow wire terminals on the switch side of the connector. With the clutch lever pulled in, continuity should be indicated. With the clutch lever out, no continuity (infinite resistance) should be indicated. If this is not the case use a small screwdriver to release the clip on the underside of the switch and pull it out of the clutch lever bracket **(see illustration 18.8)**. Check that the plunger is not broken or seized in the switch **(see illustration)**.

3 If the switch is good, turn the ignition on and check that there is voltage at the black/orange wire terminal on the loom side of the connector, and check that there is continuity to earth (ground) in the black wire. If not check the wiring. Otherwise, check the other components in the starter circuit as described in the relevant sections of this Chapter, and check the wiring between the various components (see the *Wiring Diagrams* at the end of this Chapter).

Renewal

4 The clutch switch is mounted in the clutch lever bracket. The switch is an integral part of the handlebar switch and is not available separately. Refer to Section 18 for removal and installation of the handlebar switch.

21 Oil pressure switch

Check

1 The oil pressure warning light should come on when the ignition switch is turned ON and extinguish a few seconds after the engine is started. If the oil pressure warning light comes on whilst the engine is running, stop the engine immediately and carry out an oil level check (see *Pre-ride checks*), and if the level is correct, an oil pressure check (see Chapter 2).

2 The oil pressure switch is screwed into the top of the crankcase on the right-hand side. Remove the fuel tank (see Chapter 4). Disconnect the wiring connector from the switch **(see illustration)**. With the ignition

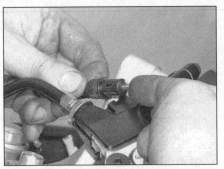

20.2 Make sure the plunger is not seized or broken

switched ON, and using an auxiliary piece of wire fitted against the connector terminal, earth (ground) the wire on the crankcase and check that the warning light comes on. If the light comes on, the switch is proven defective and must be replaced with a new one.

3 If the light still does not come on, check for voltage at the wire terminal. If there is no voltage present, check the wiring between the switch and the instrument cluster for continuity, referring to Section 2 at the beginning of the Chapter and to the wiring diagrams at the end of it.

4 If the warning light comes on whilst the engine is running, yet the oil pressure is satisfactory, remove the wire from the oil pressure switch. With the wire detached and the ignition switched ON the light should be out. If it is illuminated, the wire between the switch and instrument cluster must be earthed (grounded) at some point. If the wiring is good, the switch must be assumed faulty and be replaced with a new one.

Removal

5 The oil pressure switch is screwed into the top of the crankcase on the right-hand side. Remove the throttle bodies (see Chapter 4).

6 Disconnect the wiring connector from the switch **(see illustration 21.2)**.

7 Unscrew the switch and withdraw it from the crankcase. Discard the sealing washer – a new one should be used.

Installation

8 Install the switch using a new sealing washer and tighten it to the torque setting specified

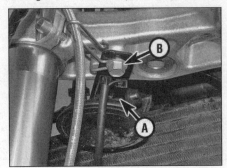

22.2a Horn wiring connectors (A) and mounting bolt (B) – Daytona

21.2 Disconnecting the wiring connector from the oil pressure switch (arrowed)

at the beginning of the Chapter. Connect the wiring connector **(see illustration 21.2)**.

9 Install the throttle bodies (see Chapter 4).

10 Run the engine and check that the switch operates correctly without leakage.

22 Horn

Check

1 If the horn doesn't work, first check the fuse (see Section 5) and the battery (see Section 3).

2 The horn is mounted on the underside of the bottom yoke on Daytona models and on the left-hand end of the radiator on Street Triple models **(see illustrations)**.

3 Disconnect the wiring connectors from the horn. Using two jumper wires, apply battery voltage directly to the terminals on the horn. If the horn doesn't sound, replace it with a new one.

4 If the horn sounds, check for voltage at the black/blue wire terminal with the ignition switch on. If there is voltage check for continuity in the purple/black wire to the horn button, then in the black/yellow wire from the horn button to earth, referring to Section 2 at the beginning of this Chapter and to the wiring diagrams at the end of it, and check the horn button itself in the switch housing (see Section 18). If there was no voltage at the black/blue wire terminal check it for continuity between the connector and the ignition switch.

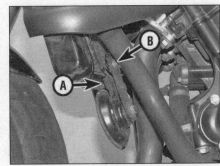

22.2b Horn wiring connectors (A) and mounting bolt (B) – Street Triple

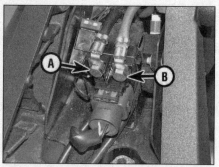

23.3 Black starter motor lead (A) and red battery lead (B) – Daytona

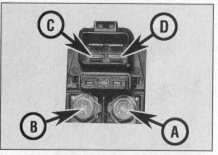

23.4 Starter motor lead terminal (A), battery lead terminal (B), black wire terminal (C), white/red wire terminal (D)

23.8 Displace the relay and disconnect the wiring connector

Renewal

5 The horn is mounted on the underside of the bottom yoke on Dayton models and on the left-hand end of the radiator on Street Triple models **(see illustrations 22.2a or b)**.
6 Disconnect the wiring connectors, then unscrew the bolt and remove the horn.
7 Install the horn and securely tighten the bolt, securing the front brake hose guide with it on Daytona models. Connect the wiring connectors.

23 Starter relay

Check

1 If the starter circuit is faulty, first check the main and starter circuit fuses (see Section 5) and the starter circuit relay (see Section 16).
2 To access the relay, on Daytona models raise or remove the fuel tank (see Chapter 7), and on Street Triple models remove the seat (see Chapter 4).
3 Remove the plastic cover **(see illustration 5.1a or b)**. Unscrew the nut securing the black starter motor lead to the relay; position the lead away from the terminal **(see illustration)**. With the ignition switch ON, the engine kill switch in the RUN position, the transmission in neutral, and the clutch lever pulled in, press the starter button. The relay should be heard to click. If the relay doesn't click, switch the ignition OFF and remove the relay as described below; then test it as follows.

4 Set a multimeter to the ohms x 1 scale and connect it across the relay's starter motor and battery lead terminals **(see illustration)**. Using a fully-charged 12 volt battery and two insulated jumper wires, connect the battery positive (+) terminal to the white/red wire terminal on the relay and the battery negative (–) terminal to the black wire terminal on the relay. At this point the relay should be heard to click and the multimeter read 0 ohms (continuity). If this is the case the relay is proved good. If the relay does not click when battery voltage is applied and indicates no continuity (infinite resistance) across its terminals, it is faulty and must be replaced with a new one.
5 If the relay is good, check for battery voltage at the white/red wire terminal on the loom side of the wiring connector with the ignition switch ON, the engine kill switch in the RUN position, the transmission in neutral, the clutch lever pulled in and the starter button pressed. If voltage is present, check the black wire for continuity to earth. If no voltage was present, check the other components and their wiring and connectors in the starter circuit from the battery to the relay (see *Wiring Diagrams* at the end of this Chapter).

Renewal

6 To access the relay, on Daytona models raise or remove the fuel tank (see Chapter 7), and on Street Triple models remove the seat (see Chapter 4).
7 Disconnect the battery negative (–) lead (see Section 3).
8 Remove the plastic cover and detach the starter motor and battery leads, noting which fits where **(see illustration 5.1a or b)**. Displace

the relay from its mount and disconnect the wiring connector **(see illustration)**. If required remove the main fuse and its spare.
9 Installation is the reverse of removal. The red lead from the battery goes on the left-hand terminal marked B (as viewed with the relay mounted), the black lead to the starter motor on the right-hand terminal marked M. Make sure the terminal nuts are securely tightened. Connect the negative (–) lead to the battery.

24 Starter motor removal and installation

Removal

1 The starter motor is mounted on the crankcase, behind the cylinder block. Disconnect the battery negative (–) lead (see Section 3). On Daytona models remove the left-hand fairing side panel (see Chapter 7).
2 Remove the throttle bodies (see Chapter 4). On Street Triple models from VIN 560477 release the trim clip and unscrew the nut securing the frame trim piece and remove it **(see illustrations)**, then remove the front sprocket cover (see Chapter 6).
3 Disconnect the wiring connector from the oil pressure switch **(see illustration 21.2)**. On Street Triple models from VIN 560477 detach the engine sub-harness wiring connector bracket from the engine – it is secured by one of the crankcase breather cover bolts.
4 Peel back the rubber terminal cover and undo the screw securing the lead to the starter motor **(see illustration)**. Detach the lead.

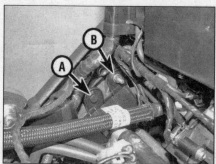

24.2a Release the trim clip (A) and unscrew the nut (B)

24.2b Release and remove the trim piece

24.4 Lift the rubber cover, then undo the screw (arrowed) and detach the lead

24.5a Unscrew the bolts . . .

24.5b . . . then draw the starter motor out of the engine . . .

24.5c . . . and remove from the left-hand side

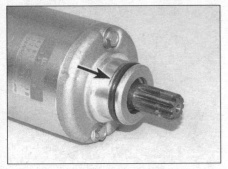

24.7 Fit a new O-ring (arrowed) and smear it with grease

25.2 Make some alignment marks between the housing and the end covers

25.3a Unscrew the two long bolts (arrowed), noting the O-rings . . .

5 Unscrew the two bolts securing the starter motor **(see illustration)** - on Street Triple models from VIN 560477 note how the rear bolt secures the CKP sensor connector bracket. Draw the starter motor out of the crankcase, using a screwdriver to lever it out if necessary, then remove it **(see illustrations)**.
6 Remove the O-ring on the end of the motor and discard it as a new one must be used **(see illustration 24.7)**.

Installation

7 Fit a new O-ring on the end of the starter motor, making sure it is seated in its groove, and smear it with grease **(see illustration)**.
8 Manoeuvre the motor into position and slide it into the crankcase **(see illustration 25.4b)**. Ensure that the starter motor teeth mesh correctly with those of the starter idle/ reduction gear. Install the mounting bolts,

on Street Triple models from VIN 560477 securing the CKP sensor connector bracket with the rear bolt, and tighten them to the torque setting specified at the beginning of the Chapter **(see illustration 25.4a)**.
9 Connect the lead to the starter motor and secure it with the screw. Fit the rubber cover over the terminal.
10 Connect the oil pressure switch wiring connector. On Street Triple models from VIN 560477 fit the engine sub-harness wiring connector bracket onto the crankcase breather cover.
11 Install the throttle bodies (see Chapter 4).
12 Connect the battery negative (–) lead (see Section 3). On Daytona models install the left-hand fairing side panel (see Chapter 7). On Street Triple models from VIN 560477 install the front sprocket cover (see Chapter 6), then fit the frame trim piece and

secure it with the nut and trim clip **(see illustrations 24.2b and a)**.

25 Starter motor overhaul

Disassembly

1 Remove the starter motor (see Section 24).
2 Make some alignment marks between the housing and both end covers **(see illustration)**.
3 Unscrew the two long bolts, then remove the front cover from the motor **(see illustrations)**. Remove the tabbed washer from the cover **(see illustration)**.
4 Slide the shim off the armature shaft **(see illustration)**. Hold the armature in place and draw the main housing off, noting that the

25.3b . . . and remove the front cover . . .

25.3c . . . and its tabbed washer

25.4a Slide the shim off the shaft

25.4b Draw the main housing off the armature

25.5 Draw the armature out of the cover

25.6 Check the brushes (arrowed) for wear and damage

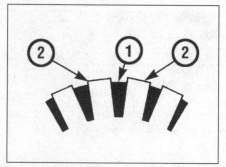

25.7 Check the commutator bars and make sure the mica (1) is below the bars (2)

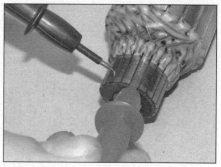

25.8a There should be continuity between the bars . . .

25.8b . . . and no continuity between the bars and the shaft

attraction of the magnets will hold it in place **(see illustration)**.
5 Draw the armature out of the rear cover **(see illustration)**.

Inspection

Note: *No replacement parts are available from Triumph for the starter motor. If the following checks indicate a worn or faulty internal component, seek the advice of a Triumph dealer or auto electrical specialist before buying a new starter motor.*

6 The parts of the starter motor that are most likely to wear are the brushes **(see illustration)**. No specification is given for the minimum length, but anything over 5 mm should be serviceable. Also check the brushes are not cracked, chipped, or otherwise damaged. Make sure each brush is securely connected to its wire, and the wire is securely connected to its terminal. Make sure the springs in the brush housings are good.

7 Inspect the commutator bars for scoring, scratches and discoloration. The bars can be cleaned and polished with crocus cloth – do not use sandpaper or emery paper. After cleaning, wipe away any residue with a cloth soaked in electrical system cleaner or denatured alcohol. Make sure the insulation material between each of the bars is below the bars themselves **(see illustration)** – if necessary carefully scrape some away.

8 Using an ohmmeter or a continuity test light, check for continuity between the commutator bars **(see illustration)**. Continuity should exist between each bar and all of the others. Also, check for continuity between the commutator bars and the armature shaft **(see illustration)**.

There should be no continuity (infinite resistance) between the commutator and the shaft. If the checks indicate otherwise, the armature is defective.

9 Check there is no continuity between the terminal and the rear cover **(see illustration)**.

25.9a Check there is no continuity between the terminal and the cover . . .

25.9c . . . and between the cover and each negative brush

Check for continuity between the terminal and each positive brush **(see illustration)**. Check for continuity between the cover and each negative brush **(see illustration)**.

10 Check the oil seal and bearing in the front cover **(see illustration)**. Check the bush in

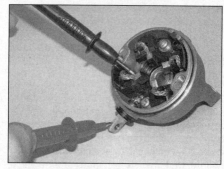

25.9b . . . and there is continuity between the terminal and each positive brush . . .

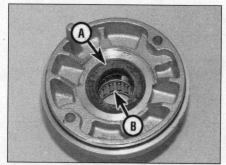

25.10a Check the front cover oil seal (A) and bearing (B) . . .

25.10b ... rear cover bush (arrowed) ...

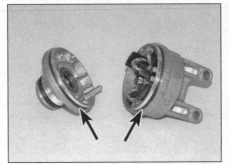

25.10c ... and the cover sealing rings (arrowed)

25.14a Secure each brush in its housing using crocodile clips as shown ...

25.14b ... then fit the armature

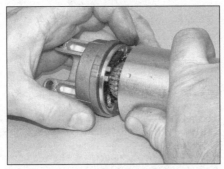

25.15 Carefully fit the housing over the armature making sure it locates correctly

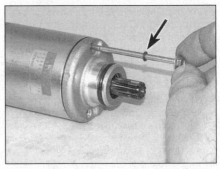

25.17 Make sure the O-ring (arrowed) is fitted under the head of each bolt

the rear cover **(see illustration)**. Inspect the covers for signs of cracks or wear, and make sure the sealing rings are in good condition **(see illustration)**.
11 Inspect the magnets in the main housing and the housing itself for cracks.
12 Check the starter shaft teeth and the idle/reduction gear in the engine for worn, cracked, chipped and broken teeth.

Reassembly

13 Make sure the sealing ring is in place on the rim of each cover **(see illustration 25.10c)**.
14 Using crocodile clips over the brush wire and the rim of the cover secure each brush so it is held retracted in the housing **(see illustration)**. Fit the armature into the rear cover, seating the shaft in its bush **(see illustration)**. Remove the crocodile clips – check that each brush locates against the commutator.
15 Identify the rear end of the main housing – it has an indented tab that locates between the two posts on the rear cover **(see illustration 25.2)**. Grasp the armature to prevent it being draw out of the rear cover and carefully fit the main housing over it, rear end first, aligning the marks made on removal, and making sure the tab locates between the posts **(see illustration)**. Side the shim onto the shaft **(see illustration 25.4a)**.
16 Fit the tabbed washer into the front cover, locating the tabs between the raised ribs **(see illustration 25.3c)**. Fit the cover over the shaft and onto the housing, aligning the marks made

on removal and locating the post between the magnets **(see illustration 25.3b)**.
17 Check the marks made on removal are correctly aligned, then fit the long bolts with their O-rings and tighten them **(see illustration)**.
18 Install the starter motor (see Section 24).

26 Charging system testing

1 If the performance of the charging system is suspect, the system as a whole should be checked first, followed by testing of the individual components. **Note:** *Before beginning the checks, make sure the battery is fully charged and that all system connections are clean and tight.*
2 Checking the output of the charging system and the performance of the various components within the charging system requires the use of a multimeter (with voltage, current and resistance checking facilities). If a multimeter is not available, the job of checking the system should be left to a Triumph dealer or specialist.
3 When making the checks, follow the procedures carefully to prevent incorrect connections or short circuits resulting in irreparable damage to electrical system components.

Leakage test

Caution: Always connect an ammeter in series, never in parallel with the battery,

otherwise it will be damaged. Do not turn the ignition ON or operate the starter motor when the ammeter is connected – a sudden surge in current will blow the meter's fuse.
4 Make sure the ignition switch is OFF. Disconnect the negative (–) lead from the battery (see Section 3).
5 Set the multimeter to the amps function and connect its negative (–) probe to the battery negative (–) terminal, and positive (+) probe to the disconnected negative (–) lead **(see illustration)**. Always set the meter to a high amps range initially and then bring it down to the mA (milli amps) range; if there is a high current flow in the circuit it may blow the meter's fuse.
6 No current flow should be indicated. If current leakage is indicated (generally greater than 1 mA), there is a short circuit in the wiring, although if an alarm is fitted remember to take its current draw into account. Using the wiring diagrams at the

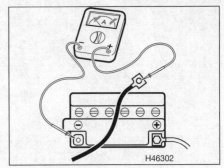

26.5 Checking the charging system leakage rate – connect the ammeter as shown

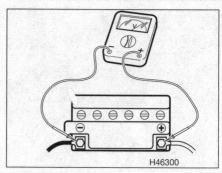

26.9 Checking the charging system output – connect the voltmeter as shown

27.2a Alternator and regulator/rectifier wiring connectors (arrowed) – Daytona to VIN 381274

27.2b Alternator wiring connector – Daytona from VIN 381275

end of this Chapter, systematically disconnect individual electrical components, checking the meter each time until the source is identified.

7 If no leakage is indicated, disconnect the meter and connect the negative (–) lead to the battery.

Output test

8 Start the engine and warm it up to normal operating temperature. On Daytona models remove the rider's seat (see Chapter 7). On Street Triple models remove the seat (see Chapter 7).

9 To check the regulated voltage output, allow the engine to idle and connect a multimeter set to the 0 to 20 volts DC scale (voltmeter) across the terminals of the battery – positive (+) lead to battery positive (+) terminal, negative (–) lead to battery negative (–) terminal **(see illustration)**. Increase engine speed to 4000 rpm and note the reading obtained. The regulated voltage should be around 13.5 to 15.0V. If the voltage is zero or below the limit, check the alternator first (Section 27), then the regulator/rectifier if necessary (Section 28). If the reading is above the limit check the regulator/rectifier (see Section 28).

HAYNES HiNT *Clues to a faulty regulator are constantly blowing bulbs, with brightness varying considerably with engine speed, and battery overheating.*

27 Alternator

1 The alternator rotor is mounted on the left-hand end of the crankshaft and the stator is located inside the left-hand engine cover. Disconnect the battery negative (–) lead (see Section 3). On Daytona models remove the left-hand fairing side panel (see Chapter 7). To access the wiring connector raise or remove the fuel tank (see Chapter 4).

Testing

2 Refer to Step 1, then trace the alternator wiring from the top of the left-hand engine cover and disconnect it at the connector with the three black wires **(see illustrations)**.

3 Using a multimeter set to the ohms scale, connect the meter probes to one pair of terminals at a time on the alternator side of the wiring connector and measure the resistance between the terminals. Make a note of the three readings obtained. Now check for continuity between each terminal and ground (earth).

4 If the stator coil windings are in good condition the three readings should be as specified at the beginning of the Chapter, and there should be no continuity (infinite resistance) between any of the terminals and ground (earth). If not, the alternator stator coil assembly is probably faulty and should be taken to a Triumph dealer or specialist for further assessment. **Note:** *Before condemning the stator coils, check the fault is not due to a loose wire in the connector or damaged wiring between the connector and coils. In some cases stators can be rewound.*

Removal

5 If the bike is on its sidestand drain the engine oil (see Chapter 1). On Street Triple models from VIN 560477 remove the throttle bodies (see Chapter 4), then release the trim clip and unscrew the nut securing the frame trim piece and remove it **(see illustrations 24.2a and b)**, then remove the front sprocket cover (see Chapter 6). Refer to Step 1, then trace the alternator wiring from the top of the left-hand engine cover and disconnect it at the connectors – one is for the stator, the other for the crankshaft position senor, which is part of the stator, and on Street Triple models from VIN 560477 the connector is clipped to a bracket secured by the starter motor rear mounting bolt. Free the wiring from any clips or ties and feed it through to the cover, noting its routing.

6 Working in a criss-cross pattern, evenly slacken the engine cover bolts then remove them **(see illustration)**. Note the relay/fairing

27.2c Alternator and regulator/rectifier wiring connectors (arrowed) – Street Triples to VIN 560476

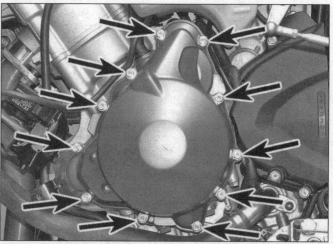

27.6 Unscrew the bolts (arrowed) and remove the cover

27.8 Withdraw the shaft and remove the gear

27.9 Using a rotor holder while unscrewing the bolt

27.10a Fit the puller onto the rotor . . .

bracket on Daytona models and the coolant hose guide on Street Triples. On all models note the bolt with the copper washer – a new washer should be used on installation.

7 Draw the cover off, noting that it will be held by the attraction of the magnets, and be prepared to catch any residual oil. Discard the gasket as a new one must be used. Note the two locating pins and remove them for safekeeping if loose.

8 Withdraw the shaft from the idle/reduction gear and remove the gear **(see illustration)**.

9 To remove the rotor bolt it is necessary to stop the crankshaft from turning. Triumph produces a Service Tool (Part No. T3880375) to do this, or alternatively a number of different rotor straps are commercially available (make sure you select the correct type), one type of which is shown **(see illustration)**. Clean the rotor with solvent to remove all traces of oil. Fit the strap, making sure it is clear of the crankshaft position (CKP) sensor triggers. If a rotor holding strap or tool is not available, and the engine is in the frame, place the transmission in gear and have an assistant apply the rear brake. Unscrew the bolt and remove the washer.

10 To remove the rotor from the crankshaft

taper it is necessary to use a rotor puller. Triumph produces a service tool (Part No. T3880203) to do this, or alternatively a number of rotor pullers are commercially available (make sure you select the correct type), one type of which is shown **(see illustrations)**. The puller should come with a thrust pad or pads to fit over the end of the crankshaft, inside the inner rim of the rotor, to protect the end of the shaft. Fit the pad, then thread the puller body onto the rotor and tighten the centre bolt against the pad. Hold the rotor as before to prevent it turning, or use a spanner on any flats provided on the puller body, and turn the centre bolt clockwise until the rotor is displaced.

11 Draw off the rotor, bringing the starter driven gear with it, or if it stays in place slide it off afterwards. Note the location of the Woodruff key in the crankshaft – remove it for safekeeping if it is loose **(see illustration)**. Take care not to damage the CKP sensor triggers on the rotor.

12 To remove the stator/CKP sensor assembly, unscrew the bolts securing them, and the bolt securing the wiring clamp, then remove the assembly, noting how the wiring grommet fits **(see illustration)**.

27.10b . . . then hold the rotor and operate the puller

Installation

13 Apply a suitable sealant to the stator wiring grommet, then fit the stator/CKP sensor assembly into the cover, aligning the grommet with the cut-out **(see illustration 27.12)**. Clean the stator, sensor and wiring clamp bolts and apply threadlock, then tighten them to the torque settings specified at the beginning of the Chapter.

14 Clean the tapered end of the crankshaft and the corresponding mating surface on the inside of the rotor with a suitable solvent **(see**

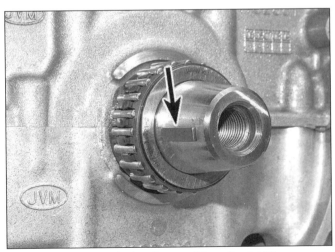

27.11 Remove the key (arrowed) from its slot if loose

27.12 Alternator stator, CKP sensor and wiring clamp bolts (arrowed)

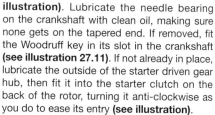

27.14a Clean the tapered section (A) and lubricate the bearing (B)

27.14b Fit the driven gear into the starter clutch

27.15 Slide the rotor onto the shaft, locating its cut-out over the key

illustration). Lubricate the needle bearing on the crankshaft with clean oil, making sure none gets on the tapered end. If removed, fit the Woodruff key in its slot in the crankshaft **(see illustration 27.11)**. If not already in place, lubricate the outside of the starter driven gear hub, then fit it into the starter clutch on the back of the rotor, turning it anti-clockwise as you do to ease its entry **(see illustration)**.

15 Make sure that no metal objects have attached themselves to the magnet on the inside of the rotor, then align the slot on the inside of the rotor boss with the Woodruff key and slide the rotor onto the shaft **(see illustration)**.

16 Fit the rotor bolt with its washer and tighten it to the torque setting specified at the beginning of this Chapter, holding the rotor as on removal to prevent it turning **(see illustrations)**.

17 Lubricate the idle/reduction gear shaft, then locate the gear and fit the shaft through **(see illustration 27.8)**.

18 If removed, fit the cover locating pins into the crankcase, then seat the new gasket onto them **(see illustration)**. Carefully fit the cover, noting that it will be forcibly drawn on by the magnets, making sure it locates correctly onto the pins **(see illustration)**. Fit the bolts, using a new copper washer on the bolt just ahead of the wiring grommet, and securing the relay/fairing bracket on Daytona models and the coolant hose guide on Street Triples **(see illustration)**. Tighten the bolts evenly in a criss-cross pattern to the specified torque setting **(see illustration 27.6)**.

19 Feed the wiring back to its connectors, making sure it is correctly routed and secured by any clips or ties, and reconnect it. On Street Triple models from VIN 560477 install

the front sprocket cover (see Chapter 6), then fit the frame trim piece and secure it with the nut and trim clip **(see illustrations 24.2b and a)**, then install the throttle bodies (see Chapter 4).

20 Replenish the engine oil if drained (see Chapter 1 and *Pre-ride Checks*).

21 Install the fuel tank (see Chapter 4). Connect the battery negative (–) lead and install the seat, and on Daytona models the fairing side panel (see Chapter 7).

28 Regulator/rectifier

Testing

1 Triumph provides no test data for the regulator/rectifier. If the output test in Section 26 indicates a fault, take the unit to a Triumph dealer for further assessment.

2 To check the power supply, on Daytona models to VIN 381274 and Street Triple models to VIN 560476 raise or remove the fuel tank, and on Daytona models from VIN 381275 refer to Steps 8 and 9 and remove the regulator/rectifier. Check for constant battery voltage at the brown wire terminal(s) in the loom side of the 4-pin connector on Daytona models and Street Triple models to VIN 560476, and at the black/red wire terminal in the top connector on the regulator/rectifier on Street Triple models from Vin 560477 **(see illustration 27.2a or c, 28.9b or 28.4)**. If there

27.16a Fit the bolt and washer . . .

27.16b . . . and tighten the bolt to the specified torque

27.18a Fit the gasket onto the pins (arrowed) . . .

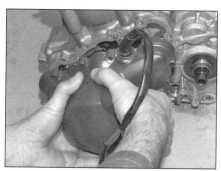

27.18b . . . then carefully fit the cover

27.18c Fit a new copper washer onto the bolt shown

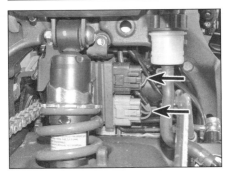

28.4 Regulator/rectifier wiring connectors (arrowed) – Street Triples from VIN 560477

28.5a Regulator/rectifier mounting bolts (arrowed) – Daytona up to VIN 381274 and Street Triples to VIN 560476

28.5b Regulator/rectifier mounting bolts (arrowed) – Street Triples from VIN 560477

is none check for continuity in the wire(s), referring to the wiring diagrams at the end of the chapter for its circuit. Also check for continuity to earth in the black wire(s).

Removal and installation

Daytona to VIN 381274 and all Street Triples

3 The regulator/rectifier is mounted on a plate just ahead of the rear shock absorber.
4 On Daytona models and Street Triple models to VIN 560476 raise or remove the fuel tank (see Chapter 4), then disconnect the regulator/rectifier wiring connectors **(see illustration 27.2a or b)**. On Street Triple models from VIN 560477 disconnect the wiring connectors from the regulator/rectifier **(see illustration)**.
5 Undo the two bolts securing the bracket to the frame and manoeuvre it out it, on Daytona models and Street Triple models to VIN 560476 noting the routing of the wiring **(see illustrations)**.

6 If required undo the nuts, withdraw the bolts, and detach the regulator/rectifier from the bracket.
7 Installation is the reverse of removal.

Daytona models from VIN 381275

8 Remove the right-hand cockpit trim panel (see Chapter 7).

28.9a Lift the regulator/rectifier out . . .

9 Undo the turn signal bolt, lift the regulator/rectifier out it, and disconnect the wiring connectors **(see illustrations)**.
10 If required undo the nuts, withdraw the bolts, and detach the regulator/rectifier from the bracket.
11 Installation is the reverse of removal.

28.9b . . . and disconnect the wiring

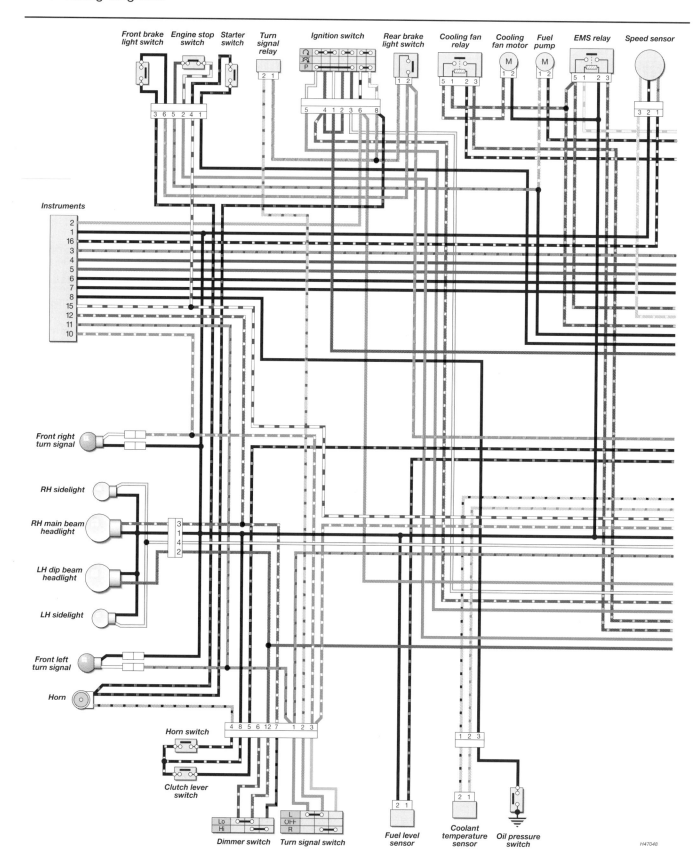

Daytona 675 (up to VIN 300525)
Refer to later diagram for fuel pump relay modification

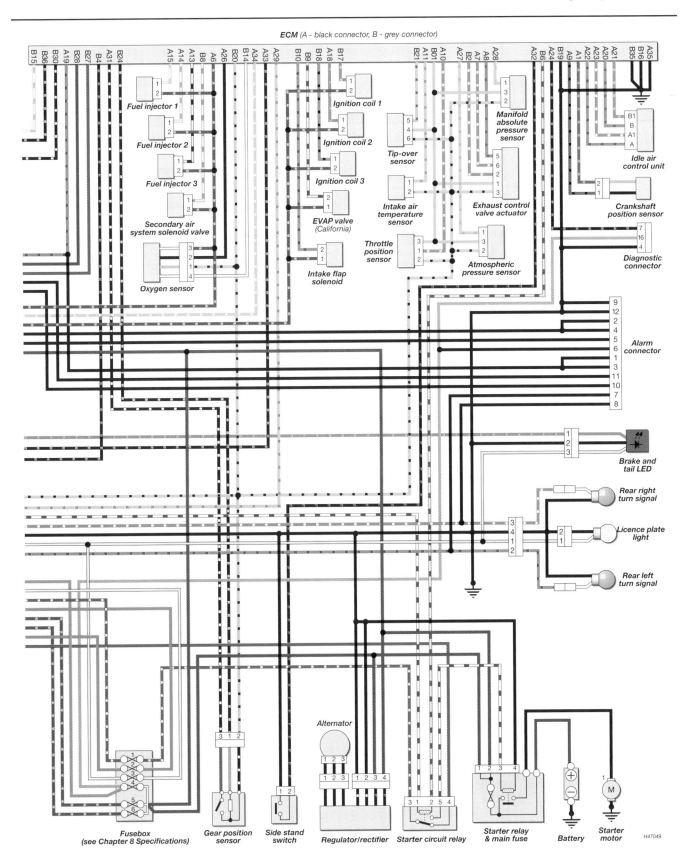

ECM (A - black connector, B - grey connector)

Fuel injector 1

Fuel injector 2

Fuel injector 3

Secondary air
system solenoid valve

Oxygen sensor

Ignition coil 1

Ignition coil 2

Ignition coil 3

EVAP valve
(California)

Intake flap
solenoid

Tip-over
sensor

Intake air
temperature
sensor

Throttle
position
sensor

Manifold
absolute
pressure
sensor

Exhaust control
valve actuator

Atmospheric
pressure sensor

Idle air
control unit

Crankshaft
position sensor

Diagnostic
connector

Alarm
connector

Brake and
tail LED

Rear right
turn signal

Licence plate
light

Rear left
turn signal

Alternator

Fusebox
(see Chapter 8 Specifications)

Gear position
sensor

Side stand
switch

Regulator/rectifier

Starter circuit relay

Starter relay
& main fuse

Battery

Starter
motor

H47049

Daytona 675 (up to VIN 300525)
Refer to later diagram for fuel pump relay modification

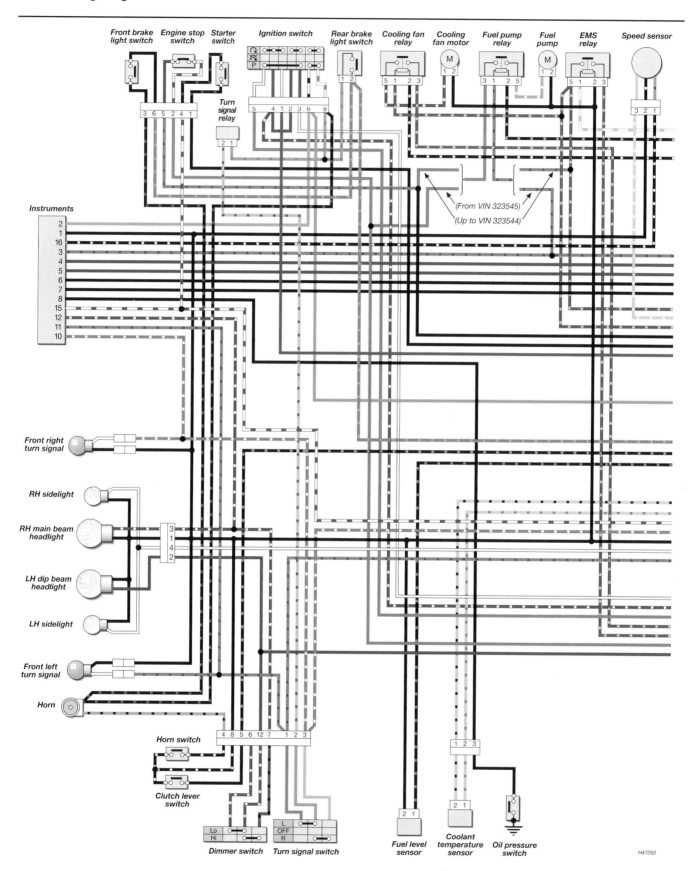

Daytona 675 (from VIN 300526) and Daytona R

H47050

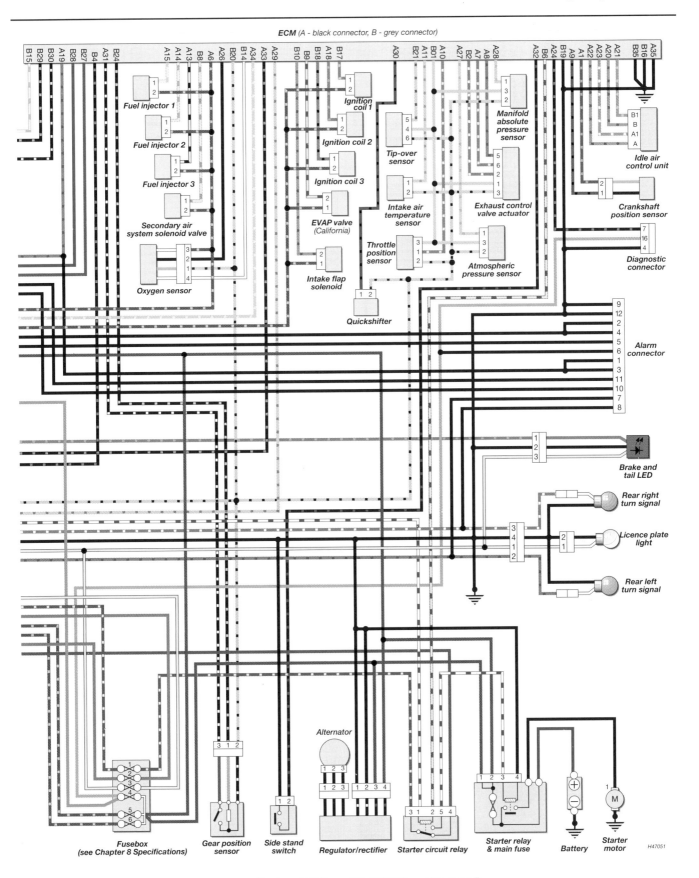

ECM (A - black connector, B - grey connector)

Fuel injector 1

Fuel injector 2

Fuel injector 3

Secondary air system solenoid valve

Oxygen sensor

Ignition coil 1

Ignition coil 2

Ignition coil 3

EVAP valve (California)

Intake flap solenoid

Quickshifter

Tip-over sensor

Intake air temperature sensor

Throttle position sensor

Manifold absolute pressure sensor

Exhaust control valve actuator

Atmospheric pressure sensor

Idle air control unit

Crankshaft position sensor

Diagnostic connector

Alarm connector

Brake and tail LED

Rear right turn signal

Licence plate light

Rear left turn signal

Fusebox (see Chapter 8 Specifications)

Gear position sensor

Side stand switch

Alternator

Regulator/rectifier

Starter circuit relay

Starter relay & main fuse

Battery

Starter motor

H47051

Daytona 675 (from VIN 300526) and Daytona R

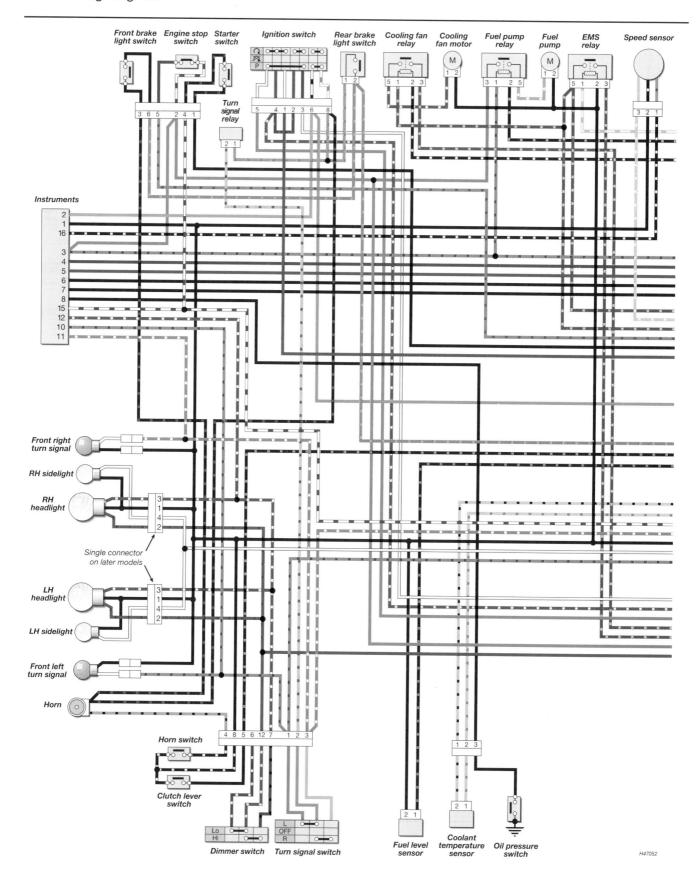

Street Triple and Street Triple R (up to VIN 560476)

H47052

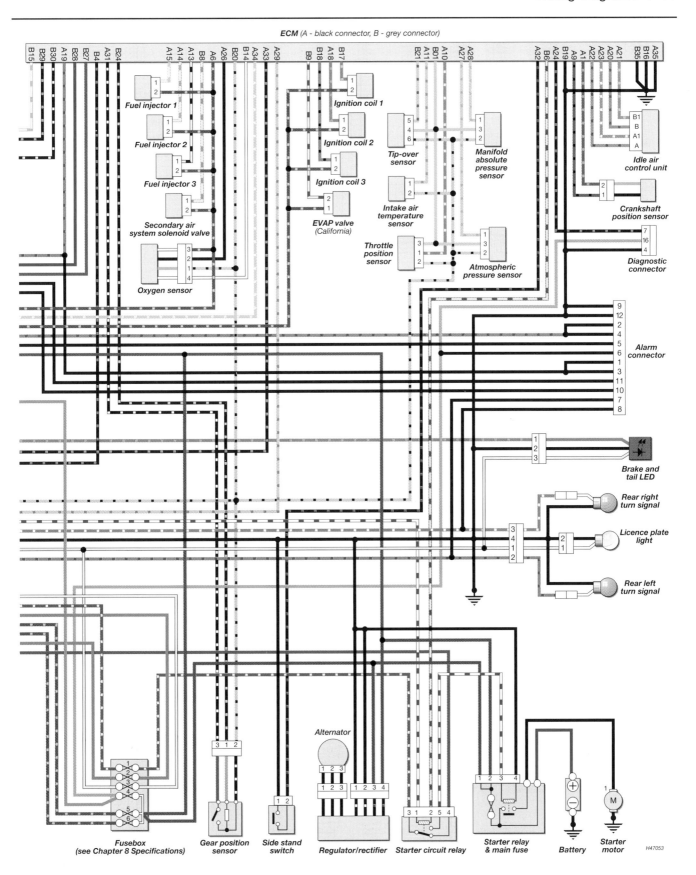

Street Triple and Street Triple R (up to VIN 560476)

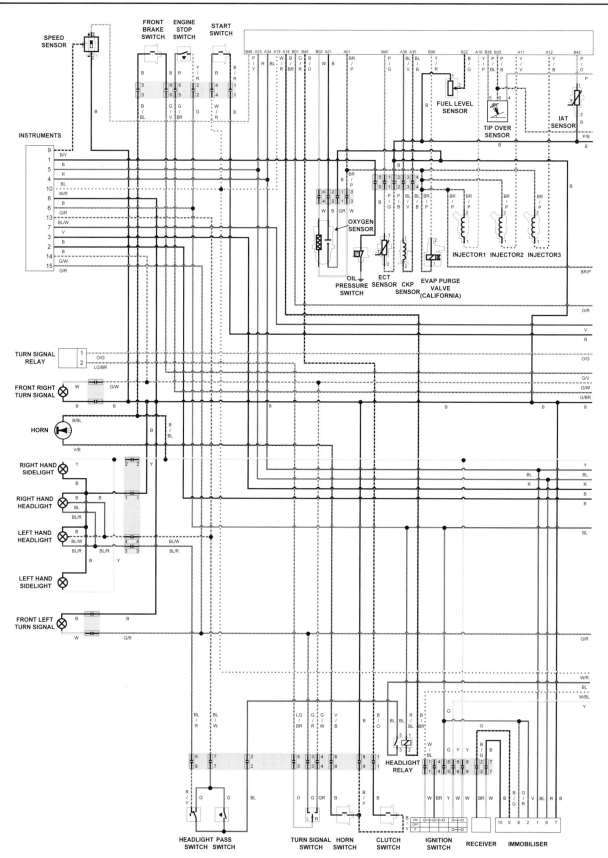

Street Triple and Street Triple R/RX (from VIN560477) without ABS

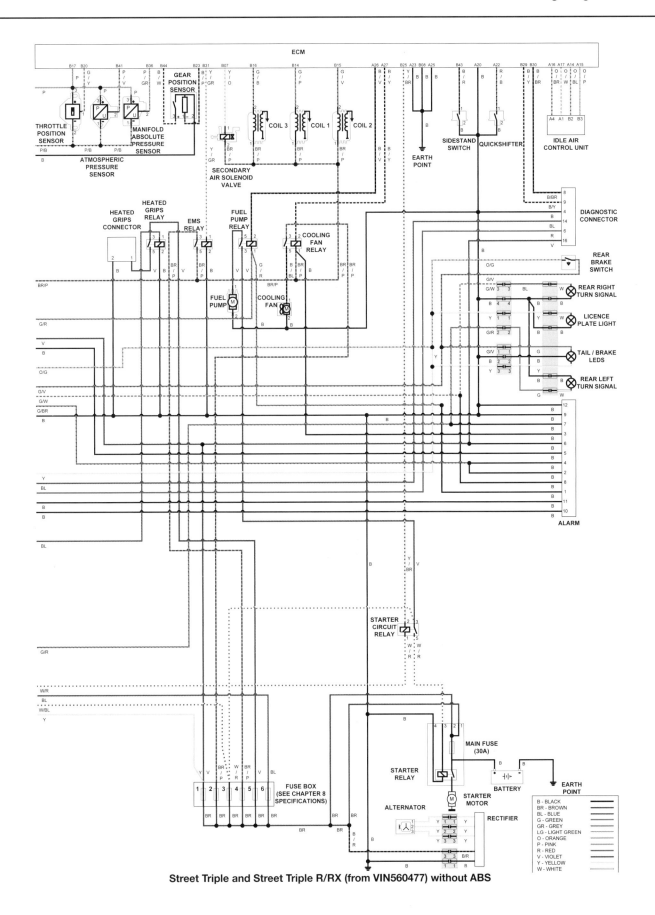

Street Triple and Street Triple R/RX (from VIN560477) without ABS

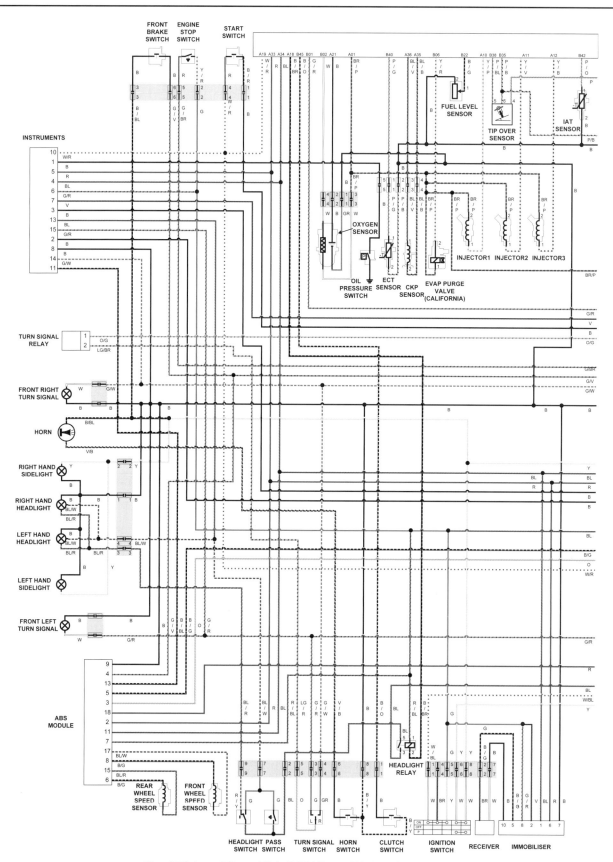

Street Triple and Street Triple R/RX (from VIN560477) with ABS

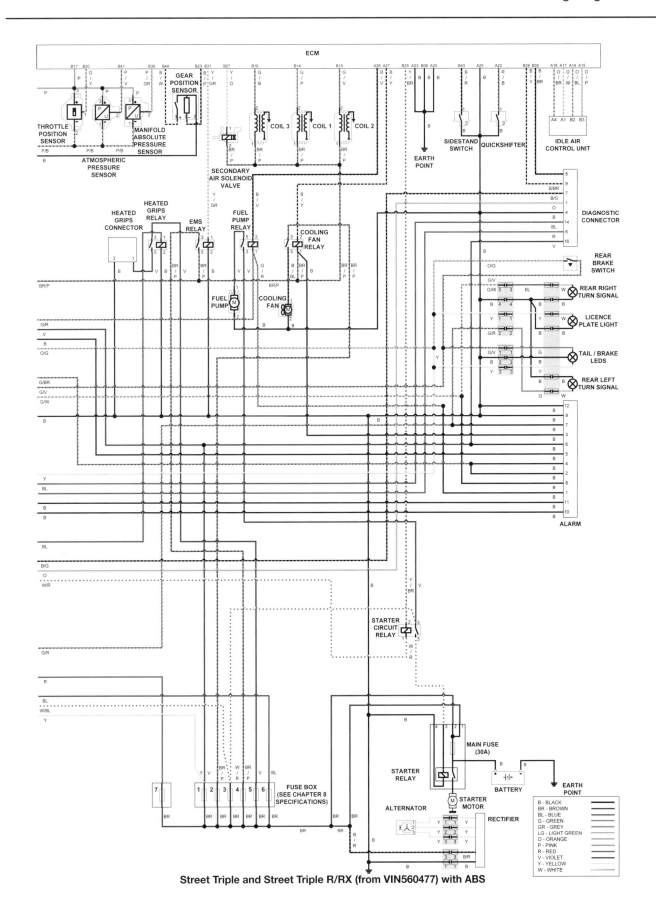

Street Triple and Street Triple R/RX (from VIN560477) with ABS

Buying tools

A toolkit is a fundamental requirement for servicing and repairing a motorcycle. Although there will be an initial expense in building up enough tools for servicing, this will soon be offset by the savings made by doing the job yourself. As experience and confidence grow, additional tools can be added to enable the repair and overhaul of the motorcycle. Many of the specialist tools are expensive and not often used so it may be preferable to hire them, or for a group of friends or motorcycle club to join in the purchase.

As a rule, it is better to buy more expensive, good quality tools. Cheaper tools are likely to wear out faster and need to be renewed more often, nullifying the original saving.

⚠️ **Warning: To avoid the risk of a poor quality tool breaking in use, causing injury or damage to the component being worked on, always aim to purchase tools which meet the relevant national safety standards.**

The following lists of tools do not represent the manufacturer's service tools, but serve as a guide to help the owner decide which tools are needed for this level of work. In addition, items such as an electric drill, hacksaw, files, soldering iron and a workbench equipped with a vice, may be needed. Although not classed as tools, a selection of bolts, screws, nuts, washers and pieces of tubing always come in useful.

For more information about tools, refer to the Haynes *Motorcycle Workshop Practice Techbook* (Bk. No. 3470).

Manufacturer's service tools

Inevitably certain tasks require the use of a service tool. Where possible an alternative tool or method of approach is recommended, but sometimes there is no option if personal injury or damage to the component is to be avoided. Where required, service tools are referred to in the relevant procedure.

Service tools can usually only be purchased from a motorcycle dealer and are identified by a part number. Some of the commonly-used tools, such as rotor pullers, are available in aftermarket form from mail-order motorcycle tool and accessory suppliers.

Maintenance and minor repair tools

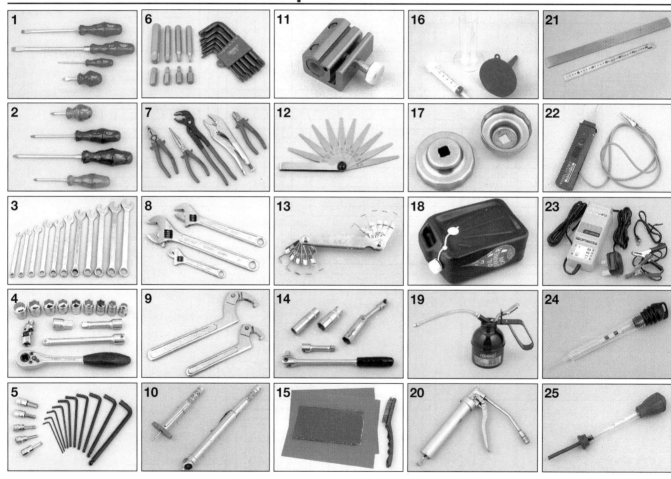

1 Set of flat-bladed screwdrivers
2 Set of Phillips head screwdrivers
3 Combination open-end and ring spanners
4 Socket set (3/8 inch or 1/2 inch drive)
5 Set of Allen keys or bits

6 Set of Torx keys or bits
7 Pliers, cutters and self-locking grips (Mole grips)
8 Adjustable spanners
9 C-spanners
10 Tread depth gauge and tyre pressure gauge

11 Cable oiler clamp
12 Feeler gauges
13 Spark plug gap measuring tool
14 Spark plug spanner or deep plug sockets
15 Wire brush and emery paper

16 Calibrated syringe, measuring vessel and funnel
17 Oil filter adapters
18 Oil drainer can or tray
19 Pump type oil can
20 Grease gun

21 Straight-edge and steel rule
22 Continuity tester
23 Battery charger
24 Hydrometer (for battery specific gravity check)
25 Anti-freeze tester (for liquid-cooled engines)

Repair and overhaul tools

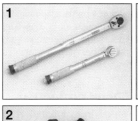 1
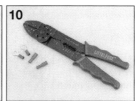 4
 7
 10
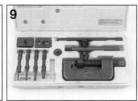 13

 2
 5
 8
 11
 14

 3
 6
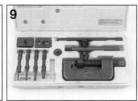 9
 12
 15

1 Torque wrench (small and mid-ranges)
2 Conventional, plastic or soft-faced hammers
3 Impact driver set
4 Vernier gauge
5 Circlip pliers (internal and external, or combination)
6 Set of cold chisels and punches
7 Selection of pullers
8 Breaker bars
9 Chain breaking/riveting tool set
10 Wire stripper and crimper tool
11 Multimeter (measures amps, volts and ohms)
12 Stroboscope (for dynamic timing checks)
13 Hose clamp (wingnut type shown)
14 Clutch holding tool
15 One-man brake/clutch bleeder kit

Specialist tools

 1
 4
 7
 10
 13

 2
 5
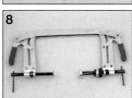 8
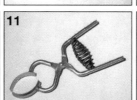 11
 14

 3
 6
 9
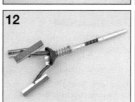 12
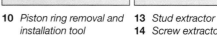
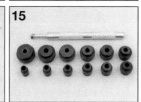 15

1 Micrometers (external type)
2 Telescoping gauges
3 Dial gauge
4 Cylinder compression gauge
5 Vacuum gauges (left) or manometer (right)
6 Oil pressure gauge
7 Plastigauge kit
8 Valve spring compressor (4-stroke engines)
9 Piston pin drawbolt tool
10 Piston ring removal and installation tool
11 Piston ring clamp
12 Cylinder bore hone (stone type shown)
13 Stud extractor
14 Screw extractor set
15 Bearing driver set

1 Workshop equipment and facilities

The workbench

● Work is made much easier by raising the bike up on a ramp - components are much more accessible if raised to waist level. The hydraulic or pneumatic types seen in the dealer's workshop are a sound investment if you undertake a lot of repairs or overhauls (see illustration 1.1).

1.1 Hydraulic motorcycle ramp

● If raised off ground level, the bike must be supported on the ramp to avoid it falling. Most ramps incorporate a front wheel locating clamp which can be adjusted to suit different diameter wheels. When tightening the clamp, take care not to mark the wheel rim or damage the tyre - use wood blocks on each side to prevent this.
● Secure the bike to the ramp using tie-downs (see illustration 1.2). If the bike has only a sidestand, and hence leans at a dangerous angle when raised, support the bike on an auxiliary stand.

1.2 Tie-downs are used around the passenger footrests to secure the bike

● Auxiliary (paddock) stands are widely available from mail order companies or motorcycle dealers and attach either to the wheel axle or swingarm pivot (see illustration 1.3). If the motorcycle has a centrestand, you can support it under the crankcase to prevent it toppling whilst either wheel is removed (see illustration 1.4).

1.3 This auxiliary stand attaches to the swingarm pivot

1.4 Always use a block of wood between the engine and jack head when supporting the engine in this way

Fumes and fire

● Refer to the Safety first! page at the beginning of the manual for full details. Make sure your workshop is equipped with a fire extinguisher suitable for fuel-related fires (Class B fire - flammable liquids) - it is not sufficient to have a water-filled extinguisher.
● Always ensure adequate ventilation is available. Unless an exhaust gas extraction system is available for use, ensure that the engine is run outside of the workshop.
● If working on the fuel system, make sure the workshop is ventilated to avoid a build-up of fumes. This applies equally to fume build-up when charging a battery. Do not smoke or allow anyone else to smoke in the workshop.

Fluids

● If you need to drain fuel from the tank, store it in an approved container marked as suitable for the storage of petrol (gasoline) (see illustration 1.5). Do not store fuel in glass jars or bottles.

1.5 Use an approved can only for storing petrol (gasoline)

● Use proprietary engine degreasers or solvents which have a high flash-point, such as paraffin (kerosene), for cleaning off oil, grease and dirt - never use petrol (gasoline) for cleaning. Wear rubber gloves when handling solvent and engine degreaser. The fumes from certain solvents can be dangerous - always work in a well-ventilated area.

Dust, eye and hand protection

● Protect your lungs from inhalation of dust particles by wearing a filtering mask over the nose and mouth. Many frictional materials still contain asbestos which is dangerous to your health. Protect your eyes from spouts of liquid and sprung components by wearing a pair of protective goggles (see illustration 1.6).

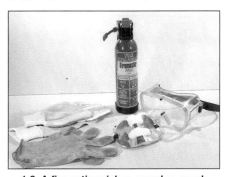

1.6 A fire extinguisher, goggles, mask and protective gloves should be at hand in the workshop

● Protect your hands from contact with solvents, fuel and oils by wearing rubber gloves. Alternatively apply a barrier cream to your hands before starting work. If handling hot components or fluids, wear suitable gloves to protect your hands from scalding and burns.

What to do with old fluids

● Old cleaning solvent, fuel, coolant and oils should not be poured down domestic drains or onto the ground. Package the fluid up in old oil containers, label it accordingly, and take it to a garage or disposal facility. Contact your local authority for location of such sites or ring the oil care hotline.

OIL CARE

Note: It is antisocial and illegal to dump oil down the drain. To find the location of your local oil recycling bank in the UK, call 03708 506 506 or visit www.oilbankline.org.uk

In the USA, note that any oil supplier must accept used oil for recycling.

2 Fasteners - screws, bolts and nuts

Fastener types and applications

Bolts and screws

● Fastener head types are either of hexagonal, Torx or splined design, with internal and external versions of each type **(see illustrations 2.1 and 2.2)**; splined head fasteners are not in common use on motorcycles. The conventional slotted or Phillips head design is used for certain screws. Bolt or screw length is always measured from the underside of the head to the end of the item **(see illustration 2.11)**.

2.1 Internal hexagon/Allen (A), Torx (B) and splined (C) fasteners, with corresponding bits

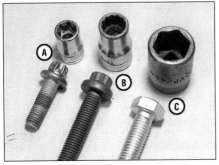

2.2 External Torx (A), splined (B) and hexagon (C) fasteners, with corresponding sockets

● Certain fasteners on the motorcycle have a tensile marking on their heads, the higher the marking the stronger the fastener. High tensile fasteners generally carry a 10 or higher marking. Never replace a high tensile fastener with one of a lower tensile strength.

Washers (see illustration 2.3)

● Plain washers are used between a fastener head and a component to prevent damage to the component or to spread the load when torque is applied. Plain washers can also be used as spacers or shims in certain assemblies. Copper or aluminium plain washers are often used as sealing washers on drain plugs.

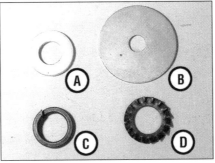

2.3 Plain washer (A), penny washer (B), spring washer (C) and serrated washer (D)

● The split-ring spring washer works by applying axial tension between the fastener head and component. If flattened, it is fatigued and must be renewed. If a plain (flat) washer is used on the fastener, position the spring washer between the fastener and the plain washer.

● Serrated star type washers dig into the fastener and component faces, preventing loosening. They are often used on electrical earth (ground) connections to the frame.

● Cone type washers (sometimes called Belleville) are conical and when tightened apply axial tension between the fastener head and component. They must be installed with the dished side against the component and often carry an OUTSIDE marking on their outer face. If flattened, they are fatigued and must be renewed.

● Tab washers are used to lock plain nuts or bolts on a shaft. A portion of the tab washer is bent up hard against one flat of the nut or bolt to prevent it loosening. Due to the tab washer being deformed in use, a new tab washer should be used every time it is disturbed.

● Wave washers are used to take up endfloat on a shaft. They provide light springing and prevent excessive side-to-side play of a component. Can be found on rocker arm shafts.

Nuts and split pins

● Conventional plain nuts are usually six-sided **(see illustration 2.4)**. They are sized by thread diameter and pitch. High tensile nuts carry a number on one end to denote their tensile strength.

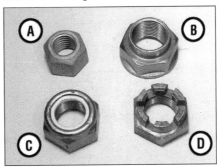

2.4 Plain nut (A), shouldered locknut (B), nylon insert nut (C) and castellated nut (D)

● Self-locking nuts either have a nylon insert, or two spring metal tabs, or a shoulder which is staked into a groove in the shaft - their advantage over conventional plain nuts is a resistance to loosening due to vibration. The nylon insert type can be used a number of times, but must be renewed when the friction of the nylon insert is reduced, ie when the nut spins freely on the shaft. The spring tab type can be reused unless the tabs are damaged. The shouldered type must be renewed every time it is disturbed.

● Split pins (cotter pins) are used to lock a castellated nut to a shaft or to prevent slackening of a plain nut. Common applications are wheel axles and brake torque arms. Because the split pin arms are deformed to lock around the nut a new split pin must always be used on installation - always fit the correct size split pin which will fit snugly in the shaft hole. Make sure the split pin arms are correctly located around the nut **(see illustrations 2.5 and 2.6)**.

2.5 Bend split pin (cotter pin) arms as shown (arrows) to secure a castellated nut

2.6 Bend split pin (cotter pin) arms as shown to secure a plain nut

Caution: If the castellated nut slots do not align with the shaft hole after tightening to the torque setting, tighten the nut until the next slot aligns with the hole - never slacken the nut to align its slot.

● R-pins (shaped like the letter R), or slip pins as they are sometimes called, are sprung and can be reused if they are otherwise in good condition. Always install R-pins with their closed end facing forwards **(see illustration 2.7)**.

2.7 Correct fitting of R-pin. Arrow indicates forward direction

Circlips (see illustration 2.8)

● Circlips (sometimes called snap-rings) are used to retain components on a shaft or in a housing and have corresponding external or internal ears to permit removal. Parallel-sided (machined) circlips can be installed either way round in their groove, whereas stamped circlips (which have a chamfered edge on one face) must be installed with the chamfer facing away from the direction of thrust load **(see illustration 2.9)**.

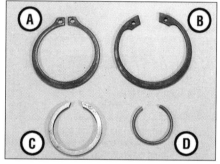

2.8 External stamped circlip (A), internal stamped circlip (B), machined circlip (C) and wire circlip (D)

● Always use circlip pliers to remove and install circlips; expand or compress them just enough to remove them. After installation, rotate the circlip in its groove to ensure it is securely seated. If installing a circlip on a splined shaft, always align its opening with a shaft channel to ensure the circlip ends are well supported and unlikely to catch **(see illustration 2.10)**.

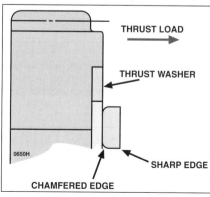

2.9 Correct fitting of a stamped circlip

THRUST LOAD

THRUST WASHER

SHARP EDGE

CHAMFERED EDGE

0650H

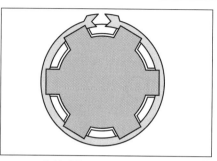

2.10 Align circlip opening with shaft channel

● Circlips can wear due to the thrust of components and become loose in their grooves, with the subsequent danger of becoming dislodged in operation. For this reason, renewal is advised every time a circlip is disturbed.
● Wire circlips are commonly used as piston pin retaining clips. If a removal tang is provided, long-nosed pliers can be used to dislodge them, otherwise careful use of a small flat-bladed screwdriver is necessary. Wire circlips should be renewed every time they are disturbed.

Thread diameter and pitch

● Diameter of a male thread (screw, bolt or stud) is the outside diameter of the threaded portion **(see illustration 2.11)**. Most motorcycle manufacturers use the ISO (International Standards Organisation) metric system expressed in millimetres, eg M6 refers to a 6 mm diameter thread. Sizing is the same for nuts, except that the thread diameter is measured across the valleys of the nut.
● Pitch is the distance between the peaks of the thread **(see illustration 2.11)**. It is expressed in millimetres, thus a common bolt size may be expressed as 6.0 x 1.0 mm (6 mm thread diameter and 1 mm pitch). Generally pitch increases in proportion to thread diameter, although there are always exceptions.
● Thread diameter and pitch are related for conventional fastener applications and the accompanying table can be used as a guide. Additionally, the AF (Across Flats), spanner or socket size dimension of the bolt or nut **(see illustration 2.11)** is linked to thread and pitch specification. Thread pitch can be measured with a thread gauge **(see illustration 2.12)**.

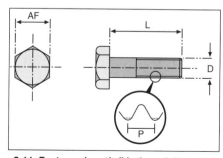

2.11 Fastener length (L), thread diameter (D), thread pitch (P) and head size (AF)

AF

L

D

P

2.12 Using a thread gauge to measure pitch

AF size	Thread diameter x pitch (mm)
8 mm	M5 x 0.8
8 mm	M6 x 1.0
10 mm	M6 x 1.0
12 mm	M8 x 1.25
14 mm	M10 x 1.25
17 mm	M12 x 1.25

● The threads of most fasteners are of the right-hand type, ie they are turned clockwise to tighten and anti-clockwise to loosen. The reverse situation applies to left-hand thread fasteners, which are turned anti-clockwise to tighten and clockwise to loosen. Left-hand threads are used where rotation of a component might loosen a conventional right-hand thread fastener.

Seized fasteners

● Corrosion of external fasteners due to water or reaction between two dissimilar metals can occur over a period of time. It will build up sooner in wet conditions or in countries where salt is used on the roads during the winter. If a fastener is severely corroded it is likely that normal methods of removal will fail and result in its head being ruined. When you attempt removal, the fastener thread should be heard to crack free and unscrew easily - if it doesn't, stop there before damaging something.
● A smart tap on the head of the fastener will often succeed in breaking free corrosion which has occurred in the threads **(see illustration 2.13)**.
● An aerosol penetrating fluid (such as WD-40) applied the night beforehand may work its way down into the thread and ease removal. Depending on the location, you may be able to make up a Plasticine well around the fastener head and fill it with penetrating fluid.

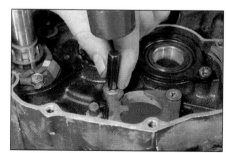

2.13 A sharp tap on the head of a fastener will often break free a corroded thread

● If you are working on an engine internal component, corrosion will most likely not be a problem due to the well lubricated environment. However, components can be very tight and an impact driver is a useful tool in freeing them **(see illustration 2.14)**.

2.14 Using an impact driver to free a fastener

● Where corrosion has occurred between dissimilar metals (eg steel and aluminium alloy), the application of heat to the fastener head will create a disproportionate expansion rate between the two metals and break the seizure caused by the corrosion. Whether heat can be applied depends on the location of the fastener - any surrounding components likely to be damaged must first be removed **(see illustration 2.15)**. Heat can be applied using a paint stripper heat gun or clothes iron, or by immersing the component in boiling water - wear protective gloves to prevent scalding or burns to the hands.

2.15 Using heat to free a seized fastener

● As a last resort, it is possible to use a hammer and cold chisel to work the fastener head unscrewed **(see illustration 2.16)**. This will damage the fastener, but more importantly extreme care must be taken not to damage the surrounding component.

Caution: Remember that the component being secured is generally of more value than the bolt, nut or screw - when the fastener is freed, do not unscrew it with force, instead work the fastener back and forth when resistance is felt to prevent thread damage.

2.16 Using a hammer and chisel to free a seized fastener

Broken fasteners and damaged heads

● If the shank of a broken bolt or screw is accessible you can grip it with self-locking grips. The knurled wheel type stud extractor tool or self-gripping stud puller tool is particularly useful for removing the long studs which screw into the cylinder mouth surface of the crankcase or bolts and screws from which the head has broken off **(see illustration 2.17)**. Studs can also be removed by locking two nuts together on the threaded end of the stud and using a spanner on the lower nut **(see illustration 2.18)**.

2.17 Using a stud extractor tool to remove a broken crankcase stud

2.18 Two nuts can be locked together to unscrew a stud from a component

● A bolt or screw which has broken off below or level with the casing must be extracted using a screw extractor set. Centre punch the fastener to centralise the drill bit, then drill a hole in the fastener **(see illustration 2.19)**. Select a drill bit which is approximately half to three-quarters the diameter of the fastener

2.19 When using a screw extractor, first drill a hole in the fastener . . .

and drill to a depth which will accommodate the extractor. Use the largest size extractor possible, but avoid leaving too small a wall thickness otherwise the extractor will merely force the fastener walls outwards wedging it in the casing thread.
● If a spiral type extractor is used, thread it anti-clockwise into the fastener. As it is screwed in, it will grip the fastener and unscrew it from the casing **(see illustration 2.20)**.

2.20 . . . then thread the extractor anti-clockwise into the fastener

● If a taper type extractor is used, tap it into the fastener so that it is firmly wedged in place. Unscrew the extractor (anti-clockwise) to draw the fastener out.

⚠ *Warning: Stud extractors are very hard and may break off in the fastener if care is not taken - ask an engineer about spark erosion if this happens.*

● Alternatively, the broken bolt/screw can be drilled out and the hole retapped for an oversize bolt/screw or a diamond-section thread insert. It is essential that the drilling is carried out squarely and to the correct depth, otherwise the casing may be ruined - if in doubt, entrust the work to an engineer.
● Bolts and nuts with rounded corners cause the correct size spanner or socket to slip when force is applied. Of the types of spanner/socket available always use a six-point type rather than an eight or twelve-point type - better grip

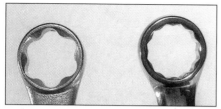

2.21 Comparison of surface drive ring spanner (left) with 12-point type (right)

is obtained. Surface drive spanners grip the middle of the hex flats, rather than the corners, and are thus good in cases of damaged heads **(see illustration 2.21)**.

● Slotted-head or Phillips-head screws are often damaged by the use of the wrong size screwdriver. Allen-head and Torx-head screws are much less likely to sustain damage. If enough of the screw head is exposed you can use a hacksaw to cut a slot in its head and then use a conventional flat-bladed screwdriver to remove it. Alternatively use a hammer and cold chisel to tap the head of the fastener around to slacken it. Always replace damaged fasteners with new ones, preferably Torx or Allen-head type.

HAYNES HINT

A dab of valve grinding compound between the screw head and screwdriver tip will often give a good grip.

Thread repair

● Threads (particularly those in aluminium alloy components) can be damaged by overtightening, being assembled with dirt in the threads, or from a component working loose and vibrating. Eventually the thread will fail completely, and it will be impossible to tighten the fastener.

● If a thread is damaged or clogged with old locking compound it can be renovated with a thread repair tool (thread chaser) **(see illustrations 2.22 and 2.23)**; special thread

2.22 A thread repair tool being used to correct an internal thread

2.23 A thread repair tool being used to correct an external thread

chasers are available for spark plug hole threads. The tool will not cut a new thread, but clean and true the original thread. Make sure that you use the correct diameter and pitch tool. Similarly, external threads can be cleaned up with a die or a thread restorer file **(see illustration 2.24)**.

2.24 Using a thread restorer file

● It is possible to drill out the old thread and retap the component to the next thread size. This will work where there is enough surrounding material and a new bolt or screw can be obtained. Sometimes, however, this is not possible - such as where the bolt/screw passes through another component which must also be suitably modified, also in cases where a spark plug or oil drain plug cannot be obtained in a larger diameter thread size.

● The diamond-section thread insert (often known by its popular trade name of Heli-Coil) is a simple and effective method of renewing the thread and retaining the original size. A kit can be purchased which contains the tap, insert and installing tool **(see illustration 2.25)**. Drill out the damaged thread with the size drill specified **(see illustration 2.26)**. Carefully retap the thread **(see illustration 2.27)**. Install the

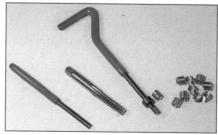

2.25 Obtain a thread insert kit to suit the thread diameter and pitch required

2.26 To install a thread insert, first drill out the original thread . . .

2.27 . . . tap a new thread . . .

2.28 . . . fit insert on the installing tool . . .

2.29 . . . and thread into the component . . .

2.30 . . . break off the tang when complete

insert on the installing tool and thread it slowly into place using a light downward pressure **(see illustrations 2.28 and 2.29)**. When positioned between a 1/4 and 1/2 turn below the surface withdraw the installing tool and use the break-off tool to press down on the tang, breaking it off **(see illustration 2.30)**.

● There are epoxy thread repair kits on the market which can rebuild stripped internal threads, although this repair should not be used on high load-bearing components.

Thread locking and sealing compounds

● Locking compounds are used in locations where the fastener is prone to loosening due to vibration or on important safety-related items which might cause loss of control of the motorcycle if they fail. It is also used where important fasteners cannot be secured by other means such as lockwashers or split pins.

● Before applying locking compound, make sure that the threads (internal and external) are clean and dry with all old compound removed. Select a compound to suit the component being secured - a non-permanent general locking and sealing type is suitable for most applications, but a high strength type is needed for permanent fixing of studs in castings. Apply a drop or two of the compound to the first few threads of the fastener, then thread it into place and tighten to the specified torque. Do not apply excessive thread locking compound otherwise the thread may be damaged on subsequent removal.

● Certain fasteners are impregnated with a dry film type coating of locking compound on their threads. Always renew this type of fastener if disturbed.

● Anti-seize compounds, such as copper-based greases, can be applied to protect threads from seizure due to extreme heat and corrosion. A common instance is spark plug threads and exhaust system fasteners.

3 Measuring tools and gauges

Feeler gauges

● Feeler gauges (or blades) are used for measuring small gaps and clearances (see illustration 3.1). They can also be used to measure endfloat (sideplay) of a component on a shaft where access is not possible with a dial gauge.

● Feeler gauge sets should be treated with care and not bent or damaged. They are etched with their size on one face. Keep them clean and very lightly oiled to prevent corrosion build-up.

3.1 Feeler gauges are used for measuring small gaps and clearances - thickness is marked on one face of gauge

● When measuring a clearance, select a gauge which is a light sliding fit between the two components. You may need to use two gauges together to measure the clearance accurately.

Micrometers

● A micrometer is a precision tool capable of measuring to 0.01 or 0.001 of a millimetre. It should always be stored in its case and not in the general toolbox. It must be kept clean and never dropped, otherwise its frame or measuring anvils could be distorted resulting in inaccurate readings.

● External micrometers are used for measuring outside diameters of components and have many more applications than internal micrometers. Micrometers are available in different size ranges, eg 0 to 25 mm, 25 to 50 mm, and upwards in 25 mm steps; some large micrometers have interchangeable anvils to allow a range of measurements to be taken. Generally the largest precision measurement you are likely to take on a motorcycle is the piston diameter.

● Internal micrometers (or bore micrometers) are used for measuring inside diameters, such as valve guides and cylinder bores. Telescoping gauges and small hole gauges are used in conjunction with an external micrometer, whereas the more expensive internal micrometers have their own measuring device.

External micrometer

Note: *The conventional analogue type instrument is described. Although much easier to read, digital micrometers are considerably more expensive.*

● Always check the calibration of the micrometer before use. With the anvils closed (0 to 25 mm type) or set over a test gauge

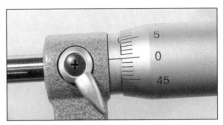

3.2 Check micrometer calibration before use

(for the larger types) the scale should read zero (see illustration 3.2); make sure that the anvils (and test piece) are clean first. Any discrepancy can be adjusted by referring to the instructions supplied with the tool. Remember that the micrometer is a precision measuring tool - don't force the anvils closed, use the ratchet (4) on the end of the micrometer to close it. In this way, a measured force is always applied.

● To use, first make sure that the item being measured is clean. Place the anvil of the micrometer (1) against the item and use the thimble (2) to bring the spindle (3) lightly into contact with the other side of the item (see illustration 3.3). Don't tighten the thimble down because this will damage the micrometer - instead use the ratchet (4) on the end of the micrometer. The ratchet mechanism applies a measured force preventing damage to the instrument.

● The micrometer is read by referring to the linear scale on the sleeve and the annular scale on the thimble. Read off the sleeve first to obtain the base measurement, then add the fine measurement from the thimble to obtain the overall reading. The linear scale on the sleeve represents the measuring range of the micrometer (eg 0 to 25 mm). The annular scale

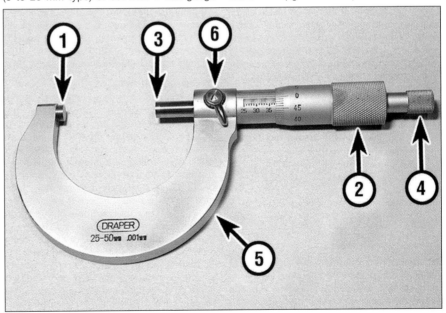

3.3 Micrometer component parts

1 Anvil	3 Spindle	5 Frame
2 Thimble	4 Ratchet	6 Locking lever

on the thimble will be in graduations of 0.01 mm (or as marked on the frame) - one full revolution of the thimble will move 0.5 mm on the linear scale. Take the reading where the datum line on the sleeve intersects the thimble's scale. Always position the eye directly above the scale otherwise an inaccurate reading will result.

In the example shown the item measures 2.95 mm (see illustration 3.4):

Linear scale	2.00 mm
Linear scale	0.50 mm
Annular scale	0.45 mm
Total figure	2.95 mm

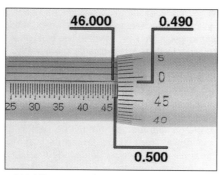

3.5 Micrometer reading of 46.99 mm on linear and annular scales . . .

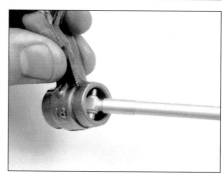

3.7 Expand the telescoping gauge in the bore, lock its position . . .

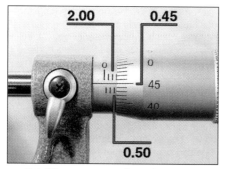

3.4 Micrometer reading of 2.95 mm

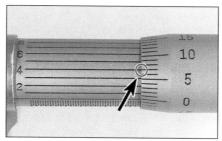

3.6 . . . and 0.004 mm on vernier scale

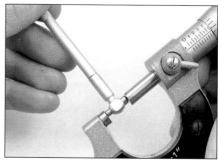

3.8 . . . then measure the gauge with a micrometer

Most micrometers have a locking lever (6) on the frame to hold the setting in place, allowing the item to be removed from the micrometer.
● Some micrometers have a vernier scale on their sleeve, providing an even finer measurement to be taken, in 0.001 increments of a millimetre. Take the sleeve and thimble measurement as described above, then check which graduation on the vernier scale aligns with that of the annular scale on the thimble. **Note:** *The eye must be perpendicular to the scale when taking the vernier reading - if necessary rotate the body of the micrometer to ensure this.* Multiply the vernier scale figure by 0.001 and add it to the base and fine measurement figures.

In the example shown the item measures 46.994 mm (see illustrations 3.5 and 3.6):

Linear scale (base)	46.000 mm
Linear scale (base)	00.500 mm
Annular scale (fine)	00.490 mm
Vernier scale	00.004 mm
Total figure	46.994 mm

Internal micrometer

● Internal micrometers are available for measuring bore diameters, but are expensive and unlikely to be available for home use. It is suggested that a set of telescoping gauges and small hole gauges, both of which must be used with an external micrometer, will suffice for taking internal measurements on a motorcycle.
● Telescoping gauges can be used to

measure internal diameters of components. Select a gauge with the correct size range, make sure its ends are clean and insert it into the bore. Expand the gauge, then lock its position and withdraw it from the bore (see illustration 3.7). Measure across the gauge ends with a micrometer (see illustration 3.8).
● Very small diameter bores (such as valve guides) are measured with a small hole gauge. Once adjusted to a slip-fit inside the component, its position is locked and the gauge withdrawn for measurement with a micrometer (see illustrations 3.9 and 3.10).

Vernier caliper

Note: *The conventional linear and dial gauge type instruments are described. Digital types are easier to read, but are far more expensive.*
● The vernier caliper does not provide the precision of a micrometer, but is versatile in being able to measure internal and external diameters. Some types also incorporate a depth gauge. It is ideal for measuring clutch plate friction material and spring free lengths.
● To use the conventional linear scale vernier, slacken off the vernier clamp screws (1) and set its jaws over (2), or inside (3), the item to be measured (see illustration 3.11). Slide the jaw into contact, using the thumb-wheel (4) for fine movement of the sliding scale (5) then tighten the clamp screws (1). Read off the main scale (6) where the zero on the sliding scale (5) intersects it, taking the whole number to the left of the zero; this provides the base measurement. View along the sliding scale and select the division which

3.9 Expand the small hole gauge in the bore, lock its position . . .

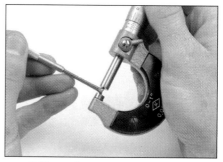

3.10 . . . then measure the gauge with a micrometer

lines up exactly with any of the divisions on the main scale, noting that the divisions usually represents 0.02 of a millimetre. Add this fine measurement to the base measurement to obtain the total reading.

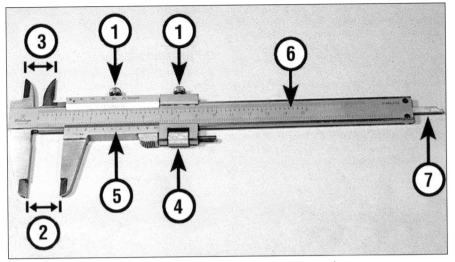

3.11 Vernier component parts (linear gauge)

1 Clamp screws   3 Internal jaws   5 Sliding scale   7 Depth gauge
2 External jaws   4 Thumbwheel   6 Main scale

In the example shown the item measures 55.92 mm **(see illustration 3.12)**:

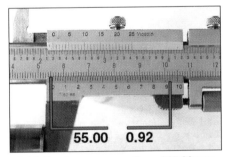

3.12 Vernier gauge reading of 55.92 mm

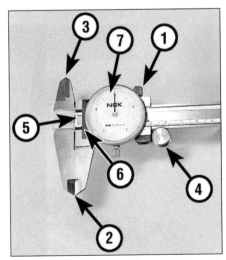

3.13 Vernier component parts (dial gauge)

1 Clamp screw
2 External jaws
3 Internal jaws
4 Thumbwheel
5 Main scale
6 Sliding scale
7 Dial gauge

Base measurement	55.00 mm
Fine measurement	00.92 mm
Total figure	55.92 mm

● Some vernier calipers are equipped with a dial gauge for fine measurement. Before use, check that the jaws are clean, then close them fully and check that the dial gauge reads zero. If necessary adjust the gauge ring accordingly. Slacken the vernier clamp screw (1) and set its jaws over (2), or inside (3), the item to be measured **(see illustration 3.13)**. Slide the jaws into contact, using the thumbwheel (4) for fine movement. Read off the main scale (5) where the edge of the sliding scale (6) intersects it, taking the whole number to the left of the zero; this provides the base measurement. Read off the needle position on the dial gauge (7) scale to provide the fine measurement; each division represents 0.05 of a millimetre. Add this fine measurement to the base measurement to obtain the total reading.

In the example shown the item measures 55.95 mm **(see illustration 3.14)**:

Base measurement	55.00 mm
Fine measurement	00.95 mm
Total figure	55.95 mm

3.14 Vernier gauge reading of 55.95 mm

Plastigauge

● Plastigauge is a plastic material which can be compressed between two surfaces to measure the oil clearance between them. The width of the compressed Plastigauge is measured against a calibrated scale to determine the clearance.

● Common uses of Plastigauge are for measuring the clearance between crankshaft journal and main bearing inserts, between crankshaft journal and big-end bearing inserts, and between camshaft and bearing surfaces. The following example describes big-end oil clearance measurement.

● Handle the Plastigauge material carefully to prevent distortion. Using a sharp knife, cut a length which corresponds with the width of the bearing being measured and place it carefully across the journal so that it is parallel with the shaft **(see illustration 3.15)**. Carefully install both bearing shells and the connecting rod. Without rotating the rod on the journal tighten its bolts or nuts (as applicable) to the specified torque. The connecting rod and bearings are then disassembled and the crushed Plastigauge examined.

3.15 Plastigauge placed across shaft journal

● Using the scale provided in the Plastigauge kit, measure the width of the material to determine the oil clearance **(see illustration 3.16)**. Always remove all traces of Plastigauge after use using your fingernails.

> *Caution: Arriving at the correct clearance demands that the assembly is torqued correctly, according to the settings and sequence (where applicable) provided by the motorcycle manufacturer.*

3.16 Measuring the width of the crushed Plastigauge

Dial gauge or DTI (Dial Test Indicator)

● A dial gauge can be used to accurately measure small amounts of movement. Typical uses are measuring shaft runout or shaft endfloat (sideplay) and setting piston position for ignition timing on two-strokes. A dial gauge set usually comes with a range of different probes and adapters and mounting equipment.

● The gauge needle must point to zero when at rest. Rotate the ring around its periphery to zero the gauge.

● Check that the gauge is capable of reading the extent of movement in the work. Most gauges have a small dial set in the face which records whole millimetres of movement as well as the fine scale around the face periphery which is calibrated in 0.01 mm divisions. Read off the small dial first to obtain the base measurement, then add the measurement from the fine scale to obtain the total reading.

In the example shown the gauge reads 1.48 mm (see illustration 3.17):

Base measurement	1.00 mm
Fine measurement	0.48 mm
Total figure	1.48 mm

3.17 Dial gauge reading of 1.48 mm

● If measuring shaft runout, the shaft must be supported in vee-blocks and the gauge mounted on a stand perpendicular to the shaft. Rest the tip of the gauge against the centre of the shaft and rotate the shaft slowly whilst watching the gauge reading (see illustration 3.18). Take several measurements along the length of the shaft and record the

3.18 Using a dial gauge to measure shaft runout

maximum gauge reading as the amount of runout in the shaft. Note: The reading obtained will be total runout at that point - some manufacturers specify that the runout figure is halved to compare with their specified runout limit.

● Endfloat (sideplay) measurement requires that the gauge is mounted securely to the surrounding component with its probe touching the end of the shaft. Using hand pressure, push and pull on the shaft noting the maximum endfloat recorded on the gauge (see illustration 3.19).

3.19 Using a dial gauge to measure shaft endfloat

● A dial gauge with suitable adapters can be used to determine piston position BTDC on two-stroke engines for the purposes of ignition timing. The gauge, adapter and suitable length probe are installed in the place of the spark plug and the gauge zeroed at TDC. If the piston position is specified as 1.14 mm BTDC, rotate the engine back to 2.00 mm BTDC, then slowly forwards to 1.14 mm BTDC.

Cylinder compression gauges

● A compression gauge is used for measuring cylinder compression. Either the rubber-cone type or the threaded adapter type can be used. The latter is preferred to ensure a perfect seal against the cylinder head. A 0 to 300 psi (0 to 20 Bar) type gauge (for petrol/gasoline engines) will be suitable for motorcycles.

● The spark plug is removed and the gauge either held hard against the cylinder head (cone type) or the gauge adapter screwed into the cylinder head (threaded type) (see illustration 3.20). Cylinder compression is measured with the engine turning over, but not running. The

3.20 Using a rubber-cone type cylinder compression gauge

gauge will hold the reading until manually released.

Oil pressure gauge

● An oil pressure gauge is used for measuring engine oil pressure. Most gauges come with a set of adapters to fit the thread of the take-off point (see illustration 3.21). If the take-off point specified by the motorcycle manufacturer is an external oil pipe union, make sure that the specified replacement union is used to prevent oil starvation.

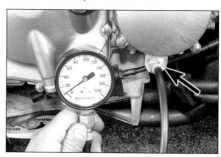

3.21 Oil pressure gauge and take-off point adapter (arrow)

● Oil pressure is measured with the engine running (at a specific rpm) and often the manufacturer will specify pressure limits for a cold and hot engine.

Straight-edge and surface plate

● If checking the gasket face of a component for warpage, place a steel rule or precision straight-edge across the gasket face and measure any gap between the straight-edge and component with feeler gauges (see illustration 3.22). Check diagonally across the component and between mounting holes (see illustration 3.23).

3.22 Use a straight-edge and feeler gauges to check for warpage

3.23 Check for warpage in these directions

● Checking individual components for warpage, such as clutch plain (metal) plates, requires a perfectly flat plate or piece or plate glass and feeler gauges.

4 Torque and leverage

What is torque?

● Torque describes the twisting force about a shaft. The amount of torque applied is determined by the distance from the centre of the shaft to the end of the lever and the amount of force being applied to the end of the lever; distance multiplied by force equals torque.
● The manufacturer applies a measured torque to a bolt or nut to ensure that it will not slacken in use and to hold two components securely together without movement in the joint. The actual torque setting depends on the thread size, bolt or nut material and the composition of the components being held.
● Too little torque may cause the fastener to loosen due to vibration, whereas too much torque will distort the joint faces of the component or cause the fastener to shear off. Always stick to the specified torque setting.

Using a torque wrench

● Check the calibration of the torque wrench and make sure it has a suitable range for the job. Torque wrenches are available in Nm (Newton-metres), kgf m (kilograms-force metre), lbf ft (pounds-feet), lbf in (inch-pounds). Do not confuse lbf ft with lbf in.
● Adjust the tool to the desired torque on the scale **(see illustration 4.1)**. If your torque wrench is not calibrated in the units specified, carefully convert the figure (see Conversion Factors). A manufacturer sometimes gives a torque setting as a range (8 to 10 Nm) rather than a single figure - in this case set the tool midway between the two settings. The same torque may be expressed as 9 Nm ± 1 Nm. Some torque wrenches have a method of locking the setting so that it isn't inadvertently altered during use.

4.1 Set the torque wrench index mark to the setting required, in this case 12 Nm

● Install the bolts/nuts in their correct location and secure them lightly. Their threads must be clean and free of any old locking compound. Unless specified the threads and flange should be dry - oiled threads are necessary in certain circumstances and the manufacturer will take this into account in the specified torque figure. Similarly, the manufacturer may also specify the application of thread-locking compound.
● Tighten the fasteners in the specified sequence until the torque wrench clicks, indicating that the torque setting has been reached. Apply the torque again to double-check the setting. Where different thread diameter fasteners secure the component, as a rule tighten the larger diameter ones first.
● When the torque wrench has been finished with, release the lock (where applicable) and fully back off its setting to zero - do not leave the torque wrench tensioned. Also, do not use a torque wrench for slackening a fastener.

Angle-tightening

● Manufacturers often specify a figure in degrees for final tightening of a fastener. This usually follows tightening to a specific torque setting.
● A degree disc can be set and attached to the socket **(see illustration 4.2)** or a protractor can be used to mark the angle of movement on the bolt/nut head and the surrounding casting **(see illustration 4.3)**.

4.2 Angle tightening can be accomplished with a torque-angle gauge . . .

4.3 . . . or by marking the angle on the surrounding component

Loosening sequences

● Where more than one bolt/nut secures a component, loosen each fastener evenly a little at a time. In this way, not all the stress of the joint is held by one fastener and the components are not likely to distort.
● If a tightening sequence is provided, work in the REVERSE of this, but if not, work from the outside in, in a criss-cross sequence **(see illustration 4.4)**.

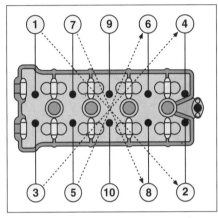

4.4 When slackening, work from the outside inwards

Tightening sequences

● If a component is held by more than one fastener it is important that the retaining bolts/nuts are tightened evenly to prevent uneven stress build-up and distortion of sealing faces. This is especially important on high-compression joints such as the cylinder head.
● A sequence is usually provided by the manufacturer, either in a diagram or actually marked in the casting. If not, always start in the centre and work outwards in a criss-cross pattern **(see illustration 4.5)**. Start off by securing all bolts/nuts finger-tight, then set the torque wrench and tighten each fastener by a small amount in sequence until the final torque is reached. By following this practice,

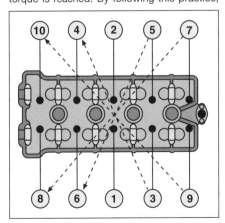

4.5 When tightening, work from the inside outwards

the joint will be held evenly and will not be distorted. Important joints, such as the cylinder head and big-end fasteners often have two- or three-stage torque settings.

Applying leverage

● Use tools at the correct angle. Position a socket wrench or spanner on the bolt/nut so that you pull it towards you when loosening. If this can't be done, push the spanner without curling your fingers around it **(see illustration 4.6)** - the spanner may slip or the fastener loosen suddenly, resulting in your fingers being crushed against a component.

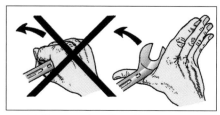

4.6 If you can't pull on the spanner to loosen a fastener, push with your hand open

● Additional leverage is gained by extending the length of the lever. The best way to do this is to use a breaker bar instead of the regular length tool, or to slip a length of tubing over the end of the spanner or socket wrench.
● If additional leverage will not work, the fastener head is either damaged or firmly corroded in place (see Fasteners).

5 Bearings

Bearing removal and installation

Drivers and sockets

● Before removing a bearing, always inspect the casing to see which way it must be driven out - some casings will have retaining plates or a cast step. Also check for any identifying markings on the bearing and if installed to a certain depth, measure this at this stage. Some roller bearings are sealed on one side - take note of the original fitted position.
● Bearings can be driven out of a casing using a bearing driver tool (with the correct size head) or a socket of the correct diameter. Select the driver head or socket so that it contacts the outer race of the bearing, not the balls/rollers or inner race. Always support the casing around the bearing housing with wood blocks, otherwise there is a risk of fracture. The bearing is driven out with a few blows on the driver or socket from a heavy mallet. Unless access is severely restricted (as with wheel bearings), a pin-punch is not recommended unless it is moved around the bearing to keep it square in its housing.

● The same equipment can be used to install bearings. Make sure the bearing housing is supported on wood blocks and line up the bearing in its housing. Fit the bearing as noted on removal - generally they are installed with their marked side facing outwards. Tap the bearing squarely into its housing using a driver or socket which bears only on the bearing's outer race - contact with the bearing balls/rollers or inner race will destroy it **(see illustrations 5.1 and 5.2)**.
● Check that the bearing inner race and balls/rollers rotate freely.

5.1 Using a bearing driver against the bearing's outer race

5.2 Using a large socket against the bearing's outer race

Pullers and slide-hammers

● Where a bearing is pressed on a shaft a puller will be required to extract it **(see illustration 5.3)**. Make sure that the puller clamp or legs fit securely behind the bearing and are unlikely to slip out. If pulling a bearing

5.3 This bearing puller clamps behind the bearing and pressure is applied to the shaft end to draw the bearing off

off a gear shaft for example, you may have to locate the puller behind a gear pinion if there is no access to the race and draw the gear pinion off the shaft as well **(see illustration 5.4)**.

> **Caution: Ensure that the puller's centre bolt locates securely against the end of the shaft and will not slip when pressure is applied. Also ensure that puller does not damage the shaft end.**

5.4 Where no access is available to the rear of the bearing, it is sometimes possible to draw off the adjacent component

● Operate the puller so that its centre bolt exerts pressure on the shaft end and draws the bearing off the shaft.
● When installing the bearing on the shaft, tap only on the bearing's inner race - contact with the balls/rollers or outer race with destroy the bearing. Use a socket or length of tubing as a drift which fits over the shaft end **(see illustration 5.5)**.

5.5 When installing a bearing on a shaft use a piece of tubing which bears only on the bearing's inner race

● Where a bearing locates in a blind hole in a casing, it cannot be driven or pulled out as described above. A slide-hammer with knife-edged bearing puller attachment will be required. The puller attachment passes through the bearing and when tightened expands to fit firmly behind the bearing **(see illustration 5.6)**. By operating the slide-hammer part of the tool the bearing is jarred out of its housing **(see illustration 5.7)**.
● It is possible, if the bearing is of reasonable weight, for it to drop out of its housing if the casing is heated as described opposite.

5.6 Expand the bearing puller so that it locks behind the bearing . . .

5.7 . . . attach the slide hammer to the bearing puller

If this method is attempted, first prepare a work surface which will enable the casing to be tapped face down to help dislodge the bearing - a wood surface is ideal since it will not damage the casing's gasket surface. Wearing protective gloves, tap the heated casing several times against the work surface to dislodge the bearing under its own weight **(see illustration 5.8)**.

5.8 Tapping a casing face down on wood blocks can often dislodge a bearing

● Bearings can be installed in blind holes using the driver or socket method described above.

Drawbolts

● Where a bearing or bush is set in the eye of a component, such as a suspension linkage arm or connecting rod small-end, removal by drift may damage the component. Furthermore, a rubber bushing in a shock absorber eye cannot successfully be driven out of position. If access is available to a engineering press, the task is straightforward. If not, a drawbolt can be fabricated to extract the bearing or bush.

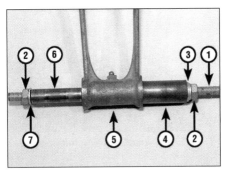

5.9 Drawbolt component parts assembled on a suspension arm

1 Bolt or length of threaded bar
2 Nuts
3 Washer (external diameter greater than tubing internal diameter)
4 Tubing (internal diameter sufficient to accommodate bearing)
5 Suspension arm with bearing
6 Tubing (external diameter slightly smaller than bearing)
7 Washer (external diameter slightly smaller than bearing)

5.10 Drawing the bearing out of the suspension arm

● To extract the bearing/bush you will need a long bolt with nut (or piece of threaded bar with two nuts), a piece of tubing which has an internal diameter larger than the bearing/ bush, another piece of tubing which has an external diameter slightly smaller than the bearing/bush, and a selection of washers **(see illustrations 5.9 and 5.10)**. Note that the pieces of tubing must be of the same length, or longer, than the bearing/bush.
● The same kit (without the pieces of tubing) can be used to draw the new bearing/bush back into place **(see illustration 5.11)**.

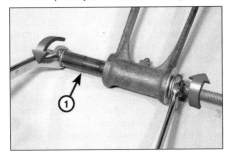

5.11 Installing a new bearing (1) in the suspension arm

Temperature change

● If the bearing's outer race is a tight fit in the casing, the aluminium casing can be heated to release its grip on the bearing. Aluminium will expand at a greater rate than the steel bearing outer race. There are several ways to do this, but avoid any localised extreme heat (such as a blow torch) - aluminium alloy has a low melting point.
● Approved methods of heating a casing are using a domestic oven (heated to 100°C) or immersing the casing in boiling water **(see illustration 5.12)**. Low temperature range localised heat sources such as a paint stripper heat gun or clothes iron can also be used **(see illustration 5.13)**. Alternatively, soak a rag in boiling water, wring it out and wrap it around the bearing housing.

> ⚠ **Warning: All of these methods require care in use to prevent scalding and burns to the hands. Wear protective gloves when handling hot components.**

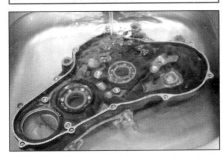

5.12 A casing can be immersed in a sink of boiling water to aid bearing removal

5.13 Using a localised heat source to aid bearing removal

● If heating the whole casing note that plastic components, such as the neutral switch, may suffer - remove them beforehand.
● After heating, remove the bearing as described above. You may find that the expansion is sufficient for the bearing to fall out of the casing under its own weight or with a light tap on the driver or socket.
● If necessary, the casing can be heated to aid bearing installation, and this is sometimes the recommended procedure if the motorcycle manufacturer has designed the housing and bearing fit with this intention.

● Installation of bearings can be eased by placing them in a freezer the night before installation. The steel bearing will contract slightly, allowing easy insertion in its housing. This is often useful when installing steering head outer races in the frame.

Bearing types and markings

● Plain shell bearings, ball bearings, needle roller bearings and tapered roller bearings will all be found on motorcycles (see illustrations 5.14 and 5.15). The ball and roller types are usually caged between an inner and outer race, but uncaged variations may be found.

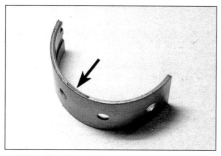

5.14 Shell bearings are either plain or grooved. They are usually identified by colour code (arrow)

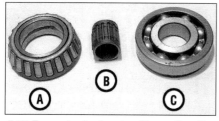

5.15 Tapered roller bearing (A), needle roller bearing (B) and ball journal bearing (C)

● Shell bearings (often called inserts) are usually found at the crankshaft main and connecting rod big-end where they are good at coping with high loads. They are made of a phosphor-bronze material and are impregnated with self-lubricating properties.
● Ball bearings and needle roller bearings consist of a steel inner and outer race with the balls or rollers between the races. They require constant lubrication by oil or grease and are good at coping with axial loads. Taper roller bearings consist of rollers set in a tapered cage set on the inner race; the outer race is separate. They are good at coping with axial loads and prevent movement along the shaft - a typical application is in the steering head.
● Bearing manufacturers produce bearings to ISO size standards and stamp one face of the bearing to indicate its internal and external diameter, load capacity and type (see illustration 5.16).
● Metal bushes are usually of phosphor-bronze material. Rubber bushes are used in suspension mounting eyes. Fibre bushes have also been used in suspension pivots.

5.16 Typical bearing marking

Bearing fault finding

● If a bearing outer race has spun in its housing, the housing material will be damaged. You can use a bearing locking compound to bond the outer race in place if damage is not too severe.
● Shell bearings will fail due to damage of their working surface, as a result of lack of lubrication, corrosion or abrasive particles in the oil (see illustration 5.17). Small particles of dirt in the oil may embed in the bearing material whereas larger particles will score the bearing and shaft journal. If a number of short journeys are made, insufficient heat will be generated to drive off condensation which has built up on the bearings.

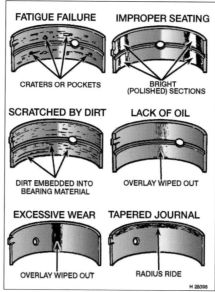

5.17 Typical bearing failures

● Ball and roller bearings will fail due to lack of lubrication or damage to the balls or rollers. Tapered-roller bearings can be damaged by overloading them. Unless the bearing is sealed on both sides, wash it in paraffin (kerosene) to remove all old grease then allow it to dry. Make a visual inspection looking to dented balls or rollers, damaged cages and worn or pitted races (see illustration 5.18).
● A ball bearing can be checked for wear by listening to it when spun. Apply a film of light oil to the bearing and hold it close to the ear - hold the outer race with one hand and spin the

5.18 Example of ball journal bearing with damaged balls and cages

5.19 Hold outer race and listen to inner race when spun

inner race with the other hand (see illustration 5.19). The bearing should be almost silent when spun; if it grates or rattles it is worn.

6 Oil seals

Oil seal removal and installation

● Oil seals should be renewed every time a component is dismantled. This is because the seal lips will become set to the sealing surface and will not necessarily reseal.
● Oil seals can be prised out of position using a large flat-bladed screwdriver (see illustration 6.1). In the case of crankcase seals, check first that the seal is not lipped on the inside, preventing its removal with the crankcases joined.

6.1 Prise out oil seals with a large flat-bladed screwdriver

● New seals are usually installed with their marked face (containing the seal reference code) outwards and the spring side towards the fluid being retained. In certain cases, such as a two-stroke engine crankshaft seal, a double lipped seal may be used due to there being fluid or gas on each side of the joint.

● Use a bearing driver or socket which bears only on the outer hard edge of the seal to install it in the casing - tapping on the inner edge will damage the sealing lip.

Oil seal types and markings

● Oil seals are usually of the single-lipped type. Double-lipped seals are found where a liquid or gas is on both sides of the joint.
● Oil seals can harden and lose their sealing ability if the motorcycle has been in storage for a long period - renewal is the only solution.
● Oil seal manufacturers also conform to the ISO markings for seal size - these are moulded into the outer face of the seal **(see illustration 6.2)**.

6.2 These oil seal markings indicate inside diameter, outside diameter and seal thickness

7   Gaskets and sealants

Types of gasket and sealant

● Gaskets are used to seal the mating surfaces between components and keep lubricants, fluids, vacuum or pressure contained within the assembly. Aluminium gaskets are sometimes found at the cylinder joints, but most gaskets are paper-based. If the mating surfaces of the components being joined are undamaged the gasket can be installed dry, although a dab of sealant or grease will be useful to hold it in place during assembly.
● RTV (Room Temperature Vulcanising) silicone rubber sealants cure when exposed to moisture in the atmosphere. These sealants are good at filling pits or irregular gasket faces, but will tend to be forced out of the joint under very high torque. They can be used to replace a paper gasket, but first make sure that the width of the paper gasket is not essential to the shimming of internal components. RTV sealants should not be used on components containing petrol (gasoline).
● Non-hardening, semi-hardening and hard setting liquid gasket compounds can be used with a gasket or between a metal-to-metal joint. Select the sealant to suit the application: universal non-hardening sealant can be used on virtually all joints; semi-hardening on joint faces which are rough or damaged; hard setting sealant on joints which require a permanent bond and are subjected to high temperature and pressure. **Note:** *Check first if the paper gasket has a bead of sealant*

impregnated in its surface before applying additional sealant.
● When choosing a sealant, make sure it is suitable for the application, particularly if being applied in a high-temperature area or in the vicinity of fuel. Certain manufacturers produce sealants in either clear, silver or black colours to match the finish of the engine. This has a particular application on motorcycles where much of the engine is exposed.
● Do not over-apply sealant. That which is squeezed out on the outside of the joint can be wiped off, whereas an excess of sealant on the inside can break off and clog oilways.

Breaking a sealed joint

● Age, heat, pressure and the use of hard setting sealant can cause two components to stick together so tightly that they are difficult to separate using finger pressure alone. Do not resort to using levers unless there is a pry point provided for this purpose **(see illustration 7.1)** or else the gasket surfaces will be damaged.
● Use a soft-faced hammer **(see illustration 7.2)** or a wood block and conventional hammer to strike the component near the mating surface. Avoid hammering against cast extremities since they may break off. If this method fails, try using a wood wedge between the two components.

> **Caution: If the joint will not separate, double-check that you have removed all the fasteners.**

7.1 If a pry point is provided, apply gently pressure with a flat-bladed screwdriver

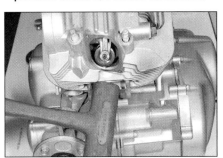

7.2 Tap around the joint with a soft-faced mallet if necessary - don't strike cooling fins

Removal of old gasket and sealant

● Paper gaskets will most likely come away complete, leaving only a few traces stuck

Most components have one or two hollow locating dowels between the two gasket faces. If a dowel cannot be removed, do not resort to gripping it with pliers - it will almost certainly be distorted. Install a close-fitting socket or Phillips screwdriver into the dowel and then grip the outer edge of the dowel to free it.

on the sealing faces of the components. It is imperative that all traces are removed to ensure correct sealing of the new gasket.
● Very carefully scrape all traces of gasket away making sure that the sealing surfaces are not gouged or scored by the scraper **(see illustrations 7.3, 7.4 and 7.5)**. Stubborn deposits can be removed by spraying with an aerosol gasket remover. Final preparation of

7.3 Paper gaskets can be scraped off with a gasket scraper tool . . .

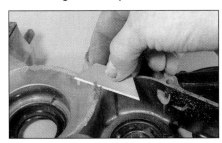

7.4 . . . a knife blade . . .

7.5 . . . or a household scraper

7.6 Fine abrasive paper is wrapped around a flat file to clean up the gasket face

7.7 A kitchen scourer can be used on stubborn deposits

the gasket surface can be made with very fine abrasive paper or a plastic kitchen scourer **(see illustrations 7.6 and 7.7)**.

● Old sealant can be scraped or peeled off components, depending on the type originally used. Note that gasket removal compounds are available to avoid scraping the components clean; make sure the gasket remover suits the type of sealant used.

8 Chains

Breaking and joining final drive chains

● Drive chains for all but small bikes are continuous and do not have a clip-type connecting link. The chain must be broken using a chain breaker tool and the new chain securely riveted together using a new soft rivet-type link. Never use a clip-type connecting link instead of a rivet-type link, except in an emergency. Various chain breaking and riveting tools are available, either as separate tools or combined as illustrated in the accompanying photographs - read the instructions supplied with the tool carefully.

 Warning: The need to rivet the new link pins correctly cannot be overstressed - loss of control of the motorcycle is very likely to result if the chain breaks in use.

● Rotate the chain and look for the soft link. The soft link pins look like they have been

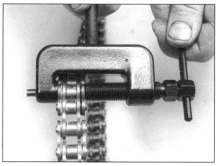

8.1 Tighten the chain breaker to push the pin out of the link . . .

8.2 . . . withdraw the pin, remove the tool . . .

8.3 . . . and separate the chain link

deeply centre-punched instead of peened over like all the other pins **(see illustration 8.9)** and its sideplate may be a different colour. Position the soft link midway between the sprockets and assemble the chain breaker tool over one of the soft link pins **(see illustration 8.1)**. Operate the tool to push the pin out through the chain **(see illustration 8.2)**. On an O-ring chain, remove the O-rings **(see illustration 8.3)**. Carry out the same procedure on the other soft link pin.

> **Caution: Certain soft link pins (particularly on the larger chains) may require their ends to be filed or ground off before they can be pressed out using the tool.**

● Check that you have the correct size and strength (standard or heavy duty) new soft link - do not reuse the old link. Look for the size marking on the chain sideplates **(see illustration 8.10)**.

● Position the chain ends so that they are engaged over the rear sprocket. On an O-ring

8.4 Insert the new soft link, with O-rings, through the chain ends . . .

8.5 . . . install the O-rings over the pin ends . . .

8.6 . . . followed by the sideplate

chain, install a new O-ring over each pin of the link and insert the link through the two chain ends **(see illustration 8.4)**. Install a new O-ring over the end of each pin, followed by the sideplate (with the chain manufacturer's marking facing outwards) **(see illustrations 8.5 and 8.6)**. On an unsealed chain, insert the link through the two chain ends, then install the sideplate with the chain manufacturer's marking facing outwards.

● Note that it may not be possible to install the sideplate using finger pressure alone. If using a joining tool, assemble it so that the plates of the tool clamp the link and press the sideplate over the pins **(see illustration 8.7)**. Otherwise, use two small sockets placed over

8.7 Push the sideplate into position using a clamp

8.8 Assemble the chain riveting tool over one pin at a time and tighten it fully

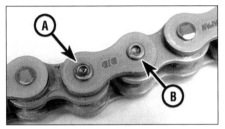

8.9 Pin end correctly riveted (A), pin end unriveted (B)

the rivet ends and two pieces of the wood between a G-clamp. Operate the clamp to press the sideplate over the pins.

● Assemble the joining tool over one pin (following the maker's instructions) and tighten the tool down to spread the pin end securely **(see illustrations 8.8 and 8.9)**. Do the same on the other pin.

 Warning: Check that the pin ends are secure and that there is no danger of the sideplate coming loose. If the pin ends are cracked the soft link must be renewed.

Final drive chain sizing

● Chains are sized using a three digit number, followed by a suffix to denote the chain type **(see illustration 8.10)**. Chain type is either standard or heavy duty (thicker sideplates), and also unsealed or O-ring/X-ring type.

● The first digit of the number relates to the pitch of the chain, ie the distance from the centre of one pin to the centre of the next pin **(see illustration 8.11)**. Pitch is expressed in eighths of an inch, as follows:

8.10 Typical chain size and type marking

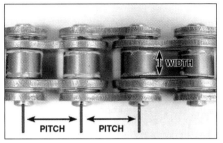

8.11 Chain dimensions

Sizes commencing with a 4 (eg 428) have a pitch of 1/2 inch (12.7 mm)
Sizes commencing with a 5 (eg 520) have a pitch of 5/8 inch (15.9 mm)
Sizes commencing with a 6 (eg 630) have a pitch of 3/4 inch (19.1 mm)

● The second and third digits of the chain size relate to the width of the rollers, again in imperial units, eg the 525 shown has 5/16 inch (7.94 mm) rollers **(see illustration 8.11)**.

9 Hoses

Clamping to prevent flow

● Small-bore flexible hoses can be clamped to prevent fluid flow whilst a component is worked on. Whichever method is used, ensure that the hose material is not permanently distorted or damaged by the clamp.

a) A brake hose clamp available from auto accessory shops **(see illustration 9.1)**.
b) A wingnut type hose clamp **(see illustration 9.2)**.

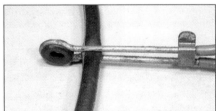

9.1 Hoses can be clamped with an automotive brake hose clamp . . .

9.2 . . . a wingnut type hose clamp . . .

c) Two sockets placed each side of the hose and held with straight-jawed self-locking grips **(see illustration 9.3)**.
d) Thick card each side of the hose held between straight-jawed self-locking grips **(see illustration 9.4)**.

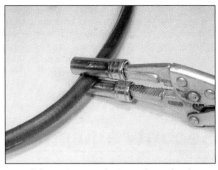

9.3 . . . two sockets and a pair of self-locking grips . . .

9.4 . . . or thick card and self-locking grips

Freeing and fitting hoses

● Always make sure the hose clamp is moved well clear of the hose end. Grip the hose with your hand and rotate it whilst pulling it off the union. If the hose has hardened due to age and will not move, slit it with a sharp knife and peel its ends off the union **(see illustration 9.5)**.

● Resist the temptation to use grease or soap on the unions to aid installation; although it helps the hose slip over the union it will equally aid the escape of fluid from the joint. It is preferable to soften the hose ends in hot water and wet the inside surface of the hose with water or a fluid which will evaporate.

9.5 Cutting a coolant hose free with a sharp knife

Introduction

In less time than it takes to read this introduction, a thief could steal your motorcycle. Returning only to find your bike has gone is one of the worst feelings in the world. Even if the motorcycle is insured against theft, once you've got over the initial shock, you will have the inconvenience of dealing with the police and your insurance company.

The motorcycle is an easy target for the professional thief and the joyrider alike and the official figures on motorcycle theft make for depressing reading; on average a motor-cycle is stolen every 16 minutes in the UK!

Motorcycle thefts fall into two categories, those stolen 'to order' and those taken by opportunists. The thief stealing to order will be on the look out for a specific make and model and will go to extraordinary lengths to obtain that motorcycle. The opportunist thief on the other hand will look for easy targets which can be stolen with the minimum of effort and risk.

Whilst it is never going to be possible to make your machine 100% secure, it is estimated that around half of all stolen motorcycles are taken by opportunist thieves. Remember that the opportunist thief is always on the look out for the easy option: if there are two similar motorcycles parked side-by-side, they will target the one with the lowest level of security. By taking a few precautions, you can reduce the chances of your motorcycle being stolen.

Security equipment

There are many specialised motorcycle security devices available and the following text summarises their applications and their good and bad points.

Once you have decided on the type of security equipment which best suits your needs, we recommended that you read one of the many equipment tests regularly carried out by the motorcycle press. These tests

Ensure the lock and chain you buy is of good quality and long enough to shackle your bike to a solid object

compare the products from all the major manufacturers and give impartial ratings on their effectiveness, value-for-money and ease of use.

No one item of security equipment can provide complete protection. It is highly recommended that two or more of the items described below are combined to increase the security of your motorcycle (a lock and chain plus an alarm system is just about ideal). The more security measures fitted to the bike, the less likely it is to be stolen.

Lock and chain

Pros: *Very flexible to use; can be used to secure the motorcycle to almost any immovable object. On some locks and chains, the lock can be used on its own as a disc lock (see below).*

Cons: *Can be very heavy and awkward to carry on the motorcycle, although some types*

will be supplied with a carry bag which can be strapped to the pillion seat.

● Heavy-duty chains and locks are an excellent security measure **(see illustration 1)**. Whenever the motorcycle is parked, use the lock and chain to secure the machine to a solid, immovable object such as a post or railings. This will prevent the machine from being ridden away or being lifted into the back of a van.

● When fitting the chain, always ensure the chain is routed around the motorcycle frame or swingarm **(see illustrations 2 and 3)**. Never merely pass the chain around one of the wheel rims; a thief may unbolt the wheel and lift the rest of the machine into a van, leaving you with just the wheel! Try to avoid having excess chain free, thus making it difficult to use cutting tools, and keep the chain and lock off the ground to prevent thieves attacking it with a cold chisel. Position the lock so that its lock barrel is facing downwards; this will make it harder for the thief to attack the lock mechanism.

Pass the chain through the bike's frame, rather than just through a wheel . . .

. . . and loop it around a solid object

U-locks

Pros: Highly effective deterrent which can be used to secure the bike to a post or railings. Most U-locks come with a carrier which allows the lock to be easily carried on the bike.

Cons: Not as flexible to use as a lock and chain.

● These are solid locks which are similar in use to a lock and chain. U-locks are lighter than a lock and chain but not so flexible to use. The length and shape of the lock shackle limit the objects to which the bike can be secured **(see illustration 4)**.

Disc locks

Pros: Small, light and very easy to carry; most can be stored underneath the seat.

Cons: Does not prevent the motorcycle being lifted into a van. Can be very embarrassing if

U-locks can be used to secure the bike to a solid object – ensure you purchase one which is long enough

you forget to remove the lock before attempting to ride off!

● Disc locks are designed to be attached to the front brake disc. The lock passes through one of the holes in the disc and prevents the wheel rotating by jamming against the fork/brake caliper **(see illustration 5)**. Some are equipped with an alarm siren which sounds if the disc lock is moved; this not only acts as a theft deterrent but also as a handy reminder if you try to move the bike with the lock still fitted.

● Combining the disc lock with a length of cable which can be looped around a post or railings provides an additional measure of security **(see illustration 6)**.

Alarms and immobilisers

Pros: Once installed it is completely hassle-free to use. If the system is 'Thatcham' or 'Sold Secure-approved', insurance companies may give you a discount.

Cons: Can be expensive to buy and complex to install. No system will prevent the motorcycle from being lifted into a van and taken away.

● Electronic alarms and immobilisers are available to suit a variety of budgets. There are three different types of system available: pure alarms, pure immobilisers, and the more expensive systems which are combined alarm/immobilisers **(see illustration 7)**.
● An alarm system is designed to emit an audible warning if the motorcycle is being tampered with.
● An immobiliser prevents the motorcycle being started and ridden away by disabling its electrical systems.
● When purchasing an alarm/immobiliser system, check the cost of installing the system unless you are able to do it yourself. If the motorcycle is not used regularly, another consideration is the current drain of the system. All alarm/immobiliser systems are powered by the motorcycle's battery; purchasing a system with a very low current drain could prevent the battery losing its charge whilst the motorcycle is not being used.

A typical disc lock attached through one of the holes in the disc

A disc lock combined with a security cable provides additional protection

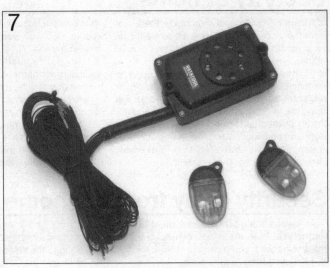

A typical alarm/immobiliser system

Indelible markings can be applied to most areas of the bike – always apply the manufacturer's sticker to warn off thieves

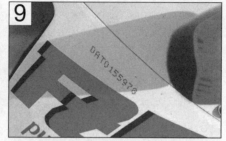

Chemically-etched code numbers can be applied to main body panels . . .

. . . again, always ensure that the kit manufacturer's sticker is applied in a prominent position

Security marking kits

Pros: *Very cheap and effective deterrent. Many insurance companies will give you a discount on your insurance premium if a recognised security marking kit is used on your motorcycle.*

Cons: *Does not prevent the motorcycle being stolen by joyriders.*

● There are many different types of security marking kits available. The idea is to mark as many parts of the motorcycle as possible with a unique security number **(see illustrations 8, 9 and 10)**. A form will be included with the kit to register your personal details and those of the motorcycle with the kit manufacturer. This register is made available to the police to help them trace the rightful owner of any motorcycle or components which they recover should all other forms of identification have been removed. Always apply the warning stickers provided with the kit to deter thieves.

Ground anchors, wheel clamps and security posts

Pros: *An excellent form of security which will deter all but the most determined of thieves.*

Cons: *Awkward to install and can be expensive.*

● Whilst the motorcycle is at home, it is a good idea to attach it securely to the floor or a solid wall, even if it is kept in a securely locked garage. Various types of ground anchors, security posts and wheel clamps are available for this purpose **(see illustration 11)**. These security devices are either bolted to a solid concrete or brick structure or can be cemented into the ground.

Permanent ground anchors provide an excellent level of security when the bike is at home

Security at home

A high percentage of motorcycle thefts are from the owner's home. Here are some things to consider whenever your motorcycle is at home:
● Where possible, always keep the motorcycle in a securely locked garage. Never rely solely on the standard lock on the garage door, these are usual hopelessly inadequate. Fit an additional locking mechanism to the door and consider having the garage alarmed. A security light, activated by a movement sensor, is also a good investment.

● Always secure the motorcycle to the ground or a wall, even if it is inside a securely locked garage.
● Do not regularly leave the motorcycle outside your home, try to keep it out of sight wherever possible. If a garage is not available, fit a motorcycle cover over the bike to disguise its true identity.
● It is not uncommon for thieves to follow a motorcyclist home to find out where the bike is kept. They will then return at a later date. Be aware of this whenever you are returning

home on your motorcycle. If you suspect you are being followed, do not return home, instead ride to a garage or shop and stop as a precaution.
● When selling a motorcycle, do not provide your home address or the location where the bike is normally kept. Arrange to meet the buyer at a location away from your home. Thieves have been known to pose as potential buyers to find out where motorcycles are kept and then return later to steal them.

Security away from the home

As well as fitting security equipment to your motorcycle here are a few general rules to follow whenever you park your motorcycle.
● Park in a busy, public place.
● Use car parks which incorporate security features, such as CCTV.

● At night, park in a well-lit area, preferably directly underneath a street light.
● Engage the steering lock.
● Secure the motorcycle to a solid, immovable object such as a post or railings with an additional lock. If this is not possible,

secure the bike to a friend's motorcycle. Some public parking places provide security loops for motorcycles.
● Never leave your helmet or luggage attached to the motorcycle. Take them with you at all times.

Lubricants and fluids

A wide range of lubricants, fluids and cleaning agents is available for motor-cycles. This is a guide as to what is available, its applications and properties.

Four-stroke engine oil

● Engine oil is without doubt the most important component of any four-stroke engine. Modern motorcycle engines place a lot of demands on their oil and choosing the right type is essential. Using an unsuitable oil will lead to an increased rate of engine wear and could result in serious engine damage. Before purchasing oil, always check the recommended oil specification given by the manufacturer. The manufacturer will state a recommended 'type or classification' and also a specific 'viscosity' range for engine oil.

● The oil 'type or classification' is identified by its API (American Petroleum Institute) rating. The API rating will be in the form of two letters, e.g. SG. The S identifies the oil as being suitable for use in a petrol (gasoline) engine (S stands for spark ignition) and the second letter, ranging from A to J, identifies the oil's performance rating. The later this letter, the higher the specification of the oil; for example API SG oil exceeds the requirements of API SF oil. **Note:** *On some oils there may also be a second rating consisting of another two letters, the first letter being C, e.g. API SF/CD. This rating indicates the oil is also suitable for use in a diesel engines (the C stands for compression ignition) and is thus of no relevance for motorcycle use.*

● The 'viscosity' of the oil is identified by its SAE (Society of Automotive Engineers) rating. All modern engines require multigrade oils and the SAE rating will consist of two numbers, the first followed by a W, e.g. 10W/40. The first number indicates the viscosity rating of the oil at low temperatures (W stands for winter – tested at –20°C) and the second number represents the viscosity of the oil at high temperatures (tested at 100°C). The lower the number, the thinner the oil. For example an oil with an SAE 10W/40 rating will give better cold starting and running than an SAE 15W/40 oil.

● As well as ensuring the 'type' and 'viscosity' of the oil match the recommendations, another consideration to make when buying engine oil is whether to purchase a standard mineral-based oil, a semi-synthetic oil (also known as a synthetic blend or synthetic-based oil) or a fully-synthetic oil. Although all oils will have a similar rating and viscosity, their cost will vary considerably; mineral-based oils are the cheapest, the fully-synthetic oils the most expensive with the semi-synthetic oils falling somewhere in-between. This decision is very much up to the owner, but it should be noted that modern synthetic oils have far better lubricating and cleaning qualities than traditional mineral-based oils and tend to retain these properties for far longer. Bearing in mind the operating conditions inside a modern, high-revving motorcycle engine it is highly recommended that a fully synthetic oil is used. The extra expense at each service could save you money in the long term by preventing premature engine wear.

● As a final note always ensure that the oil is specifically designed for use in motorcycle engines. Engine oils designed primarily for use in car engines sometimes contain additives or friction modifiers which could cause clutch slip on a motorcycle fitted with a wet-clutch.

Two-stroke engine oil

● Modern two-stroke engines, with their high power outputs, place high demands on their oil. If engine seizure is to be avoided it is essential that a high-quality oil is used. Two-stroke oils differ hugely from four-stroke oils. The oil lubricates only the crankshaft and piston(s) (the transmission has its own lubricating oil) and is used on a total-loss basis where it is burnt completely during the combustion process.

● The Japanese have recently introduced a classification system for two-stroke oils, the JASO rating. This rating is in the form of two letters, either FA, FB or FC – FA is the lowest classification and FC the highest. Ensure the oil being used meets or exceeds the recommended rating specified by the manufacturer.

● As well as ensuring the oil rating matches the recommendation, another consideration to make when buying engine oil is whether to purchase a standard mineral-based oil, a semi-synthetic oil (also known as a synthetic blend or synthetic-based oil) or a fully-synthetic oil. The cost of each type of oil varies considerably; mineral-based oils are the cheapest, the fully-synthetic oils the most expensive with the semi-synthetic oils falling somewhere in-between. This decision is very much up to the owner, but it should be noted that modern synthetic oils have far better lubricating properties and burn cleaner than traditional mineral-based oils. It is therefore recommended that a fully synthetic oil is used. The extra expense could save you money in the long term by preventing premature engine wear, engine performance will be improved, carbon deposits and exhaust smoke will be reduced.

● Always ensure that the oil is specifically designed for use in an injector system. Many high quality two-stroke oils are designed for competition use and need to be pre-mixed with fuel. These oils are of a much higher viscosity and are not designed to flow through the injector pumps used on road-going two-stroke motorcycles.

Transmission (gear) oil

● On a two-stroke engine, the transmission and clutch are lubricated by their own separate oil bath which must be changed in accordance with the Maintenance Schedule.
● Although the engine and transmission units of most four-strokes use a common lubrication supply, there are some exceptions where the engine and gearbox have separate oil reservoirs and a dry clutch is used.
● Motorcycle manufacturers will either recommend a monograde transmission oil or a four-stroke multigrade engine oil to lubricate the transmission.
● Transmission oils, or gear oils as they are often called, are designed specifically for use in transmission systems. The viscosity of these oils is represented by an SAE number, but the scale of measurement applied is different to that used to grade engine oils. As a rough guide a SAE90 gear oil will be of the same viscosity as an SAE50 engine oil.

Shaft drive oil

● On models equipped with shaft final drive, the shaft drive gears are will have their own oil supply. The manufacturer will state a recommended 'type or classification' and also a specific 'viscosity' range in the same manner as for four-stroke engine oil.
● Gear oil classification is given by the number which follows the API GL (GL standing for gear lubricant) rating, the higher the number, the higher the specification of the oil, e.g. API GL5 oil is a higher specification than API GL4 oil. Ensure the oil meets or

exceeds the classification specified and is of the correct viscosity. The viscosity of gear oils is also represented by an SAE number but the scale of measurement used is different to that used to grade engine oils. As a rough guide an SAE90 gear oil will be of the same viscosity as an SAE50 engine oil.
● If the use of an EP (Extreme Pressure) gear oil is specified, ensure the oil purchased is suitable.

Fork oil and suspension fluid

● Conventional telescopic front forks are hydraulic and require fork oil to work. To ensure the forks function correctly, the fork oil must be changed in accordance with the Maintenance Schedule.
● Fork oil is available in a variety of viscosities, identified by their SAE rating; fork oil ratings vary from light (SAE 5) to heavy (SAE 30). When purchasing fork oil, ensure the viscosity rating matches that specified by the manufacturer.
● Some lubricant manufacturers also produce a range of high-quality suspension fluids which are very similar to fork oil but are designed mainly for competition use. These fluids may have a different viscosity rating system which is not to be confused with the SAE rating of normal fork oil. Refer to the manufacturer's instructions if in any doubt.

Brake and clutch fluid

● All disc brake systems and some clutch systems are hydraulically operated. To ensure correct operation, the hydraulic fluid must be changed in accordance with the Maintenance Schedule.
● Brake and clutch fluid is classified by its DOT rating with most motorcycle manufacturers specifying DOT 3 or 4 fluid. Both fluid types are glycol-based and can be mixed together without adverse effect; DOT 4 fluid exceeds the requirements of DOT 3

fluid. Although it is safe to use DOT 4 fluid in a system designed for use with DOT 3 fluid, never use DOT 3 fluid in a system which specifies the use of DOT 4 as this will adversely affect the system's performance. The type required for the system will be marked on the fluid reservoir cap.
● Some manufacturers also produce a DOT 5 hydraulic fluid. DOT 5 hydraulic fluid is silicone-based and is not compatible with the glycol-based DOT 3 and 4 fluids. Never mix DOT 5 fluid with DOT 3 or 4 fluid as this will seriously affect the performance of the hydraulic system.

Coolant/antifreeze

● When purchasing coolant/antifreeze, always ensure it is suitable for use in an aluminium engine and contains corrosion inhibitors to prevent possible blockages of the internal coolant passages of the system. As a general rule, most coolants are designed to be used neat and should not be diluted whereas antifreeze can be mixed with distilled water to provide  a coolant solution of the required strength. Refer to the manufacturer's instructions on the bottle.
● Ensure the coolant is changed in accordance with the Maintenance Schedule.

Chain lube

● Chain lube is an aerosol-type spray lubricant specifically designed for use on motorcycle final drive chains. Chain lube has two functions, to minimise friction between the final drive chain and sprockets and to prevent corrosion of the chain. Regular use of a good-quality chain lube will extend the life of the drive chain and sprockets and thus maximise the power being transmitted from the transmission to the rear wheel.
● When using chain lube, always allow some time for the solvents in the lube to evaporate before riding the motorcycle. This will minimise the amount of lube which will

'fling' off from the chain when the motorcycle is used. If the motorcycle is equipped with an 'O-ring' chain, ensure the chain lube is labelled as being suitable for use on 'O-ring' chains.

Degreasers and solvents

● There are many different types of solvents and degreasers available to remove the grime and grease which accumulate around the motorcycle during normal use. Degreasers and solvents are usually available as an aerosol-type spray or as a liquid which you apply with a brush. Always closely follow the manufacturer's instructions and wear eye protection during use. Be aware that many solvents are flammable and may give off noxious fumes; take adequate precautions when using them (see Safety First!).

● For general cleaning, use one of the many solvents or degreasers available from most motorcycle accessory shops. These solvents are usually applied then left for a certain time before being washed off with water.

Brake cleaner is a solvent specifically designed to remove all traces of oil, grease and dust from braking system components. Brake cleaner is designed to evaporate quickly and leaves behind no residue.

Carburettor cleaner is an aerosol-type solvent specifically designed to clear carburettor blockages and break down the hard deposits and gum often found inside carburettors during overhaul.

Contact cleaner is an aerosol-type solvent designed for cleaning electrical components. The cleaner will remove all traces of oil and dirt from components such as switch contacts or fouled spark plugs and then dry, leaving behind no residue.

Gasket remover is an aerosol-type solvent designed for removing stubborn gaskets from engine components during overhaul. Gasket remover will minimise the amount of scraping required to remove the gasket and therefore reduce the risk of damage to the mating surface.

Spray lubricants

● Aerosol-based spray lubricants are widely available and are excellent for lubricating lever pivots and exposed cables and switches. Try to use a lubricant which is of the dry-film type as the fluid evaporates, leaving behind a dry-film of lubricant. Lubricants which leave behind an oily residue will attract dust and dirt which will increase the rate of wear of the cable/ lever.

● Most lubricants also act as a moisture dispersant and a penetrating fluid. This means they can also be used to 'dry out' electrical components such as wiring connectors or switches as well as helping to free seized fasteners.

Greases

● Grease is used to lubricate many of the pivot-points. A good-quality multi-purpose grease is suitable for most applications but some manufacturers will specify the use of specialist greases for use on components such as swingarm and suspension linkage bushes. These specialist greases can be purchased from most motorcycle (or car) accessory shops; commonly specified types include molybdenum disulphide grease, lithium-based grease, graphite-based grease, silicone-based grease and high-temperature copper-based grease.

Gasket sealing compounds

● Gasket sealing compounds can be used in conjunction with gaskets, to improve their sealing capabilities, or on their own to seal metal-to-metal joints. Depending on their type, sealing compounds either set hard or stay relatively soft and pliable.

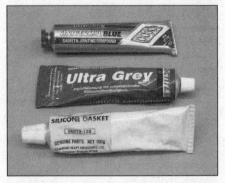

● When purchasing a gasket sealing compound, ensure that it is designed specifically for use on an internal combustion engine. General multi-purpose sealants available from DIY stores may appear visibly similar but they are not designed to withstand the extreme heat or contact with fuel and oil encountered when used on an engine (see 'Tools and Workshop Tips' for further information).

Thread locking compound

● Thread locking compounds are used to secure certain threaded fasteners in position to prevent them from loosening due to vibration. Thread locking compounds can be purchased from most motorcycle (and car) accessory shops. Ensure the threads of the both components are completely clean and dry before sparingly applying the locking compound (see 'Tools and Workshop Tips' for further information).

Fuel additives

● Fuel additives which protect and clean the fuel system components are widely available. These additives are designed to remove all traces of deposits that build up on the carburettors/injectors and prevent wear, helping the fuel system to operate more efficiently. If a fuel additive is being used, check that it is suitable for use with your motorcycle, especially if your motorcycle is equipped with a catalytic converter.

● Octane boosters are also available. These additives are designed to improve the performance of highly-tuned engines being run on normal pump-fuel and are of no real use on standard motorcycles.

Conversion factors

Length (distance)

Inches (in)	x 25.4	= Millimetres (mm)	x 0.0394	= Inches (in)
Feet (ft)	x 0.305	= Metres (m)	x 3.281	= Feet (ft)
Miles	x 1.609	= Kilometres (km)	x 0.621	= Miles

Volume (capacity)

Cubic inches (cu in; in^3)	x 16.387	= Cubic centimetres (cc; cm^3)	x 0.061	= Cubic inches (cu in; in^3)
Imperial pints (Imp pt)	x 0.568	= Litres (l)	x 1.76	= Imperial pints (Imp pt)
Imperial quarts (Imp qt)	x 1.137	= Litres (l)	x 0.88	= Imperial quarts (Imp qt)
Imperial quarts (Imp qt)	x 1.201	= US quarts (US qt)	x 0.833	= Imperial quarts (Imp qt)
US quarts (US qt)	x 0.946	= Litres (l)	x 1.057	= US quarts (US qt)
Imperial gallons (Imp gal)	x 4.546	= Litres (l)	x 0.22	= Imperial gallons (Imp gal)
Imperial gallons (Imp gal)	x 1.201	= US gallons (US gal)	x 0.833	= Imperial gallons (Imp gal)
US gallons (US gal)	x 3.785	= Litres (l)	x 0.264	= US gallons (US gal)

Mass (weight)

Ounces (oz)	x 28.35	= Grams (g)	x 0.035	= Ounces (oz)
Pounds (lb)	x 0.454	= Kilograms (kg)	x 2.205	= Pounds (lb)

Force

Ounces-force (ozf; oz)	x 0.278	= Newtons (N)	x 3.6	= Ounces-force (ozf; oz)
Pounds-force (lbf; lb)	x 4.448	= Newtons (N)	x 0.225	= Pounds-force (lbf; lb)
Newtons (N)	x 0.1	= Kilograms-force (kgf; kg)	x 9.81	= Newtons (N)

Pressure

Pounds-force per square inch (psi; lbf/in^2; lb/in^2)	x 0.070	= Kilograms-force per square centimetre (kgf/cm^2; kg/cm^2)	x 14.223	= Pounds-force per square inch (psi; lbf/in^2; lb/in^2)
Pounds-force per square inch (psi; lbf/in^2; lb/in^2)	x 0.068	= Atmospheres (atm)	x 14.696	= Pounds-force per square inch (psi; lbf/in^2; lb/in^2)
Pounds-force per square inch (psi; lbf/in^2; lb/in^2)	x 0.069	= Bars	x 14.5	= Pounds-force per square inch (psi; lbf/in^2; lb/in^2)
Pounds-force per square inch (psi; lbf/in^2; lb/in^2)	x 6.895	= Kilopascals (kPa)	x 0.145	= Pounds-force per square inch (psi; lbf/in^2; lb/in^2)
Kilopascals (kPa)	x 0.01	= Kilograms-force per square centimetre (kgf/cm^2; kg/cm^2)	x 98.1	= Kilopascals (kPa)
Millibar (mbar)	x 100	= Pascals (Pa)	x 0.01	= Millibar (mbar)
Millibar (mbar)	x 0.0145	= Pounds-force per square inch (psi; lbf/in^2; lb/in^2)	x 68.947	= Millibar (mbar)
Millibar (mbar)	x 0.75	= Millimetres of mercury (mmHg)	x 1.333	= Millibar (mbar)
Millibar (mbar)	x 0.401	= Inches of water (inH$_2$O)	x 2.491	= Millibar (mbar)
Millimetres of mercury (mmHg)	x 0.535	= Inches of water (inH$_2$O)	x 1.868	= Millimetres of mercury (mmHg)
Inches of water (inH$_2$O)	x 0.036	= Pounds-force per square inch (psi; lbf/in^2; lb/in^2)	x 27.68	= Inches of water (inH$_2$O)

Torque (moment of force)

Pounds-force inches (lbf in; lb in)	x 1.152	= Kilograms-force centimetre (kgf cm; kg cm)	x 0.868	= Pounds-force inches (lbf in; lb in)
Pounds-force inches (lbf in; lb in)	x 0.113	= Newton metres (Nm)	x 8.85	= Pounds-force inches (lbf in; lb in)
Pounds-force inches (lbf in; lb in)	x 0.083	= Pounds-force feet (lbf ft; lb ft)	x 12	= Pounds-force inches (lbf in; lb in)
Pounds-force feet (lbf ft; lb ft)	x 0.138	= Kilograms-force metres (kgf m; kg m)	x 7.233	= Pounds-force feet (lbf ft; lb ft)
Pounds-force feet (lbf ft; lb ft)	x 1.356	= Newton metres (Nm)	x 0.738	= Pounds-force feet (lbf ft; lb ft)
Newton metres (Nm)	x 0.102	= Kilograms-force metres (kgf m; kg m)	x 9.804	= Newton metres (Nm)

Power

Horsepower (hp)	x 745.7	= Watts (W)	x 0.0013	= Horsepower (hp)

Velocity (speed)

Miles per hour (miles/hr; mph)	x 1.609	= Kilometres per hour (km/hr; kph)	x 0.621	= Miles per hour (miles/hr; mph)

Fuel consumption*

Miles per gallon, Imperial (mpg)	x 0.354	= Kilometres per litre (km/l)	x 2.825	= Miles per gallon, Imperial (mpg)
Miles per gallon, US (mpg)	x 0.425	= Kilometres per litre (km/l)	x 2.352	= Miles per gallon, US (mpg)

Temperature

Degrees Fahrenheit = (°C x 1.8) + 32   Degrees Celsius (Degrees Centigrade; °C) = (°F - 32) x 0.56

It is common practice to convert from miles per gallon (mpg) to litres/100 kilometres (l/100km), where mpg x l/100 km = 282

About the MOT Test

In the UK, all vehicles more than three years old are subject to an annual test to ensure that they meet minimum safety requirements. A current test certificate must be issued before a machine can be used on public roads, and is required before a road fund licence can be issued. Riding without a current test certificate will also invalidate your insurance.

For most owners, the MOT test is an annual cause for anxiety, and this is largely due to owners not being sure what needs to be checked prior to submitting the motorcycle for testing. The simple answer is that a fully roadworthy motorcycle will have no difficulty in passing the test.

This is a guide to getting your motorcycle through the MOT test. Obviously it will not be possible to examine the motorcycle to the same standard as the professional MOT tester, particularly in view of the equipment required for some of the checks. However, working through the following procedures will enable you to identify any problem areas before submitting the motorcycle for the test.

It has only been possible to summarise the test requirements here, based on the regulations in force at the time of printing. Test standards are becoming increasingly stringent, although there are some exemptions for older vehicles. More information about the MOT test can be obtained from the TSO publications, *How Safe is your Motorcycle* and *The MOT Inspection Manual for Motorcycle Testing*.

Many of the checks require that one of the wheels is raised off the ground. If the motorcycle doesn't have a centre stand, note that an auxiliary stand will be required. Additionally, the help of an assistant may prove useful.

Certain exceptions apply to machines under 50 cc, machines without a lighting system, and Classic bikes - if in doubt about any of the requirements listed below seek confirmation from an MOT tester prior to submitting the motorcycle for the test.

Check that the frame number is clearly visible.

Electrical System

Lights, turn signals, horn and reflector

● With the ignition on, check the operation of the following electrical components. **Note:** *The electrical components on certain small-capacity machines are powered by the generator, requiring that the engine is run for this check.*

a) *Headlight and tail light. Check that both illuminate in the low and high beam switch positions.*
b) *Position lights. Check that the front position (or sidelight) and tail light illuminate in this switch position.*
c) *Turn signals. Check that all flash at the correct rate, and that the warning light(s) function correctly. Check that the turn signal switch works correctly.*
d) *Hazard warning system (where fitted). Check that all four turn signals flash in this switch position.*
e) *Brake stop light. Check that the light comes on when the front and rear brakes are independently applied. Models first used on or after 1st April 1986 must have a brake light switch on each brake.*
f) *Horn. Check that the sound is continuous and of reasonable volume.*

● Check that there is a red reflector on the rear of the machine, either mounted separately or as part of the tail light lens.
● Check the condition of the headlight, tail light and turn signal lenses.

Headlight beam height

● The MOT tester will perform a headlight beam height check using specialised beam setting equipment **(see illustration 1)**. This equipment will not be available to the home mechanic, but if you suspect that the headlight is incorrectly set or may have been maladjusted in the past, you can perform a rough test as follows.
● Position the bike in a straight line facing a brick wall. The bike must be off its stand, upright and with a rider seated. Measure the height from the ground to the centre of the headlight and mark a horizontal line on the wall at this height. Position the motorcycle 3.8 metres from the wall and draw a vertical

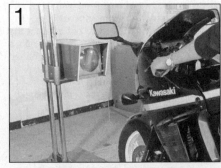

Headlight beam height checking equipment

line up the wall central to the centreline of the motorcycle. Switch to dipped beam and check that the beam pattern falls slightly lower than the horizontal line and to the left of the vertical line **(see illustration 2).**

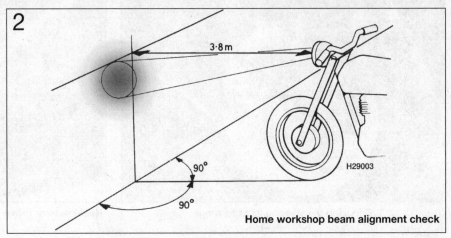

Home workshop beam alignment check

Exhaust System and Final Drive

Exhaust

● Check that the exhaust mountings are secure and that the system does not foul any of the rear suspension components.
● Start the motorcycle. When the revs are increased, check that the exhaust is neither holed nor leaking from any of its joints. On a linked system, check that the collector box is not leaking due to corrosion.

● Note that the exhaust decibel level ("loudness" of the exhaust) is assessed at the discretion of the tester. If the motorcycle was first used on or after 1st January 1985 the silencer must carry the BSAU 193 stamp, or a marking relating to its make and model, or be of OE (original equipment) manufacture. If the silencer is marked NOT FOR ROAD USE, RACING USE ONLY or similar, it will fail the MOT.

Final drive

● On chain or belt drive machines, check that the chain/belt is in good condition and does not have excessive slack. Also check that the sprocket is securely mounted on the rear wheel hub. Check that the chain/belt guard is in place.
● On shaft drive bikes, check for oil leaking from the drive unit and fouling the rear tyre.

Steering and Suspension

Steering

● With the front wheel raised off the ground, rotate the steering from lock to lock. The handlebar or switches must not contact the fuel tank or be close enough to trap the rider's hand. Problems can be caused by damaged lock stops on the lower yoke and frame, or by the fitting of non-standard handlebars.
● When performing the lock to lock check, also ensure that the steering moves freely without drag or notchiness. Steering movement can be impaired by poorly routed cables, or by overtight head bearings or worn bvearings. The tester will perform a check of the steering head bearing lower race by mounting the front wheel on a surface plate, then performing a lock to

lock check with the weight of the machine on the lower bearing **(see illustration 3)**.
● Grasp the fork sliders (lower legs) and attempt to push and pull on the forks

Front wheel mounted on a surface plate for steering head bearing lower race check

(see illustration 4). Any play in the steering head bearings will be felt. Note that in extreme cases, wear of the front fork bushes can be misinterpreted for head bearing play.
● Check that the handlebars are securely mounted.
● Check that the handlebar grip rubbers are secure. They should by bonded to the bar left end and to the throttle cable pulley on the right end.

Front suspension

● With the motorcycle off the stand, hold the front brake on and pump the front forks up and down **(see illustration 5)**. Check that they are adequately damped.

Checking the steering head bearings for freeplay

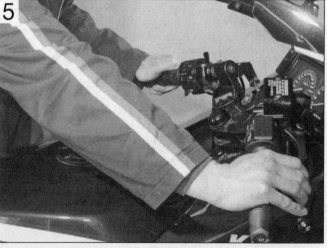

Hold the front brake on and pump the front forks up and down to check operation

Inspect the area around the fork dust seal for oil leakage (arrow)

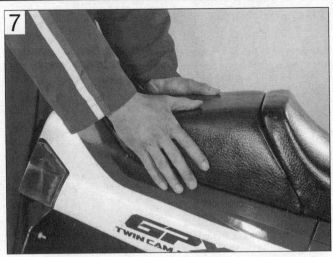

Bounce the rear of the motorcycle to check rear suspension operation

Checking for rear suspension linkage play

● Inspect the area above and around the front fork oil seals **(see illustration 6)**. There should be no sign of oil on the fork tube (stanchion) nor leaking down the slider (lower leg). On models so equipped, check that there is no oil leaking from the anti-dive units.

● On models with swingarm front suspension, check that there is no freeplay in the linkage when moved from side to side.

Rear suspension

● With the motorcycle off the stand and an assistant supporting the motorcycle by its handlebars, bounce the rear suspension **(see illustration 7)**. Check that the suspension components do not foul on any of the cycle parts and check that the shock absorber(s) provide adequate damping.

● Visually inspect the shock absorber(s) and check that there is no sign of oil leakage from its damper. This is somewhat restricted on certain single shock models due to the location of the shock absorber.

● With the rear wheel raised off the ground, grasp the wheel at the highest point and attempt to pull it up **(see illustration 8)**. Any play in the swingarm pivot or suspension linkage bearings will be felt as movement. **Note:** Do not confuse play with actual suspension movement. Failure to lubricate suspension linkage bearings can lead to bearing failure **(see illustration 9)**.

● With the rear wheel raised off the ground, grasp the swingarm ends and attempt to move the swingarm from side to side and forwards and backwards - any play indicates wear of the swingarm pivot bearings **(see illustration 10)**.

Worn suspension linkage pivots (arrows) are usually the cause of play in the rear suspension

Grasp the swingarm at the ends to check for play in its pivot bearings

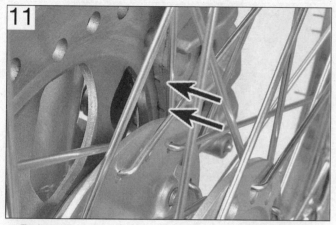

Brake pad wear can usually be viewed without removing the caliper. Most pads have wear indicator grooves (arrowed) and some also have indicator tangs or cut-outs.

On drum brakes, check the angle of the operating lever with the brake fully applied. Most drum brakes have a wear indicator pointer or scale.

Brakes, Wheels and Tyres

Brakes

● With the wheel raised off the ground, apply the brake then free it off, and check that the wheel is about to revolve freely without brake drag.
● On disc brakes, examine the disc itself. Check that it is securely mounted and not cracked.
● On disc brakes, view the pad material through the caliper mouth and check that the pads are not worn down beyond the limit (see illustration 11).
● On drum brakes, check that when the brake is applied the angle between the operating lever and cable or rod is not too great (see illustration 12). Check also that the operating lever doesn't foul any other components.
● On disc brakes, examine the flexible hoses from top to bottom. Have an assistant hold the brake on so that the fluid in the hose is under pressure, and check that there is no sign of fluid leakage, bulges or cracking. If there are any metal brake pipes or unions, check that these are free from corrosion and damage. Where a brake-linked anti-dive system is fitted, check the hoses to the anti-dive in a similar manner.
● Check that the rear brake torque arm is secure and that its fasteners are secured by self-locking nuts or castellated nuts with split-pins or R-pins (see illustration 13).
● On models with ABS, check that the self-check warning light in the instrument panel works.
● The MOT tester will perform a test of the motorcycle's braking efficiency based on a calculation of rider and motorcycle weight. Although this cannot be carried out at home, you can at least ensure that the braking systems are properly maintained. For hydraulic disc brakes, check the fluid level, lever/pedal feel (bleed of air if its spongy) and pad material. For drum brakes, check adjustment, cable or rod operation and shoe lining thickness.

Wheels and tyres

● Check the wheel condition. Cast wheels should be free from cracks and if of the built-up design, all fasteners should be secure. Spoked wheels should be checked for broken, corroded, loose or bent spokes.
● With the wheel raised off the ground, spin the wheel and visually check that the tyre and wheel run true. Check that the tyre does not foul the suspension or mudguards.
● With the wheel raised off the ground, grasp the wheel and attempt to move it about the axle (spindle) (see illustration 14). Any play felt here indicates wheel bearing failure.

Brake torque arm must be properly secured at both ends

Check for wheel bearing play by trying to move the wheel about the axle (spindle)

Checking the tyre tread depth

Tyre direction of rotation arrow can be found on tyre sidewall

Castellated type wheel axle (spindle) nut must be secured by a split pin or R-pin

Two straightedges are used to check wheel alignment

- If the tyre sidewall carries a direction of rotation arrow, this must be pointing in the direction of normal wheel rotation **(see illustration 16)**.
- Check that the wheel axle (spindle) nuts (where applicable) are properly secured. A self-locking nut or castellated nut with a split-pin or R-pin can be used **(see illustration 17)**.
- Wheel alignment is checked with the motorcycle off the stand and a rider seated. With the front wheel pointing straight ahead, two perfectly straight lengths of metal or wood and placed against the sidewalls of both tyres **(see illustration 18)**. The gap each side of the front tyre must be equidistant on both sides. Incorrect wheel alignment may be due to a cocked rear wheel (often as the result of poor chain adjustment) or in extreme cases, a bent frame.

- Check the tyre tread depth, tread condition and sidewall condition **(see illustration 15)**.
- Check the tyre type. Front and rear tyre types must be compatible and be suitable for road use. Tyres marked NOT FOR ROAD USE, COMPETITION USE ONLY or similar, will fail the MOT.

General checks and condition

- Check the security of all major fasteners, bodypanels, seat, fairings (where fitted) and mudguards.

- Check that the rider and pillion footrests, handlebar levers and brake pedal are securely mounted.

- Check for corrosion on the frame or any load-bearing components. If severe, this may affect the structure, particularly under stress.

Sidecars

A motorcycle fitted with a sidecar requires additional checks relating to the stability of the machine and security of attachment and swivel joints, plus specific wheel alignment (toe-in) requirements. Additionally, tyre and lighting requirements differ from conventional motorcycle use. Owners are advised to check MOT test requirements with an official test centre.

Preparing for storage

Before you start

If repairs or an overhaul is needed, see that this is carried out now rather than left until you want to ride the bike again.

Give the bike a good wash and scrub all dirt from its underside. Make sure the bike dries completely before preparing for storage.

Engine

● Remove the spark plug(s) and lubricate the cylinder bores with approximately a teaspoon of motor oil using a spout-type oil can **(see illustration 1)**. Reinstall the spark plug(s). Crank the engine over a couple of times to coat the piston rings and bores with oil. If the bike has a kickstart, use this to turn the engine over. If not, flick the kill switch to the OFF position and crank the engine over on the starter **(see illustration 2)**. If the nature on the ignition system prevents the starter operating with the kill switch in the OFF position, remove

the spark plugs and fit them back in their caps; ensure that the plugs are earthed (grounded) against the cylinder head when the starter is operated **(see Illustration 3)**.

> ⚠️ **Warning: It is important that the plugs are earthed (grounded) away from the spark plug holes otherwise there is a risk of atomised fuel from the cylinders igniting.**

> **HAYNES HiNT** *On a single cylinder four-stroke engine, you can seal the combustion chamber completely by positioning the piston at TDC on the compression stroke.*

● Drain the carburettor(s) otherwise there is a risk of jets becoming blocked by gum deposits from the fuel **(see illustration 4)**.

● If the bike is going into long-term storage, consider adding a fuel stabiliser to the fuel in the tank. If the tank is drained completely, corrosion of its internal surfaces may occur if left unprotected for a long period. The tank can be treated with a rust preventative especially for this purpose. Alternatively, remove the tank and pour half a litre of motor oil into it, install the filler cap and shake the tank to coat its internals with oil before draining off the excess. The same effect can also be achieved by spraying WD40 or a similar water-dispersant around the inside of the tank via its flexible nozzle.

● Make sure the cooling system contains the correct mix of antifreeze. Antifreeze also contains important corrosion inhibitors.

● The air intakes and exhaust can be sealed off by covering or plugging the openings. Ensure that you do not seal in any condensation; run the engine until it is hot,

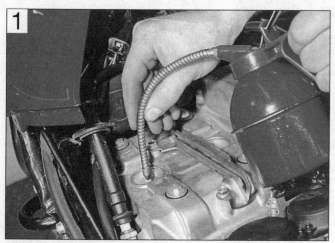

Squirt a drop of motor oil into each cylinder

Flick the kill switch to OFF . . .

. . . and ensure that the metal bodies of the plugs (arrows) are earthed against the cylinder head

Connect a hose to the carburettor float chamber drain stub (arrow) and unscrew the drain screw

Exhausts can be sealed off with a plastic bag

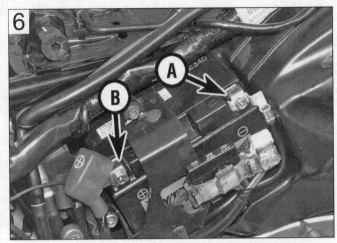

Disconnect the negative lead (A) first, followed by the positive lead (B)

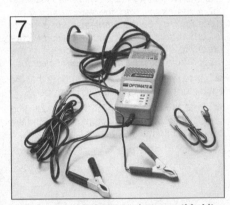

Use a suitable battery charger - this kit also assess battery condition

then switch off and allow to cool. Tape a piece of thick plastic over the silencer end(s) (see illustration 5). Note that some advocate pouring a tablespoon of motor oil into the silencer(s) before sealing them off.

Battery

● Remove it from the bike - in extreme cases of cold the battery may freeze and crack its case (see illustration 6).

● Check the electrolyte level and top up if necessary (conventional refillable batteries). Clean the terminals.
● Store the battery off the motorcycle and away from any sources of fire. Position a wooden block under the battery if it is to sit on the ground.
● Give the battery a trickle charge for a few hours every month (see illustration 7).

Tyres

● Place the bike on its centrestand or an auxiliary stand which will support the motorcycle in an upright position. Position wood blocks under the tyres to keep them off the ground and to provide insulation from damp. If the bike is being put into long-term storage, ideally both tyres should be off the ground; not only will this protect the tyres, but will also ensure that no load is placed on the steering head or wheel bearings.
● Deflate each tyre by 5 to 10 psi, no more or the beads may unseat from the rim, making subsequent inflation difficult on tubeless tyres.

Pivots and controls

● Lubricate all lever, pedal, stand and footrest

pivot points. If grease nipples are fitted to the rear suspension components, apply lubricant to the pivots.
● Lubricate all control cables.

Cycle components

● Apply a wax protectant to all painted and plastic components. Wipe off any excess, but don't polish to a shine. Where fitted, clean the screen with soap and water.
● Coat metal parts with Vaseline (petroleum jelly). When applying this to the fork tubes, do not compress the forks otherwise the seals will rot from contact with the Vaseline.
● Apply a vinyl cleaner to the seat.

Storage conditions

● Aim to store the bike in a shed or garage which does not leak and is free from damp.
● Drape an old blanket or bedspread over the bike to protect it from dust and direct contact with sunlight (which will fade paint). This also hides the bike from prying eyes. Beware of tight-fitting plastic covers which may allow condensation to form and settle on the bike.

Getting back on the road

Engine and transmission

● Change the oil and replace the oil filter. If this was done prior to storage, check that the oil hasn't emulsified - a thick whitish substance which occurs through condensation.
● Remove the spark plugs. Using a spout-type oil can, squirt a few drops of oil into the cylinder(s). This will provide initial lubrication as the piston rings and bores comes back into contact. Service the spark plugs, or fit new ones, and install them in the engine.

● Check that the clutch isn't stuck on. The plates can stick together if left standing for some time, preventing clutch operation. Engage a gear and try rocking the bike back and forth with the clutch lever held against the handlebar. If this doesn't work on cable-operated clutches, hold the clutch lever back against the handlebar with a strong elastic band or cable tie for a couple of hours (see illustration 8).
● If the air intakes or silencer end(s) were blocked off, remove the bung or cover used.
● If the fuel tank was coated with a rust

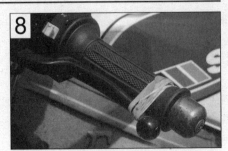

Hold clutch lever back against the handlebar with elastic bands or a cable tie

preventative, oil or a stabiliser added to the fuel, drain and flush the tank and dispose of the fuel sensibly. If no action was taken with the fuel tank prior to storage, it is advised that the old fuel is disposed of since it will go off over a period of time. Refill the fuel tank with fresh fuel.

Frame and running gear

● Oil all pivot points and cables.
● Check the tyre pressures. They will definitely need inflating if pressures were reduced for storage.
● Lubricate the final drive chain (where applicable).
● Remove any protective coating applied to the fork tubes (stanchions) since this may well destroy the fork seals. If the fork tubes weren't protected and have picked up rust spots, remove them with very fine abrasive paper and refinish with metal polish.
● Check that both brakes operate correctly. Apply each brake hard and check that it's not possible to move the motorcycle forwards, then check that the brake frees off again once released. Brake caliper pistons can stick due to corrosion around the piston head, or on the sliding caliper types, due to corrosion of the slider pins. If the brake doesn't free after repeated operation, take the caliper off for examination. Similarly drum brakes can stick

due to a seized operating cam, cable or rod linkage.
● If the motorcycle has been in long-term storage, renew the brake fluid and clutch fluid (where applicable).
● Depending on where the bike has been stored, the wiring, cables and hoses may have been nibbled by rodents. Make a visual check and investigate disturbed wiring loom tape.

Battery

● If the battery has been previously removal and given top up charges it can simply be reconnected. Remember to connect the positive cable first and the negative cable last.
● On conventional refillable batteries, if the battery has not received any attention, remove it from the motorcycle and check its electrolyte level. Top up if necessary then charge the battery. If the battery fails to hold a charge and a visual checks show heavy white sulphation of the plates, the battery is probably defective and must be renewed. This is particularly likely if the battery is old. Confirm battery condition with a specific gravity check.
● On sealed (MF) batteries, if the battery has not received any attention, remove it from the motorcycle and charge it according to the information on the battery case - if the battery fails to hold a charge it must be renewed.

Starting procedure

● If a kickstart is fitted, turn the engine over a couple of times with the ignition OFF to distribute oil around the engine. If no kickstart is fitted, flick the engine kill switch OFF and the ignition ON and crank the engine over a couple of times to work oil around the upper cylinder components. If the nature of the ignition system is such that the starter won't work with the kill switch OFF, remove the spark plugs, fit them back into their caps and earth (ground) their bodies on the cylinder head. Reinstall the spark plugs afterwards.
● Switch the kill switch to RUN, operate the choke and start the engine. If the engine won't start don't continue cranking the engine - not only will this flatten the battery, but the starter motor will overheat. Switch the ignition off and try again later. If the engine refuses to start, go through the fault finding procedures in this manual. **Note:** *If the bike has been in storage for a long time, old fuel or a carburettor blockage may be the problem. Gum deposits in carburettors can block jets - if a carburettor cleaner doesn't prove successful the carburettors must be dismantled for cleaning.*
● Once the engine has started, check that the lights, turn signals and horn work properly.
● Treat the bike gently for the first ride and check all fluid levels on completion. Settle the bike back into the maintenance schedule.

This Section provides an easy reference-guide to the more common faults that are likely to afflict your machine. Obviously, the opportunities are almost limitless for faults to occur as a result of obscure failures, and to try and cover all eventualities would require a book. Indeed, a number have been written on the subject.

Successful troubleshooting is not a mysterious 'black art' but the application of a bit of knowledge combined with a systematic and logical approach to the problem. Approach any troubleshooting by first accurately identifying the symptom and then checking through the list of possible causes, starting with the simplest or most obvious and progressing in stages to the most complex.

Take nothing for granted, but above all apply liberal quantities of common sense.

The main symptom of a fault is given in the text as a major heading below which are listed the various systems or areas which may contain the fault. Details of each possible cause for a fault and the remedial action to be taken are given, in brief, in the paragraphs below each heading. Further information should be sought in the relevant Chapter.

1 Engine doesn't start or is difficult to start

- [ ] Starter motor doesn't rotate
- [ ] Starter motor rotates but engine does not turn over
- [ ] Starter works but engine won't turn over (seized)
- [ ] No fuel flow
- [ ] Engine flooded
- [ ] No spark or weak spark
- [ ] Compression low
- [ ] Stalls after starting
- [ ] Rough idle

2 Poor running at low speed

- [ ] Spark weak
- [ ] Fuel/air mixture incorrect
- [ ] Compression low
- [ ] Poor acceleration

3 Poor running or no power at high speed

- [ ] Firing incorrect
- [ ] Fuel/air mixture incorrect
- [ ] Compression low
- [ ] Knocking or pinking
- [ ] Miscellaneous causes

4 Overheating

- [ ] Engine overheats
- [ ] Firing incorrect
- [ ] Fuel/air mixture incorrect
- [ ] Compression too high
- [ ] Engine load excessive
- [ ] Lubrication inadequate
- [ ] Miscellaneous causes

5 Clutch problems

- [ ] Clutch slipping
- [ ] Clutch not disengaging completely

6 Gearchange problems

- [ ] Doesn't go into gear, or lever doesn't return
- [ ] Jumps out of gear
- [ ] Overselects

7 Abnormal engine noise

- [ ] Knocking or pinking
- [ ] Piston slap or rattling
- [ ] Valve noise
- [ ] Other noise

8 Abnormal driveline noise

- [ ] Clutch noise
- [ ] Transmission noise
- [ ] Final drive noise

9 Abnormal frame and suspension noise

- [ ] Front end noise
- [ ] Shock absorber noise
- [ ] Brake noise

10 Oil pressure warning light comes on

- [ ] Engine lubrication system
- [ ] Electrical system

11 Excessive exhaust smoke

- [ ] White smoke
- [ ] Black smoke
- [ ] Brown smoke

12 Poor handling or stability

- [ ] Handlebar hard to turn
- [ ] Handlebar shakes or vibrates excessively
- [ ] Handlebar pulls to one side
- [ ] Poor shock absorbing qualities

13 Braking problems

- [ ] Brakes are spongy, don't hold
- [ ] Brake lever or pedal pulsates
- [ ] Brakes drag

14 Electrical problems

- [ ] Battery dead or weak
- [ ] Battery overcharged

1 Engine doesn't start or is difficult to start

Starter motor doesn't rotate

- ☐ Engine kill switch OFF.
- ☐ Fuse blown. Check main, ignition, starter circuit and engine management fuses (Chapter 8).
- ☐ Battery voltage low. Check and recharge battery (Chapter 8).
- ☐ Starter motor defective. Make sure the wiring to the starter is secure. Make sure the starter relay clicks when the starter button is pushed. If the relay clicks, then the fault is in the wiring or motor.
- ☐ Starter relay or starter circuit relay faulty. Check as described in Chapter 8.
- ☐ Starter button not contacting. The contacts could be wet, corroded or dirty. Disassemble and clean the switch (Chapter 8).
- ☐ Wiring open or shorted. Check all wiring connectors to make sure that they are dry, tight and not corroded. Also check for broken or frayed wires and wiring insulation that can cause a short to ground (earth) (see wiring diagrams, Chapter 8).
- ☐ Ignition switch defective. Check the switch as described in Chapter 8. Replace the switch with a new one if it is defective.
- ☐ Engine kill switch defective. Check for wet, dirty, corroded or broken contacts. Clean or renew the switch as necessary (Chapter 8).
- ☐ Faulty neutral, sidestand or clutch switch. Check the wiring to each switch and the switch itself as described in Chapter 8.

Starter motor rotates but engine does not turn over

- ☐ Starter clutch defective. Inspect and repair or renew (Chapter 2).
- ☐ Damaged idler or starter gears. Inspect and renew the damaged parts (Chapter 2).

No fuel flow

- ☐ No fuel in tank.
- ☐ Fuel tank breather hose obstructed.
- ☐ Fuel pump faulty, or strainer and/or filter is blocked (see Chapter 4).
- ☐ Fuel hose clogged, or connector not properly fitted onto union.
- ☐ Fuel injector clogged or faulty. For all of the injectors to be clogged, either a very bad batch of fuel with an unusual additive has been used, or some other foreign material has entered the tank. Many times after a machine has been stored for many months without running, the fuel turns to a varnish-like liquid.

Engine flooded

- ☐ Fuel injector stuck open. The Triumph diagnostic tool is required to check the injectors (see Chapter 4).
- ☐ Starting technique incorrect. Under normal circumstances (i.e., if the fuel injection system is sound) the machine should start with no throttle, whatever the temperature.

No spark or weak spark

- ☐ Ignition switch OFF.
- ☐ Engine kill switch turned to the OFF position.
- ☐ Battery voltage low. Check and recharge the battery as necessary (Chapter 8).
- ☐ Spark plugs dirty, defective or worn out. Locate reason for fouled plugs using spark plug condition chart on the inside rear cover and follow the plug maintenance procedures (Chapter 1).
- ☐ Ignition coil wiring faulty or connector loose. Check condition and connector fitting (Chapter 1).
- ☐ Electronic control module (ECM) defective. Check it, referring to Chapter 4 for details.
- ☐ Crankshaft position sensor defective. Check it, referring to Chapter 4 for details.
- ☐ Ignition coil(s) defective. Check the coils, referring to Chapter 4.
- ☐ Ignition or kill switch shorted. This is usually caused by water, corrosion, damage or excessive wear. The switches can be disassembled and cleaned with electrical contact cleaner. If cleaning does not help, renew the switches (Chapter 8).
- ☐ Wiring shorted or broken in the ignition and starting circuit. Make sure that all connectors are clean, dry and tight. Look for chafed and broken wires (Chapters 4 and 8).

Compression low

- ☐ Spark plugs loose. Remove the plugs and inspect their threads. Reinstall and tighten to the specified torque (Chapter 1).
- ☐ Cylinder head not sufficiently tightened down. If the cylinder head is loose, then there's a chance that the gasket or head is damaged. Tighten the cylinder head bolts to the correct torque in the proper sequence (Chapter 2).
- ☐ Incorrect valve clearance. If the valve is not closing completely then engine pressure will leak past the valve. Check and adjust the valve clearances (Chapter 1).
- ☐ Cylinder liner and/or piston worn. Excessive wear will cause compression pressure to leak past the rings. This is usually accompanied by worn rings as well. A top-end overhaul is necessary (Chapter 2).
- ☐ Piston rings worn, weak, broken, or sticking. Broken or sticking piston rings usually indicate a lubrication or fuelling problem that causes excess carbon deposits to form on the pistons and rings. Top-end overhaul is necessary (Chapter 2).
- ☐ Piston ring-to-groove clearance excessive. This is caused by excessive wear of the piston ring lands. Piston renewal is necessary (Chapter 2).
- ☐ Cylinder head gasket damaged. If the head is allowed to become loose, or if excessive carbon build-up on the piston crown and combustion chamber causes extremely high compression, the head gasket may leak. Retorquing the head is not always sufficient to restore the seal, so gasket renewal is necessary (Chapter 2).
- ☐ Cylinder head warped. This is caused by overheating or improperly tightened head bolts. Machine shop resurfacing or head renewal is necessary (Chapter 2).
- ☐ Valve spring broken or weak. Caused by component failure or wear; the springs must be renewed (Chapter 2).
- ☐ Valve not seating properly. This is caused by a bent valve (from over-revving or improper valve adjustment), burned valve or seat (improper combustion) or an accumulation of carbon deposits on the seat (from combustion or lubrication problems). The valves must be cleaned and/or renewed and the seats serviced if possible (Chapter 2).

Stalls after starting

- ☐ Ignition malfunction. See Chapter 4.
- ☐ Fuel injection or engine management system malfunction. See Chapter 4.
- ☐ Fuel contaminated. The fuel can be contaminated with either dirt or water, or can change chemically if the machine is allowed to sit for several months or more. Drain the tank, fuel hoses and fuel rail (Chapter 4).
- ☐ Intake air leak. Check for loose throttle body-to-intake manifold connections or a leaking gasket (Chapter 4).
- ☐ Idle air control unit faulty. The unit can only be checked using the Triumph diagnostic tool (see Chapter 4).

1 Engine doesn't start or is difficult to start (continued)

Rough idle

- [ ] Ignition malfunction. See Chapter 4.
- [ ] Idle air control unit faulty. The unit can only be checked using the Triumph diagnostic tool (see Chapter 4).
- [ ] Throttle bodies not synchronised (see Chapter 1).
- [ ] Fuel injection or engine management system malfunction. See Chapter 4.

- [ ] Fuel contaminated. The fuel can be contaminated with either dirt or water, or can change chemically if the machine is allowed to sit for several months or more. Drain the tank, fuel hoses and fuel rail (Chapter 4).
- [ ] Intake air leak. Check for loose throttle body-to-intake duct connections or loose duct bolts or failed O-ring (Chapter 4).
- [ ] Air filter clogged. Fit a new air filter element (Chapter 1).

2 Poor running at low speeds

Spark weak

- [ ] Battery voltage low. Check and recharge battery (Chapter 8).
- [ ] Spark plugs fouled, defective or worn out. Refer to Chapter 1 for spark plug maintenance.
- [ ] Ignition coil faulty or loose wiring. Check condition. Renew if cracks or deterioration are evident (Chapter 4).
- [ ] Electronic control module (ECM) defective. Check it, referring to Chapter 4 for details.

Fuel/air mixture incorrect

- [ ] Fuel injector clogged or fuel injection system malfunction (see Chapter 4).
- [ ] Air filter clogged, poorly sealed or missing (Chapter 1).
- [ ] Air filter housing poorly sealed. Look for cracks, holes or loose clamps and renew or repair defective parts.
- [ ] Fuel tank breather hose obstructed.
- [ ] Intake air leak. Check for loose throttle body-to-intake duct connections or loose duct bolts or failed O-ring (Chapter 4).
- [ ] Idle air control unit faulty. The unit can only be checked using the Triumph diagnostic tool (see Chapter 4).
- [ ] Fuel injection or engine management system malfunction. See Chapter 4.

Compression low

- [ ] Spark plugs loose. Remove the plugs and inspect their threads. Reinstall and tighten to the specified torque (Chapter 1).
- [ ] Cylinder head not sufficiently tightened down. If the cylinder head is loose, then there's a chance that the gasket or head is damaged. Tighten the cylinder head bolts to the correct torque in the proper sequence (Chapter 2).
- [ ] Incorrect valve clearance. If a valve is not closing completely then engine pressure will leak past the valve. Check and adjust the valve clearances (Chapter 1).
- [ ] Cylinder liner and/or piston worn. Excessive wear will cause compression pressure to leak past the rings. This is usually accompanied by worn rings as well. A top-end overhaul is necessary (Chapter 2).
- [ ] Piston rings worn, weak, broken, or sticking. Broken or sticking piston rings usually indicate a lubrication or fuelling problem that causes excess carbon deposits to form on the pistons and rings. Top-end overhaul is necessary (Chapter 2).
- [ ] Piston ring-to-groove clearance excessive. This is caused by excessive wear of the piston ring lands. Piston renewal is necessary (Chapter 2).
- [ ] Cylinder head gasket damaged. If the head is allowed to become loose, or if excessive carbon build-up on the piston crown and combustion chamber causes extremely high compression, the head gasket may leak. Retorquing the head is not always sufficient to restore the seal, so gasket renewal is necessary (Chapter 2).
- [ ] Cylinder head warped. This is caused by overheating or improperly tightened head bolts. Machine shop resurfacing or head renewal is necessary (Chapter 2).
- [ ] Valve spring broken or weak. Caused by component failure or wear; the springs must be renewed (Chapter 2).
- [ ] Valve not seating properly. This is caused by a bent valve (from over-revving or improper valve adjustment), burned valve or seat (improper combustion) or an accumulation of carbon deposits on the seat (from combustion or lubrication problems). The valves must be cleaned and/or renewed and the seats serviced if possible (Chapter 2).

Poor acceleration

- [ ] Intake air leak. Check for loose throttle body-to-intake duct connections or loose duct bolts or failed O-ring (Chapter 4).
- [ ] Timing not advancing. The ECM or a sensor in the engine management system may be defective. If so, they must be renewed as they can't be repaired. The systems can only be checked using the Triumph diagnostic tool – see Chapter 4 for details.
- [ ] Throttle bodies not synchronised (see Chapter 1).
- [ ] Engine oil viscosity too high. Using a heavier oil than that recommended in Pre-ride checks can damage the oil pump or lubrication system and cause drag on the engine.
- [ ] Brakes dragging. Usually caused by debris which has entered the brake piston seals, or from a warped disc or bent axle. Repair as necessary (Chapter 6).
- [ ] On Daytona models faulty intake air duct flap or faulty exhaust control valve (Chapter 4).

3 Poor running or no power at high speed

Firing incorrect

☐ Air filter restricted. Clean or renew the filter (Chapter 1).
☐ Spark plugs fouled, defective or worn out. See Chapter 1 for spark plug maintenance.
☐ Ignition coil or wiring defective. See Chapters 1 and 4 for details of the ignition system.
☐ Incorrect spark plugs. Wrong type, heat range or cap configuration. Check and install correct plugs listed in Chapter 1.
☐ Electronic control module (ECM) defective. Check it, referring to Chapter 4 for details.

Fuel/air mixture incorrect

☐ Fuel injector clogged or fuel injection system malfunction (see Chapter 4).
☐ Air filter clogged, poorly sealed or missing (Chapter 1).
☐ Air filter housing poorly sealed. Look for cracks, holes or loose clamps and renew or repair defective parts.
☐ Fuel tank breather hose obstructed.
☐ Intake air leak. Check for loose throttle body-to-intake duct connections or loose duct bolts or failed O-ring (Chapter 4).
☐ Idle air control unit faulty. The unit can only be checked using the Triumph diagnostic tool (see Chapter 4).
☐ Fuel injection or engine management system malfunction. See Chapter 4.

Compression low

☐ Spark plugs loose. Remove the plugs and inspect their threads. Reinstall and tighten to the specified torque (Chapter 1).
☐ Cylinder head not sufficiently tightened down. If the cylinder head is loose, then there's a chance that the gasket or head is damaged. Tighten the cylinder head bolts to the correct torque in the proper sequence (Chapter 2).
☐ Incorrect valve clearance. If the valve is not closing completely then engine pressure will leak past the valve. Check and adjust the valve clearances (Chapter 1).
☐ Cylinder liner and/or piston worn. Excessive wear will cause compression pressure to leak past the rings. This is usually accompanied by worn rings as well. A top-end overhaul is necessary (Chapter 2).
☐ Piston rings worn, weak, broken, or sticking. Broken or sticking piston rings usually indicate a lubrication or fuelling problem that causes excess carbon deposits to form on the pistons and rings. Top-end overhaul is necessary (Chapter 2).
☐ Piston ring-to-groove clearance excessive. This is caused by excessive wear of the piston ring lands. Piston renewal is necessary (Chapter 2).
☐ Cylinder head gasket damaged. If the head is allowed to become loose, or if excessive carbon build-up on the piston crown and combustion chamber causes extremely high compression, the head gasket may leak. Retorquing the head is not always sufficient to restore the seal, so gasket renewal is necessary (Chapter 2).
☐ Cylinder head warped. This is caused by overheating or improperly tightened head bolts. Machine shop resurfacing or head renewal is necessary (Chapter 2).
☐ Valve spring broken or weak. Caused by component failure or wear; the springs must be renewed (Chapter 2).
☐ Valve not seating properly. This is caused by a bent valve (from over-revving or improper valve adjustment), burned valve or seat (improper combustion) or an accumulation of carbon deposits on the seat (from combustion or lubrication problems). The valves must be cleaned and/or renewed and the seats serviced if possible (Chapter 2).

Knocking or pinking

☐ Carbon build-up in combustion chamber. Use of a fuel additive that will dissolve the adhesive bonding the carbon particles to the crown and chamber is the easiest way to remove the build-up. Otherwise, the cylinder head will have to be removed and decarbonised (Chapter 2).
☐ Incorrect or poor quality fuel. Old or improper grades of fuel can cause detonation. This causes the piston to rattle, thus the knocking or pinking sound. Drain old fuel and always use the recommended fuel grade.
☐ Spark plug heat range incorrect. Uncontrolled detonation indicates the plug heat range is too hot. The plug in effect becomes a glow plug, raising cylinder temperatures. Install the proper heat range plug (Chapter 1).
☐ Improper air/fuel mixture. This will cause the cylinders to run hot, which leads to detonation. Clogged injectors or an air leak can cause this imbalance, as could a fault in the engine management system which controls the fuel injection. See Chapter 4.

Miscellaneous causes

☐ Throttles don't open fully. Check the cable and the twistgrip, and then the throttle bodies themselves (Chapters 1 and 4).
☐ Clutch slipping. May be caused by loose or worn clutch components. Refer to Chapter 2 for clutch overhaul procedures.
☐ Timing not advancing. The ECM or a sensor in the engine management system may be defective. If so, they must be renewed with new ones, as they can't be repaired. The system can only be checked using the Triumph diagnostic tool – see Chapter 4 for details.
☐ Engine oil viscosity too high. Using a heavier oil than the one recommended in Chapter 1 can damage the oil pump or lubrication system and cause drag on the engine.
☐ Brakes dragging. Usually caused by debris which has entered the brake piston seals, or from a warped disc or bent axle. Repair as necessary.
☐ On Daytona models faulty intake air duct flap or faulty exhaust control valve (Chapter 4).

4 Overheating

Engine overheats

☐ Coolant level low. Check and add coolant (Pre-ride checks).
☐ Leak in cooling system. Check cooling system hoses and radiator for leaks and other damage. Repair or renew parts as necessary (Chapter 3).
☐ Thermostat sticking open or closed. Check and renew as described in Chapter 3.
☐ Faulty radiator cap. Remove the cap and have it pressure tested.
☐ Coolant passages clogged. Drain and flush the system, then refill with fresh coolant (Chapter 1).
☐ Water pump defective. Remove the pump and check the components (Chapter 3).
☐ Clogged radiator fins. Clean them by blowing compressed air through the fins from the rear of the radiator.
☐ Cooling fan not cutting in. Cooling fan or fan relay fault (Chapter 3). Coolant temperature sensor faulty or ECM faulty (Chapter 4)

Firing incorrect

☐ Air filter restricted. Clean or renew filter (Chapter 1).
☐ Spark plugs fouled, defective or worn out. See Chapter 1 for spark plug maintenance.
☐ HT coil or wiring defective. See Chapters 1 and 4 for details of the ignition system.
☐ Incorrect spark plugs. Wrong type, heat range or cap configuration. Check and install correct plugs listed in Chapter 1.
☐ Electronic control module (ECM) defective. Check it, referring to Chapter 4 for details.

Fuel/air mixture incorrect

☐ Fuel injector clogged or fuel injection system malfunction (see Chapter 4).
☐ Air filter clogged, poorly sealed or missing (Chapter 1).
☐ Air filter housing poorly sealed. Look for cracks, holes or loose clamps and renew or repair defective parts.
☐ Fuel tank breather hose obstructed.
☐ Intake air leak. Check for loose throttle body-to-intake duct connections or loose duct bolts or failed O-ring (Chapter 4).
☐ Idle air control unit faulty. The unit can only be checked using the Triumph diagnostic tool (see Chapter 4).
☐ Fuel injection or engine management system malfunction. See Chapter 4.

Compression too high

☐ Carbon build-up in combustion chamber. Use of a fuel additive that will dissolve the adhesive bonding the carbon particles to the piston crown and chamber is the easiest way to remove the build-up. Otherwise, the cylinder head will have to be removed and decarbonised (Chapter 2).
☐ Improperly machined head surface or installation of incorrect gasket during engine assembly.

Engine load excessive

☐ Clutch slipping. Can be caused by damaged, loose or worn clutch components. Refer to Chapter 2 for overhaul procedures.
☐ Engine oil level too high. The addition of too much oil will cause pressurisation of the crankcase and inefficient engine operation. Check Specifications and drain to proper level (Chapter 1).
☐ Engine oil viscosity too high. Using a heavier oil than the one recommended in Pre-ride checks can damage the oil pump or lubrication system as well as cause drag on the engine.
☐ Brakes dragging. Usually caused by debris which has entered the brake piston seals, or from a warped disc or bent axle. Repair as necessary.

Lubrication inadequate

☐ Engine oil level too low. Friction caused by intermittent lack of lubrication or from oil that is overworked can cause overheating. The oil provides a definite cooling function in the engine. Check the oil level (Pre-ride checks).
☐ Poor quality engine oil or incorrect viscosity or type. Oil is rated not only according to viscosity but also according to type. Some oils are not rated high enough for use in this engine. Change to the correct oil (Pre-ride checks).

Miscellaneous causes

☐ Modification to exhaust system. Most aftermarket exhaust systems cause the engine to run leaner, which make them run hotter. Before installing an accessory exhaust system, always check with the exhaust manufacturer or Triumph themselves, as you may well need an adjustment to the engine management system, which can only be done using a diagnostic tool.

5 Clutch problems

Clutch slipping

☐ Insufficient clutch cable freeplay. Check and adjust (Chapter 1).
☐ Friction plates worn or warped. Overhaul the clutch assembly (Chapter 2).
☐ Plain plates warped (Chapter 2).
☐ Clutch springs broken, sagged or weak. Replace the springs with new ones (Chapter 2).
☐ Clutch release mechanism defective. Remove the clutch cover and check the mechanism (Chapter 2).
☐ Clutch centre or housing unevenly worn. This causes improper engagement of the plates. Renew the damaged or worn parts (Chapter 2).

Clutch not disengaging completely

☐ Excessive clutch cable freeplay. Check and adjust (Chapter 1).
☐ Clutch plates warped or damaged. This will cause clutch drag, which in turn will cause the machine to creep. Overhaul the clutch assembly (Chapter 2).

☐ Clutch spring tension uneven. Usually caused by a sagged or broken spring. Check and renew the springs as a set (Chapter 2).
☐ Engine oil deteriorated. Old, thin, worn out oil will not provide proper lubrication for the plates, causing the clutch to drag. Change the oil and filter (Chapter 1).
☐ Engine oil viscosity too high. Using a heavier oil than recommended can cause the plates to stick together, putting a drag on the engine. Change to the correct weight oil (Pre-ride checks).
☐ Clutch housing sleeve seized on input shaft. Lack of lubrication, severe wear or damage can cause the sleeve to seize on the shaft. Overhaul of the clutch, and perhaps transmission, may be necessary to repair the damage (Chapter 2).
☐ Clutch release mechanism defective. Remove the clutch cover and check the mechanism (Chapter 2).
☐ Loose clutch centre nut. Causes housing and centre misalignment putting a drag on the engine. Engagement adjustment continually varies. Overhaul the clutch assembly (Chapter 2).

6 Gearchange problems

Doesn't go into gear or lever doesn't return

☐ Clutch not disengaging. See above.
☐ Selector fork(s) bent or seized. Often caused by dropping the machine or from lack of lubrication. Overhaul the transmission (Chapter 2).
☐ Gear pinion(s) stuck on shaft. Most often caused by a lack of lubrication or excessive wear in transmission bearings and bushings. Overhaul the transmission (Chapter 2).
☐ Selector drum binding. Caused by lubrication failure or excessive wear. Renew the drum and bearing (Chapter 2).
☐ Gearchange lever return spring weak or broken (Chapter 2).
☐ Gearchange lever broken. Splines stripped out of lever or shaft, caused by allowing the lever to get loose or from dropping the machine. Renew necessary parts (Chapter 2).
☐ Gearchange mechanism stopper arm broken or worn. Full engagement and rotary movement of selector drum results. Renew the arm (Chapter 2).
☐ Stopper arm spring broken. Allows arm to float, causing sporadic gearchange operation. Renew spring (Chapter 2).

☐ Gearchange mechanism selector arm pawl broken or worn. The selector arm pawls aren't engaging correctly with the pins on the selector drum cam plate. Check the entire mechanism (Chapter 2).

Jumps out of gear

☐ Selector fork(s) worn. Overhaul the transmission (Chapter 2).
☐ Gear groove(s) worn. Overhaul the transmission (Chapter 2).
☐ Gear dogs or dog slots worn or damaged. The gears should be inspected and renewed. No attempt should be made to service the worn parts.

Overselects

☐ Stopper arm spring weak or broken (Chapter 2).
☐ Gearchange shaft return spring post broken or distorted (Chapter 2).
☐ Gearchange mechanism stopper arm broken or worn. Full engagement and rotary movement of selector drum results. Renew the arm (Chapter 2).

7 Abnormal engine noise

Knocking or pinking

☐ Carbon build-up in combustion chamber. Use of a fuel additive that will dissolve the adhesive bonding the carbon particles to the piston crown and chamber is the easiest way to remove the build-up. Otherwise, the cylinder head will have to be removed and decarbonised (Chapter 2).

☐ Incorrect or poor quality fuel. Old or improper fuel can cause detonation. This causes the pistons to rattle, thus the knocking or pinking sound. Drain the old fuel and always use the recommended grade fuel (Chapter 4).

☐ Spark plug heat range incorrect. Uncontrolled detonation indicates that the plug heat range is too hot. The plug in effect becomes a glow plug, raising cylinder temperatures. Install the proper heat range plug (Chapter 1).

☐ Improper air/fuel mixture. This will cause the cylinders to run hot and lead to detonation. Clogged injectors or an air leak can cause this imbalance. See Chapter 4.

Piston slap or rattling

☐ Cylinder-to-piston clearance excessive. Caused by improper assembly. Inspect and overhaul top-end parts (Chapter 2).

☐ Connecting rod bent. Caused by over-revving, trying to start a badly flooded engine or from ingesting a foreign object into the combustion chamber. Renew the damaged parts (Chapter 2).

☐ Piston pin or piston pin bore worn or seized from wear or lack of lubrication. Renew damaged parts (Chapter 2).

☐ Piston ring(s) worn, broken or sticking. Overhaul the top-end (Chapter 2).

☐ Piston seizure damage. Usually from lack of lubrication or overheating. Renew the pistons and cylinder liners, as necessary (Chapter 2).

☐ Connecting rod upper or lower end clearance excessive. Caused by excessive wear or lack of lubrication. Renew worn parts.

Valve noise

☐ Incorrect valve clearances. Adjust the clearances by referring to Chapter 1.

☐ Valve spring broken or weak. Check and renew weak valve springs (Chapter 2).

☐ Camshaft or cylinder head worn or damaged. Lack of lubrication at high rpm is usually the cause of damage. Insufficient oil or failure to change the oil at the recommended intervals are the chief causes. Since there are no replaceable bearings in the head, the head itself will have to be renewed if there is excessive wear or damage (Chapter 2).

Other noise

☐ Cylinder head gasket leaking.

☐ Exhaust pipe leaking at cylinder head connection. Caused by improper fit of pipe(s), loose nuts or broken gasket(s). All exhaust fasteners should be tightened evenly and carefully. Failure to do this will lead to a leak. If there is still a leak after tightening, remove the downpipe assembly and install new gaskets (Chapter 4).

☐ Crankshaft runout excessive. Caused by a bent crankshaft (from over-revving) or damage from a top-end component failure. Can also be attributed to dropping the machine on either of the crankshaft ends.

☐ Engine mounting loose. Tighten all engine mounts in the order stated to the correct torque settings (Chapter 2).

☐ Crankshaft bearings worn (Chapter 2).

☐ Camchain, guide blades or tensioner worn. Renew according to the procedure in Chapter 2.

8 Abnormal driveline noise

Clutch noise
- [ ] Clutch housing/friction plate clearance excessive (Chapter 2).
- [ ] Loose or damaged clutch pressure plate and/or bolts (Chapter 2).

Transmission noise
- [ ] Bearings worn. Also includes the possibility that the shafts are worn. Overhaul the transmission (Chapter 2).
- [ ] Gears worn or chipped (Chapter 2).
- [ ] Metal chips jammed in gear teeth. Probably pieces from a broken clutch, gear or selector mechanism that were picked up by the gears. This will cause early bearing failure (Chapter 2).

- [ ] Engine oil level too low. Causes a howl from transmission. Also affects engine power and clutch operation (Pre-ride checks).

Final drive noise
- [ ] Chain not adjusted properly (Chapter 1).
- [ ] Front or rear sprocket loose. Tighten fasteners (Chapter 5).
- [ ] Sprockets worn. Renew sprockets and chain (Chapter 5).
- [ ] Sprocket coupling or hub assembly bearings worn, or loose axle nut, or damaged cush drive. Check and tighten or renew, according to model (Chapter 5).

9 Abnormal frame and suspension noise

Front end noise
- [ ] Low fork oil level or improper viscosity. This can sound like spurting and is usually accompanied by irregular fork action (Chapter 5).
- [ ] Spring weak or broken. Makes a clicking or scraping sound. Fork oil, when drained, will have a lot of metal particles in it (Chapter 5).
- [ ] Steering head bearings loose or damaged. Clicks when braking. Check and adjust or renew as necessary (Chapters 1 and 5).
- [ ] Fork yokes loose. Make sure all clamp bolts are tightened to the specified torque (Chapter 5).
- [ ] Fork tube bent. Good possibility if machine has been dropped. Replace tube with a new one (Chapter 5).
- [ ] Front axle bolt or axle clamp bolts loose. Tighten them to the specified torque (Chapter 6).
- [ ] Loose or worn wheel bearings. Check and renew if necessary (Chapter 6).

Shock absorber noise
- [ ] Fluid level incorrect. Indicates a leak caused by defective seal. Shock will be covered with oil. Renew shock or seek advice on repair from a Triumph dealer or suspension specialist (Chapter 5).
- [ ] Defective shock absorber with internal damage. This is in the body of the shock and can't be remedied. The shock must be replaced with a new one (Chapter 5).

- [ ] Bent or damaged shock body. Replace the shock with a new one (Chapter 5).
- [ ] Loose or worn suspension linkage components. Check and renew if necessary (Chapter 5).

Brake noise
- [ ] Squeal caused by pad shim not installed or positioned correctly (where fitted) (Chapter 6).
- [ ] Squeal caused by dust on brake pads. Usually found in combination with glazed pads. Clean using brake cleaning solvent (Chapter 6).
- [ ] Contamination of brake pads. Oil, brake fluid or dirt causing brake to chatter or squeal. Clean or renew pads (Chapter 6).
- [ ] Pads glazed. Caused by excessive heat from prolonged use or from contamination. Do not use sandpaper, emery cloth, carborundum cloth or any other abrasive to roughen the pad surfaces as abrasives will stay in the pad material and damage the disc. A very fine flat file can be used, but pad renewal is suggested as a cure (Chapter 6).
- [ ] Disc warped. Can cause a chattering, clicking or intermittent squeal. Usually accompanied by a pulsating lever and uneven braking. Renew the disc (Chapter 6).
- [ ] Loose or worn wheel bearings. Check and renew if necessary (Chapter 6).

10 Oil pressure warning light comes on

Engine lubrication system
- [ ] Engine oil pump defective, blocked oil strainer gauze or failed relief valve. Carry out an oil pressure check (Chapter 2).
- [ ] Engine oil level low. Inspect for leak or other problem causing low oil level and add recommended oil (Pre-ride checks).
- [ ] Engine oil viscosity too low. Very old, thin oil or an improper weight of oil used in the engine. Change to correct oil (Chapter 1).
- [ ] Camshaft or journals worn. Excessive wear causing drop in oil pressure. Renew cam and/or cylinder head (Chapter 2). Abnormal

wear could be caused by oil starvation at high rpm from low oil level or improper weight or type of oil.
- [ ] Crankshaft and/or bearings worn. Same problems as above. Check and renew crankshaft and/or bearings (Chapter 2).

Electrical system
- [ ] Oil pressure switch defective. Check the switch according to the procedure in Chapter 8. Renew it if it is defective.
- [ ] Oil pressure warning light circuit defective. Check for pinched, shorted, disconnected or damaged wiring (Chapter 8).

11 Excessive exhaust smoke

White smoke

- [ ] Piston oil ring worn. The ring may be broken or damaged, causing oil from the crankcase to be pulled past the piston into the combustion chamber. Replace the rings with new ones (Chapter 2).
- [ ] Cylinders worn, cracked, or scored. Caused by overheating or oil starvation. Install new liners (Chapter 2).
- [ ] Valve stem seal damaged or worn. Remove valves and replace seals with new ones (Chapter 2).
- [ ] Valve guide worn. Perform a complete valve job (Chapter 2).
- [ ] Engine oil level too high, which causes the oil to be forced past the rings. Drain oil to the proper level (Chapter 1 and *Pre-ride checks*).
- [ ] Head gasket broken between oil return and cylinder. Causes oil to be pulled into the combustion chamber. Renew the head gasket and check the head for warpage (Chapter 2).
- [ ] Abnormal crankcase pressurisation, which forces oil past the rings. Clogged breather is usually the cause.

Black smoke

- [ ] Air filter clogged. Clean or renew the element (Chapter 1).
- [ ] Fuel injection system or idle air control unit malfunction (Chapter 4). These systems can only be checked using the Triumph diagnostic tool. Refer to Chapter 4 for further information.
- [ ] Fuel pressure too high. Check the fuel pressure regulator (Chapter 4).

Brown smoke

- [ ] Fuel pump faulty or pressure regulator stuck open (Chapter 4).
- [ ] Throttle body-to-intake manifold bolts loose or gasket broken (Chapter 4).
- [ ] Air filter poorly sealed or not installed (Chapter 1).
- [ ] Fuel injection system malfunction (Chapter 4).

12 Poor handling or stability

Handlebar hard to turn

- [ ] Steering head bearing adjuster nut too tight. Check adjustment as described in Chapter 1.
- [ ] Bearings damaged. Roughness can be felt as the bars are turned from side-to-side. Renew bearings and races (Chapter 5).
- [ ] Races dented or worn. Denting results from wear in only one position (e.g. straight-ahead), from a collision or hitting a pothole or from dropping the machine. Renew races and bearings (Chapter 5).
- [ ] Steering stem lubrication inadequate. Causes are grease getting hard from age or being washed out by high pressure car washes. Disassemble steering head and repack bearings (Chapter 5).
- [ ] Steering stem bent. Caused by a collision, hitting a pothole or by dropping the machine. Renew damaged part. Don't try to straighten the steering stem (Chapter 5).
- [ ] Front tyre air pressure too low (*Pre-ride checks*).

Handlebar shakes or vibrates excessively

- [ ] Tyres worn or out of balance (Chapter 6).
- [ ] Swingarm bearings worn. Renew worn bearings (Chapter 5).
- [ ] Wheel rim(s) warped or damaged. Inspect wheels for runout (Chapter 6).
- [ ] Wheel bearings worn. Worn front or rear wheel bearings can cause poor tracking. Worn front bearings will cause wobble (Chapter 6).
- [ ] Handlebar clamp bolts loose (Chapter 5).
- [ ] Fork clamp bolts loose in yoke(s). Tighten them to the specified torque (Chapter 5).
- [ ] Engine mounting bolts loose. Will cause excessive vibration with increased engine rpm (Chapter 2).

Handlebar pulls to one side

- [ ] Frame bent. Definitely suspect this if the machine has been dropped. May or may not be accompanied by cracking near the bend. Renew the frame (Chapter 5).
- [ ] Wheels out of alignment. Caused by improper location of axle spacers or from bent steering stem or frame (Chapter 5).
- [ ] Swingarm bent or twisted. Caused by age (metal fatigue) or impact damage. Renew the arm (Chapter 5).
- [ ] Steering stem bent. Caused by impact damage or by dropping the motorcycle. Renew the steering stem (Chapter 5).
- [ ] Fork tube bent. Disassemble the forks and renew the damaged parts (Chapter 5).
- [ ] Fork oil level uneven. Check and add or drain as necessary (Chapter 5).

Poor shock absorbing qualities

- [ ] Too hard:
    - a) *Fork oil level too high (Chapter 5).*
    - b) *Fork oil viscosity too high. Use a lighter oil.*
    - c) *Fork tube bent. Causes a harsh, sticking feeling (Chapter 5).*
    - d) *Rear shock shaft or body bent or damaged (Chapter 5).*
    - e) *Fork internal damage (Chapter 5).*
    - f) *Rear shock internal damage.*
    - g) *Tyre pressure too high (Pre-ride checks).*
- [ ] Too soft:
    - a) *Fork or shock oil insufficient and/or leaking (Chapter 5).*
    - b) *Fork oil level too low (Chapter 5).*
    - c) *Fork oil viscosity too light (Chapter 5).*
    - d) *Fork springs weak or broken (Chapter 5).*
    - e) *Rear shock internal damage or leakage (Chapter 5).*

13 Braking problems

Brakes are spongy, don't hold

☐ Air in brake line. Caused by inattention to master cylinder fluid level or by leakage. Locate problem and bleed brakes (Chapter 6).
☐ Pad or disc worn (Chapters 1 and 6).
☐ Brake fluid leak. Locate leak and renew faulty seals or hose as necessary (Chapter 6).
☐ Contaminated pads. Caused by contamination with oil, grease, brake fluid, etc. Renew the pads. Clean disc thoroughly with brake cleaner (Chapter 6).
☐ Brake fluid deteriorated. Fluid is old or contaminated. Drain system, replenish with new fluid and bleed the system (Chapter 6).
☐ Master cylinder internal parts worn or damaged causing fluid to bypass (Chapter 6).
☐ Master cylinder bore scratched by foreign material or broken spring. Repair or renew master cylinder (Chapter 6).
☐ Disc warped. Renew disc(s) (Chapter 6).

Brake lever or pedal pulsates

☐ Disc warped. Renew disc(s) (Chapter 6).

☐ Axle bent. Renew axle (Chapter 6).
☐ Brake caliper bolts loose (Chapter 6).
☐ Brake caliper slider pins damaged or sticking (rear caliper only), causing caliper to bind. Lubricate the sliders or renew them if they are corroded or bent (Chapter 6).
☐ Wheel warped or otherwise damaged (Chapter 6).
☐ Wheel bearings damaged or worn (Chapter 6).

Brakes drag

☐ Master cylinder piston seized. Caused by wear or damage to piston or cylinder bore (Chapter 6).
☐ Lever balky or stuck. Check pivot and lubricate (Chapter 6).
☐ Brake caliper binds (sliding type caliper only). Caused by corrosion or inadequate lubrication or damage on caliper slider pins (Chapter 6).
☐ Brake caliper piston seized in bore. Caused by wear or ingestion of dirt past deteriorated seal (Chapter 6).
☐ Brake pad damaged. Pad material separated from backing plate. Usually caused by faulty manufacturing process or from contact with chemicals. Renew pads (Chapter 6).
☐ Pads improperly installed (Chapter 6).

14 Electrical problems

Battery dead or weak

☐ Battery faulty. Caused by sulphated plates which are shorted through sedimentation. Also, broken battery terminal making only occasional contact (Chapter 8).
☐ Battery cables making poor contact (Chapter 8).
☐ Load excessive. Caused by addition of high wattage lights or other electrical accessories.
☐ Ignition switch defective. Switch either earths (grounds) internally or fails to shut off system. Renew the switch (Chapter 8).
☐ Regulator/rectifier defective (Chapter 8).
☐ Alternator defective (Chapter 8).

☐ Wiring faulty. Wiring earthed (grounded) or connections loose in ignition, charging or lighting circuits (Chapter 8).

Battery overcharged

☐ Regulator/rectifier defective. Overcharging is noticed when battery gets excessively warm (Chapter 8).
☐ Battery defective. Replace battery with a new one (Chapter 8).
☐ Battery amperage too low, wrong type or size. Install manufacturer's specified amp-hour battery to handle charging load (Chapter 8).

A

ABS (Anti-lock braking system) A system, usually electronically controlled, that senses incipient wheel lockup during braking and relieves hydraulic pressure at wheel which is about to skid.

Aftermarket Components suitable for the motorcycle, but not produced by the motorcycle manufacturer.

Allen key A hexagonal wrench which fits into a recessed hexagonal hole.

Alternating current (ac) Current produced by an alternator. Requires converting to direct current by a rectifier for charging purposes.

Alternator Converts mechanical energy from the engine into electrical energy to charge the battery and power the electrical system.

Ampere (amp) A unit of measurement for the flow of electrical current. Current = Volts ÷ Ohms.

Ampere-hour (Ah) Measure of battery capacity.

Angle-tightening A torque expressed in degrees. Often follows a conventional tightening torque for cylinder head or main bearing fasteners **(see illustration).**

Angle-tightening con-rod bolts

Antifreeze A substance (usually ethylene glycol) mixed with water, and added to the cooling system, to prevent freezing of the coolant in winter. Antifreeze also contains chemicals to inhibit corrosion and the formation of rust and other deposits that would tend to clog the radiator and coolant passages and reduce cooling efficiency.

Anti-dive System attached to the fork lower leg (slider) to prevent fork dive when braking hard.

Anti-seize compound A coating that reduces the risk of seizing on fasteners that are subjected to high temperatures, such as exhaust clamp bolts and nuts.

API American Petroleum Institute. A quality standard for 4-stroke motor oils.

Asbestos A natural fibrous mineral with great heat resistance, commonly used in the composition of brake friction materials. Asbestos is a health hazard and the dust created by brake systems should never be inhaled or ingested.

ATF Automatic Transmission Fluid. Often used in front forks.

ATU Automatic Timing Unit. Mechanical device for advancing the ignition timing on early engines.

ATV All Terrain Vehicle. Often called a Quad.

Axial play Side-to-side movement.

Axle A shaft on which a wheel revolves. Also known as a spindle.

B

Backlash The amount of movement between meshed components when one component is held still. Usually applies to gear teeth.

Ball bearing A bearing consisting of a hardened inner and outer race with hardened steel balls between the two races.

Bearings Used between two working surfaces to prevent wear of the components and a build-up of heat. Four types of bearing are commonly used on motorcycles: plain shell bearings, ball bearings, tapered roller bearings and needle roller bearings.

Bevel gears Used to turn the drive through 90°. Typical applications are shaft final drive and camshaft drive **(see illustration).**

Bevel gears are used to turn the drive through 90°

BHP Brake Horsepower. The British measurement for engine power output. Power output is now usually expressed in kilowatts (kW).

Bias-belted tyre Similar construction to radial tyre, but with outer belt running at an angle to the wheel rim.

Big-end bearing The bearing in the end of the connecting rod that's attached to the crankshaft.

Bleeding The process of removing air from an hydraulic system via a bleed nipple or bleed screw.

Bottom-end A description of an engine's crankcase components and all components contained there-in.

BTDC Before Top Dead Centre in terms of piston position. Ignition timing is often expressed in terms of degrees or millimetres BTDC.

Bush A cylindrical metal or rubber component used between two moving parts.

Burr Rough edge left on a component after machining or as a result of excessive wear.

C

Cam chain The chain which takes drive from the crankshaft to the camshaft(s).

Canister The main component in an evaporative emission control system (California market only); contains activated charcoal granules to trap vapours from the fuel system rather than allowing them to vent to the atmosphere.

Castellated Resembling the parapets along the top of a castle wall. For example, a castellated wheel axle or spindle nut.

Catalytic converter A device in the exhaust system of some machines which converts certain pollutants in the exhaust gases into less harmful substances.

Charging system Description of the components which charge the battery, ie the alternator, rectifer and regulator.

Circlip A ring-shaped clip used to prevent endwise movement of cylindrical parts and shafts. An internal circlip is installed in a groove in a housing; an external circlip fits into a groove on the outside of a cylindrical piece such as a shaft. Also known as a snap-ring.

Clearance The amount of space between two parts. For example, between a piston and a cylinder, between a bearing and a journal, etc.

Coil spring A spiral of elastic steel found in various sizes throughout a vehicle, for example as a springing medium in the suspension and in the valve train.

Compression Reduction in volume, and increase in pressure and temperature, of a gas, caused by squeezing it into a smaller space.

Compression damping Controls the speed the suspension compresses when hitting a bump.

Compression ratio The relationship between cylinder volume when the piston is at top dead centre and cylinder volume when the piston is at bottom dead centre.

Continuity The uninterrupted path in the flow of electricity. Little or no measurable resistance.

Continuity tester Self-powered bleeper or test light which indicates continuity.

Cp Candlepower. Bulb rating commonly found on US motorcycles.

Crossply tyre Tyre plies arranged in a criss-cross pattern. Usually four or six plies used, hence 4PR or 6PR in tyre size codes.

Cush drive Rubber damper segments fitted between the rear wheel and final drive sprocket to absorb transmission shocks **(see illustration).**

Cush drive rubbers dampen out transmission shocks

D

Decarbonisation The process of removing carbon deposits - typically from the combustion chamber, valves and exhaust port/system.

Degree disc Calibrated disc for measuring piston position. Expressed in degrees.

Detonation Destructive and damaging explosion of fuel/air mixture in combustion chamber instead of controlled burning.

Dial gauge Clock-type gauge with adapters for measuring runout and piston position. Expressed in mm or inches.

Diaphragm The rubber membrane in a master cylinder or carburettor which seals the upper chamber.

Diaphragm spring A single sprung plate often used in clutches.

Direct current (dc) Current produced by a dc generator.

Diode An electrical valve which only allows current to flow in one direction. Commonly used in rectifiers and starter interlock systems.

Disc valve (or rotary valve) A induction system used on some two-stroke engines.

Double-overhead camshaft (DOHC) An engine that uses two overhead camshafts, one for the intake valves and one for the exhaust valves.

Drivebelt A toothed belt used to transmit drive to the rear wheel on some motorcycles. A drivebelt has also been used to drive the camshafts. Drivebelts are usually made of Kevlar.

Driveshaft Any shaft used to transmit motion. Commonly used when referring to the final driveshaft on shaft drive motorcycles.

E

Earth return The return path of an electrical circuit, utilising the motorcycle's frame.

ECU (Electronic Control Unit) A computer which controls (for instance) an ignition system, or an anti-lock braking system.

EGO Exhaust Gas Oxygen sensor. Sometimes called a Lambda sensor.

Electrolyte The fluid in a lead-acid battery.

EMS (Engine Management System) A computer controlled system which manages the fuel injection and the ignition systems in an integrated fashion.

Endfloat The amount of lengthways movement between two parts. As applied to a crankshaft, the distance that the crankshaft can move side-to-side in the crankcase.

Endless chain A chain having no joining link. Common use for cam chains and final drive chains.

EP (Extreme Pressure) Oil type used in locations where high loads are applied, such as between gear teeth.

Evaporative emission control system Describes a charcoal filled canister which stores fuel vapours from the tank rather than allowing them to vent to the atmosphere. Usually only fitted to California models and referred to as an EVAP system.

Expansion chamber Section of two-stroke engine exhaust system so designed to improve engine efficiency and boost power.

F

Feeler blade or gauge A thin strip or blade of hardened steel, ground to an exact thickness, used to check or measure clearances between parts.

Final drive Description of the drive from the transmission to the rear wheel. Usually by chain or shaft, but sometimes by belt.

Firing order The order in which the engine cylinders fire, or deliver their power strokes, beginning with the number one cylinder.

Flooding Term used to describe a high fuel level in the carburettor float chambers, leading to fuel overflow. Also refers to excess fuel in the combustion chamber due to incorrect starting technique.

Free length The no-load state of a component when measured. Clutch, valve and fork spring lengths are measured at rest, without any preload.

Freeplay The amount of travel before any action takes place. The looseness in a linkage, or an assembly of parts, between the initial application of force and actual movement. For example, the distance the rear brake pedal moves before the rear brake is actuated.

Fuel injection The fuel/air mixture is metered electronically and directed into the engine intake ports (indirect injection) or into the cylinders (direct injection). Sensors supply information on engine speed and conditions.

Fuel/air mixture The charge of fuel and air going into the engine. See Stoichiometric ratio.

Fuse An electrical device which protects a circuit against accidental overload. The typical fuse contains a soft piece of metal which is calibrated to melt at a predetermined current flow (expressed as amps) and break the circuit.

G

Gap The distance the spark must travel in jumping from the centre electrode to the side electrode in a spark plug. Also refers to the distance between the ignition rotor and the pickup coil in an electronic ignition system.

Gasket Any thin, soft material - usually cork, cardboard, asbestos or soft metal - installed between two metal surfaces to ensure a good seal. For instance, the cylinder head gasket seals the joint between the block and the cylinder head.

Gauge An instrument panel display used to monitor engine conditions. A gauge with a movable pointer on a dial or a fixed scale is an analogue gauge. A gauge with a numerical readout is called a digital gauge.

Gear ratios The drive ratio of a pair of gears in a gearbox, calculated on their number of teeth.

Glaze-busting see **Honing**

Grinding Process for renovating the valve face and valve seat contact area in the cylinder head.

Gudgeon pin The shaft which connects the connecting rod small-end with the piston. Often called a piston pin or wrist pin.

H

Helical gears Gear teeth are slightly curved and produce less gear noise that straight-cut gears. Often used for primary drives.

Helicoil A thread insert repair system. Commonly used as a repair for stripped spark plug threads **(see illustration)**.

Installing a Helicoil thread insert

Honing A process used to break down the glaze on a cylinder bore (also called glaze-busting). Can also be carried out to roughen a rebored cylinder to aid ring bedding-in.

HT (High Tension) Description of the electrical circuit from the secondary winding of the ignition coil to the spark plug.

Hydraulic A liquid filled system used to transmit pressure from one component to another. Common uses on motorcycles are brakes and clutches.

Hydrometer An instrument for measuring the specific gravity of a lead-acid battery.

Hygroscopic Water absorbing. In motorcycle applications, braking efficiency will be reduced if DOT 3 or 4 hydraulic fluid absorbs water from the air - care must be taken to keep new brake fluid in tightly sealed containers.

I

lbf ft Pounds-force feet. An imperial unit of torque. Sometimes written as ft-lbs.

lbf in Pound-force inch. An imperial unit of torque, applied to components where a very low torque is required. Sometimes written as in-lbs.

IC Abbreviation for Integrated Circuit.

Ignition advance Means of increasing the timing of the spark at higher engine speeds. Done by mechanical means (ATU) on early engines or electronically by the ignition control unit on later engines.

Ignition timing The moment at which the spark plug fires, expressed in the number of crankshaft degrees before the piston reaches the top of its stroke, or in the number of millimetres before the piston reaches the top of its stroke.

Infinity (∞) Description of an open-circuit electrical state, where no continuity exists.

Inverted forks (upside down forks) The sliders or lower legs are held in the yokes and the fork tubes or stanchions are connected to the wheel axle (spindle). Less unsprung weight and stiffer construction than conventional forks.

J

JASO Quality standard for 2-stroke oils.

Joule The unit of electrical energy.

Journal The bearing surface of a shaft.

K

Kickstart Mechanical means of turning the engine over for starting purposes. Only usually fitted to mopeds, small capacity motorcycles and off-road motorcycles.

Kill switch Handebar-mounted switch for emergency ignition cut-out. Cuts the ignition circuit on all models, and additionally prevent starter motor operation on others.

km Symbol for kilometre.

kmh Abbreviation for kilometres per hour.

L

Lambda (λ) sensor A sensor fitted in the exhaust system to measure the exhaust gas oxygen content (excess air factor).

Lapping see Grinding.
LCD Abbreviation for Liquid Crystal Display.
LED Abbreviation for Light Emitting Diode.
Liner A steel cylinder liner inserted in a aluminium alloy cylinder block.
Locknut A nut used to lock an adjustment nut, or other threaded component, in place.
Lockstops The lugs on the lower triple clamp (yoke) which abut those on the frame, preventing handlebar-to-fuel tank contact.
Lockwasher A form of washer designed to prevent an attaching nut from working loose.
LT Low Tension Description of the electrical circuit from the power supply to the primary winding of the ignition coil.

M

Main bearings The bearings between the crankshaft and crankcase.
Maintenance-free (MF) battery A sealed battery which cannot be topped up.
Manometer Mercury-filled calibrated tubes used to measure intake tract vacuum. Used to synchronise carburettors on multi-cylinder engines.
Micrometer A precision measuring instrument that measures component outside diameters **(see illustration)**.

Tappet shims are measured with a micrometer

MON (Motor Octane Number) A measure of a fuel's resistance to knock.
Monograde oil An oil with a single viscosity, eg SAE80W.
Monoshock A single suspension unit linking the swingarm or suspension linkage to the frame.
mph Abbreviation for miles per hour.
Multigrade oil Having a wide viscosity range (eg 10W40). The W stands for Winter, thus the viscosity ranges from SAE10 when cold to SAE40 when hot.
Multimeter An electrical test instrument with the capability to measure voltage, current and resistance. Some meters also incorporate a continuity tester and buzzer.

N

Needle roller bearing Inner race of caged needle rollers and hardened outer race. Examples of uncaged needle rollers can be found on some engines. Commonly used in rear suspension applications and in two-stroke engines.
Nm Newton metres.
NOx Oxides of Nitrogen. A common toxic pollutant emitted by petrol engines at higher temperatures.

O

Octane The measure of a fuel's resistance to knock.
OE (Original Equipment) Relates to components fitted to a motorcycle as standard or replacement parts supplied by the motorcycle manufacturer.
Ohm The unit of electrical resistance. Ohms = Volts ÷ Current.
Ohmmeter An instrument for measuring electrical resistance.
Oil cooler System for diverting engine oil outside of the engine to a radiator for cooling purposes.
Oil injection A system of two-stroke engine lubrication where oil is pump-fed to the engine in accordance with throttle position.
Open-circuit An electrical condition where there is a break in the flow of electricity - no continuity (high resistance).
O-ring A type of sealing ring made of a special rubber-like material; in use, the O-ring is compressed into a groove to provide the sealing action.
Oversize (OS) Term used for piston and ring size options fitted to a rebored cylinder.
Overhead cam (sohc) engine An engine with single camshaft located on top of the cylinder head.
Overhead valve (ohv) engine An engine with the valves located in the cylinder head, but with the camshaft located in the engine block or crankcase.
Oxygen sensor A device installed in the exhaust system which senses the oxygen content in the exhaust and converts this information into an electric current. Also called a Lambda sensor.

P

Plastigauge A thin strip of plastic thread, available in different sizes, used for measuring clearances. For example, a strip of Plastigauge is laid across a bearing journal. The parts are assembled and dismantled; the width of the crushed strip indicates the clearance between journal and bearing.
Polarity Either negative or positive earth (ground), determined by which battery lead is connected to the frame (earth return). Modern motorcycles are usually negative earth.
Pre-ignition A situation where the fuel/air mixture ignites before the spark plug fires. Often due to a hot spot in the combustion chamber caused by carbon build-up. Engine has a tendency to 'run-on'.
Pre-load (suspension) The amount a spring is compressed when in the unloaded state. Preload can be applied by gas, spacer or mechanical adjuster.
Premix The method of engine lubrication on older two-stroke engines. Engine oil is mixed with the petrol in the fuel tank in a specific ratio. The fuel/oil mix is sometimes referred to as "petroil".
Primary drive Description of the drive from the crankshaft to the clutch. Usually by gear or chain.
PS Pfedestärke - a German interpretation of BHP.
PSI Pounds-force per square inch. Imperial measurement of tyre pressure and cylinder pressure measurement.
PTFE Polytetrafluroethylene. A low friction substance.
Pulse secondary air injection system A process of promoting the burning of excess fuel present in the exhaust gases by routing fresh air into the exhaust ports.

Q

Quartz halogen bulb Tungsten filament surrounded by a halogen gas. Typically used for the headlight **(see illustration)**.

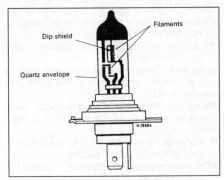

Quartz halogen headlight bulb construction

R

Rack-and-pinion A pinion gear on the end of a shaft that mates with a rack (think of a geared wheel opened up and laid flat). Sometimes used in clutch operating systems.
Radial play Up and down movement about a shaft.
Radial ply tyres Tyre plies run across the tyre (from bead to bead) and around the circumference of the tyre. Less resistant to tread distortion than other tyre types.
Radiator A liquid-to-air heat transfer device designed to reduce the temperature of the coolant in a liquid cooled engine.
Rake A feature of steering geometry - the angle of the steering head in relation to the vertical **(see illustration)**.

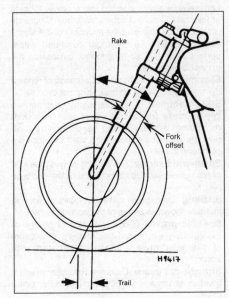

Steering geometry

Rebore Providing a new working surface to the cylinder bore by boring out the old surface. Necessitates the use of oversize piston and rings.

Rebound damping A means of controlling the oscillation of a suspension unit spring after it has been compressed. Resists the spring's natural tendency to bounce back after being compressed.

Rectifier Device for converting the ac output of an alternator into dc for battery charging.

Reed valve An induction system commonly used on two-stroke engines.

Regulator Device for maintaining the charging voltage from the generator or alternator within a specified range.

Relay A electrical device used to switch heavy current on and off by using a low current auxiliary circuit.

Resistance Measured in ohms. An electrical component's ability to pass electrical current.

RON (Research Octane Number) A measure of a fuel's resistance to knock.

rpm revolutions per minute.

Runout The amount of wobble (in-and-out movement) of a wheel or shaft as it's rotated. The amount a shaft rotates 'out-of-true'. The out-of-round condition of a rotating part.

S

SAE (Society of Automotive Engineers) A standard for the viscosity of a fluid.

Sealant A liquid or paste used to prevent leakage at a joint. Sometimes used in conjunction with a gasket.

Service limit Term for the point where a component is no longer useable and must be renewed.

Shaft drive A method of transmitting drive from the transmission to the rear wheel.

Shell bearings Plain bearings consisting of two shell halves. Most often used as big-end and main bearings in a four-stroke engine. Often called bearing inserts.

Shim Thin spacer, commonly used to adjust the clearance or relative positions between two parts. For example, shims inserted into or under tappets or followers to control valve clearances. Clearance is adjusted by changing the thickness of the shim.

Short-circuit An electrical condition where current shorts to earth (ground) bypassing the circuit components.

Skimming Process to correct warpage or repair a damaged surface, eg on brake discs or drums.

Slide-hammer A special puller that screws into or hooks onto a component such as a shaft or bearing; a heavy sliding handle on the shaft bottoms against the end of the shaft to knock the component free.

Small-end bearing The bearing in the upper end of the connecting rod at its joint with the gudgeon pin.

Spalling Damage to camshaft lobes or bearing journals shown as pitting of the working surface.

Specific gravity (SG) The state of charge of the electrolyte in a lead-acid battery. A measure of the electrolyte's density compared with water.

Straight-cut gears Common type gear used on gearbox shafts and for oil pump and water pump drives.

Stanchion The inner sliding part of the front forks, held by the yokes. Often called a fork tube.

Stoichiometric ratio The optimum chemical air/fuel ratio for a petrol engine, said to be 14.7 parts of air to 1 part of fuel.

Sulphuric acid The liquid (electrolyte) used in a lead-acid battery. Poisonous and extremely corrosive.

Surface grinding (lapping) Process to correct a warped gasket face, commonly used on cylinder heads.

T

Tapered-roller bearing Tapered inner race of caged needle rollers and separate tapered outer race. Examples of taper roller bearings can be found on steering heads.

Tappet A cylindrical component which transmits motion from the cam to the valve stem, either directly or via a pushrod and rocker arm. Also called a cam follower.

TCS Traction Control System. An electronically-controlled system which senses wheel spin and reduces engine speed accordingly.

TDC Top Dead Centre denotes that the piston is at its highest point in the cylinder.

Thread-locking compound Solution applied to fastener threads to prevent slackening. Select type to suit application.

Thrust washer A washer positioned between two moving components on a shaft. For example, between gear pinions on gearshaft.

Timing chain See **Cam Chain**.

Timing light Stroboscopic lamp for carrying out ignition timing checks with the engine running.

Top-end A description of an engine's cylinder block, head and valve gear components.

Torque Turning or twisting force about a shaft.

Torque setting A prescribed tightness specified by the motorcycle manufacturer to ensure that the bolt or nut is secured correctly. Undertightening can result in the bolt or nut coming loose or a surface not being sealed. Overtightening can result in stripped threads, distortion or damage to the component being retained.

Torx key A six-point wrench.

Tracer A stripe of a second colour applied to a wire insulator to distinguish that wire from another one with the same colour insulator. For example, Br/W is often used to denote a brown insulator with a white tracer.

Trail A feature of steering geometry. Distance from the steering head axis to the tyre's central contact point.

Triple clamps The cast components which extend from the steering head and support the fork stanchions or tubes. Often called fork yokes.

Turbocharger A centrifugal device, driven by exhaust gases, that pressurises the intake air. Normally used to increase the power output from a given engine displacement.

TWI Abbreviation for Tyre Wear Indicator. Indicates the location of the tread depth indicator bars on tyres.

U

Universal joint or U-joint (UJ) A double-pivoted connection for transmitting power from a driving to a driven shaft through an angle. Typically found in shaft drive assemblies.

Unsprung weight Anything not supported by the bike's suspension (ie the wheel, tyres, brakes, final drive and bottom (moving) part of the suspension).

V

Vacuum gauges Clock-type gauges for measuring intake tract vacuum. Used for carburettor synchronisation on multi-cylinder engines.

Valve A device through which the flow of liquid, gas or vacuum may be stopped, started or regulated by a moveable part that opens, shuts or partially obstructs one or more ports or passageways. The intake and exhaust valves in the cylinder head are of the poppet type.

Valve clearance The clearance between the valve tip (the end of the valve stem) and the rocker arm or tappet/follower. The valve clearance is measured when the valve is closed. The correct clearance is important - if too small the valve won't close fully and will burn out, whereas if too large noisy operation will result.

Valve lift The amount a valve is lifted off its seat by the camshaft lobe.

Valve timing The exact setting for the opening and closing of the valves in relation to piston position.

Vernier caliper A precision measuring instrument that measures inside and outside dimensions. Not quite as accurate as a micrometer, but more convenient.

Wet liner arrangement

VIN Vehicle Identification Number. Term for the bike's engine and frame numbers.

Viscosity The thickness of a liquid or its resistance to flow.

Volt A unit for expressing electrical "pressure" in a circuit. Volts = current x ohms.

W

Water pump A mechanically-driven device for moving coolant around the engine.

Watt A unit for expressing electrical power. Watts = volts x current.

Wear limit see **Service limit**

Wet liner A liquid-cooled engine design where the pistons run in liners which are directly surrounded by coolant **(see illustration)**.

Wheelbase Distance from the centre of the front wheel to the centre of the rear wheel.

Wiring harness or loom Describes the electrical wires running the length of the motorcycle and enclosed in tape or plastic sheathing. Wiring coming off the main harness is usually referred to as a sub harness.

Woodruff key A key of semi-circular or square section used to locate a gear to a shaft. Often used to locate the alternator rotor on the crankshaft.

Wrist pin Another name for gudgeon or piston pin.

Note: *References throughout this index are in the form - "Chapter number" • "Page number"*

Note: *References throughout this index are in the form - "Chapter number" • "Page number"*

Note: *References throughout this index are in the form - "Chapter number" • "Page number"*

Preserving Our Motoring Heritage

< The Model J Duesenberg
Derham Tourster.
Only eight of these
magnificent cars were
ever built – this is the
only example to be found
outside the United States
of America

Almost every car you've ever loved, loathed or desired is gathered under one roof at the Haynes Motor Museum. Over 300 immaculately presented cars and motorbikes represent every aspect of our motoring heritage, from elegant reminders of bygone days, such as the superb Model J Duesenberg to curiosities like the bug-eyed BMW Isetta. There are also many old friends and flames. Perhaps you remember the 1959 Ford Popular that you did your courting in? The magnificent 'Red Collection' is a spectacle of classic sports cars including AC, Alfa Romeo, Austin Healey, Ferrari, Lamborghini, Maserati, MG, Riley, Porsche and Triumph.

A Perfect Day Out

Each and every vehicle at the Haynes Motor Museum has played its part in the history and culture of Motoring. Today, they make a wonderful spectacle and a great day out for all the family. Bring the kids, bring Mum and Dad, but above all bring your camera to capture those golden memories for ever. You will also find an impressive array of motoring memorabilia, a comfortable 70 seat video cinema and one of the most extensive transport book shops in Britain. The Pit Stop Cafe serves everything from a cup of tea to wholesome, home-made meals or, if you prefer, you can enjoy the large picnic area nestled in the beautiful rural surroundings of Somerset.

> John Haynes O.B.E.,
Founder and
Chairman of the
museum at the wheel
of a Haynes Light 12.

< The 1936 490cc
sohc-engined
International
Norton – well known
for its racing success

The Museum is situated on the A359 Yeovil to Frome road at Sparkford, just off the A303 in Somerset. It is about 40 miles south of Bristol, and 25 minutes drive from the M5 intersection at Taunton.
Open 9.30am - 5.30pm (10.00am - 4.00pm Winter) 7 days a week, *except Christmas Day, Boxing Day and New Years Day*
Special rates available for schools, coach parties and outings Charitable Trust No. 292048